COGNITIVE PROCESSES
IN ANIMAL BEHAVIOR

COGNITIVE PROCESSES IN ANIMAL BEHAVIOR

Edited by

STEWART H. HULSE
Johns Hopkins University

HARRY FOWLER
University of Pittsburgh

WERNER K. HONIG
Dalhousie University

 LAWRENCE ERLBAUM ASSOCIATES, PUBLISHERS
1978   Hillsdale, New Jersey

DISTRIBUTED BY THE HALSTED PRESS DIVISION OF
JOHN WILEY & SONS
New York   Toronto   London   Sydney

Lawrence Erlbaum Associates, Inc., Publishers
62 Maria Drive
Hillsdale, New Jersey 07642

Distributed solely by Halsted Press Division
John Wiley & Sons, Inc., New York

Library of Congress Cataloging in Publication Data

Main entry under title:
Cognitive processes in animal behavior.

   Based on papers from a conference held June 1976
at Dalhousie University, Halifax, Nova Scotia.
   Includes bibliographical references and indexes.
Stewart H.   II. Fowler, Harry, 1934–
III.   Honig, Werner K.
QL785.C53   156'.3   78-14522
ISBN 0-470-26484-5

Printed in the United States of America

lw
4-30-80

Contents

Preface

At the meetings of the Psychonomic Society in Boston in November 1974, the three of us had the opportunity to discuss some current developments in the field of animal learning and behavior. Research in this province had long been characterized by a stimulus–response (S–R) tradition which had as its basis many historical and philosophical antecedents. These included an early emphasis on reflex physiology as a source of theoretical models for learning; a biological continuity suggesting that the apparently "simple" or mechanistic principles of animal learning could be applied to man; and a behavioristic metatheory which argued against introspection and the study of mentalistic processes—such as cognition—which could not be tied to direct observation and measurement. It was apparent to us, however, that many of the principles of animal learning had turned out not to be so simple after all, suggesting an important limitation to the strict application of an S–R approach. Furthermore, we found ourselves and those sharing our interests attacking problems which seemed to stem more and more from the general domain of cognition, such as higher-order association, memory, and concept formation. Clearly, we were using with increasing frequency some of the techniques and models of our colleagues in the field of human cognition and information processing. The time seemed proper for an organized discussion of matters, and so we undertook to bring together some fellow psychologists whose work reflected the state of affairs as we saw it. Accordingly, an appropriate group gathered at a conference in June 1976 at Dalhousie University in Halifax, Nova Scotia, Canada. This book is a collection of chapters based on the papers read at that conference.

Many of our friends in some other spheres of experimental psychology may find no small measure of irony in our endeavor. For years, those who worked on problems in human learning—memory is an excellent example— borrowed heavily from strict S–R models of behavior patterned after those developed in animal learning. But with the advent of psycholinguistics and mathematical learning theory, and especially with the appearance of the computer both as a tool and as a ready-made model for human thought, memory, and attention, S–R approaches were largely discarded. Their contributions had been absorbed. Now, it may be the turn of us animal psychologists to reverse the principle of biological continuity and borrow ideas and methods from our neighbors in human cognitive psychology.

By such steps, progress takes place. Certainly the question of the limits of animal intelligence is very old, and our work may reflect a current renewal of interest in comparative cognition. Others have already made important contributions to this topic, broadly conceived, through such books as Wilson's *Sociobiology,* Thorpe's *Animal nature and human nature,* and Griffin's *The question of animal awareness.* Not everyone, including these authors (and some of the contributors to this volume) would agree on the defining properties of a field of comparative cognition, however, and some may question whether in fact it does—or should—exist. But we view the material in this book to be part of an approach, however loosely defined, that deems the study of the cognitive capacities of animals other than man to be a worthwhile enterprise. Perhaps our work will help to cross-fertilize the production of still newer and fresher views of the commonalities and differences among organisms.

Following an introductory essay in which Honig discusses a metatheoretical and philosophical approach to the problem of cognition in animals, succeeding chapters are arranged, topically, from basic associative processes to higher mental operations. Thus, Rescorla, Hearst, Bolles,and Fowler discuss problems derived from models of association; Mackintosh, Wagner, Honig, and Riley and Roitblat describe their work on attention, memory, and the processing of stimulus information; whereas Church, Hulse, Olton, Menzel, and Premack deal with time, spatial, and serial organization of behavior, and concept formation. Because the topic at hand is hardly unidimensional, the order of chapters is somewhat arbitrary, and many could fit several locations in the book.

There are many who deserve the thanks of both the editors and the other contributors. First and foremost, we thank both the National Research Council of Canada and Dalhousie University for the financial support that made the conference possible. We are also greatly indebted to Dalhousie University, especially the faculty, students, and staff of the Psychology Department, for acting as such gracious hosts during the four days that we were their guests in Halifax. Finally, we owe a special debt of gratitude to Larry Erlbaum, who, with a welcome wry twist, helped shepherd our efforts into print.

STEWART H. HULSE
HARRY FOWLER
WERNER K. HONIG

**COGNITIVE PROCESSES
IN ANIMAL BEHAVIOR**

1 On the Conceptual Nature of Cognitive Terms: An Initial Essay

Werner K. Honig
Dalhousie University

In this book, cognitive terms are used in the description, analysis, and explanation of animal behavior. They do not describe behavior in the narrow sense of referring to specific observable events; they are not part of the "data language" of experimental psychology. To say that an animal chooses between two stimuli, runs to a particular location, or reduces its rate of responding in the presence of a specific signal is quite different from saying that it *remembers* one or another stimulus, *knows* the location of food, or *associates* two events. Much of the present essay is concerned with the difference between these two kinds of description. Terms of the latter kind are more and more being used in summary descriptions of behavior, but often they refer to states or processes that enter into the determination of behavior.

It is therefore important to clarify the conceptual status of cognitive terms within the psychology of animal behavior. In the first part of this essay, I will make such an attempt, particularly with respect to their role in concept formation, explanation, and theory construction. But even when the status of cognitive terms has been discussed, the nature of their "content" will not have been specified. Is it possible to distinguish cognitive concepts from others that also lie outside the data language of psychology? I will discuss this question in the second part of the chapter.

In the chapters that follow, many contributors argue in favor of the use of cognitive terms within the vocabulary appropriate to their particular areas of research. I do not want to anticipate their arguments, nor do I intend to review the empirical findings which they use to support them. The present discussion concerns conceptual rather than empirical aspects of the material in this book. It is neither an overview of the contents, nor an introduction to particular

1

chapters. I intend to raise general questions and issues that are within that domain of the philosophy of science which is relevant to a cognitive description and explanation of behavior. An evaluation of empirical material in cognitive terms requires an understanding of the conceptual issues that are raised by the use of such terms. Conceptual issues facing psychologists who want to employ cognitive concepts should be understood before the empirical material on which these concepts are based can be evaluated.

I. SOME CATEGORIES OF PSYCHOLOGICAL TERMS

Terms whose function is other than to provide an immediate account of observed behavior and the conditions under which it occurs, are generally concepts. Such concepts may have different functions and attributes; they may be *descriptive, explanatory, theoretical*, or *mental*. These functions or attributes are not mutually exclusive, although a rough set of distinctions will be useful. A concept may simply be used to summarize or to provide a category for a set of related primary accounts of behavior. Cognitive concepts often play this *descriptive* role. The events of interest are often observed under critical test conditions, and the concepts derived from such observations are *dispositional* concepts (Hempel, 1952). Closely related or parallel test conditions can be used as a set of convergent operations (Garner, Hake, & Eriksen, 1956) to provide the empirical basis of particular concepts. It can be argued that most or all cognitive concepts are dispositional terms, but a defense of this point would take us too far afield.

A concept can be used within the paradigm for scientific explanation that is generally accepted in the philosophy of science (Hempel & Oppenheim, 1948). No concept by itself comprises an explanation; *explanatory* concepts are used in explanatory statements. In an explanation one or more statements must be general and law-like; at least one other, more specific statement describes a set of specific conditions. From such a set of statements, others can be deduced which will describe or predict particular observations. In the absence of such a deductive procedure, the observation of interest has not been explained.

It is generally accepted within psychology that many concepts are *theoretical* in nature because they refer to entities which are not observable. Such entities are assumed to possess particular attributes which make then useful within a system of theoretical terms, often of a deductive nature. Such terms are often known as constructs. They are "constructed" on the basis of a set of data. They derive support from the predictions that are confirmed within the deductive system in which they participate.

Mental, or subjective terms are presumably part of the particular domain of psychology. Basically, they are descriptive of "private" experience, rather than "public" events. Mental terms have been used both as explanatory and theoretical terms, although this route toward explanation in psychology has not been accepted by behaviorists. Cognitive terms can be mental terms if they refer to private experience, but clearly they need not be limited to such a reference.

To which of these categories of concepts do cognitive terms belong? I believe that they can and do belong to all of them, depending on their function. We shall see that they can be used to *describe* sets of related observations in the realm of animal learning and behavior. If cognitive terms possess attributes beyond those specified in the defining observations, they can be *theoretical* terms as well. I will also suggest uses of cognitive terms which endow them with *explanatory* capacity. And finally it is reasonable, and perhaps even obvious, to argue that many cognitive terms were originally adopted from our vocabulary of *mental* experience.

It runs counter to the behavioristic tradition to suppose that any conceptual term could play such a variety of roles. According to the philosophy of science that until recently dominated experimental psychology, terms either described behavior as part of the "data language" of psychology, or they entered deductive systems as theoretical terms used for the explanation of behavior. Cognitive terms were suspect as part of the data language because they did not provide an immediate description of behavior, and because their mental or subjective connotations were contrary to behavioristic principles. The explanation of behavior could presumably be accomplished with other, more "behavioral" terms, which rendered cognitive concepts unnecessary.

In my view, the functions of terms cannot always be so neatly divided between the empirical and the theoretical. Even a descriptive vocabulary involves classification and abstraction to some degree. A particular term will play quite a different role depending on its relationship to the data on which it is based, and on its function within the laws or principles that encompass the generalities of scientific discourse. In an ideal science, these roles can perhaps be clearly separated. But the fact that we cannot do so with cognitive terms in psychology is not a sufficient reason to reject them.

II. SOME FUNCTIONS OF COGNITIVE TERMS

A. Description and Conceptualization

Some descriptions of behavior deal only with the characteristics of observed behavior, while others provide a conceptualization, which is based upon complex behavioral interactions and contingencies. Descriptions of the latter kind emerge from the observation of behavior, but they are at least partly theoretical in nature, because they refer to some state or process which is not directly observable. It may be useful to identify a continuum that extends from the "more observable" and thus "less theoretical" to the more theoretical and thus less observable.

1. At one level, we can observe a performance that is not under the immediate control of stimuli presented by the experimenter, and which is not exemplified by a simple, specific behavior pattern, but which is appropriate to the experimental contingencies. For example, Olton and I have both (rather independently) proposed the notion of a "working memory." In some learning situations, animals need to remember an event, or a set of events, to perform efficiently during a given trial. They also need to terminate the memory of these events in order to perform well on a later trial. In Olton's work, rats are placed on a central platform of an eight-arm radial maze. Each arm is baited at the end with a bit of food. Rats readily learn to obtain this food in an exhaustive fashion; they run down every arm before returning to any. On subsequent trials the rat shows little or no interference from previous trials; the working memory has presumably been canceled, or reset. The concept of working memory provides a framework for the description of behavior that is systematic but not under the control of a sensory cue, such as a scent mark. However, it does not *explain* the behavior; on the contrary, it summarizes in a more abstract way those observations which now stand in need of explanation.

Other examples similar in kind are the "internal" clock of the rat described by Church in Chapter 10 and the division of attention between the elements of a sample in a matching-to-sample task noted for pigeons by Riley and Roitblat in Chapter 9. These authors would, I think, agree that these concepts are not explanations, as such, of "timing behavior" or of the differences in performance on trials involving elements and compounds as stimuli. In fact, Church's chapter is largely devoted to experiments which specify the operation of the cognitive device. They elucidate the workings of the clock rather than citing them to explain behavior. Certainly one may eventually propose theoretical mechanisms for the operation of the clock, for the division of attention between stimuli, or for the registration of events in a working memory, but these concepts are not in themselves meant to accomplish this task.

2. Concepts like the above classify and characterize a particular set of behavioral observations. We proceed to a second level of conceptualization, at which terms of this kind are more theoretical, because the observed behavior is more widely separated from its presumed determining conditions. The behavior is used as an indicator of a process that has already taken place. A good example is the concept of association. In Chapter 3, Hearst describes a study by Browne in which pigeons were exposed to pairing of a key light with food but without the opportunity to peck at either. When these restrictions were removed, the pigeons pecked at the key more often during the course of autoshaping (which again involved pairings of these stimuli) than did other birds who had earlier experienced random or negative correlations between key light and food. Clearly, something not obvious to the experimenter happened to the birds during the

initial pairings, and this influenced the later criterion behavior. This process can be called the formation of an association. However, this too serves as a descriptive conceptualization rather than an explanation of the process.

Another example of this sort is the "cognitive map" proposed by Menzel in Chapter 13; see also Menzel, 1973. A young chimpanzee is carried around a field by an experimenter, and is able to view another person hiding food in clumps of grass, under leaves, etc., in a number of different places. The chimpanzee is then released from his cage after an interval, and with remarkable accuracy he visits the places where the food has been hidden. He does not retrace the experimenter's route during the hiding of the food, but generally follows a shorter, more direct path. Clearly, the chimpanzee must have learned a great deal from his initial observations. This learning is manifested in the absence of the experimenter, and while the chimp is moving on his own, rather than clinging to the experimenter. Clearly a process is at work which cannot be encompassed by a description of the chimpanzee's behavior during the test phase. That behavior is the result of such a process. But this process − the development or use of a cognitive map − summarizes a set of observations rather than explaining them. If we learn enough about the formation of association, the use of cognitive maps, etc., such concepts may become useful for the explanation of behavior in other situations. I will return to this issue.

3. At a third level of conceptualization, the concepts are again inferred from the observation of behavior, but in addition the concepts are endowed with active processes. This is the most "theoretical" level of conceptualization. In his chapter, Wagner provides a number of good examples; let us take the "rehearsal" of a prior event by the rabbit. In one study (Wagner, Rudy, & Whitlow, 1973), rabbits received discriminative eyelid conditioning with stimulus A (which was a CS+) and stimulus B (which was a CS−). Then they were started on simple acquisiton with a third, independent stimulus C. A few seconds after each reinforced C trial, a further trial with A or B was presented. For some animals, this trial was congruent with previous training − A was followed by the US and B was not. For others, the event was incongruent, or "surprising"; the US was omitted after A and presented after B. The rabbits that received incongruent trials conditioned much more slowly with stimulus C. Since the critical events *followed* each C trial, Wagner argues that they must have interfered with some rehearsal or consolidation process which followed the paired presentations of C and the US. In this case, the cognitive process is postulated very indirectly − through the relative rates of the acquisition of a response to which it contributes. But "active" characteristics are ascribed to the process because it appears to be necessary for learning, and it is subject to disruption by events which are not expected. The conceptualization in this case is both rich and complex. Nonetheless, this experiment identifies a particular process that can be subjected to

further analysis at the hand of appropriate further experiments. However, the concept of rehearsal does not *in itself* explain the differential speeds of learning which comprise its empirical basis.

B. Conceptualization and Explanation

I have stressed the descriptive aspects of concepts which are based on sets of particular experimental procedures and results. Such concepts incorporate processes or states which are not directly observable, but which are inferred from the data at hand. If they are not observable, such processes must be theoretical, and this in turn suggests that the concept into which they are incorporated should play some role in the explanation and not just the description of behavior. The philosophy of science adopted by many experimental psychologists ascribes explanatory functions to theoretical terms. But I have already suggested that some of the theoretical concepts put forward in this book don't "explain anything." Rather, they characterize complex relationships between behavior and its governing circumstances. How can cognitive concepts serve an explanatory function as well?

As I suggested earlier, the theoretical nature of a concept and its potential explanatory function are not necessarily linked. Explanations can, for example, be devised without the use of theoretical terms. Dallenbach and his associates (e.g., Supa, Cotzin, & Dallenbach, 1944) showed that blind people avoid obstacles by using auditory cues produced by their own movements. This explanation of "facial vision" replaced that theoretical concept, which had been invoked to characterize the ability of the blind to avoid obstacles. On the other hand, we have seen in the previous section that theoretical concepts can be formulated independently of any explanatory function.

Psychologists who have tried to link theory to explanation have at times introduced theoretical terms for the exclusive purpose of explaining a set of data, but without reference to any defining observations. These terms tend to be empirically rather vacuous, since no independent assessment of their validity is immediately available. I tried to show in the previous section that the cognitive concepts in question are not of this kind. The main effort has generally been the determination of the functional characteristics of the states or processes in question.

Church uses most of his chapter to delineate the characteristics of the internal clock. Riley and Roitblat (Chapter 9) ask whether the selective attention that is the topic of their chapter can be "cued" by a priming stimulus in advance of each trial. Olton has tested the capacity of working memory in the rat by increasing the number of arms in a radial maze. These characteristics are studied "in their own right," as it were, and not as part of an effort to provide the concepts with explanatory power. The usefulness of such concepts will, of course, be enhanced if they can participate in the explanation of behavior, but the enterprise of formulating them on the basis of the kinds of data reviewed in the last section need not be abandoned if they do not do so immediately.

Under what conditions, then, does a concept possess explanatory power? An explanation is a set of general and specific statements from which particular observations can be deduced and/or predicted. If this set of statements accomplishes no more than the "prediction" of the data which led to the formulation of the theoretical terms contained in those statements in the first place, then the explanation is rather trivial. If, however, the theoretical terms permit the deduction or prediction of observations outside the set of the observations which led to their original formulation, then I suggest that the terms have true explanatory potential. In other words, the attributes ascribed to the states or processes represented by a concept should be useful in the prediction of data outside the definition of the concept. Such attributes may be suggested by the defining observations themselves. But they may also arise by analogy with concepts from other fields of research. For example, the similarity of cognitive concepts formulated independently on the basis of work with humans and animals may make it possible to extrapolate attributes from one set to the other. Such attributes may also emerge from a set of convergent operations, which suggest that a concept is richer than the observations based on any particular operation would imply. Attributes could also be suggested by work at a different empirical level. If the process in question is thought to reflect neurophysiological correlates, then those correlates may possess attributes which can be "translated" into a set of further behavioral observations.

Can the concepts offered in this book generate predictions in any of these ways? The pursuit of a cognitive approach would be a sorry undertaking if they could not. Wagner ascribes particular characteristics to the process of rehearsal in the rabbit; it is short term, as it tends to be in humans. From this it is predicted that if incongruent trials follow by a fair length of time the conditioning trials that provide the critical data, interference from the incongruent trials will be eliminated. This prediction has, in fact, been confirmed (Wagner et al., 1973). But the brief nature of the rehearsal was not inherent in the concept of rehearsal as a process that was originally identified with a separate set of observations.

In Chapter 5 on cognitive associations in instrumental conditioning, Fowler identifies a dimension of "discrepancy" between an outcome signalled by a stimulus (e.g., no food, delivery of shock), and the outcome produced by the response (e.g., food, absence of shock). This dimension is identified on the basis of one set of studies. He then predicts that if there is little discrepancy between the signalled outcome and the real outcome, the signal will block the effect of the outcome, even though the two may involve different motivational systems. Thus, Fowler predicts that the suppressing effect of a conditioned aversive stimulus upon drinking in the rat will be reduced (through blocking) when the shock reinforcer is preceded by a signal for the absence of food, but will be enhanced when the shock is preceded by a signal for the delivery of food. Fowler's theoretical structure is used for the prediction of data that lie outside the original identification of a dimension of discrepancy.

Two general observations follow from my analysis of explanatory function. The first is that at the present stage of a cognitive analysis of animal behavior, the terms are used in the first instance to identify complex and orderly behavior in such a way as to facilitate further study and analysis. Their initial function is *not* the explanation of behavior. This is, of course, contrary to the more traditional approach to theoretical terms, according to which the *only* defensible function of such terms is their participation in the explanation of behavior. But this restrictive view does not reflect the way in which a cognitive analysis is generally carried out.

The second observation is that explanatory power is more likely to accrue to those terms that are located toward the "theoretical" end of the dimension sketched in the previous section. This is fairly obvious. If a set of observations leads to the inference that an active process must have been going on at another time or in a different set of circumstances, then it is likely that such a process will have characteristics not "required" by the original set of observations. I have cautioned against the *assumption* within the philosophy of psychological science that theoretical status and explanatory power are uniformly and directly correlated. But, in fact, it is likely that more abstract, "theoretical" terms are richer in structure, that they can be more readily related to other disciplines, and that they may have additional "inessential" attributes leading to the prediction of behavioral phenomena that are outside the range of defining observations.

III. ON THE IDENTIFICATION OF "COGNITIVE" CONCEPTS

To this point I have discussed the conceptual status of cognitive terms, but this does not necessarily distinguish them from other classes or concepts in psychology. On what basis do we identify a concept as "cognitive," rather than "perceptual," "developmental," "motivational," or whatever? Our answer to this question must at best be sketchy, since our understanding of cognitive states and processes is far from complete. However, one generalization that is valid for many cognitive behaviors is that they can provide information about the environment that is not otherwise available when the behavior occurs. Cognitive behavior reflects order in the environment, although it is not under the immediate control of the stimuli or the circumstances that provide the basis for that order. However, the information not immediately available from the environment can, in principle, be reconstructed by observing the cognitive behavior of interest.

A. Information Contained in Cognitive Behavior

If the preceding generalization is correct, then the observer can obtain information about the environment from cognitive behavior, provided that he knows the rules relating that behavior to the determining conditions. Language, of course, provides the clearest example. But less complex and sophisticated behaviors can be used to the same effect. If orderly behavior reflects the passage of time (Church, Chapter 10), the observer could set an external clock by observing the animal. Behavior can also provide information about the location of food which is not visible (Menzel, Chapter 13), or about the progressive increase or decrease in the size of reward across a series of trials (Hulse, Chapter 11). The observation of one of Olton's rats from the middle to the end of a trial in a radial maze provides information about the arms that the rat visited before the observation began (since each arm is visited only once), but not about the order in which those arms were entered.

These examples suggest that cognitive behavior often requires a memory for past events — not only the long-term memory essential for all kinds of learning, but the ability to maintain information in the short run so that appropriate behavior will occur when the determining conditions are no longer present. Furthermore, the environmental order which governs the behavior may be transformed into quite a different order in the behavior itself. It is not a new observation that respone dimensions differ from the stimulus dimensions that govern the responses in question. In the cases under discussion here, an entire pattern of stimulus events or conditions is translated by the organism into a specific pattern of behaviors, and this process presumably requires not only the storage but also the reprocessing of the information available from the environment.

Perhaps the most striking form of reprocessing is seen in the use of symbols. This is well illustrated by Premack in his chapter and his recent book (Premack, 1977). He asked his chimpanzee subject, Sarah, to provide a color token to complete the sentence "... is the color of chocolate." She chose the token for *brown*. Neither this token, nor the token for *chocolate* was brown. The stimuli governing the criterion behavior, namely the color(s) of brown and chocolate, are separated from that behavior by a symbolic relationship. If the experimenter knew the meaning of the tokens he could derive information from Sarah's behavior if he did not already know the color of chocolate. Premack suggests that the animal must have an internal representation of colors and of chocolate to overcome the separation in circumstances between the physical stimuli and the appropriate responses.

In many other cases, however, cognitive behaviors observed in a single subject do not reflect environmental circumstances in a direct manner. Many procedures described in this book actually involve simple criterion behaviors under the

direct control of a particular stimulus. The acquisition, extinction, and maintenance of such behavior may be used to reflect experiences with that same stimulus, or with other stimuli at other times and possibly in other circumstances.
The chapters by Wagner (7), Fowler (5), Rescorla (2), Hearst (3), Bolles (4), and
Mackintosh (6), among others, provide many examples. Indeed, Rescorla interprets conditioning as a process that reflects the informational relationships
among stimuli rather than simple contiguity. But these relationships are reflected
in behavioral differences between different groups of subjects, not by an orderly
set of responses within a single animal.

I have already described a study by Wagner and his associates in which the
rate of conditioning was modulated by experience with congruent and incongruent events following each trial. In his analysis of blocking, Mackintosh describes a set of comparisons among groups who received criterion trials in which
the "blocked" stimulus alone was presented. When this stimulus was earlier introduced together with an initial training or preconditioned stimulus, some
animals experienced a change in the value of the reinforcer. For others, this
change occurred only after one or more compound trials. Mackintosh and his
associates observed blocking only when the change was not correlated with the
introduction of the blocked stimulus. The criterion trials provided an assessment of the control gained by the blocked stimulus on the previous trials, and
Mackintosh concluded that on the earlier trials, the rats would learn to ignore
stimuli that predict no change in reinforcement.

In cases like these, criterion behaviors differ although the immediate conditions of stimulation are the same. Again, the differences reflect environmental
treatments or experiences that are separated from the criterion behavior in time
or circumstance. The animal appears to "process" such experiences, although
this processing is not evident from its behavior at the time. But the question
arises to what extent the general descriptions that I have provided really sort out
cognitive processes from others. Are there not other paradigms which involve a
separation between determining conditions and the criterion behavior, but which
may not reflect true cognitive processes? Is trace conditioning, for example, a
cognitive procedure? In this case, the behavior is under the direct but not immediate control of environmental events. How about experiments on the partial
reinforcement effect? All subjects receive criterion trials without reinforcement,
and these reflect the prior experience of the animal with different reinforcement
programs. In this case, the effect of those environmental circumstances is indirect. Does this reflect a cognitive process?

There is no ready answer to questions like these, although a cognitive processing of relationships among events may well underlie much of the animal's behavior. The partial reinforcement effect, for example, could well be analyzed in
cognitive terms; indeed, Capaldi (1971) suggests that the rat retains a memory of
the sequence of events experienced during previous trials. The lack of a clear
answer points up both the strengths and weaknesses of the analysis I have sug-

gested. The analysis is plausible because it places cognitive process and cognitive behavior within the general framework of a functional and experimental analysis of behavior (not necessarily in the operant sense of that phrase). There is nothing magical or mysterious about the relevant experimental or criterion behaviors, and thus cognitive processes remain within the realm of *behavioral* identification and analysis. We do not need a new kind of psychology to deal with cognitive events.

On the other hand, it can be argued that this functional analysis lacks substance. Other kinds of behavior also can inform the experimenter about the organism's external or internal environment. Traditionally, these behaviors have been placed within the domains of perception and motivation, not cognition. Indeed, cognitive processes seem more clearly defined by the exclusion of immediate control of behavior by environmental conditions than by the inclusion of the "meat," or "essence," of cognitive functioning. A positive description of cognitive mechanisms or processes common to the defining observations still seems to be lacking.

B. The Search for a Cognitive "Content" of Cognitive Terms

In my view, such a positive description will not be provided by further, more detailed, or even more insightful descriptions of experimental procedures or paradigms. The distinctive characteristics of cognitive processes will be more directly established only by the mechanisms which are observed or assumed to explain the behavior − in short, by theory. As I indicated earlier in this essay, cognitive concepts can initially be established on a behavioral basis. The functional nature of the definitions limits the meanings of the concepts to the range of observations upon which they are based. More detailed and more incisive experiments may then elucidate the causal and possibly the neural bases of cognitive functioning. Once the cognitive functions are understood well enough so that they can participate in explanations and in theories, it becomes sensible to ask whether they make contact with entities at a different level. This contact might provide cognitive concepts with a distinctive cognitive content that would be independent of their functionally defined characteristics.

One approach to the search for such content is the argument by analogy. Behaviorists used such a strategy to explain indirect, or "remote," control of behavior. Real stimuli and real responses, and the stimuli produced by real responses, were thought to have theoretical counterparts "inside" the organism. These counterparts were subject to the same laws as observable S−R relationships, and cognitive functions might in this way be explained. A good example is the fractional anticipatory goal response proposed by Hull (1930) and later adopted by Amsel (1958) to encompass frustration and to explain the effects of partial reinforcement. Sensory preconditioning, which is evidence for a direct association between stimuli, can be explained on a similar basis but in a rather contrived way — by the operation of hypothetical responses which produce hypothetical stimuli which, in turn, have a hypothetical mediating function. Short-term memory in animals might also be accomplished through mediating chains of stimuli and responses.

In my view, this strategy does not suffice to cope with the analysis of cognitive processes. For one thing, the data which are now available are simply too rich and complex. An analysis of rehearsal processes, attention, cognitive mapping, concept attainment, and so forth, is probably beyond the scope of even an extended S—R system. The whole point of the enterprise, namely the construction of a fairly "tight" system for making specific predictions, would be lost among the many assumptions and unspecified variables required to make it work at all. But more important to me is the argument that it is gratuitous to assume that the S—R paradigm, initially adopted to provide a *description* of the orderly aspects of behavior, should be adopted as a theory for the explanation of behavior. The effect of a magnet is not explained by assuming that there are little magnets operating inside the real magnet, although in fact little magnets do result from the cutting up of a big magnet. The mechanisms used for breathing are not reproduced in miniature at the point where oxygen is exchanged for carbon dioxide as blood passes through the lungs. Most explanations in science involve discontinuities in mechanism. One does not normally use the terms and concepts established for the description of phenomena in order to explain them, even if they are recast as theoretical terms when they are endowed with an explanatory function.

A second approach to the search for distinctive characteristics of cognitive concepts would be reductionistic. The physiological analysis of many psychological functions has made great strides in recent years, and the search for physiological correlates of cognitive functions could be very exciting. The effort would be great, and it will probably take a long time to determine whether the physiology of cognition differs from the physiology of other psychological processes. If large amounts of neural tissue are destroyed, it is difficult to separate motor and sensory deficits from a reduction in cognitive functioning. And the electrical or chemical stimulation of small parts of the brain tends to elicit specific reflexive or consummatory responses. Small, carefully placed lesions, together with recording from individual cells or groups of cells in the same area, may provide a more promising approach to the localization of cognitive functions. In a recent article, Olton (1977) reviews research on the hippocampus with respect to localization in space by the rat. Animals with lesions in the fornix suffer very specific deficits in the radial arm maze that he uses for the study of working memory. Furthermore, single neurons of the hippocampus are active only when the animal is in a particular position in his apparatus. This kind of analytic approach may well serve as a model for the analysis of other cognitive functions in physiological terms.

A third approach is the use of terms arising from human experience and action as theoretical concepts. Psychologists working in human memory, cognition, and information processing do this quite productively. Some terms like rehearsal, symbolization, and attention have already been mentioned in this essay. While the work described in this book provides functional definitions, people are also capable of giving more direct, subjective accounts of such mental processes. Other serious analyses carried out with humans are founded on concepts of imagery, subjective organization, scanning, and so forth. Processes of this kind were long held to be scientifically inaccessible. But since the accounts derived from the S–R position seem in the long run not to have captured the essence of cognitive functioning in humans, more "subjective" concepts and terms were adopted. Even with humans, of course, the firm data remain behavioral. But there is a vocabulary common both to the functional analyses of complex behavior and to the subjective descriptions of one's perception, knowledge, and memory of the environment. This may well be the language that best captures the essential character of cognitive concepts.

If psychologists were consistent in applying the principle of biological continuity among species, they would find it easier to adopt concepts based on human experience to characterize behavior in other species and to suggest theoretical formulations. The principle of continuity implies the possibility of moving in both directions along the phylogenetic continuum. Traditionally, psychologists have started with a S–R analysis founded on animal behavior and have moved "up" the scale for the analysis of human behavior. The study of cognitive processes in animals may open the way to movement in the other direction. Once the behavioral analysis has been soundly established, subjective or mentalistic concepts arising from human experience can perhaps be used for explanation or theory. This could lead to the prediction of other cognitive behavior, and it would provide cognitive concepts with a distinctive content. Perhaps a comparative psychology of cognitive processes would be established. Indeed, the chapters by Hulse (11), Honig (8), Church (10), Menzel (13), and Premack (14) are a start in this direction.

If a biologist were to discover a process that at first seems distinctly human, he would not hesitate to seek corresponding processes in other animal species. The notion of biological continuity would almost make this mandatory. Psychologists should consider adopting the same freedom with respect to those distinctly human behaviors. In the area of language, such attempts have recently been successful, at least with chimpanzees. But the sorts of language that chimps have learned from psychologists were imposed on them; they did not evolve naturally. Other states, processes, and capacities are much more likely to occur naturally among animals. Working memory, associative capacity, rehearsal, geographical representation, and so forth, might have emerged simply as part of the animal's psychological structure in the course of evolution. Their survival value would be important in an environment that is for the most part orderly and consistent, and where significant events are frequently correlated but often separated in space and time as well.

ACKNOWLEDGMENTS

I am indebted to all of the contributors to this book for having provided me with the background necessary for the writing of this chapter, both through their stimulating ideas and their many incisive experiments. I do not pretend to represent their views in an adequate way; indeed, I expect that their opinions would in some cases differ from mine. Nonetheless, I hope that this chapter may provide a background which is relevant to an appreciation of their work.

Stewart Hulse and Harry Fowler, my coeditors, have given me much helpful advice in the writing and preparation of the final draft. I have also received many valuable comments from Alex Rosenberg, Richard Smith, James W. Clark, Philip Dunham, and Jeffrey Willner, who read an earlier version.

I dedicate this work to my father, Richard M. Honig. As a jurist and scholar, he was the first to make it clear to me that concepts are more interesting and more important than objects.

REFERENCES

Amsel, A. The role of frustrative nonreward in noncontinuous reward situations. *Psychological Bulletin*, 1958, *55*, 102–119.

Capaldi, E. J. Memory and learning: A sequential viewpoint. In W. K. Honig & P. H. R. James (Eds.), *Animal memory*. New York: Academic Press, 1971, pp. 111–154.

Garner, W. R., Hake, H. W., & Eriksen, C. W. Operationism and the concept of perception. *Psychological Review*, 1956, *63*, 149–159.

Hempel, C. G. *Fundamentals of concept formation in empirical science. International enclyclopedia of unified science*, Vol. 2, No. 7. Chicago: University of Chicago Press, 1952.

Hempel, C. G., & Oppenheim, P. Studies in the logic of explanation. *Philosophy of Science*, 1948, *15*, 135–175.

Hull, C. L. Knowledge and purpose as habit mechanisms. *Psychological Review*, 1930, *37*, 511–525.

Menzel, E. W. Chimpanzee spatial memory organization. *Science*, 1973, *182*, 943–954.

Olton, D. S. Spatial memory. *Scientific American*, 1977, *236*, 82–98.

Premack, D. *Intelligence in ape and man*. Hillsdale, New Jersey: Lawrence Erlbaum Associates, 1977.

Supa, M., Cotzin, M., & Dallenbach, K. M. "Facial vision": the perception of obstacles by the blind. *Americal Journal of Psychology*, 1944, *57*, 133–183.

Wagner, A. R., Rudy, J. W., & Whitlow, J. W. Rehearsal in animal conditioning. *Journal of Experimental Psychology*, 1973, *97*, 407–426.

2 Some Implications of a Cognitive Perspective On Pavlovian Conditioning

Robert A. Rescorla
Yale University

The intention of this paper is to describe some research from our laboratory which was suggested by a cognitive view of Pavlovian conditioning. With a few notable exceptions (e.g., Tolman, 1932; Zener, 1937) Pavlovian conditioning has historically been viewed as the most mechanistic and least cognitive of learning processes. Although it has often been used as an explanatory device to account for apparently cognitive aspects of complex behaviors, Pavlovian conditioning has itself been less frequently described in cognitive terms. It is the contention of this paper that such a description can potentially encourage novel and interesting experimentation.

The description of conditioning adopted here, while attributable to no particular author, is clearly in the spirit of that given by Tolman (1932). We view Pavlovian conditioning as the learning of relations among environmental events which occur outside the organism's control. As a result of the environment arranging a relation between two stimulus events, the organism undergoes learning which in turn is reflected by a change in its behavior. Typically one event [the conditioned stimulus (CS)] is initially neutral and one [the unconditioned stimulus (US)] is initially potent, and typically the change in behavior observed is a modification of the response to the CS. But from the present viewpoint the essential feature is that the organism learns about interevent relations. This description of conditioning differs in many ways from those commonly employed; some of those differences will be discussed later. However, for the present, we will emphasize three aspects of this description which generated the three lines of research described below.

First, although characterizing Pavlovian conditioning as a modification resulting from relations arranged among events, the present description fails to specify any particular relations as critical. In this regard it departs from most traditional descriptions which emphasize temporal contiguity as the central relation involved in Pavlovian conditioning. This lack of specification is intentional because it suggests the important possibility that a wide range of relations may participate in Pavlovian conditioning. The first line of research described below begins an exploration of this possibility that the organism does indeed represent relations among worldly events with a richness far greater than sensitivity only to contiguity would imply.

Second, the present description of the learning which occurs in Pavlovian conditioning does not refer in detail to the organism's responding. Traditionally, the response has been the central organizing theme in discussions of Pavlovian conditioning. Indeed, Pavlovian preparations are normally described in terms of the response measured, e.g., salivary, cardiac, flexion, suppression, etc. But the above description neglects the response in favor of emphasizing the underlying learning from which that response stems. It is, of course, a well-rehearsed comment that cognitive accounts fail to anticipate the particular behaviors which will result from learning. In the second section below it is argued that this supposed failing is not without its virtues.

Third, the present description of conditioning seems to suggest that the organism learns about the events being related. In describing conditioning as learning about relations among events, we are encouraged to ask how the events themselves are represented. The present view suggests the possibility that the organism has a fairly rich knowledge of the events, a possibility to which the third section below speaks.

None of these features of a cognitive viewpoint can be rigorously deduced from an existing theory. Indeed, there has never been a fully developed cognitive theory of conditioning. Instead we have been offered, since Tolman, an orientation to the study of learning. The sections below constitute an argument that this orientation has some value.

I.   RELATIONS LEARNED IN PAVLOVIAN CONDITIONING

As noted above, Pavlovian conditioning has often been described in terms of a particular interevent relation: temporal contiguity of the CS and US. This relation is obviously a potent one, and it has often been thought that all Pavlovian learning could ultimately be deduced from the presence or absence of temporal coincidences. However, the description of conditioning used here suggests that attention to temporal contiguity should not preclude the study of other relations.

Much of the work which has come from our laboratory over the last several years can be seen as an attempt to expand the domain of interevent relations studied in Pavlovian settings. For instance, the contingency view of conditioning

(Rescorla, 1967) argues that descriptions in terms of contiguous occurrence of CS and US fail to capture the sophistication of the organism's sensitivity to relations. According to that view, the organism does not simply tabulate the number of times a CS is followed closely in time by a US. Rather it is sensitive to "informational" relations among events, as though asking the CS to accurately forecast the occurrence of the US. Thus this view attributes to the animal a broader perspective in developing excitatory Pavlovian conditioning: such conditioning occurs when the CS and US are positively correlated in time, so that the CS provides information that the likelihood of a US occurrence is temporarily increased. Equally, this view provides a place for the historically disreputable notion of inhibition: Inhibitory conditioning occurs when the CS and US are negatively correlated, so the CS provides information that the likelihood of the US is temporarily decreased.

This view of conditioning remains controversial. Some authors have continued to argue for the primacy of event contiguity (e.g., Gormezano & Kehoe, 1975). Even our own molecular theory (e.g., Rescorla & Wagner, 1972) has attempted to deduce sensitivity to such global event relations from individual instances of contiguity. It is not my intention here to review the kinds of data which the contingency view has generated nor to pursue the controversy over its accuracy. Rather, my point is that a more general cognitive outlook on Pavlovian conditioning encourages the exploration of various interevent relations. The contingency position is a small step in the direction of considering the role of some of those relations.

In the same spirit, the rest of this section emphasizes the possibility of studying another kind of interevent relation. One feature which both contiguity and contingency share is that they may be described in purely temporal terms, without reference to the qualitative properties of the events involved. With either of these relations, one of the events could be replaced by a qualitatively unrelated event of similar temporal extent without disrupting the relation. Indeed, this replaceability of one event by another has sometimes been seen as central to Pavlovian conditioning. But it is clear that other than temporal relations can be arranged among events. For instance, spatial relations, although studied extensively in instrumental learning, have only recently received exploration in the Pavlovian setting (e.g., Testa, 1975).

Moreover, as Rescorla and Holland (1976) note, many of the relations that can obtain among events refer to the qualitative properties of those events themselves. A prominent example is the relation of interevent similarity. One cannot arrange a similarity relation among events without reference to the qualitative properties of the events. It is abundantly clear that the organism is sensitive to interevent similarities and intuitively it seems plausible that such similarities should affect the formation of associations among the events. But relatively little attention has been paid to the possibility that relations of this sort participate in the formation of Pavlovian associative connections.

As a first step in exploring this possibility, we have recently asked whether arranging a similarity relation among two events modulates the success with which their contiguous presentation establishes conditioning. We describe the results here as an example that such relations are indeed effective and warrant further exploration with Pavlovian preparations. As such they illustrate the value of a cognitive view which encourages the study of many interevent relations.

A.   A Second-Order Conditioning Design

To address this question, we have made use of a second-order conditioning paradigm. This paradigm differs from simple Pavlovian conditioning in that the reinforcer used is not originally potent but rather has become so by virtue of its own past history. Thus in this procedure a neutral S_2 is regularly followed by an S_1 which has reinforcing power only because it has previously been paired with a US. We have argued elsewhere that such second-order conditioning has many analytic advantages in the study of Pavlovian associations, but in the present context one feature is particularly salient. Because we can select both S_1 and S_2 from a broad range of stimulus events, we have considerably greater freedom to arrange relations among events. Instead of searching the world for a US which is similar to some CS, we can pick two stimuli which are similar and convert one of them into a reinforcer. This brings under the control of the experimenter a considerable portion of the relation being studied because it potentially allows him to disentangle similarity among stimuli from other intrinsic properties of the individual stimulus events.

In principle, the design of this sort of experiment is straightforward. One simply performs second-order conditioning with similar stimuli and compares it with the conditioning obtained with dissimilar stimuli. But the actual experiments must be considerably more elaborate in order to avoid various trivial interpretations of the outcomes. For instance, we need to be sure that the actual events picked as S_1 and S_2 do not produce the observed outcome simply because a particular S_1 is more potent than another or because one S_2 is generally more conditionable than another. Our concern here is with the effect of the similarity *relationship* between S_1 and S_2, not with the potencies of the individual events themselves. Equally important, since learning theories have traditionally interpreted the effects of stimulus similarity in terms of generalization, we need to be sure that any observed superiority of second-order conditioning with similar stimuli is not attributable to that well-documented phenomenon. We are concerned with effects upon the formation of associations, not upon simple performance.

A design which goes some distance toward satisfying these objectives was employed in the two experiments to be described. We selected two pairs of stimuli such that the within-pair similarity was greater than that between pairs. One pair consisted of two tones, T_1 and T_2, which differed in pitch and rate of interruption; the second pair consisted of two lights, L_1 and L_2, which differed in intensity, location, and rate of interruption. One member of each pair, L_1 and T_1, was converted into a reinforcer by repeated pairing with a US. Then four second-order conditioning groups were formed. Two groups received T_2 as the second-order stimulus and two received L_2. One of each of these pairs had their second-order CS followed by L_1 and in addition received separate nonreinforced presentations of T_1. The other of each pair received T_1 as the reinforcer and in addition separate presentations of L_1. These design relations are shown in Fig. 1.

Three features of this design are worth noting. First, since in different groups each first-order CS serves as the reinforcer for each second-order CS, simple differences in potency between L_1 and T_1 or conditionability between L_2 and T_2 can be readily detected. Evidence that the similarity among events, rather than their individual properties, is important would take the form of T_2 being especially conditionable by T_1 rather than by L_2, and L_2 being especially conditionably by L_1 rather than by T_1.

Second, since all animals receive first-order conditioning with both T_1 and L_1, we can anticipate equivalent amounts of stimulus generalization to the target second-order stimuli. For instance, whether T_2 is followed by T_1 or L_1 during second-order conditioning, it should receive similar amounts of stimulus generalization from T_1. Thus a pattern of results like that described above could not readily be interpreted simply in terms of differential stimulus generalization.

Third, during the second-order conditioning portion of such a design, animals with the same target stimulus all receive the same individual events; they differ only in their relations. Consequently, any effects of the mere presence of a similar event during second-order conditioning should not be differential. That

FIRST-ORDER	SECOND-ORDER
$T_1+,\ L_1+$	$T_2 \longrightarrow T_1$, L_1
$T_1+,\ L_1+$	$T_2 \longrightarrow L_1$, T_1
$T_1+,\ L_1+$	$L_2 \longrightarrow T_1$, L_1
$T_1+,\ L_1+$	$L_2 \longrightarrow L_1$, T_1

FIG. 1.   Design of the second-order conditioning experiments for the study of stimulus-similarity effects upon association.

is, any group differences must result from the different temporal relations arranged among the same stimuli. This is the kind of evidence normally interpreted to mean there are differences in associative learning. Indeed, this procedure, which uses multiple reinforcers only one of which is paired with the CS, accomplishes many of the same goals achieved by a discriminative conditioning procedure, which uses multiple CSs only one of which is paired with the reinforcer.

We report here the application of this design with two conditioning preparations, conditioned suppression based upon an aversive US and conditioned activity based upon appetitive US.

B. Conditioned Suppression

In the conditioned suppression experiment (Rescorla & Furrow, 1977), four groups of eight rats each received initial bar-press training in a standard operant chamber until they were steady responders for food on a VI 2-min schedule. They then received first-order conditioned suppression training designed to convert T_1 and L_1 into fear elicitors but to leave the target second-order stimulus relatively neutral. The T_1 was a 250-Hz tone interrupted at the rate of one per second and L_1 was a two per second flashing of the normally off 6-W houselight. Each presentation of these stimuli was 30 sec long and terminated in a 1/2-mA 1/2-sec footshock. For the initial two days of first-order conditioning each stimulus was presented and reinforced twice while the animal engaged in bar pressing. Thereafter, a discrimination procedure was introduced during each day of which six nonreinforced 30-sec presentations of the target second-order CS were intermingled with one reinforced presentation each of tone (T_1+) and light (L_1+). This treatment continued until the initial generalization to the future second-order CS was attenuated. For those subjects for which the second-order stimulus was T_2 (steady 1,800-Hz tone) this stage was 4 days long; suppression to L_2 (steady illumination of a signal light located over the food magazine) was initially greater and required 14 days to eliminate. By the end of first-order training, all animals had substantial fear of T_1 and L_1 but little fear of their target second-order CS.

The animals were then ready to enter the phase of interest: second-order conditioning of T_2 and L_2. In order to slow second-order conditioning sufficiently to permit exposure of any differences due to similarity, a trace conditioning procedure was employed. In this procedure a 30-sec period without any stimulus intervened between the presentation of the 30-sec S_2 and the 30-sec S_1. On each day, the animals received three second-order conditioning trials with their designated first-order reinforcers, as shown in Fig. 1. Of course, on those trials no shock was delivered. In addition, each animal received three nonreinforced presentations of the other first-order CS. Finally, to maintain the value of the first-order stimuli, a single separate reinforced presentation of T_1

and L_1 was given on each day. Most of these trials were included to maintain equal numbers of presentations of the individual events across groups. Our main concern, however, was with the development of fear to the various second-order CSs.

The left-hand panels of Fig. 2 show the course of this second-order conditioning. This figure displays the suppression elicited by the second-order CS, as indexed by a ratio of the form $A/(A+B)$. Here A is the response rate during the CS and B the rate in a comparable period prior to CS onset. This ratio has the property that it yields a low value for very suppressive stimuli and one around .5 for stimuli which leave the behavior unaffected. The top left-hand panel shows the results of conditioning to T_2 when either L_1 or T_1 was the reinforcer; the bottom left-hand panel shows the comparable results for L_2.

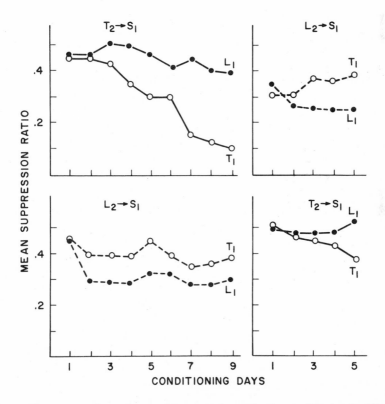

FIG. 2.   Mean suppression ratio over the course of second-order conditioning. In different pairs of groups either T_2 or L_2 served as the second-order stimuli whereas either T_1 or L_1 served as the first-order stimuli. The left-hand panels show the first phase of second-order conditioning; the right-hand panels show the results for the same groups with the second-order stimuli interchanged. (From Rescorla & Furrow, 1977. Copyright 1977 by the American Psychological Association. Reprinted by permission.)

When T_2 was followed by T_1, substantial second-order conditioning resulted; however, following that same stimulus with L_1 yielded very little suppression. Conversely, when L_2 was the target, more substantial conditioning was produced by the L_1 reinforcer than by T_1. Thus the judgment as to which reinforcer is the more powerful depends upon the target stimulus being conditioned. Furthermore, the pattern of data is such that relative amounts of learning are predicted by the similarity relations among S_2 and S_1: Similar stimuli produced more second-order conditioning.

To further check on these results, we interchanged treatments among groups following the collection of these data. Animals who had received second-order conditioning with T_2 were then given first-order discrimination and second-order conditioning with L_2. Similarly, those who had previously received L_2 were subjected to these treatments with T_2. Within each treatment, half the animals receiving a similar S_2 and S_1 had previously received dissimilar events and half had previously received similar events. The results of these additional treatments are shown in the right-hand panels of Fig. 2. These results substantially replicate those of the earlier phase of the experiment. When L_2 was the target CS, L_1 was a superior reinforcer; however, when T_2 was the target, T_1 was superior. Consequently, the results of this experiment provide initial support for a facilitative effect of interevent similarity in conditioning.

It should be commented that the levels of conditioning observed in this experiment were not large. Indeed, none of the groups receiving dissimilar stimuli showed reliable conditioning. The low levels of conditioning were intentionally produced by the use of a trace procedure. It seems possible that such conditions of minimal contiguity are especially likely to reveal a similarity effect, but we have no data on that point.

C. Appetitive Conditioning

In order to provide evidence on the generality of these effects, we have also employed this same design with a Pavlovian preparation using a food US. In this preparation (see Holland & Rescorla, 1975a) rats are conditioned in operant chambers with the levers removed. Conditioning consists of response-independent pairings of tones and lights with food pellets. One may use various measures to determine that the organism has learned associations from such treatments, measures ranging from general activity to detailed descriptions of response topography. Moreover, as will be discussed in more detail in the next section, the behavioral consequence of these associations seems to vary depending upon the particular CS employed. However, one consistent consequence is that a CS paired with food comes to provoke food-magazine-oriented behaviors. Moreover, if that CS is then paired with a neutral stimulus, it too provokes magazine behaviors. Consequently, the present study employed that measure in an attempt to assess the importance of interevent similarity.

Four groups of eight rats each were initially given first-order Pavlovian conditioning with two 10.5-sec stimuli, each containing a delivery of two 45-mg Noyes pellets during the last .5-sec. On each of 13 days the animals received two reinforced presentations of a flashing houselight mounted on the rear wall of the cage 25 cm above the grid floor (L_1), and two reinforced presentations of an interrupted 250-Hz tone (T_1). Intermingled with these trials were four non-reinforced presentations of a target second-order CS. For half the animals this was an 1,800-Hz steady tone (T_2) and for half it was a steady light mounted below the level of the cage (L_2). By the end of this first-order discrimination training, substantial conditioning was evident to T_1 and L_1, but T_2 and L_2 evoked little behavior.

Then second-order conditioning was begun. During each of 7 days, three second-order conditioning trials were given. These consisted of a 10-sec presentation of either T_2 or L_2 followed immediately by a 10.5-sec presentation of either T_1 or L_1. For any given animal the S_2 and S_1 were constant from trial to trial; however, each pairing was represented across groups. In addition, three nonreinforced presentations of the other first-order CS were given, as was one reinforced presentation of each first-order stimulus. As before, these additional trials match the frequencies of events across groups and maintain the values of the first-order stimuli.

Throughout conditioning, the behavior was monitored by an observational procedure. Trials were recorded on videotape and the responding subsequently classified into behavioral categories which are described in detail in the next section. For the purposes of this experiment, only those behaviors involved in approach to the food magazine were tabulated. During each 10-sec stimulus, an observer made eight recordings of the animal's behavior, at 1.25-sec intervals paced by an auditory signal.

Figure 3 displays the percentages of such observations which were classified as magazine-oriented behaviors for the second-order trials on the final day of conditioning. At the left of the figure are displayed the responses to the T_2, separated according to whether T_1 or L_1 was the reinforcer. The right are the comparable results from L_2. It is clear that T_2 and L_2 were not equivalent in the level of magazine responding they produced. This outcome agrees with other observations from our laboratory. Of more interest, for each second-order CS, the amount of conditioning was dependent upon the reinforcer. For T_2, pairings with T_1 produced more conditioning than did pairings with L_1; for L_2 the effectiveness of the reinforcers was reversed, with L_1 providing more conditioning than did T_1. Thus these results are in agreement with those from the conditioned suppression experiment reported above: Similar stimuli generated more second-order conditioning than did dissimilar stimuli.

Together, these two studies provide some empirical support for the proposition that the organism is sensitive to the qualitative relation among events when it forms Pavlovian associations. In themselves, of course, the results

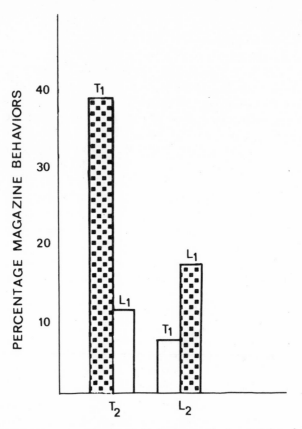

FIG. 3.   Mean percentage magazine-directed behaviors on the terminal day of second-order conditioning. Either T_2 or L_2 served as the second-order stimulus, whereas either T_1 or L_1 was the first-order stimulus used as a reinforcer.

are preliminary. They explore only one relation and, although the results are consistent, they are relatively small in magnitude. But they do encourage additional investigation of other relations. In this connection it may be noted that the relation of similarity may occupy a special place. Many of the relations which involve qualitative properties of the events may ultimately be reducible to similarity or shared elements. For this reason the similarity relation may serve not only as a model but also as a general rubric for a broad class of relations.

The kinds of investigation reported in this section have, of course, both historical theoretical and empirical antecedents. For instance, Testa (1975) has recently described some compatible results for first-order conditioning within a conditioned suppression paradigm. More impressively, there is now a substantial amount of research using illness-inducing agents which suggests that qualitative relations among the events being associated may determine the success of temporal contiguity.

One may note, however, several advantages of the present studies. First, they provide a somewhat more controlled context in which to investigate relations among qualitative features of events. For instance, the presentation of several reinforcing events to the same animal reduces the plausibility of various non-associative accounts which can be given for much of the currently available data (cf. Rescorla & Holland, 1976). Such alternatives have continued to plague previous reports (Foree & LoLordo, 1975).

More importantly, the use of second-order conditioning permits a flexibility of analysis not possible with unconditioned reinforcers. By making available broad classes of stimuli for investigation, it allows the study of many relations. Moreover, selection among those stimuli should permit more precise identification of those aspects of a relation among two stimuli which affect the formation of associations. It allows us to evaluate the contribution of various stimulus features, such as effective event duration or overall potency, which might otherwise be confounded with the relation of interest.

In addition to their empirical antecedents, the present experiments also have theoretical predecessors. The notion that similarity among events may be a condition of association has, of course, been frequently entertained by students of association. It is important to note, however, that "association by similarity" has historically referred not to the conditions governing the formation of associations but rather to the conditions of recall. In its historical usage, that phrase is actually closer to the modern concept of stimulus generalization. Although recognizing this difference, Köhler (1941) argued that perhaps similarity also affects the formation of associations. This argument was part of Köhler's general claim that perceptual features of events affect learning and that the formation of associations cannot proceed independently of the content of the items being associated. Moreover, Köhler reported paired-associate experiments with humans which are, in their logical design, very similar to those reported here for Pavlovian conditioning. He too found that similarity seemed to facilitate the effects of contiguity.

Experiments like these are only a small beginning. But perhaps they will call attention to the important problem of exploring various relations among stimuli. And perhaps they suggest a technique which facilitates that exploration.

II.   RELATION BETWEEN LEARNING AND RESPONDING

A second prominent feature of the present description of Pavlovian conditioning is characteristic of most cognitive views. The organism is seen as learning relations among events and then generating its behavior based upon that learning. Knowledge about the world is explicitly separated from the behavioral index of that knowledge. Of course, a learning-performance distinction is not limited to cognitive approaches, but it is central to such orientations.

One consequence of that distinction is that we are encouraged to look broadly at behavior in an attempt to identify the learning which has occurred. It is most common in Pavlovian conditioning experiments to use a particular type of behavior during a particular time as the index of learning. We normally anticipate that as a result of CS-US pairings the behavior during the CS will change so as to be more like that during the US. But the present view sees such changes as only one possible index of the organism's learning. If our interest lies in detecting the organism's knowledge about interevent relations, then any behaviors which are differential as a result of exposure to a relation are potentially of interest. Responses which are apparently unrelated to the UR or which occur at times other than the CS also deserve examination. Indeed, changes other than in the ability of stimuli to evoke responses, such as changes in their reinforcing power, are also of interest as potential indices of Pavlovian conditioning.

A related consequence of such an explicit learning-performance distinction will occupy our attention in this section. This view suggests that many features of the conditioning situation may influence the manner in which the same Pavlovian conditioning is exhibited in performance. We are, of course, accustomed to the idea that the US determines the nature of the observed CR. That influence is usually ascribed to differences in the learning which different USs produce. The present view suggests that there are other determinants of performance, determinants which modulate the exhibition of otherwise common learning. We describe below one such example, the nature of the CS.

A. CS as a Determinant of Performance

Several cognitive theorists (e.g., Bindra, 1974; Bolles, 1972; Tolman, 1932) have argued that the detailed features of the CS may affect the nature of the response observed in Pavlovian conditioning. However, aside from the recent studies of autoshaping (see Hearst & Jenkins, 1974) and scattered casual reports from early experiments on conditioning, there is little systematic evidence on this point. Consequently, to emphasize the value of the present approach, we have begun to explore this possibility in more detail. Our question is whether similar Pavlovian learning about relations among events might result in widely different index behaviors, behaviors determined in part by the nature of the CS employed.

We took as our starting point a rather unsettling observation we had made in the course of some activity-conditioning experiments (Holland & Rescorla, 1975a). Those experiments used an appetitive-conditioning procedure like that described in the preceding section but they measured the general activity of the rat during the CS. Upon pairing tone CSs with food USs, we observed rather standard acquisition curves, with increases in general activity similar to those reported by others (e.g., Zamble, 1967). However, when we paired light CSs with that same food, we found little or no activity increases during the CS.

One obvious possibility was that the animals had only poorly learned the light-food relation. But that possibility was easily discarded because of the results of a subsequent phase of the experiment which provided an alternative index of the animal's knowledge of the CS-US relation. That same light proved very effective as a reinforcer for establishing second-order conditioning to an antecedent neutral tone. Moreover, the light's reinforcing power was dependent upon its own history of pairing with the food. Thus we had evidence that the animal had learned both the light-food and the tone-food relation, but apparently the behaviors evoked by those CSs were sufficiently different that only the latter learning was indexed by general activity. Those results suggested an important dependency of the CR upon the CS, but they were very indirect. Consequently, Holland (1977) has recently carried out a series of experiments employing direct behavioral observations in an attempt to identify the different behaviors underlying the general activity results.

Holland's first experiment employed a discriminative-conditioning paradigm so as to permit observation of the behaviors to CSs when they were either followed by food or were nonreinforced. Conditioning was carried out in standard operant chambers with the levers removed. Those chambers were mounted on the previously used activity devices, which consisted of two horizontal plywood plates, separated by self-centering ball bearings. A metal plumbob was suspended from the upper plate so as to hang inside a metal ring. When the animal showed activity, the top plate moved slightly, causing the bob to strike the ring; those contacts were recorded as activity counts. Four such apparatuses were placed in sound attenuating shells. The front doors of the shells were left open, and a 6-W jewel lamp over the magazine was continuously illuminated, so as to permit observation of the animal's behavior.

Two groups of eight rats each received initial magazine training and pre-testing of the stimuli to be conditioned. They then received eight sessions of discriminative conditioning with two 45-mg Noyes pellets as the US. During each session, all animals received four 10.5-sec presentations each of a two per second flashing of the houselight (mounted on the rear wall of the shell 25 cm above the grid floor) and of a steady 1,800-Hz tone. For the animals in Group L—T+ the final .5 sec of the tone was accompanied by the delivery of the food, but the light was nonreinforced. For Group L+T— the reinforcement contingencies were reversed.

Throughout the experiment an observer recorded the animal's behavior using a checklist procedure modeled on that of Shettleworth (1975) but adapted to preliminary observations in our laboratory. Each rat was observed twice during each stimulus presentation; for each observation the behavior was classified into one of six categories: (1) any locomotion, including rapid circling and darting, was labeled "perambulate"; (2) any time the rat's front paws were off the grid and he was not grooming, it was recorded "rearing"; (3) passive sitting with the head in the food magazine was called "magazine"; (4) rapid and jerky movements of the head (usually in and around the food magazine) were labeled "head-jerk"; (5) head jerking also accompanied by rapid movement of the hindquarters was labeled "head-jerk/hind.' Finally, (6) all other behaviors, including grooming, were labeled "quiet." Only one behavior was recorded for each observation; but in addition the organism's orientation was noted. These categories were standardized with a second observer and could be rapidly judged with good interobserver reliability [see Holland (1977) for further details of procedure].

In this experiment, as in our previous work, tones paired with food rapidly developed the ability to increase general activity; nonreinforced tones, as well as both reinforced and nonreinforced lights, failed to increase activity. But the data of principle interest are the detailed behavioral observations. These are shown over the course of conditioning in Fig. 4. Looking first at the behavior of Group L–T+ during the reinforced tone (lower-right panel), notice that three behaviors, all primarily oriented toward the food magazine, predominated: head jerking,

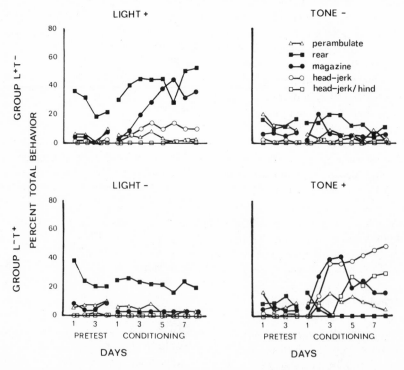

FIG. 4.   Observational data from pretest and discrimination training in Groups L+T– (upper panels) and L–T+ (lower panels). The responses to the reinforced and nonreinforced stimuli are displayed separately. The dependent variable is the percentage of all observations which fall in a given behavior category. (From Holland, 1977. Copyright 1977 by the American Psychological Association. Reprinted by permission.)

head-jerk/hind, and passive magazine behavior. Early in conditioning the passive magazine behavior grew rapidly, but as conditioning progressed it gave way to the more vigorous head-jerk/hind behavior. Rearing and perambulate were infrequent responses to the conditioned tone. That these magazine-directed behaviors were the result of tone-food pairing is confirmed by their failure to appear as responses to the nonreinforced tone in Group L+T− (upper-right panel).

A quite different pattern of behaviors was observed for Group L+T− during the reinforced light (upper-left panel). Both passive magazine responses and rearing grew during conditioning of the light, whereas there was little change in the other behaviors. Again, however, these changes depended upon the light being paired with food; the frequency of these behaviors was less during the nonreinforced light of Group L−T+ (lower-left panel). Comparison between the two stimuli which were reinforced indicates that rearing and passive magazine behaviors were more frequent in the reinforced light than in the reinforced tone; the converse was true for head jerking and head-jerk/hind behaviors.

Two other differential behaviors, which are not shown in this figure, should also be mentioned. First, the reinforced tone tended to provoke an immediate startle and circling response at its onset, whereas none of the other stimuli did. Second, although Fig. 4 ignores the temporal distribution of behaviors within the CS, it is worth noting that differences among stimuli appear in temporal pattern as well as in overall frequency.

A trial-by-trial analysis of the activity measure and the occurrence of these behaviors reveals the reason for our failure to see activity increases during reinforced lights. It is predominantly rapid lateral movements, such as head jerking, walking, head-jerk/hind, and the initial startle response, which produce activity counts. Passively sitting in front of the magazine and rearing have little effect upon our activity device.

Thus this experiment confirmed our initial suspicion that different CSs, although paired with the same US, come to provoke different behavior patterns. With both the light and the tone there is substantial evidence of learning, but one must look to different behavioral indices to see that learning.

Before commenting more on the implications of such findings, however, it is important to speak to one potentially uninteresting interpretation. It is possible that by its mere presence a stimulus may constrain the responses which an animal can make. For instance, the stimulus may elicit an unconditioned response which interacts with the response established by conditioning to produce the observed behavior. If the stimuli differ in the nature of that unconditoned response (as the pretest data shown in Fig. 4 suggest they do), then different overt responses would be expected. To examine this possibility, Holland presented all animals at the end of the experiment with a nonreinforced compound stimulus consisting of the light and tone together. During that test all animals received the same physical stimulus; but, of course, they differed in which component had previously been paired with food. Nevertheless, the responses observed during those compounds were quite distinctive and depended upon which component had been conditioned. Indeed, the organism's reaction to the compound was very similar to that evoked by the trained component presented singly. Thus, these data suggest that the mere physical presence of one or the other stimulus together with the unconditioned responses it controls, is not importantly responsible for the differences in CRs observed here.

B.   Evidence for Common Associative Learning with Different CSs

From the present point of view, the interesting feature of the Holland data is the possibility that they display different behaviors based upon the same underlying associative structure. That is, they suggest that the translation of the organism's Pavlovian learning into performance is affected by the properties of the CS. However, the claim that these different behaviors result from a common associative learning is based largely upon a procedural similarity: both the light and tone were repeatedly followed by food. Although it is plausible to interpret this procedural similarity as establishing similar learning, it remains possible that the actual learning does differ. For instance, some authors have suggested the plausible idea that reinforcers should be viewed as events with multiple components (e.g., Estes, 1969). Moreover, various aspects of a conditioning situation might influence which of those US features participate in the association (cf. Konorski, 1967). Thus it is possible that different CSs might be especially associable with different features. In that case, the light and the tone might select different features of the reinforcer for participation in their respective associations; consequently, what the animal learns about the US might be different when different CSs are used. Differences in behavior evoked by those different CSs would then simply reflect the acknowledged fact that the CR depends upon the US.

This is an interesting alternative possibility which Holland (1977) attempted to evaluate in two further experiments. Both of these experiments followed the orientation of the present view by providing alternative measures of the learning which results from tone-food and light-food pairings. The first evaluated learning in terms of the ability of the CS to block conditioning to another CS, whereas the second employed second-order conditioning as a procedure for detecting the success of first-order conditioning. Because these experiments not only bear on the present issue but also give some general information about conditioning, they are briefly described here.

1. *Blocking.* In a standard blocking experiment, two groups of animals receive a compound stimulus, *AB,* which is followed by reinforcement. However, for one group, *A* has previously been singly presented and paired with reinforcement. For that group the addition of *B* and the continuation of the same

reinforcement results in little conditioning of B (e.g., Kamin, 1968, 1969). On the other hand, a group without previous A reinforcement gains substantial conditioning to B as a result of AB reinforcement. Various theoretical accounts are available for this phenomenon, but current theories all appeal to the observation that in the first group B is redundant because the reinforcement is already well predicted by A. Those interpretations all receive support from the observation that changes in the reinforcer which occur at the same time as B is introduced enable B to acquire conditioning (e.g., Kamin, 1969). When AB is followed by a different reinforcer than was used with A alone, then B becomes informative and develops conditioning.

The issue in the present context is whether a light and tone which evoke disparate responses following their pairing with food can nevertheless play the roles of A and B, successfully blocking each other. To the degree that their functional reinforcers are the same and the underlying learning therefore similar, blocking would be expected to occur; to the degree that their different responses are attributable to selection of different aspects of the reinforcer, blocking might fail.

To examine this question, Holland trained three groups of rats with different initial conditioning treatments. Two treatments (Groups L+T— and L—T+) were intended to establish one stimulus as an excitor (A) and leave the other stimulus "neutral" to play subsequently the role of B. These animals received four 10.5-sec presentations each of the 1,800-Hz tone and the flashing houselight. For one group, the light was paired with food and the tone nonreinforced; the roles of the stimuli were reversed in the other group. A third group served as a control with neither stimulus reinforced; these animals received the same light and tone presentations and additionally four deliveries of pellets explicitly unpaired with those stimuli. This initial conditioning phase continued for eight sessions.

In the second phase of the experiment, all animals received 4 days of compound stimulus conditioning on each of which eight 10.5-sec presentations of the light-tone compound were reinforced. Finally, to assess conditioning of the individual stimuli, two test sessions were given, during each of which there were four nonreinforced light and four nonreinforced tone presentations.

This experiment measured both general activity and the detailed behaviors described above. However, the introduction of the videotape system described in the previous section resulted in three changes from Holland's first experiment. First, there was a loss of resolution, making difficult the distinction between head-jerk and head-jerk/hind behaviors; consequently, these behaviors were no longer separated and the latter label was not employed. Second, in order to protect the low-light TV camera from direct exposure to the houselight CS, a black mask was placed over the houselight. Unfortunately this also changed the stimulus presented to the subject and resulted in a changed CR topography during the light, which took the form of a reduction in the relative proportion of rearing in favor of more frequent passive magazine behavior. Nevertheless, clearly distinctive behavior patterns remained to the light and tone. Finally, permanent records of the sessions permitted more detailed temporal measurement, so that eight observations were made for each animal in each CS.

The observational data from the last day of initial conditioning and the 8 days of compound conditioning are shown for each group in the left-hand panels of Fig. 5. The patterns at the end of initial conditioning are reminiscent of those from the previous experiment. The trained tone in Group L—T+ showed more passive magazine behavior and some rearing. Behaviors to the nonreinforced stimuli in all three groups were quite low and are not shown to avoid cluttering the figure. With the institution of compound stimulus conditioning, those groups with previous element conditioning responded as they had to their trained element alone, thus continuing to display differential behaviors. This confirms the observation mentioned earlier that the response to the identical compound depends upon which element has been conditioned. The animals without prior

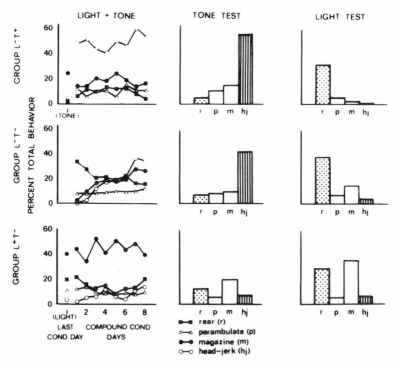

FIG. 5.   Observational data from the blocking experiment. The left-hand panels show the results for the final day of initial conditioning and for each day of compound stimulus conditioning. The middle- and right-hand panels show the results for the nonreinforced test session. The data from groups with prior tone reinforcement, prior light reinforcement and unpaired food presentations are shown in the upper, bottom, and middle rows, respectively. (From Holland, 1977. Copyright 1977 by the American Psychological Association. Reprinted by permission.)

element conditioning (Group L–T–) showed evidence of learning during this phase of the experiment. That learning was exhibited as a compromise between the behavior patterns of the other two groups: intermediate levels of head jerking, passive magazine, and rearing.

The results of most interest are those of the nonreinforced test presentations of tone and light which followed compound-stimulus conditioning. These are shown in the middle and right-hand panels of Fig. 5. During this test the animals in the control group (L–T–) showed evidence that some conditioning had occurred to both the tone and light. Moreover, the conditioning was evidenced by the occurrence of the appropriate distinctive behaviors to those stimuli. That is, the tone promoted head jerking whereas the light generated passive magazine behavior. Neither of those responses was as large as the comparable behaviors to the separately trained stimuli in the experimental groups, suggesting the possibility of overshadowing. Most important, however, these responses in the control group were larger than those evoked by the added (B) elements of the experimental groups. That is, the control group showed more head jerking to the tone than did Group L+T–, suggesting blocking of conditioning to the tone by prior conditioning of the light; similarly, the light produced more magazine behavior in the control group than in Group L–T+, suggesting blocking of conditioning to the light in the latter group. Despite the fact that the light and tone evoked quite different behaviors, the prior conditioning of one stimulus allowed it to block conditioning to the other. This outcome argues for substantial commonality in the learning established to these stimuli.

This conclusion is supported by the patterns of two other behaviors (not shown in Fig. 5) which occur only during the tone: general activity and the startle response produced by tone onset. Prior conditioning with the light enabled it to block the development of both those behaviors to the tone as a result of compound stimulus conditioning in Group L+T–.

Three further comments should be made about the results of this experiment. First, they suggest that the peripheral response is not critical for the occurence of blocking. Most blocking experiments use stimuli which evoke similar CRs and so fail to disentangle the occurrence of a particular response from the history of pairing with a particular reinforcer. The present data indicate that a response need not be evoked by A for it to block the development of that response to B on $AB+$ trials. A related finding has been reported by Blanchard and Honig (1976). Such outcomes are a particular instance of the general theme of most cognitive approaches, that responding need not be intimately involved in Pavlovian conditioning. The present instance is of particular interest since it applies to the rules governing the effectiveness of a reinforcer.

Second, it is worth noting that the test results were very well forecast by the animal's behavior during the compound stimulus phase of the experiment. Throughout that phase the differential history of element conditioning in the various groups remained obvious in their response to the compound. This observation suggests that situations like the present one, in which different elements of a compound evoke different conditioned responses, could be very useful analytically. They permit us to track continuously the conditioning of the individual elements during compound stimulus conditioning itself, making less necessary the potentially disruptive test presentations of the elements. One may note a similar consequence of a sequential-compound stimulus used by Fowler (see Chapter 5).

Finally, the development of distinctive response patterns to the stimuli in Group L–T– warrants some comment. That result speaks to another class of alternative interpretations of the present results. One might entertain the possibility that when any CS precedes a US delivery, that CS to some extent modifies the nature of the UR. If so, then light and tone, when separately presented prior to food, could result in the food provoking different URs and thus generating different conditioning. However, in Group L–T– of the present experiment, a common stimulus event preceded food; yet the behaviors which were later controlled by the elements of that stimulus were quite distinctive. That outcome suggests that the differential behaviors controlled by light and tone in these experiments do not originate from such a UR modification.

The important point about the present experiment here, however, is its implication for the similarity in the learning responsible for the behaviors evoked by the tone and light. To the degree that blocking can be used as an alternative measure of conditioning, these data suggest commonality of conditioning for these stimuli.

2. *Second-order conditioning.* Holland (1977) also examined another measure of the learning gained by these light and tones. Following our earlier work, he used the ability of these stimuli to serve as reinforcers for the second-order conditioning of a third stimulus as an index of their learning. He reasoned that if their disparate behaviors stem from common learning, then when used as reinforcers in a second-order conditioning paradigm they might produce comparable behaviors to an antecedent signal. On the other hand, to the degree that they govern different learning, the light and tone might condition different behaviors to an antecedent stimulus. Consequently, he attempted to second-order condition an interrupted 250-Hz tone with each of these stimuli.

For this purpose two groups of rats were given a treatment much like that of the similarity experiments reported in the first section of this paper. They initially received first-order discriminative conditioning, designed to establish conditioning to the light and to the 1,800-Hz (high) tone but to leave the 250-Hz (low) tone relatively neutral for use in the subsequent phase. During each of 11 first-order-conditioning days, each animal received two reinforced presentations each of the light and the 1,800-Hz tone together with four non-reinforced presentations of the low tone. As in previous experiments, the reinforced stimuli were 10.5 sec long with food delivered during the final .5 sec.

Then second-order conditioning began, during each day of which eight animals received three pairings of the 10-sec low tone with the high tone; seven animals received three pairings of the low tone with the light. To equate the occurrence of individual stimuli across the groups, each animal also received three non-reinforced presentations of the other first-order CS. Finally, a single reinforced presentation of each first-order CS was given to maintain the values of those stimuli. Second-order conditioning continued for ten days.

Throughout the experiment, responding to the light and high tone was clearly differential, along the lines of previous experiments. The only point requiring comment is that the mask used to shield the camera from the house-light in the preceding experiment was moved so as to reinstitute direct visual access to the light for the rat. That change resulted in the return of substantial rearing during the first-order light.

The results of more interest, those from the second-order conditioning of the low tone, are shown in Fig. 6. The left-hand panel displays the behaviors conditioned when the light was the reinforcer; those resulting from the high-tone reinforcer are shown on the right. The course of conditioning in these two groups showed a remarkably similar pattern. Both displayed an initial increase in passive-magazine responding, followed by a gradual loss of this behavior. Both also showed a slower but more substantial rise in the frequency of head jerking, again followed by a loss. And finally, both showed a slower and less substantial rise in both perambulation and rearing.

These data suggest that the light was the more potent reinforcer, with each behavior developing somewhat earlier in conditioning. But aside from differences

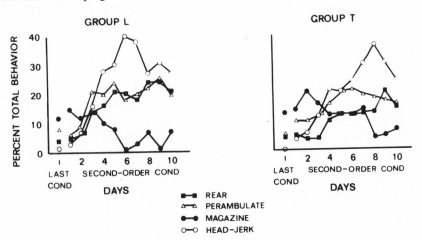

FIG. 6.   Observational data from second-order conditioning of a low tone. The left-hand panel displays the results when light was the reinforcer; the right-hand panel shows the results obtained from using a high tone as the reinforcer. (From Holland, 1977. Copyright 1977 by the American Psychological Association. Reprinted by permission.)

in rate of learning, the outcomes of second-order conditioning with these two very different response evokers were highly similar in overall pattern. It appears as though the response during the low tone was determined by its properties, not the responses controlled by the various reinforcers. Of course, our particular observational categories may have neglected some behavioral differences, but these results are consistent with the tone and light controlling similar learning.

It is worth noting several further points about these second-order conditioning results. First, several of the indices of second-order conditioning showed a peak level of responding and then fell off as pairing continued. This result is not surprising in the context of previous second-order conditioning results (e.g., Rescorla, 1973). Many second-order conditioning experiments result in the eventual development of conditioned inhibition.

Second, this experiment suggests a way in which we might hope to solve a difficult problem raised by the general pattern of results reported in this section. If different CSs result in different conditioned responses, how can one compare the levels of conditioning which they control? Surely we cannot take any one response as a measure; just as surely we cannot compare the frequencies of responses with different topographies. However, by using these stimuli to condition a common third stimulus perhaps we can at least measure their reinforcing power in common terms. That is, second-order conditioning may provide a way of converting into comparable behavioral units amounts of conditioning which are otherwise reflected in incommensurate units.

The third point suggests a limitation on that conclusion. Notice that the present experiment is parallel in design to the similarity studies described in the first section of this paper. Apparently, in the present case the high tone and flashing light were different enough in individual salience to mask any S_2-S_1 similarity effect. But the previous results suggest that under some circumstances such similarity will modulate the effectiveness of S_1 as a reinforcer. That outcome argues for caution in assessing the comparability of conditioning among first-order stimuli based upon their ability to produce second-order conditioning of any one target stimulus.

Finally, these results provide some information on the nature of second-order conditioning itself. We have elsewhere (Rescorla, 1973) distinguished among several possible associative bases for second-order conditioning: S_2-S_1 associations, S_2-US associations, and associations between S_2 and the conditioned response evoked by S_1. On the basis of various kinds of data, some of which are mentioned in the next section, we have argued that neither S_2-S_1 nor S_2-US associations provide a complete account of second-order conditioning. Rather, we have suggested that during such conditioning S_2 becomes associated with the reaction evoked by S_1. But the present results argue against any simple notion that the peripheral response observed to the first-order CS is directly associated with the second-order CS. Despite evoking different responses, light and high tone established similar second-order behavior to the low tone. Moreover, this data pattern also seems incompatible with an interpretation in terms of S_2-S_1 associations in which S_2 simply makes use of the response currently controlled by S_1 in the manner of a mediated chain.

One interpretation which remains consistent with these data is that any S_1 comes to evoke an emotional or affective response. Second-order conditioning might particularly result in the establishment of that emotional reaction to S_2. That is, following second-order conditioning the organism may recall that some positive (or negative) experience occurred following S_2 without encoding either the details of what occasioned that experience or what overt behaviors were performed. The overt response then observed to S_2 would be determined by the same factors which are operative in producing first-order behavior, e.g., the nature of the CS. This issue is further discussed below.

3. *Some further implications.* As a set, the experiments in this section suggest that although pairing various CSs with a common US produces similar learning, that learning may be very differently reflected in behavior. This observation has several implications for the study of conditioning.

First, it casts a different light on the historically important issue of the similarity between the response to the CS and that to the US. If CRs vary with the properties of the CS, then their similarity to the UR will also vary. Thus any conclusion about CR-UR similarity may turn out to be highly specific to the CS being studied. This point has been made by a number of authors (e.g., Konorski, 1967), usually in the service of defending one position or another on the issue of CR-UR similarity. In the context of the present cognitive view of conditioning, variation in the similarity between the CR and UR is not at all surprising.

Second, the observation that the exhibition of learning is dependent upon the CS must make one skeptical of any one response as a measure of conditioning. It suggests the distressing possibility that different response measures would give different answers to questions about the relative amounts of conditioning controlled by different CSs. Even well-counterbalanced conditioning experiments like the similarity designs reported here or their counterparts in the toxicosis literature may give misleading information if only one response measure is employed. To a substantial extent this is the point made by Zener (1937), when he argued for broader observation of behavior during Pavlovian CSs. But the issue goes beyond simply missing the CR to some stimuli; it makes any evaluation of relative amounts of conditioning difficult. At the very least the results encourage multiple assessments of association.

Finally, we should acknowledge that our discussion has followed in the cognitive tradition of pointing to response variability but failing to specify why particular responses are the province of particular CSs. This remains an unsatisfactory state of affairs but one which the present preparation may offer some hope of improving. This preparation gives us an independent variable which reliably manipulates the CR. That should be a substantial step forward in the attempt to analyze the way in which Pavlovian associations are mapped into behavior. Moreover, because this preparation admits of a wide range of stimuli and a richness of description of responses to those stimuli, it should have special flexibility in approaching the problem. We have begun to explore this problem, but our results are too scattered to suggest many general principles, let alone the bases for those principles. I will just mention very briefly something of what we do know on the basis of Holland's initial work.

In our situation, stimulus modality is very important. A range of auditory stimuli give predominantly head-jerking and initial startle response as CRs but fail to support large amounts of rearing. Visual stimuli, on the other hand, give relatively fewer head-jerking and startle responses. Second, intermittency of the CS has little apparent effect upon the nature of the CR. Third, with visual stimuli, both the degree of diffuseness and the place of localization matter. Localized stimuli tend to promote rearing, especially if the source is located above the animal. Finally, within the ranges so far studied, stimulus intensity seems unimportant.

One can, of course, entertain many hypotheses about the bases for appearance of various CRs. For instance, some components of the conditioned behaviors described here seem forecast by the unconditioned response to the CS on its first presentation. Rearing to the light and startle to the tone are responses of this sort. Responses like these, which are augmented by the arranging of conditioning relations, might encourage the view that conditioning enhances the orienting response (e.g., Sokolov, 1963). Alternatively, one might suppose that one result of Pavlovian conditioning is to endow the CS with various instrumentally rewarding or punishing properties. The observed response to a CS might then be governed by the animal's attempt to enhance or minimize exposure to that CS. Such an exhibition of Pavlovian conditioning through the execution of instrumental performance seems to capture part of what Tolman (1932) and Zener (1937) had in mind when they described the Pavlovian CR as "appropriate." More recent versions have been suggested by Mowrer (1960) and Bindra (1974), among others. Or, it might be, as has recently been suggested in the context of autoshaping, that the CS comes to substitute for the US in such a way that the organism behaves toward it in the same way it would if the CS were a reinforcer.

These are samples of some of the more detailed hypotheses which would acknowledge the dependence of the CR upon the nature of the CS. The present data are not particularly well suited to choosing among these nor to differentiating them from a variety of other accounts. Indeed, it seems unlikely that all features of the CR share a common origin. The mapping of Pavlovian associations into behavior is likely to be multiply determined. It is one contribution of more cognitive approaches to conditioning to point to the disengagement of the underlying learning from the exhibition of any particular response, and hence to encourage the study of just such problems.

III.   REPRESENTATION OF THE REINFORCER

The description of Pavlovian conditioning given here refers to the learning of relations among events. This suggests that the organism must also represent those events themselves. That suggestion is consistent with a traditional cognitive orientation which attributes to the animal a fairly rich memory for the events of its world. That attribution is particularly frequent in the conceptualization of the reinforcer. For instance, Tolman (1932) made clear his assumption that the organism learns *about* the reinforcer, not simply *because* of the reinforcer. The features of the reinforcer not only determine whether or not learning occurs, they also participate in the content of that learning. More recently, Irwin (1971) has emphasized the centrality of the notion of expectancy in a cognitive orientation. By this he means not simply that the organism behaves in advance of an event but also that it anticipates the particular event in some detail. These views suggest that individual event representations participate in the learning and consequently in the production of behavioral outcomes of conditioning experiments. Behavior is generated both because the organism knows a relation (e.g., it expects one event to be followed by another) and because it has knowledge of and feelings toward the event itself (e.g., it is highly valued). Consequently, one would anticipate that changes in either the knowledge about the relation or in the value of the event representations themselves would modify the organism's behavior. It is the latter possibility that interests us here.

Tolman's laboratory, of course, generated many attempts to test this sort of proposition for the performance of instrumentally learned behaviors. Considerable subsequent work has borne out the initial findings of the sensitivity of instrumental performance to reward values and changes in those values. By far the most frequent class of accounts for such sensitivity has involved an appeal to differences in the associative structure of an underlying Pavlovian conditioning which is presumed to modulate instrumental performance. That is, for instrumental performance the notion of reinforcer representation has frequently been analyzed not in terms of event learning but rather in terms of Pavlovian associations. But until quite recently there have been very few studies of event representation and its importance in the Pavlovian situation itself, where such an appeal seems less satisfactory.

In recent years, our laboratory has approached this problem with a number of Pavlovian preparations. Our general strategy has been to intrude after the completion of Pavlovian conditioning so as to modify aspects of the reinforcer representation, while leaving the organism's knowledge of relations as unchanged as possible. To this point we have largely attempted to change the reinforcing power of the US after conditioning.

In one series of studies we first carried out Pavlovian fear conditioning with aversive USs such as a shock or a loud klaxon and then separately treated the reinforcer (Rescorla, 1973). For instance, we presented the klaxon repeatedly in an attempt to make it less aversive; we knew that doing this prior to conditioning would reduce its subsequent reinforcing power. Of interest here is the observation that this also reduced the fear controlled by a CS previously paired with that klaxon. Similarly, we have found ways to augment the reinforcing power of shock prior to its use in conditioning; when administered after a CS has been paired with the shock, these techniques also increased the fear controlled by that CS. Thus procedures designed to enhance or degrade the representation of aversive reinforcers can, at least with some reinforcers, also modify the behavior previously conditioned by those reinforcers.

A related set of experiments has suggested that changes in the reinforcer representation participate not only in conditioning but also in extinction. Rescorla and Heth (1975) found that the simple application of an unsignalled shock was often sufficient to reinstate to a previously trained and extinguished CS a substantial portion of its fear response. On the basis of experiments designed to rule out a number of common alternative interpretations, they suggested that part of the decrement observed during extinction is attributable to degradation of the reinforcer representation. That degradation can be reversed by simple reexposure to the reinforcer, independently of the presentation of CSs.

Moreover, results of these sorts are not confined to aversive reinforcers. Holland and Rescorla (1975b) have reported that the activity which is conditioned to a CS signaling food delivery undergoes modification if that food is subsequently reduced in value by its being paired with high-speed rotation. Consequently, there has been developing a pattern of data which suggests that the reinforcer is represented and participates in the association underlying many examples of Pavlovian conditioning.

One striking feature of these results has been our failure to find parallel outcomes within second-order conditioning paradigms. Various attempts at modifying the reinforcer (i.e., the first-order CS) in that paradigm have had little impact upon second-order responding (Rizley & Rescorla, 1972; Holland & Rescorla, 1975a). Similarly, alterations in the original reinforcer for the first-order CS have been ineffective in modifying second-order performance, although they concurrently affect first-order responding. These findings have suggested a difference in the reinforcer encoding to which we will return later.

Rather than review in detail this pattern of data, I want to emphasize one example of it. In this example, the reinforcer was modified not by a manipulation normally thought to involve learning but rather by changes in the motivational state of the animal. The intention in describing the following two experiments is fourfold. First, they illustrate the data pattern briefly described above. Second, they permit us to note the way in which a cognitive view introduces motivation into the performance of Pavlovian conditioning and to provide some evidence relevant to that view. Third, they give some initial information on the detail with which the reinforcer is encoded. And finally, they point to a general limitation on the power of changes in reinforcer representation to change Pavlovian performance.

The first of these two experiments was reported by Holland and Rescorla (1975b). Using the general activity device described previously, we carried out first-order Pavlovian appetitive conditioning in two groups of rats (designated 1-S and 1-D) by pairing a 1,800-Hz tone with a two-pellet reinforcer. We also ran two other groups (2-S and 2-D) which received that tone followed by a flashing light which had itself previously been paired with food. Thus in two groups the tone came to produce activity through first-order conditioning, and in two it did so through second-order conditioning. Since all groups had received the history of light-food pairings, they were alike except in whether first- or second-order conditioning had been carried out with the tone. After completing conditioning, one group from each pair was satiated (as indicated by the S in the group designation). This was accomplished by making standard laboratory chow constantly available in the home cage, as well as by providing access to a dish of the Noyes-pellet reinforcer prior to each testing session. The other group from each pair (labeled with a D) continued on deprivation. While under these motivational conditions, each animal received nonreinforced test presentations of the tone CS.

Figure 7 shows the tone-generated activity counts at the end of conditioning and over the course of extinction testing. Terminal acquisition performance was substantial and reasonably similar for the first- and second-order CSs. However, satiation during testing markedly reduced the activity occasioned by the first-order CS (Group 1-S vs. 1-D). That effect upon first-order CSs was immediate, grew during testing, and then declined as extinction occurred. More surprisingly, there was no comparable effect upon performance to the second-order CS (Group 2-S vs. 2-D). Indeed, second-order conditioning was sufficiently well maintained that under conditions of satiation, responding to it exceeded responding to the first-order CS. The right-hand portion of Fig. 7 shows the results of additional testing after redeprivation. Here, too, first-order conditioning showed a sensitivity to motivational changes while second-order conditioning did not. For the first-order CS, extinction while sated had a smaller decremental effect upon subsequent performance while hungry.

These results indicate that a change in the motivational state that reduces the desirability of the primary reinforcer depressed first-order responding. This outcome is consistent with the notion that the reinforcer representation participates in Pavlovian performance. However, the absence of an effect on second-order performance raises the possibility that the current value of neither the original reinforcer nor of the first-order CS participates importantly in the execution of second-order responding. That conclusion is consonant with the other evidence alluded to above, that experimental changes in the first-order CS and in the original reinforcer likewise fail to modify second-order responding.

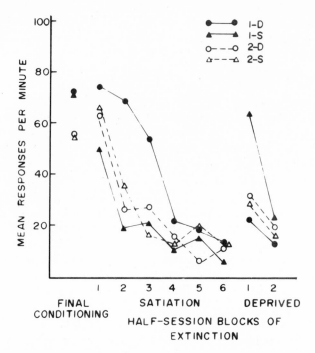

FIG. 7.   Mean number of activity counts per minute produced by the tone CS on the final day of conditioning, during the satiation test session, and during a second test under re-deprivation. Open symbols represent second-order CSs; closed symbols, first-order CSs. Triangles indicate satiated animals during the middle phase. (From Holland & Rescorla, 1975b. Copyright 1975 by the American Psychological Association. Reprinted by permission.)

For the moment, let us concentrate on the finding from first-order condition-ing. The notion of a reinforcer representation is vague and not well developed; however, it does suggest that somehow the organism encodes various features of the reinforcing event. Indeed, unless one can demonstrate that the organism forms representations in the sense that different reinforcers leave different representations, then the notion has little conceptual value. So it is important to know whether details of the reinforcer are encoded; this is presumably what Tolman meant when he suggested that animals learn about reinforcers. One approach to this problem is to ask whether motivational changes are selective in their action upon different reinforcer representations. Satiation on a par-ticular reinforcer should selectively change the value of its representation com-pared with that of other reinforcers and hence differentially depress conditioning established by it.

The preceding attempt to change motivation was, of course, quite blunt, modifying the general hunger state of the organism. To provide initial evidence on the details of the reinforcer representation and on the specificity of action of motivational changes, we recently pressed the animal somewhat. We used two positive reinforcers which generate similar CRs but which differ in their own stimulus properties. Following conditioning with both reinforcers, we provided unlimited access to one of them and subsequently tested the various CSs. Our hope was to find, in line with the casual report of Zener (1937), that both the reinforcer representation and the motivational manipulation would be sufficiently selective so as to differentially modify the response to the antecedent CSs.

To accomplish this, three groups of rats received conditioning in the activity chambers. A 10.5-sec 1,800-Hz tone and a 10.5-sec flashing light served as CSs, whereas the delivery of two Noyes pellets or of .5 ml of 8% sucrose served as the USs. The apparatus was modified by mounting a small well on the wall of the chamber opposite the food magazine; a tube permitted a solenoid-operated valve to deliver sucrose into that well. For half the animals the light was paired with food and the tone with sucrose; the other half received the reverse relations. All animals received four presentations of each CS, all reinforced, on each of five conditioning days. The animals were then divided into three groups differing in satiation treatment. Group S was given free access to sucrose by mounting two Richter tubes, each filled with 100 ml of 8% sucrose, in the home cage. A second group (F) was given free access to a dish of Noyes pellets, placed in the home cage so as to be continuously replenished from a reservoir. In addition, both of these groups had ad lib access to the standard laboratory chow and to water. The third, control, group (C) remained on 80% deprivation during this phase of the experiment. After six days of these treatments, all animals received three test days in the activity chambers, each involving four nonreinforced presentations each of the light and tone.

Finally, to evaluate the success of the satiation procedures, a consumption test was administered in the home cage on the next day. Animals were permitted 5-min access to either 10 ml of 8% sucrose or 100 Noyes pellets. Pellet intake was 69, 40.5, and 11.6 for the deprived-control, sucrose-sated, and pellet-sated animals, respectively. Sucrose intake for the same groups was 9.7, 2.1, and 8.4 ml, respectively. Thus these treatments produced differential consumption patterns, although neither complete selectively nor complete satiation was achieved.

The results of principal interest, those from the activity tests with the CSs, are shown in Fig. 8. This figure displays responding over the three test days to CSs previously paired with either a food pellet or sucrose reinforcer. As in previous experiments, the light CS produced less activity than did the tone, but that difference is ignored here because the pattern of results was similar for both stimuli. For those control animals maintained on deprivation during testing (C), responding was quite similar during the CS previously paired with sucrose and that previously paired with food, suggesting that the two reinforcers were reasonably equivalent in reinforcing value. Responding during the CS which had

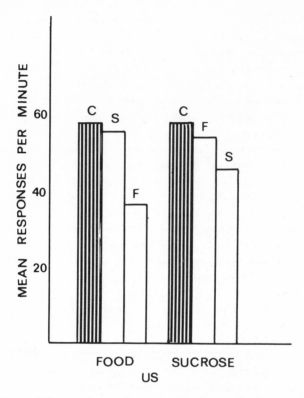

FIG. 8.   Mean activity counts per minute over the three extinction test sessions. Conditioning had been carried out either with a Noyes pellet or a sucrose US. Testing was done under either continued deprivation (C), sucrose (S) satiation or Noyes pellet (F) satiation.

previously been paired with food was slightly depressed in the animals given free access to sucrose (S), but substantially more depressed in those given free access to food (F). A comparable pattern was observed for the CS previously paired with sucrose, free access to sucrose being more detrimental. Thus satiation had a detrimental effect which was largely specific to the CSs previously paired with the now sated reinforcer; but there also appears to be a small nonspecific effect. The latter may reflect the common access to laboratory chow.

In this experiment we also used the video system to monitor the kinds of behavior patterns described in previous experiments. Those results will not be given in detail here, but two points should be mentioned. First, the behavior patterns generated by sucrose and food were very similar, except for the orientation of magazine-directed behaviors. In this situation, differences in the behaviors were governed by the nature of the CS as well as of the reinforcer. Second and more relevant in the present context, the effects of satiation upon those behaviors were in agreement with the effects upon general activity. Free access to a reinforcer had a selective effect but it also had a small nonselective consequence.

Together, these two experiments provide information on the way in which motivation interacts with Pavlovian conditioning. They make implausible a number of common descriptions of the action of motivation. For instance, they do not seem consonant with an interpretation in terms of a general "energizing" or amplifying action of drive. Such a consequence of changes in deprivation should be relatively nonspecific, so as to produce changes in the response to various CSs, including ones whose power comes from other primary reinforcers or through second-order conditioning. Similarly, an account of the present data cannot be given entirely in terms of decrements induced by the stimulus change which accompanies changes in deprivation. That change should apply equally to all of the various CSs. But these results are, of course, consistent with the kind of motivational theory suggested by Tolman (1932) and by Young (1959) in which motivational changes affect the organism's evaluation of the reinforcer representation. Since the current evaluation of that representation participates in generating performance, behavior changes with the specific motivational state. Such an account gains in plausibility from the demonstration that details of the reinforcer are stored in memory.

There is, however, one aspect of these data which does not fit so well with that approach. Although satiation depressed responding to the CSs, its effect was actually surprisingly small. Even in the case of first-order conditioned stimuli, the data of Fig. 7 and 8 suggest that substantial responding remained under satiation, at least early in testing. Similar observations have been made in the case of instrumental performance (e.g., Morgan, 1974). Animals have often been observed to engage in antecedent instrumental behavior which is disproportionate to the value they currently place on the reinforcer.

One interpretation of such incompleteness of the effects of satiation is that we have not fully reduced the organism's desire for the reinforcer. It is notoriously difficult to actually stop the animal from eating by simple satiation techniques. The consumption results given above attest to this difficulty. Furthermore, once conditioning has occurred, even a minimal reinforcer might be sufficient to maintain substantial responding. Thus one possibility is that our changes in the organism's evaluation of the reinforcer were incomplete.

A second possibility is suggested, however, by an observation which we noted earlier: the insensitivity of second-order conditioning to motivational changes. We commented that this kind of observation has been taken by us (e.g., Rescorla, 1973) as implying a difference in the encoding of reinforcers in first- and second-order conditioning. Reinforcers have many features, presumably not all of which are fully encoded in the organism's representation. Indeed, it seems plausible that features of the reinforcer might partially compete for participation in that representation. Thus an unconditioned stimulus may have potent stimulus properties, evoke various peripheral responses, and result in an emotional-evaluative change in the organism. During first-order conditioning, each of these might partially share in the representation of the reinforcer. However, the reinforcing CS used in second-order conditioning has, by the nature of stimuli we select to play that role, only insubstantial stimulus properties of its own. Its principle feature is that it can produce a potent emotional reaction in the organism; it then seems plausible that this emotion contributes heavily to the representation of that reinforcer. That is, it seems possible that after second-order conditioning the organism has learned only that its own emotional reaction followed the CS. After first-order conditioning, however, it may also remember some of the more salient stimulus features of the reinforcer.

Whatever the value of such an account, the behavioral response to a second-order Pavlovian CS seems better preserved under satiation. But notice that second-order conditioning may also participate even in our supposedly first-order conditioning paradigms. In the present situation so-called first-order conditioning consists of following a CS with the delivery of food. That treatment provides ample opportunity for the participation of second-order conditioning in the training of the CS. The food has various visual, tactile, and olfactory properties which have presumably acquired conditioning because of the ultimate primary reinforcement. These stimuli are well-placed to provide substantial second-order conditioning of our CS. Moreover, once first-order conditioning begins to occur to a CS, it seems possible that temporally later portions of that CS could act as reinforcers for second-order conditioning of temporally earlier portions. In cases of this sort we might never be able to observe pure first-order conditioning. As a consequence, we might never be able to completely eliminate responding simply by satiation. Although the animal might evaluate the reinforcer as (say) unattractive, the CS might make it recall not only that reinforcer but also its previous evaluation and emotional reaction; perhaps the latter can sustain responding.

One source of support for such an interpretation of the incompleteness of satiation-produced decrement in first-order responding is the parallel from other techniques attempting to change the reinforcer representation. In all of the experiments which we mentioned earlier in this section, postconditioning manipulations designed to change that representation had effects upon responding to the first-order CS; but in all those effects were incomplete. Thus it is not simply incomplete satiation that produces this pattern.

Overall, the experiments described here and elsewhere in this series emphasize the value of the idea that the organism forms a representation of the reinforcer, a representation that participates in the production of the CR. Furthermore, these experiments give some support to the notion that this representation is reasonably detailed. And they suggest that motivational variables may act through that representation rather than on associations themselves. But they also suggest that some of the responding involved in conditioning may depend upon other than stimulus features of the reinforcer representation.

IV. A FINAL COMMENT ON THE DESCRIPTION OF CONDITIONING

The description of Pavlovian conditioning given here departs in many ways from that commonly given in textbooks. A typical description might be paraphrased as follows: In Pavlovian conditioning a US which regularly evokes a UR is arranged to follow a CS which initially fails to evoke that response. With repeated pairings, however, the CS also comes to evoke that response.

This description seems to derive from the reflex tradition in physiology, in the context of which one views conditioning as the addition of a new stimulus into an existing reflex system. In contrast, the description used here, which emphasizes the learning of relations among events, derives more from the association tradition in psychology.

One of the important features of the reflex definition is its emphasis upon the response. In the very definition of conditioning, three response restrictions are imposed: The US must evoke a response, the CS must initially fail to do so, and the consequence of conditioning must be that the CS evoke a response closely resembling that to the US. None of these restrictions appears in the present description of conditioning. From the present viewpoint, the issue is whether the organism's behavior changes as a result of exposing it to some interevent relation. Whether the events themselves originally evoke responses is irrelevant, except insofar as it may create difficulties in detecting the occurrence of conditioning. Moreover, there is no particular interest in one behavior change as compared with other possible consequences of arranging the relation.

A related consequence of the reflex definition is that it encourages the identification of learning with responding. As a consequence, it seems most at home with an S-R, rather than an S-S, view of conditioning. More importantly, it encourages us to blur the distinction between learning and performance. As noted above, this distinction which is commonly accepted for instrumental behavior has been less generally applied to Pavlovian conditioning. But the separation between underlying associative knowledge and behavior is at the heart of the cognitive description given here.

Because of its interest in the association as a separate theoretical entity, the present view focuses attention on a broad class of relations to be studied. Perhaps it is the concentration on responding which has directed attention away from those possibilities and has permitted those studying Pavlovian conditioning to feel satisfied with the relation of contiguity.

But probably the most important difference between the present view and that of the reflex tradition lies in the place which Pavlovian conditioning is thought to occupy in the study of learning. Our view is that Pavlovian conditioning is an example of associative learning generally, that much of what we learn by its study will be applicable to various examples of associative learning. For that reason, we are at pains not to segregate it from other examples of associative learning by the application of definitional restrictions. By contrast, the reflex tradition has often emphasized what demarcates Pavlovian conditioning from other forms of learning.

There are two issues surrounding this demarcation, one substantive and one strategic. The substantive issue is whether those forms of Pavlovian conditioning which meet more stringent, response-based criteria follow different principles than examples of conditioning permitted under a broader description, such as that given here. That issue is far from settled, but in my opinion, one would be hard pressed to find present evidence of any basic differences. Indeed, there is little reason, other than historical precedence, to anticipate that the particular restrictions which are commonly applied should isolate a unitary form of learning. The strategic issue concerns which approach will be more fruitful in the study of conditioning. Researchers will differ on this point, but it is my view that placing Pavlovian conditioning within a broader context is primarily responsible for the current resurgence of interest in it as a learning process.

ACKNOWLEDGMENTS

This research was supported by various grants from the National Science Foundation. Technical assistance was provided by Sherri Bruno and Joan Bombace. Special thanks are due to Peter Holland both for many helpful comments and for permission to use his dissertation data.

REFERENCES

Bindra, D. A motivational view of learning, performance, and behavior modification. *Psychological Review,* 1974, *81,* 199–213.

Blanchard, R., & Honig, W. K. Surprise value of food determines its effectiveness as a reinforcer. *Journal of Experimental Psychology: Animal Behavior Processes,* 1976, *2,* 67–74.

Bolles, R. C. Reinforcement, expectancy, and learning. *Psychological Review,* 1972, *79,* 304–409.

Estes, W. K. New perspectives on some old issues in association theory. In N. J. Mackintosh and W. K. Honig (Eds.) *Fundamental issues in associative learning.* Halifax, Canada: Dalhousie University Press, 1969.

Foree, D. D., & LoLordo, V. M. Stimulus-reinforcer interactions in the pigeon: the role of electric shock and the avoidance contingency. *Journal of Experimental Psychology: Animal Behavior Processes,* 1975, *1,* 39–46.

Gormezano, I., & Kehoe, E. J. Classical conditioning: some methodological conceptual issues. In W. K. Estes (Ed.), *Hanbook of Learning and Cognitive Processes,* Vol. 2. Hillsdale, New Jersey: Lawrence Erlbaum Associates, 1975.

Hearst, E., & Jenkins, H. M. *Sign-tracking: The stimulus-reinforcer relations and directed action.* Austin, Texas: Psychonomic Society, 1974.

Holland, P. C. Conditioned stimulus as a determinant of the form of the Pavlovian conditioned response. *Journal of Experimental Psychology: Animal Behavior Processes,* 1977, *3,* 77–104.

Holland, P. C., & Rescorla, R. A. Second-order conditioning with food unconditioned stimulus. *Journal of Comparative and Pysiological Psychology,* 1975, *88,* 459–467 (a).

Holland, P. C., & Rescorla, R. A. The effects of two ways of devaluing the unconditioned stimulus after first- and second-order appetitive conditioning. *Journal of Experimental Psychology: Animal Behavior Processes,* 1975, *1,* 355–363 (b).

Irwin, F. W. *Intentional behavior and motivation.* Philadelphia: Lippincott, 1971.

Kamin, L. J. Attention-like processes in classical conditioning. In M. R. Jones (Ed.) *Miami symposium on the prediction of behavior: aversive stimulation.* Miami, Florida: University of Miami Press, 1968.

Kamin, L. J. Predictability, surprise, attention, and conditioning. In B. A. Campbell and R. M. Church (Eds.) *Punishment and aversive behavior.* New York: Appleton-Century-Crofts, 1969.

Kohler, W. On the nature of associations. *Proceedings of the American Philosophical Society,* 1941, *84,* 489–502.

Konorski, J. *Integrative Activity of the Brain.* Chicago: University of Chicago Press, 1967.

Morgan, M. J. Resistance to satiation. *Animal Behavior,* 1974, 22, 449–466.

Mowrer, O. H. *Learning theory and behavior.* New York: Wiley, 1960.

Rescorla, R. A. Pavlovian conditioning and its proper control procedures. *Psychological Review,* 1967, *74,* 71–80.

Rescorla, R. A. Second-order conditioning: Implications for theories of learning. In F. J. McGuigan and D. B. Lumsden (Eds.) *Contemporary approaches to conditioning and learning.* Washington, D.C.: V.H. Winston, 1973.

Rescorla, R. A., & Furrow, D. R. Stimulus similarity as a determinant of Pavlovian conditioning. *Journal of Experimental Psychology: Animal Behavior Processes,* 1977, *3,* 203–215.

Rescorla, R. A., & Heth, C. D. Reinstatement of fear to an extinguished conditioned stimulus. *Journal of Experimental Psychology: Animal Behavior Processes,* 1975, *1,* 88–96.

Rescorla, R. A., & Holland, P. C. Some behaviorial approaches to the study of learning. In E. Bennett and M. R. Rozensweig, (Eds.) *Neural Mechanisms of Learning and Memory.* Cambridge, Massachusetts: MIT Press, 1976.

Rescorla, R. A., & Wagner, A. R. A theory of Pavlovian conditions: variations in the effectiveness of reinforcement and nonreinforcement. In A. Black and W. R. Prokasy (Eds.) *Classical Conditioning II.* New York: Appleton-Century-Crofts, 1972.

Rizley, R. C., & Rescorla, R. A. Associations in second-order conditioning and sensory preconditioning. *Journal of Comparative and Physiological Psychology,* 1972, *81,* 1–11.

Shettleworth, S. J. Reinforcement and the organization of behavior in Golden Hamsters: hunger, environment, and food reinforcement. *Journal of Experimental Psychology: Animal Behavior Processes,* 1975, *1,* 56–87.

Sokolov, Y. N. *Perception and the conditioned reflex.* Oxford, England: Pergamon Press, 1963.

Testa, T. J. Effects of similarity of location and temporal intensity pattern of conditioned and unconditioned stimuli on the acquisition of conditioned suppression in rats. *Journal of Experimental Psychology: Animal Behavior Processes,* 1975, *1,* 114–121.

Tolman, E. C. *Purposive behavior in animals and men.* New York: Appleton-Century, 1932.

Young, P. T. The role of   affective processes in learning and motivation. *Psychological Review,* 1959, *66,* 104–125.

Zamble, E. Classical conditioning of excitement anticipatory to food reward. *Journal of Comparative and Physiological Psychology,* 1967, *63,* 526–529.

Zener, K. The significance of behavior accompanying conditioned salivary secretion for theories of the conditioned response. *American Journal of Psychology,* 1937, *50,* 384–403.

3 Stimulus Relationships and Feature Selection in Learning and Behavior

Eliot Hearst
Indiana University

I. INTRODUCTION

Much contemporary research in the field of animal learning is characterized by a shift away from extremely behavioristic, response-centered approaches. If the material in this book provides any yardstick, the use of abstractions and inferences that go well beyond simple relationships among observables is more frequent and acceptable now than it was 10 or 20 years ago. This swing of the pendulum toward more flexible interpretations of animal learning seems to have its roots in the belief that highly descriptive or associationistic approaches, which scrupulously avoid the postulation of mechanisms intervening between environmental stimulus and observable response, have not provided us with many truly significant or novel insights and are unlikely to do so in the future.

The work described in the present chapter reflects, I think, this shift in the climate of opinion. The research bears on some old issues and controversies in learning theory, but examines them within the context of recent methods, concepts, and specific findings. For example, 30 or 40 years ago, the major learning theorists argued about the question of what is learned during a conditioning experiment. In general, expectancy or cognitive theories conceived learning more flexibly than did response-centered theories. The former theories viewed learning as mainly a matter of gaining knowledge about relationships among stimulus events; registration or perception of the fact that one event invariably follows another, or bears some other type of relation to the second event, was stressed in the analysis of learning, rather than the specific responses a subject comes to perform when these events occur. On the other hand, response-centered theories conceived learning as a matter of developing links between specific actions and preceding or subsequent stimuli, with contiguity operating as the major factor to produce strong or weak links between stimuli and responses. According to this general view, in Pavlovian conditioning a dog learns to *salivate* to a buzzer, and in operant conditioning a pigeon acquires a *key-pecking* response for food reinforcement in the presence of certain stimuli. Pushed to their extreme, response-centered approaches presume that only a movement or glandular secretion can be learned, whereas a stimulus sequence or relationship cannot.

Over the past several years research in my laboratory has focused on the use of unrestrained subjects (pigeons or rats) that are exposed to various types of relationships between certain environmental events (CSs and USs) in a Skinner Box. Although we measure directed movements (e.g., approach-withdrawal, contact responses) of the subjects with respect to the location of various stimuli in the chamber, no particular actions are required for presentation of the US in most of the experiments. Thus the procedures conform to a Pavlovian-conditioning paradigm, but the experimental setting and the responses studied are historically more typical of experiments in operant conditioning (Hearst, 1975a, 1975b). Stated simply, such arrangements permit us to determine how various aspects of a subject's behavior will change depending on the specific properties of CS and US and on the nature of the CS-US relationship that the experimenter establishes.

At least three major themes of our research resemble those of other chapters in this volume and ought to be stressed at the outset. One theme involves the relative importance of stimulus-reinforcer and response-reinforcer relations. Another theme pertains to the value of making a learning-performance distinction, and the final theme concerns conceptualization of stimulus events as potential sources of information. A few comments on each of these themes seem appropriate before any specific research is discussed.

A. Stimulus-Reinforcer vs. Response-Reinforcer Relations

Like many experimenters who study Pavlovian or operant conditioning, we have been interested in the relative roles of stimulus-stimulus (e.g., CS-US) and response-stimulus correlations during original learning and subsequent performance. Whether the procedure used in a standard animal learning experiment is Pavlovian or operant, a response is acquired that occurs in some consistent temporal relation with certain prior stimuli and a subsequent reinforcer. Many writers have emphasized the role of the response-reinforcer relation, particularly in the control of operant behavior. However, even in a standard operant experiment, the conditioned response may be directed toward a lever or key for reasons other than the response-reinforcer correlation. *Stimulation* from the lever or key is necessarily (though implicitly) correlated with the reinforcer, and this correlation may be as important or more important than the explicitly programmed correlation between a lever-press or key-peck *response* and the reinforcer. As we will see, studies of what Hearst and Jenkins (1974) called "sign tracking" demonstrate that subjects will usually direct their behavior toward any easily localizable signal that bears a high positive correlation with the reinforcer. In these cases, learning of a CS-US relationship seems to precede and guide the appearance of the particular skeletal movements that constitute the observable conditioned response (cf. Lajoie & Bindra, 1976).

The question of the relative importance of stimulus-reinforcer and response-reinforcer relationships resembles closely the issue raised by Bolles (Chapter 4) in his discussion of stimulus learning vs. response learning, and by Rescorla (Chapter 2) in his defense of a cognitive view of Pavlovian conditioning that stresses the learning of interevent relations rather than the acquisition of very specific CRs to the CS. Of historic interest in this connection is the opinion of Spence (1950) that *both* S-S and S-R associations are probably established during learning, and that the differences between cognitive and S-R theories are highly exaggerated. Similarly, several contributors to the present volume seem to regard the question of the relative importance of S-S vs. S-R associations in different learning tasks as a basic issue that is open to direct experimental attack. One can study the influence of various relations among stimuli and responses without a commitment to the kinds of extreme positions sometimes taken on related points in the 1930s and 1940s.

B. Learning vs. Performance

A second major theme of this chapter concerns the value of making an explicit distinction between learning and performance. Although an old issue, the question of whether learning can occur in the absence of (1) overt behavioral change, or (2) definite reinforcement of some kind, still seems fundamental and experimentally meaningful. Of course, this problem provided the rationale for many experiments (e.g., studies of latent learning) performed by cognitively inclined theorists in the 1930s and 1940s. Since a great deal of human learning in and out of the classroom apparently takes place without overt behavioral change and without the presentation of explicit reinforcing stimuli, it seems reasonable to expect that nonhuman subjects possess similar capabilities to some degree.

Rescorla's contribution to this volume (Chapter 2) also argues strongly for a separation of learning and performance. The distinction implies that an experimenter will often be forced to rely on various assays of performance after the presumed learning experience has occurred—in order to detect whether or what the subjects have learned from it—rather than to rely on observable behavioral changes (e.g., conventional Pavlovian CRs) during the learning phase itself. The development of sensitive postconditioning assays may challenge the ingenuity of the experimenter, but once he is willing to pursue the possibility that important forms of learning may proceed without behavioral change, many strategies come to mind. Some of these detection techniques are essentially the same as those used for assessing conditioned inhibition in situations where various performance measures during original learning are not revealing (see Hearst, 1972; Hearst, Besley & Farthing, 1970; Rescorla, 1969). Contributors to the present volume offer other possible techniques. For example, Rescorla (Chapter 2) notes the advantages of higher-order-conditioning procedures in this connection, and Menzel (Chapter 13) and Premack (Chapter 14) describe tasks that were developed to map knowledge or information presumably possessed by the subject, but not easily revealed by traditional response measures. There is nothing mentalistic or nonbehavioral about these tasks and observations, even though their implementation may result from the experimenter's desire to test some hypothesis concerning internal processes, transformations, or representations.

Consider a recent comment of Skinner, which contrasts strongly with the views about the learning-performance distinction expressed in my and several other chapters of this book. He said that "The distinction [between learning or competence and performance] was useful in early studies of learning because the changes in performance then observed were rather erratic. Since it was assumed that learning was an orderly process, there appeared to be a discrepancy, but it was resolved by supposing that learning was not very accurately revealed in the behavior the organism displayed. . . . Improved techniques have revealed an orderly relation between performance and contingencies and have eliminated the need to appeal to a separate inner learning process or to competence (Skinner, 1974, p. 66)."

This statement seems to imply two dubious conclusions: That we now possess the necessary techniques to measure learning at the very time it is occurring (cf. Shimp, 1975, 1976), and that learning involves nothing more than a change in the subject's overt responding, which results from the application of reinforcement contingencies. The general attitude expressed in the quotation discourages research aimed at detecting evidence of learning in the absence of observable behavioral change—just as Skinner's view that "inhibition" is just another word for low response strength discouraged the experimental separation of learned inhibitory effects from other kinds of decremental phenomena (see Boakes & Halliday, 1972). In a subsequent section of this chapter, I will describe studies which demonstrate that subjects learn something about stimulus relations even though they display no evidence of overt CRs to the CS during initial conditioning. Dependence on measures of various observable behaviors during initial conditioning would have led to the conclusion that no learning had occurred.

Another relevant point is that workers in the field of operant conditioning rarely attempt to study the phenomenon of "learning," in the sense that the word would be used by many psychologists. Tolman (cited in Premack, 1965, p. 164) once commented that the lever-pressing arrangement is an uninteresting one for studying general laws of learning because acquisition occurs so quickly;

what happens after the first or second reinforced lever press, he said, involves changes in performance. As Premack pointed out, Tolman's comment could be interpreted as a very perceptive one, because some of the steps taken to make the subject susceptible to reinforcement in the Skinner Box situation—e.g., training it to eat from the food magazine—are not a very explicit part of any empirical or theoretical analysis. Skinnerians have tended to stress the investigation of steady-state performance, rather than transitions from one state to another, such as the changes that occur during learning. For example, the initial conditioning of the pigeon's key peck by means of hand shaping (or, more recently, autoshaping) is often regarded as preliminary to the investigation of really important behavioral effects, rather than as of great significance in itself.

C. Information, Feature Selection, and Context

A third major theme of the present chapter involves our view that the stimulus presented by the experimenter is best regarded as a source of information, whose features, dimensions, or elements may exert differential behavioral control depending on the temporal, spatial, or historical context in which the stimulus is embedded. Exactly what a subject learns about different aspects of a conditioned stimulus is a function of the following: (1) the type of correlation (e.g., positive or negative) between the presence or absence of some feature of the stimulus and the US; (2) the reliability, redundancy, and salience of other predictors of reinforcement in the situation; (3) the properties of the specific CSs and USs employed in the experiment; and (4) various perceptual factors that facilitate learning of relationships between CS and US, perhaps along the lines implied by the classic Gestalt laws of organization. The idea that stimulus elements compete for control of behavior—since not all information provided by the stimulus can or need be processed by the organism—is closely related to the concept of selective attention, which appears in one form or another in several chapters of this book (e.g., Mackintosh, Chapter 6; Riley and Roitblat, Chapter 9) and is a concept that guides much current research in human cognitive psychology.

In their analysis of the phenomenon of sign tracking, to be discussed in more detail shortly, Hearst and Jenkins (1974) concluded that the perception or registration of correlations between stimulus events, somewhat akin to what Tolman and Brunswik (1935) referred to as the "causal texture of the environment," is a crucial factor in many, if not all, learning tasks. Situations for studying sign tracking allow experimental analysis of various issues raised by cognitive psychologists in their criticisms of response-centered theories. Writers such as Tolman (1932) and Woodworth (1958), in addition to the Gestalt psychologists, have presented views similar to some of those expressed in the present chapter, but the findings I will describe do not seem to follow directly from the specific theories which they offered. Nevertheless, it seems unfortunate that many of us who received training along strongly behavioristic lines have had little or no exposure to the views of these writers. In my opinion, several of the major issues and alternative explanations that they raised deserve careful consideration.

II. AUTOSHAPING, THE FEATURE-POSITIVE EFFECT, AND SIGN TRACKING

Autoshaping and the feature-positive effect were used by Hearst and Jenkins (1974; see also Hearst, 1975a) to illustrate the more general phenomenon of sign tracking. Autoshaping refers to the conditioning of contact responses directed at a localized stimulus (usually some standard manipulandum, like a rat lever or pigeon key) that signals the delivery of an appetitive reinforcer. A typical experiment employs a Pavlovian-conditioning procedure in which presentations of the stimulus and reinforcer occur independently of the subject's behavior. For example, Brown and Jenkins (1968) made grain presentations contingent only on a prior stimulus (8-sec illumination of a standard pigeon key). As pairings of CS (key illumination) and US (grain) continued, birds first showed increases in activity during the CS, then oriented toward the lighted key, and eventually began to approach and peck directly at it.

Since Brown and Jenkins' initial work, autoshaping has been reported in studies employing a variety of species, CSs, responses, reinforcers and general situations. There is also a negative counterpart to the standard finding. Not only do pigeons approach and contact a localized visual stimulus that signals an appetitive reinforcer, but they also position themselves relatively far from the same stimulus when it signals that the reinforcer is *not* going to occur (Hearst & Franklin, 1977; Wasserman, Franklin, & Hearst, 1974). It is worth pointing out that if measurement of behavior had been limited only to signal contacts (i.e., key pecks), the development of withdrawal behavior to this negatively correlated signal would not have been detected. In that case one might have falsely concluded that subjects had not learned the negative relationship between signal and reinforcer.

Two additional facts about autoshaping, all described more extensively in Hearst and Jenkins (1974), are pertinent to points that will arise later in this chapter. First of all, autoshaping does not emerge at all or is relatively weak when other stimuli in the situation (auditory or visual) predict the arrival of a reinforcer as well as does the CS. Thus, autoshaping develops to the extent that the CS is a nonredundant, or "informative," predictor of the reinforcer. Second, the type of behavior directed at the CS generally depends on the kind of US with which it is correlated. A pigeon's key pecks at a food-predictive signal are evenly spaced, brief, and forceful, whereas its pecks at a water-predictive signal are irregularly spaced, sustained, and relatively weak; birds seem to be "eating" the former signal, and "sipping" or "drinking" the latter. Analogously, rats gnaw or lick a CS (insertion of a lighted lever into the chamber) that predicts food, but sniff or "explore" the same CS when it signals electrical stimulation of the lateral hypothalamus. Thus, within certain limits, the type of behavior directed at the CS is appropriate to the type of reinforcer with which it is correlated. Cognitively inclined theorists would use such data as evidence in favor of their view that the subject has come to "expect" a certain event after the CS, and as evidence against an alternative view that conceives reinforcers as mere strengtheners of immediately preceding responses.

In addition to autoshaping, the feature-positive effect (FPE) played an important role in Hearst and Jenkins' analysis. This phenomenon was first reported by Jenkins and Sainsbury (1969, 1970) in pigeon experiments that employed small circles, stars, and gaps in a solid line as features projected on a response key. The FPE refers to the superior discrimination learning shown by subjects for whom the specific feature that distinguishes positive from negative trials appears on the positive trials (feature positive, FP), as compared to the learning shown by subjects for whom the feature appears on the negative trials (FN). In the FP case subjects generally learn the discrimination quickly; they respond on positive trials and soon stop responding on negative trials. Furthermore, their behavior is very specifically directed toward the feature rather than toward other parts of the display—even though responses aimed directly at the feature are not required for reinforcement. In pigeon experiments the development of pecking at the feature on the FP discrimination precedes elimination of responding to the negative display. On the other hand, in the FN case subjects often fail to learn the discrimination at all, or their efficiency is markedly inferior to that of FP subjects. For the FN birds, pecks at the feature occur infrequently and soon disappear, but pecks continue at other parts of the display—parts common to positive and negative trials.

Figure 1 presents an illustration of typical findings with FP and FN arrangements from my laboratory. Each discrimination-learning trial consisted of illumination of *all three keys* in a standard pigeon chamber. The "feature" was a key illuminated by a color different from the color that appeared on the other two keys during feature-present trials and on all three keys during feature-absent trials. For example, the FP discrimination might involve one red key and two green keys as the positive, reinforced display (the red color shifting randomly from one key to another on successive positive trials), and three green keys as the negative, nonreinforced display. The two types of display would be reversed in reinforcement outcome for the FN arrangement.

As Fig. 1 indicates, the FP discrimination, which required pecking at feature-present but not at feature-absent displays, was acquired by all subjects, regardless of whether the discrimination was in force during the first or second phase of the experiment. Furthermore, *within* the feature-present display of the FP discrimination, each subject began to track (peck at) the feature before mastering the successive discrimination. On the other hand, in the FN arrange-

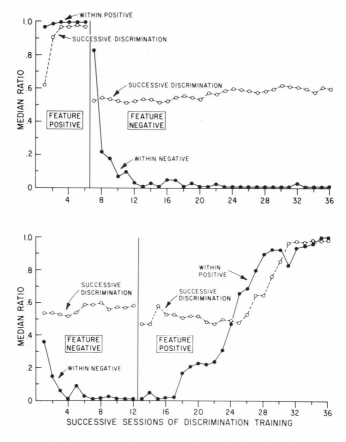

FIG. 1.   Median discrimination ratios for groups trained with a distinguishing feature (key color) either on positive, i.e., reinforced trials (feature positive) or on negative, i.e., nonreinforced trials (feature negative). The index for the development of the *successive discrimination* (positive vs. negative *displays*) is the ratio of the number of responses on the positive display to the total number of responses on both displays; this index approaches 1.0 as responses on the negative display approach zero. The index for the development of a discrimination between common and feature key colors *within* the display containing both key colors is given by the ratio of the number of responses on the feature key to the total number of responses on that display. On positive trials the first peck at any key after 5 sec produced grain. All negative trials lasted 5 sec. After initial exposure to either the feature-positive or feature-negative condition, subjects were switched to the other condition. (From Hearst, 1975a.)

ment learning of the discrimination between the feature-present and feature-absent displays was poor or nonexistent—even in birds that had formerly mastered the FP discrimination and had at that time presumably learned to "attend to" the feature. [See Hearst (1975a) for additional details and results of these experiments.]

The FPE has been obtained with a variety of responses, organisms, reinforcers, and kinds of features. It appears in both operant- and Pavlovian-conditioning situations. Although Fig. 1 presents an example of the FPE from an operant paradigm, most of my own research has involved Pavlovian arrangements. A later section of this chapter will briefly review some of the work done by others, present recent data concerning the FPE from our laboratory, indicate some factors that seem to influence the effect, and reassess earlier analyses of it. I will also attempt to list several phenomena observed in human experimentation that appear related to the FPE.

Hearst and Jenkins (1974) discussed the above two phenomena—autoshaping and the FPE—in terms of the subject's tracking of stimulus elements that have the highest positive correlation with the occurrence of the reinforcer. The evocation of directed approach and contact behavior by such environmental features presumably facilitates discrimination learning in the FP case, because the feature that is the best predictor of forthcoming reinforcement is present only on positive trials. In the FN discrimination the environmental features that bear the highest positive correlation with occurrences of the reinforcer are the elements common to the two stimulus displays. Since they appear on both positive and negative trials, tracking of these elements retards or prevents acquisition of the discrimination between displays.

The term *sign tracking* was coined to cover these and several other effects in animal and human learning. Sign tracking refers to behavior (e.g., eye movements, bodily orientation, approach, signal contact) that is directed toward or away from a feature of the environment (a sign) as a result of the relation between that environmental feature and another (the reinforcer, in a typical experiment). Besides exploring a phenomenon that is interesting in its own right, studies of sign tracking provide useful arrangements for assessing the relative behavioral control exerted by stimulus-reinforcer and response-reinforcer correlations—a topic to which we now turn.

III. WHAT IS LEARNED IN SIGN TRACKING: STIMULUS-STIMULUS VS. RESPONSE-STIMULUS RELATIONS

The original development of CS-contact behavior in the autoshaping situation depends on the type of relationship that exists between the CS and US. For example, little or no key pecking develops in pigeons exposed to: (1) CS-only trials (i.e., no grain presented); (2) a continuously illuminated key and occasional presentations of grain; or (3) variants of Rescorla's (1967) truly random control procedure, in which the CS and US are independently presented. However, when a positive contingency between the CS and US is in effect, autoshaping occurs even in situations where the unconditioned level of key pecking is virtually zero and even where there is no evidence of any generalized pecking at the illuminated response key as a result of prior training to eat from the lighted magazine (Wasserman et al., 1974). The occurrence of the first key peck is mainly controlled by the positive relationship between the CS and US, rather than by "nonassociative" factors.

However, as soon as such directed movements toward the CS begin to occur with regularity, they are fortuitously associated with delivery of the reinforcer. The eventual strength and persistence of signal-directed behavior in the situation may depend as much on close temporal conjunctions between acquired *responses* and the reinforcer as on the explicitly programmed positive contingency between *signal* and reinforcer. We are faced with a problem similar to the one that was a focus of controversy in the 1930s and 1940s: Is perception of the positive relation between CS and US responsible for the persistent behavior directed at the CS, or is the behavior directed at the CS maintained and strengthened by the reinforcer that consistently follows it? Or are both important?

Two general methods can be used to assess the separate effects of stimulus-reinforcer and response-reinforcer correlations. The first involves procedures that pit a response-reinforcer relation against a stimulus-reinforcer relation. The omission procedure, introduced into autoshaping research by Williams and Williams (1969), illustrates this method. The scheduled US is omitted if the target response occurs during the CS. Thus, while maintaining a positive stimulus-reinforcer correlation (all USs occur immediately after CS), the experimenter makes certain that the reinforcer never occurs in conjunction with the specified movement (negative response-reinforcer correlation). If the response remains strong even when its occurrence cancels the US, then a primary role for the stimulus-reinforcer correlation would be demonstrated and the Law of Effect challenged.

The second general method for evaluating the relative contributions of stimulus-reinforcer and response-reinforcer correlations entails arrangements in which the subject is physically prevented from approaching or contacting the two stimuli while they are presented in some relationship to each other. A barrier may be inserted between the subject and the CS or US locations, or the subject may be harnessed in a place from which CS and US are visible but inaccessible. If actual occurrences of approach, contact, and consummatory responses are not necessary either for the learning of stimulus-reinforcer relations or for the development of tendencies to approach and contact the CS, then mere exposure of subjects to some positive contingency between the CS and US should produce the immediate or very rapid appearance of approach and contact behavior in a subsequent test phase with the CS and US both accessible. The basic rationale and various aspects of these kinds of experiments are similar to those underlying classic studies of latent learning (see reviews by MacCorquodale & Meehl, 1954, and Thistlethwaite, 1951). Positive evidence for latent learning was used to support a cognitive approach to learning (e.g., Tolman's theory), and to argue against the necessity for overt behavioral change and reinforcement in learning.

Results of experiments employing these two general methods are described in detail in Hearst (1975a). Therefore I will provide only a brief summary of that work here, supplemented by some new findings from recent research.

A. Omission Procedures

1. Autoshaped key pecking in pigeons.   Williams and Williams (1969) found that pigeons continued to peck a key on many trials even though a single peck canceled the grain delivery scheduled at the end of any trial; therefore, the subjects lost a large number of the reinforcers that they would have received had they not responded. Although these results indicate that the positive contingency between the CS and US is more important than conjunctions of the response and US in producing and maintaining autoshaped key pecking, response-reinforcer conjunctions appear to have some influence, too. Birds peck a key less frequently under the omission procedure than during standard autoshaping (e.g., Hearst, 1975a; Schwartz & Williams, 1972). This response reduction is probably not due to the partial pairings of CS and US (i.e., changes in the *stimulus*-reinforcer correlation) that occur during the omission procedure; Blaine Peden and I have found that when the US is explicitly programmed to follow the CS on only 25% to 50% of the CS presentations, autoshaped behavior is generally maintained at levels equal to or higher than those for 100% schedules.

The "long box" experiments performed by Herbert Jenkins (see Hearst & Jenkins, 1974, p. 11) also support the conclusion that stimulus-reinforcer correlations are more important than response-reinforcer correlations in autoshaping. In Jenkins' research, approach toward and pecking of a food-predictive key light that was located 3 ft (.9 m) away from the grain magazine developed and persisted even though this behavior always caused complete or partial loss of food: Grain presentations lasted only 4 sec and the food tray had frequently dropped out of reach by the time the bird managed to return to it. This experimental arrangement provides a spatial analog to Williams and Williams' (1969) procedure, since the frequency of CS-directed behavior was negatively correlated with the amount of grain obtained.

2. Approach movements.   The term sign tracking refers to a variety of directed movements governed by the spatial location of the CS. Are separate components of a total pattern of movements differentially sensitive to the omission contingency? In the case of pigeons, Wessells (1974) suggested that autoshaped key pecking develops and persists mainly because prepecking behaviors (e.g., orientation or approach toward the CS) occur in conjunction with the reinforcer. In other words, pecking is not independent of prior orientation and approach; and if orientation and approach are correlated with the reinforcer, they may bring about pecking because of the normal sequential structure of a pigeon's appetitive behavior.

In Wessells' experiment, grain was canceled on every trial during which the subject "approached" the key (i.e., moved into the front left corner of a standard chamber in which illumination of the left key served as the CS). Wessells reported that approach responses toward the CS disappeared on this procedure. Therefore, he argued that response-reinforcer relations, especially those involving prepecking behaviors, are probably more important in autoshaping and the omission-for-pecking effect than Williams and Williams (1969) and Schwartz and Williams (1972) had recognized.

Only two subjects were included in Wessells' experiment, and approach responses were judged by the experimenter rather than recorded in some automatic fashion. Blaine Peden and Michael Browne have collaborated with me on a series of experiments that are similar to those of Wessells, but which involve a substantial number of birds and a more objective measure of "approach to the CS" (Peden, Browne, & Hearst, 1977). In one of our experiments, the response key was mounted on the left wall of an experimental chamber 35 cm from the grain magazine and houselight. Whenever the pigeon entered an area within 25 cm from the key, an approach response was automatically recorded by means of switches beneath the hinged floor. When the omission-for-approach procedure was in effect, the key light was immediately terminated and grain delivery was canceled if the pigeon made an approach response during the CS. One group of birds was placed on the omission procedure from the beginning of the experiment, whereas another group started on a standard autoshaping procedure and then was switched to the omission procedure.

Figure 2 shows that even after 40 sessions on the omission-for-approach treatment (Sessions 36-40), the mean percentage of grain presentations lost per session because of persisting approach responses was 41% (range = 14-78%) for birds given no prior autoshaping. Although the extent of the effect was variable from subject to subject, approach responses never disappeared in any of the six birds. The five birds in the group given prior autoshaping (not shown in Fig. 2) yielded very similar data during the omission-for-approach phase. Each of the two groups lost an average of 49% of the total 2000 reinforcers possible during their 40 sessions on the omission procedure.

Thus the arrangement of a negative contingency between CS-approach behavior and US delivery produced effects that closely parallel those resulting from the establishment of a negative contingency between CS contacts (key pecking) and US delivery. The probability of an approach response was reduced compared to its level during autoshaping, but the response persisted strongly despite the contingent penalty. As with a key-pecking response, the positive

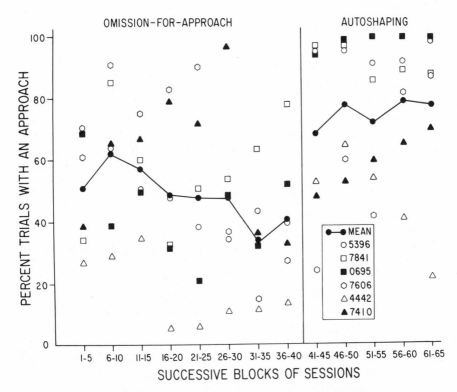

FIG. 2.   Percentage of trials with a key-approach response, over successive blocks of sessions, for six pigeons that were first exposed to an omission procedure for 40 sessions. During those sessions an approach response to CS canceled the grain scheduled to occur at the end of that trial. During the last 25 sessions (autoshaping) all CSs were followed by grain regardless of the bird's behavior. Both individual and group mean data are indicated in the figure. (From Hearst, 1975a.)

contingency between signal and US proved to be a more crucial determinant of performance than any response-reinforcer correlation. Results from omission experiments argue against the Law of Effect as an overriding principle of learning, in the sense that Thorndike proposed it and Skinner employs it (for a further discussion of the applicability of their theories, see Hearst & Jenkins, 1974, pp. 26-30).

The data in our omission-for-approach experiments were inconsistent with Wessells' findings concerning the importance of correlations between prepecking behaviors and grain delivery in the autoshaping situation. He was able to eliminate CS-approach behavior via an omission procedure, whereas we were not. In an attempt to discover the source of this discrepancy, we performed another experiment that adhered to the details of Wessells' study in all major aspects. "Approach toward the CS," judged by the experimenter according to Wessells' rules, canceled reinforcement in ten subjects, some of which had received prior autoshaping and some of which had not. Two different experimenters (Peden and Evans) ran different subjects in each group. We were not able to replicate Wessells' findings; eight of ten subjects continued to approach the CS on more than 70% of the daily trials over the last 5 days of a 15-day exposure to the omission procedure, and the other two subjects approached on more than 35% of the trials.

In another experiment we varied the distance of the CS from the US in an elongated version of the long box used to obtain the data in Fig. 2; in this new box the CSs could appear at either end of the chamber. The CS involved illumination of either a standard key light or a food magazine light, and these CSs were either near to (less than 10 cm) or far from (approximately 60 cm) the magazine that delivered grain. Thus the experiment factorially combined type of CS (key light or magazine light) and CS-US proximity (near or far). Omission-for-approach procedures were in force from the start of training and approach responses were measured automatically by switches beneath the floor near the appropriate CS. Over the last five sessions of the 20-session experiment, birds with either kind of "near CS" lost approximately 90% of the possible food deliveries, and those with either kind of "far CS" lost approximately 65%. Other studies performed in our laboratory indicate that, without the omission contingency, approach responses toward both the near and far CSs generally occur on more than 95% of the trials. Therefore, introduction of a negative response-reinforcer correlation has definite but relatively small effects on the strength of sign tracking. The stimulus-reinforcer relation plays a more powerful role, especially when the CS and US are close to each other.

This series of experiments (Peden et al., 1977) suggests that, rather than merely omitting reinforcement for approach behavior, Wessells may have inadvertently delivered grain while his birds were looking at some specific feature of the environment or perhaps he inadvertently reinforced specific competing movements of his subjects. In fact, he noticed the development of stereotyped behaviors in his birds and remarked that acquisition of such behaviors "incompatible with approaching toward the key may be an essential condition for the effectiveness of this negative contingency procedure" in eliminating approach behavior. Our use of an automatic rather than subjective criterion for approach seems to make this outcome much less likely.

3. Feature-positive discriminations. According to Hearst and Jenkins' (1974) analysis of sign tracking, both autoshaping and the FPE reflect the operation of very similar basic mechanisms. If this view is correct, then the omission procedure ought to produce effects in FP-discrimination situations that parallel the effects described for autoshaping arrangements. Subjects should persist in contacting the distinctive feature, i.e., the aspect of the environment that bears the highest positive correlation with the reinforcer, even though such behavior cancels the delivery of a scheduled reinforcer.

In my laboratory [see Jenkins (1973) for analogous results obtained with an operant procedure], we have examined the effects of adding an omission contingency to a FP discrimination in which key pecks were not required for grain delivery. Except for the absence of a key-peck requirement, the procedure was quite similar to that described earlier in this chapter for the three-key arrangement that produced the FPE shown in Fig. 1. Specific details of this FP-omission procedure, and results for both FP and FN discriminations without the inclusion of an omission contingency, are described in Hearst (1975a, pp. 237–242, 251–252). From the outset of training on the FP-omission arrangement, all positive trials lasted 6 sec and ended with the delivery of grain unless the subject had pecked the feature key during the trial. All negative trials also lasted 6 sec but were never followed by grain.

After the first session, birds pecked frequently on positive trials and confined their responding almost exclusively to the feature key. They hardly ever pecked on negative trials. As in standard autoshaping experiments, pecking quickly developed to the environmental feature that bore the highest positive correlation with the reinforcer, even though no response of any kind was required for delivery of the reinforcer and even though a peck at the feature key prevented delivery of a reinforcer. Out of a maximum of 25 possible grain deliveries, the median number of daily reinforcers declined from 24.5 on Day 1 to approximately 6 or 7 on Days 5 to 14. Only two of the nine birds obtained more than 50% of the maximum possible number of reinforcers over the last 10 days of the experiment (Days 5 to 14). Six of the nine subjects lost more than 73% of this maximum over the same 10 days.

It is important to note that, in both the FP-omission and the FN arrangement, pecks at the feature key were never followed by grain, whereas pecks at the other key color were followed by grain 50% of the time. (Half the daily trials were scheduled for reinforcement and half for nonreinforcement.) Therefore the fact that the feature signaled grain in the FP-omission arrangement and signaled no grain in the FN arrangement provides the only plausible basis for our finding that the feature was pecked (tracked) in the former case and hardly ever pecked in the latter. The effects of adding an omission contingency in Jenkins' (1973) operant study of the FPE and in our discriminative autoshaping experiment demonstrate that the role of the feature as a signal for food or no food is the crucial factor influencing the tendency of subjects to peck at it. Therefore, contrary to Jenkins and Sainsbury's (1969, 1970) original explanation of the FPE in terms of response-reinforcer conjunctions occurring for pecks directed at common vs. distinctive features, Hearst and Jenkins (1974, p. 23) concluded that in the FP case "pecking the feature results mainly from the perception of the feature's relation to reinforcement." A response-centered account cannot explain why pecks at the feature persist on the omission procedure, since only other behaviors could be followed by the reinforcer. "Perception of [the feature-reinforcer] relationship precedes and steers behavior toward the distinctive feature (Hearst & Jenkins, 1974, p. 24)."

4. Additional comment on omission effects.   Finally, a few cautious words seem warranted concerning the generality of response maintenance on omission procedures. There is a real question as to how persistent various target behaviors will be across different species, stimuli, reinforcers, responses, and experimental situations. A review of the literature is beyond the scope of this chapter, but several experimenters have reported that "autoshaped" responses can be eliminated in some organisms and situations by means of omission contingencies. We discussed above our inability to replicate Wessells' (1974) influential findings along these lines. Peden et al. (1977) reviewed other reports of response elimination by the omission procedure and pointed out that, in several of these studies, strong autoshaping was not actually demonstrated in the absence of an explicit response-reinforcer contingency (i.e., in these experiments a response immediately produced the US). If powerful approach and contact behavior toward CS (sign tracking) cannot be demonstrated in a given situation without inclusion of some explicit contingency for such behavior, then that situation is probably not an ideal one for studying the effects of an omission contingency on sign-tracking behavior. Of course, one would want to understand why sign tracking did not develop strongly in these situations, but that is presumably a somewhat different question. Hearst and Jenkins (1974) and Hearst (1975a) have indicated several situational factors that influence or limit the development and persistence of sign tracking, and future research will undoubtedly add other factors to the list.

B. Overt Movements and the Learning of Stimulus Relationships

The second general method for separating stimulus-reinforcer and response-reinforcer correlations in sign tracking involves prevention of certain directed movements during initial presentations of the CS and US; subjects merely "observe" the stimulus-stimulus relations. Can learning of a relationship between two stimuli take place in the absence of overt approach, contact, and consummatory responses?

A series of experiments performed by Browne (1974, 1976) at Indiana University evaluated the role of overt movements and access to food in the development of sign tracking. Browne's general scheme permitted pigeons to observe presentations of the CS (key light) and the US (activation of the grain magazine) at times when access to both the CS and the US (in some experiments) or only to the US (in other experiments) was blocked by placement of a transparent plastic cover in front of the appropriate stimuli. After this observation period, the CS and the US were both made available to the subject and the CS signaled the US. The acquisition of autoshaped key pecking was examined as a function of the type of CS-US contingency to which the subject had been exposed during the prior observation phase.

In his main experiment Browne first trained birds to eat from the lighted magazine and then blocked it with a transparent cover; whenever the food tray was raised, grain was visible to the subject but not accessible. The key always remained accessible, however, and any pecks at it were recorded. For three training sessions different groups of birds were exposed to different relationships between CS and "US" (the different treatments are described in the caption accompanying Fig. 3). Then, for all subjects, the cover in front of the magazine opening was removed, three grain deliveries were given, and standard autoshaping was immediately instituted.

As shown in Fig. 3, birds that had observed a positive contingency between CS and "US" pecked sooner and more frequently during the autoshaping (TEST) sessions than did subjects in the other groups. The median trial of the first key peck was 9.5, 27.5, 61.5, 56.0, and 83.5 for the positive, "US"-only, zero,

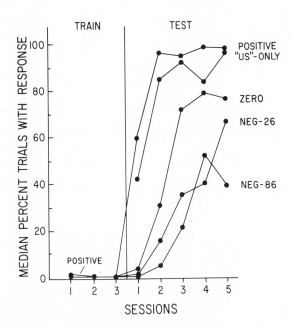

FIG. 3.   Acquisition of autoshaped key pecking over five sessions (test) for five experimental groups. During the preceding phase (train) the different groups had observed different correlations between an accessible 6-sec key light and visible but inaccessible grain: *positive* correlation (every key light followed by "US"); *zero* correlation (key light and "US" presented according to independent VI 60-sec schedules); *negative-26* ("US" never occurred within a 26-sec period following onset of the key light); *negative-86* ("US" never occurred within an 86-sec period following onset of the key light); and *"US"-only* (no key light, but "US" presented on a VI 60-sec schedule). (From Browne, 1976.)

negative-26, and negative-86 groups, respectively. During the observation phase, periodic visual observation of the subjects by the experimenter revealed no consistent movements toward or away from the lighted key; when monitored, birds typically were crouching in front of the magazine during CSs.

A subsequent experiment, which employed microswitches under separate floor sections to obtain objective measures of approach and withdrawal movements with respect to the lighted key in positive and negative subjects during the observation phase, also yielded no evidence for the conditioning of specific directed movements during that phase. Nevertheless, when the cover in front of the magazine was subsequently removed and all birds received key light-food pairings, subjects in the positive group approached the key significantly more often than the negative birds.

Other experimenters have obtained results that nicely complement Browne's conclusions. Parisi and Matthews (1975) found that a group of pigeons receiving pairings of key lights and magazine-operation cues during a phase when both the key light and magazine were blocked made more responses during a subsequent autoshaping phase than a group receiving random presentations of key light and magazine cues during the blockage phase. Deeds and Frieman (Note 1) trained all their subjects to eat from the grain magazine while at 75% of free-feeding weight; then they satiated the subjects and exposed different groups to different treatments involving key light presentations and food delivery. During this satiation phase, birds in the various treatment groups showed no differences in eating, pecking, or approach behavior; they ate and pecked the key on fewer than 2% of the trials. Then all subjects were returned to their 75% weight levels and placed on a standard autoshaping procedure. Subjects that had been exposed to a positive CS-US correlation while satiated acquired the key pecking response significantly faster than birds previously exposed to a zero or negative correlation between CS and US.

Furthermore, Boakes and Ismail (Note 2) reported evidence of stimulus-stimulus learning in subjects that had not received any magazine training (i.e., had never even been placed in the experimental chamber) before introduction of either correlated (100% pairings of key lights and an *empty* but illuminated food hopper) or random presentations of these two stimuli. During subsequent autoshaping, birds that had been exposed to the correlated condition pecked significantly sooner than the random birds. Evidently, learning of a relationship between key illumination and magazine cues can occur even when subjects have never received food in the situation. This result argues against general explanations of Browne's and Deeds and Frieman's findings in terms of secondary reinforcement accruing to magazine cues during initial magazine training. The experiment of Boakes and Ismail is of course similar to research on the topic of sensory preconditioning (see Seidel, 1959, for a review)—another phenomenon often used by S-S theorists to point up weaknesses in response-centered theories of learning.

All these findings indicate that subjects can certainly learn about a stimulus sequence or relationship during a period of exposure to it. There is little or no evidence suggesting that specific overt responses must appear during this period in order for such experience to be effective. As already suggested at several points in this chapter, the learning of relationships between stimuli seem quite possible—even for pigeons—in the absence of definite primary or secondary reinforcement and observable behavioral changes.

C. Stimulus Properties, Perceptual Factors, and Associative Relations

An interest in stimulus relationships inevitably leads one to wonder about the specific factors which may influence the ease of learning a particular relationship and may control the level and type of performance that is eventually achieved. Experiments along these lines are likely to focus on what many researchers would label "perceptual" factors in learning. Of course, workers with a cognitive or Gestalt orientation have always regarded the topics of perception, learning, and memory as closely related, in contrast to experimentalists operating within a more behavioristic, response-centered tradition. Recall the Gestaltist's view that their basic laws of organization apply equally well to perception and learning, and Tolman's and Woodworth's extensive use of perceptual processes in their approaches to learning.

This general attitude fosters analysis of the effects of such specific factors as (1) the similarity of the events entering into a relationship, (2) their temporal and spatial proximity, (3) their salience and localizability, and (4) the patterning or overall structure of the distributed stimulus events. Since temporal contiguity assumes a major role in most approaches to learning and memory, this factor has already received extensive attention from investigators of every theoretical persuasion. Numerous experiments have, for example, involved variation of the interstimulus and intertrial intervals in Pavlovian conditioning. A summary of such work would be inappropriate here, but with respect to the theme of this book a conclusion expressed by Jenkins (1970) and Staddon (1972), as a result of work on reinforcement schedules in pigeons, is noteworthy. They concluded that *relative temporal proximity*—which takes into account the structure or organization of events in time, including the *relation* between trial duration, temporal locus of reinforcement delivery, and length of the intertrial interval—is probably a more important factor than contiguity in any absolute sense (see Hearst & Franklin, 1977; Rescorla, 1967).

However, analysis of the other variables mentioned above seems to have been neglected in past research with animals. While arguing in favor of the study of a broader variety of inter-event relations in Pavlovian conditioning, Rescorla (this volume, Chapter 2; see Rescorla & Holland, 1976) also comments on similar gaps in our knowledge. A few examples of conclusions from recent relevant studies will indicate several directions that research along these lines might take.

Although some of the findings are tentative, they support Rescorla's argument that the above factors are important and deserve further experimental attention.

Close spatial proximity of the visual CS and the grain magazine promotes sign tracking behavior in the pigeon. [See Peden et al. (1977); Karpicke, Christoph, Peterson, & Hearst (1977) present some related material concerning positive and negative conditioned suppression in the rat.] Furthermore, compact "clusters" containing the common and distinctive elements employed in a FN discrimination yield better learning of that discrimination than displays on which the elements are distributed over a wider area (Sainsbury, 1971a). Probably relevant to these findings is the point that, in the natural environment of most organisms, stimuli which predict biologically important events are almost always located at approximately the same place in space as those events (e.g., the visual or olfactory cues associated with food, and the food itself).

Similarity of the visual properties (e.g., color) of CS and US events is also of some importance in promoting acquisition of autoshaped behavior (Sperling, Perkins, & Duncan, 1977; Steinhauer, Davol, & Lee, 1976). In addition, the modality of the CS (presumably in relation to the US) has large effects on the kinds of behavior that appear in an autoshaping situation, and perhaps on the rate of learning a particular CS-US relationship. Jenkins (see Hearst & Jenkins, 1974, p. 9) found that pigeons will track the location of auditory signals for food, but the effect is weaker and more variable than in the case of localized visual signals. In my laboratory, we have had even less success than Jenkins in obtaining consistent tracking of auditory signals, although we used a situation quite similar to his. Nevertheless, we have often observed consistent head-bobbing movements, "listening" behavior, or magazine-approach responses during an auditory (clicker) CS for food.

Obviously, subjects acquire anticipatory or preparatory behavior to both visual and auditory stimuli, but pecking movements and approaches toward the signal are much more common forms of behavior to a visual stimulus. However, the apparent advantage of visual signals over auditory signals in the autoshaping situation may occur not because of any intrinsic properties of the different modalities, but because of differences in the localizability of the particular visual and auditory stimuli that have so far been employed. It is not easy to assess the localizability of a signal or to define the conditions of an appropriate visual-auditory comparison. Furthermore, a plastic key provides direct "behavior support" (Tolman, 1932) for a response like pecking, whereas an auditory signal does not.

Therefore, as Rescorla (Chapter 2) similarly reports for rats presented with visual or auditory food signals, different predictors of the same reinforcer in a Pavlovian conditioning paradigm will not necessarily evoke the same set of behaviors—particularly in situations that involve the use of unrestrained subjects and the measurement of skeletal movements of the whole organism rather than autonomic responses. Depending on the specific properties of CS and US, and their relationship to each other, detection of learning may require analysis of several different responses. If the experimenter confined himself to a single measure of the "CR" he might falsely conclude that learning had not occurred. The same potential danger also exists on operant procedures that involve measurement of only one type of response.

IV. THE FEATURE-POSITIVE EFFECT REVISITED

The findings summarized above and in Hearst (1975a) convinced us that, at least in pigeons which are placed on typical autoshaping or feature-discrimination procedures, the learning of a relation between some localizable environmental feature and a reinforcer precedes and guides the development of behavior directed at that feature. Although this conclusion seemed of systematic importance, we were uncertain about its empirical generality and its specific theoretical implications. Recent research in our laboratory, along with work on the FPE reported by others, suggests that the phenomenon occurs in a variety of situations that are quite different from the arrangements used in earlier studies. I would like to introduce and describe some of this recent work, even though the distinct possibility will remain that these various examples of the FPE are only superficially related to each other and will require separate analysis.

Most researchers in the field of animal learning who have come across papers on the FPE probably regard it as an interesting experimental curiosity, which may appear in pigeons pecking at small objects like circles, dots, or stars, but which is unlikely to occur in other organisms performing other responses to other types of stimuli in other situations. Even for the pigeon, there is not very much solid information available about specific factors that control the magnitude of the FPE and there is much vagueness about exactly what a "feature" is. Features have been selected by guesswork or intuition on the part of the experimenter rather than by any strict quantitative or qualitative rules; researchers in the area often joke that you cannot tell whether a stimulus element (a line on the key, a black dot) is really a feature until you have actually performed an experiment with that element and have successfully obtained the FP superiority. Furthermore, since both human and nonhuman subjects can obviously learn a variety of FN discriminations (for example, those involved in Pavlov's conditioned-inhibition paradigm, which involves reinforcement of stimulus A and non-reinforcement of compound stimulus AX), it is very unlikely that experimenters will routinely obtain a FPE as massive as the effects reported by members of Jenkins' laboratory. In the studies performed by Jenkins and his colleagues, only one out of approximately 50 pigeons ever mastered a FN discrimination, whereas a large majority of the FP birds did.

Despite inevitable exceptions and limitations, FN learning may still prove to be typically slower and, at asymptote, less efficient and more variable than FP learning. Is it relevant that students and colleagues cannot easily generate examples from everyday life or naturalistic observation in which the *presentation* of some discrete environmental event simply signals the absence of a reinforcer, as in the FN case? A fundamental behavioral bias or principle—perhaps traceable to specific aspects of the innate organization of our nervous systems or to details of our typical past experiences—may be operating and may underlie not only the FPE but also various other related effects obtained in experiments on human sensory processing, learning, decision making, and problem solving. I will list some of these phenomena at the end of this chapter.

A. Species Generality: Humans, Too

Although few published studies concerning the FPE conform closely to the procedures originally employed and analyzed by Jenkins and Sainsbury (1969, 1970), a FP superiority has been reported in the discrimination learning of pigeons (Farthing, 1971; Hearst, 1975a; Jenkins, 1973; Jenkins & Sainsbury, 1969, 1970; Sainsbury, 1971a; Siegel, 1970), rats (Halgren, 1974; Reberg & LeClerc, 1977; Crowell, Lupo, Bernhardt, & Kubiak, Note 3; Reberg & LeClerc, Note 4; an experiment with rats by Lea, 1974, may be related to the FPE, but is not clearly an instance of it), cats (Diamond, Goldberg, & Neff, 1962), and young and adult human beings (Bitgood, Segrave, & Jenkins, 1976; Norton, Muldrew, & Strub, 1971; Sainsbury, 1971b, 1973; Newman, Note 5).

Some of our recent research with human subjects seems worthy of mention here. In one set of experiments involving the learning of successive discriminations in college students, Joseph Newman and I used a discrete-trial operant procedure in which displays, each consisting of several different symbols projected on a row of keys, were presented to the subjects, who were asked to identify correct and incorrect displays by touching and not touching them, respectively. For the FP subjects a display was "correct" whenever a particular symbol (e.g., a triangle) appeared on any key; whenever no triangle was present anywhere, the display was "incorrect." The conditions were reversed for the FN subjects. In most of our studies a clear FPE occurred: little or no learning of the FN discrimination and relatively good learning of the FP discrimination within the 72-trial limit of the experiments. There was occasional but not consistent evidence of sign tracking (e.g., touching the triangle in the FP case).

In another experiment designed and supervised by Newman, college students had to learn a simultaneous discrimination. Index cards containing two trigrams (meaningless combinations of three letters, such as TBX or ZAQ) were presented to subjects every 5 sec. They were told that one of each pair of trigrams was "good" and the other "not good" and that their task was to discover the rule differentiating the two. For FP subjects, the presence of a particular letter (a specific vowel for one subexperiment, a specific consonant for another subexperiment) in one of the trigrams made it the correct choice, whereas for FN subjects the correct trigram was the one without that particular letter. On each trial the subjects stated whether they thought the trigram on the left or right was the good one, and they were told whether they were correct immediately after every trial. In the instructions preceding the start of training, subjects were asked to inform the experimenter as soon as they thought they had discovered the rule and then to verbalize it.

In each of the two FP subgroups (vowel and consonant: $n = 8$) the median number of trials to criterion (a statement of the correct rule) was 35.5 trials. Of the 16 FP subjects, 12 reached the criterion within the 60-trial limit of the experiment, but only one of the 16 FN subjects ever learned. It was common for subjects in the FN groups to report that after choosing the wrong trigram they rehearsed only the other (correct) member of the pair. They focused on information contained in the positive trigram and ignored information contained in the negative trigram.

Successive-discrimination experiments with single trigrams also yielded a large FPE. In addition, we conducted experiments in which (a) informative feedback was delayed until various times after the end of a trial, or (b) subjects had to spell aloud their choices. Under these conditions we hoped that subjects would be more likely to notice and take into account information contained in the wrong trigram. However, such changes made little or no difference in the extent of the FPE.

Thus, in these studies at least, the FPE is remarkably large in adult human subjects. In the FN case, noticing that the "clue" required to solve the problem appears on incorrect displays is very rare.

B. Situational and Procedural Generality

There seems no doubt that various specific properties of features, displays, common elements, and background or contextual stimuli—as well as interactions between these constituents of the total situation—will prove critical for obtaining a clearcut FPE. The problem of defining a feature appears related to the *integrality* vs. *separability* of stimulus dimensions (Garner, 1970; see also Riley and Roitblat, this volume, Chapter 9) and the *symmetry* vs. *asymmetry* of discriminative stimuli (Jenkins & Sainsbury, 1969, 1970). The general problem is pertinent to points raised by Gibson (1969), Jakobson, Fant, and Halle (1969), and Tversky (1977) in their discussions of distinctive features in perceptual learning, speech perception, and similarity relations. In our laboratory we frequently find it difficult to design FPE research, or to conceive new "features" for possible study, without somehow invoking the old (and unfortunately vague) Gestalt laws of perceptual organization (e.g., figure-ground, proximity and similarity, and goodness or simplicity; see Hearst, 1975a, pp. 242–243, and Sainsbury, 1971a).

Several recent findings with pigeons and rats have suggested more generality for the FPE than we had actually anticipated across situations and procedural manipulations. On the other hand, a few studies, apparently very similar to prior successful ones, have failed to produce a FPE. Although detailed descriptions and analysis of these experiments are not possible or appropriate in this chapter, selective comments about certain points should help the reader gain some perspective concerning the generality of the FPE.

1. Appetitive vs. aversive reinforcers.   Most demonstrations of the FPE have involved positive reinforcers. However, Reberg and LeClerc (1977) obtained a robust FPE in a conditioned suppression experiment. While responding on a VI 1-min schedule, two groups of rats (FP) received 60-sec presentations of a compound stimulus (AX, with the elements of the compound stimulus being a flashing light, L, and an intermittent tone, T) followed by shock, and 60-sec presentations of one of the two elements, A, never followed by shock. For one FP group stimulus A was the light, and for the other group it was the tone. The two groups of FN subjects received presentations of A (either the light or tone, depending on the group) followed by shock, and presentations of AX never followed by shock.

Figure 4 presents a summary of Reberg and LeClerc's results. The two FP groups acquired the discrimination between AX and A considerably faster than their FN counterparts. There was appreciable learning of the FN discrimination in this experiment, especially in the group (lower right in Fig. 4) that had the light as the feature. Nevertheless, it is clear that the FP superiority is not limited to pigeon subjects and food reinforcement.

2. Type of feature.   Reberg and LeClerc's study also showed that the FPE can be obtained without the use of localized visual displays, as has been typical of pigeon experiments. However, in one pigeon experiment Brown and Jenkins (cited in Jenkins & Sainsbury, 1969, p. 158) did observe a FPE with an auditory stimulus (a burst of tone) as the distinguishing feature and illumination of the response key as the element common to positive and negative trials. Under this arrangement, the FN subjects eventually reached reasonably good levels of performance, although their learning was relatively slow compared to the FP group—as in Reberg and LeClerc's study and in the studies by Halgren (1974) and Diamond et al. (1962). Using an auditory feature with rats that received appetitive reinforcers, Halgren obtained FP learning that was superior to FN learning, whereas Diamond et al. reported superior FP learning in cats placed on discriminations that involved an auditory feature and shock avoidance training.

In my laboratory Sarah Bottjer has obtained a consistent FPE with a new type of feature, *US delivery* preceding CS+ or CS- presentations. She noticed that part of Terry and Wagner's (1975; see also Wagner, this volume, Chapter 7) design could be conceptualized as involving FP vs. FN treatments in different

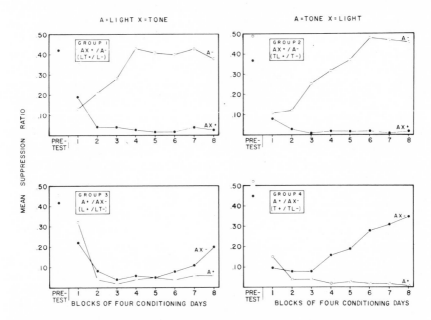

FIG. 4.   Mean ratios of conditioned suppression [(number of bar presses during the 60-sec periods of stimulus *A* or *AX*) divided by (number of bar presses during the 60-sec periods immediately preceding *A* or *AX* plus the number of bar presses during *A* or *AX*)] for two FP groups (top panels) and two FN groups (bottom panels) over successive 4-day blocks of training. For the groups on the left, stimulus *A* was a light, whereas for the groups on the right it was a tone. The points plotted as pretest values were obtained during unreinforced presentations of *AX* and *A* on the last two days of VI training prior to introduction of the *AX* vs. *A* discrimination. (From Reberg & LeClerc, 1977.)

subgroups, with an aversive pretrial US serving as the feature in a rabbit-eyelid-conditioning paradigm. Although Terry and Wagner's data indicated a FP superiority, particularly with an 8-sec US-CS interval, they did not offer an extensive analysis of that portion of their experiment. Since my colleagues are likely to pursue any phenomenon that seems to resemble the FPE, Bottjer has performed two somewhat different experiments which are analogs of the Terry and Wagner study but which involve an appetitive US. Both experiments revealed a significant FPE. Even though the second experiment yielded a more powerful FPE than the first experiment, the procedure of the first experiment was somewhat simpler and only that experiment will be briefly described here.

The left and right keys of a standard pigeon chamber were used, and 6-sec illumination of either key was followed by grain delivery 50% of the time (i.e., a partial-reinforcement autoshaping procedure was in effect). Preceding each key illumination was a 6-sec "preparatory" interval consisting either of (1) a 3-sec clicking sound, *A*, plus simultaneous grain presentation, *X*, followed by 3 sec of no stimulation, or (2) a 3-sec clicking sound, *A*, followed by 3 sec of no stimulation. Thus grain presentation, X, served as the feature and, in the FP case, AX presentations were followed by reinforced key illuminations and A presentations by nonreinforced key illuminations. In the FN case, of course, the reinforcement outcomes following A and AX presentations were reversed.

Various measures of discrimination learning (e.g., sessions required to reach a certain key-pecking discrimination ratio; approach-withdrawal difference scores for positive vs. negative trials) revealed significantly more rapid acquisition of differential behavior during illuminations of the key in the six FP subjects than in the six FN subjects (see Fig. 5). Furthermore, at the beginning of training there was no bias in favor of more key pecks during key illuminations after AX presentations than after A presentations; in fact, the top panel in Fig. 5 shows that, if anything, the opposite occurred. We had been worried about this possibility when setting up an appetitive analog to Terry and Wagner's (1975) eyelid-conditioning procedure; and, as a matter of fact, we included a preparatory stimulus (the clicker) on all trials to minimize the likelihood that FP subjects would be better "prepared" for positive trials than FN subjects and could therefore initiate pecking faster. Terry and Wagner's subjects were not prepared for trials that were preceded by no US, but our subjects received a "ready signal" on all trials.

3. Sequential presentation of elements.   Besides the use of food delivery as a feature, Bottjer's experiment differed from almost all prior studies of the FPE in another significant way: The feature was presented prior to a trial rather than at the same time. William Wolff and I have also obtained a clear FP superiority in a discrimination involving a temporally prior feature. This research employed a second key color as the feature; pigeons received trials of white-only and green-white key illuminations. Presentations of each color were 6 sec long. After four sessions of nondifferential pretraining with 50% reinforcement on both kinds of trials, discrimination sessions began. Positive trials were followed by food, whereas negative trials were not. When the distinguishing feature (green) preceded positive trials (FP), subjects pecked both colors on positive trials and seldom pecked on white-only trials. Other subjects, for whom green preceded positive trials (FP), *seldom pecked green* but pecked white on both positive and negative trials. In the data analysis, discrimination ratios were calculated by the formula: (key pecks during positive white trials) divided by (total key pecks during both positive and negative white trials). None of the eight FN birds ever attained a discrimination ratio above .90 until Day 18 of the experiment, whereas five of the six FP subjects attained this ratio at least once by Day 10.

Thus the FP superiority was substantial and reliable in Bottjer's and Wolff's pigeon experiments with a temporally prior feature, regardless of whether the feature was food delivery or the illumination of a differently colored key. Results paralleling those of Wolff have also been reported by Manzone and

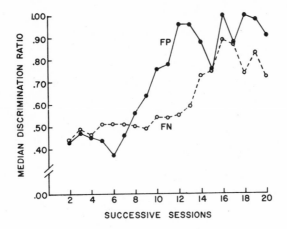

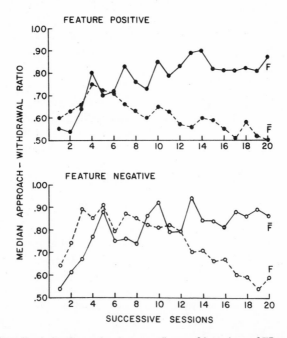

FIG. 5.   Median discrimination ratios (top panel) over 20 sessions of FP or FN training in which prior grain delivery served as the feature distinguishing positive and negative trials. Discrimination ratios were calculated by dividing the total number of key pecks to CS+ by the total number of key pecks to both CS+ and CS−. In the bottom set of panels median approach-withdrawal ratios (total time spent on the same side as the key light divided by total trial time) are supplied for feature (F) and nonfeature ($\overline{\text{F}}$) trials in each group; F trials correspond to trials labeled AX in the text, and $\overline{\text{F}}$ trials to trials labeled A. [For additional details concerning the rationale and experimental technique for obtaining approach-withdrawal ratios, see Hearst (1975a, pp. 222–225).]

D'Andrea (Note 6) in an appetitive *operant*-discrimination task, and one of their colleagues, Bruce Campbell, has since replicated and extended their major findings. Recently we were pleased to learn that Reberg and LeClerc (Note 4) have obtained analogous results in a conditioned suppression arrangement with rats. Like the Reberg and LeClerc (1977) study described above, they used visual and auditory stimuli in this research; however, the visual stimulus was now the offset of a houselight and the auditory stimulus was a 75-db white noise. They obtained significantly better FP than FN learning for three different temporal arrangements of AX trials: (a) 60-sec presentations of X and A began and terminated simultaneously (as in the Reberg & LeClerc, 1977, study); (b) X preceded A by 60 sec and also overlapped it for 60 sec; and (c) a 60-sec presentation of X preceded but did not overlap A.

4. Size, salience, and overshadowing.   Our opinion is that the relative size and salience of the feature are important determinants of the FPE. Back in 1967 I performed my first experiment on what I later realized was a comparison of FP vs. FN learning and I failed to obtain a FPE (Hearst, 1969). The discriminative stimuli involved a completely white key vs. a white key containing a black line that bisected it, and I now suspect that, among other things, the salience and size of the feature had something to do with my failure to secure an effect like Jenkins and Sainsbury's (1969, 1970). A recent study by Morris (1977) strongly supports this speculation, since line length was found to be directly related to the efficiency of FN learning. Using dark black dots on a white background, Strub, Gfellner, and Norton (Note 7) also failed to obtain a FPE in pigeons, and their procedures were even more similar to Jenkins and Sainsbury's than was my 1969 procedure.

Jenkins (personal communication, October, 1970) remarked that his comparable experiments involved a black dot that was not of "extremely high contrast," since the entire display was front lighted and had a transparent plastic covering on it to prevent the bird from marking the display with its beak. William Wolff and I are currently performing a series of experiments in which the intensity and color of the background are well controlled and varied by means of carefully prepared slides, a Carousel projector, and a relatively sophisticated optical system (instead of the conventional miniprojectors used in most pigeon work.) Our hope is, of course, to define salience in terms of the relationship between background and feature and to examine the magnitude of the FPE as a function of feature salience. No definite conclusions from these experiments are available yet, and therefore we cannot provide strong empirical support for our opinion that feature salience is an important factor in FP vs. FN differences—an outcome that seems likely both on the basis of common sense and various formal models of discrimination learning.

Thus we are implying that the degree to which certain elements of the display overshadow other elements is important in determining the magnitude and existence of the FPE. This speculation is related to Pavlov's remark that "the rate of formation of conditioned inhibition depends, again, on the character and relative intensity of the additional stimulus in comparison with the conditioned stimulus (Pavlov, 1927, p. 75)." He presented examples of stimuli that failed to act as strong conditioned inhibitors and examples of other stimuli that easily assumed this function. It also seems worth reiterating Mackintosh's conclusion (this volume, Chapter 6) that salience and predictiveness apparently interact to determine how animals evaluate the relative significance of the elements of a compound CS and learn to attend to them selectively. Although his research mainly involved "blocking" procedures, Mackintosh's results are likely to have definite implications for the FPE.

C. General Observations on the Feature-Positive Effect

Despite considerable differences in experimental procedure, reinforcers, stimulus properties and arrangements, and type of subject, a substantial number of studies have revealed a strong FPE. Several experiments yielded virtually no learning of the FN discrimination, in contrast to the excellent performance quickly achieved on the FP procedure, whereas in other experiments subjects eventually did acquire the FN discrimination but at significantly slower rates than for the FP discrimination. Most failures to obtain a FP superiority seem to have involved the use of distinctive features that were very salient; in such cases FP and FN learning apparently progress at approximately the same rate.

The paradigmatic case of a pigeon pecking at displays that differ only in the presence or absence of a relatively small, localizable visual feature may prove helpful toward our eventual understanding of the results obtained in other, more complicated situations which have yielded a FPE. Even though, on operant procedures, the bird is not required to peck at any particular element of the displays—or, on autoshaping procedures, to peck anywhere at all—it consistently pecks at the distinctive feature in the FP case and usually at some common element of the displays in the FN case. In both cases the feature of the environment that bears the highest positive correlation with the reinforcer is the target of the bird's directed behavior. The bird seems to be telling us which aspect of the environment it considers the "cause" of grain delivery. In this sense, the approach and contact responses of the pigeon—what we have called sign tracking —provide us with overt behavioral measures of how the subject selectively assesses the causal texture of its environment. Stated more objectively, sign tracking tells us how strongly the subject is controlled by various external cues. The power and persistence of the pigeon's tendency to track highly reliable predictors of food are indicated by the development and maintenance of such tracking even when it is penalized by loss of reinforcement, as in the FP-omission arrangement. Findings with the omission procedure provide strong arguments against response-centered explanations of the FPE (see also Jenkins, 1973), and favor approaches that emphasize the perception or registration of stimulus relationships.

Nevertheless, I think it would be premature to attempt a theoretical integration of all the FPE work on the basis of research involving the pigeon paradigm. Even for the pigeon, we know relatively little about the factors that control the magnitude or existence of the FPE. Furthermore, the above analysis in terms of sign tracking cannot be simply extended to (a) situations with diffuse stimuli, sequential presentation of elements, or verbal materials and (b) situations in which FN learning readily occurs. We might speculate that sign tracking in the pigeon reveals fundamental processes of feature selection or hypothesis testing which characterize many organisms and situations, but which are not so directly measurable in other arrangements as in the standard pigeon paradigm. However, until more information is accumulated, it seems wise to continue to entertain the possibility that various examples of the FPE are only superficially related and may eventually require separate analysis.

Some workers (e.g., Jenkins, 1973; Reberg & LeClerc, 1977; Reberg & LeClerc, Note 4) have tried to indicate how the Rescorla-Wagner (1972) model might handle various aspects of the FPE. The model does seem to make the general prediction that FP discriminations should be acquired more quickly than FN discriminations, because in the latter case the feature must acquire considerable inhibitory strength in order for responding on negative trials to disappear. In the FP case, the development of conditioned inhibition is not necessary for discrimination learning since mere loss of excitation by the common element would be sufficient to produce response elimination on negative trials. However, Jenkins (1973) pointed out some problems that the model encounters when applied to the specific results he has obtained in pigeon experiments.

The results of studies concerning the FPE are compatible in several ways with the main points of Mackintosh's contribution to this volume (Chapter 6). He concludes that (1) the presence of better predictors of reinforcement interferes with conditioning to poor predictors of the same reinforcer, and (2) subjects learn to ignore relatively poor predictors. Mackintosh also presents data demonstrating that salience overrides or interacts with predictiveness in experiments on blocking, and we noted that salience may have analogous effects in determining the extent of the FPE. However, "salience" itself requires a stricter definition than tacitly used in the past, which is not an easy goal to achieve. Furthermore, it is not clear how Mackintosh's general conclusions would predict the massive asymmetries between FP and FN learning that have been reported in several experiments. A highly reliable predictor of *non*reinforcement is not one that ought to be "ignored," as I understand his arguments, and yet that outcome seems to characterize several instances of the FPE which we have described above. In order to explain the FPE, a general asymmetry between positive- and negative-contingency learning may have to be assumed (see, for example, Baker, 1974), whereby stimulus elements with the greatest excitatory strength somehow exert more selective control not only in comparison to poor predictors of reinforcement but also in comparison to elements highly correlated with nonreinforcement. Relevant here is the sizable literature covering studies of the relative "weights" of positive and negative stimuli in animal discrimination learning. For a summary of methods used in such experiments, and for comments on the somewhat inconsistent results obtained, see Hearst (1971) and Stevens and Wixon (1976).

Theorists with a cognitive orientation would probably tend to interpret the FPE along the lines suggested by Tolman's views about reinforcement. He believed that "reinforcers" are *emphasizers*, which determine the specific aspects of the environment that will interest the subject and attract its attention. According to this general view, hungry pigeons receiving food in an autoshaping situation, rats experiencing shocks in a CER situation, and cooperative human subjects achieving success on certain trials in a concept-formation experiment, test various hypotheses about events or features that are possibly related to the outcomes. They eventually respond mainly on the basis of which environmental aspects are best correlated with these emphasizers. Similarly, in contemporary cognitive psychology, incentives like money are considered to act as sources of information that highlight facts or relationships which would be valuable for the subject to learn, rehearse, or recode.

These approaches imply that we could easily remove the FPE, and perhaps obtain a FNE, if we suggested to our human subjects that critical information is contained in incorrect items; establishment of such a set would encourage the subjects to focus their attention on features to which they apparently do not attend very much under normal conditions. (Newman, Note 5, reports several experiments that support such a prediction.) An animal analog to this type of manipulation is not obvious, however, unless pretraining on various FN discriminations would yield positive transfer to relatively hard discriminations of this kind. In any event, the type of cognitive approach outlined above, while perhaps of heuristic value, seems currently too vague to predict the specific details of the various experimental results described in this paper.

In animal studies there is an asymmetry in the FP and FN procedures that may contribute to the FP superiority which is usually obtained. The only discrete stimulus events that are programmed to occur in these experiments are presentations of the conditioned (or discriminative) stimuli and the reinforcer. On *AX* (feature) trials in the FP case, the stimuli immediately preceding and following the trial are different (the ITI condition before a trial; the reinforcer after a trial), whereas pretrial and posttrial stimuli are the same for *AX* trials in the FN case (the ITI condition before and after). In the FN case nonreinforcement is indicated merely by a return to the ITI condition, and thus no salient new event occurs after a feature trial in the FN case. Perhaps if a discrete cue (e.g., a distinctive noise; a brief blackout; magazine illumination but with inaccessible grain) were arranged to follow negative trials in the FN case, learning of the FN discrimination would be promoted (see Zanich & Fowler, 1975, who would apparently predict the same outcome but for a different reason).

Along the lines of our suggestion, a Gestalt psychologist might have argued that, in most of the above-mentioned animal experiments, FP learning is easier because both the feature and its temporally contiguous outcome (US) stand out against a common background and are relatively brief events, mainly visual and with sudden onsets—factors that would facilitate their organization and grouping—whereas in the FN case organizational factors of this kind are not present on AX trials to promote "association" of the feature and the outcome. According to this logic, perceptual factors would be expected to interact with predictability to create the FPE, a general conclusion supported by many of the findings that we have summarized in this chapter.

D. The FPE and Related Phenomena in Humans

Over the past few years, I have been making a list of various results and phenomena, observed in either human or animal experimentation, which seem related to the FPE. My decision rules for including an item on the list are not very strict, and I would not like to be forced to justify every entry (on days of great optimism, almost everything seems related to the FPE). I admit that it is probably unwise to conceive various other effects and issues in relation to a phenomenon that is itself not very well analyzed or understood, and for which no comprehensive theoretical framework currently exists. However, the list has been useful for me in suggesting experiments, and, to conclude the chapter, I would like to give some examples of items from human research on the list. In my opinion, they represent pieces of a puzzle whose solution will have theoretical importance for a variety of phenomena in the fields of learning, perception, and memory. Space limitations preclude more than a mere listing, and I leave to the reader the task of determining the distinctive and common features that probably governed my choice of particular items.

1. The relative effectiveness of positive and negative instances in concept learning (see Bourne, Ekstrand, Lovallo, Kellogg, Hiew, & Yaroush, 1976).

2. Differential depth of processing or differential rehearsal of right vs. wrong items (e.g., Kausler, Majcher, & Conover, 1975).

3. Number of stages, transformations, or conditionalizing operations in the formation of abstract representations (e.g., presence-absence decisions in Chase & Clark, 1971).

4. Preferences for positive vs. negative information (see Posner, 1973, pp. 113-116 for a summary).

5. Visual search for present vs. absent target features (see Neisser, 1967, for a summary).

6. Differential retention of words associated with questions producing positive vs. negative answers (Craik & Tulving, 1975).

7. Biased judgments of the extent of contingency, correlation, or causality between events (e.g., Chapman & Chapman, 1971; Jenkins & Ward, 1965; Ward & Jenkins, 1965).

8. Probability learning and the subject's attention to positive vs. negative outcomes (for general findings and developmental effects, see Estes, 1976).

V. CONCLUDING COMMENTS

In this research, two phenomena, autoshaping and the feature-positive effect, served as vehicles for analyzing some issues similar to those which have traditionally separated cognitive and response-centered approaches to learning. Data from omission and response-prevention experiments show that the subject's learning of a relationship between stimuli is more important in accounting for the two phenomena than is learning of associations between specific overt responses and stimuli. Such findings support perception-centered rather than response-centered theories and indicate the value of making an explicit distinction between learning and performance. However, the generality of these conclusions needs further assessment by means of research that carefully examines the relative importance of stimulus-reinforcer and response-reinforcer correlations in a variety of Pavlovian and operant conditioning situations.

Several recent studies were described or mentioned in which both children and adult human beings display a clear feature positive effect. This outcome suggests that analogous findings with pigeons and rats may apply more broadly than we previously suspected. Under a variety of conditions, it is considerably easier for subjects to learn that some specific feature of a compound stimulus is a signal for reinforcement than to learn that the feature is a signal for nonreinforcement. This difference between positive- and negative-contingency learning may disappear if the feature is very intense or salient. Successful theories of selective attention or discrimination learning will eventually have to encompass this apparent asymmetry in the way positive and negative information are processed.

The present approach to Pavlovian and operant conditioning embraces the distinction between learning and performance, the perception of relationships among stimuli, and the notion of feature selection. Such an approach will not appeal to workers who believe that, in order to maintain its integrity and utility, the psychology of animal learning must focus almost exclusively on observable stimuli and responses and avoid the postulation of organismic processes or mechanisms that are not directly measurable. Valuable research can certainly be performed within both kinds of framework, but in my opinion, a relatively comprehensive theory of learning and behavior—one that will apply to both animals and humans—is more likely to emerge from the less rigid type of general approach outlined in this and almost every other chapter of the present volume.

ACKNOWLEDGMENTS

The preparation of this chapter and the animal research connected with it were supported by U.S. National Institute of Mental Health Research Grant No. MH-19300. In addition to the students and other colleagues mentioned as collaborators in the text, I would like to thank Carol Daniels Smith, Dexter Gormley, John Karpicke, Lynn Sternberg, and Edward Walker for their generous assistance, advice, and encouragement.

NOTES

1. Deeds, W., & Frieman, J. Latent learning of auto shaping: Stimulus-reinforcer learning in the nondeprived pigeon. Paper presented at the meeting of the Midwestern Psychological Association, Chicago, May 1977.
2. Boakes, R. A., & Ismail, R. B. An effect similar to sensory preconditioning in autoshaping of key pecking in pigeons. Unpublished manuscript, 1971. (Available from R. A. Boakes, Laboratory of Experimental Psychology, University of Sussex, Brighton, England.)
3. Crowell, C. R., Lupo, J. V., Bernhardt, T., & Kubiak, P. Feature-positive and feature-negative discrimination learning in the rat. Paper presented at the meeting of the Midwestern Psychological Association, Chicago, May 1976.
4. Reberg, D., & LeClerc, R. Pavlovian discriminations based on distinguishing stimuli (Research Bulletin No. 367: ISSN 0316-4675). London, Canada: University of Western Ontario, Dept. of Psychology, May 1976.
5. Newman, J. The feature-positive effect in human subjects. Unpublished manuscript, 1976. (Available from J. Newman, Department of Psychology, Indiana University, Bloomington, Indiana 47401.)
6. Manzone, T. A., & D'Andrea, T. The effect of CS predictiveness in a phenomenon similar to autoshaping. Paper presented at the meeting of the Eastern Psychological Association, New York, April 1975.
7. Strub, H., Gfellner, B., & Norton, G. R. Equivalent discrimination acquisition under feature-positive and feature-negative conditions. Paper presented at the meeting of the Psychonomic Society, San Antonio, Texas, November, 1970.

REFERENCES

Baker, A. G. Conditioned inhibition is not the symmetrical opposite of conditioned excitation: A test of the Rescorla-Wagner model. *Learning and Motivation,* 1974, *5,* 369–379.

Bitgood, S. C., Segrave, K. & Jenkins, H.M. Verbal feedback and the feature-positive effect in children. *Journal of Experimental Child Psychology,* 1976, *21,* 249–255.

Boakes, R. A., & Halliday, M. S. *Inhibition and learning.* New York: Academic Press, 1972.

Bourne, L. E., Ekstrand, B. R., Lovallo, W. R., Kellogg, R. T., Hiew, C. C., & Yaroush, R. A. Frequency analysis of attribute identification. *Journal of Experimental Psychology: General,* 1976, *105,* 294–312.

Brown, P. L., & Jenkins, H. M. Auto-shaping of the pigeon's key peck. *Journal of the Experimental Analysis of Behavior*, 1968, *11*, 1–8.

Browne, M. P. *Auto-shaping and the role of primary reinforcement and overt movements in the acquisition of stimulus-stimulus relations*. Unpublished doctoral dissertation, Indiana University, 1974.

Browne, M. P. The role of primary reinforcement and overt movements in autoshaping in the pigeon. *Animal Learning and Behavior*, 1976, *4*, 287–292.

Chapman, L. J., & Chapman, J. P. Associatively based illusory correlation as a source of psychodiagnostic folklore. In L. D. Goodstein and R. I. Lanyon (Eds.), *Readings in personality assessment*. New York: Wiley, 1971.

Chase, W. G., & Clark, H. Semantics in the perception of verticality. *British Journal of Psychology*, 1971, *62*, 311–326.

Craik, F. I., & Tulving, E. Depth of processing and the retention of words in episodic memory. *Journal of Experimental Psychology: General*, 1975, *104*, 268–294.

Diamond, I. T., Goldberg, J. M., & Neff, W. D. Tonal discrimination after ablation of auditory cortex. *Journal of Neurophysiology*, 1962, *25*, 223–235.

Estes, W. K. The cognitive side of probability learning. *Psychological Review*, 1976, *83*, 37–64.

Farthing, G. W. Discrimination of compound stimuli involving the presence or absence of a distinctive visual feature. *Journal of the Experimental Analysis of Behavior*, 1971, *16*, 327–336.

Garner, W. R. The stimulus in information processing. *American Psychologist*, 1970, *25*, 350–358.

Gibson, E. J. *Principles of perceptual learning and development*. New York: Appleton-Century-Crofts, 1969.

Halgren, C. R. Latent inhibition in rats: Associative or nonassociative? *Journal of Comparative and Physiological Psychology*, 1974, *86*, 74–78.

Hearst, E. Excitation, inhibition, and discrimination learning. In N.J. Mackintosh and W. K. Honig (Eds.), *Fundamental issues in associative learning*. Halifax, Canada: Dalhousie University Press, 1969.

Hearst, E. Differential transfer of excitatory versus inhibitory pretraining to intradimensional discrimination learning in pigeons. *Journal of Comparative and Physiological Psychology*, 1971, *75*, 206–215.

Hearst, E. Some persistent problems in the analysis of conditioned inhibition. In R. A. Boakes and M. S. Halliday (Eds.), *Inhibition and learning*. New York: Academic Press, 1972.

Hearst, E. Pavlovian conditioning and directed movements. In G. Bower (Ed.), *The psychology of learning and motivation* (Vol. 9). New York: Academic Press, 1975. (a)

Hearst, E. The classical-instrumental distinction: Reflexes, voluntary behavior, and categories of associative learning. In W. K. Estes (Ed.), *Handbook of learning and cognitive processes* (Vol. 2: Conditioning and behavior theory.) Hillsdale, New Jersey: Lawrence Erlbaum Associates, 1975. (b)

Hearst, E., Besley, S., & Farthing, G. W. Inhibition and the stimulus control of operant behavior. *Journal of the Experimental Analysis of Behavior*, 1970, *14*, 373–409.

Hearst, E., & Franklin, S. Positive and negative relations between a signal and food: Approach-withdrawal behavior to the signal. *Journal of Experimental Psychology: Animal Behavior Processes*, 1977, *3*, 37–52.

Hearst, E., & Jenkins, H. M. *Sign-tracking: The stimulus-reinforcer relation and directed action*. Austin, Texas: Psychonomic Society, 1974.

Jakobson, R., Fant, C. G. M., & Halle, M. *Preliminaries to speech analysis: The distinctive features and their correlates*. Cambridge, Massachusetts: MIT Press, 1969.

Jenkins, H. M. Sequential organization in schedules of reinforcement. In W. N. Schoenfeld (Ed.), *The theory of reinforcement schedules.* New York: Appleton-Century-Crofts, 1970.

Jenkins, H. M. Noticing and responding in a discrimination based on a distinguishing element. *Learning and Motivation,* 1973, *4,* 115–137.

Jenkins, H. M., & Sainsbury, R. S. The development of stimulus control through differential reinforcement. In N. J. Mackintosh and W. K. Honig (Eds.), *Fundamental issues in associative learning.* Halifax, Canada: Dalhousie University Press, 1969.

Jenkins, H. M., & Sainsbury, R. S. Discrimination learning with the distinctive feature on positive or negative trials. In D. Mostofsky (Ed.), *Attention: Contemporary theory and analysis.* New York: Appleton-Century-Crofts, 1970.

Jenkins, H. M., & Ward, W. C. The judgment of contingency between responses and outcomes. *Psychological Monographs: General and Applied,* 1965, *79,* No. 1 (Whole No. 594).

Karpicke, J., Christoph, G., Peterson, G., & Hearst, E. Signal location and positive vs. negative conditioned suppression in the rat. *Journal of Experimental Psychology: Animal Behavior Processes,* 1977, *3,* 105–118.

Kausler, D., Majcher, L. L., & Conover, J. Schematic exemplars as items in multiple-item recognition learning. *Bulletin of the Psychonomic Society,* 1975, *6,* 472–474.

Lajoie, J., & Bindra, D. An interpretation of autoshaping and related phenomena in terms of stimulus-incentive contingencies alone. *Canadian Journal of Psychology,* 1976, *30,* 157–173.

Lea, S. E. G. The non-occurrence of a stimulus as a signal. *Quarterly Journal of Experimental Psychology,* 1974, *26,* 616–621.

MacCorquodale K., & Meehl, P. E., Edward C. Tolman. In W. K. Estes, S. Koch, K. MacCorquodale. P. E. Meehl, C. G. Mueller, W. N. Schoenfeld, and W. S. Verplanck (Eds.), *Modern learning theory.* New York: Appleton-Century-Crofts, 1954.

Morris, R. C. Spatial variables and the feature-positive effect. *Learning and Motivation,* 1977, *8,* 194–212.

Neisser, U. *Cognitive psychology.* New York: Appleton-Century-Crofts, 1967.

Norton, G. R., Muldrew, D., & Strub, H. Feature-positive effect in children. *Psychonomic Science,* 1971, *23,* 317–318.

Parisi, T., & Matthews, T. J. Pavlovian determinants of the auto-shaped key peck response. *Bulletin of the Psychonomic Society,* 1975, *6,* 527–529.

Pavlov, I. P. *Conditioned reflexes.* London and New York: Oxford University Press, 1927.

Peden, B., Browne, M. P., & Hearst, E. Persistent approaches to a signal for food despite food omission for approaching. *Journal of Experimental Psychology: Animal Behavior Processes,* 1977, *3,* 377–399.

Posner, M. I. *Cognition: An introduction.* Glenview, Illinois: Scott, Foresman, 1973.

Premack, D. Reinforcement theory. In D. Levine (Ed.), *Nebraska symposium on motivation* (Vol. 13). Lincoln, Nebraska: University of Nebraska Press, 1965.

Reberg, D., & LeClerc, R. A feature positive effect in conditioned suppression. *Animal Learning and Behavior,* 1977, *5,* 143–147.

Rescorla, R. A. Pavlovian conditioning and its proper control procedures. *Psychological Review,* 1967, *74,* 71–80.

Rescorla, R. A. Pavlovian conditioned inhibition. *Psychological Bulletin,* 1969, *72,* 77–94.

Rescorla, R. A., & Holland, P. C. Some behavioral approaches to the study of learning. In M. R. Rosenzweig and E. L. Bennett (Eds.), *Neural mechanisms of learning and memory.* Cambridge, Massachusetts: MIT Press, 1976.

Rescorla, R. A., & Wagner, A. R. A theory of Pavlovian conditioning: Variations in the effectiveness of reinforcement and nonreinforcement. In A. H. Black and W. F. Prokasy (Eds.), *Classical conditioning II: Current research and theory.* New York: Appleton-Century-Crofts, 1972.

Sainsbury, R. S. Effect of proximity of elements on the feature-positive effect. *Journal of the Experimental Analysis of Behavior*, 1971, *16*, 315–325. (a)

Sainsbury, R. S. The "feature positive effect" and simultaneous discrimination learning. *Journal of Experimental Child Psychology*, 1971, *11*, 347–356. (b)

Sainsbury, R. S. Discrimination learning utilizing positive or negative cues. *Canadian Journal of Psychology*, 1973, *27*, 46–57.

Schwartz, B., & Williams, D. R. The role of the response-reinforcer contingency in negative automaintenance. *Journal of the Experimental Analysis of Behavior*, 1972, *17*, 351–357.

Seidel, R. J. A review of sensory preconditioning. *Psychological Bulletin*, 1959, *56*, 58–73.

Shimp, C. P. Perspectives on the behavioral unit: Choice behavior in animals. In W. K. Estes (Ed.), *Handbook of learning and cognitive processes* (Vol. 2: Conditioning and behavior theory). Hillsdale, New Jersey: Lawrence Erlbaum Associates, 1975.

Shimp, C. P. Organization in memory and behavior. *Journal of the Experimental Analysis of Behavior*, 1976, *26*, 113–130.

Siegel, R. K. *Discrimination learning between and within complex displays.* Unpublished doctoral dissertation, Dalhousie University, 1970. [Summarized in R. Hinde and J. Stevenson-Hinde (Eds.), *Constraints on learning.* New York: Academic Press, 1973, p. 204].

Skinner, B. F. *About behaviorism.* New York: Knopf, 1974.

Spence, K. W. Cognitive versus stimulus-response theories of learning. *Psychological Review*, 1950, *57*, 159–172.

Sperling, S. E., Perkins, M., & Duncan, H. Stimulus generalization from feeder to response key in the acquisition of autoshaped pecking. *Journal of the Experimental Analysis of Behavior*, 1977, *27*, 469–478.

Staddon, J. E. R. Temporal control and the theory of reinforcement schedules. In R. M. Gilbert and J. R. Millenson (Eds.), *Reinforcement: Behavioral analysis.* New York: Academic Press, 1972.

Steinhauer, G., Davol, G., & Lee, A. Acquisition of the autoshaped key peck as a function of preliminary magazine training. *Journal of the Experimental Analysis of Behavior*, 1976, *25*, 355–359.

Stevens, D. A., & Wixon, D. R. Stimulus quality and assessments of relative importance of S+ and S−. *Journal of Experimental Psychology: Animal Behavior Processes*, 1976, *2*, 214–220.

Terry, W. S., & Wagner, A. Short-term memory for "surprising" vs. "expected" unconditioned stimuli in Pavlovian conditioning. *Journal of Experimental Psychology: Animal Behavior Processes*, 1975, *104*, 122–133.

Thistlethwaite, D. A critical review of latent learning and related experiments. *Psychological Bulletin*, 1951, *48*, 97–129.

Tolman, E. C. *Purposive behavior in animals and men.* New York: Century, 1932.

Tolman, E. C., & Brunswik, E. The organism and the causal texture of the environment. *Psychological Review*, 1935, *42*, 43–77.

Tversky, A. Features of similarity. *Psychological Review*, 1977, *84*, 327–352.

Ward, W. C., & Jenkins, H. M. The display of information and the judgment of contingency. *Canadian Journal of Psychology*, 1965, *19*, 231–241.

Wasserman, E. A., Franklin, S., & Hearst, E. Pavlovian appetitive contingencies and approach vs. withdrawal to conditioned stimuli in pigeons. *Journal of Comparative and Physiological Psychology*, 1974, *86*, 616–627.

Wessells, M. G. The effects of reinforcement upon the prepecking behaviors of pigeons in the auto-shaping experiment. *Journal of the Experimental Analysis of Behavior*, 1974, *21*, 125–144.

Williams, D. R., & Williams, H. Auto-maintenance in the pigeon: Sustained pecking despite contingent nonreinforcement. *Journal of the Experimental Analysis of Behavior*, 1969, *12*, 511–520.

Woodworth, R. S. *Dynamics of behavior*. New York: Holt, 1958.

Zanich, M. L., & Fowler, H. Primary and secondary reinforcers as distinctive cues which acquire information value in partial-reinforcement discrimination training. *Learning and Motivation*, 1975, *6*, 299–313.

4 The Role of Stimulus Learning in Defensive Behavior

Robert C. Bolles
University of Washington

A consensus seems to be emerging: What animals learn in instrumental situations is the relationship between their behavior and its programmed consequences. Thus, if a biologically significant event, S*, such as food or shock, is programmed to follow some response, R, such as pressing a bar, we can attribute changes in the animal's behavior specifically to a learned R-S* association: The animal learns that bar pressing is followed by food or that bar pressing is followed by shock. This view of instrumental learning has been advocated by such diverse theoretical writers as Irwin (1971), Mackintosh (1974), and Seligman and Johnston (1973). It is an attractive view. It is compatible with a cognitive orientation, and it seems to be consistent with a variety of experimental findings.

Much of the evidence that has been cited in support of this R-S* interpretation, curiously, comes from aversive situations. For example, Mackintosh (1974) appears to take at face value that animals can learn to avoid shock as evidence for learned R-S* associations of the form: response-no shock. Learning in the punishment paradigm is taken as evidence for the learning of associations of the form: response-shock. The main argument of this chapter is that the changes in behavior that occur in aversive situations *cannot* be taken at face value. Just as we have become sensitive to the frequent failures of programmed consequences to control appetitive behaviors (see Hearst, Chapter 3), so should we be sensitive to such failures in the control of defensive behaviors. The reason in each case is that the behavior tends to be dominated by the S-S* contingencies that are implicit in the learning situation, so S-S* learning obscures whatever R-S* learning might otherwise occur. My principal message is that S-S* factors play a large and important part in the control of defensive behavior, just as they do in certain appetitive situations. I am not proposing that all learning in aversive situations is S-S*, only that a large part of it is.

I will consider first the case of avoidance behavior, and I will begin by describing some of the experimental work that initially impressed me with the power of S-S* contingencies and the relative frailty of R-S* contingencies in controlling avoidance behavior.

I. AVOIDANCE: SITUATIONAL FACTORS

The most salient fact about avoidance learning, the one thing that comes out most clearly in the literature, is that avoidance learning occurs much more readily in some situations than in others. In the one-way apparatus the rat needs only a handful of trials, 10 or so, to master the problem. There are situations, such as the jump-out apparatus in which the rat avoids shock by jumping out of the shock compartment, where performance increases reliably after a single training trial. On the other hand, if the rat is required to press a bar to avoid shock, it may still be performing poorly after 1,000 trials. This bad showing is reflected both in poor prospects for ultimate success, i.e., a low level of asymptotic performance, and in a slow rate of learning, i.e., a gradual approach to the asymptote. There are, in addition, other avoidance situations in which the rat approaches some intermediate asymptotic level in some intermediate number of trials.

The differences between the learning curves obtained in different situations are really quite remarkable. These differences dwarf the effects of the experimental variables usually manipulated in avoidance-learning experiments. Thus, while parameters such as the properties of the shock, the properties of the warning signal, the kind of rat, or various experimental contingencies can be shown to have reliable effects on performance in this or that situation, all such effects are rather puny compared with the enormous differences that are typically found between different situations. I suspect that if all the avoidance-learning data ever reported could be combined and subjected to a gigantic analysis of variance, we would find that about 80% of the total variance would be attributable to situational factors, and only about 10% could be attributed to all the other parameters that are usually considered to be of theoretical interest. (The remaining 10% would be error variance.) The existence of these great situational differences is, I repeat, the most salient fact about avoidance learning.

Several points should be noted about the different learning curves characteristically found in different situations. One is that they reflect a more or less continuous spectrum of learnabilities. It is not the case that avoidance proceeds well except in certain situations such as the Skinner Box. Nor is it the case that learning proceeds normally in most situations but with peculiar facility in the one-way apparatus. In the past various statements of what might be called "special hypotheses" have been advanced to account for the level of performance typically found in one situation or another. For example, it has been suggested that the rat does poorly in the Skinner Box because the freezing that occurs there effectively competes with bar pressing. This is probably a good hypothesis, but it is incomplete. To have any real power, it would have to be expanded to indicate why so little freezing occurs in the shuttlebox, and why freezing produces still less competition with running in the one-way apparatus. Another special hypothesis to deal with the latter problem is that the rat in the shuttlebox is handicapped, relative to the one-way animal, because it is required on every trial to return to a previously dangerous place. This is also a plausible notion, but as it stands it provides no account of the extremely poor performance of rats in the Skinner Box. It is clear that any such special hypothesis, "special" in the sense of having been formulated to account for the rate of learning typically found in a particular situation, cannot be expected to deal with the broad spectrum of differential performance found across the range of different situations. No doubt a combination of such special hypotheses coluld be pressed into service to cover the entire spectrum. Finding a general hypothesis that will do the whole job in a more systematic and satisfying manner provides a more pleasing prospect, however.

It may be noted that generations of psychologists were trained to believe that to understand learning in general it was sufficient to study learning in some particular situation. The maze, the runway and the Skinner Box all seemed suitable at one time or another. We were assured that it was only necessary to study systematically the acquisition of any "convenient" operant, a total understanding of learning would follow. But the spectrum of different learnabilities indicates that there are not very many convenient operants for the study of avoidance learning. The one-way situation is not convenient because learning there is too fast. The Skinner Box is not convenient because learning is too slow and because the behavior usually never does come under experimental control.[1] The only "convenient" operant turns out to be running in the shuttlebox. It should not be surprising, therefore, to discover that the bulk of the systematic studies of avoidance learning have investigated this response. It is therefore apparently not a matter of selecting any convenient operant; we are almost stuck with running in the shuttlebox if we want a response whose performance improves at a moderate rate and in a consistent manner. This state of affairs is nice for those who wish to investigate running in the shuttlebox, but where does it leave those of us who are more concerned with understanding learning processes in general? And where

---

[1]Typically, the median animal in a group shows a little learning, but a few animals may perform moderately well, and a few may perform dismally. To be honest about it, though, many experimenters have gradually evolved a set of conditions and parameters with which they can obtain middling bar-press avoidance performance. The relevant parameters seem to include weak and intermittent shock, long and loud auditory warning cues, female rats, lots of response-feedback, and appropriate positioning of the bar. Little of this laboratory wisdom is in the literature, unfortunately, and there is, moreover, a serious disparity between the practical importance of such parameters and their systematic theoretical treatment. For example, I know of no explanation for why females do better than males; the major learning theories provide no insight on the matter. The fact remains that bar-press avoidance training is too uncertain a business to be useful in clarifying general learning processes.

does it leave our theoretical accounts of avoidance behavior? Again, we appear to need a general hypothesis that will account systematically for the whole spectrum of performances found in different avoidance situations.

It may be noted that poor performance in a learning task can arise from lack of response availability. In operant terms, the response simply does not occur frequently enough for the reinforcement contingency to be effectively applied. This mechanism does not help us much. Granted that there are differences in operant level and in the level at which responses occur in the absence of a response contingency, these differences nevertheless do not account for the different learning curves. Even in the bar-press situation, the avoidance response may occur on 15 to 20% of the trials, and, of course, bar pressing typically occurs as an escape response on all the other trials and is then subject to contingencies that are supposed to reinforce it. Nonetheless, performance is usually poor. It appears then that the failure here is a failure of learning, i.e., a failure of the reinforcement contingencies to be effective, and not merely the unavailability of the response. The cases of situations where responses have similar initial strengths before training and quite different strengths after training point to the same conclusion. I once reported a case where of three responses of comparable initial strength, one (running) was quickly acquired, another (turning around) was acquired at a modest rate, and the third (standing up) gradually disappeared (Bolles, 1969). Similar results were reported by Wahlsten (1972) who found that although different strains of mice had quite distinctive defensive behaviors, there was no connection between the initial strengths of these behaviors and how rapidly they were acquired as avoidance responses. Apparently, then, we need an explanatory device that will account, not just for the unconditioned incidence of different behaviors, but for the differential reinforcability of different behaviors.

It might be objected that there is already in the public domain of learning theory a perfectly acceptable explanation for all of the troubles so far described. Differential learning can be accounted for, it might be argued, by the long-familiar fear-reduction hypothesis of avoidance learning. The argument might go like this: In the one-way situation the animal runs from a region of high fear to one of low fear. In the shuttlebox it runs from a new fear to an old one; the overall reduction in fear level is considerably less, so the amount of reinforcement is correspondingly less. In the Skinner Box the small amount of fear reduction effected by the termination of the warning cue is masked by the large amount of residual fear constantly elicited by the unchanging environmental cues. The main virtue of such an analysis is that it preserves the old two-factor theory, and keeps avoidance learning within the accepted boundaries of S-R reinforcement theory. Basically, it is a conservative argument. The main fault with it is its circularity. There now seems little hope of monitoring the level of fear that is presumed to maintain avoidance responding in a manner which is independent of the avoidance response itself (Rescorla & Solomon, 1967). In other words, the only reason the fear-reduction theorist thinks bar pressing produces little reduction in total fear level is that he has so much trouble reinforcing bar pressing. The argument is not wholly circular; given certain assumptions, it is possible to manipulate fear level by means of apparatus cues and intertrial intervals (e.g., McAllister & McAllister, 1971). So two-factor theory could probably be kept alive, but a more promising approach would be to seek a new and more attractive account of the differential learning that occurs in different situations.

I suggested one possibility a few years ago (Bolles, 1970). The idea was that the frightened animal has a limited repertoire of relatively fixed species-specific defensive reactions (SSDRs), which provide the behavioral elements out of which avoidance behavior must be built. In the case of the rat, its SSDRs are mainly fleeing the situation and freezing. If the rat is required to make an avoidance response that takes it completely out of the frightening situation, it will perform very well. If it is required to make a response that keeps it in the frightening situation, it will perform poorly—except under special circumstances. The SSDR hypothesis had the merit of calling attention specifically to the problem of differential learning, and it provided some perspective over the entire spectrum. It was primarily a descriptive device, a way of looking at avoidance behavior, because it was a conjecture about the conditions under which avoidance learning occurs, and not primarily a theoretical statement about the learning process per se. I suggested (Bolles, 1970) that an avoidance response would be learned if it was compatible with one of the animal's SSDRs and that it would be learned to the extent that incompatible SSDRs were suppressed by unavoided shocks. Therefore, the basic response-learning mechanism was punishment. This was supplemented by a positive reinforcement safety-signal mechanism, which I will discuss shortly.

II. AVOIDANCE: FREEZING BEHAVIOR

Everything looked good for the SSDR hypothesis; it was generally well received. But the critical case was freezing. Freezing is an SSDR for the rat, so it ought to be quickly learned. Its acquisition should require only that fleeing attempts are punished. (Such learning would have confounded two-factor theory, however, because the freezing response does not appear to effect any change in fear-eliciting cues, so it is not clear how freezing could reduce the prevailing level of fear.) When we did the study (Bolles & Riley, 1973), we found that rats were very quickly freezing about 97% of the time.[2] We had dispelled the two-factor, inadequate-reinforcement argument, and appeared to have put the SSDR

---

[2]Because freezing is a prolonged or continuously occurring response rather than a discrete response, like running in the shuttlebox or pressing a bar, its strength is best assessed by a percentage-of-time measure. This character of the behavior also required us to use a Sidman avoidance procedure. Brief shocks occurred every 5 sec if the rat was active. Shock was prevented by freezing and was reinstated following 15 sec of activity. Other animals were run under punishment conditions where 15 sec of freezing produced shock; activity avoided shock.

hypothesis on a solid foundation. But there was something odd about the freezing data. We had expected that the animals reinforced for freezing would resume freezing sooner following an unavoided shock than the animals that were punished for freezing. Whether the learning mechanism operated positively to strengthen freezing in the avoidance animals, or negatively to suppress activity in the punishment animals, there should have been a difference with which the two groups resumed freezing after a shock elicited unconditioned responding. But there was no difference. A careful analysis of this and other aspects of the data finally convinced Riley and me that there was no response learning here at all. Freezing behavior, which appeared at a high level in the avoidance group and at a much lower level in the punishment group, and which appeared, therefore, to be under the control of the contingencies programmed for these groups, was actually totally controlled by the density of shocks the animals were receiving. The behavior could be described this way: The avoidance group froze almost all the time because shock never disrupted it; long bouts of freezing could run their normal course. The punishment group would have frozen almost all the time, too, but could not because frequent shocks kept disrupting it. The incidence of freezing appeared to be totally dependent on when and how frequently shocks occurred, and quite independent of the contingencies that we had arranged between the behavior and its consequences. Freezing is a respondent and not an operant!

In an unpublished follow-up study, Riley and I examined the possibility that these surprising results were an artifact of the disrupting, activity-eliciting effects of shock (shock always breaks up freezing). We gave extended Pavlovian training in another situation where a tone was repeatedly paired with shock. Then the basic freezing study was repeated making the tone rather than shock the aversive event. All animals, whether run under punishment, avoidance, or noncontingent conditions, froze about 60% of the time. The different contingencies were quite ineffective in controlling freezing. Freezing is indeed a respondent.

Here we had a curious state of affairs. We had hoped to show that freezing was one of the most readily reinforceable of avoidance responses. What we found instead was that although it occurs at a high level and in some functional sense it solves the rat's problem with respect to shock just as, presumably, it solves some of the rat's problems in nature (we have recently found that cats are less likely to attack rats that hold still), it is not a learnable response in any real sense. We were familiar with the idea that some animals solve some problems without benefit of learning. Ameba do not have to learn to eat, nor do humans have to learn to breathe. But we had assumed, along with everyone else, that our phylogenetic neighbor, the rat, had to learn to defend itself, and that it did so by learning in one way or another to respond in adaptive ways to specific cues.

The freezing study does begin to make sense when viewed in another light. What it shows, fundamentally, is that rats have this marvelously adaptive freezing response which works so well that they can defend themselves automatically. They do not have to learn to freeze, nor perhaps can they. But they defend themselves well enough anyway. We do not have to teach the rat to freeze; all we have to do is frighten it, and it will freeze by itself. Perhaps, the broad-range biological advantages of this behavior are so great that it has become functionally isolated from the rat's learning mechanisms. And perhaps defensive behavior in general is too important a matter for the rat for such behavior to be functionally dependent upon response learning.

Even so, there is a very important sense in which freezing, as well as other defensive behaviors in the rat, depends on learning. But this critical learning is not consequence-related response learning of the familiar operant variety, it is stimulus learning. We may suppose that our rats that froze so persistently in the freezing study did not freeze when they were safely back in their living cages. They only froze to a noteworthy extent in our experimental situation. Thus, this behavior obviously depended on experience, but it was the experience with shock in the situation that counted, and not any experience with the relationship between a particular behavior and its consequences.

This point has now been documented more systematically in a study by Bolles and Collier (1976). Groups of rats were given shock in two boxes, one of which had a large square shape and the other an oblong shape of about the same area. After receiving shock in one box the animals were picked up and immediately placed either in the same box where they had been shocked or in the other one. Then the incidence of freezing was recorded. We found that the median rat froze 20 times as much during the next 15 min when returned to the shock box as when placed in the other box. Freezing, therefore, seems to be dependent primarily on apparatus cues that have been associated with shock. It does not seem to be a reaction that depends on a persisting physiological state; the rat does not freeze just because it is full of adrenalin or because it is driven by autonomic arousal. It is the situation and not the state of the rat that produces freezing. We also found that, other things being equal, more freezing occurred in the square box than in the long box (more running was observed in the long box). Thus, freezing seems to be dependent primarily on the stimulus configuration confronting the animal: If environmental cues have been recently paired with shock, and if these cues provide little stimulus support for alternative behaviors, such as running, then we find persistent freezing in the situation. But if the environmental cues have not been associated with shock, of if they provide support for alternative behaviors, then little freezing is seen. In other words, freezing seems to be largely controlled by environmental stimuli and by what these stimuli signify. Freezing appears to be dependent mainly on stimulus learning rather than response learning.

III. AVOIDANCE: STIMULUS LEARNING EFFECTS

If it is helpful to conceive of defensive behavior in the freezing experiments as being primarily respondent in character, perhaps such an analysis can also help to clarify the behavior that occurs in other avoidance-learning situations. In this section I will consider a number of stimulus-produced effects that appear

in different situations. Some stimulus factors may be conceived as innately eliciting particular behaviors, such as freezing or running (as in the square- vs. long-
box study). Another possibility is that learning occurs in the avoidance situation,
but it is stimulus learning, i.e., learning about the significance of stimuli. If we
program shocks in a given situation, the rat may simply learn that shocks occur
in this situation. This may be all the rat has to learn to perform adequately in
some situations such as the one-way and the jump-out apparatus. The issue may
be put this way: If we have taught a rat that it is dangerous over here and that it
is safe over there, is it also necessary to teach the rat to run from here to there?
Or can it get there all by itself?

It is tempting to suppose that if response learning (i.e., operant conditioning)
plays little part in the appearance of behavior in these situations, it may also
play little part in other situations such as the Skinner Box where, as we have already noted, reinforcement contingencies have been found to be peculiarly
ineffective. In short, perhaps the rat's behavior in most avoidance-learning situations is, at least initially, governed by stimulus learning rather than response
learning. Some recent research supports such an analysis of shuttlebox avoidance.
Bolles, Moot, and Nelson (1976) measured the latency of avoidance responses
in the shuttlebox and found no change in latency over trial blocks. The probability of avoidance increased in an orderly manner but avoidance responding
appeared to be stationary in time. Different experimental manipulations affected
mean latency, but under no condition did the latency of responding on avoidance trials show any change. It is as if the running response is a unit of behavior
that is not subject to modification during the course of avoidance learning. All
that really counts is whether or not the rat runs. Whether it runs or not depends,
perhaps, on whether it makes the rather abstract discrimination that its present
side of the box is dangerous and the "other side" is safe. We may suppose that
this perceptual learning takes about 100 trials, and that, as the perception becomes more certain, the fixed running response becomes more probable.

In another study (Moot, Nelson, & Bolles, 1974) rats were trained in a
shuttlebox that was black on one end and white on the other Weisman, Denny,
and Zerbolio (1967) had found poor learning in such a situation and had attributed it to their rats not being able to discount the black-white spatial cues, which
they must do, according to their theory, if they are to learn to relax following
a run. However, we found poor learning in this situation only when intertrial
responses were prevented with a door, and we argued that the door prevented
the rat from learning the abstraction of this side vs. the other side. Such a perception appears to require that the rat be free to explore the apparatus between
trials. This argument is admittedly somewhat tenuous, but no matter how the
data are construed, they appear to show that stimulus learning of some sort can
be more important than response learning—even in the shuttlebox. The shuttlebox is an interesting test case because it is one situation in which there appears
to be good evidence for response learning.

In another study (Bolles & Nelson, 1975), groups of rats were trained in a
one-way apparatus with very long intertrial intervals, up to 3 hours. We found

that under conditions where animals were required to spend the long ITI in the dangerous part of the apparatus, i.e., the shock side of the apparatus, there was almost no learning of the running avoidance response. This seems odd at first sight because there was a distinctive CS that was repeatedly associated with shock. The response occurred on every trial as an escape, and the response was supposedly reinforced by its programmed consequences. Yet there was little avoidance responding. We suggested that the reason for this apparent failure of learning was that during the long ITI the dangerous part of the apparatus became perceived as a safe place (it was safe for some time). Then when the animal was frightened by the CS, it merely remained in this safe place. Once again, it looks like the rat's defensive behavior is more dependent upon stimulus contingencies embedded in the experimental situation than it is on any response learning per se.

The paper by Bolles and Nelson (1975) also described a relatively unstudied kind of avoidance response. Animals were confined to a small box which had a hardware-cloth "cupola" above the ceiling. Floor shock could be escaped or avoided by leaping up into the cupola, but the cupola was too small for the rat to do more than hang there momentarily. It had to fall back into the box and await the next trial. We found rapid avoidance acquisition and a high level of performance in this situation, comparable to that obtained in the one-way situation. The reason for the fast learning in the two situations may be intuited as the same, namely, the dangerous part of the apparatus is readily discriminable from the safe part, and the rat is permitted to go from the one to the other, at least temporarily. Incidentally, one practical advantage of the cupola situation is that animals do not have to be handled between trials as in the one-way task, nor does a trial have to be arbitrarily terminated by the removal of a shelf as in the automated jump-up box.

To return to the problem presented by the broad spectrum of differential learnabilities, this brief sketch of stimulus-learning effects has already suggested some mechanisms to deal with it. The rapid acquisition of running in the one-way situation has been conventionally attributed to the large amount of reinforcement (fear reduction) that is contingent on the occurrence of running. This view of the behavior was plausible, and it was consistent with the finding that the avoidance contingency is far more important in establishing avoidance in this situation than either termination of the warning signal or escaping shock on nonavoidance trials.[3] My view of it is that the one-way procedure makes it very easy for the rat to distinguish one region that is always dangerous and another region that is always safe. The avoidance contingency per se is irrelevant;

---

[3]These three response contingencies define the typical discrete trial avoidance learning procedure. A review of relevant studies (Bolles, 1975) suggests that in the rapid-learning situations, the avoidance contingency is all-important. Moving across the spectrum to situations like the shuttlebox, the three contingencies make comparable-sized contributions to response acquisition. At the other end of the spectrum, i.e., the Skinner box, there are fewer data, but a recent unpublished study from my laboratory indicated that none of the three contingencies made an appreciable contribution to the modest amount of bar-press avoidance that our animals showed.

it is an artifact created by the geometry of the situation. The study by Bolles and Nelson (1975), cited earlier, in which we found poor one-way performance with a very long ITI indicates that it is the spatial location of dangerous and safe regions, and not the avoidance of shock, that really controls the behavior The cupola and other kinds of jump-up apparatus can be dealt with in the same way: in principle, they require only that the animal go from a shock-associated region to a shock-free region. The learning that occurs need only involve associating different places with the occurrence and nonoccurrence of shock. In short, it is stimulus learning.

The reason shuttlebox avoidance is learned more slowly than one-way avoidance is, I suggest, that the shuttlebox provides no really safe place. The rat must learn that safety is "over there." This is a difficult concept to express in behavioral language, and it must be a relatively difficult abstraction for the rat to make, too, because it characteristically takes a fair number of trials.

There remains the troublesome case of bar-press avoidance, and the perennial question of why it is so difficult to train. The answer I would suggest at this point is that bar-press acquisition is slow and uncertain precisely because it is ordinarily not assisted by any kind of stimulus-learning mechanism. The situation itself encourages freezing, so the rat's SSDRs are all nonfunctional, and it can solve the problem only by recourse to learning about the consequences of bar pressing. It seems that when confronted by a situation it cannot flee and in which freezing is of no avail, it is in a poor position to engage in response learning. So its performance is poor. But perhaps the proper emphasis is to note that some response learning does typically occur. Response learning is possible, I assume, and the conditions that appear to promote it will now be discussed. This section can be concluded by observing that although a good deal of research needs to be done before the whole spectrum of differential learnabilities can be seen in a coherent pattern, it seems likely that S-S* learning mechanisms will be an important part of the picture.

IV. AVOIDANCE: RESPONSE LEARNING EFFECTS

Many avoidance responses are peculiarly resistant to control by the contingencies that have conventionally been assumed to be important in avoidance learning (the evidence is reviewed by Bolles, 1975). A notorious example is the CS-termination contingency, which has long had the theoretical burden of explaining most of avoidance learning, but whose importance has not been well documented empirically except in the case of the shuttlebox. Perhaps the reason for this discrepancy is that the real S* for response learning is an event that is something different from CS termination, but which is correlated with it, such as the presentation of a safety signal. Typically, the stimulus conditions that exist when the CS goes off have the special property that they signal a period of time which is free from shock, and it may well be this safety-signal aspect of these conditions, rather than the correlated termination of the CS, that provides the main source of reinforcement for response learning in the avoidance paradigm.

Two experimenters have tried to test this idea. In an unpublished study, S.A. Moot established a response-produced safety-signal in the shuttlebox situation and then used this safety signal as an additional source of reinforcement in a bar-press avoidance situation. The animals trained under these conditions learned the bar-press response much faster than various kinds of control animals. Morris (1975) has reported the same thing: A safety signal previously established in a Pavlovian situation was effective in reinforcing running in a shuttlebox. The shuttlebox response was acquired with remarkable rapidity. Thus we have the attractive possibility that safety signals may be an important source of reinforcement for a number of different avoidance responses. it should be emphasized, however, that these studies showing the efficacy of preestablished safety signals do not prove that such a learning mechanism is operative in the normal avoidance-learning situation. Normally, the safety signal must be established during the course of avoidance training, and it now seems likely that the effective establishment of a safety signal requires a substantial number of trials, perhaps 50 or 100. Therefore we cannot reasonably expect such a mechanism to play any part in situations such as one-way avoidance, where the response is quickly acquired, or even much of a part in situations such as the shuttlebox, where the response is acquired with moderate speed. Thus, it seems likely that while the safety-signal reinforcement effect exists and can generate genuine response learning with the avoidance paradigm, it does not serve an important function in most avoidance-learning situations.

It might be supposed that the safety signal S^* would be an important factor in bar-press avoidance (because the response is only slowly learned and because there are no powerful S-S learning effects). It has been known for some time that bar-press avoidance learning is especially poor if the experimental situation provides no stimulus event which is immediately contingent upon a bar press response (e.g., Bolles & Popp, 1964). In that study rats trained on Sidman avoidance in a bar-press situation that minimized response feedback performed much more poorly than rats trained with a loud click whenever they pressed the bar. Perhaps, then, the response feedback served to reinforce responding (response learning) because this feedback click signaled a period of time free from shock (stimulus learning). There is some irony in the possibility that even in a case where response learning does play an important part in avoidance behavior, it does so only by virtue of earlier and more basic stimulus learning.[4]

---

[4]The same was true, of course, in classical two-factor theory. Instrumental behavior was reinforced only by virtue of the prior conditioning of fear to the CS. The irony applies to the more modern cognitive version that avoidance depends on the animal learning that its response is followed by an absence of shock. This kind of $R-S^*$ mechanism is now beginning to appear unpromising.

Let me say a few words at a more general level about the relationship between stimulus learning and response learning. As I noted in the introduction, an instrumental learning experiment is one that is defined by an explicit contingency between some response, R, and some biologically important S*, such as shock. For example, the contingency might be that every response prevents shock. Once we have gained control of the animal's behavior, i.e., once it has become responsive to the particular contingency, we are inclined to attribute this control to the contingency. We think of the contingency as *causing* the behavior to be expressed. The trouble with this inference is that operant control is always established in a specific situation, and there are nearly always some cues, S, in the situation that are correlated with S*. These implicit and largely unintended S-S* contingencies are not well defined initially, but once the animal is responding regularly, they may have just as much reality as the explicit and intended R-S* contingency. Thus, once we have gained control over the animal's behavior, we may suppose that the R-S* contingency is exercising the control, but we cannot be sure that the critical factor is not some S-S* contingency that is embedded in the experimental situation. I am using the term "response learning" to refer to the case where a behavior is really attributable specifically to an R-S* contingency, and "stimulus learning" to the case where a behavior is actually controlled by an S-S* contingency. Recent findings in certain areas such as autoshaping, and particularly omission training (Williams & Williams, 1969), indicate that even in situations that have conventionally beeen regarded as R-S*, S-S contingencies can play a more important role in the determination of behavior than R-S* contingencies. Work from my laboratory (Bolles, 1975), indicates that in many avoidance-learning situations, R-S* contingencies may have only a weak influence upon the rat's behavior. Thus, many avoidance responses seem to depend primarily upon existent but poorly defined S-S* contingencies rather than upon well defined but relatively ineffectual R-S* contingencies.

The question of response learning vs. stimulus learning bears an interesting relationship to the older question of whether learning is S-R or cognitive. Once upon a time all learning was assumed to be S-R. At that time stimulus learning as it is defined here was inconceivable; all learning was some variety of response learning. In instrumental learning, the S-R contingency was all-important; for all theorists the contiguity of S and R was necessary for learning (for Guthrie it was also sufficient), and the S* merely reinforced the mythical S-R connection. Even in Pavlovian conditioning, where there was an explicit S-S* contingency, the critical factor was, ironically, the implicit or embedded S-R contingency. Except for Pavlov (1927) and Rescorla (1967), nearly everyone after John B. Watson believed that the important contingency, like the conditioning itself, was S-R. The S* merely elicited the R. It is only now that we have begun to accept the idea that not all learning is S-R—now that an important part of learning is seen as S-S—that it becomes meaningful to ask whether any particular learning, or what part of the total learning, is S-S. Note also that if some particular behavior is shown to be an instance of response learning, we have the option of regarding it either in the old way, as S-R, or in the new cognitive way as the expression of an R-S* expectancy (Bolles, 1972; Irwin, 1971). On the other hand, if the behavior proves to be due to S-S learning, the option of an S-R explanation is lost, and we must have recourse to some kind of S-S, information-processing explanation of the behavior.

A final word about terminology: It takes a little care nowadays to find a neutral terminology with which to describe the results of a learning experiment. It has become so easy and natural to say "the rat learned to press the bar" or "the rat learned to run." But this style reflects the usage of an era that is rapidly passing. It was an era in which there was little doubt about what was learned—the response was learned as it became "connected" to a stimulus. The main theoretical issue was what mechanism produced or strengthened the connection. Except to the few followers of Tolman, it *was* theoretically neutral to say "the rat learned to run." Today, when there is little consensus about what the substance of learning is, such a statement is not neutral. But it is like the language of sexism; although I know it is tainted, I cannot always keep from using it. The safest approach is probably to keep the accent on performance, as I have tried to do here. It should be kept in mind, though, that in using the language of performance to describe the outcome of a learning experiment, I am not necessarily making the old learning-performance distinction, but simply emphasizing the current uncertainty about what learning is.

V. PUNISHMENT: RESPONSE VS. STIMULUS LEARNING

The question of response vs. stimulus learning is an old, familiar issue in the punishment literature. The question arose when Thorndike and other early theorists began to doubt the efficacy of the punishment procedure. The theoretical question was put into experimental focus by the demonstration of Estes (1944) that punishing a response with weak shock might not weaken the response any more than, or in any way different from, giving animals noncontingent shocks. The possibility existed that a response was weakened by shock only because shock conditions fear to some environmental stimuli, and this fear elicits behaviors that compete with the punished response. Thus, even though the punishment procedure is defined by an explicit R-S* contingency, the change in the animal's behavior might be due entirely to implicit S-S* contingencies embedded in the situation. Couched in more modern terms, the question is whether punishment produces R-S* learning—does the animal learn that some response is followed by shock—or does the S* merely establish some subset of environmental cues as danger signals that evoke innate SSDRs such as freezing, which interfere with the expression of the index response.

The question has been fairly extensively studied, particularly by Church and his students (Church, 1969), but their work has not settled the matter because it has not yielded entirely consistent results. Evidence for response learning, i.e., a genuine punishment effect, is sometimes obtained, but sometimes it is not. Our first study on the problem (Bolles, Uhl, Wolfe & Chase, 1975) used the technique of Church, Wooten, and Matthews (1970) in which two groups of rats were occasionally punished for bar pressing in the presence of a cue. The difference between the groups was that for one of them there were additional noncontingent shocks given in the absence of the cue. These noncontingent shocks were scheduled at approximately the same rate as during the periods of punishment, so for this group the punishment cue signalled no change in the overall density of shock. Thus, it conveyed no S-S* information; it indicated only when the punishment contingency was in effect, and it conveyed information only about the R-S* contingency. Church et al. found essentially no suppression by the cue under these conditions, nor did we, at least not initially. But ultimately, in 90 sessions, we obtained good suppression by the cue, indicating that response learning did occur. By contrast, the control group, for which the cue signalled both the punishment contingency and an increase in the overall density of shock, showed strong suppression right from the beginning of training. Our conclusion was that under these conditions stimulus learning occurs very rapidly, with the first few shocks, and that response learning occurs only with extended training. Stimulus learning can evidently be a very powerful factor in the punishment situation.

This conclusion was pleasing (because it was consistent with my assessment of the avoidance situation), but it was not wholly convincing. For one thing, it is possible, with a little theoretical sophistry, to contend that even when it appeared we had response learning we really did not. Perhaps the rat merely learned about a new complex danger signal, namely, the sight of the bar in the presence of the cue, and withdrew from this stimulus complex in the only way it could, by leaving the bar. We need a procedure that separates fearful stimuli from dangerous responses.

Perhaps a more serious consideration is the discriminability of the punishment contingency. Like Church et al., we had punished pressing only occasionally, on a sparse VI-2 schedule. Perhaps closer or more frequent contact of punishment with the response would have produced evidence of more rapid response learning. To examine these possibilities we conducted a second experiment, using another procedure. Rats were trained on a special manipulandum, which they could either press like a bar or pull out from the wall. They were trained to pull and press approximately equally to obtain food, and then one or the other response was punished. As expected, the results of this study (for a preliminaty report, see Bolles, Holtz, & Dunn, 1976) indicated that stimulus learning predominated initially—both the punished and the unpunished responses were strongly suppressed. But when one response was punished on an FR-10 schedule, it took only about 10 shocks (100 responses) for differential suppression to emerge (the unpunished response recovered its initial strength). Thus, response learning was obtained relatively quickly with this procedure and these parameters. In a follow-up study, we have discovered that the discriminability of the punishment contingency is indeed an important parameter. When one of the two responses was punished on an FR-25 schedule, the emergence of differential suppression was roughly half as fast. And when the punishment schedule was FR-4, we found differential suppression right at the outset. We seem to have discovered a set of procedures that not only provides a demonstration of response learning that ought to satisfy the most dedicated and critical stimulus-learning theorist but also produces response learning very rapidly. Indeed, I must admit to considerable surprise at the rapidity with which response learning emerged. I hoped to find none, I expected to find a little, but I was not prepared for such a wealth of it. The question now is why these procedures facilitate response learning, as compared with the typical bar-press punishment procedure. Perhaps an answer lies in the fact that we had some difficulty in establishing the baseline behavior of two responses on one manipulandum. About 14 days of training were necessary to establish the baseline, and perhaps this preliminary training served as response-differentiation experience which then made it relatively easy for the animals to associate one response with its new consequence, shock.

Whatever the answer may be to this puzzle, it seems clear that both stimulus learning and response learning can occur in the punishment situation. It no longer seems profitable to defend an either-or position. The better question now—now that an important place for stimulus learning in the control of defensive behavior seems assured—is this: What are the factors that promote stimulus learning and what are the factors that facilitate response learning? How do we change the balance between stimulus and response factors in defensive behavior?

If stimulus learning is so important in regulating defensive behavior, then there are two sets of questions that demand our attention. One set of questions concerns how the regulation is achieved. Does an S-S* expectancy "motivate" defensive behavior? Does it merely establish the S term as something to be approached or withdrawn from? Does it establish the S as a secondary reinforcer or punisher? Or is behavior controlled in some manner besides that suggested by the old trilogy of motivation, elicitation, and reinforcement?

The second set of questions deals with establishing danger signals and safety signals. It no longer suffices to say that such cues are established by conditioning, unless there is some additional statement telling us what kind of process conditioning is. So far, I have been relatively noncommital on the question; I have referred to S-S* learning without endowing such learning with any conceptual properties except that it must ultimately depend upon an S-S* contingency. Nor do I intend to become any more adventurous at this point. But I would like to conclude by discussing one theoretical aspect of S-S* learning.

VI. THE BASIS OF STIMULUS LEARNING

In a recent paper (Bolles, 1976), I have made a distinction between what I will call the *content* of learning and the *basis* of learning. The question of content is concerned with what kinds of elements are associated, or what kinds of information are assimilated, when learning occurs. The contents of learning might be stimuli and responses (S-R), cues and consequences (S-S), or responses and consequences (R-S). The question of the basis of learning is concerned with what the associative law is that provides the basis for a particular instance of learning. Whatever elements or pieces of information may be associated with what, what is the principle which determines that the association will be formed? For example, contiguity can serve as a powerful basis for learning. It is usually easy to associate contiguous events. But contiguity does not provide a sufficient account. With the human subject, a "set" to learn particular contents can override contiguity, or permit the subject to associate noncontiguous elements. Mackintosh (1974) has argued persuasively for the importance of "attention" in determining what an animal will or will not learn. The conditioned taste aversion literature illustrates, apparently, certain fairly specific cues and consequences being associated in defiance of the law of contiguity. The basis for this learning may be labeled "stimulus relevance." Lett (1975) has shown that discrimination learning over long delays is possible in rats, provided the experimental situation is used as a "context" to define the relevant contents to be associated. In his contribution to this book, Rescorla (Chapter 2) shows how "similarity" can be a basis for associative learning in animals. Each of these factors—context, relevance, attention, similarity—can be a basis for learning and can, on occasion, overrule the powerful law of contiguity.

For some time I have been intrigued by the idea that "predictiveness" can serve as a basis for learning. In this view, a danger signal becomes established by virtue of predicting shock, not because it occurs at the same time as shock. This conception was supported by earlier work of Rescorla (e.g., Rescorla, 1968), but more recently Rescorla and Wagner (1972) have reinstated contiguity as the basis of fear conditioning. Indeed, according to their model, contiguity becomes the sole basis of fear conditioning. Further problems for the predictiveness concept arise from Ayres's (1966) failure to demonstrate the Egger and Miller informativeness principle in fear conditioning and from Kamin's (1965) failure to find fear conditioning with even short delays using a trace-conditioning procedure. We begin to suspect that while other bases may exist for other kinds of learning, contiguity may rule supreme over fear learning.

But there is another possibility. Perhaps the contiguity principle is important, but other bases can also play a part in fear learning if their effects are not masked by contiguity-based learning. In other words, perhaps contiguity serves to preempt other varieties of fear learning. It was to test this possibility that we began to examine the trace conditioning of fear (Bolles, Collier, & Bouton,

1975). The trace procedure eliminates contiguity, but unfortunately it also seems to preclude fear conditioning. We tested Mowrer and Lamoreaux's (1951) hypothesis that the failure of conditioning here was due to the animal confusing the interstimulus interval (ISI) with the ITI. We found that inserting a filler, a second CS, in the ISI gap to mark it off from the ITI resulted in substantial fear conditioning to the first CS (and to the filler too, of course) in a suppression test. Indeed, we found that the trace decrement was virtually gone. We also found that without the filler the trace decrement disappears by itself with continued conditioning experience (64 pairings), but at this point other effects, such as inhibition of delay, begin to emerge to complicate the measurement of fear conditioning.

Nancy Marlin, working in my laboratory, seems to have discovered another way to overcome the trace deficit. Rather than marking the brief ISI with a filler to make it distinctive, she marked the ITI. A brief tone stimulus was presented at the beginning of the long ITI, i.e., immediately following shock. It is not clear how the introduction of this brief safety signal can be effective; shock offset should overshadow it by providing ample information about the forthcoming period of safety. Perhaps shock itself cannot serve well as a safety signal. In any case, the tone cue does seem to be effective in the sense that it permits the animal to process information about the CS-US contingency.

Once we have reliable techniques for obtaining trace conditioning, we will be free of contiguity. (Contiguity is not necessarily a bad thing, but it is a nuisance when one wants to examine other associative principles.) Then we will be in a position to examine other possible bases for S-S* learning; we will be able to determine just what kinds of information can go into S-S associations. And then we should begin to see how the processing of information about the environment controls an animal's defensive behavior.

ACKNOWLEDGMENTS

The preparation of this paper and some of the research described were supported by Research Grant GB-40314 from the National Science Foundation.

REFERENCES

Ayres, J. J. B. Conditioned suppression and the information hypothesis. *Journal of Comparative and Physiological Psychology*, 1966, *62*, 21–25.

Bolles, R. C. Avoidance and escape learning: Simultaneous acquisition of different response. *Journal of Comparative and Physiological Psychology*, 1969, *68*, 355–358.

Bolles, R. C. Species-specific defense reactions and avoidance learning. *Psychological Review*, 1970, *71*, 32–48.

Bolles, R. C. Reinforcement, expectancy, and learning. *Psychological Review,* 1972, *79,* 394–409.

Bolles, R. C. *Theory of Motivation* (2nd ed.) New York: Harper & Row, 1975.

Bolles, R. C. Some relationships between learning and memory. In R. T. Davis (Ed.), *Encoding processes in animal memory.* Hillsdale, New Jersey: Lawrence Erlbaum Associates, 1976.

Bolles, R. C., & Collier, A. C. The effect of predictive cues on freezing behavior in rats. *Animal Learning and Behavior,* 1976, *4,* 6–8.

Bolles, R. C., Collier, A. C. & Bouton, M. A. Overcoming the trace decrement in classical fear conditioning. Paper presented at the Psychonomic Society Meeting, 1975.

Bolles, R. C., Holtz, R. & Dunn, T. Stimulus learning and response learning in a punishment situation. Paper presented at EPA, 1976.

Bolles, R. C., Moot, S. A., & Nelson, K. A note on the invariance of response latency in shuttlebox avoidance learning. *Learning and Motivation,* 1976, *7,* 108–116.

Bolles, R. C. & Nelson, K. The role of intertrial interval in the learning of two simple avoidance tasks. *Animal Learning and Behavior,* 1975, *3,* 157–160.

Bolles, R. C. & Popp, R. J. Parameters affecting the acquisition of Sidman avoidance. *Journal of the Experimental Analysis of Behavior.* 1964, *7,* 315–321.

Bolles, R. C. & Riley, A. L. Freezing as an avoidance response: Another look at the operant-respondent distinction. *Learning and Motivation.* 1973, *4,* 268–275.

Bolles, R. C., Uhl, C. N., Wolfe, M. & Chase, P. B. Stimulus learning vs. response learning in a discriminated punishment situation. *Learning and Motivation,* 1975, *6,* 439–447.

Church, R. M. Response suppression. In B.A. Campbell and R. M. Church (Eds.),*Punishment and aversive behavior.* New York: Appleton-Century-Crofts, 1969.

Church, R. M., Wooten, C. L. & Matthews, T. J. Contingency between responses and an aversive event in the rat. *Journal of Comparative and Physiological Psychology,* 1970, *72,* 476–485.

Estes, W. K. An experimental analysis of punishment. *Psychological Monographs,* 1944, *57,* (No 263).

Irwin, F. W. *Intentional behavior and motivation,* Philadelphia: Lippincott, 1971.

Kamin, L. J. Temporal and intensity characteristics of the conditioned stimulus. In W. F. Prokasy (Ed.), *Classical conditioning.* New York: Appleton-Century-Crofts, 1965.

Lett, B. T. Long delay learning in the T-maze. *Learning and Motivation,* 1975, *6,* 80–90.

Mackintosh, N. J. *The psychology of animal learning.* New York: Academic Press, 1974.

McAllister, W. R. & McAllister, D. E. Behavioral measurement of conditioned fear. In F. R. Brush (Ed.), *Aversive conditioning and learning.* New York: Academic Press, 1971.

Moot, S. A., Nelson, K. & Bolles, R. C. Avoidance learning in a black and white shuttlebox. *Bulletin of the Psychonomic Society,* 1974, *4,* 501–502.

Morris, R. G. M. Preconditioning of reinforcing properties to an exteroceptive feedback stimulus. *Learning and Motivation,* 1975, *6,* 289–298.

Mowrer, O. H., & Lamoreaux, R. R. Conditioning and conditionality (discrimination). *Psychological Review,* 1951, *58,* 196–212.

Rescorla, R. A. Pavlovian conditioning and its proper control procedure. *Psychological Review,* 1967, *74,* 71–80.

Rescorla, R. A. Probability of shock in the presence and absence of CS in fear conditioning. *Journal of Comparative and Physiological Psychology,* 1968, *66,* 1–5.

Rescorla, R. A. & Solomon, R. L. Two-process learning theory: Relationships between Pavlovian conditioning and instrumental learning. *Psychological Review,* 1967, *74,* 151–184.

Rescorla, R. A. & Wagner, A. R. A theory of Pavlovian conditioning: Variations in the effectiveness of reinforcement and nonreinforcement. In A. H. Black & W. F. Prokasy (Eds.) *Classical conditioning II: current research and theory.* New York: Appleton-Century-Crofts, 1972.

Seligman, M. E. P. & Johnston, J. C. A cognitive theory of avoidance learning. In F. J. McGuigan & D. B. Lumsden (Eds.), *Contemporary Approaches to Conditioning and Learning.* New York: Wiley, 1973.

Wahlsten, D. Phenotypic and genetic relations between initial response to electric shock and rate of avoidance learning in rats. *Behavior Quarterly,* 1972, *2,* 211–249.

Weisman, R. G., Denny, M. R. & Zerbolio, D. J. Discrimination based on differential non-shock confinement in a shuttlebox. *Journal of Comparative and Physiological Psychology,* 1967, *63,* 34–38.

Williams, D. R. & Williams, H. Auto-maintenance in the pigeon: sustained pecking despite contingent non-reinforcement. *Journal of the Experimental Analysis of Behavior,* 1969, *12,* 511–520.

5 Cognitive Associations as Evident in the Blocking Effects of Response-Contingent CSs

Harry Fowler
University of Pittsburgh

I. INTRODUCTION

This chapter describes a program of research that, in its initial conception, was not the least bit concerned with cognitive functioning in animals — let alone an argument favoring these processes in nonprimates, such as the rat. An attitude dismissing, or even disavowing, animal cognition has long been prevalent among investigators. It reflects a heritage stemming from Descartes' dualistic philosophy (on mind and body) and the reaction of the behavioristic school. Mentalistic processes are not to be considered in the analysis of behavior; instead, the bodily reactions of the organism should be studied directly. Adopting this posture, the investigator can ensure public observation and replication of his data and, in so doing, promote the use of a scientific method.

A behavioristic approach has also influenced the animal-learning theorist in his efforts to assimilate the facts of his science, namely, the functional relationships between observable stimulus and response events. As a matter of recourse and strategy, the learning theorist has typically assumed (1) that the process underlying learned reactions entails the formation of an association, or "bond," and (2) that the elements which are associated are functionally equivalent or isomorphic to those designated in the observed S–R relationship. This has proved an effective strategy because the learning process is operationalized in terms of observable stimulus and response events, and thus the theorist has a "handle" on the conceptual process which he is attempting to describe: Changes in behavior will reflect operation of the process prompted by certain antecedent stimuli, and therefore the process itself is subject to empirical assessment.

The above position, although convenient and operationally sound, should not deter us from considering that the learning process may entail something other than an association or bond (see Mackintosh, Chapter 6), or that the association formed is between, say, different stimulus elements, rather than between a stimulus and a response. From the standpoint of a behavioristic philosophy, the singular difficulty with a position espousing a cognitive or a S–S relationship is that the inferred associative process is devoid of a behavioral referent. Thus, subject to Guthrie's criticism of the rat's being "buried in thought," cognitive theory seems to lose by default. But inasmuch as this limitation is by reason of philosophy and the lack of performance rules (for a similar critique of S–R theory, see Bolles, 1972), it clearly does not deny a cognitive or other type of process. Indeed, to the extent that one is confronted by findings which are not amenable to and even defy description in terms of S–R bonds, then one has, by exclusion, evidence for a learning process which is of a different form.

The present chapter provides evidence of the above nature, and suggests that we are obliged to entertain cognitive interpretations to account more fully for the learning and performance of lower animals. Such a thesis, as we shall argue, is not restricted to Pavlovian conditioning situations where the experimenter structures a stimulus contingency or a S–S relationship independently of the animal's behavior. It applies as well to instrumental- and operant-conditioning arrangements where a reinforcer or some other stimulus consequence is contingent upon a designated response to the situation, or to specific antedating stimuli. The argument is, of course, not new. Psychologists, both past and present (e.g., Tolman, 1932; Woodworth, 1947; Bolles, 1972), have suggested that the control of instrumental responding is attributable in part to the expectancy or cognitive association which the animal forms between a discriminative stimulus (S^D) for the response and the reinforcer for that response (or between contextual cues and the reinforcer, or even between response-produced feedback and the reinforcer). To investigate this S–S type of relationship, contemporary psychologists (e.g., Trapold & Overmier, 1972) have often resorted to a Pavlovian-to-instrumental transfer design where a CS, first established in Pavlovian conditioning on the basis of one reinforcer, is employed in instrumental conditioning as the S^D for a response subject to the same reinforcer. The rationale for this design is relatively straightforward. Given that the S^D–reinforcer association is part of what the animal has to learn in instrumental conditioning, the preconditioning of that S^D as a CS for the same reinforcer should enhance learning of the instrumental response, despite the fact that such a response or any variant of it was not present in Pavlovian conditioning, and is not facilitated by any conditioned motor response elicited by the S^D as a CS.

The present research also incorporates a Pavlovian-to-instrumental transfer paradigm, but with a slightly different twist: The CS first established in Pavlovian conditioning is employed in instrumental conditioning as a response—contingent event. Thus, depending upon its correlation with the Pavlovian reinforcer and the affective nature of that reinforcer, the CS, when produced by the instrumental response, is operationally equivalent to either a conditioned reinforcer or a conditioned punisher (as with conditioned appetitive and aversive excitors, respectively). As one might expect, response—contingent CSs are rather influential in determing the rate at which the instrumental response is learned, but evidently not by way of any direct, backward-acting effect which the CS exerts on the response, nor by way of any conditioned motor reaction which the CS may produce. The present findings suggest that this is so because, for a variety of training conditions, they indicate that a conditioned reinforcer does not facilitate, but rather suppresses the instrumental response, and a conditioned punisher, rather than suppressing, actually facilitates the response. In the following description of our research, we shall argue that a resolution of these seemingly paradoxical effects is achieved only through an interpretation that focuses on the manner in which the subject processes or "interprets" the CS in relation to the instrumental reinforcer. Even so, such a cognitive interpretation can take on quite different forms, as will be evident in a recounting of the history of our research.

II. PAVLOVIAN-TO-INSTRUMENTAL TRANSFER: BACKGROUND AND METHODOLOGY

The present research had its origin in earlier work by the author (e.g., Fowler & Wischner, 1969; Fowler, 1971b) showing that mild shock punishment for the correct, food-reinforced response in a visual T-maze discrimination would facilitate learning. This "shock-right" facilitation effect was largely attributable to the shock's function as a highly discernible stimulus, or "distinctive cue." Contingent upon one response, right or wrong, the shock stimulus would reduce the similarity of the discriminative-stimulus compounds (including background cues) constituting the reinforced and nonreinforced alternatives; and in this manner it would reduce the generalization of conditioned—reward and conditioned—nonreward effects between the alternatives, and thereby facilitate performance. Consistent with this interpretation, the facilitation effect was shown to be dependent on discrimination difficulty. It did not generally occur in easy (e.g., light-dark) discriminations where the stimulus alternatives were highly discriminable (e.g., Wischner & Fowler, 1964; Wischner, Fowler, & Kushnick, 1963). On the other hand, it consistently occurred in more difficult (e.g., bright-dim) discriminations where a cue effect of the shock could be potentiated (e.g., Fowler & Wischner, 1965). Furthermore, when the aversive component of the shock experience was reduced by the administration of sodium amytal (Fowler, Goldman, & Wischner, 1968), the facilitation observed in a difficult discrimination was found to be an *increasing* S-shaped function of shock intensity, consistent with the Weber principle on the discriminable-cue properties (e.g., the intensity) of a stimulus. Subsequent research (Fago & Fowler, 1972) showed that the same facilitating effect and intensity relationship could also be obtained with a nonaversive white-noise stimulus used in place of shock for either the correct or incorrect response.

Given that our prior research had separated the stimulus component of punishment from its aversive, or fear-producing, component, we turned our attention to the latter property. Our intent, however, was not do demonstrate a suppressing or interfering effect of punishment; rather, it was to evaluate the extent to which fear and its *feedback* component could contribute to the facilitating stimulus effect observed for shock. To do so required, of course, that the fear reaction itself be isolated. The means for this manipulation were apparent in our prior findings on the cue effects of noise (Fago & Fowler, 1972). Because the facilitating effect of this stimulus, like that for shock, was an S-shaped function of its intensity, one could use Pavlovian aversive conditioning to establish a weak noise stimulus (with minimal cue value and no inherent aversiveness) as a conditioned fear excitor, that is, as a stimulus which had "acquired distinctiveness" (cf. Goss, 1955) through conditioned fear and its feedback component. In turn, this CS could be administered contingent upon the food-reinforced response to provide "fear-right" training, analogous to the prior shock-right and noise-right procedures. In this way, we could study the cue effects of a conditioned punisher independently of the vehicle stimulus serving as the CS.

Pursuing the above approach, we initiated a study (Fowler, Fago, Domber, & Hochhauser, 1973) in which, for different groups of rats, a relatively weak and brief (70-db, .2-sec) white-noise stimulus was differentially correlated with a moderate (.5-mA, .2-sec) shock-US in Pavlovian training (conducted in a separate chamber) so as to establish the noise as either a conditioned fear excitor (CS+), a nonfunctional stimulus (CS0), or a conditioned fear inhibitor (CS−). Then, in subsequent T-maze training on a difficult bright-dim discrimination, the CS was presented contingent upon the food-reinforced response. In this experiment, as in all subsequent research, the CS0 group served as a general control for the noise and shock experiences of Pavlovian conditioning. Accordingly, following Rescorla's (1967) contingency argument, the CS0 group received CS and US presentations in an uncorrelated fashion, as contrasted with the positive correlation used for the CS+ group. The CS− group, for which CS and US presentations were negatively correlated (cf. Rescorla, 1969), served as a control for the specific type of reaction conditioned to noise for the CS+ group. As a signal for the absence of shock, the CS− could be expected to produce a conditioned reaction of "relief" or "relaxation" (e.g., Denny, 1971). Hence, to the extent that the feedback component of this reaction produced a cue effect comparable to that for fear, one could expect just as much if not more facilitation for the CS− as

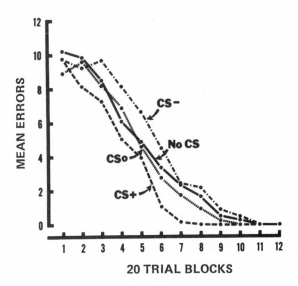

FIG. 1.   Mean errors over the course of training for groups of rats receiving either an aversive CS+, CS0, CS— or no CS contingent upon the food-reinforced response in a difficult visual discrimination. (From Fowler, Fago, Domber, & Hochhauser, 1973.)

for the CS+ group. Indeed, as a safety signal, a response—contingent CS— should also function as a conditioned reinforcer for the response (e.g., LoLordo, 1969). Finally, to evaluate a distinctive-cue effect of the weak noise stimulus itself, possibly amplified as a result of a sensitization effect in which orienting responses (and their feedback) were augmented during Pavlovian conditioning, a fourth group comprised of subjects from each of the three Pavlovian conditions received no CS in discrimination training.

There were other features of the experimental design but, for the moment, let us consider the basic findings. Fig. 1, which depicts the rate of error elimination for the groups, shows that there was no difference in learning between the CS0 and no-CS groups (nor between subgroups of the no-CS condition). This indicated that the weak noise stimulus did not itself produce a facilitating effect. Furthermore, as expected, the CS+ group was facilitated, showing a more rapid elimination of errors and fewer trials to criterion than both the CS0 and no-CS controls. However, the CS— group showed poorer performance than both the CS+ group and the two controls. To our way of thinking, there was no basis by which this effect could have occurred. Conceivably, as a result of a less pronounced cue effect and a relatively weak conditioned—reinforcing effect, the CS— could produce less facilitation than the CS+, but surely it would not retard performance.

When the above results first became apparent, we modified the design of the experiment and, in the course of several replications, evaluated three different conditioning procedures for establishing a CS—: (1) a differential procedure in which the CS was explicitly unpaired with the shock-US, (2) a "conditioned-inhibition" (within-subjects) procedure in which the CS (tone 1) was presented immediately following a CS+ (tone 2) but with the shock-US absent, and (3) a backward-conditioning procedure in which the CS was presented 2 sec after the shock-US. These variations, of course, did not enter into the CS+ procedure, which always involved a forward order of CS and US presentations. However, they did affect the CS0 procedure, as this procedure represented a balanced combination of the CS+ and CS– procedures, e. g., an intermixing of both forward and backward training. These procedural variations did not alter the contingency rules for establishing a CS– or a CS0. With each training procedure, the CS– was always negatively correlated with the occurrence of shock, and the CS0 uncorrelated with the shock, as compared with the positive correlation used for the CS+. As is indicated in the left panel of Fig. 2, which presents mean errors to criterion as a function of CS–US correlation, the three procedural variations produced virtually identical results: Whereas the CS+ facilitated learning, the CS– always retarded learning relative to the CS0 control. (Corresponding data points with horizontal blips designate means for respective no-CS groups. Note that there is a slight, albeit nonsignificant, cue effect of the noise or tone CS.)

There was one other feature of the design important to the interpretation of the CS– outcome. In planning the experiment, we were sensitive to the possibility that an aversive CS– might not be effective in an appetitive discrimination be-

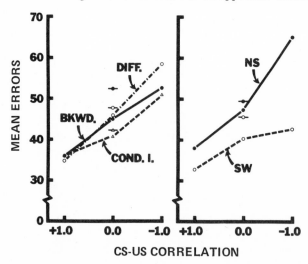

FIG. 2.   Mean errors to criterion as a function of CS–US correlation for groups which received either differential, forward–backward or conditioned–inhibition Pavlovian training (left panel); and for subgroups of these training conditions which received either no shock (NS) or shock for the wrong, i.e., nonreinforced, response (SW) in discrimination training (right panel). Corresponding data points with a horizontal blip designate means for respective no-CS controls. (From Fowler, Fago, Domber, & Hochhauser, 1973.)

cause there presumably would be little if any fear present to enable the CS— to function as a conditioned fear *inhibitor*. For this reason, each replication of the study had involved a factorial design in which, in addition to a specific CS, or no CS, for the food-reinforced response, the subjects received either shock-punishment (.2 sec, .25 mA) or no shock for the wrong, i.e., nonreinforced, response. With the difficult discrimination that we used, the fear produced by the "shock-wrong" treatment could generalize to the similar correct alternative with the result that a fear inhibition effect of the CS— would be potentiated. The right panel of Fig. 2 shows that, relative to the no-shock (NS) treatment, the shock-wrong (SW) treatment had the general effect of reducing errors, and to some extent it attenuated the CS+ and CS— effects. However, it clearly did not eliminate these effects. This outcome argued strongly against a distinctive-cue function of the CSs as based on their respective conditioned reactions and feedback components. Indeed, even when a conditioned—relief or safety effect of the CS— was potentiated by training in a fearful (SW) context, the CS— still retarded learning. Relatedly, when the fear produced by the CS+ in the reinforced alternative was matched by shock-produced fear in the nonreinforced alternative, thereby promoting an *added-equivalence* effect by which discrimination learning could be retarded, the CS+ still facilitated learning.

Confronted with the above findings, we considered the different kinds of reactions that might have been established in Pavlovian and/or instrumental conditioning to produce the observed effects. For example, it was conceivable that in instrumental conditioning the CS+ (which was administered midway in the arm) excited the animal into fleeing and running faster and therefore receiving the food sooner than CS0 and CS— subjects. For the latter group, such an effect would be far less pronounced considering that the CS— could elicit a conditioned response of relaxing. It was also possible that in Pavlovian conditioning CS+ training, as compared with CS0 and CS—training, caused the animal to become more sensitive, or attentive, to stimuli, and therefore in discrimination training the CS+ animal was better able to detect the S^D and associate its instrumental response with this stimulus and the food reinforcer. A simple test of these response explanations was provided as part of an unpublished doctoral dissertation by Edward A. Domber (1971). In addition to presenting aversive CSs (+, 0 and —) contingent upon the food-reinforced response for some groups of subjects (CS/Right), Domber presented the CSs contingent upon the nonreinforced response for other groups of subjects (CS/-Wrong). If the observed CS/Right effects were due to the kinds of reactions and effects suggested, then a similar outcome would occur with the CS/Wrong procedure: The CS+ would produce more immediate *non*reinforcement, or it would better alert the subjects to the S^Δ and the instrumental-response outcome of nonreinforcement and, in either or both of these ways, it would facilitate discrimination performance.

The results of Domber's (1971) study are indicated by the dashed functions of Fig. 3 and, for comparison purposes, the data for the NS subjects of our

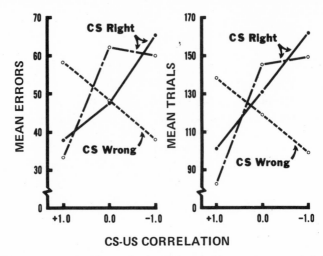

FIG. 3.   Mean errors and trials to criterion (left and right panels, respectively) as a function of CS–US correlation for groups which received the CS contingent upon either the Right (reinforced) or Wrong (nonreinforced) response. The dashed functions show the data of the present experiment; the solid-line function, the comparable data of our original experiment (Fowler et al., 1973). (Adapted from Domber, 1971.)

original study (Fowler et al., 1973) are indicated by the solid-line function. Despite the spuriously high error score for Domber's CS_0/Right group as compared with that of our original study, or even with Domber's CS_0/Wrong control, Fig. 3 shows that the effects obtained for the CS+/Right and CS–/Right groups of the two studies matched quite well on measures of both errors and trials to criterion. More importantly, Domber's results showed that the outcome for the CS/Wrong procedure was just the opposite of that for the CS/Right procedure. Contingent upon the nonreinforced response, the CS+ retarded and the CS– facilitated discrimination learning, with these effects being symmetric to that for the CS_0 control.

Given the equal and opposite effects observed for the two response contingencies, one could not reasonably attribute our findings to specific behaviors that were conditioned to and elicited by the CS in Pavlovian and in instrumental conditioning. To do so, one would have to conceive of a response to the CS+ which, when occasioned in the food-reinforced alternative, would be effective in facilitating performance, but when occasioned in the nonreinforced alternative would be *equally* effective in retarding performance. Furthermore, such a response would have to be matched by an *exact* counterresponse to the CS–, one which would be comparable in the strength of its effect in each alternative but just the *opposite* in function. Processes may work this way but individual responses do not.

III. ASSESSMENT OF THE CS'S SIGNALING
AND AFFECTIVE PROPERTIES

The findings of our initial experiments were not without parallel. In a series of studies investigating the effects of Pavlovian appetitive (Ap) on instrumental aversive (Av) conditioning, Overmier and Bull (1970; see also Overmier & Payne, 1971) reported that an ApCS+ (a signal for food), when used as a discriminative stimulus for shock in a hurdle-jump avoidance task, would facilitate learning, wheras an ApCS− (a signal for the absence of food) similarly employed would retard such learning. These and related observations indicating better conditioning (or less interference in the conditioning) of an AvCS+, when the CS was first established as an ApCS+ rather than as an ApCS−, led Overmier and his associates to argue for a general "cue" effect of the CS. Specifically, they suggested that a CS, once established as a cue (say, a CS+) for one type of reinforcer (e.g., food), could easily be switched to the same kind of cue for a qualitatively different reinforcer (e.g., shock).

We were inclined to agree with the above interpretation, particularly in light of our observation showing that the effect of an AvCS− was relatively independent of any fear motivation (as provided by the shock-wrong treatment) and thus was apparently associative in nature. Therefore, on the basis of both our own findings and those reported by Overmier and his colleagues, we suggested that Pavlovian conditioning could be viewed as a dual-learning process comprised of both primary and secondary stimulus associations: Depending upon the correlation between the CS and the US (cf. Rescorla, 1967), the primary associative property of the CS should be to signal either the presence (CS+) or absence (CS−) of the US. In addition, but as a secondary and more transient "motivational" property, the CS should acquire a specific affective value characterizing the nature (Ap or Av) or the particular US that is present. Jointly, these two properties would enable the CS to function as a signal for either the presence or absence of an affectively positive (e.g., food) or an affectively negative (e.g., shock) event and thereby control motor and emotional responses specific to the US.

By assuming that the CS's affective property was relatively transient and dependent on the characteristics of the US presently available, it followed that such a property could be rapidly extinguished and even converted to a new value in the presence of a qualitatively different reinforcer, *while leaving the CS's original signaling value largely intact.* Applied to our transfer findings, this interpretation argued, then, that AvCSs in an Ap choice discrimination would quickly lose their Av affect and would come to function as signals for the presence (CS+) or absence (CS−) of the new, Ap reinforcer. Hence, if the AvCSs were presented for the food-reinforced response, the AvCS+ (as transformed) could facilitate learning by mediating the presence of the Ap reinforcer, whereas the AvCS− could retard learning by signaling the reinforcer's absence.

However, if the AvCSs were presented for the nonreinforced response, their effects should be reversed. In this case, the transformed AvCS+ could retard learning by inappropriately signaling the presence of the Ap reinforcer, whereas the AvCS– could facilitate learning by appropriately mediating the reinforcer's absence.

The above interpretation, through its emphasis on transfer of the CS's signaling property, appeared to handle our data rather well. However, it obviously needed some independent corroborating evidence. Particularly helpful would be findings indicating (1) that the affective component of the AvCS was not only rapidly extinguished relative to the CS's signaling property, but was actually transformed to a new value in the presence of a qualitatively different reinforcer, and (2) that the signaling property of the AvCS, as transformed, would in fact mediate presence or absence of the Ap reinforcer in discrimination training. With these goals in mind, we initiated two, independent lines of research, which were designed to assess the component properties of the CS.

A. Transformation of the CS's Affective Property

Based on our assumption that the affective property of the CS was dependent on the characteristics (e.g., quality, and intensity or magnitude) of the US presently available, it seemed reasonable that any transformation of this property would be influenced by the strength of the reinforcers employed in both Pavlovian and instrumental conditioning. Therefore, to assess the rate at which the CS's original Av affect might be transformed to a value consistent with the new Ap reinforcer in discrimination training, we conducted a pair of parametric studies investigating the effects of US-shock intensity in Pavlovian conditioning and Ap reward magnitude in discrimination training. In this research, we attempted to monitor the signaling and affective components of the CS by utilizing choice and speed measures of performance as respective indices of associative and "motivational" effects.

1.   Variation in US intensity (Experiment 1).   The first study in the series (Ghiselli & Fowler, 1976) factorially varied US-shock intensity from 0 to 240 V (in 60-V steps of a matched impedance system) together with differential between subjects training designed to establish white noise for different groups of rats as either an AvCS+, CS0 or CS–. Then, as in our original study (Fowler et al., 1973), the CS was presented contingent upon the food-reinforced response in a difficult (bright-dim) T-maze discrimination, with the nagnitude of the food reinforcer held constant at two pellets for all subjects.

Assessment of the animal's speed of running in the CS arm of the T maze at the very start of discrimination training provided clear evidence of differential Av conditioning effects. Relative to the performance of the AvCS0 control, the

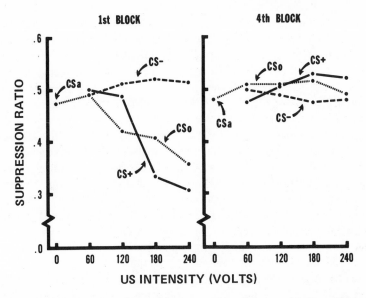

FIG. 4.   Mean suppression ratios for the CS+, CS0, CS– and CS-alone (CSa) groups on the first five–trial block (left panel) and fourth five–trial block (right panel) of respective correct-response (CS) and error (no-CS) trials, as a function of US intensity. (From Ghiselli & Fowler, 1976.)

AvCS+ suppressed and the AvCS– facilitated speeds, with these effects being stronger with stronger US intensities. However, because we could not determine an absolute level of suppression (or of facilitation) from these relative speed effects, we devised a ratio measure of speed suppression. This ratio took the familiar form, $A/(A + B)$, where A referred to the subject's speed of running in the CS (reinforced) arm of the T maze and B referred to its speed on comparable trials in the no-CS (nonreinforced) arm. Note that because the CS was very brief (.2 sec), we could not measure suppression during the CS. Instead, our measure was of speed of running throughout arm, i.e., from choice to entry into the goal.

Figure 4 presents the suppression ratios as a function of US intensity for the CS+, CS0 and CS– groups, as well as for a CS-alone (CSa) control which received presentations of just the CS (0-V US) during Pavlovian conditioning. The left panel, which shows the ratio data based on the first 5 CS and first 5 no-CS trials for each subject, indicates effects comparable to those obtained with our speed measure. Relative to the nonsuppression baseline (a ratio of .5), the CS+ suppressed and the CS– actually facilitated performance (i.e., produced ratios significantly greater than .5). Furthermore, these effects were amplified by stronger US intensities. Although generally intermediate to the CS+ and CS– groups, as least at the higher US intensities, the CS0 group also showed increasing suppression as a function of US intensity. This suggested either a conditioned aversive effect for the CS0 and/or a sensitization effect in which orienting responses to the CS were amplified by stronger shock USs and, in turn, exerted stronger external-inhibition effects (cf. Pavlov, 1927) on speed or running.

The more important results for our purposes are those depicted in the right panel of Fig. 4, which presents the ratio data based on the fourth block of 5 CS and 5 no-CS trials for each subject. As indicated, the initial aversive effects of the CSs completely extinguished within some 16 to 20 CS presentations. (This outcome matches the results of CER studies using comparable shock intensities; cf. Annau & Kamin, 1961). However, the extinction effect was accompanied by an additional effect, as the CS+ and CS− groups were now reversed. In fact, relative to the nonsuppression baseline as well as to the overall performance of the controls, the CS+ reliably facilitated and the CS− reliably suppressed speed of running. Moreover, these effects were also amplified by stronger US intensities. These findings were particularly impressive because they indicated that very early in discrimination training the animal learned to speed up in the presence of the CS+ and to slow down in the presence of the CS−, as if the CSs were now signaling the presence or absence of the new, Ap reinforcer. The significance of these reversed speed effects is best illustrated by drawing a comparison with the rate of discrimination (choice) learning observed in our original study (see Fig. 1). Within 20 CS and 20 no-CS trials, or roughly 40 discrimination trials given the initial chance level of choice responding, the CSs in the present study were apparently functioning as signals for the Ap reinforcer even though choice learning (as shown in Fig. 1) was far from evident. Indeed, it was as if, once the CSs were transformed, differences in choice learning emerged thereafter. Such an

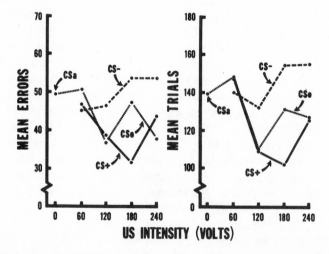

FIG. 5.   Mean errors and trials to criterion (left and right panels, respectively) for the CS+, CS0, CS− and CS-alone (CSa) groups, as a function of US intensity. (Adapted from Ghiselli & Fowler, 1976.)

outcome was consistent with a mediational function of the CSs in bringing forth in the response chain the effect of reinforcement (or signaled nonreinforcement) at the goal.

Like the results of our initial study, those of the present study showed that choice learning was facilitated by the CS+ and retarded by the CS— relative to the CS0 control. However, there was an interesting parallel to the speed data regarding US-intensity effects. As Fig. 5 indicates, both errors and trials to criterion were *increasingly reduced* by the CS+ and *increasingly amplified* by the CS— across stronger US intensities up to 180 v (.75 mA). Only at the strongest US intensity (240 V; 1.0 mA) was the retarding effect of the CS— constrained and the facilitating effect of the CS+ attenuated — but not reversed. The latter effect was not surprising. Rather, it would have been surprising if a response—contingent CS+ based on a strong, 1.0-mA shock-US did not produce some suppression of the reinforced response, in opposition to the CS's potential facilitating effect as a transformed signal for the Ap reinforcer. These choice data and the preceding speed data were easily reconciled with our interpretation. If the CS's signaling property was the basis by which the animal predicted the presence or absence of the US, then it stood to reason, with the low range of US intensities employed, that the greater the intensity of the US, the greater would be its impact and detectability and hence, within limits, the stronger would be the signaling effect of the CS established in Pavlovian conditioning. To this extent, then, both the choice and speed data would show stronger transfer effects with stronger USs.

2. Variation in reward magnitude (Experiment 2). With our US-intensity results in hand, we were eager to determine whether our Av-to-Ap transfer effects would be comparably influenced by the magnitude of the Ap reinforcer used in discrimination training. Our reasoning was that the original Av affect of the CS might be more rapidly overcome (or "counterconditioned") with a larger reward magnitude and, in turn, lead to more rapid or more pronounced transfer of the CS's signaling property. To evaluate this possibility, we conducted a study (Fowler, Goodman, & Zanich, 1977) in which, on the basis of a moderate (120-V) shock-US, a weak (70-db) white-noise stimulus was established for different groups of rats as either an AvCS+, CS0 or CS—. Then, in discrimination training, the CS was presented contingent upon a designated correct response for which the magnitude of food reinforcement was factorially varied at 0, 1, 2, and 4 pellets. The 0-pellet condition, which extended the magnitude dimension to its lower limit, was for the purpose of assessing a "dynamogenic" effect of the AvCSs, that is, a facilitating effect based on the emotional excitement or arousal produced by the AvCSs themselves.

As in the prior US-intensity study (Experiment 1), absolute and ratio measures of speed of running in the present study showed that at the beginning of discrimination training the CS+ suppressed and the CS— facilitated performance relative to the CS0 control. These effects, which were common to all of the

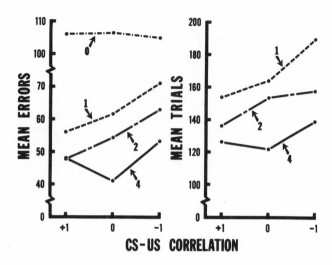

FIG. 6.   Mean errors and trials to criterion (left and right panels, respectively) as a function of CS—US correlation for groups which received either 0, 1, 2, or 4 pellets of food reward for a designated correct response. The data for the 0-pellet subjects are restricted to errors because of a 200 trial cutoff. (From Fowler, Goodman, & Zanich, 1977.)

reward-magnitude conditions including the 0-pellet condition, also extinguished very rapidly. Somewhat surprisingly, however, both the initial effects of the CSs and their rates of extinction were unaffected by reward magnitude, even though larger rewards themselves produced faster running virtually from the start of training. Also, due apparently to the relatively weak (.5-mA) shock-US that we had employed in Pavlovian conditioning, there was no detectable reversal of CS effects on speed of running prior to the onset of choice learning.

Similar interaction effects (or the lack of them) were apparent in our choice measures. Figure 6 shows that "errors" for the 0-pellet subjects, i.e., responses to the no-CS alternative over 200 imposed trials (or at any stage of training), were unaffected by CS—US correlation. In contrast, both errors and trials to criterion for the reinforced (1- to 4-pellet) subjects were reduced by the CS+ and increased by the CS—relative to the CS0 control. But, as Fig. 6 shows, these effects did not interact with reward magnitude (with the exception that in the 4-pellet case a CS+ effect was absent, possibly as a result of a "floor" effect). These findings indicated that our transfer effects, although independent of a dynamogenic effect of the CSs, were very much dependent upon the presence of food reinforcement. However, the fact that reward magnitude could influence rate of discrimination learning for the reinforced subjects, as shown, and yet not interact with CS—US correlation seemed at odds with our interpretation. Surely, one could expect transformation of the CS's affective property from Av to Ap to be modulated by the magnitude of the Ap reinforcer. On second thought, though, perhaps not.

If the CS's signaling property was dependent on the correlation between the CS and the US, as we had originally assumed, and was influenced by US intensity only insofar as detectability of the US was concerned, as Experiment 1 had indicated, then such a property might well reflect and be restricted to a binary or nominal (1, 0; yes, no) processing of information by the animal. Were this the case, AvCSs functioning as transformed signals for the Ap reinforcer would provide information about the presence or absence of the food reinforcer but not about its magnitude. Viewed in this fashion, the transfer effects would be independent of reward magnitude even though this variable itself affected rate of learning. On this assumption, then, we turned our attention to the mechanism by which the AvCSs could function as signals for the Ap reinforcer.

B. Mediational Tests of the CS's Signaling Property

Because all of our prior studies had employed a relatively difficult, bright-dim discrimination to investigate Av-to-Ap transfer, there were two possible interpretations of the mechanism by which the AvCSs operated to influence discrimination learning. One interpretation was that the AvCSs mediated the presence or absence of the Ap reinforcer directly *within* the instrumental-response chain. That is, as transformed signals for the Ap reinforcer, the AvCSs produced expectancies of the presence or absence of the reinforcer early in the chain and thereby "secondarily reinforced" or "nonreinforced" the instrumental response. In contrast, the second interpretation stressed a *between-chain* mediational effect by which the AvCSs, as signals for the Ap reinforcer, could modulate discriminability of the stimulus alternatives — particularly in a difficult discrimination where performance is regulated largely by generalization effects between highly similar discriminative-stimulus compounds. This interpretation argued as follows: When the AvCS+ as a transformed signal for the Ap reinforcer was presented in the *correct* alternative (or when the AvCS— as a signal for nonreinforcement was presented in the *incorrect* alternative), the expectancy generated by the CS would be appropriate to the outcome in that alternative and therefore, by way of its contrast with the outcome and the expectancy formed in the no-CS alternative, it would produce an added-distinctiveness effect. Hence, generalization effects between the alternatives would be reduced and discrimination performance would be facilitated. On the other hand, when the AvCS+ as a signal for reinforcement was presented in the *incorrect* alternative (or when the AvCS— as a signal for nonreinforcement was presented in the *correct* alternative), the expectancy generated by the CS would not only be inappropriate to the outcome in that alternative, but it would be similar to the outcome and the expectancy formed in the no-CS alternative. Consequently, it would produce an added-equivalence effect by which generalization effects would be amplified and discrimination performance retarded.

1. Within- vs. between-chain mediation (Experiment 3).

To evaluate the two interpretations of the CS's mediational function, as well as to assess the generality of our transfer effects, we ran a study (Goodman & Fowler, 1976) in which AvCSs (+, 0, and −) based on a moderate (.5mA) shock-US were administered for different groups of rats contingent upon either the food-reinforced (CS/Right) or nonreinforced (CS/Wrong) response in an easy, light-dark discrimination. In an easy discrimination, where the alternatives are already highly discriminable, an added-distinctiveness effect of the AvCSs would be largely precluded. Thus, a between-chain mediational interpretation would predict that the facilitation effects previously observed for the CS+/Right and CS−/Wrong subjects (see Fig. 3) would be reduced if not eliminated. On the other hand, it was conceivable that an added-equivalence effect of the CSs would operate equally well if not better in any easy discrimination. And, if so, the retardation effects previously observed for the CS+/Wrong and CS−/Right subjects (see Fig. 3) would be maintained or even augmented. According to a between-chain interpretation, then, it would follow that in an easy discrimination the transfer effects, if at all present, would be restricted predominately to retardation effects, i.e., for the CS+/Wrong and CS−/Right subjects. By contrast, a within-chain mediational interpretation would predict the same effects and *symmetrical* relationships, as had been observed previously, because the CS's

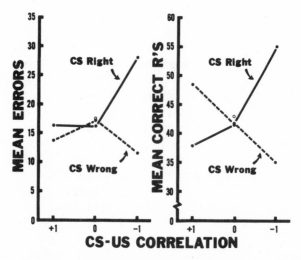

FIG. 7. Mean errors and correct responses, i.e., reinforced trials, to criterion (left and right panels, respectively) as a function of CS−US correlation for groups which received the CS contingent upon either the Right (reinforced) or Wrong (nonreinforced) response. Open data points designate means for no-CS controls. (From Goodman & Fowler, 1976.)

within-chain effect would not be affected by dissimilarity of the stimulus alternatives.

The results of our easy discrimination problem are shown in Fig. 7, which presents mean errors and mean *correct responses* to criterion, i.e., the number of reinforced trials required to reach criterion, for CS groups of the two response contingencies. (Open data points designate means for subjects which received one or another of the three CS treatments in Pavlovian conditioning but no CS in discrimination training. As in our initial research, these no-CS controls were included to check on a discriminability effect of the weak noise stimulus serving as the CS.) The right panel of Fig. 7 shows that the results obtained with the correct-response measure were basically the same as those obtained in our prior difficult discriminations. Relative to both the CS0 and no-CS controls, the CS+ facilitated (i.e., reduced the number of reinforced trials to criterion) and the CS— retarded (i.e., increased trials) for CS/Right subjects, with these effects being just the reverse for CS/Wrong subjects. With the error measure, however, the outcome was somewhat different: The left panel of Fig. 7 shows that, whereas the difference between CS— groups of the two response contingencies was maintained, the difference between CS+ groups was eliminated. Hence, by comparison with both our prior findings (cf. Fig. 3) and those depicted by the correct-response measure of the present study, the effect of the CS+ treatment was to *increase* errors for CS/Right subjects and to *decrease* errors for CS/Wrong subjects, with the resultant outcome being one of no difference.

The error effect for the CS+ groups was the first indication in our choice measures of an aversive or suppressing effect of an AvCS+ based on a moderate (.5-mA) shock-US. Evidently, in opposition to its effect as a transformed signal for the Ap reinforcer, the AvCS+ also suppressed the choice response upon which it was contingent or, via a higher—order conditioning effect, induced an avoidance of the discriminative stimulus with which it was associated.[1] This outcome would not have been apparent in our prior difficult discriminations because the suppression or avoidance associated with one stimulus alternative would generalize to the other highly similar alternative. Therefore, a specific avoidance effect would be obscured. The occurrence of such an effect in the present easy discrimination did not affect our judgment regarding interpretations of the AvCS's function as a mediator for the Ap reinforcer. Contrary to a between-chain interpretation, the transfer effects were not restricted to retardation effects. Instead, for respective CS groups of the two response contingencies, the observed effects were still quite symmetric. Whatever outcome prevailed when the CS was contingent upon one response was exactly reversed and statistically comparable

---

[1]The basis for a higher—order conditioning effect should be apparent. In Pavlovian conditioning, the CS is established as a first-order CS (CS_1); then, in discrimination training, the discriminative stimulus (CS_2) occurs in forward order to the response-contingent CS, allowing responses produced by CS_1 to be conditioned to CS_2.

in size when that CS was contingent upon the other response. All that the underlying aversive effect of the CS+ accomplished was to comparably offset the symmetrically opposite effects which the CS+ exerted when functioning as a signal for Ap reinforcement in the correct and incorrect arms. Thus, the present results argued in favor of the AvCS's role as a within-chain mediator of Ap reinforcement and, as such, afforded the basis for an additional test.

2. Locus of the CS within the chain (Experiment 4). An interpretation stressing the AvCS's role as a within-chain mediator of reinforcement implies that the magnitude of transfer will be regulated by the locus of the CS within the response chain leading to either reinforcement or nonreinforcement. Administered immediately after choice, the CS should better mediate, i.e., bring forward in the chain, the presence or absence of the Ap reinforcer than when administered in conjunction with reinforcement or nonreinforcement at the goal. In the latter case, the CS's mediational effect would be attenuated, if not eliminated, both by the CS's delay relative to choice and by the presence or absence of the actual reinforcer. In all of our prior studies, we had administered the AvCSs at an intermediate position (Locus 2) in the T-maze arm. To evaluate the CS's within-chain effect, we conducted a study (Fowler, Goodman, & DeVito, 1977), which duplicated the training conditions and response contingencies of the prior study (Experiment 3) but instead presented the AvCSs for different groups of rats at a position either just after choice (Locus 1) or immediately prior to food reinforcement or nonreinforcement in the goal (Locus 3).

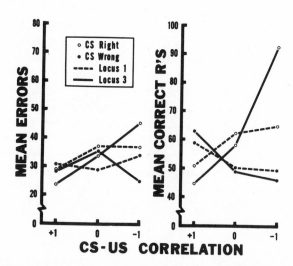

FIG. 8.   Mean errors and correct responses to criterion (left and right panels, respectively) as a function of CS–US correlation for groups which received the CS either immediately after choice (Locus 1) or at the food cup in the goal (Locus 3) contingent upon either the Right or Wrong response. (From Fowler, Goodman, & DeVito, 1977.)

As Fig. 8 shows, the overall pattern of results for the CS/Right and CS/Wrong groups of the present study was comparable to that observed in Experiment 3. Whereas the effects of the two response contingencies were constrained for CS+ groups in the error measure (left panel), the correct-response measure (right panel) showed that the CS+ facilitated, and the CS— retarded, discrimination learning relative relative to the CS0 control for CS/Right subjects, with these effects being just the reverse for CS/Wrong subjects. The striking aspect, however, of the correct-response data was that the interaction between response contingency and CS—US correlation was more pronounced for Locus 3 than for Locus 1 subjects. In fact, separate assessments of the contingency by correlation interaction for Locus 1 and Locus 3 subjects indicated that the interaction was significant only for the latter subjects. The error data showed basically the same effects. The Locus 1 functions were virtually flat, whereas the Locus 3 functions interacted and, with the exception of the CS+/Wrong group, showed the same pattern of results as obtained with the correct-response measure.

These results seriously challenged our signaling interpretation. We had progressed to the point where the only viable interpretation of the CS's function as a transformed signal for the Ap reinforcer was as a within-chain mediator; yet, the present results required us to conclude that the CS's mediational function was more, it not only, effective when the CS was presented late in the chain.[2] Conceivably, the difference in outcome for Loci 1 and 3 could be attributed to the CS's initial aversive property, that is, the possibility that the suppressing effect of an AvCS+ (or the reinforcing effect of an AvCS—) would be less pronounced — and thus less opposing of the CS's transformed signaling effect — when the CS was administered at Locus 3, distal to the choice response. But even so, how was one to account for the existence of any transfer effects at Locus 3? At this position, a mediational effect of the CS as a transformed signal for the Ap reinforcer would *also* be attenuated by the CS's delay relative to the choice response — as well as by the presence or absence of the Ap reinforcer. Most troublesome in the latter respect was the pronounced retardation effect observed for the Locus 3, CS—/Right subjects (see Fig. 8). These subjects had received the CS— contiguous with food reinforcement in the goal, and therefore on the basis of our signaling interpretation we could only conclude that the animal had heeded the CS— (as a signal for the *absence* of the Ap reinforcer) over the Ap reinforcer itself! But surely this could not be so, at least not by our interpretation. We could hardly argue that an AvCS was transformed in affect on the basis of the Ap reinforcer and, at the same time, that the animal paid little or no attention to that reinforcer.

Confronted with the above results, we were led to consider a radically different interpretation of our findings, one which acknowledged a contrast between what

---

[2]In actuality, a comparison of *z*-score transforms of the data from the present study and from Experiment 3, where the CS was presented at Locus 2, indicated a graded progression of effects from Locus 1 to Locus 3.

the subject had learned to expect on the basis of the CS in Pavlovian conditioning and what it actually received as an outcome contingent upon that CS in discrimination training. In particular, the observation that an AvCS— at Locus 3 in the reinforced arm would apparently "overshadow" the Ap reinforcer and exert a pronounced retardation effect suggested to us that our transfer effects were none other than blocking effects (e.g., Kamin, 1968, 1969).

IV. REINTERPRETATION: ACROSS—REINFORCEMENT BLOCKING EFFECTS

Our blocking interpretation was specifically patterned after Rescorla and Wagner's (1972; Wagner & Rescorla, 1972) reinforcement—limit, or "discrepancy," theory of conditioning. In its basic form, this theory posits that the conditioning of a single stimulus element, or of elements in compound, is a function of the size and the direction of the discrepancy between the particular US outcome obtained (i.e., the "limit" of conditioning which the US can support) and the expectancy which is produced by the CS or CS compound. To accommodate our across-reinforcement transfer effects, all that the theory required was an additional but quite reasonable assumption: Ap and Av reinforcers and the expectancies generated by CSs based on these reinforcers are functionally related and can be scaled on a common dimension, e.g., a positive-to-negative incentive or a "good-bad" outcome dimension.

Given the above interpretation, the effects of our CS/Right and CS/Wrong procedures fell readily into place. When AvCSs were presented contingent upon the food-reinforced response, i.e., *in the presence of the S^D*, the good outcome of food reinforcement would produce little "surprise" or a relatively small discrepancy as compared with the good outcome (absence of shock) predicted by the AvCS—. Hence, the AvCS— would effectively block the association of food reinforcement and the S^D, and discrimination learning would be retarded. However, by contrast with the bad outcome (presence of shock) predicted by the AvCS+, the good outcome of food reinforcement would produce considerable surprise or a relatively large *positive* discrepancy. Thus, the AvCS+ would "counterblock" or, to use Rescorla and Wagner's term, it would "supercondition" the reinforcer's association with the S^D (cf. Rescorla, 1971, Experiment 1; Wagner, 1969b). On the other hand, if the AvCSs were presented for the non-reinforced response, i.e., *in the presence of the S^Δ*, their effects would be reversed. As a negative-incentive or frustrating condition (i.e., by comparison with food for the reinforced response), the outcome of nonreinforcement would produce relatively little discrepancy as compared with the similarly bad (shock) outcome predicted by the AvCS+. Thus the AvCS+ would block the association of non-reinforcement and the S^Δ, and discrimination learning would be retarded (cf. Suiter & LoLordo, 1971). By contrast, however, with the good outcome (safety) predicted by the AvCS—, the bad outcome of nonreinforcement would produce a relatively large *negative* discrepancy. Consequently, the AvCS— would counterblock the association of nonreinforcement and the S^{Δ}, and discrimination learning would be facilitated (cf. Mackintosh & Turner, 1971).

In brief, then, our reinterpretation argued that our AV-to-Ap transfer findings reflected the across-reinforcement blocking and counterblocking of both excitatory conditioning to the S^{D} and inhibitory conditioning to the S^{Δ}. With this blocking interpretation, it mattered little that the CS in our procedure was response—contingent and hence operationally equivalent to either a conditioned reinforcer (as with the AvCS—) or a conditioned punisher (as with the AvCS+). Rather, what our findings suggested was that, to the extent that the CSs functioned in these ways, their response effects (and underlying associations, e.g., S^{D}–R and/or R—CS) were relatively insignificant by comparison with the effects of the CS's association with the instrumental-response outcome of reinforcement or nonreinforcement.[3] Furthermore, it was of little consequence to a blocking interpretation that the CS was contingent upon a response to a discriminative stimulus and thus, in combination with that stimulus, formed a sequential, say, S^{D}-then-CS compound.

A similar procedure had actually been used by Kamin (1968) in his initial investigations of blocking. In that research, Kamin showed that blocking would occur not only when the preconditioned stimulus (a CS+) was presented simultaneously with an added stimulus and was followed by reinforcement, but also when the CS+ was presented briefly (for 5 sec) during the terminal portion of an added 3-min stimulus that was followed by reinforcement. On the other hand, if the preconditioned stimulus was presented briefly during the *initial* portion (cf. Locus 1) of an added 3-min stimulus that likewise terminated in reinforcement, blocking was attenuated; that is, conditioning occurred to the added stimulus (cf. our S^{D}) at a normal rate. In this light, the findings of Experiment 4 on the effects of administering an AvCS— at either Locus 1 or Locus 3 in the *food-reinforced* arm matched Kamin's results exactly. Collectively, the results of that study, like Kamin's findings, highlighted the significance of the CS's temporal relationship to the reinforcer (or US) in determining a blocking effect and, in addition, indicated that such a relationship was important in both the blocking *and* counterblocking of excitatory *and* inhibitory conditioning.

The findings of our other experiments, in which the AvCSs had been administered at Locus 2 (typically in the reinforced arm), were also consistent with a blocking interpretation, particularly when one considered the nature and the relationship of elements in the S^{D}—CS—reinforcer sequence. Clearly, it was reasonable to expect, as a result of Pavlovian conditioning, that the AvCSs would at first exert differential suppressing effects on speed of running in the reinforced

---

[3]See Bolles' contribution in this volume (Chapter 4) for a similar conclusion regarding the response associations that are formed in avoidance conditioning and punishment training.

arm — or, more explicitly, in the presence of the visual S^D, which extended throughout the arm into the goal (cf. Experiment 1). It was also reasonable to expect that these effects would be complemented by a higher—order, aversive conditioning effect to the S^D based on its association with the AvCS+. Thus, some avoidance of the S^D arm, i.e., increased errors, would be likely in an easy discrimination (e.g., Experiment 3), but not necessarily in a difficult discrimination where the effect could generalize to the similar S^Δ (e.g., Experiment 1). However, in the course of training, these second—order, conditioned aversive effects would be outweighed by the CS's effect in blocking (CS—) or counterblocking (CS+) the *primary reinforcer's* association with the S^D. Initially, these blocking effects would occur to the S^D at the goal, i.e., at the point of reinforcement, but with further training they would "backchain" down the arm to the S^D at the choice point. In this light, the reversal of CS effects on speed of running in the presence of the S^D (cf. Experiment 1) was nothing more than an early indication of the blocking and counterblocking effects that were developing to the S^D at the choice point. Accordingly, the speed effects of the CSs would parallel the choice effects and, within limits, both would be augmented by stronger USs. This would follow because stronger shock-USs would produce stronger conditioning effects and thus more divergent values for the AvCS+ and AvCS—. Consequently, when contrasted with a particular magnitude of Ap reinforcement in discrimination training, these stronger CSs would produce a wider range of contrast effects, and would lead therefore to more pronounced blocking and counterblocking effects.

In contrast to the outcome of Experiment 1 showing a positive relationship between Av-to-Ap transfer and US intensity, the results of Experiment 2 indicated that the transfer effects, although dependent upon Ap reinforcement, were independent of reward magnitude. From the standpoint of a discrepancy interpretation of blocking, however, this was as it should have been. In the Pavlovian-conditioning phase of Experiment 2, the AvCSs were set at specific values (+, 0, and —) on the basis of a specific US intensity. Therefore, at fixed values, they would yield constant differences among CS+, CS0 and CS— groups when contrasted with whatever magnitude of food reinforcement that was used in discrimination training. In the vernacular of Rescorla and Wagner's (1972) reinforcement-limit theory, *lambda* (the limit of reinforcement) would vary as a function of reward magnitude but the values of the AvCS compounds, being fixed for CS+, CS0, and CS— groups, would yield additive, i.e., noninteractive, differences. By comparison, the no-reinforcement or 0-pellet condition of Experiment 2 would not provide the basis for a conditioning effect and therefore, to the extent that our measures of performance were at all sensitive, they would show only differential suppressing effects of the AvCSs — as indeed had been observed for the 0-pellet subjects in the speed data of that study.

V. BLOCKING AND COUNTERBLOCKING ("SUPERCONDITIONING") TESTS

In spite of what appeared to be a very good match of theory and data, we had a few reservations about our reinterpretation. For one thing, all of the published research on blocking had employed qualitatively the same reinforcer (Ap or Av) in both single-element preconditioning and in compound conditioning. Thus, there was a question in our minds as to whether one could formally demonstrate an across-reinforcement blocking effect, that is, in a Pavlovian-to-Pavlovian transfer paradigm. For another, the published research on blocking had shown that shifts in the magnitude or intensity of a particular reinforcer from preconditioning to compound conditioning would attenuate blocking (e.g., Kamin, 1968, 1969; Feldman, 1971; Neely & Wagner, 1974). Was it not reasonable, therefore, to expect that a change in the *quality* of the reinforcer would also attenuate blocking? Indeed, from the standpoint of Kamin's surprise interpretation of blocking (which had treated surprise virtually as an all-or-none factor), the receipt of a food reinforcer following a CS that had been established on the basis of a shock reinforcer — even a CS that was negatively correlated with the shock — would be surprising and should, therefore, preclude a blocking effect. Confronted with these possibilities, our purpose became twofold: (1) to employ the standard within-reinforcement (e.g., Ap-to-Ap) blocking manipulation in our Pavlovian-to-instrumental paradigm, and in this manner provide a test which would oppose signaling and discrepancy interpretations of our findings, and (2) to evaluate blocking and counterblocking effects based on qualitatively different reinforcers in a Pavlovian-to-Pavlovian transfer paradigm.

A. Within-Reinforcement Transfer: Signaling vs. Discrepancy Interpretations (Experiments 5 and 6)

In view of our first objective, we conducted a study (Zanich & Fowler, 1978) assessing the effects of Pavlovian Ap conditioning on Ap discrimination learning, that is, where an ApCS was utilized as a response—contingent event. In this study, rats first received magazine training in an operant chamber (with the manipulandum absent), followed by Pavlovian conditioning in which response—independent food was differentially correlated with a brief and moderate (.5-sec, 80-db) white-noise stimulus, so as to establish this stimulus for different groups as an ApCS+, CS0 or CS−. In addition, to check on the effectiveness of the ApCS0 control, we included a fourth group which received only food presentations in Pavlovian conditioning, and thus was designated a US-alone control. Then, comparable to our prior research, the CS (or a novel white-noise stimulus in the case of the US-alone controls) was presented at Locus 3 contingent upon the food-reinforced response in a moderately difficult (bright-dim) T-maze discrimination.

The experiment was especially suited to comparing signaling and discrepancy interpretations of our findings. If a signaling interpretation were correct, the ApCS+ would essentially function as a conditioned reinforcer to produce the same, if not a larger, facilitating effect as had been observed for an AvCS+. According to the interpretation, both CSs would signal the presence of the reinforcer, but the affective value of the ApCS would already be appropriate to that reinforcer. Similarly, the ApCS− should function as a conditioned non-reinforcer to produce the same, if not a larger, retarding effect as had been observed for an AvCS−. On the other hand, if a discrepancy interpretation were correct, the effects of the ApCSs would be just the opposite of those observed for their AvCS counterparts. Based on the discrepancy between the good out-come of food reinforcement and the expectancy produced by the CS, the ApCS+, in signaling a good outcome, should block and the ApCS−, in signaling a bad (no−food) outcome, should counterblock the reinforcer's association with the S^D. Thus, it would follow from a discrepancy interpretation that the ApCS+ would operate as though it were a conditioned *nonreinforcer* to retard learning, and the ApCS− as though it were a conditioned *reinforcer* to facilitate learning.

To vary the differences in outcome predicted by the two interpretations, we also manipulated the magnitude of Ap reinforcement. Following magazine training for all subjects at 1 pellet per delivery, the food reinforcer in Pavlovian condition-ing was factorially varied at 2 and 4 pellets, with the magnitude of food reward in discrimination training being the same as that which a subject had received as the US in Pavlovian conditioning.[4] With this manipulation, a signaling interpreta-tion would predict that the respective facilitating and retarding effects of an ApCS+ and an ApCS− would be greater with a 4-pellet than with a 2-pellet reinforcer because of the affective strengths and hence conditioned−reinforcing and conditioned−nonreinforcing effects of the CSs would be greater (cf. D'Amato, 1955). Likewise, a discrepancy interpretation would predict a positive relation-ship between reinforcement magnitude and the respective blocking and counter-blocking effects of an ApCS+ and an ApCS−. However, there was an interesting corollary to the prediction: The CS+ groups of the 2- and 4-pellet conditions should show comparably retarded (blocked) discrimination learning because in both cases the discrepancy between the magnitude of reinforcement obtained and that which the CS predicts is exactly the same, namely, zero. In contrast, there should be a marked difference in the faciliated performance of the CS− groups because the discrepancy between expecting the *absence* of a particular magnitude of reinforcement (e.g., 2-pellet frustration) and actually receiving

---

[4]Note the upward shift in reinforcement magnitude from magazine training to Pavlovian conditioning. This feature was designed to preclude a blocking effect of the magazine click, or of contextual cues, on the development of noise as a CS+, a potentially serious problem.

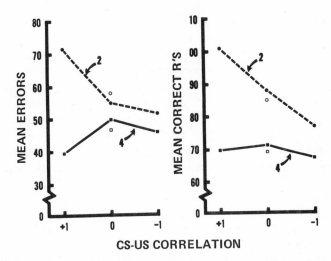

FIG. 9.   Mean errors and correct responses to criterion (left and right panels, respectively) as a function of CS—US correlation for groups which received either a 2- or a 4-pellet food reinforcer in both Pavlovian conditioning and instrumental discrimination training. Corresponding open data points designate means for respective US-alone controls. (From Zanich & Fowler, 1978. Copyright 1978 by the American Psychological Association. Reprinted by permission.)

that reinforcement magnitude (i.e., the "joy" of 2 pellets) in essence doubles as reinforcement magnitude doubles.

Figure 9 shows that the findings for the 2-pellet subjects were entirely consistent with a discrepancy interpretation: The ApCS+, although *operationally* equivalent to a conditioned reinforcer, retarded discrimination learning whereas the ApCS—, the operational equivalent of a conditioned nonreinforcer, facilitated learning as compared with both the CS0 and US-alone controls. (Means for the latter subjects are designated by corresponding open data points.) However, the findings for the 4-pellet subjects did not show any reliable effects; for these subjects, the CS—US correlational functions for both the error and correct-response data were basically flat. In light of the outcome for the 2-pellet subjects, we could hardly attribute the lack of effects for the 4-pellet subjects to the ineffectiveness of our procedures. Some other factor, or factors, had to have operated to offset the blocking and counterblocking effects evident in the 2-pellet case. One obvious interpretation (in line with a signaling interpretation) was that ApCSs based on a relatively large (i.e., 4-pellet) reinforcer were sufficiently potent as conditioned reinforcers and conditioned nonreinforcers to offset the respective blocking and counterblocking effects of an ApCS+ and an ApCS—. Likewise, it was possible that higher—order conditioning effects were more pronounced with the stronger, 4-pellet CSs. In this case, a reward or nonreward expectancy would be conditioned to the S^D by way of its forward association with the CS. In turn, the response tendencies associated with these effects (i.e., approach or withdrawal; cf. Bindra, 1974) would influence the choice response and would work against a blocking or counterblocking effect of the CS.

There was still another interpretation of the 4-pellet outcome. We had employed a moderately difficult bright-dim discrimination because of our concern with reward—magnitude effects and the related fact that such effects are typically constrained in an easy discrimination (cf. Reynolds, 1949; Hochhauser & Fowler, 1975). Thus, it was possible that the blocking effects of the stronger, 4-pellet CSs had been offset by their discriminability effects. Compared with the outcome of no food, as well as with the expectancy of no food which the animal formed in the incorrect arm, a strong (i.e., 4-pellet) signal for food in the correct arm could produce an added-distinctiveness effect by which generalization effects between the alternatives would be reduced, and hence discrimination learning facilitated. On the other hand, a strong signal for the absence of food in the *correct* alternative could produce an added-equivalence effect by which generalization effects would be enhanced, and thus discrimination learning retarded. This interpretation was the same as that which we had earlier assessed in Experiment 3, only now our reference was to the expectancies produced by ApCSs rather than by AvCSs. For the latter, we could only presume at the time that they would function as transformed signals for the Ap reinforcer. In the case of strong ApCSs, however, the suggested discriminability effects were quite reasonable because they had independently been shown in other research to operate for the Ap reinforcer itself: Larger magnitudes of food reward would facilitate learning in a difficult discrimination merely on the basis on their distinctive stimulus features and associated consummatory feedback (Hochhauser & Fowler, 1975; see also Zanich & Fowler 1975). Thus, it was not unlikely that the expectancies generated by strong ApCSs would have a similar function.

To evaluate the different interpretations of the 4-pellet findings, we replicated the experiment using an easy, light-dark discrimination. If discriminability effects of the ApCSs were responsible for the anomalous 4-pellet outcome, then such effects would be attenuated in an easy discrimination where the stimulus alternatives are already highly discriminable. However, if the 4-pellet findings reflected conditioned—reinforcing and/or higher—order conditioning effects of the ApCSs, then these effects would reappear in an easy discrimination because, clearly, they are not dependent upon a difficult discrimination. Figure 10 shows that, with an easy discrimination, the outcome for the 4-pellet subjects was consistent with a discrepancy interpretation: whereas the ApCS+ blocked (retarded) learning, the ApCS— counterblocked (facilitated) learning as compared with the CS0 control. Furthermore, the overall pattern of results was now in line with specific predictions of a discrepancy interpretation. As earlier noted, this interpretation requires that discrimination learning for the CS+ groups of the 2- and 4-pellet conditions be comparably blocked because, for both groups, there is no discrepancy between the magnitude of reinforcement obtained and that ex-

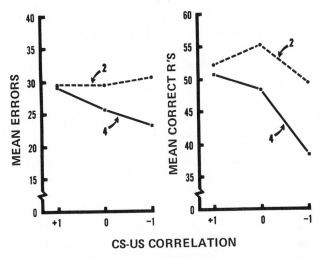

FIG. 10.   Mean errors and correct responses to criterion (left and right panels, respectively) as a function of CS–US correlation for groups which received either a 2- or a 4-pellet food reinforcer in both Pavlovian conditioning and instrumental training on an easy discrimination. (From Zanich & Fowler, 1978. Copyright 1978 by the American Psychological Association. Reprinted by permission.)

pected. On the other hand, some difference should exist between CS0 groups due merely to the difference in the magnitude of the instrumental reinforcer (i.e., +4 vs. +2). By comparison, however, the difference between CS— groups should be relatively large because the discrepancy between expecting the absence of 4 pellets and receiving 4 pellets is appreciably larger than that between expecting the absence of the 2 pellets and receiving 2 pellets (cf. +8 vs. +4). Figure 10 shows that the relationship of the CS–US correlational functions for the 2- and 4-pellet subjects matched these predictions rather well.

Although it is true that the CS–US correlational functions for the 2-pellet subjects were virtually flat and indicated neither a blocking nor a counterblocking effect, this outcome was not unreasonable. Given the weaker conditioning (i.e., reinforcement) base for the 2-pellet CSs, our easy discrimination test may have been relatively insensitive to the weaker effects of these CSs. Furthermore, there appeared to be another factor responsible for the 2-pellet outcome. The correct-response data of Fig. 10 show that the CS–US correlational functions for the 2- and 4-pellet subjects are partially quadratic: *Both* of the CS+ groups show far fewer correct responses to criterion than would be expected on the basis on a linear extrapolation of the means for their respective CS0 and CS— groups. This common effect suggests, then, that a conditioned—reinforcing and/or higher—order conditioning effect of the ApCS+ also operated to partially offset a blocking effect of the CS+ (and thus produce the relatively flat function observed for the 2-pellet subjects). This outcome was not without parallel for it matched the results of our prior studies (Experiments 3 and 4) assessing the effects of AvCSs in an easy discrimination. It will be recalled that, in those experiments, an apparent blocking or counterblocking effect of the AvCS+ was also offset, in part, by the CS's condition—suppressing and/or higher—order aversive conditioning effect (see Fig. 7 and 8).

B. Across-Reinforcement Transfer in a Purely Pavlovian Paradigm (Experiment 7)

With the above findings clearly favoring a discrepancy interpretation of our prior transfer results, it remained for us to accomplish our second objective, namely, to demonstrate across-reinforcement blocking and counterblocking effects in a Pavlovian-to-Pavlovian transfer paradigm. In this research, we also wanted to show that such effects would develop to the initial stimulus of an overlapping sequential compound — the arrangement characteristic of the S^D-then-CS compound used in our discrimination research. Therefore, we employed a condition-suppression (CER) methodology patterned after our discrimination method. Rats that were both hungry and thirsty first received magazine training in an operant chamber at 1 pellet per delivery, followed by Pavlovian conditioning in which response—independent food at 4 pellets per delivery was differentially correlated with a 5-sec flashing light so as to establish this event (stimulus A) as an ApCS+, CS_0 or CS— for different groups. For other subjects, the food-US was presented without A to provide a US-alone (USa) control. Then, in a different type of chamber with a different set of explicity arranged background cues (to match our Pavlovian-to-instrumental transfer research), the subjects received on-baseline aversive conditioning to a 20-sec clicker (stimulus B) which was administered 15 sec prior to the 5-sec A stimulus, with the two events being coterminous and followed immediately by a .5-sec, 1.0-mA shock-US. To avoid a confounding effect of the food-based ApCS in CER training, baseline responding consisted of a steady rate of licking maintained by continuous water reinforcement.

With the sequential B-then-A compound presentation that we used, a blocking or counterblocking effect of A on B could easily be monitored by measuring conditioned suppression to the B-alone portion of the compound. In fact, our primary interest was in assessing the animal's *initial* reaction to B, so as to provide a parallel to our discrimination assessment of the animal's choice (as opposed to running) response to the S^D. However, because the conditioning of suppression is extremely rapid in a CER paradigm (and is relatively unstable with US-shock intensities much less than 1.0 mA), we also employed the B-then-A compound presentation in CER extinction. Our purpose was to show that, in spite of rapid and complete suppression to B for all groups during CER acquistion, differential amounts of conditioning had occurred to B based on the blocking or counterblocking effect of A, and these would be reflected in CER extinction.

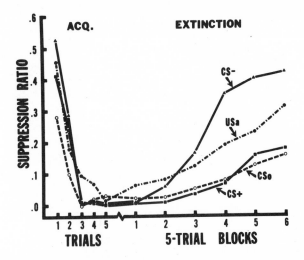

FIG. 11.   Mean suppression, over the course of CER acquisition and extinction, to the initial 5 sec of B in a sequential B-then-A compound presentation for the ApCS+, CS0, CS– and USa groups. (Adapted from Goodman, 1976.)

The relevant findings of the present study, part of a dissertation by Joel H. Goodman (1976), are shown in Fig. 11 which depicts group mean suppression ratios, over the course of 5 CER acquisition trials and 30 CER extinction trials, to the intial 5 sec of B (analogous to an animal's initial reaction to an S^D). Suppression scores are based on the ratio, CS/(CS + preCS), where CS designates responding in the first 5 sec of B and preCS designates mean responding over successive 5-sec intervals of a 20-sec period immediately preceding the CS. As expected, conditioning was too rapid to allow any group differences to emerge, but for one important exception: The CS0 control showed pronounced suppression to B on the very first conditioning trial, *prior* to presentation of the shock-US. This effect, which indicates a strong unconditioned reaction to B for the CS0 subjects, was also reflected in the more rapid acquisition of suppression by this group (cf. trial 2) and in a relatively protracted rate of extinction. Despite this bias for the CS0 control, the data for the other groups showed that the extinction of suppression to B was equally protracted for the CS+ group but, in contrast, was very rapid for the CS– group. Furthermore, these effects were symmetric to the extinction performance of the USa control. Thus, apart from the performance of the CS0 group (which in fact differed reliably from the USa control), the extinction data indicated that the ApCS–, as a signal for a bad outcome, had restricted (blocked) aversive conditioning to B, whereas the ApCS+, as a signal for a good outcome, had enhanced (counterblocked) aversive conditioning to B. These results, then, provided an appropriate parallel to our discrimination findings on choice performance.

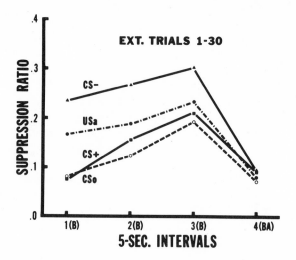

FIG. 12. Mean suppression ratios for the ApCS+, CS0, CS−, and USa groups throughout extinction, as a function of successive 5-sec intervals of B including the terminal BA portion of the compound. (Adapted from data presented in Goodman, 1976.)

There were other similarities as well. Group differences in extinction to B are summarized in Fig. 12 which presents the suppression ratios as a function of successive 5-sec intervals of B, including the terminal BA portion of the compound. This comparison shows that, whereas the same group effects were present throughout the B-alone portion of the compound, suppression for all of the groups weakened over successive intervals of B prior to the onset of A. This indicates either a stronger ("pseudo") conditioning effect to the onset of B (based on the similarly abrupt onset of the shock reinforcer) and/or a learned "safety" effect with time spent in B. (The latter would follow because stimulus A could serve as a highly discernible temporal cue for shock in CER acquisition.) Importantly, the decreased suppression over time in B was significantly more pronounced for the ApCS+ group suggesting that, for this group, B was also subject to a higher−order *appetitive* conditioning effect based on its forward association with the ApCS+. This finding was in line with our prior discrimination results and with Konorski and Szwejkowska's (1956) findings indicating that an ApCS+, as compared to an ApCS−, is relatively difficult to recondition into an AvCS+. Hence, to the extent that temporally later portions of B were subject to higher−order Ap conditioning based on their more contiguous association with the ApCS+, they would be "protected" from aversive conditioning based on the shock US.

That an offsetting higher−order conditioning effect would be relatively weak and restricted to the later portions of B is not surprising when one considers the relative reinforcing strengths of an ApCS+ and an Av US. Also, the effective interstimulus interval for Av conditioning seems far more extensive than that for

Ap conditioning based on exteroceptive CSs (see, e.g., McAllister & McAllister, 1971), and presumably such a difference would hold as well for higher—order Ap conditioning. This account is not rendered any less plausible in the absence of a comparable higher—order *inhibitory* conditioning effect for the ApCS— group (by which one could expect *less* weakening of suppression to the later portions of *B*). The absence of such an effect may suggest (1) that one cannot readily obtain a higher—order inhibitory conditioning effect, (2) that it is undetectable in the absence of an Ap excitor, or (3) that if it occurs (e.g., Rescorla, 1976) it is far less pronounced than a higher—order excitatory conditioning effect. Whichever the case, the purely classical data of the present study provide a close match with the findings of our prior, easy discrimination studies (Experiments 3, 4, and 6). It will be recalled that those studies, in addition to demonstrating a blocking or counterblocking effect of the CS, consistently indicated a higher—order excitatory conditioning effect of the CS+ (based on either an Ap or an Av reinforcer) but not a higher—order inhibitory conditioning effect of the CS—.

The data shown in Fig. 12 for the *BA* portion of the compound are also important in the interpretation of the present findings. As indicated, the occurrence of *A* in compound with *B* produced relatively marked but virtually identical suppression for all groups despite pronounced differences in suppression to *B* alone. This outcome indicates that the observed differences in suppression to *B* cannot be ascribed to differences in suppression to *A* alone; that is, the possibility that the ApCS+ produced greater conditioned (or unconditioned) suppression than the ApCS— and that, in turn, these differences were transmitted to *B* by way of its forward association with *A*. Had this been the case, suppression to the *BA* portion of the compound would have been more pronounced for the ApCS+ than for the ApCS— group; clearly, though, this was not the case. Rather, what the *BA* compound data suggest is just the reverse: That, in line with the Rescorla-Wagner (1972) interpretation, the value of the *BA* compound reflects a summation of the values of the individual elements; and that, given the observed differences in suppression to *B*, suppression to *A* was if anything more pronounced with the ApCS— than with the ApCS+. Although the present experiment was not designed to make this comparison, it should be apparent that such a difference is equally in line with Konorski and Szwejkowska's (1956) findings on the relative ease of reconditioning an ApCS—, as compared to an ApCS+, into a CS+ for shock.

VI. CONCLUSIONS AND IMPLICATIONS

The uniformity of our findings across discrimination and CER methodologies suggests several conclusions regarding both (1) the kinds of association that are formed in instrumental as well as in Pavlovian conditioning — to which we shall address specific comment in a later section — and (2) the manner in which the animal processes information within and across reinforcement systems. On the latter point, our findings seem clear in establishing not only that Ap and Av reinforcers and the CSs based on these reinforcers are functionally related, but that the animal processes the CS through a central-motive or an expectancy state characterizing the incentive (e.g., good-bad) features of its associated US outcome. Although the basis for this interpretation has earlier been elaborated, its theoretical support and significance as a cognitive interpretation should be made clear, particularly with respect to the nature of blocking effects.

A. S–R vs. S–S Interpretations of Blocking

Prior investigators (e.g., Brown & Wagner, 1964; Wagner, 1969a; Linden & Hallgren, 1973) have argued in a vein very similar to ours insofar as they have suggested that processes based on Av and Ap reinforcers, e.g., fear and frustration, are functionally related. However, the interpretation which they have offered of their findings has been cast within the mold of S–R theory, and therefore it has relied on an implicitly peripheral, mediating response: Overt behaviors that are associated with and occasioned by the affective properties of an emotional *reaction* (e.g., fear), which is conditioned to one stimulus or situation, can be mediated by the similar affective properties of another emotional *reaction* (e.g., frustration), which is conditioned to a different stimulus or situation.

The present findings are not amenable to a mediating-response interpretation for there is little if any meaningful way in which such an interpretation can be applied to a blocking paradigm. The closest that one comes to this interpretation is by arguing that our sequential B-then-A compound procedure allows responses to the preconditioned A stimulus to become associated with the added B stimulus (e.g., through higher—order conditioning) and that, in turn, these responses mediate the effect of the US via their similarity to the UR. However, this interpretation cannot possibly account for the obtained findings. If anything, it would have to predict that in our CER paradigm, for example, a preestablished ApCS– (a conditioned frustrative stimulus) would enhance aversive conditioning to B because B, by way of its association with the ApCS–, can elicit a frustrative reaction which is affectively similar to the shock-produced response of fear. (Or that, in our discrimination paradigm, a response—contingent AvCS–, a safety signal, would facilitate conditioning to the S^D by mediating, through conditioned "relief," the affectively similar response of "joy" occasioned by the Ap reinforcer.) Quite apart from the absence in our research of any evidence of higher—order *inhibitory* conditioning (upon which the above effects would be based) the fact that the ApCS– blocked Av conditioning to the added B stimulus in CER training (and that the AvCS– blocked Ap conditioning to the S^D in discrimination training) is clearly counter to this interpretation.

The foregoing analysis is instructive because it highlights an important but relatively unacknowledged feature of blocking phenomena. By their very nature, they are opposed to any S–R interpretation which focuses on the relationship or similarity of a preestablished CR and the UR, whether the point of focus is either a peripheral motor response or an emotional reaction. Even though a CR, at full strength (i.e., at *lambda,* cf. Rescorla & Wagner, 1972) and appropriate to the US, can occur to the preconditioned *A* stimulus, it still occurs in a *contiguous* relationship with the added *B* stimulus. On this basis alone, it should condition to that stimulus — or even on the basis of reinforcement, considering that the preestablished CS (say, a CS+) can function as a second-order reinforcer. In fact, the same holds true for the UR. To say, as some theorists (e.g., Rescorla & Wagner, 1972) have, that the US can lose its "effectiveness" as a reinforcer (because it is already signaled by the preconditioned *A* stimulus) does not in any way deny the *effect* of that US in producing a UR; nor does it deny that the UR will occur in a contiguous relationship with the added B stimulus. In so many words, it acknowledges that conditioning to *B* will not occur unless the US is discrepant from the subject's *expectation.* [5]

To our way of thinking, the preceding observations would be sufficient to reject S—R theory outright were it not for one other consideration. Attentional theorists, like Sutherland and Mackintosh (1971), have argued that blocking is not due to a failure of S—R contiguity or reinforcement as such, but rather to a limitation in the animal's ability to process more than one stimulus at a time. By their interpretation, the animal learns in preconditioning to attend to the *A* stimulus because, by virtue of its correlation with the reinforcer, it obtains significance for the animal. Therefore, when this preconditioned stimulus, say, an AvCS+, is presented in compound CER conditioning, the animal attends selectively to it and ignores the added *B* stimulus with the result that conditioning to *B* is "blocked." However, this interpretation cannot account for the present findings (see also Dickinson, 1977) showing an across-reinforcement *counterblocking* effect, that is, an enhancement of Av conditioning to *B* by an ApCS+ in CER training (or of Ap conditioning to the S^D by an AvCS+ in discrimination training). Clearly a CS+ for food in preconditioning will obtain significance for the animal, and therefore in compound CER conditioning this stimulus should command attention over the added *B* stimulus, and hence it should block rather than, as observed, counterblock conditioning to *B*. (The presence of a qualitatively different reinforcer in CER conditioning does not alter this conclusion. The ApCS+ should still be selectively attended to and, in the process, it should be reconditioned to a signal for shock.) The same difficulty is evident with a *within-reinforcement* counterblocking effect, that is, the enhancement which results to *B* when a CS— established on the basis of one reinforcer is employed in compound

---

[5]In this regard, it should be made clear that the present interpretation differs from Rescorla and Wagner's (1972) as theirs was apparently cast as an S—R interpretation. However, for a liberalized and more cognitively toned interpretation of their position, see Rescorla (1972). Also, for empirical evidence indicating that blocking is independent of peripheral CRs, see Rescorla's contribution in this volume (Chapter 2).

excitatory conditioning with B involving the same reinforcer (cf. Experiments 5 and 6; Rescorla, 1971; Wagner, 1969b).

The foregoing considerations argue, then, that an interpretation of blocking based on selective attention is itself inadequate, and therefore unable to sustain S–R theory. Acknowledging the above and other difficulties, Mackintosh (1975a, b; see also Chapter 6, in this volume) has modified his conceptualization of attention and has proposed that animals attend to and ignore stimuli, not to the extent that they have already learned to attend to one and, as a result, ignore the other, but rather to the extent that they perceive the stimuli as better or poorer *predictors* of reinforcement. In particular, Mackintosh proposes that the learning-rate parameter for a given stimulus (cf. *alpha* or "attention" in the linear-operator type of model used by Rescorla & Wagner, 1972) will increase to the extent that the stimulus better predicts the occurrence of a reinforcer, as compared with other stimuli in the situation, and will decrease (leading to an apparent blocking effect) when the stimulus signals no change in reinforcement from that anticipated on the basis of the other stimuli present. This neoattentional interpretation, however, cannot salvage S–R theory. By its very emphasis on the nature of the CS as a "predictor," the interpretation itself assumes a cognitive character. Furthermore, to account for the observed across-reinforcement blocking and counterblocking effects, the interpretation must additionally assume that in compound CER training, for example, the ApCS+ as a signal for food is a poorer predictor, whereas the ApCS− as a signal for no food is better predictor of the shock reinforcer than is the added B stimulus. It should be apparent that this assumption also posits that Ap and Av reinforcers and the CSs based on these reinforcers are functionally related and can be scaled on a common (e.g., incentive) dimension. Hence, by its own nature and that of the present analysis and results, a neoattentional interpretation, like a discrepancy interpretation, is committed to the view that the CS produces a central-motive or a "predictive" state reflecting the affective properties of its associated US outcome.

B. Levels of Cognitive and "Motivational" Processing

By its emphasis on "central-motive" states, the preceding discussion should not be taken to indicate that nonprimates, such as the rat, are capable of forming cognitive associations relating solely to the general affective (i.e., good-bad) properties of a reinforcer. There is other evidence which argues compellingly that the animal, if encouraged to do so, will process information pertaining to the more specific features of the reinforcer.

Trapold (1970) and Trapold and Overmier (1972; see also Rescorla, Chapter 2) have shown that the rat can form an expectancy which is specific to the particular kind of Ap reinforcement that is employed: When the rat is subjected to a conditional discrimination – which involves the reinforcement of different S–R associations (i.e., S_1-R_1 reinforcement, S_2-R_2 reinforcement) – learning is facilitated by the use of qualitatively different Ap reinforcers (food and sucrose) for each association, as opposed to one or the other reinforcer for both. Like our own discrimination findings, these findings cannot be ascribed solely to the added-distinctiveness effects of different reinforcers for the different associations. Trapold and Overmier have also shown that the learning of a conditional discrimination involving different reinforcers (i.e., S_1-R_1 food, S_2-R_2 sucrose) is facilitated by prior Pavlovian conditioning entailing a consistent (S_1-food, S_2-sucrose) relationship of CS and US events, but is retarded by an inconsistent (S_1-sucrose, S_2-food) relationship. These results are equally unamenable to an S–R interpretation.

Recently, Capaldi, Hovancik, and Friedman (1976) have presented comparable evidence indicating that the rat can form an expectancy which is specific to the quantity of Ap reinforcement that is used: When rats are trained on a discrete-trial procedure to approach and press a lever for either a small or a large magnitude of food reward (1 or 5 pellets), their performance is facilitated by the presentation of a CS which in prior Pavlovian training has been associated with the same reward magnitude as used in instrumental training, but is retarded by a CS previously associated with the other reward magnitude – even though this other reward magnitude may have been larger. Appropriately enough, Capaldi et al. (1976) interpret these and related performance effects as indicating that it is not the absolute magnitude of reward which is associated with the CS that is critical, but rather the *relationship* between the reward magnitude received in training and testing and that which is expected on the basis of the CS. Our own findings on the effects of magnitude of Ap reinforcement in Pavlovian-to-instrumental transfer (Experiments 5 and 6) complement these results rather well.

Taken together with our findings, the above results and similar findings based on the use of discriminably different Av reinforcers (see Overmier, Bull, & Trapold, 1971) suggest different levels, or stages, or cognitive processing. Evidently, the rat (or dog, in the Overmier et al. study) can process CS-produced information pertaining not only to the general affective properties of an outcome (i.e., whether the reinforcer, by way of its presence or absence, is either good or bad), but also the specific kind of Ap or Av affect, as well as the magnitude of affect that will or will not be occasioned – and, undoubtedly, other more perceptually based properties of the reinforcer relating to its form of presentation (e.g., several pieces vs. a single chunk; see Wolfe & Kaplon, 1941) and its location in space (see Strain, 1953; also, Olton, Chapter 12). Presumably, the level or depth at which the animal processes information within this affectively structured "tree" will be determined largely by the demands of the training situation. Although this possibility has not been assessed in any single study, for example, by within- and between-subject training comparisons, it is noteworthy that animals in the Capaldi et al. (1976) and Trapold and Overmier (1972) research were "forced" to compare quantitative or qualitative variations in the reinforcer and to associate these variations with different CSs. In contrast, the present research required that the animal learn only about the presence or absence of a particular reinforcer prior to its receipt of the same or a qualitatively different reinforcer in subsequent training.

Given that the attributes or "levels" of a reinforcer can be processed, one is led to ask whether the animal can form an expectancy regarding the mere presence or absence of the reinforcer, that is, independently of its affective nature and presumed significance. This is essentially the hypothesis which we originally advanced to account for the results of our across-reinforcement (Av-to-Ap) transfer studies. The CS, based on its correlation with the reinforcer, would function as a signal for the presence (CS+) or absence (CS−) of that reinforcer, or even of a qualitatively different reinforcer. Clearly, this interpretation finds no support in the results of our within-reinforcement (Ap-to-Ap) transfer studies (Experiments 5 and 6) nor, for that matter, in the results of a traditional, i.e., within-reinforcement, blocking study (e.g., Kamin, 1968, 1969). Like a mediating-response interpretation, a general cue or signaling interpretation of the CS's properties argues that the preconditioned A stimulus, say a CS+ for the reinforcer, should function as a mediator for that reinforcer when used in a sequential (or even a simultaneous) compound procedure, and should therefore facilitate rather than block conditioning to the added B stimulus. Of course, the rejection of our original interpretation does not deny the possibility of a general signaling property of the CS; nor does it deny the findings of others on this subject. However, it does encourage one to question whether the reported findings are substantial.

As noted earlier, Overmier and his colleagues (Overmier & Bull, 1970; Overmier & Payne, 1971) have argued for a general cue effect of the CS on the basis of findings showing that an ApCS+, when used as a signal for shock in a hurdle-jump avoidance task, will facilitate learning, and that an ApCS− similarly applied will retard such learning. An examination of their methodology, as detailed in Overmier and Payne (1971), suggests, however, that their findings are also amenable to a blocking interpretation. In their hurdle-jump avoidance task, their ApCS (a tone) was presented in conjunction with a new and highly salient visual stimulus which had not been present in preliminary escape training, namely, the raising of a "drop gate" which was used in avoidance training to prevent intertrial hurdle-jumping responses. As such, the bad outcome of shock would produce a large negative discrepancy by contrast with the good (food) outcome predicted by the ApCS+, and hence the ApCS+ would counterblock Av conditioning to the salient visual S^D (i.e., raising of the gate) with the result that avoidance learning would be facilitated. By comparison, the ApCS− in predicting a bad (no-food) outcome would generate relatively little discrepancy with the bad outcome of shock, and thus it would block Av conditioning to the visual S^D with the result that avoidance learning would be retarded. This analysis is not hindered by the simultaneous occurrence of the visual S^D and the tone CS. Even though signals for good and bad outcomes, the ApCSs would, by prior conditioning, control responses appropriate to obtaining food, and not to avoiding shock. In fact, the visual S^D could even come to overshadow the tone CS, as animals in an escape-avoidance task will quickly learn to await (i.e., orient and attend to) the operation of a gate.

In light of the reinterpretation of our original findings and the possibility of the same for those reported by Overmier and his colleagues (see also Bacon & Bindra, 1967; Braud, 1971), there would appear to be little if any evidence which clearly substantiates a general cue or signaling property of the CS. Even the findings reported by Konorski and Szwejkowska (1956) on the difficulty of reconditioning a CS+ for one reinforcer into a CS+ for another stand in opposition to this interpretation. One is led therefore to the tentative conclusion that, although animals can process information about the general and more specific affective features of a reinforcer, and its relation to other stimuli in the environment, they do not process information about — or at least they do not display any knowledge of — the presence or absence of the reinforcer independently of its affective significance. By this conclusion, we do not mean to deny the learning of "simple" stimulus relationships as are evident in phenomena such as sensory preconditioning. Rather, we would caution that even biologically "neutral" stimuli can obtain significance through their curiosity or sensory-reinforcing properties (cf. Fowler, 1967, 1971a). Our interpretation essentially follows Spence (1956) in assuming that reinforcement (cf. affect) is necessary for Pavlovian conditioning, but in the restricted sense of causing the animal to attend to the properties of the reinforcer and its relationship to other events (see Fowler & Siegel, 1971).

The above issue is an interesting one because it raises the parallel issue of a learning-performance distinction in the context of cognitive theory, and therefore it draws attention to the manner in which the animal can translate its cognition into action — or to counter Guthrie, "climb its way out of thought." In view of the above evidence (or lack of it) on a general cue or signaling property of the CS, and what we have traditionally been taught about the defining operation of a US, we seem to be confronted with the view that the "motivational" or *eliciting* action of a reinforcer is essentially built into the reinforcer (or is potentiated by conditions of deprivation) and is transmitted to the CS *as part of* the information pertaining to the general and more specific affective features of the reinforcer. This possibility is well enough recognized and, indeed, is even accepted in our description of a CS+ as a conditioned *excitor.* But what about a conditioned *inhibitor?* Must its action be somehow indirectly transmitted by excitors such as contextual or background cues that are explicitly or inadvertently paired with the US? Perhaps not if one examines the methodological basis for Av-to-Ap transfer findings.

In all of our discrimination studies, apart from the very first study (Fowler et al., 1973) where, for half of the subjects, shock punishment was presented for the incorrect response in Ap discrimination training (so as to potentiate the action of an AvCS–), there was no experimentally induced form of Av or fear motivation present for the AvCS– animals in instrumental discrimination learning. Furthermore, it is unlikely that any fear generalized from Pavlovian Av conditioning to Ap discrimination training as the two training situations were discriminably different and could, in fact, be described as involving a shock vs. food discrimination. Our subjects always received nondifferential pretraining entailing continuous food reinforcement in the T maze *prior* to Av conditioning in a distinctive chamber (and in a different room), and then Ap discrimination training in the T maze. How, then, is one to account for the action of an AvCS– which, when presented in the reinforced alternative, would apparently function as a good (i.e., safety) signal to block the association of food reinforcement and the S^D, and when presented in the nonreinforced alternative would similarly function to counterblock the association of nonreinforcement and the S^Δ?

One can, of course, resort to the argument that the experimenter himself provides the basis for generalized fear merely by transporting the animal to both the Av and Ap training apparatuses, or that a different or changed training situation, even one where Ap reinforcement is present, will elicit fear as the animal is naturally jittery. But is it reasonable to expect this fear to persist beyond a single trial or two when the animal is confronted with a *familiar* situation in which it has previously received continuous Ap reinforcement (as in nondifferential pretraining) and in which it never receives an Av reinforcer? We obviously cannot deny this possibility but there is another possibility that is suggested by the present findings: If Ap and Av reinforcers and the CSs based on these reinforcers share a commonality on the basis of good and bad outcomes or, at a more central level, through the activation of "pleasure" and "pain" centers, then quite possibly their motivational properties are also shared. In short, what has traditionally been cast as the inhibitor of one center might well function, either independently or in conjunction with an antipodal form of motivation, as an excitor of the other center, and thus in a dual or interrelated manner (cf. Konorski, 1967, 1972).

Currently, we do not have any evidence on this possibility other than the fact that an AvCS– was operative in the present research in the absence of apparent Av motivation. There are, however, ways of assessing this view. For example, in our research, one could administer Ap pretraining *after* Pavlovian Av conditioning to ensure that the effect of the AvCS– in discrimination training was not due to general (or generalized) fear. Alternatively, one could assess the effects of ApCSs that are administered on baseline in an avoidance task (cf. Grossen, Kostansek, & Bolles, 1969) for animals which, at the time of testing, are neither food nor water deprived – or, better yet, are even prefed and watered. The latter would be a stringent test considering the performance decrement that should result with the absence during testing of any Ap "drive" stimuli. However, were these or similar experiments to work, our understanding of the motivational functions of cognitive associations and their conditioned-stimulus mediators would surely be enhanced.

C. Stimulus—Reinforcer Associations in Instrumental Conditioning

Our discussion to this point has emphasized a cognitive processing of CS and US events, but it has not addressed the issue of how a CS works as a response—contingent event. It would do us well in concluding this chapter to take stock of what the present findings have to offer on the effects of a response—contingent CS and, by implication, the kinds of association that are formed in instrumental as well as in Pavlovian conditioning.

As argued at the outset of this chapter, the present findings stand in opposition to any interpretation which would stress the reinforcement or direct strengthening of an instrumental-response association. The observed effects of our response—contingent CSs have, with little exception, been consistently counter to those anticipated on the basis of the CS's potential function as either a conditioned reinforcer or a conditioned punisher. Rather than strengthening choice and approach responses occasioned in the presence of the S^D, a response—contingent ApCS+ suppressed these behaviors, whereas a response—contingent AvCS+, rather than suppressing the behaviors, actually facilitated them. By establishing these effects as blocking and counterblocking effects, the present findings are significant not only in degrading response connections (i.e., involving the S^D or CS or both) and in highlighting a stimulus relation between the CS and the primary reinforcers, but also in implicating a direct association between the primary reinforcer and the S^D. That is to say, the apparent nature of blocking as a stimulus-learning phenomenon argues that the action of the primary reinforcer, like that of our response—contingent CS, is relatively independent of any association directly involving the instrumental response.

Our conclusion might be questioned on the basis of whether our discrimination findings actually demonstrate that the blocked (or counterblocked) effect of the Ap reinforcer is specific to the S^D or, as others (e.g., Williams, 1975) would seem to suggest, to the instrumental response itself. On this rather tenuous *theoretical* issue of "stimulus vs. reinforcement control" of the response, we would argue that the action of a reinforcer can never be independent of the stimulus context in which it is presented, and that the weight of the process must still lie with the S^D. Furthermore, we would point out that the observation of comparable blocking effects in the Pavlovian analogue of our discrimination methodology must be taken to implicate the reinforcer's association with the S^D rather than with any instrumental response, and therefore the burden of proof lies with the response theorist. Indeed, confronted with our findings and those of others, the response theorist seems to be caught in a peculiar bind. Hyde (1976), for example, has convincingly demonstrated that in the absence of primary reinforcement a response—contingent ApCS+ will facilitate the learning of an instrumental response, presumably by "secondarily reinforcing" the response in the presence of the S^D or of contextual cues. However, when primary reinforcement is also employed, as in the present research, the presumed response

—strengthening effect of the primary reinforcer (as well as that of the response—contingent CS) is blocked! That such an outcome should result from the *addition* of a primary reinforcer can only be viewed as contesting the importance, if not the principle, or a response—reinforcer relationship.

There are other effects of a response—contingent CS which should be acknowledged in evaluating the kinds of association that are formed in instrumental conditioning. Both the within- and across-reinforcement paradigms of our Pavlovian-to-instrumental transfer studies showed that, with an easy discrimination, a response—contingent CS+ would exert an ancillary effect in opposition to its blocking effect. As argued in the interpretation of these findings, this opposed effect can be attributed either to a direct, response effect (i.e., a conditioned—reinforcing or a conditioned—punishing effect) of the CS+ or to its effect in promoting higher—order excitatory conditioning to the S^D. Although the choice between these two alternatives cannot be resolved on the basis of the obtained discrimination findings, the parallel observation of higher—order excitatory conditioning in our purely Pavlovian paradigm comparably serves to implicate an association between the S^D and the CS, rather than any association involving the instrumental response. Indeed, in view of our evidence regarding the primary reinforcer's association with the S^D, it would seem unlikely that the CS's association could be otherwise. We are not here arguing that higher—order conditioning necessarily involves stimulus learning — although this possibility is not so far removed (see, e.g., Rescorla, Chapter 2) — but rather that in instrumental conditioning the animal processes a relationship between the S^D and a response—contingent CS as well as, if not better than, that between its instrumental response and the CS.

The above point may be illustrated by drawing a comparison between conditioned—reinforcing and higher—order conditioning effects in our CER paradigm, that is, where an ApCS+ as the preconditioned A stimulus was presented *contingent* upon the added B stimulus and the suppression which this stimulus produced. In this paradigm, the observed effect of the ApCS+ was actually counter to that which could be expected on the basis of a conditioned—reinforcing property of the CS, a property which surely would not be revoked merely because of the Pavlovian nature of the paradigm. As will be recalled, suppression to the added B stimulus weakened over successive intervals of B prior to the onset of the preconditioned A stimulus, with this effect being significantly more pronounced for the ApCS+ group. However, a conditioned—reinforcing or response—strengthening effect of the ApCS+ argues that the observed suppression to B should be maintained if not strengthened, rather than increasingly attenuated over successive intervals of B. Viewed in this manner, our CER paradigm effectively opposes conditioned—reinforcing and higher—order conditioning effects of the ApCS+, with the outcome clearly favoring the latter.

In sum and substance, then, our findings argue that the animal's response in instrumental conditioning is governed primarily by stimulus—reinforcer associations. In the present case, where a preestablished CS, say, an ApCS+, is presented contingent upon that response, there are three such associations: the higher–order association between the S^D and the CS (or second–order reinforcer); the reinforcement association between the S^D and the US (or primary reinforcer); and the preestablished (i.e., "blocking") association between the CS and the US. Given the nature of these associations and the relationship of their elements, the outcome of our procedure and of others can easily be understood. When the CS occurs at the end of the response chain in proximal relation to the US, i.e., when the CS–US interval is short, the animal will readily detect this relationship and therefore the CS, in predicting the US, will block the primary reinforcer's association with the S^D. Consequently, the animal's response will be predominantly controlled by a relatively weak second–order association – that between the S^D and the CS. Of course, if the CS were omitted and hence a blocking effect eliminated, the reinforcement association would operate as is normally the case, and thus the S^D would control performance through the expectancy of the US which it would produce. On the other hand, if the CS were retained and the US were omitted, thereby eliminating a blocking effect as well, the S^D–CS association would again be potentiated, enabling the S^D to control the animal's response. In fact, if the CS were presented early in the chain, not only would it enhance this association, i.e., through a shorter S^D–CS interval, but it would control *ongoing* performance through the preestablished expectancy which it would produce. We would argue that this is basically the manner in which a response–contingent ApCS+ operates as a "conditioned reinforcer" to promote the learning of a new response.

ACKNOWLEDGMENTS

The preparation of this article and the research that it describes were supported in part by Grants MH-08482 and MH-24115 from the National Institute of Mental Health, United States Public Health Service. A special note of appreciation is owing to the students who were involved in the research; their names are duly noted in its reporting.

REFERENCES

Annau, Z., & Kamin, L. J. The conditioned emotional response as a function of intensity of the US. *Journal of Comparative and Physiological Psychology,* 1961, *54,* 428–432.
Bacon, W. E., & Bindra, D. The generality of the incentive-motivational effects of classical conditioned stimuli in instrumental learning. *Acta Biologiae Experimentalis,* 1967, *27,* 185–197.

Bindra, D. A motivational view of learning, performance, and behavior modification. *Psychological Review*, 1974, *81*, 199–213.

Bolles, R. C. Reinforcement, expectancy and learning. *Psychological Review*, 1972, *79*, 394–409.

Braud, W. G. Effectiveness of "neutral," habituated, shock-related, and food-related stimuli as CSs for avoidance learning in goldfish. *Conditional Reflex*, 1971, *6*, 153–156.

Brown, R. T., & Wagner, A. R. Resistance to punishment and extinction following training with shock or nonreinforcement. *Journal of Experimental Psychology*, 1964, *68*, 503–507.

Capaldi, E. D., Hovancik, J. R., & Friedman, F. Effects of expectancies of different reward magnitudes in transfer from noncontingent pairings to instrumental performance. *Learning and Motivation*, 1976, *7*, 197–210.

D'Amato, M. R. Secondary reinforcement and magnitude of primary reinforcement. *Journal of Comparative and Physiological Psychology*, 1955, *48*, 378–380.

Denny, M. R. Relaxation theory and experiments. In F. R. Brush (Ed.), *Aversive conditioning and learning*. New York: Academic Press, 1971, pp. 235–295.

Dickinson, A. Appetitive-aversive interactions: Superconditioning of fear by an appetitive CS. *Quarterly Journal of Experimental Psychology*, 1977, *29*, 71–83.

Domber, E. A., Jr. Facilitation and retardation of instrumental appetitive learning by prior Pavlovian aversive conditioning. Unpublished doctoral dissertation, University of Pittsburgh, 1971.

Fago, G., & Fowler, H. Facilitated discrimination learning as effected by response-contingent neutral and aversive stimuli. *Learning and motivation*, 1972, *3*, 20–30.

Feldman, J. M. Added cue control as a function of reinforcement predictability. *Journal of Experimental Psychology*, 1971, *91*, 318–325.

Fowler, H. Satiation and curiosity: Constructs for a drive and incentive-motivational theory of exploration. In K. W. Spence and J. T. Spence (Eds.), *The psychology of learning and motivation* (Vol. 1). New York: Academic Press, 1967, pp. 157–227.

Fowler, H. Implications of sensory reinforcement. In R. Glaser (Ed.), *The nature of reinforcement*. New York: Academic Press, 1971, pp. 151–195. (a)

Fowler, H. Suppression and facilitation by response-contingent shock. In F. R. Brush (Ed.), *Aversive conditioning and learning*. New York: Academic Press, 1971, pp. 537–604. (b)

Fowler, H., Fago, G. C., Domber, E. A., & Hochhauser, M. Signaling and affective functions in Pavlovian conditioning. *Animal Learning and Behavior*, 1973, *1*, 81–89.

Fowler, H., Goldman, L., & Wischner, G. J. Sodium amytal and the shock-right intensity function for visual discrimination learning. *Journal of Comparative and Physiological Psychology*, 1968, *65*, 155–159.

Fowler, H., Goodman, J. H., & DeVito, P. L. Across-reinforcement blocking effects in a mediational test of the CS's general signaling property. *Learning and Motivation*, 1977, *8*, 507–519.

Fowler, H., Goodman, J. H., & Zanich, M. L. Pavlovian aversive to instrumental appetitive transfer: Evidence for across-reinforcement blocking effects. *Animal Learning and Behavior*, 1977, *5*, 129–134.

Fowler, H., & Siegel, A. W. Attention. In L. C. Deighton (Ed.), *The encyclopedia of education* (Vol. 1). New York: Macmillan, 1971, pp. 390–396.

Fowler, H., & Wischner, G. J. Discrimination performance as affected by problem difficulty and shock for either the correct or incorrect response. *Journal of Experimental Psychology*, 1965, *69*, 413–418.

Fowler, H., & Wischner, G. J. The varied functions of punishment in discrimination learning. In B. A. Campbell and R. M. Church (Eds.), *Punishment and aversive behavior*. New York: Appleton-Century-Crofts, 1969, pp. 375–420.

Ghiselli, W. B., & Fowler, H. Signaling and affective functions of conditioned aversive stimuli in an appetitive choice discrimination: US intensity effects. *Learning and Motivation*, 1976, *7*, 1–16.

Goodman, J. H. Blocking and counterblocking ("superconditioning") effects across reinforcement systems in a conditioned-emotional-response paradigm. Unpublished doctoral dissertation, University of Pittsburgh, 1976.

Goodman, J. H., & Fowler, H. Transfer of the signaling properties of aversive CSs to an instrumental appetitive discrimination. *Learning and Motivation*, 1976, *7*, 446–457.

Goss, A. E. A stimulus-response analysis of the interaction of cue-producing and instrumental responses. *Psychological Review*, 1955, *62*, 20–31.

Grossen, N. E., Kostansek, D. J., & Bolles, R. C. Effects of appetitive discriminative stimuli on avoidance behavior. *Journal of Experimental Psychology*, 1969, *81*, 340–343.

Hochhauser, M., & Fowler, H. Cue effects of drive and reward as a function of discrimination difficulty: Evidence against the Yerkes-Dodson law. *Journal of Experimental Psychology: Animal Behavior Processes*, 1975, *104*, 261–269.

Hyde, T. S. The effect of Pavlovian stimuli on the acquisition of a new response. *Learning and Motivation*, 1976, *7*, 223–239.

Kamin, L. J. "Attention-like" processes in classical conditioning. In M. R. Jones (Ed.), *Miami symposium on the prediction of behavior: Aversive stimulation.* Miami, Florida: University of Miami Press, 1968, pp. 9–31.

Kamin, L. J. Predictability, surprise, attention, and conditioning. In B. A. Campbell and R. M. Church (Eds.), *Punishment and aversive behavior.* New York: Appleton-Century-Crofts, 1969, pp. 279–296.

Konorski, J. *Integrative activity of the brain.* Chicago: University of Chicago Press, 1967.

Konorski, J. Some ideas concerning physiological mechanisms of so-called internal inhibition. In R. A. Boakes and M. S. Halliday (Eds.), *Inhibition and learning.* New York: Academic Press, 1972, pp. 341–357.

Konorski, J., & Szwejkowska, G. Reciprocal transformations of heterogeneous conditioned reflexes. *Acta Biologiae Experimentalis*, 1956, *17*, 141–165.

Linden, D. R., & Hallgren, S. O. Transfer of approach responding between punishment and frustrative nonreward sustained through continuous reinforcement. *Learning and Motivation*, 1973, *4*, 207–217.

LoLordo, V. M. Positive conditioned reinforcement from aversive situations. *Psychological Bulletin*, 1969, *72*, 193–203.

Mackintosh, N. J. A theory of attention: Variations in the associability of stimuli with reinforcement. *Psychological Review*, 1975, *82*, 276–298. (a)

Mackintosh, N. J. Blocking of conditioned suppression: Role of the first compound trial. *Journal of Experimental Psychology: Animal Behavior Processes*, 1975, *1*, 335–343. (b)

Mackintosh, N. J., & Turner, C. Blocking as a function of novelty of CS and predictability of UCS. *Quarterly Journal of Experimental Psychology*, 1971, *23*, 359–366.

McAllister, W. R., & McAllister, D. E. Behavioral measurement of conditioned fear. In F. R. Brush (Ed.), *Aversive conditioning and learning.* New York: Academic Press, 1971, pp. 105–179.

Neely, J. H., & Wagner, A. R. Attenuation of blocking with shifts in reward: The involvement of schedule-generated contextual cues. *Journal of Experimental Psychology*, 1974, *102*, 751–763.

Overmier, J. B., & Bull, J. A., III. Influences of appetitive Pavlovian conditioning upon avoidance behavior. In J. H. Reynierse (Ed.), *Current issues in animal learning: A colloquium.* Lincoln, Nebraska: University of Nebraska Press, 1970, pp. 117–141.

Overmier, J. B., Bull, J. A., III, & Trapold, M. A. Discriminative cue properties of different fears and their role in response selection in dogs. *Journal of Comparative and Physiological Psychology*, 1971, *76*, 478–482.

Overmier, J. B., & Payne, R. J. Facilitation of instrumental avoidance learning by prior appetitive Pavlovian conditioning to the cue. *Acta Neurobiologiae Experimentalis,* 1971, *31,* 341–349.

Pavlov, I. P. *Conditioned reflexes.* (Translation by G. V. Anrep.) London and New York: Oxford University Press, 1927.

Rescorla, R. A. Pavlovian conditioning and its proper control procedures. *Psychological Review,* 1967, *74,* 71–80.

Rescorla, R. A. Pavlovian conditioned inhibition. *Psychological Bulletin,* 1969, *72,* 77–94.

Rescorla, R. A. Variation in the effectiveness of reinforcement and nonreinforcement following prior inhibitory conditioning. *Learning and Motivation,* 1971, *2,* 113–123.

Rescorla, R. A. Informational variables in Pavlovian conditioning. In G. H. Bower (Ed.), *The psychology of learning and motivation* (Vol. 6). New York: Academic Press, 1972, pp. 1–46.

Rescorla, R. A. Second-order conditioning of Pavlovian conditioned inhibition. *Learning and Motivation,* 1976, *7,* 161–172.

Rescorla, R. A., & Wagner, A. R. A theory of Pavlovian conditioning: Variations in the effectiveness of reinforcement and nonreinforcement. In A. H. Black and W. F. Prokasy (Eds.), *Classical conditioning II: Current research and theory.* New York: Appleton-Century-Crofts, 1972, pp. 64–99.

Reynolds, B. The acquisition of a black-white discrimination habit under two levels of reinforcement. *Journal of Experimental Psychology,* 1949, *39,* 760–769.

Spence, K. W. *Behavior theory and conditioning.* New Haven, Connecticut: Yale University Press, 1956.

Strain, E. R. Establishment of an avoidance gradient under latent learning conditions. *Journal of Experimental Psychology,* 1953, *46,* 391–399.

Suiter, R. D., & LoLordo V. M. Blocking of inhibitory Pavlovian conditioning in the conditioned emotional response procedure. *Journal of Comparative and Physiological Psychology,* 1971, *76,* 137–144.

Sutherland, N. S., & Mackintosh, N. J. *Mechanisms of animal discrimination learning.* New York: Academic Press, 1971.

Tolman, E. C. *Purposive behavior in animals and men.* New York: Century, 1932.

Trapold, M. A. Are expectancies based upon different positive reinforcing events discriminably different? *Learning and Motivation,* 1970, *1,* 129–140.

Trapold, M. A., & Overmier, J. B. The second learning process in instrumental learning. In A. H. Black and W. F. Prokasy (Eds.), *Classical conditioning II: Current research and theory.* New York: Appleton-Century-Crofts, 1972, pp. 427–452.

Wagner, A. R. Frustrative nonreward: A variety of punishment. In B. A. Campbell and R. M. Church (Eds.), *Punishment and aversive behavior.* New York: Appleton-Century-Crofts, 1969, pp. 157–181. (a)

Wagner, A. R. Stimulus selection and a "modified continuity theory." In G. H. Bower and J. T. Spence (Eds.), *The psychology of learning and motivation* (Vol. 3). New York: Academic Press, 1969, pp. 1–40. (b)

Wagner, A. R., & Rescorla, R. A. Inhibition in Pavlovian conditioning: Application of a theory. In R. A. Boakes and M. S. Halliday (Eds.), *Inhibition and learning.* London: Academic Press, 1972, pp. 301–336.

Williams, B. A. The blocking of reinforcement control. *Journal of the Experimental Analysis of Behavior,* 1975, *24,* 215–225.

Wischner, G. J., & Fowler, H. Discrimination performance as affected by duration of shock for either the correct or incorrect response. *Psychonomic Science,* 1964, *1,* 239–240.

Wischner, G. J., Fowler, H., & Kushnick, S. A. Effect of strength of punishment for "correct" or "incorrect" responses on visual discrimination performance. *Journal of Experimental Psychology,* 1963, *65,* 131–138.

Wolfe, J. B., & Kaplon, M. D. Effect of amount of reward and consummative activity on learning in chickens. *Journal of Comparative Psychology*, 1941, *31*, 353–361.

Woodworth, R. S. Reinforcement of perception. *American Journal of Psychology*, 1947, *60*, 119–124.

Zanich, M. L., & Fowler, H. Primary and secondary reinforcers as distinctive cues which acquire information value in partial-reinforcement discrimination training. *Learning and Motivation*, 1975, *6*, 299–313.

Zanich, M. L., & Fowler, H. Transfer from Pavlovian appetitive to instrumental appetitive conditioning: Signaling versus discrepancy interpretations. *Journal of Experimental Psychology: Animal Behavior Processes*, 1978, *4*, 37–49.

6

Cognitive or Associative Theories of Conditioning: Implications of an Analysis of Blocking

N. J. Mackintosh
University of Sussex

I. INTRODUCTION

When applied to theories of animal learning and behavior, the term "cognitive" is usually defined by contrast or exclusion: A cognitive theory is one which rejects certain assumptions of the theoretical tradition which has long dominated the study of animal behavior, namely, S—R theory. In opening my chapter with this remark, I do not intend to set up a target for subsequent attack. My intention is rather to use the antithesis with S—R theory as a way of distinguishing some of the strands that go to make up cognitive theory. If I am correct in supposing that cognitive theories have been defined by contrast in this way, it is probable that there will be as many different cognitive theories as there are assumptions within S—R theory which someone may choose to challenge. It will be well to understand which one we are talking about on any given occasion.

It seems reasonable to suggest that the fundamental assumption of S—R theory has been that learning and knowledge reflect the formation of associations or bonds between representations of events in the brain. This associationist view, stemming ultimately from British associationist philosophy, has provoked opposition of equally distinguished ancestry. Modern heirs to the European rationalist tradition have questioned whether the full complexity of behavior can ever be accounted for by an associationist analysis. Organisms, it is said, are not just systems of connections, passively forming links or bonds between events that happen to occur together: They structure their experience, actively organizing it into a coherent, meaningful whole.

I do not intend to resolve a dispute of such long standing in a brief chapter such as this. Instead, I wish to reduce the problem to more manageable proportions by distinguishing two aspects of the dispute. An opponent of association theory might either be arguing that the theory was clearly inadequate to account for any of the more interesting aspects of behavior, such as those considered elsewhere in this volume by Menzel and Premack (Chapters 13 and 14, respectively), or wondering whether it should even be granted a limited field of application, for example, to such a trivial example of learned behavior as simple conditioning. I do not wish to discuss the first of these two questions, but only the second. My concern is with the issue of whether associative theory provides an adequate account of conditioning.

There is a certain air of paradox about posing such a question. Conditioning experiments are usually defined as arrangements of relationships between events whose association is evidenced by appropriate changes in the subject's behavior. If association theory cannot explain conditioning, what can it explain? The cognitive theorist's argument is, perhaps, better understood not as questioning whether conditioning is properly defined as a form of associative learning, but rather as a rejection of the form of theory provided by traditional associationists. Once again it will be useful to view cognitive theory as a reaction to the assumptions of S–R theory. If the fundamental assumption of S–R theory is a commitment to associationism, the most prominent assumption is that associations are formed only between specific classes of event, for the S–R theorist between responses and antecedent stimuli. Thus the most prominent version of cognitive learning theory has been that which assumes that associations are formed between other classes of event, usually between stimuli and stimuli but sometimes between responses and subsequent stimuli.

The position adopted by S–R theory on this issue, although intelligible when viewed in historical perspective, seems so intrinsically implausible that it need not detain us. One may wonder, indeed, whether a more liberal attitude to the question of what events can be associated is sufficient to characterize a theory as cognitive. It would, of course, be unprofitable to wrangle over the choice of terms to describe our theories. Moreover, as Rescorla's contribution to this volume (Chapter 2) admirably shows, this more liberal attitude opens up for consideration a whole host of interesting questions which hardly arise within the context of S–R theory. Nevertheless, in what follows I shall simply take it for granted that an adequate theory of conditioning is not bound by the assumption that conditioning consists in the strengthening of stimulus–response associations.

There is a more interesting limitation to the traditional associationist view of conditioning provided by S–R theory, a limitation not overcome by any extension of the range of events which may be associated. This traditional view has always adopted a very simple-minded attitude to the question of what are the conditions for the establishment of associations. One or two simple principles of reinforcement, such as contiguity or effect, have usually beeen thought sufficient to explain the occurrence of conditioning under some circumstances and its absence under others. Given the satisfaction of these conditions, associations are formed automatically and mechanically.

As we shall see, one of the most salient features of conditioning is that it does not proceed automatically by the action of these particular principles of reinforcement. Strict temporal contiguity between CS and US, for example, is neither sufficient nor necessary for the establishment of reliable conditioning. It is increasingly clear that traditional associationist theories have ignored many of the most interesting issues that should concern the student of conditioning. The question is how we should modify our theories of association in order to deal with these issues. It is possible to discern two strategies. The first suggests that at the core of conditioning there is a simple associative process whereby representations of contiguous events are linked together, but insists that this system be supplemented by additional processes in order to encompass problematic data. Thus one might want to elaborate the notion of the representation of conditional and unconditional stimuli; allow that the organism has a memory which permits the association of events quite widely separated in time; admit possible complications arising from limitations of perception or attention. However, these are regarded as complexities superimposed on a basically simple associative process. The alternative is to reject the view that the associative process is just a matter of connecting contiguous events and to argue that an adequate view of conditioning will require a fundamentally more complex associative structure.

II. BLOCKING AS A PROBLEM FOR ASSOCIATION THEORY

It is time to turn from this rather abstract discussion to a consideration of experimental data. Why should it be doubted that Pavlovian or instrumental conditioning is a matter of simple associative learning? One reason is that simple associative systems are generally assumed to register the coincident occurrence of events. There is, however, a great deal of evidence showing that the course of conditioning is not simply dependent on the number of times a particular stimulus and reinforcer have occurred together, but is also affected by the subject's past experience with that stimulus and reinforcer, by the presence of other stimuli signaling that reinforcer, and by the subject's past experience with those other stimuli. One of the most convincing demonstrations of this point is Kamin's blocking experiment (e.g., Kamin, 1969).

In the basic experiment, rats are conditioned to a compound CS, consisting of two elements, A and B, paired with the delivery of a brief shock as the US. Conditioning is measured by the suppression of ongoing appetitively rewarded lever pressing when the CS is presented. Control animals normally show marked suppression to either A or B when they are presented alone; but animals previously conditioned to one of the stimuli alone as a signal for shock show little or no suppression to the other after compound training. That is to say, after initial conditioning to A alone in Stage 1, a series of compound trials in Stage 2 during which A and B are repeatedly paired with shock may produce no evidence that B has been associated with the shock.

The most immediately obvious explanation of this blocking effect is, I think, to suppose that rats have a limited capacity to process incoming stimuli. To the extent that they are fully occupied attending to the pretrained stimulus A, they will fail to attend to the added element B and therefore will fail to associate it with reinforcement. The virtue of this explanation is that it enables us to preserve a relatively simple associative theory. The failure of association is regarded as a perceptual failure and requires us only to supplement, not to modify, our associative theory.

Kamin himself toyed with the "primitive hunch" that blocking was "a consequence of a kind of 'competition for attention' between the previously conditioned and the new element (Kamin, 1969, p. 62)." He soon, however, rejected it. The problem, as Kamin noted, is that blocking depends not only upon stimulus A having been established as a signal for reinforcement, but upon the fact that the same reinforcement continues after the addition of stimulus B. Blocking occurs only when B signals no change in reinforcement.

One illustration of this important point is provided by an experiment by Fowler (this volume, Chapter 5) in which he shows that if animals are initially trained with stimulus A signaling the delivery of food, and are then conditioned to AB signaling shock, pretraining with A, so far from blocking the conditioning of suppression to B, tends to enhance it. Similar results have been obtained in our laboratory by Dickinson (e.g., Dickinson, 1977). It can hardly be doubted that establishing a stimulus as a signal for food will ensure that hungry rats will attend to it. It is clear therefore that biasing attention to one element of a compound stimulus does not prevent animals attending to the other.

Kamin himself concluded that the redundancy of the added element, B, was critical for the occurrence of blocking on the basis of experiments in which the addition of B signaled some change in the shock delivered. When shock intensity was increased from Stage 1 to Stage 2, for example, significant conditioning accrued to B. In a second experiment, he showed that the addition of a second shock 5 sec after the end of each compound trial was also sufficient to attenuate blocking.

This last observation promises to shed some light on the processes involved in blocking. How does the second, unpredicted shock serve to attenuate blocking? What is its precise role in producing reliable conditioning to the added element, B? Several explanations have been suggested. The simplest, on the face of it, is that implied by Rescorla and Wagner (1972): The second shock acts as a US to reinforce, across a trace interval, conditioning to B. The central proposition of their model is that a US will reinforce conditioning only to the extent that it is unpredicted. They explain the occurrence of blocking, therefore, by noting that the first shock, because it is already reliably predicted by A, is no longer able to reinforce further conditioning on compound trials. The second shock, however, because it is unpredicted, can act as a normally effective reinforcer. Kamin (1969) proffered a related, although clearly distinct, explanation. He also assumed that blocking was a consequence of the first shock losing its ability to reinforce further conditioning as it became fully predicted by A, but suggested that the second shock, rather than itself acting to reinforce conditioning to B somehow restored the reinforcing properties of the *first* shock. A third, rather less interesting possibility is that the attenuation of blocking produced by a change in reinforcement is a consequence of generalization decrement. It is possible that conditioning trials in Stage 1 do not establish A alone, the nominal CS, as a signal for reinforcement, but rather A together with traces of preceding reinforcements. Thus the reinforcer used in Stage 1 would become part of the stimulus complex signaling further reinforcement, and a change in the conditions of reinforcement might disrupt suppression and hence permit further conditioning to B. Although not necessarily plausible in all experimental situations, there is good evidence that generalization decrement is responsible for some failures of blocking (e.g., Neely & Wagner, 1974).

III. ANALYSIS OF THE ATTENUATION OF BLOCKING BY SURPRISING CHANGES IN REINFORCEMENT

A. The Basic Phenomenon

We have undertaken a number of experiments in an attempt to evaluate these explanations (Dickinson, Hall, & Mackintosh, 1976; Mackintosh, Bygrave, & Picton, 1977). All of our experiments, like those of Kamin, have employed conditioned suppression in rats. However, in one series (Dickinson et al.) hungry rats were trained to press a lever for food on a variable-interval schedule, whereas in the other (Mackintosh et al.) thirsty rats licked at a water tube. The procedure for the former experiments was relatively standard. Two 100-sec CS trials were given in each 50-min session, with conditioning conducted on the baseline, i.e., while subjects continued to lever press for food. In the latter set of experiments, the CS was 60 sec long and only one trial was given in each daily 10-min session. Conditioning was conducted off the baseline and subjects received two or three recovery sessions before being tested for suppression to the CS. A major advantage of this second procedure is that it is easy to obtain significant conditioning to the elements of a compound CS in a single conditioning trial; this enabled us to schedule only one or two compound trials with a view to locating, with some precision, the effect of a surprising shock.

Using either procedure, we have been able to replicate Kamin's original finding: the addition of an unexpected second shock on compound trials shortly after the first shock significantly attenuates the blocking observed in a control group. Dickinson et al. (1976, Experiment 1) conditioned two groups of rats to a light. For the experimental group, the light terminated with a single shock; for the control group, a second, identical shock occurred 8 sec after the first on each trial. After 12 such trials to the light alone, both groups received eight compound trials on each of which a clicker was added to the light and a second shock occurred 8 sec after the first. The control group, already expecting this second shock after the light, showed no evidence of conditioning to the clicker: their suppression ratio[1] on the first test trial to the clicker alone was .51; the experimental group, originally conditioned with a single shock and thus surprised by the addition of a second shock on compound trials, was significantly more suppressed with a ratio of .41.

Mackintosh et al. (1977, Experiment 1) gave thirsty rats four conditioning trials to a light alone signaling a single shock, followed by two trials to a tone-light compound. For the control group (TL+), the compound CS also signaled a single shock; for the experimental group (TL+10+) a second shock was added 10 sec after the first, but only on the first compound trial. Over five nonreinforced test trials to the tone alone, the control group had an average suppression ratio of .26, the experimental group a ratio of .11. The difference was significant.[2]

These two results establish the generality of Kamin's original observations. Taking the argument one step further, Dickinson et al. (1976) were able to show that blocking of conditioning to the added element was attenuated not only by the addition of an unexpected second shock, but also by the temporary post-

---

[1]Conditioned suppression is measured by calculating a ratio of the form $a/(a + b)$, where a represents the rate of responding (lever pressing or licking) during the CS and b represents the rate of responding during an equivalent period of time immediately preceding the CS. Thus a ratio of .50 signifies equal rates of responding both before and during the CS, i.e., no differential suppression to the CS, whereas a ratio of .00 signifies no responding during the CS, i.e., complete suppression.

---

[2]The absolute values of the suppression ratios differ rather markedly between these two experiments – even though in both cases a significant *attenuation* of blocking was observed in the group surprised by the added shock. Several differences in procedure were presumably responsible for this difference. The procedures emplyed by Mackintosh et al. (1977) were, as noted above, designed to ensure significant conditioning in a single compound trial. Since there is little evidence of any blocking at all on the first compound trial (Mackintosh, 1975b), it is only to be expected that the control group should show a considerable level of conditioning to the added element.

ponement of an *expected* second shock on compound trials. A third group in their first experiment also received clicker-light compound trials with a second shock occurring 8 sec after the first on each trial. On their initial trials to the light alone, however, the second shock had occurred 4 sec after the first on each trial. On their first test trial to the clicker alone this group had a suppression ratio of .38, showing marginally (albeit not significantly) more conditioning to the clicker than the experimental group surprised by the addition of a second shock. Thus the postponement of a second shock from 4 to 8 sec after the first is also a surprising event capable of attenuating blocking.

B. Generalization Decrement

Having established that our procedures were adequate to replicate Kamin's findings, we were in a position to analyse the effect further. The first possibility which we examined was that the surprising change in reinforcement attenuates blocking by disrupting suppression to the pretrained element A through some process of generalization decrement. One way of testing this notion, at least in its simplest form, is to see whether the effect of adding a second shock on compound trials depends on the time interval separating first and second shocks. If the surprising second shock affects blocking by disrupting suppression on subsequent compound trials, it should not matter much whether it occurs very shortly after the preceding compound trial or only after a much longer interval. In order to test this, a third group was run in the experiment by Mackintosh et al. (1977) already described. In addition to the control group (TL+) and the experimental group surprised by a second shock 10 sec after the first (TL+10+), the third group received a second shock 100 sec after the first on the first compound trial (TL+100+). The results of the five nonreinforced test trials to the tone (the stimulus added in compound training) are shown in Fig. 1. As we have already noted, Group TL+10+ was substantially more suppressed to the tone than the control Group TL+. It is also apparent that there was no significant attenuation of blocking in Group TL+100+, for subjects in this group were no more suppressed than the control group. Thus, although a second shock 10 sec after the first attenuated blocking, one 100 sec later failed to do so. These results are consistent with those reported by Gray and Appignanesi (1973). Using a presumably less potent surprising event (a very brief presentation of the compound CS), these investigators observed an attenuation of blocking only when the surprising event occurred within 5 sec of the end of a compound trial.

It is obvious enough that we might have observed significant attenuation of blocking at the longer interval had we employed different parameters (more compound trials, a stronger shock, an intertrial interval shorter than 24 hr). This does not affect the important conclusion that the attenuation of blocking observed for Group TL+10+ in our situation is not attributable to generalization decrement.

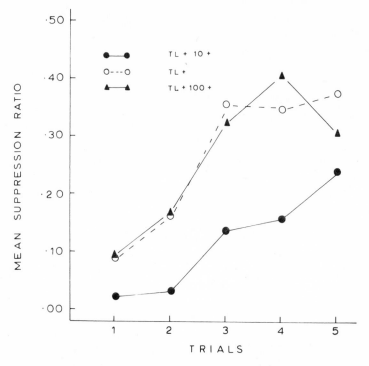

FIG. 1.   Supression ratios to the tone over five nonreinforced test trials. Results of Experiment 1 by Mackintosh et al. (1977).

A second test of the importance of generalization decrement, similar to that used by Neely and Wagner (1974), can be provided by interspersing, throughout Stage 2, trials to the compound stimulus, *AB*, with retraining trials to *A* alone. With this procedure, it is possible to program a surprising change in reinforcement either after each compound trial, or after each retraining trial (or after both or neither). The design we employed (Dickinson et al., 1976, Experiment 2) is shown in Table 1. After conditioning to the light in Stage 1, subjects received

TABLE 1
Design of Experiment 2 by Dickinson et al. (1976)[a]

Group	Stage 1	Stage 2
S (surprise)	L+4+	L+4+, CL+8+
GD (generalization decrement)	L+8+	L+4+, CL+8+
S-GD (surprise and generalization decrement)	L+4+	L+8+, CL+8+
C (control)	L+8+	L+8+, CL+8+

[a]L, light; C, clicker; +4+, double shock with 4-sec intershock interval; +8+, double shock with 8-sec intershock interval.

two trials a day throughout Stage 2, with the first trial of each day being a re-training trial to the light and the second a clicker-light compound trial. Through-out the experiment, all trials terminated with two shocks, separated by either 4 or 8 sec. Surprise was defined as a change in this intershock interval from Stage 1 to Stage 2. As can be seen from Table 1, one group (S) was surprised only on compound trials, one (GD) was surprised only on retraining trials to the light, one (S-GD) was surprised on both kinds of trial, and the final, control group (C) on neither. If a process of generalization decrement were responsible for attenuating blocking, we should expect that a change in reinforcement on the first (i.e., retraining) trial of each day in Stage 2 would disrupt suppression on the second trial and thus permit additional conditioning to the clicker present on that trial. The results of test trials to the clicker, shown in Fig. 2, provide no support for this suggestion. Surprising subjects on the retraining trial to the light alone had essentially no effect on suppression to the clicker; surprising subjects on the second (i.e., compound) trial of each day, on the other hand, significantly attenuated the blocking of conditioning to the clicker. This effect, it should be noted, was rather less marked in Group S-GD than in Group S. For Group S-GD, of course, the interval before the second shock was changed from Stage 1 to Stage 2 both on the retraining and on the compound trial. One might expect this to have decreased the extent to which subjects were surprised on compound trials.

We may conclude, therefore, that although some cases of attenuation of blocking may be attributable to generalization decrement, this is not true of the significant effects observed in our experiments. With our procedures, the surpris-

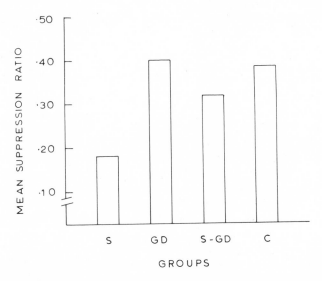

FIG. 2. Suppression ratios to the clicker over four nonreinforced test trials for the groups described in Table 1. Results of Experiment 2 by Dickinson et al. (1976).

ing addition or postponement of a second shock must occur on compound trials, and relatively shortly after the end of the trial, if it is to attenuate blocking. The reasonable inference is that the surprising change in reinforcement increases conditioning to the added element only if it is paired with, or predicted by, that element.

C. Surprise Provides the Source of Reinforcement

This conclusion seems entirely consistent with the proposition that the role of the surprising shock is to reinforce conditioning to the added element. Certainly this appears to be the simplest account of the case where a second shock is added on compound trials. It is perhaps less easily applied to the case where the surprise consists of the postponement of an expected second shock, but can certainly not be ruled out by these data.

How may we decide whether a surprising event is actually reinforcing conditioning to the added element, as Rescorla and Wagner's model suggests, or, as Kamin suggested, somehow enabling the nominal US (the first shock) to play its normal reinforcing role? One way would be to use a surprising event which could not by any reasonable argument be thought capable of reinforcing conditioning. Instead of adding an unexpected second shock, we could omit an expected one.

We have run this experiment twice, once (Mackintosh et al., 1977, Experiment 2) with thirsty rats licking at a water tube and once (Dickinson et al., 1976, Experiment 3) with hungry rats lever pressing for food. In both experiments, the omission of an expected second shock on compound trials reliably attenuated the blocking of conditioning to the added element. The results of the more substantial of the two experiments, that by Dickinson et al., are shown in Fig. 3. The experiment had a factorial design: subjects received either a single shock or two shocks (separated by an 8-sec interval) on each trial in Stage 1; then, each of these groups was divided into two for compound training in Stage 2, with half receiving a single shock on compound trials and the other half two shocks. We thus compared the effects of adding and of omitting a second shock. As can be seen in Fig. 3, by comparison with the appropriate control groups, both operations significantly attenuated blocking. Furthermore, there was no suggestion in these data that one operation was more effective than the other.

That the omission of an expected second shock can attenuate blocking implies that an effective surprise need not be an event that itself reinforces conditioning to the added element. It is improbable, therefore, that the attenuation produced by the addition of an unexpected second shock, or by the postponement of an expected one, is due to the reinforcing effect of that shock. We cannot, of course, rule out the possibility that an extra shock may have some direct reinforcing effect, but as Fig. 3 suggests, with the parameters employed here, the effect of adding a second shock is no greater than that of omitting one, and it

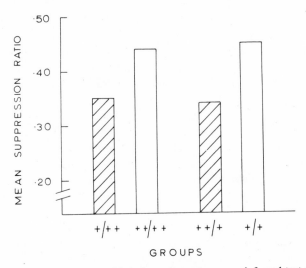

FIG. 3.   Suppression ratios to the added element over two nonreinforced test trials. Group +/++ was surprised by the addition, and Group ++/+ by the omission, of a second shock on compound trials. Group ++/++ received two shocks on each trial throughout Stages 1 and 2, while Group +/+ received only a single shock. Results of Experiment 3 by Dickinson et al. (1976).

seems reasonable to suggest that both operations attenuate blocking in the same way. Rather than directly providing the reinforcement for conditioning to the added element, they somehow enable the first shock to act as an effective reinforcer.

D. Surprise Restores the Reinforcing Properties of the US

This conclusion is a restatement of the thesis suggested originally by Kamin (1969). He argued that the predictability of the first shock stripped it of its reinforcing properties, which were then restored by the unpredicted occurrence of the second shock. Kamin went on the elaborate two possible ways in which this might happen. According to the first suggestion, an unexpected event may "provoke the animal into a 'backward scanning' of its memory store of recent stimulus input; only as a result of such a scan can an association between CS and US be formed (Kamin, 1969, p. 60)." As a "plausible alternative," however, Kamin also suggested that "the effect of the unpredicted, extra shock is to 'alert' the animal in such a way that it is more 'attentive' or sensitive to *subsequent* events, i.e., to the following compound trials. . . .The extra shock does not increase the amount of conditioning taking place to the superimposed CS element on the first compound trial, but it *does* increase the amount of such conditioning taking place on all subsequent compound trials (Kamin, 1969, p. 61)."

As Kamin (1969, p. 63) pointed out, "there is no obvious experimental difficulty presented by the problem of 'localizing' the effect of the extra shock." But he also reported that his attempts to perform the necessary experiments had been bedevilled by problems and artifacts to the point where "one begins to suspect the logical framework within which this particular set of experiments has been cast (p. 63)." The first requirement for localizing the effect is a preparation which produces measurable levels of conditioning in a single trial. Since our procedure for the suppression of licking does just this, we hoped we might be able to make some progress in answering Kamin's question. As it turns out, our results suggest that neither of his alternative analyses is correct, and this conclusion may explain some of the problems he encountered.

Of we wish to know whether a surprising additional shock attenuates blocking on the first compound trial or only on subsequent compound trials, we surely need only to compare the effects of a surprising shock in animals given a single compound trial and in animals given two compound trials. Animals given a single compound trial may be either surprised or not surprised on that trial; those given two compound trials are either surprised or not surprised on the *first* trial. If the surprise acts retroactively, its effect will be seen both in the one-trial and in the two-trial group; if proactively only in the two-trial group. In our experimental test (Mackintosh et al., 1977, Experiment 3), the two-trial groups were further divided, with half of the subjects receiving a single shock on their second compound trial and half receiving two shocks. The complete design of the experiment is shown in Table 2. By giving some animals a surprising additional shock on the second compound trial, we provided an additional test of the retroactive interpretation.

After conditioning, all subjects received six nonreinforced test trials to the added element, the tone. The results are shown in Fig. 4. These results may be summarized by saying that they offer no support for the retroactive interpretation. For animals given a single compound trial, there was no difference in suppression to the tone between those given a single shock on this trial (TL+) and

TABLE 2
Design of Experiment 3 by Mackintosh et al. (1977)[a]

	Stage 1	Stage 2	
Group	(4 trials)	Trial 1	Trial 2
TL+	L+	TL+	–
TL++	L+	TL++	–
TL+ TL+	L+	TL+	TL+
TL+ TL++	L+	TL+	TL++
TL++ TL+	L+	TL++	TL+
TL++ TL++	L+	TL++	TL++

[a]T, tone; L, light; +, single shock; ++, double shock separated by 10-sec intershock interval.

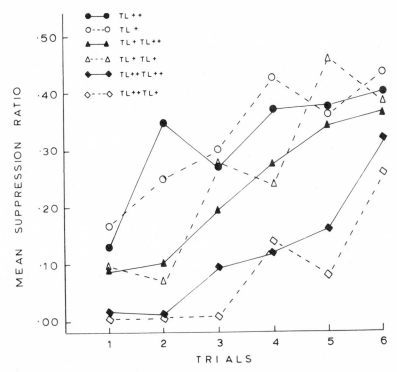

FIG. 4.   Suppression ratios to the tone over six nonreinforced test trials for the groups described in Table 2. Results of Experiment 3 by Mackintosh et al. (1977).

those surprised by the addition of a second shock (TL++). Equally, if we consider animals given two compound trials, then those treated alike on the first compound trial showed no effect of any difference in treatment on the second compound trial: Group TL+TL++ was not significantly more suppressed than Group TL+TL+, nor was Group TL++TL++ more suppressed than Group TL++TL+. The major effect shown in Fig. 4 is that animals surprised on their first compound trial (TL++TL++ and TL++TL+) were significantly more suppressed than those given no surprise on that trial (TL+TL++ TL+TL+). This latter pair of groups was only marginally (but nonetheless significantly) more suppressed than subjects given a single compound trial.

If these results rule out Kamin's retroactive interpretation of surprise, are we to accept a proactive interpretation? Certainly the effect of the extra shock is proactive in the sense that it appears to attenuate blocking only on subsequent compound trials. But Kamin's own proactive interpretation, although no doubt able to explain the results of this particular experiment, appears to suffer from the grave disadvantage of closely resembling a generalization decrement analysis, and has therefore already been ruled out by our earlier results. A surprising shock cannot attenuate blocking simply by alerting subjects on the following trial, for this implies that its temporal relationship to the preceding trial would be irrelevant. But as we have seen, a second shock occurring 10 sec after a compound trial will attenuate blocking while one occurring 100 sec after the trial fails to do so.

Our second experiment on generalization decrement is particularly damaging to Kamin's proactive analysis. In that experiment (see Table 1 and Fig. 2 above) we preceded each compound trial to AB with a retraining trial to A alone. Blocking was attenuated by a surprising change in reinforcement on compound trials but not by a change on retraining trials. Kamin's proactive account predicts precisely the opposite outcome. It is clear that in our situation at least blocking is attenuated only by surprising changes in reinforcement that occur shortly after the presentation of the added element.

E. Surprise Maintains the Associability of the CS

We seem to have created a dilemma. The surprising event does not act retro-actively to produce conditioning to the added element on the compound trial just past. On the other hand, it does not act in the sort of proactive manner envisaged by Kamin (1969) to alert the subject to subsequent events, for it must have occurred on one compound trial in order to attenuate blocking on the next. The dilemma arises, I believe, only because we have tacitly accepted one of the assumptions implicit in both the Rescorla and Wagner (1972) and Kamin accounts of blocking. This is the assumption that the cause of blocking is the ineffectiveness of a predicted US as a reinforcer, and that the role of a surprising change in reinforcement is somehow to provide or restore the normal process of reinforcement. It is very difficult to see how our results can be interpreted if we start from this assumption. They do, however, make sense if we start from a quite different assumption: The occurrence of blocking reflects not on the effectiveness of the US but on that of the added CS. We know that blocking occurs when the added element signals no change in reinforcement, and that it is attenuated when the conditions of reinforcement on AB compound trials differ significantly from those in force during initial training to A alone. Perhaps, then, blocking occurs when animals learn to ignore a stimulus which signals no change in reinforcement, and is attenuated when animals do not ignore a stimulus which does signal a significant change (Mackintosh, 1975a).

Although this might be classed as an attentional analysis of blocking, it is to be sharply distinguished from the account traditionally provided by theories of selective attention (e.g., Sutherland & Mackintosh, 1971). According to the latter, blocking is a consequence of competition between A and B for a limited attentional capacity. The present view implies no direct competition for attention. On the first compound trial, subjects are assumed to attend normally to the added element, B. They will continue to attend and condition to B provided that it signals some change in reinforcement; but if B predicts nothing not already predicted by A alone, they will cease to attend to it and no further conditioning to B will occur.

There is, in fact, good evidence that blocking develops during the course of compound trials in just this way. By using a sensitive measure of learning, Kamin was able to show that significant conditioning accrued to the added element in his standard blocking design. In other words, even when the reinforcer was the same, blocking was not complete (a conclusion amply confirmed in subsequent studies and by the conditioning evident for many of our control groups in the present research; see, e.g., Fig. 2 and 4). Kamin further found that animals given a single AB compound trial showed as much conditioning to B as those given eight, implying that conditioning to B was largely confined to the first compound trial. Some experiments of our own (Mackintosh, 1975b) are entirely consistent with Kamin's conclusion, for we also found that animals given eight compound trials showed no more suppression to the added B element than those given a single trial. In these experiments, moreover, conditioning to B appeared to proceed quite normally on this first compound trial: Animals pretrained to A alone before their single trial to the AB compound showed as much suppression to B as those given no pretraining. In other words, we found no evidence of blocking on the first compound trial. According to the present analysis, blocking occurs when subjects learn to ignore a redundant stimulus. On the first compound trial, when B is a novel stimulus, animals attend normally to it; only when they have had the opportunity to learn that B is redundant do they cease to attend and condition to it. Blocking therefore is a multitrial phenomenon.

If conditioning to the added element proceeds normally on the first compound trial, it is easy to see why we were unable to detect any effect of a surprising second shock on that trial: if no blocking occurs, there is no blocking to attenuate. Furthermore, if the reinforcer delivered on the first compound trial is the same as that delivered on pretraining trials, the redundancy of the added element produces blocking on subsequent trials. If, however, there is some unexpected change in reinforcement on the first trial, even though the change is not itself sufficient to reinforce conditioning to the added element, B, it may be sufficient to ensure that B is not treated as redundant and hence is not ignored on subsequent trials.

My conclusion, therefore, is that a surprising change in reinforcement does not affect the status of the US, as Kamin supposed, but rather that of the added CS. Surprise ensures that the added element B signals some event not already predicted by A alone, and hence it interferes with the process of learning to ignore B which would otherwise produce blocking. On this view, the nature of the reinforcer delivered on the first compound trial assumes critical importance. Subjects attend to B on the first trial; if B signals some change in reinforcement, they will continue to attend to B on subsequent trials. If, however, there is no change in reinforcement on this trial, they will tend to ignore B on subsequent trials *and hence may fail to attribute any subsequent change to the presence of*

B. A final experiment tested this analysis by manipulating the temporal relationship between the introduction of the new element and the scheduling of surprise: for one group surprise was scheduled on the first compound trial; for a second group surprise did not occur until the second compound trial.

The experiment employed the conditioned suppression of licking and all general procedures, stimuli, shocks, etc., were identical to those used in the earlier series (Mackintosh et al., 1977). Forty-eight rats were divided into four groups of 12 which received the treatments shown in Table 3. In Stage 1, all four groups received four conditioning trials to a light paired with a single shock; in Stage 2, two groups (TL++TL+ and TL+TL+) received an additional light trial followed by two trials to a tone-light compound, while the remaining two groups (TL+TL++TL+ and TL+TL+TL+) received three compound trials. For one group in each pair, a surprising second shock was programmed to occur on the second trial of Stage 2, 10 sec after the first shock. For Group TL++TL+, of course, the second trial of Stage 2 was their *first* compound trial, while for Group TL+TL++ TL+, it was their second compound trial.

At the end of conditioning, all four groups received two recovery days followed by five nonreinforced test trials to the tone at a rate of one trial per day. The results of these test trials are shown in Fig. 5.

It is apparent that animals surprised on their first compound trial (Group TL++TL+) were more suppressed to the tone than any of the remaining groups, which showed relatively similar levels of suppression. A Kruskal-Wallis analysis of variance of mean suppression ratios over the five test trials revealed a significant overall difference between the four groups ($H = 12.56, p < .01$); subsequent Mann-Whitney tests revealed that Group TL++TL+ differed from each of the remaining three groups ($Us \leq 27, p < .02$) but that the latter groups did not differ from one another. With the parameters employed here, therefore, blocking is attenuated by a surprising change in reinforcement only if that change occurs on the first compound trial.

TABLE 3
Experimental Design[a]

Group	Stage 1 (4 trials)	Stage 2		
		Trial 1	Trial 2	Trial 3
TL++ TL+	L+	L+	TL++	TL+
TL+ TL+	L+	L+	TL+	TL+
TL+ TL++ TL+	L+	TL+	TL++	TL+
TL+ TL++ TL+	L+	TL+	TL+	TL+

[a]T, tone; L, light; +, single shock; ++, double shock separated by 10-sec intershock interval.

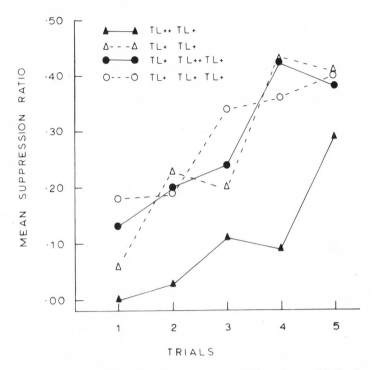

FIG. 5.   Suppression ratios to the tone over five nonreinforced test trials for the groups described in Table 3. Results of an experiment comparing the effects of a surprising extra shock scheduled on the first or on the second compound trial.

These results are reminiscent of those obtained in an earlier experiment by Mackintosh and Turner (1971). In that study, we employed Kamin's procedure of increasing shock intensity on compound trials in order to attenuate the blocking of conditioning to the added element. After conditioning to a noise signaling a 1-mA shock in Stage 1, rats received four trials in Stage 2 with a noise–light compound signaling a 4-mA shock. For one group, however, an additional four compound trials were interposed between Stages 1 and 2 during which the compound signaled only the 1-mA shock. Animals in this group showed significantly less suppression to the light than did those for whom the addition of the light had coincided with the increase in shock intensity. Here also, therefore, blocking was reliably attenuated when reinforcement was changed on the first compound trial; but if the surprising change in reinforcement was delayed until the fifth compound trial, it was relatively ineffective in producing conditioning to the added element. Thus in both experiments, if the new element signaled no change in reinforcement when it was first introduced, blocking was hardly attenuated by a subsequent change in reinforcement. This is entirely consistent with the proposition that animals learn to ignore a stimulus signaling no change in reinforcement, and that this is the major process responsible for blocking.

IV. CONCLUSIONS AND IMPLICATIONS

I have chosen to analyze the phenomenon of blocking in some detail, but I think it important to recognize that blocking is only one example of a central and pervasive feature of conditioning. It is a special case of the general rule that the availability of a better predictor of reinforcement may detract from conditioning to a poorer predictor. In the standard blocking experiment, A is a better predictor of reinforcement than B because it has already been established as a signal for that reinforcer. Other procedures for varying the relative predictive value of A and B have similar effects. If A is better correlated with reinforcement than B (Wagner, 1969) or more salient than B (Kamin, 1969; Mackintosh, 1976), its presence may significantly interfere with the course of conditioning to B. Moreover, it is easy enough to show that prior, reinforced experience with one element of a compound CS, the manipulation responsible for blocking, may be less effective than relative validity or relative salience in determing the course of conditioning to the two elements of the compound. Consider the following case: in Stage 1, stimulus A is imperfectly correlated with reinforcement, as only 50% of trials are reinforced ($A+$, $A-$); in Stage 2, while A continues to be imperfectly correlated, B is added on reinforced trials only ($AB+$, $A-$) and is thus perfectly correlated with the availability of reinforcement. If conditioning to B were blocked by the presence of the previously trained A stimulus, subjects would fail to solve the discrimination problem posed by Stage 2. Indeed, the solution of this problem requires, on the contrary, that the better predictor B take control away from the previously trained A stimulus, and this is what happens (e.g., Hall, Mackintosh, Goodall, & Martello, 1977). Hall et al. also found that a similar outcome would occur if B was simply a more salient stimulus than A. If rats were initially conditioned to a faint tone signaling shock and were subsequently given compound trials on which a bright light was added to the tone, then although the tone was as well correlated with reinforcement as the light, and benefited from a longer history of reinforcement, it rapidly lost control over responding in favor of the more salient light.

The phenomenon of blocking appears, therefore, to be only one example of a more general interaction between the elements of a compound CS. In any given instance, not all of the elements will be established as reliable signals for reinforcement. The course of conditioning to one element of a compound depends not only on the salience or correlation of that element with the reinforcer, but also on the salience and current and past correlation of the other element with that reinforcer.

What implications does this conclusion hold for our theories of conditioning? It is clear that conditioning cannot be regarded simply as a matter of registering coincident events. If it were, our task as psychologists trying to understand conditioning might be simpler, but our subjects' success in understanding the world they live in would be very much poorer. By conditioning selectively to good predictors of reinforcement, at the expense of poor predictors, animals succeed in attributing events of consequence to their most probable causes. Without this selectivity built into it, the animal's general associative system would be at the mercy of chance conjunctions of events. It would be unable to distinguish between the true cause of the occurrence of a particular reinforcer and other events which are only coincidentally related to that reinforcer (Mackintosh, 1977).

It is one thing, however, to say that the information-processing machinery that an animal brings to the world is designed to attribute effects to their true causes rather than to coincidentally antecedent events. But this tells us relatively little about the nature of that machinery. We know, it is true, that we can reject any theory which seeks to reduce conditioning to a simple matter of associating all paired events. But we do not necessarily know what to put in its place. We do not even know, to hark back to a distinction which I drew at the beginning of this chapter, whether we must reject as completely inadequate any simple associative theory of conditioning, or whether it will be possible to salvage such a theory by supplementary principles of suitable complexity.

My own preference is for the second alternative. I assume that the basic associative process is a simple one that registers the coincident occurrence of events. In addition to this process of associative learning, however, an additional learning process evaluates the relative predictiveness of potential CSs for a certain reinforcer and thus determines the probability that the relationship between a given CS and US will actually be stored as an association between them. We may, if we wish, call this process one of learning to attend to or ignore particular stimuli, although it would be less misleading, however cumbersome, to say that it is a system determining the associability of a particular class of stimuli with a particular class of reinforcers (see Mackintosh, 1975a).

One reason for preferring this solution is that there is good, independent evidence that we need some such principle of attention or variable associability. Experiments on acquired distinctiveness in discrimination learning or latent inhibition in classical conditioning imply that the probability of forming a new association between a stimulus and a reinforcer is significantly affected by the subject's past experience of the predictive value of that stimulus (Mackintosh, 1975a). Given this evidence, it seems reasonable to determine whether some such principle of variable associability will also serve to explain the selectivity of conditioning and discrimination learning observed in experiments on blocking and overshadowing.

Learning to attend to or ignore stimuli, or learning to regard them as probable or improbable causes of particular reinforcers, does not obviously reflect the workings of a simple associative process. In this sense, I should like to argue that an adequate theory of conditioning will need to call on nonassociative principles as well as a basic associative process. There is no reason to suppose, however, that these nonassociative principles must be unduly elaborate. What is needed is a system for evaluating the relative predictive value of different stimuli. Rescorla and Wagner (1972) have proposed a simple and elegant way of representing the predictive value of a stimulus and it does not require much ingenuity to use this representation in a rather different way (see Mackintosh, 1975a) to affect the attentional value or associability of a stimulus. Wagner himself, in his contribution to this volume (Chapter 7), has proposed an alternative, even simpler rule for modifying the effectiveness (including the associability) of a CS, based on a general theory of habituation. He views habituation itself as an associative process whereby a given context or set of background stimuli can become established as a signal for the occurrence of a given CS; in effect, he retains an associative theory of conditioning, albeit a relatively elaborate one involving two distinct associative processes. Thus, whereas I assume that the present effectiveness of a CS as a signal for a particular reinforcer depends upon its relative predictive value as a signal for that reinforcer in the past, Wagner assumes that it depends on how well that CS has previously been predicted by the present context. In one case the associability of the CS depends upon its earlier consequences; in the other on its earlier antecedents. It is too early to say which of these accounts will prove more adequate to explain the sorts of data that I have been considering; it should not prove too difficult, however, to distinguish between two such apparently different approaches.

ACKNOWLEDGMENTS

This research was supported by a grant from the U. K. Science Research Council. The experiments presented in this chapter and the writing of the chapter itself owe a very great deal to numerous discussions with A. Dickinson.

REFERENCES

Dickinson, A. Appetitive-aversive interactions: Superconditioning of fear by an appetitive CS. *Quarterly Journal of Experimental Psychology*, 1977, *29*, 71–84.

Dickinson, A., Hall, G., & Mackintosh, N. J. Surprise and the attenuation of blocking. *Journal of Experimental Psychology: Animal Behavior Processes*, 1976, *2*, 313–322.

Gray, T., & Appignanesi, A. A. Compound conditioning: Elimination of the blocking effect. *Learning and Motivation*, 1973, *4*, 374–380.

Hall, G., Mackintosh, N. J., Goodall, G., & Martello, M. Loss of control by a less valid or less salient stimulus compounded with a better predictor of reinforcement. *Learning and Motivation*, 1977, *8*, 145–158.

Kamin, L. J. Selective association and conditioning. In N. J. Mackintosh and W. K. Honig (Eds.), *Fundamental issues in associative learning*. Halifax, Canada: Dalhousie University Press, 1969, p. 42–64.

Mackintosh, N. J. A theory of attention: Variations in the associability of stimuli with reinforcement. *Psychological Review*, 1975, *82*, 276–298. (a)

Mackintosh, N. J. Blocking of conditioned suppression: Role of the first compound trial. *Journal of Experimental Psychology: Animal Behavior Processes,* 1975, *1,* 335–345. (b)

Mackintosh, N. J. Overshadowing and stimulus intensity. *Animal Learning and Behavior,* 1976, *4,* 186–192.

Mackintosh, N. J. Conditioning as the perception of causal relations. In R. E. Butts and J. Hintikka (Eds.), *Foundational problems in the special sciences.* Dordrecht, Netherlands: Reidel, 1977, p. 241–250.

Mackintosh, N. J., Bygrave, D. J., & Picton, B. M. B. Locus of the effect of a surprising reinforcer in the attenuation of blocking. *Quarterly Journal of Experimental Psychology,* 1977, *29,* 327–336.

Mackintosh, N. J., & Turner, C. Blocking as a function of novelty of CS and predictability of UCS. *Quarterly Journal of Experimental Psychology,* 1971, *23,* 359–366.

Neely, J. H., & Wagner, A. R. Attenuation of blocking with shifts in reward: The involvement of schedule-generated contextual cues. *Journal of Experimental Psychology,* 1974, *102,* 751–763.

Rescorla, R. A., & Wagner, A. R. A theory of Pavlovian conditioning: Variations in the effectiveness of reinforcement and nonreinforcement. In A. H. Black and W. F. Prokasy (Eds.), *Classical conditioning II: Current research and theory.* New York: Appleton-Century-Crofts, 1972, p. 64–99.

Sutherland, N. S., & Mackintosh, N. J. *Mechanisms of animal discrimination learning.* New York: Academic Press, 1971.

Wagner, A. R. Stimulus validity and stimulus selection in associative learning. In N. J. Mackintosh and W. K. Honig (Eds.), *Fundamental issues in associative learning.* Halifax, Canada: Dalhousie University Press, 1969, p. 90–122.

7 Expectancies and the Priming of STM

Allan R. Wagner
Yale University

I. EXPECTANCIES AND THE PRIMING OF STM

One of the most consistent themes in our theories of learning and memory is that the individual's "expectations" influence what is learned in any training situation. This theme is surely most evident in treatments of human learning. Thus, for example, when an individual is instructed via a natural-language text, we can observe that the subject acquires information that is not literally presented, but is implied on the basis of prior knowledge (e.g., Schank, 1975). The same kind of observation can be made when the individual is instructed in a variety of perceptual modes (e.g., Bartlett, 1932). It is thus common to assume that the environment is scanned and learned about in relationship to cognitive schemata (e.g., Bobrow & Norman, 1975), knowledge "frames" (Minsky, 1975), or "scripts" (Schank, 1975).

In treatments of animal learning, at least those following Morgan (1894) and Hobhouse (1915), we have been more reluctant to grant such a pervasive role to expectancies. But, in one way or another the general phenomenon has been recognized. Thus, for example, Tolman (e.g., 1932) insisted that an animal's expectations shape its perception, and hence what will be noted in the environment. And, anticipatory-goal-response theory (e.g., Spence, 1956; Amsel, 1958; Wagner, 1966) was calculated to address the same general issue by assuming that an animal's expectations may shape its response to the training environment, e.g., to promote "frustration" or not on the occasions of nonreinforcement.

A notable meeting ground for the treatment of expectancies in human and animal learning is in recent information-processing formulations (e.g., Atkinson & Wickens, 1971; Bobrow & Norman, 1975; Bower, 1975; Wagner, 1976) that suppose that "surprising" events are subjected to different degrees or different "levels" of processing than are expected events. The most common notion is that surprising events are more likely to be "rehearsed," and thus retained in memory, than are expected events. This language may appear more appropriate to the human subject than to nonarticulate animals, and might be thought to be more suited to complex learning phenomena than to the simple tasks of the animal laboratory. Then it may be instructive to appreciate that the assumptions involved have gained substantial support from investigations of animal condition-ing and habituation, and that they hold prospect of allowing us to integrate an even more substantial set of phenomena in animal as well as human memory. The differential processing of expected vs. surprising events appears to be a relatively basic behavioral phenomenon. The chapter that follows is intended to elucidate the general theoretical reasoning that is hinted at in this paragraph, to review some of the findings from our laboratory which have encouraged such reasoning, and to point to some of the prospects for further theoretical integra-tion.

II. THE PRIMING OF STM

The essential notion with which we will be concerned can be adapted to a variety of formalisms (see, e.g., Pfautz & Wagner, 1976). However, it will assist exposition and help to avoid potential misunderstandings, if we place it in the specific context of certain relatively conventional propositions of current information-processing theories. Figure 1 presents an abbreviated information-processing schematization that should suffice for this purpose.

I shall assume recognition of the major mechanisms in such schemata: An initial Sensory Register (SR) that provides a primitive sensory coding of environmental stimulation; a memory system in which we must distinguish between a Short-term Memory (STM) component and the supporting Long-term Memory structure (LTM); and a final output mechanism, the Response Generator (RG). What must be elaborated is a set of assumptions about the memory system.

We follow the reasoning of Norman (1968), Konorski (1967), Anderson and Bower (1973), Shiffrin and Schneider (1977), and others, in assuming that the memory system may be conceptualized as a large (effectively unlimited) number of representative elements (so-called gnostic units, ideas, logogens, images, etc.) interconnected via an associative network. The "structure" of this system – the representations included and their interconnections – define Long-term Memory. In contrast, the distinction between Long-term Memory and Short-term Memory involves the assumption that the representative elements may be in either an inactive or active state: The set of elements in LTM that is currently active defines Short-term Memory.

We wish to avoid here as many as possible of the questions that divide different theories, e.g., concerning the genesis of the representative elements (see Konor-ski, 1967; Anderson & Bower, 1973) and the form of the associative network

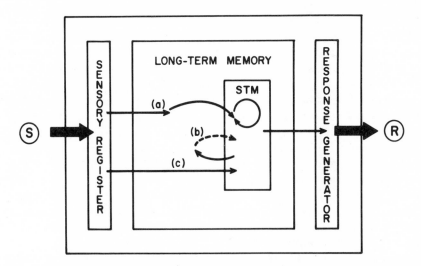

FIG. 1. An information-processing schema incorporating the assumed mechanism of priming. The labeled arrows refer to (a) a sequence for initial activation of a representation in Short-term Memory (STM) implicating "rehearsal" (designated by the looped arrow in STM); (b) a sequence for retrieving associated representations from Long-term Memory; and (c) a sequence for refreshing a prior prepresentation in STM, not implicating rehearsal. (See text.)

that connects them (see Estes, 1975; Anderson & Bower, 1973). Thus, we will simply assume that an environmental event coded by the SR may activate a representation of that event in LTM, thus "transferring" the latter into STM. And, we will allow that, as a result of the associative network, the activation of one representation in STM may lead to the activation of other representations with which it is linked, thus "retrieving" the latter into STM. These processes are meant to be suggested by the sequence of arrows labeled (a) and (b), respectively, in Fig. 1.

The critical assumptions for present purposes concern the operating characteristics of STM. An activated element is not presumed to remain in such state indefinitely, but rather is presumed to revert to inactivity. The transient nature of the activation is, of course, what suggests the label "Short-term Memory." The transience may be attributed to an intrinsic, continuous decay process (e.g., Atkinson & Shiffrin, 1968). Or it might be taken to be a stochastic product of a second characteristic of STM that is conventionally assumed. That is, it is assumed that STM has a limited capacity. Thus the activation of a new representation should tend to displace existing representations, and displacement of an element should be more probable the longer the opportunity.

A further presumption about the operating characteristics of STM is that a representation may be *maintained* active while others are not. While there are surely some unfortunate connotations of the terminology, it is common to refer to this maintenance as "rehearsal" (e.g., Wagner, Rudy, & Whitlow, 1973), or to the set of elements under maintenance as a "rehearsal buffer" (e.g., Atkinson & Shiffrin, 1968). Again, we can be indifferent to whether rehearsal is treated as a probablistic event or as a continuous variable. In either case, we can note that rehearsal should have several consequences. Most obviously, a rehearsed representation in STM should be presented longer to the Response Generator and thus potentially have an augmented influence on performance. Secondly, a rehearsed representation should have sustained opportunity to act as a retrieval cue to activate associated representations. Thirdly, apart from, and in conjunction with, the preceding point, a rehearsed representation should especially act to deny the limited capacity of STM to other representations. Finally, and perhaps most importantly, a rehearsed representation should have an enhanced influence on the subsequent state of LTM. If it is assumed that permanent associative connections are developed between representative elements only to the degree that the elements are jointly active in STM (e.g., Konorski, 1967; Shiffrin & Schneider, 1977; Wagner & Terry, 1975), then a rehearsed representation should be especially likely to form effective associations.

There are likely to be a considerable number of factors that control the occurrence of rehearsal. Rehearsal may be especially granted to representations of affectively toned events, may be more generally engaged in under states of relative arousal, and may be assumed to be directed in the human by instructions or problem solving routines (see, e.g., Shiffrin & Schneider, 1977). The notion that was anticipated, however, in the introduction, and that is of present interest, is that rehearsal is a more likely consequence of "surprising" than of "expected" events. Having provided the above theoretical background, we can now formulate this notion more precisely and in a manner that is substantially more general.

What we have assumed (e.g., Wagner, 1976; Pfautz & Wagner, 1976) is that environmental stimulation is more or less likely to be followed by a rehearsed representation in STM, depending on whether or not the stimulus on such occasion is or is not already represented in STM. When a stimulus is presented in the absence of pre-representation in STM, we assume that it activates an appropriate representation from LTM, and that this initial activation is likely to be followed by a rehearsal in STM. In Figure 1, this is the course of events that is meant to be suggested by the sequence of arrows labeled (a), with the final loop in STM denoting the assumed rehearsal. When a stimulus is presented on an occasion in which it is prerepresented in STM, we assume that although it may act to refresh the latter representation, it will not provoke rehearsal. In Fig. 1, this is the course of events that is meant to be suggested by the arrow labeled (c), which does not eventuate in a rehearsal loop in STM.

This statement covers what we wish to convey about the differential processing in STM of "expected" vs. "surprising" events, but it has more general implications. To speak of an "expected" event is to refer to an event which is presumably prerepresented in STM as a result of the retrieval action of other antedating stimuli with which it has associative connections. But, an event can presumably be prerepresented in STM as a result of a simpler set of circumstances, namely the recent presentation of the same event. In either case, the mechanism outlined in Fig. 1 supposes that the event should be less likely to be rehearsed than in the absence of prerepresentation. To adopt a language suited to these very different, but theoretically related possibilities, Wagner (1976) has distinguished between a "retrieval-generated priming" and a "self-generated priming" of STM, but with the assumption that the final influence on rehearsal, and eventual measures of performance, is indifferent to this distinction.

III. RETRIEVAL-GENERATED PRIMING

A. Blocking

The class of studies that initially drew us toward the above model has as its prototype Kamin's (e.g., 1969) original investigation of the so-called blocking phenomenon in Pavlovian conditioning. In the general case, a target Conditioned Stimulus (CS) is trained in compound with a second CS that has been experimentally pretreated so as to make it a more or less valid predictor of an Unconditioned Stimulus (US). The principal observation from such studies is that there is systematic variation in conditioned responding to the target CS, X, alone depending upon the different pretreatments of the second CS, A, even though the reinforcement schedule in the presence of X is held constant. Thus, it is well documented (e.g., Kamin, 1969; Wagner, 1969) that the greater the prior acquisition training to A, the less will be the increment in conditioned responding to X as a result of AX–US pairings, and the greater will be the decrement in conditioned responding to X as a result of AX nonreinforcements. One relevant experiment will be described to exemplify the pattern, as well as to introduce certain procedures of our laboratory.

The study was conducted by Maria Saavedra (reported in Wagner, 1976) and involved eyelid conditioning in the rabbit. Conditioned stimuli were always 1,100 msec in duration and, when reinforced, overlapped and terminated with a 100-msec, 4.5-mA shock US applied to the area surrounding the eye. The experimental design called for three different CSs. These involved a 20 per second flashing light, a 3-kHz tone, and a 60-Hz vibratory stimulus in contact with the animal's chest, in counterbalanced assignment to the different experimental conditions. Eyelid deflections were monitored and scored as CRs when they occurred during the first 1,000 msec of CS presentation.

In the initial phase of this study, rabbits were given reinforced training with two of the CSs, designated A and B, on separate trials. The intention was to highly train cue A and only weakly train cue B. This was done by administering 448 reinforcements to A and only 28 to B in a quasi-random sequence. At the end of this first phase, the subjects were separated into two matched groups and the third CS, *X,* was then reinforced in compound with one of the two pre-trained cues, i.e., either in an *AX* or *BX* compound. The third, and final, phase evaluated the degree of learning to respond to *X* as a result of the compound training. This was done by presenting a series of nonreinforced test trials to *X* alone.

Figure 2 depicts the results from the several stages of this experiment. Notice in Phase 1 (left panel) the differential acquisition to *A* and *B,* and in Phase 2 (center panel) the correspondingly higher level of responding to *AX* than to *BX* as both groups in this phase received the same number of reinforcements of *X* in one of these compounds. The important results, however, are to be seen in the final, test phase (right panel): There was less responding to *X* alone following the *AX* reinforcements than following the *BX* reinforcements.

This variation upon Kamin's blocking design did not produce as dramatic an effect as Kamin has sometimes reported (e.g., 1969). But the present design carefully controls for such differences as the overall conditioning history of the comparison groups. And, the effect is still substantial. Two test trials were included at the end of Phase 1 to *X* alone (see left panel, Fig. 2). Comparing the responding to *X* immediately before and after compound training, there was a 5% increase in Group *AX* and a 35% increase in Group *BX.*

This is the kind of finding that led Kamin (e.g., 1969) to propose that an "expected" US may promote less conditioning than a "surprising" US. The terms expected and surprising can be objectified in terms of the degree to which

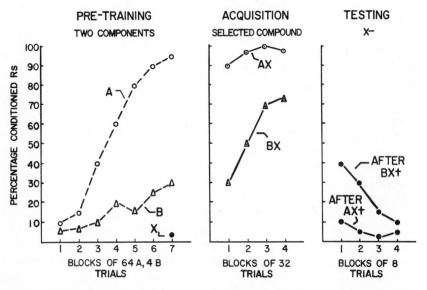

FIG. 2.   Mean percentage conditioned eyeblink responses during three stages of a "block-ing" experiment. (Reprinted from Wagner, 1976.)

the US can be assumed to be *predicted by the total aggregation of cues which precede it.* In the case of the above experiment we can thus suppose that the US was more expected when it occurred in the AX compound than when it occurred in the BX compound.

It should be apparent how the priming mechanism portrayed in Fig. 1 is calculated to predict the blocking effect seen in Fig. 2. As a result of their different numbers of pairings with the US, the A cue should have been more effective than the B cue at the time of compound training in retrieving into STM a representation of the US from LTM. The most obvious witness to the differential retrieval effects, which is presumed to occur, is the greater responding to A alone than to B alone in Phase 1 and the continued greater responding to AX than to BX in Phase 2. If the US is thus assumed to be more likely to be represented in STM *prior to* the US reinforcement which occurs in an AX vs. a BX training trial, we are led to expect that the reinforcing US will be less likely to be rehearsed in STM when it occurs. Following AX the *US* presumably does not enjoy extended processing in STM beneficial to associating X and the US.

There are now a large number of experiments concerned with the blocking effect. How well their data can *all* be accounted for in terms of variations in the effectiveness of the US event as just described is still not certain (see, e.g., Mackintosh, Chapter 6). The major theoretical alternative that has conventionally been entertained (e.g., Lashley, 1942; Mackintosh, 1975) takes the form of suggesting that cue X, rather than the US, was less likely to be processed (attended to) in the AX than in the BX compound of the preceding experiment. We need not deny this general possibility. What is clear, however, is that whether or not X will be learned about, and what will be learned, depends upon what the remaining cues signal vs. what actually occurs. Thus, for example, in a companion experiment to the one which has been described (Wagner, 1969) we observed *more* learning to X in an AX than in a BX compound, when the compounds were *nonreinforced*, and what was to be learned was extinction of conditioned responding. This is appropriate to our conception, as the absence of reinforcement should have been more surprising (less likely to have been primed in STM) following an AX than a BX compound. What appears to be the case is that the learner is instructed only in what it is not remembering, i.e., what is not already in STM.

B. Persistence in STM

If the conditions of US signaling that produce the blocking effect are influential because they alter the likelihood that the US will be rehearsed in STM, then such conditions should have a corresponding influence on other behavioral measures that are presumably reflective of the contents of STM. Accordingly, Terry and Wagner (1975) sought to answer a very simple question: Does the rabbit better remember that it has just experienced a shock US, when the US was surprising than when the US was expected? The experimental strategy was first to train subjects to respond in a distinctively different manner to a 1,100-msec vibratory CS, when an unannounced US had occurred within the past few seconds, as compared to occasions when such a US had not been recently presented. In each of two groups CS_R (a so-called releasing stimulus, marking the occasion for responding or not) was sometimes reinforced and sometimes nonreinforced according to an irregular sequence. The only reliable cue available to signal the occasions of reinforcement was the occurrence vs. nonoccurence of a shock US (a so-called preparatory stimulus) irregularly 2, 4, 8, or 16 sec prior to the time that CS_R might be reinforced. In one group the preparatory US announced the subsequent reinforcement of CS_R; in the other it announced the subsequent nonreinforcement of CS_R. In either case with extensive training the subjects learned to respond differentially on the occasions of CS_R, appropriate to the reinforcement schedule, depending upon the prior occurrence vs. non-occurrence of the preparatory US. And, the discriminative behavior was more evident the shorter was the preparatory-releaser interval. Thus, it could be assumed that the subjects were responding differentially to CS_R depending upon whether or not the US was on that occasion represented in STM.

We could now set up conditions to ask whether a preparatory US, presented some interval before CS_R, was more likely to still evidence representation in STM at the time of CS_R, if the US had been made surprising than if made expected, in the manner of the previously described blocking studies. In order to manipulate the surprisingness of the US, all subjects were further trained in a simple Pavlovian discrimination with a visual and an auditory CS, one (CS^+) being consistently reinforced with the US, the other (CS^-) being consistently nonreinforced. This training, which was conducted in separate discrimination sessions and never involved a preparatory US, culminated in consistent conditioned responding to CS^+ and negligible responding to CS^-. Thus it might be assumed that a US which was preceded by CS^+ would be expected, while a US preceded by CS^- would be surprising.

The eventual test was provided by running all subjects in the preparatory-releaser paradigm as during training, in which CS_R was sometimes preceded by a preparatory US and sometimes not. Now, however, the preparatory US was either announced by CS^+, as was the same US during discrimination training, or was announced by CS^-, as was never the case for a US during discrimination training. The results were straightforward: Subjects were reliably more likely to respond to the releasing stimulus, CS_R, as they had been trained to respond following a preparatory US (appropriate to whether or not CS_R was then reinforced) when the preparatory episode involved the sequence CS^- US as compared to CS^+ US. Figure 3 presents data to this effect from one of the series of tests that was conducted. The findings from the two subgroups are combined by expressing the percentages responding on trials involving a preparatory US as "correct deviation" from the same percentages on trials involving no preparatory US. It may be seen that this deviation systematically decreases the longer the

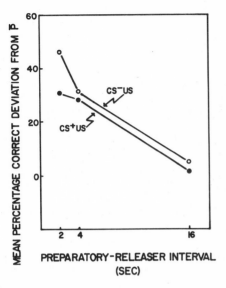

FIG. 3.   Mean percentage conditioned responding to a releasing stimulus, CS_R, following a preparatory stimulus involving either CS⁻US or CS⁺US, expressed as a "correct deviation" from the percentages following no preparatory stimulus P. (Reprinted from Terry and Wagner, 1975. Copyright 1975 by the American Psychological Association. Reprinted by permission.)

preparatory-releaser interval, and is greater when the preparatory US was preceded by CS⁻ than when it was preceded by CS⁺.

Such findings encourage us to assume that conditions of prerepresenting a US in STM do more than influence the associative learning that the US can promote. The conditions of priming influence the likelihood that a representation of the US will evidence being resident in STM a few seconds after US presentation.

C. Interference

A congenial set of conclusions follow from a related set of studies reported by Wagner, Rudy, and Whitlow (1973). In this case the essential proposition was that an expected US should be less likely than a surprising US to *interfere* with the learning about other temporally adjacent training episodes. We assume that for a CS—US association to be formed in LTM that the two events must be jointly represented in STM, and that the longer the joint representation is allowed to persist undisturbed the better will be conditioning. A posttrial episode that itself commands occupancy of the limited capacity STM should thus have more of an interference effect upon such conditioning than a posttrial episode that is less likely to command occupancy of STM. This reasoning has familiar antecedents in studies of human memory (e.g., Atkinson & Shiffrin, 1968; Tulving, 1969).

The series of experiments reported by Wagner et al. (1973) all had the same general characteristics. In Phase 1, rabbits were trained in eyelid conditioning with CS_A consistently followed by a US and CS_B consistently followed by no US ($\overline{US}$). Figure 4a shows the results of this training of four separate groups in

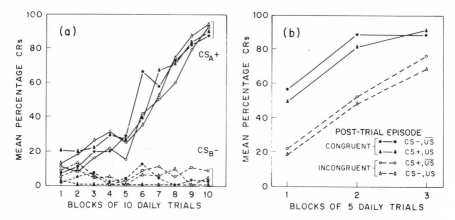

FIG. 4.   Percentage conditioned eyeblink responses in an investigation of the interference effects of different posttrial episodes (PTEs). (a) Initial discrimination learning of 4 separate groups. (b) Subsequent acquisition of responding to CS_C when the PTE was congruent or incongruent with the initial discrimination training in the manner indicated. (Reprinted from Wagner, Rudy, & Whitlow, 1973. Copyright 1973 by the American Psychological Association. Reprinted by permission.)

one experiment. This phase was necessary only to develop what could subsequently be viewed as surprising or expected Pavlovian episodes: CS_A–US and CS_B–$\overline{US}$ (congruent with original training) could be considered expected; CS_A–$\overline{US}$ and CS_B–US (incongruent with original training) could be considered surprising. In Phase 2, all animals received a series of *reinforced* trials with a new cue, CS_C, in a different modality than CS_A and CS_B, at very distributed intervals and in some cases separated by buffer trials involving the Phase 1 training trials. The important manipulation was that a short interval after each CS_C–US trial (usually 10 sec) different groups of subjects received different posttrial episodes (PTEs) involving CS_A and CS_B either reinforced or nonreinforced in a manner either congruent or incongruent with Phase 1 training.

Figure 4b depicts the acquisition of conditioned responding to CS_C in the four groups of Figure 4a. Each group received as the PTE one of the four episodes, CS_A–US, CS_B–$\overline{US}$, CS_A–$\overline{US}$, or CS_B–US. The important observation is that when the PTEs were incongruent with original training, i.e., surprising, acquisition to CS_C was depressed in relationship to the cases in which the PTEs were congruent with original training, i.e., expected. It made no reliable difference overall whether the PTE included CS_A or CS_B, or the US or $\overline{US}$. All that mattered was whether the pairing of CS and US events was congruent or incongruent with the animal's prior experience.

The remaining experiments in the series reported by Wagner et al. (1973) added appropriate details. The initial study that has been described does not uniquely indicate that the several PTEs differentially *interfered* with conditioning. Perhaps, instead, a congruent PTE facilitates conditioning. Furthermore, there are a considerable number of ways in which an experimental event might interfere with performance, for example, via some general processing disturbance, or via proactive transfer effects, as well as by interfering with rehearsal in STM. The basic experimental phenomenon seen in Fig. 4 does not distinguish among these. If an incongruent PTE commands rehearsal in a manner that a congruent PTE does not, one should observe a decrement in acquisition that is specific to just those trial CSs with which the incongruent PTE was temporally adjacent during training, and a greater decrement the shorter the trial-PTE interval.

In one of the further experiments, Wagner et al. (1973) required subjects to learn a "list" of new CS–US associations. The PTEs were inserted after some members but not others. A surprising PTE was found to interfere with conditioning to just those members of the list that it was arranged to follow. An expected PTE had no decremental effect. In another experiment involving surprising PTEs the trial-PTE interval was systematically manipulated. In brief, it was observed that the shorter the trial-PTE interval over the range of 3 to 300 sec the poorer the acquisition of responding to CS_C.

In all, the Wagner et al. (1973) studies offer abundant evidence that surprising and expected USs (or absence of USs) are differentially effective. The manner of difference, in interfering with the learning that results from contemporaneous training episodes, lends consistent support to the view that surprising events operate to command residence in STM in a way that expected events do not. When added to the findings of Terry and Wagner (1975) and the considerable literature on blocking which has been exemplified by the Saavedra study, we are encouraged to suppose that a retrieval-generated priming of STM reduces the likelihood that corresponding stimulation will be rehearsed, as suggested in the schema of Fig. 1.

IV. SELF-GENERATED PRIMING

The preceding studies were obviously concerned with the relationship between "expectancies" and learning. Some stimulus, as a result of prior training, could be assumed to retrieve representation of a consequent event into STM prior to the event's actual occurrence and thereby modify the stimulus processing that would occur. As has been pointed out, however, the conceptualization schematized in Fig. 1 treats such instances as only special cases in which the critical conditions of priming call upon relatively complex association and retrieval processes. If the formulation is correct we should be able to see it evidenced in circumstances that dispense with much of this machinery. That is, if a stimulus is less likely to occasion rehearsal in STM when its representation is already active in STM, we should be able to demonstrate the phenomenon by generating the activation more directly than in the previous studies, i.e., through the recent prior presentation of the stimulus itself. We should be able, for example, to diminish the effectiveness of a Pavlovian US by the recent prior presentation of that US (so-called self-generated priming) just as by the prior presentation of a specially trained retrieval cue.

A. Blocking

This is the line of reasoning that was followed by William Terry in a recent dissertation (Terry, 1976) conducted in our laboratory. In essence, he sought to evaluate whether or not a blocking-like effect would result, if the CS—US episodes, rather than involving another CS that would signal the US, were shortly preceded by an instance of the US itself.

In the first of several experiments reported by Terry, rabbits were trained in eyelid conditioning using procedures similar to those in the preceding studies. On each of 8 days of conditioning the subjects received eight trials with each of two CSs, with 4-min intertrial intervals and a sequence that balanced first order sequential probabilities. One of the stimuli, CS_N, was simply reinforced on each of its occasions, i.e., was involved in the sequence CS—US. The other stimulus, CS_{US}, was similarly reinforced, but was also preceded 4 sec earlier by a US, i.e., was involved in the sequence US—CS—US. What was anticipated from the priming notion was that, in a within-subject comparison of the degree of conditioning to CS_N and CS_{US}, acquisition would be diminished to the latter cue: The pretrial US should have introduced US representation into STM which could then be expected to persist over the time intervals involved (see Terry & Wagner, 1975; Wagner et al., 1973) to decrease the effectiveness of the reinforcing US when presented. Conditioned responding was evaluated on the training trials just described and on selected daily test trials, which were special in the case of CS_{US} in that the priming US was then omitted.

Figure 5 summarizes the findings. As may be seen, there was less conditioned responding to CS_{US} than to CS_N over the several blocks of training days. This was true on the training trials on which CS_{US} had just been preceded by a priming US but CS_N had not (see left panel), and equally so on the test trials when the differential priming stimulus was removed (see right panel). Such a general decrement in conditioned responding to CS_{US} as compared to CS_N is indicative of a reduced level of conditioning to the former CS. And, it is consistent with the priming formulation: A blocking-like effect should be as producible following self-generated priming of the US as following retrieval-generated priming of the US.

The data of Fig. 5, of course, do not settle the issue, any more than the simple demonstration of blocking, as seen in Fig. 2, necessarily indicates that in that case the variation in conditioning was due to differences in effectiveness of the reinforcing US. Indeed, we must entertain some of the same reasonable

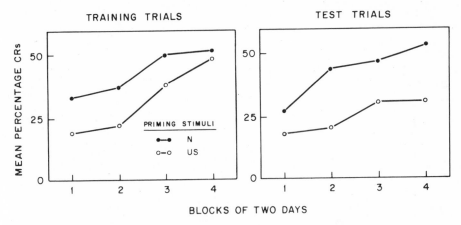

FIG. 5.   Mean percentage conditioned responding to two CSs on CS–US training trials, in which one CS was preceded by a priming stimulus (US) and the other was not (N), and on isolated test trials. (Reprinted from Terry, 1976. Copyright 1976 by the American Psychological Association. Reprinted by permission.)

alternatives, e.g., that the deficit in conditioning to CS_{US} as compared to CS_N was due to some deficit in CS processing. Perhaps the priming US acted to mask or overshadow the following CS (or all subsequent stimuli) rather than to influence uniquely the effectiveness of the subsequent, similar US.

Terry (1976) commented upon the latter possibility in relationship to the priming notion by way of two further experiments. According to the priming notion, a pretrial US will diminish the conditioning that results from a following CS–US pairing only to the degree that the pretrial and trial USs are the same, i.e., to the degree that the representation placed in Short-term Memory by the priming stimulus corresponds to the representation that would otherwise be provoked by the subsequent stimulus. Furthermore, according to the priming notion, a pretrial US should diminish conditioning only to the degree that its representation is allowed to persist in STM until the trial occasion. If representation is disrupted by presentation of "distractor" events, the priming effect, per se, should be removed, even if it then should be assumed that the distractor is occupying STM. Neither of these predictions appear to follow from the assumption that the priming US has only a more general disruptive effect on subsequent stimulus processing.

In the first of the two studies, Terry took advantage of the fact that in his experimental preparation he could arbitrarily select the area of the right or the left eye to receive the conditioning US (and from which then to record conditioned responding), and he could equally choose to use as a priming US the exact same US or one which was as equivalent as possible in all respects except that it was delivered to the other location. If the priming US is effective only to the degree that it matches the subsequent conditioning US, it should make a dif-

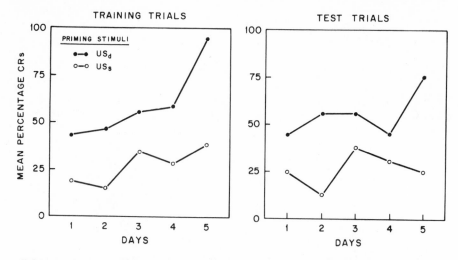

FIG. 6.   Mean percentage conditioned responding in two groups where the priming US was either the same (US$_s$) or different (US$_d$) from the subsequent conditioning US. (Reprinted from Terry, 1976. Copyright 1976 by the American Psychological Association. Reprinted by permission.)

ference whether or not the two stimuli were delivered to the same location. Alternatively, if a priming US is effective by virtue of masking or overshadowing the subsequent auditory, visual, or vibrotactual CS, it should not make any difference, everything else being equal, whether or not it was delivered to the same location as the subsequent conditioning US.

Two groups of rabbits were conditioned to a single CS according to the same general procedures as in the preceding experiment. In this case, however, each training trial was always preceded by 4 sec by a priming US. The only difference in the treatment of the two groups was whether the priming US was consistently delivered to the same eye or the different eye as the conditioning US. As in other cases, the stimulus assignments were otherwise counterbalanced, i.e., in each group half of the subjects had the priming US delivered to the right eye, half to the left; half of the subjects had the conditioning US delivered to the right eye, half to the left. What distinguished the groups, as noted, was only whether the priming US was then delivered to the same eye (designated as US$_s$) or the different eye (designated as US$_d$) as the subsequent conditioning US.

Figure 6 summarizes the percentage conditioned responding observed in the two groups on training trials and on daily test trials in which the priming US was omitted, as in the case of the preceding experiment. The data are unambiguous. There was less evidence of conditioning in the group in which the priming US was the same as the reinforcing US, as compared to that in which the priming US was different from the reinforcing US. Such specificity of effect obviously encourages the notion that a priming US uniquely alters the effectiveness of subsequent similar stimulation, i.e., the reinforcing US, while discouraging the assumption that the blocking-like effect seen in the previous study should be attributed to a more general interference effect, such as the masking or overshadowing of the CS involved.

Terry's (1976) second follow-up study reinforces this conclusion. Four groups of rabbits were conditioned. Group N had no pretrial stimuli scheduled, and simply received CS–US pairings on every trial. Group US received a priming US presentation 7 sec prior to the onset of each training trial, i.e., the sequence US–CS–US. These two groups correspond to the CS_N and CS_{US} conditions, respectively, of Terry's first experiment, but in a between-groups design. Group US+D received a priming US 7 sec before each training trial as did Group US, but in addition received a "distractor" stimulus (D) beginning 2 sec after the priming US and 5 sec before the CS–US pairing, i.e., the sequence US–D–CS–US. Finally, Group D received only the "distractor" stimulus in the same location as Group US+D, i.e., the sequence D–CS–US.

The distractor stimulus was a 1-sec, irregular sequence of auditory clicks and vibrotactual stimulation designed to have a different pattern on each occasion. The intention was to make this stimulus sufficiently salient and novel so as to command the subject's attention in STM. To the degree that this was so, and to the degree that STM can be assumed to be a limited-capacity device, D could then be supposed to act to displace representation of the priming US in Group US+D. In this case a priming deficit should not be anticipated in Group US+D as it should be in Group US.

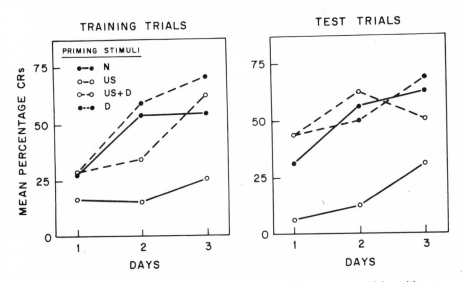

FIG. 7.   Mean percentage conditioned responding in four groups receiving either no priming stimulus (N), a priming US (US), a priming US followed by a distractor (US+D) or a distractor alone (D). (Reprinted from Terry, 1976. Copyright 1976 by the American Psychological Association. Reprinted by permission.)

The experiment comments upon alternatives to the priming notion in a manner similar to the preceding study. A deficit is expected not simply to the degree that *something* is represented in STM at the time of the CS–US trial, but to the degree that the *US* is represented. If US representation can be removed by a distractor interposed between the priming US and the CS–US trial there should be an increase in the conditioning that results. The inclusion of Group D in the design was obviously to evaluate the unlikely possibility that the distractor itself would improve conditioning, in the absence of US priming.

Figure 7 depicts the conditioned responding observed in each of the four groups over three days of training. Again, test trials were included in which the pretrial stimuli were omitted and the data from these trials are displayed separately. The pattern is obvious and consistent, however. Group US evidenced substantially less conditioning than Group N. In contrast Group US+D was not suppressed in its level of conditioned responding. There were no reliable differences among Group N, Group D, or Group US+D, but all were reliably more responsive than Group US, on training and on test trials.

Terry (1976) and Terry and Wagner (Note 1), have followed this research with several studies that add some details and have additional implications for our treatment of the priming phenomenon. The major point, however, is contained in the above studies: A blocking-like effect is observed under conditions of self-generated priming as under conditions of retrieval-generated priming. The available evidence concerning the specificity of the effect and its susceptibility to interference is consistent with the assumption that the locus of the effect is in a diminished rehearsal of the subsequent US. Presentation of a Pavlovian US does not appear to promote associative learning when that US is being remembered in STM.

B. Other Measures

The schema of Fig. 1 predicts the same range of deficits in effectiveness of a primed US in instances of self-generated priming as in instances of retrieval-generated priming. Thus we should be encouraged to look, as we specifically did in the case of surprising vs. expected USs (Terry & Wagner, 1975; Wagner et al., 1973), beyond the conditioning that is produced, to see that a primed US otherwise shows less evidence of being rehearsed by the subject than does a nonprimed US. In the case of self-generated priming, we have less evidence than in the case of retrieval-generated priming, but that which is available is equally supportive.

The rather obvious first place to look is at the unconditioned response to the US. If a primed US is less likely to be rehearsed in STM we might expect to see a less persistent or less vigorous UCR. Indeed, we might have included under the evidence relevant to retrieval-generated priming the phenomenon called "conditioned diminution of the UCR" (Kimble & Ost, 1961; Kimmel, 1966), which is a reduction in the amplitude of a UCR that can be shown to be under the control of an associated CS (e.g., the diminution is specific to occasions in which the CS precedes the US, and is "extinguished" by CS-alone presentations). Unfortunately, we have less information concerning UCR variations in our eyelid-conditioning preparation than might be expected. As a practical matter, our recording system does not capture the full UCR when set to provide sufficient amplification for discerning smaller CRs. Thus, UCR data have not been routinely available, e.g., from the above studies of Terry (1976). However, even if such data had been available, it is unlikely that they would have been informative. In unpublished studies we have observed that the amplitude of the rabbits' unconditioned eyelid response is relatively indifferent to variation in US parameters within wide ranges around those we normally employ in conditioning. From the same studies, we know that self-generated priming effects can be seen in a reduction in probability of the eyelid response to a *threshold* US, but we have not as yet collected substantial analytic data under these conditions.

The measure we have exploited is the vasoconstriction response, recorded from the ear of the rabbit under conditions of restraint identical to those in our eyelid conditioning studies. A particular advantage of this response, in addition to its potential variability in amplitude or duration, is that normally it may be evoked by any of a variety of stimuli. Thus, it becomes an easy experimental task to determine whether or not any change in responsivity, as expected from the priming notion, has the degree of stimulus specificity demanded. Two studies from a recent dissertation conducted in our laboratory by Jesse Whitlow (1975) indicate how this is the case.

In order to assess the possibility that there is a transient stimulus-specific decrement in unconditioned responding produced by recent stimulation, Whitlow (1975) presented rabbits with a series of 1-sec tones, equally often 530 Hz and 4,000 Hz. The series was arranged with successive pairs of tones being separated by 150 sec, and the members within each pair (designated as S_1 and S_2) separated by 30, 60, or 150 sec in an irregular counterbalanced order. It was expected that a refractory-like response decrement would be observed in variation in responding to S_2 as a function of the $S_1 - S_2$ interval. However, it was arranged that on half of the $S_1 - S_2$ pairs, involving each interstimulus interval, the two stimuli were the same (equally often 530 Hz or 4,000 Hz) while on the remaining pairs the two stimuli were different (equally 530 Hz followed by 4,000 Hz, or 4,000 Hz followed by 530 Hz). It was thus possible to evaluate the degree to which any decremental effect of the input stimulus (S_1) was specific to the occasions in which it matched the test stimulus (S_2) as suggested by the priming notion.

The study was run over two 2-hr sessions and involved 48 $S_1 - S_2$ pairs. There was an overall decrease in response to the respective stimuli in the pairs with repetitive stimulation (see Whitlow, 1975). But, the major data of interest can be seen in Fig. 8 which plots the averaged evoked vasoconstriction response at successive 5-sec intervals, following S_1, and then S_2, over all pairs in which the interstimulus interval was either 30, 60, or 150 sec, and separately for those pairs in which the stimuli were the same vs. different tones. The principal finding is obvious and highly reliable. When S_2 followed S_1 by 30 sec there was a substantial depression in the vasoconstriction evoked by the same as compared to the different tone. When S_2 followed S_1 by 60 sec this difference was smaller, although still quite apparent. However, when S_2 followed S_1 by 150 sec there was no longer a detectable depression in responding to S_2, as the subjects responded equivalently when S_2 was the same or different from the preceding stimulus. There is, in this preparation, evidence of a stimulus-specific response decrement that dissipates over the tested intervals in a manner congruent with our priming assumptions.

Granted this finding, it was then possible for Whitlow to ask whether or not an extraneous stimulus that should compete for occupancy of STM would act to remove the stimulus-specific response decrement in a manner analogous to

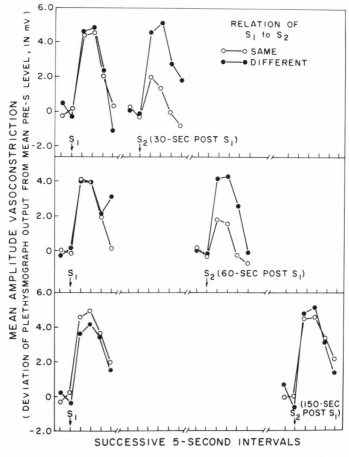

FIG. 8.   Mean average evoked responses to successive auditory stimuli, S_1 and S_2, when the two were the same or different frequencies. Plotted separately in the top, middle and bottom panels, respectively, are the responses to those stimuli separated by 30, 60, and 150 sec. (Reprinted from Whitlow, 1975. Copyright 1975 by the American Psychological Association. Reprinted by permission.)

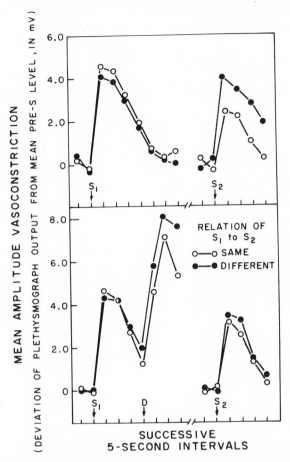

FIG. 9.   Mean average evoked responses to successive auditory stimuli, S_1 and S_2, when the two were the same or different frequencies. Plotted separately are the responses to those pairs involving no intervening stimulation (top panel) and those pairs separated by a distractor stimulus, D, as indicated (bottom panel). (Reprinted from Whitlow, 1975. Copyright 1975 by the American Psychological Association. Reprinted by permission.)

the Terry (1976) observation. The experiment was closely patterned after the previous study with the exceptions that (a) the $S_1 - S_2$ interval was consistently 60 sec, and (b) on half of each of the occasions in which S_2 was the same tone as S_1 or was different from S_1, the interval included a distractor stimulus 20 sec after S_1 and thus 40 sec prior to S_2. From the data presented in Fig. 8, it could be expected that in the absence of the distractor stimulus there would be ample stimulus-specific response decrement to S_2 at this $S_1 - S_2$ interval. The question was whether or not the distractor (which was a sequential compound of a 1-sec flashing light and a 1-sec electrotactile stimulation of the cheek) would remove the decrement, as extending the duration of the $S_1 - S_2$ interval to 150 sec had been found to do.

Figure 9 summarizes the relevant data in the same manner as Fig. 8. When there was no intervening stimulation (see top panel) the response to S_2 was reduced on occasions in which S_1 was the same stimulus relative to occasions on which S_1 was a different stimulus. When the distractor was presented between S_1 and S_2 (see bottom panel), it produced an evoked response itself, but more importantly, it removed any differential effect upon S_2 responding of the same vs. different S_1 events. These findings are what one would expect if the stimulus-specific response decrement were dependent upon a perseverating representation of the test stimulus in STM, and the distractor acted to remove such representation.

There are a variety of reasons why the unconditioned response to a stimulus might be reduced on the second of two temporally adjacent presentations. Sensory adaptation or response system fatigue are two obvious possibilities and each would lead one to expect a recovery function. Whitlow's (1975) studies are particularly informative in indicating that such accounts would not suffice. The stimulus-specificity of the decrement argues against simple response system fatigue, while the restorative effect of the distractor is outside of our notions of what might remove sensory adaptation. The distractor, furthermore, did not appear to act as a general sensitizer. It appears preferable to suppose that the refractory-like response decrement as observed by Whitlow (1975) is due to the persistence of S_1 representation in STM. We can then assume that S_2, if it is the same as S_1, will be less likely than it otherwise would be to occasion full processing (rehearsal) in STM.

V. EXTRAPOLATION

There are a considerable number of implications of the priming notion for phenomena outside of the data domain which initially provoked the formulation. In the space available I will mention just two that are particularly relevant to the overall theme of the paper. Even thus restricted, the discussion will necessarily be rather superficial. But it should suffice to indicate certain potentialities for theoretical interpretation and some promising areas for further research.

A. Distribution of Trials

First, consider the implications of the model for distribution-of-trials phenomena. What is performed and what is learned on trial n of a sequence of training trials should depend importantly on what remains in STM from preceding trials. In some situations the dependencies may be relatively complex (see, e.g., Pfautz & Wagner, 1976), but a rather simple set of expectations can be seen to be confirmed by a dissertation conducted in our laboratory by Michael Davis (1970). The study was provoked by the authoritative assertion of Thompson and Spencer (1966) that one of the nine defining characteristics of "habituation" is that it proceeds faster the shorter the intertrial interval. This is an adequate characterization of the response decrement seen with repeated stimulation at different fixed intervals, but seemed to us likely to be an oversimplification if there is any short-term, refractory-like decrement in stimulus processing as we have now seen in the Whitlow (1975) studies. Then one might well expect to see, throughout an habituation sequence, less unconditioned responding to a stimulus the shorter the time since its last presentation, i.e., the more likely it was still represented in STM. But if an habituation decrement also follows from alterations in Long-term Memory, such alterations might be *less* likely to be witnessed the shorter the intertrial interval.

Davis employed a stabilimeter device to measure the startle response of the rat to 50-msec, 4,000-Hz tones that increased the sound pressure level from 80 to 120 db. In an initial prehabituation test and an identical posthabituation test, all subjects were exposed to a series of 300 tones during which the interstimulus interval was varied among 2, 4, 8, and 16 sec in an order that equated the first-, second-, and third-order sequential probabilities. Between these two tests all subjects received an habituation series of 1,000 tone stimulations, half of the subjects with a constant 2-sec interstimulus interval, the remainder with a constant 16-sec interval.

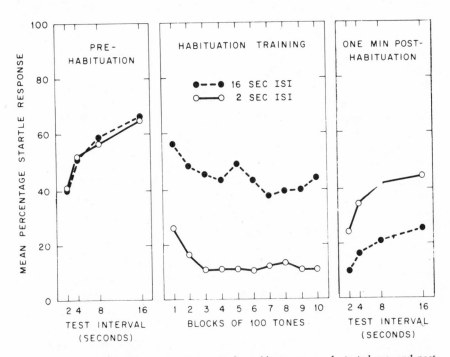

FIG. 10.   Mean percentage startle response for subjects commonly tested pre- and post-habituation at each of 4 interstimulus intervals (ISI), but segregated into separate groups with intervening habituation at either a constant 2- or 16-sec ISI. (Reprinted from Davis, 1970. Copyright 1970 by the American Psychological Association. Reprinted by permission.)

Figure 10 presents a summary of percentage startle responses during each of the three experimental phases for two groups of animals which received the post-habituation test series beginning 1 min after the habituation sequence. The important findings to be noted are as follows: (1) In each of the pre- and post-habituation test series the probability of startle on any trial n was an increasing function of the interval separating trial n from trial $n - 1$, i.e., a subject was less likely to startle the shorter the interval on that occasion; (2) During the habituation sequence with a constant 2- or 16-sec interstimulus interval in the separate groups, a similar pattern was quite evident, i.e., when the stimuli were consistently separated by 2-sec intervals there was a lower level of responding than when the stimuli were consistently separated by 16-sec intervals; (3) The striking finding, in relationship to this pattern, is that when the two habituation groups were subsequently tested again at all interstimulus intervals, the group that had received habituation exposures at 16-sec intervals was much less responsive than the group that had received habituation exposures at 2-sec intervals, and this difference was apparent at all interstimulus intervals during the posttest, e.g., whether at 2 sec, or 16 sec after the immediately preceding trial.

This pattern can be interpreted as perfectly consistent with the present notions concerning the priming of STM. When a stimulus is repeated on the occasions of S_1 and S_2, we assume that the shorter the interstimulus interval the more likely the stimulus will still be represented in STM at the time of S_2. To the degree that this is so, S_2 should be less likely to initiate the rehearsal it otherwise would in STM. Thus, it may (a) be less likely to produce a vigorous unconditioned response and (b) be less likely to produce an increment in long-term memory that would be revealed in an habituation decrement on a remote test. The subject appears to respond to S_2, and learn from S_2, only to the degree that it is not at the time remembering S_1.

It need be added that there are other possibilities for interpreting the better long-term memory with longer $S_1 - S_2$ intervals, even within our framework. It is just as likely, for example, that the shorter the $S_1 - S_2$ interval, the less learning is produced by S_1. Too soon an application of S_2 may prevent the subject from benefiting from the full rehearsal of S_1 that would otherwise have occurred. We have not as yet carried out the kinds of analytical studies that would allow us to decide among such alternatives in an habituation situation as employed by Davis. It is notable, however, that exactly the same interpretive issue has arisen in studies of human memory, and that there are some suggestive data that would locate a processing decrement on the occasion of S_2. When subjects are given a list of words, nonsense syllables, pictures, or paired associates in a paced serial fashion, and are then tested after some retention interval in recall (e.g., Greeno, 1964) or recognition (e.g., Hintzman & Block, 1970), a "spacing effect" occurs. That is, if an item is presented *twice* in the list, on the occasions of S_1 and S_2, subsequent retention performance increases as the $S_1 - S_2$ interval increases from 0 to 15 sec, while further lengthening the interval beyond 15 sec has little further beneficial effect. Hintzman (1974), after reviewing the available literature, concluded that this spacing effect is more likely to be a result of diminished processing of S_2 than a lack of full opportunity to process S_1, the shorter the S_1-S_2 interval. A major piece of evidence cited was a study by Bjork and Allen (1970) in which easy or difficult distractor tasks were inserted in the S_1-S_2 interval. Somewhat *better* retention was observed with the difficult than with the easy distractor tasks. Assuming that the more difficult task was more effective in removing S_1 representation from STM, it should thereby have produced poorer learning from S_1. It is reasonable, therefore, to assume that the increased performance with a difficult distractor task was a result of better processing of S_2, that was otherwise especially prevented by the representation of S_1 in STM. In accordance with this reasoning, Hintzman (1974) favored an "habituation" account of the spacing effect, which is very similar to the present notion of "self-generated" priming.

B. CS Processing

As a second implication of the priming notion, consider what it should tell us about CS processing in Pavlovian conditioning. In presenting data relevant to presumed variations in US processing, possible variations in CS processing were mentioned only as an alternative that needed to be discounted. However, there is no reason to suppose that what has been proposed with respect to self-generated or retrieval-generated priming is peculiar to unconditioned stimuli within a Pavlovian conditioning paradigm. Indeed, the findings of Whitlow (1975) and Davis (1970) on the short-term and long-term response decrements to repetitive stimulation should generalize as well as to either CSs or USs in Pavlovian conditioning.

A CS should be less likely to initiate rehearsal if that stimulus has recently been presented so as to still be represented in STM. Following earlier reasoning we might then expect that the priming of CS representation in STM would have at least two notable effects. If a CS has been previously associated with a US, it might, under conditions of priming, be a less effective retrieval cue than it otherwise would be. And, when a CS is first paired with a US, it might, under conditions of priming, be less likely to form association with the US than it otherwise would be. There are now data to confirm each of these expectations.

Pfautz and Wagner (1976) investigated the former possibility in rabbit eyelid conditioning by training subjects to several CSs and then presenting test occasions in which a given target CS was preceded by 2.5, 5, or 10 sec by either the same or a different CS, or was recently preceded by no stimulation. As compared to the latter condition, prior presentation of a *different* CS augmented conditioned responding to the target CS, and the more so the shorter the interstimulus interval. In contrast, the important observation was that prior presentation of the *same* CS depressed conditioned responding to the target CS, and the more so the shorter the interstimulus interval. To interpret these results, Pfautz and Wagner (1976) essentially argued that any persisting representation of a priming CS had two effects: (1) that of acting as a retrieval cue for the US representation, thus tending to facilitate conditioned responding at the time of the target CS, and (2) that of acting to prevent rehearsal, and further retrieval action, of the target CS, but only if the target CS were the same as the priming stimulus.

Primavera and Wagner (Note 2) followed the results of Pfautz and Wagner (1976) by asking whether a distractor event, interposed between the priming and target CS occasions, would remove the decremental effects seen when the two CSs are the same. The reasoning as to why this should be the case is identical to that which we have employed in discussing the Terry (1976) and Whitlow (1975) dissertations. The study is particularly important, however, in that it comments on an alternative interpretation of the effects of CS priming as seen in the Pfautz and Wagner (1976) study. The priming CS is, of course, presented by itself prior to the target CS. But, this is then a *nonreinforced* CS exposure, and could be thought to be effective because it "extinguishes" the association between that particular CS and the US. We might be reluctant to argue that an extinction effect regresses with time between the priming and target CS, as would be necessary to accommodate the temporal data of Pfautz and Wagner (1976). But then, we would be more reluctant to suppose that it could be removed by the interposition of a distractor between the priming and target CS, as follows from the present formulation. Primavera and Wagner (Note 2) used CER conditioning of rats, first pairing a 30-sec tone CS with a shock US, and then in a later session evaluating conditioned responding in terms of the suppression of drinking during a 180-sec presentation of the CS. In testing, the latter CS was preceded by different events for each of four groups of subjects: by no stimulation (Group *N*), by a 30-sec priming CS 300 sec before the target (Group CS), by the same priming CS followed 30 sec later by a distractor (Group CS+D), or by the distractor alone (Group D). The distractor in this study was the ill-specified, but effective, complex of auditory, visual, and mechanical stimulation produced by opening the door of the isolation unit enclosing each experimental chamber, for 30 sec.

Figure 11 presents the continuous drinking records of the four groups, during the sequence of testing events described. As may be seen, licking was suppressed when either the CS or the distractor was presented, to then recover. The major findings are in the licking of the four groups during the final target CS. Group CS was reliably less suppressed than Group N — the basic priming effect. In contrast, Group CS+D was *not* less suppressed than Group N — interposing the distractor between the priming and target CS removed any detectable effect of the priming CS. Finally, Group D was indistinguishable from Group N — the distractor did not itself appear to influence subsequent response to the target CS. The target CS appeared to be a less effective retrieval cue when CS representation could be assumed to have been primed in STM and not to have been displaced by the competing distractor.

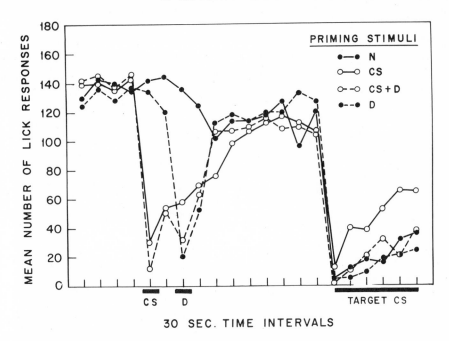

FIG. 11.   Mean number of lick responses in successive 30-sec intervals during a test sequence for 4 groups. The target CS, previously paired with a shock US, was either preceded by no stimulation (N), by a priming CS (CS), by a priming CS followed by a distractor (CS+D), or by a distractor alone (D). The labels on the abscissa indicate the occasion for each stimulus, when scheduled in the respective groups.

We have less data relevant to the question of whether or not a recent CS exposure will diminish the *association* that can result from a CS–US pairing. The obvious way to approach this question is with studies analogous to those in the Terry (1976) dissertation, concerned with US priming. We should see that a sequence of CS–CS–US will produce less evidence of conditioning than a simple sequence of CS–US, *when conditioning is assessed on CS–alone occasions* as well as in training. We should see that the depressed conditioning under the former sequence is greater when the priming CS is the same as the trial CS, as compared to when it is a different CS. And, we should see that the effects of CS priming are reduced by placing a distractor between the priming and trial CS. Unfortunately, our available data are too provisional to report at this time.

In this case, however, we are strongly encouraged by studies from other laboratories. An especially illuminating study has been reported by Best and Gemberling (1977). This study addressed a phenomenon originally reported by Kalat and Rozin (1973). The latter authors had compared the conditioned taste aversion produced by each of three treatments: One group (CS_{30}–US) received a taste CS 30 min prior to lithium chloride–induced toxicosis; a second group

(CS_{240}–US) received the same taste CS 240 min prior to toxicosis; the third group (CS_{240}–CS_{30}–US) received two exposures to the taste CS, the first 240 min and the second 30 min prior to toxicosis. As would be expected from the differential temporal relationships, Group CS_{30}–US showed more of a subsequent taste aversion than did Group CS_{240}–US. The interesting observation, however, was that although Group CS_{240}–CS_{30}–US had the same final CS–US pairing as did Group CS_{30}–US, it showed substantially less aversion to the CS, and indeed no more than was observed in Group CS_{240}–US. Kalat and Rozin (1973) interpreted these data as indicative of what they termed a "learned-safety" effect: The longer the interval that the animal was granted following a taste CS in which a noxious event did *not* occur, the more it would presumably learn that the taste was safe and hence not to be avoided. A longer safety interval was provided in Group CS_{240}–CS_{30}–US (and in Group CS_{240}–US) than in Group CS_{30}–US.

Best and Gemberling (1977) argued instead that the data might reflect a CS-priming effect, with less conditioning produced in the double CS case due to the persistence of the initial CS representation at the time of the terminal CS–US pairing. Among the data from several experiments reported by Best and Gemberling (1977), the theoretically most decisive came from double CS treatments in which the initial CS exposure was made increasingly more removed than 240 min from the final CS–US pairing. As this was done there was not a systematic decrease in taste aversion as would be expected from the learned safety view, but rather a systematic *increase* as would be expected from the priming notion. As it was made less likely that the initial CS would still be represented in STM at the time of the second CS, association of the latter CS and the US was apparently increased.

The generality of this phenomenon is made to seem more likely by the fact that there are again data from human learning that foreshadow our animal findings. Horowitz and Newman (1969) ran a paired-associate learning study, in which each stimulus–response pair took 5 sec to present, four 1-sec intervals for the stimulus term, and one 1-sec interval for the response term. In one condition the stimulus was presented four times in the trial sequence S–S–S–S–R. In the other condition the stimulus term was presented only twice separated by blank intervals (0) in the sequence S–0–0–S–R. Learning was much faster in the latter condition than in the former. When the terminal S–R pairing was preceded by recent S presentation we can assume a self-generated priming that would diminish stimulus processing necessary for associative learning.

As a final comment on the potential influences on CS processing, we should note that CS rehearsal may be affected, just as is US rehearsal, by retrieval-generated priming. Thus, for example, a CS may be less likely to form new associations with a consequent US when it is expected via the retrieval action of other stimuli than when it is surprising. CSs, of course, are not generally announced in Pavlovian conditioning by other explicit signals as are USs, but we might assume that they can become expected on the basis of contextual cues, just as we have assumed with good evidence (e.g., Blanchard & Honig, 1976; Dweck & Wagner, 1970; Sheafor, 1975) that USs can come to be signalled by contextual cues.

When discussing the Davis (1970) dissertation, we pointed to evidence that a long-term habituation effect was favored by longer interstimulus intervals. We did not, however, explicate what alterations in LTM were presumably responsible for such an effect. What we have assumed (Wagner, 1976) is that associations are formed between contextual cues and the habituating stimulus so that the contextual cues can lead to a retrieval-generated priming of STM, and thus to a relatively permanent decrement in the measured response to the stimulus. The response decrement, seen to iterated stimulation in habituation experiments, is assumed to be the consistent result of the priming of STM, although we can conceptually distinguish between that priming that may be attributed to recent presentation of the stimulus (self-generated priming) and to the signalling action of contextual cues (retrieval-generated priming). What should be obvious is that we would hold the same position with respect to iterated presentations of a potential CS in Pavlovian conditioning. We would only add that another index of the lack of rehearsal of such a stimulus is a reduction in its likelihood of being associated with a consequent US.

"Latent inhibition" is the term that is commonly used to recognize the long-term decrement in associability of an "habituated" CS. The phenomenon is powerful and easy to demonstrate (see, e.g., Lubow, 1973). From our perspective, the major question at this time is whether or not this decrement in associability, along with other measures of long-term habituation, can be shown to be dependent upon the acquired signalling value of the available contextual stimuli. There is some evidence that long-term habituation (e.g., Peeke & Vino, 1973) and latent inhibition (e.g., Anderson, O'Farrell, Formica, & Caponegri, 1969) are context specific, but there are remarkably few relevant studies.

Perhaps the most interesting prediction from the present theory is that habituation and latent inhibition should be subject to "extinction." That is, following a series of stimulus presentations in context, sufficient to produce a decrement in response or a decrement in associability on a remote test, we should be able to produce recovery by exposing the animal to the experimental environment in the absence of the habituated stimulus. The context should thus lose its ability to prime the effective stimulus representation in STM, just as would any "non-reinforced" signal.

A relevant habituation study was conducted in collaboration with Jesse W. Whitlow and Penn L. Pfautz (reported in Wagner, 1976), using the same vasomotor preparation employed by Whitlow (1975). In initial training, two groups of rabbits were subjected to a 2-hr habituation session during which a 1-sec tonal stimulus was presented on 32 occasions with a 150-sec interstimulus interval. The frequency of the habituation stimulus was for half of each group 530 Hz and for the re-

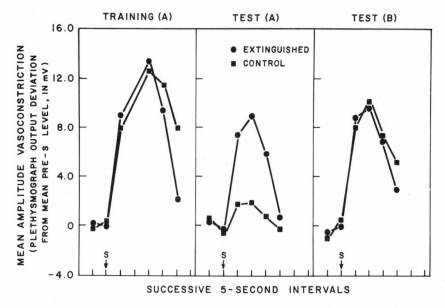

FIG. 12.   Mean average auditory evoked response in each of two groups of rabbits. The successive panels present the response to the first 2 presentations of a subsequently habituated tone A, to the first 2 exposures to the same tone on a posthabituation retention test, and finally to 2 exposures to a novel tone B. Between habituation and testing one group (Extinguished) was exposed to the experimental environment in the absence of the habituated stimulus, the other group (Control) was not. (Reprinted from Wagner, 1976.)

mainder 4,000 Hz. All subjects were returned for a retention test 2 days later. The only difference in treatment of the two groups was that on the intervening day one group (Control) was simply left in their home cages, while the other group (Extinguished) was placed in the experimental chamber, had the recording apparatus attached, and was treated identically to the previous habituation session except that no tones were presented. On the retention day all subjects received a series of 32 exposures to the previously habituated tone, as in Session 1, and then received two test exposures to the alternate frequency tone.

Figure 12 summarizes the essential data from this experiment. In each panel is presented the averaged evoked response, at 5-sec intervals preceding and following the test stimulus, for each group. The left panel indicates the initial level of responding to the to-be-habituated stimulus (designated *A*), as it shows the averaged response to the first 2 tone presentations in the training session for each of the two groups. The middle panel indicates the responding of the two groups to the comparable two tone presentations at the beginning of the retention test session. The major effect is obvious in these data. Both groups evidenced an habituation decrement in their responding on the retention day as compared to the initial stimulation. However, whereas there was a very sizeable habituation decrement (an 85% reduction in response magnitude) seen in the case of the Control Group, there was a much smaller habituation decrement (a 34% reduction in response magnitude) seen in the case of the Extinguished Group.

The test trials to the nonhabituated tonal stimulus (designated B) were included in the retention session as a gross check that the extinction manipulation had not been effective by producing some general change in vasomotor responsivity. The right panel of Fig. 12 presents the evoked response to the novel tone. It is apparent that the two groups did not differ in their response to this stimulus whereas they did differ in their response to the previously habituated tone.

Wagner, Pfautz, and Donegan (Note 3) have replicated the essential findings of the above study in two assessments of latent inhibition, in rabbit eyelid conditioning and in CER conditioning with rats. Thus, we are encouraged in our general assumptions concerning the retrieval-generated priming of STM by contextual cues. It remains an important matter for future research, however, to evaluate the generality of these assumptions in regard to various measures of habituation and latent inhibition, and to begin to isolate the controlling stimuli that are presumably implicated.

VI. CONCLUDING COMMENTS

Several years ago Robert Rescorla and I collaborated in an effort to capture certain of the process speculations of Kamin (1969) and ourselves (Rescorla, 1969; Wagner, 1969) within a quantitative equation for Pavlovian conditioning (Rescorla & Wagner, 1972; Wagner & Recorla, 1972). We were primarily concerned with the interpretations of blocking-like studies (e.g., Kamin, 1969) that suggested differential effects of surprising vs. expected USs. What we proposed is that the increment in associative strength (ΔV) that would accrue to a component CS, i, could be represented as

$$\Delta V_i = a\beta (\lambda - \overline{V}), \tag{1}$$

where a and β are rate parameters determined by the characteristics of the CS and US, respectively, λ is the asymptotic associative strenth supportable by the US, and $\overline{V}$ is the US–signaling value of the aggregation of antecedent cues. We could identify the quantity ($\lambda - \overline{V}$) with our less formal statements concerning how surprising was the US, and thus convey the notion that the more surprising, the more learning should occur.

This proposition has enjoyed some success in dealing with blocking-like studies that I have here discussed in connection with a presumed retrieval-generated priming of the US. It may lend understanding to the remaining process speculations in which I have engaged to see how they might be accommodated in the spirit of the Rescorla-Wagner model.

Consider the implication of the notion of self-generated US priming as presumably witnessed in the Terry (1976) study. What might be proposed is that

$$\Delta V_i = a\beta \left[\lambda - (\overline{V} + K)\right],   \tag{2}$$

where $\overline{V} + K$ stands for the total US representation in STM at the time of US presentation, $\overline{V}$ summarizing what is a result of the signaling value of preceding retrieval cues, K summarizing what persists from prior application of the same US; K would presumably decay with time since the last US and be reduced to negligible value by other, intervening "distractor" events.

I have suggested that we may further need to reckon with changes in CS effectiveness as a CS may also be variously prerepresented in STM by the retrieval action of situational cues or by the persistence from recent CS exposure. We could then assume that

$$\Delta V_i = a \left[l - (\overline{v} + k)\right] \beta \left[\lambda - (\overline{V} + K)\right],   \tag{3}$$

where the terms in the initial parenthetical quantity are exactly analogous to those in the latter parenthetical quantity, except that they are identified with the asymptotic conditioning that can be supported by the CS (l), the degree to which the CS is predicted by the aggregation of preceding stimuli ($\overline{v}$) and the degree of CS representation that persists in STM from prior stimulation (k). In this manner we could acknowledge that the associative learning between a CS and US is dependent on memorial factors that equivalently influence the likelihood of the individual stimuli being rehearsed on any trial.

I do not know how useful such particular algebraic formulation may be at the present time, or that the specific changes in the Rescorla-Wagner model that are suggested are the most necessary in order to bring the model in line with available data (see, e.g., Rescorla, 1974; Blough, 1975; Mackintosh, 1975). But it is instructive and esthetically pleasing that the underlying conceptualization can be so satisfactorily generalized.

ACKNOWLEDGMENTS

Preparation of this chapter and portions of the research reported were supported by National Science Foundation Grant BMS 74-20521. Among the several collaborators in the research project, special acknowledgment is due William S. Terry, Nelson Donegan, Penn L. Pfautz, and Judith Primavera for their individual and collective contributions to the present report.

NOTES

1. Terry, W. S., & Wagner, A. R. *The effects of US priming on CR performance and acquisition.* Prepublication manuscript, 1977.
2. Primavera, J., & Wagner, A. R. *The effects of CS priming on performance of the Conditioned Emotional Response.* Prepublication manuscript, 1977.
3. Wagner, A. R., Pfautz, P. L., & Donegan, N. *The extinction of stimulus-exposure effects.* Prepublication manuscript, 1977.

REFERENCES

Amsel, A. The role of frustrative nonreward in noncontinuous reward situations. *Psychological Bulletin,* 1958, *55,* 102–119.

Anderson, D. C., O'Farrell, T., Formica, R., & Caponegri, V. Preconditioning CS exposure: Variation in the place of conditioning and presentation. *Psychonomic Science,* 1969, *15,* 54–55.

Anderson, J., & Bower, G. *Human associative memory.* New York: Winston, 1973.

Atkinson, R. C., & Shiffrin, R. M. Human memory: A proposed system and its control processes. In K. W. Spence (Ed.), *The psychology of learning and motivation* (Vol. 2). New York: Academic Press, 1968.

Atkinson, R. C., & Wickens, T. D. Human memory and the concept of reinforcement. In R. Glaser (Ed.), *The Nature of Reinforcement.* New York: Academic Press, 1971.

Bartlett, F. C. *Remembering: A study in experimental and social psychology.* London and New York: Cambridge University Press, 1932.

Best, M. R., & Gemberling, G. A. The role of short-term processes in the CS preexposure effect and the delay of reinforcement gradient in long–delay taste–aversion learning. *Journal of Experimental Psychology: Animal Behavior Processes,* 1977, *3,* 253–263.

Bjork, R. A., & Allen, T. W. The spacing effect: Consolidation or differential coding? *Journal of Verbal Learning and Verbal Behavior,* 1970, *9,* 567–572.

Blanchard, R., & Honig, W. K. Surprise value of food determines its effectiveness as a reinforcer. *Journal of Experimental Psychology: Animal Behavior Processes,* 1976, *2,* 67–74.

Blough, D. S. Steady state data and a quantitative model of operant generalization and discrimination. *Journal of Experimental Psychology: Animal Behavior Processes,* 1975, *1,* 3–21.

Bobrow, D. G., & Norman, D. A. Some principles of memory schemata. In D. G. Bobrow and A. Collins (Eds.), *Representation and understanding.* New York: Academic Press, 1975.

Bower, G. H. Cognitive Psychology: An introduction. In W. K. Estes (Ed.), *Handbook of learning and cognitive processes* (Vol. 1). Hillsdale, New Jersey: Lawrence Erlbaum Associates, 1975.

Davis, M. Effects of interstimulus interval length and variability on startle-response habituation in the rat. *Journal of Comparative and Physiological Psychology,* 1970, *72,* 177–192.

Dweck, C. S., & Wagner, A. R. Situational cues and correlation between CS and US as determiners of the conditioned emotional response. *Psychonomic Science,* 1970, *18,* 145–147.

Estes, W. K. Structural aspects of associative models for memory. In C. C. Cofer (Ed.), *The Structure of Human Memory.* San Francisco: Freeman, 1975.

Greeno, J. G. Paired-associate learning with massed and spaced repetition of items. *Journal of Experimental Psychology*, 1964, *67*, 286–295.

Hintzman, D. L. Theoretical implications of the spacing effect. In R. L. Solso (Ed.), *Theories in cognitive psychology: The Loyola symposium*. Hillsdale, New Jersey: Lawrence Erlbaum Associates, 1974.

Hintzman, D. L., & Block, R. A. Memory judgments and the effects of spacing. *Journal of Verbal Learning and Verbal Behavior*, 1970, *9*, 561–566.

Hobhouse, L. T. *Mind in evolution*. London: Macmillan, 1915.

Horowitz, L. M., & Newman, W. An interrupted stimulus can facilitate P. S. learning. *Journal of Verbal Learning and Verbal Behavior*, 1969, *8*, 219–224.

Kalat, J. W., & Rozin, P. "Learned safety" as a mechanism in long delay taste-aversion learning in rats. *Journal of Comparative and Physiological Psychology*, 1973, *83*, 198–207.

Kamin, L. J. Predictability, surprise, attention and conditioning. In B. Campbell and R. Church (Eds.), *Punishment and aversive behavior*. New York: Appleton-Century-Crofts, 1969.

Kimble, G. A., & Ost, J. W. P. A conditioned inhibitory process in eyelid conditioning. *Journal of Experimental Psychology*, 1961, *61*, 150–156.

Kimmel, H. D. Inhibition of the unconditioned response in classical conditioning. *Psychological Review*, 1966, *73*, 232–240.

Konorski, J. *Integrative activity of the brain*. Chicago: Chicago University Press, 1967.

Lashley, K. S. An examination of the "continuity theory" as applied to discriminative learning. *Journal of General Psychology*, 1942, *26*, 241–265.

Lubow, R. E. Latent inhibition. *Psychological Bulletin*, 1973, *79*, 398–407.

Mackintosh, N. J. A theory of attention: Variations in the associability of stimuli with reinforcement. *Psychological Review*, 1975, *82*, 276–298.

Minsky, M. A framework for representing knowledge. In P. H. Winston (Ed.), *The psychology of computer vision*. New York: McGraw-Hill, 1975.

Morgan, C. L. *An introduction to comparative psychology*. London: Scott, 1894.

Mowrer, O. H. *Learning theory and behavior*. New York: Wiley, 1960.

Norman, D. A. Toward a theory of memory and attention. *Psychological Review*, 1968, *75*, 522–536.

Peeke, H. V. S., & Vino, G. Stimulus specificity of habituated aggression in three-spined sticklebacks (*Gasterosteus aculeatus*). *Behavioral Biology*, 1973, *8*, 427–432.

Pfautz, P. L., & Wagner, A. R. Transient variations in responding to Pavlovian conditioned stimuli have implications for the mechanism of "priming." *Animal Learning and Behavior*, 1976, *4*, 107–112.

Rescorla, R. A. Conditioned inhibition of fear. In W. K. Honig and N. J. Mackintosh (Eds.), *Fundamental issues in associative learning*. Halifax, Canada: Dalhousie University Press, 1969.

Rescorla, R. A. A model of Pavlovian conditioning. In V. S. Rusinov (Ed.), *Mechanism of formation and inhibition of conditioned reflex*. Moscow: Academy of Sciences of the USSR, 1974.

Rescorla, R. A., & Wagner, A. R. A theory of Pavlovian conditioning: Variations in the effectiveness of reinforcement and nonreinforcement. In A. H. Black and W. F. Prokasy (Eds.), *Classical conditioning II: Current theory and research*. New York: Appleton-Century-Crofts, 1972.

Schank, R. C. The role of memory in language processing. In C. Cofer (Ed.) *The structure of human memory*. San Francisco: Freeman, 1975.

Sheafor, P. J. "Pseudoconditioned" jaw movements of the rabbit reflect associations conditioned to contextual background cues. *Journal of Experimental Psychology: Animal Behavior Processes*, 1975, *1*, 245–260.

Shiffrin, R. M., & Schneider, W. Controlled and automatic information processing: II. Perceptual learning, automatic attending, and a general theory. *Psychological Review*, 1977, *84*, 127–190.

Spence, K. W. *Behavior theory and conditioning*. New Haven: Yale University Press, 1956.

Terry, W. S. The effects of priming US representation in short-term memory on Pavlovian conditioning. *Journal of Experimental Psychology: Animal Behavior Processes*, 1976, *2*, 354–370.

Terry, W. S., & Wagner, A. R. Short-term memory for "surprising" versus "expected" unconditioned stimuli in Pavlovian conditioning. *Journal of Experimental Psychology: Animal Behavior Processes*, 1975, *1*, 122–133.

Thompson, R. F., & Spencer, W. A. Habituation: A model phenomenon for the study of neuronal substrates of behavior. *Psychological Review*, 1966, *197*, 16–43.

Tolman, E. C. *Purposive Behavior in Animals and Men*. New York: Century, 1932.

Tulving, E. Retrograde amnesia in free recall. *Science*, 1969, *164*, 88–90.

Wagner, A. R. Frustration and punishment. In R. N. Haber (Ed.), *Current research in motivation*. New York: Holt, Rinehart and Winston, 1966.

Wagner, A. R. Stimulus selection and a "modified continuity theory." In G. H. Bower and J. T. Spence (Eds.), *The psychology of learning and motivation* (Vol. 3). New York: Academic Press, 1969.

Wagner, A. R. Elementary associations. In H. H. Kendler and J. T. Spence (Eds.), *Essays in neobehaviorism: A memorial volume to Kenneth W. Spence*. New York: Appleton-Century-Crofts, 1971.

Wagner, A. R. Priming in STM: An information processing mechanism for self-generated or retrieval-generated depression in performance. In T. J. Tighe and R. N. Leaton (Eds.), *Habituation: Perspectives from child development, animal behavior, and neurophysiology*. Hillsdale, New Jersey: Lawrence Erlbaum Associates, 1976, 95–128.

Wagner, A. R., & Rescorla, R. A. Inhibition in Pavlovian conditioning: Application of a theory. In R. A. Boakes and M. S. Halliday (Eds.), *Inhibition and learning*. New York: Academic Press, 1972.

Wagner, A. R., Rudy, J. W., & Whitlow, J. W. Rehearsal in animal conditioning. *Journal of Experimental Psychology*, 1973, *97*, 407–426. (Monograph).

Wagner, A. R., and Terry, W. S. Backward conditioning to a CS following an expected vs. a surprising UCS. *Animal Learning and Behavior*, 1975, *3*, 370–374.

Whitlow, J. W. Short-term memory in habituation and dishabituation. *Journal of Experimental Psychology: Animal Behavior Processes*, 1975, *1*, 189–206.

8 Studies of Working Memory in the Pigeon

Werner K. Honig
Dalhousie University

I. WORKING MEMORY, REFERENCE MEMORY, AND ASSOCIATIVE MEMORY

Several training situations have been devised in which animals have to base their discriminative behavior upon cues that terminate within a trial before they have the opportunity to make the correct response. The correct response must be guided by the memory of those cues, and the subject must generally ignore the memory of relevant stimuli from preceding trials. This situation necessitates the action of a *working memory* within each trial. It is the purpose of this chapter to review the conceptual status of working memory, especially in relation to other kinds of memory processes; to describe a few working memory procedures; to give an account of research on working memory in pigeons carried out in our laboratory; and to speculate upon an appropriate theoretical account of our results.

It is commonly agreed that learning involves at the very least the formation of associations between two or more stimuli, or between responses and stimuli which follow them. Once such associations are established, they become part of what may be called a *reference memory* of a given problem or discrimination. The reference memory, then, is the long–term maintenance of an acquired psychological structure. The factors governing the fate of reference memories in animals are assumed to be similar to those governing long-term memory in humans. Just as with human memory, there is no single, simple function to describe the forgetting of long-term reference memories. Forgetting may be very slow for highly trained subjects in a conditioning situation (Hoffman, Fleshler, & Jensen, 1963), or rather rapid in instrumental learning situations (Gleitman,

1971; Spear, 1971), especially when conflicting responses are required in separate problems. As with human long-term memory, interference and retrieval failure appear to be the primary mechanisms that underlie forgetting.

Within the present context, there are two important points to make about reference memory. First, reference memory is normally latent. Like long-term storage in human memory, reference memories are "inactive" (Lett, in press) until they are reactivated by the presentation of appropriate cues; this corresponds to retrieval or recall. Then the reference memory can control behavior. Second, a stable reference memory must be assumed for the maintenance of good performance on a problem. Sometimes poor performance due to the loss of reference memory is falsely blamed on attentional, motivational, or perceptual factors, or to an insufficient working memory. Poor performance caused by such factors may sometimes result in a deterioration of the reference memory, which is not recognized by the experimenter.

In the course of the learning process – that is, while the reference memory is being established – the events that are to be associated may not occur at the same time. In such a case, the subject must remember the first event (in a trial) when the second event occurs. I will call this kind of memory *associative memory*. Revusky (1971) and Lett (in press) call this kind of procedure "long-delay learning." It encompasses, among other procedures, delay of reinforcement for a correct choice (Lett, 1973, 1975), taste-aversion learning (Revusky & Garcia, 1970) and trace conditioning (Kamin, 1965). Operationally, associative memory differs from reference memory because it is involved in the learning process itself, not in the retention of what has been learned. When the events to be associated are contiguous, associative memory is not required to establish a reference memory. Conceptually, it is not yet clear whether reference memory and associative memory involve similar processes. Rather short delays limit effective trace conditioning, and this suggests that associative memory fails unless the memory of the CS is actively maintained between its termination and the occurrence of the UCS. On the other hand, rats will tolerate long delays of reinforcement (up to 1 hr) in some discrimination situations (Lett, 1973, 1975), and between the exposure to critical events involved in taste-aversion learning, namely drinking of a flavored solution, and poisoning by chemicals or exposure to X irradiation (Revusky & Garcia, 1970).

Lett (in press) thinks that in long-delay learning, the memory of the first event is latent until the second event occurs; the latter provides a retrieval cue which activates the former. In Lett's learning situation, this happens when the rat is fed in the start box of the maze in which that subject made the correct response minutes or even an hour earlier. Food in the maze reactivates the memory of the most recent behavior in the maze. A parallel mechanism for taste-aversion learning does not seem equally evident, but it is possible that illness leads to the reactivation of memories of what the animal consumed during the preceding few hours, and the flavor and illness can then become associated (see Lavin, 1976).

By definition, then, *associative memory* is required when a learning problem involves an interval between two significant elements *within* a trial. *Reference memory* is required to maintain performance in the face of intervals *between* trials that, short or long, are inherent in any learning procedure. *Working memory* may involve either inter- or intratrial intervals, although the latter are more common. The critical difference between working memory and the other varieties is that different stimuli govern the criterion response on different trials, so that the cue that the animal must remember varies from trial to trial. Therefore, working memory situations often involve conditional discriminations. An example may help to clarify this point.

In Grice's classic study (1948) of delay of reinforcement (an associative memory problem), rats had to learn to choose a black rather than a white alley (or vice versa) before entering a common gray holding chamber. The rats had to remember which alley they chose in order to associate it with reinforcement, but the same alley was correct on every trial. This association became part of the reference memory for the problem, and the rat could make the correct choice on each trial without any further information. A working-memory procedure might be somewhat like this: The rat is forced to run either through a black or through a white alley on each trial, before entering the gray holding chamber. If he runs through the black alley, the right goal box is baited; if he runs through the white alley, the left goal box contains food. In this procedure, the rat must remember *on each trial* which alley he encountered, and he must avoid confusion between the memory of events on that trial and the memory of corresponding events on previous trials. Now the latter procedure can be run without any associative memory requirement, if there is no delay between the rat's run through the alley and the choice of the goal box. The working memory requirement can then be introduced with such a delay. On the other hand, if such a delay is in effect from the beginning of training, then the problem involves both an associative and a working-memory requirement — the former, because the animal has to remember which color of alley he ran through in order to associate it differentially with reinforcement in one of the goal boxes, and the latter, because on a given trial, the rat has to remember which alley he encountered in order to make a choice. In most studies of working memory, the problem is learned (and the reference memory established) without an associative memory requirement. This makes it easier for the subject.

I will use a set of terms applicable to most working memory paradigms: The correct *criterion response* in each trial depends upon an *initial stimulus*; the stimulus is usually presented at the beginning of the trial, as in delayed matching to sample, but it may be the outcome of a previous trial, as in runway studies on patterned reinforcement. The initial stimulus is followed by an *interim stimulus* (or condition) during the *delay period*; this is normally the same on all trials, since it should not contain any cues for the performance of the criterion response. The criterion response follows the delay period, and it is usually a response to a *terminal stimulus*, with which the trial ends. On some occasions, the terminal stimulus may follow the criterion response and serve to reinforce it.

A number of questions can be asked of working memory, and the major purpose of this chapter is to describe research which is relevant to their answers. First, what is the temporal course of working memory? As with other memory processes, this is unlikely to be a simple or invariant decay function, but there may be absolute limits which would presumably be less than the limits of reference memory. I shall seek to show in this chapter that working memory, for pigeons, at least, is not as evanescent as many psychologists have supposed, nor is it necessarily subject to intrinsic decay of a trace. Second, what are the characteristics of a learning problem that determine the course and the limits of working memory? This is a complex matter that certainly involves the nature of the stimuli to be remembered, and is probably affected by the activity of the subject during the interim period and by the cues available when the terminal response is made. Third, how does the subject come to be governed by the memory of the stimulus appropriate for a particular trial, rather than the memory of stimuli which govern behavior on earlier trials? Fourth, what is the theoretical status of the memorial process involved in working memory?

As a partial answer to the last question, I will propose, in Section VIII, a hypothesis of working memory as an "instruction," which is generated by the animal during the initial period and is in effect until the criterion response is made. The instruction is either maintained or forgotten in an all-or-none fashion during the interim condition. It is terminated when the criterion response is made. The maintenance of the instruction may be facilitated by differential patterns of behavior, or "rehearsal," during the delay period. A detailed discussion of this hypothesis, in the light of our research, together with the evaluation of other theoretical approaches, follows in Section VIII. At this point, however, I would like to set the stage for the main body of our chapter by the description of three different procedures or paradigms for the study of working memory. All of these have contributed significantly to the descriptive and theoretical formulations of working memory as a cognitive process.

II. THREE WORKING-MEMORY PARADIGMS

A. Delayed Alternation

Patterned reinforcement in runway studies has been widely investigated, and Capaldi has argued persuasively that the control over the rate of running depends largely upon the cues available from the previous trial (e.g., Capaldi, 1966, 1967, 1971). The most explicit test of such a notion is found in delayed alternation studies. If a rat is rewarded on trial N, he will not be rewarded on trial $N + 1$, and vice versa. The memory of the reward on the former trial can serve to control speed of running on the latter. Thus, outcome of trial N is the initial stimulus for trial $N + 1$, the delay interval between trials, normally spent in the home cage, is the interim condition, and the run down the alley on trial $N + 1$ is the criterion response, usually measured in terms of speed. The terminal stimulus is the reinforcer (or lack of it) supplied at the end of the alley on trial $N + 1$.

Capaldi and Stanley (1963) ran three experiments, each showing that rats would learn, after a number of sessions, to run more slowly on trials following reinforcement than on trials following nonreinforcement when these trials alternated. They were interested in part in the effect of the intertrial interval delay during the interim period. They did not arrive at a clear-cut function relating the difference in running speeds between positive and negative trials to the length of the delay. If anything, it appeared that the best discrimination was obtained at delays of 15 sec and 20 min, with poorer performance at intermediate values. The reasons for the complex relationship are not clear, but the experiments clearly established that rats could remember the outcome of the previous trial over 20 min well enough to form a reliable discrimination.

More interesting, and perhaps more convincing with respect to working memory, was an experiment in which Capaldi (1971) showed that rats could solve the *double*–alternation problem by providing them with differential cues on the first and the second of each pair of rewarded and nonrewarded trials. Thus, on the first nonrewarded trial, the rat might be run in a black alley with a smooth floor; on the second, in a white alley with a rough floor; likewise, on the next (rewarded) trial, the rat would again be run in the black alley, and on the fourth trial (again rewarded) in the white alley; and so forth. Now the rat could master the problem by treating black-alley trials and white-alley trials as separate single-alternation problems. They simply had to remember whether they were rewarded on the previous trial in which they were run in the same alley. Capaldi showed that the animals could master this discrimination with an intertrial interval of 1½ to 2 min. They could not do so when alley colors were randomly assigned to rewarded and nonrewarded trials in the double-alternation problem.

The working memory displayed in such studies seems to be relatively insensitive to the length of the interim period, in contrast to the rapid decay obtained in delayed matching-to-sample experiments to be described below. One possible reason for this is that in runway studies rats are usually trained from the outset on a given delay condition. Thus the acquisition of the problem requires associative memory as well as the working memory needed for its performance. There seem to be few studies in which alternation is first acquired with a minimal delay which is then gradually extended. It is possible that if associative memory of more than, say, a few seconds is required for the learning of a problem, the mechanism may simply be insensitive to the passage of time (Lett, 1975). Another possible reason is that in alternation studies the animal has to remember the occurrence of reinforcement (or lack of it) on the previous trial, and may also remember his own differential running behavior. These are likely to be salient, easily remembered stimuli. Third, the animals in runway studies are generally in their home cages during the delay interval, while other subjects in the same squad are being run. The home cage environment may protect the "memory" of the previous trial, which is then reactivated when the rat is put back in the apparatus (Lett, in press).

It is of some interest that a forgetting curve was clearly obtained in a related study on delayed alternation in the T maze (Roberts, 1974). During a trial, a rat makes an initial forced choice into either the right or the left arm of the maze. In the subsequent free choice, the turn into the opposite arm is rewarded. There is a delay interval between the forced and the free choices. Roberts demonstrated a forgetting of the initial cue over the course of 3 min. It is noteworthy that the subjects were held in the start box during the interim period between runs, and returned to the home cage only between trials. Roberts' results and in some ways his method appear related to the second paradigm that I will discuss.

B. Delayed Matching to Sample

The most popular technique for the study of working memory has been delayed matching to sample (DMTS). It was introduced by Blough with pigeons (1959), and has been studied extensively with pigeons by Roberts and Grant (for a review see Roberts & Grant, 1976; also Roberts, 1972; Roberts & Grant, 1974), and in monkeys by D'Amato and his associates (D'Amato, 1973; Jarrard & Moise, 1971). The bottlenosed dolphin is also a gifted subject when auditory stimuli are used (Herman, 1975; Herman & Gordon, 1974). When pigeons are used as subjects, the sample is presented as the initial stimulus on the center key in an array of three keys. When the pigeon pecks at this stimulus, it is turned off, and after a predetermined interval during which none of the keys are lit (which we will call t), the two side keys are turned on as terminal stimuli. The stimulus displayed on one of them matches the sample and responding to it is reinforced. Pigeons are normally trained on the matching procedure with a simultaneous display of the sample and comparison stimuli to establish a reliable reference memory for the problem. Delays are then introduced, and often randomized between trials. While performance is often close to 100% with the simultaneous display or with zero values of t, it tends to deteriorate rapidly if t exceeds a few seconds.

Typical results can be seen in Fig. 1. However, Grant (1976) has recently reported a respectable performance (60 to 70% correct) with delays up to 60 sec when highly practiced subjects were used, and the initial stimulus was displayed for 8 or 14 sec. Monkeys can, with practice, remember the sample for much longer than pigeons. Apparently, delays of 2 min are achieved fairly readily, and D'Amato (1973) reports that one highly practiced monkey performed well with $t = 9$ min. Herman and Gordon also report that their bottlenosed dolphin could master delays of 2 min with no decrement in performance when they selected different auditory stimuli from a rather large "pool" of available stimuli on different problems.

Two theoretical approaches have been advanced to account for the forgetting observed in DMTS. Roberts and Grant (1976) believe that decay of the trace of the sample stimulus is primarily responsible. Their research points to such factors as the initial strength of the trace, and competition among two or more traces as determinants of working memory. D'Amato (1973) suggests that forgetting is due to a failure to distinguish the most recent sample stimulus within the set of sample stimuli. Thus, Roberts's model implies that forgetting is inevitable over a fairly short term, but that it can be retarded by building strong traces. D'Amato would not view forgetting as inevitable, but suggests that stimuli are discriminable partly on the basis of their relative recency (see also Worsham, 1975). Since relative recency of a sample stimulus declines as a function of the delay interval, discrimination is reduced, and forgetting is more likely to occur with increases of t.

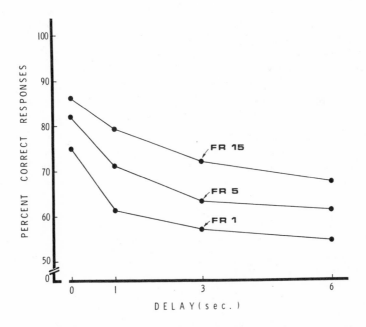

FIG. 1.   Data that are rather typical for delayed matching with pigeons. In this experiment, 1, 5, or 15 pecks to the sample stimuli were required to initiate the delay interval. Thus, sample duration increased with greater FR requirements. (From Roberts, 1972. Copyright 1972 by the American Psychological Association. Reprinted by permission.)

For both of these theories, the working memory involves a process of discrimination. In D'Amato's theory, this is quite obvious. In trace theory, traces can be viewed as persisting cues that govern choice behavior. As these traces weaken, they presumably become less discriminable, and it is well known that the more similar stimuli are, the greater is the rate of error in a discrimination. Likewise, the presence of more than one cue at a time will disrupt performance, and the theory proposed by Roberts and Grant suggests that traces from one trial persist so as to affect performance on subsequent trials.

Delayed matching is a procedure that may discourage the establishment of strong traces of initial stimuli and do little to enhance their discriminability. The specific sample stimuli are equally associated with reinforcement, because of the constraints inherent in the problem. They might be more discriminable (and thus more memorable) if there were a differential association, but this requires a different kind of experimental procedure. Furthermore, responding to the two sample stimuli is generally the same. Differential response patterns might also make the initial stimuli more memorable or more discriminable. Cohen, Looney, Brady, and Aucella (1976), working with line orientations as stimuli, found that if pigeons were required to respond to one sample stimulus on a fixed ratio to obtain the comparison stimuli, and to respond to the other with a low rate of spaced responding, acquisition of the simultaneous matching problem was greatly facilitated. The differential requirements presumably enhanced the discriminability of the sample stimuli. Perhaps delayed matching could benefit from a similar procedure.

DMTS is a procedure in which proactive interference may readily be generated, and there is some evidence for it. Worsham (1975) showed that monkeys are more likely to make more errors in a matching task if the nonmatching stimulus had been presented as the sample stimulus on the immediately preceding trial, than if some other stimulus had been presented on that trial. Furthermore, monkeys made more errors when two or three specific stimuli were used for matching than when seven stimuli comprised the sample set. With a large set, the temporal separation between repetitions of a particular stimulus increases, and confusion is less likely to occur. Herman (1975) reports somewhat similar data for the bottle-nosed dolphin. Grant (1975) also reports proactive interference, which he interprets as competition between traces.

C. Spatial Memory in Rats

Olton and Samuelson (1976) describe a very different kind of working memory paradigm, also reviewed in Olton's chapter (12). Rats are placed on a center platform of an elevated radial maze, with eight arms extending from the platform at intervals of 45°. Each arm is baited at the end, and the rat is free to explore the arms in any sequence to obtain food. In a convincing set of studies, Olton and Samuelson (1976) found that the rat will run down each arm before returning to any. In other words, during the first eight runs, the rats most often sample all the arms. (The actual long-term mean seems to be about 7.6 different arms entered in the first eight runs on each trial.) Olton describes various experiments which show that the rats don't use any obvious patterns of choices (such as going around the maze arm by arm in one or another direction), and they don't "mark" each arm that they enter to provide a cue that inhibits a second entry during a trial. His general conclusion is that the rat maintains a working memory of the arms that he has entered throughout the trial, although there is a slight tendency to repeat choices made early in a trial rather than later in a trial. If the rat is confined for a minute or so on the central platform while the arms are rebaited, several trials can be run in one session. Olton shows that the rats make no more errors at the beginnings of such trials than they do on the first trial in a session. This argues in favor of a "resetting" of the working memory between trials, so that the rat does not confuse the memory of arm entries from previous trials with those from the current trial. Elsewhere in this volume, Menzel (Chapter 13) describes interesting related research with chimpanzees.

Olton's model of working memory does not contain any notion of trace decay. Nor does it stress confusion (i.e., lack of discriminability) between arms previously entered and arms not yet entered on a given trial. It suggests that previous events are "stored" with no particular time constraints in a working memory, but that this memory, once it is no longer useful to the subject, can be reset or terminated. The research which I will now discuss has led to a formulation of working memory that has much in common with Olton's model.

III. THE ADVANCE-KEY PROCEDURE

In the research to be described in the following sections, the subject controlled aspects of the experimental program. We used an "advance procedure," which is related to the changeover procedures that were originally introduced in the study of concurrent schedules. In such a procedure, pigeons are trained on a simple successive discrimination, and then provided with an advance key, which they can peck to terminate any trial, and to initiate the next trial. In the absence of an advance-key response, the trial lasts for a predetermined duration. The pigeon quickly learns to respond to the control key during unfavorable (S−) trials, and to refrain from using it during favorable (S+) trials. This reduces the time spent in the less favorable component of the schedule. The procedure is described by Honig, Beale, Seraganian, Lander, and Muir (1972), Leyland and Honig (1975), and Honig and Beale (1976).

In our working-memory procedure, the pigeon could use an advance key during the interim stimulus. This enabled him to obtain one of two terminal stimuli, one of which was associated with a more favorable reinforcement schedule than was the interim stimulus. The other was associated with extinction. The nature of the terminal stimulus was "predicted" by the initial stimulus, which thus served as a cue for the advance response. When the onset of the advance key was delayed during the interim stimulus, the appropriate response to it depended upon the memory of the initial stimulus. Thus, a working memory of the latter was required for appropriate responding to the advance key.

A. Procedure

Pigeons were run in a standard three-key Grason-Stadler operant behavior chamber. The center key was the food key, and responding to it could procure access to a grain hopper for 4 sec at a time on a variable interval schedule. This key was illuminated by colors, or by single white lines of various orientations on a black background. These patterns were back projected by in-line digital display projectors. The left key served as the advance key. Responding to it was maintained by appropriate changes on the food key.

The trial procedure is illustrated in Fig. 2. The initial stimulus (called here the prestimulus) was presented on the food key, and lasted for 20 sec. It was either a single vertical line (S+) which was correlated with a VI 30—sec reinforcement schedule, or a single horizontal line (S-), correlated with extinction. The terminal stimulus, also called the poststimulus, was one of the same two stimuli, and lasted 60 sec. A trial that began with S+ always ended with S-, while a trial that began with S- always ended with S+. The pigeon had no control over this aspect of the program; however, he could learn the predictive relationship involved in this contingency. The interim stimulus was a plain white light on the food key. It was associated with a VI 2-min schedule, which is less favorable than the schedule associated with S+, but of course more favorable than the extinction associated with S-. After a delay interval called t, the advance key was illuminated during the interim condition with a red light. In the absence of a response to the advance key, it remained lit until the interim stimulus terminated. In the earlier phases of our program, the interim stimulus ended automatically after 60 sec, including t. Later, the duration was changed to $t + 60$ sec, as illustrated in the upper panel of Fig. 2. If the pigeon pecked the advance key, both it and the interim stimulus were turned off immediately, and the terminal stimulus appeared on the food key.

In this procedure, then, the pigeon procures, but does not determine, the terminal stimulus after t elapsed. It was to the bird's advantage to do so when the initial stimulus was S- (called an "S- trial") since this procured S+ and an improvement of the reinforcement schedule. It was to the bird's advantage not to do so when the trial began with S+ (an "S+ trial") since this procured 60 sec of extinction.

A response to the advance key occurred with a latency that ranged on any trial from zero to the maximum time that the advance key was available. (This was 60 sec in the procedure illustrated in Fig. 2, but varied somewhat when

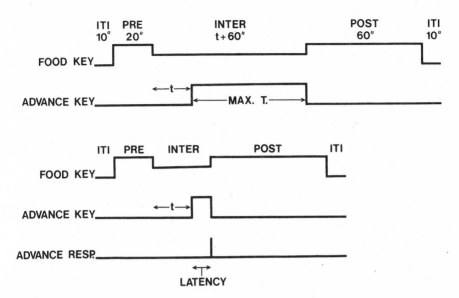

FIG. 2.   Diagram of the advance-key procedure. The upper panel represents the course of events during a trial without an advance-key response. The lower panel represents trials with an advance-key response.

other forms of the procedure were used.) Over the course of the 15 trials beginning with S+ and the 15 trials beginning with S– in each session, these latencies were separately cumulated. The index of discrimination was a *latency ratio*. Separate ratios for S+ and S– trials were derived by dividing the total latencies for each kind of trial by the maximum time that the advance key was available. With the procedure illustrated in Fig. 2, that maximum was 900 sec (15 trials of 60 sec each). Thus, a good discrimination is indicated by: (1) a latency close to 1.00 for S+ trials because the pigeon did not rapidly procure S– as the post-stimulus, if at all; and (2) a latency ratio close to zero for S– trials, because the pigeon procured S+ as the poststimulus quite rapidly. The separation of the two ratios is therefore important as an index of working memory. When working memory fails, the ratios will converge. The ratio for negative S– trials could rise to 1.0, or the ratio for S+ trials could fall to zero, or the ratios might both change so that they "meet" somewhere between these values. Since the pigeon's bias was in the direction of responding to the advance key, a decline in working memory was generally indicated by a fall in the ratio for S+ trials.[1]

---

[1]. Two pilot subjects were run on a similar program, except that trials beginning with S+ always ended with S+, and trials beginning with S– always ended with S–. For them, the appropriate latency ratios were, of course, the reverse of those indicated for the procedure described here. Results were quite comparable to those reported for the present advance-key procedure.

Three pigeons were used which had previously been run in an experiment with an advance procedure. They were adapted readily to the current program in a number of preliminary training procedures that are not recounted here. Each bird was then run for a number of sessions with a given delay interval. The value of t was increased when performance stabilized at a reasonably good level. These increases were not always consecutive; other treatments to be described later intervened from time to time. Responding to the food key was stable and appropriate to the schedule in effect. These response rates will not be further discussed. Training sessions were generally 30 trials long, with order of S+ and S- trials randomized.

B. Results

Median latency ratios were obtained for the first block of five sessions under each delay condition, the middle block, and the last block, if more than 15 sessions were run. Otherwise, data from the first and the last blocks of five sessions alone were used. These ratios are presented for S+ and for S- trials in Fig. 3 for each of the three subjects run initially under this procedure. Two features of the data emerge from Fig. 3: There was relatively little disruption in performance when delays were increased, and in general the quality of the discrimination was remarkably stable in spite of substantial increases in delay intervals. $S18$ maintained good performance even to delay intervals of 50 sec. $S11$ did not do nearly so well after the first session at this delay value; this could be due to the large increment in t imposed between 30 and 50 sec. $S17$ was not run under this condition because his performance deteriorated during an intervening manipulation.

We were particularly interested in the best performance of each bird under the various values of t. We examined the day-to-day records, and determined the five *consecutive* sessions proving the best, most stable data. The mean of the latency ratios from these sessions are shown in Fig. 4. Adjacent points at the 20-sec delay interval represent the best data before and after the program change in which the interim stimulus was extended from 60 sec including t, to $t + 60$ sec. (The data shown in Fig. 3 came from sessions preceding that change for values of $t = 20$ sec or less, and from sessions following that change for values of t greater than 20 sec.) There is no very strong suggestion in Fig. 4 that performance would deteriorate rapidly with values of t greater than 30 sec. Nevertheless, these selected data are, in a sense, less representative of the entire performance under each condition for long delays than for short ones. A bird occasionally suffered from "stretches" mediocre performance. Furthermore, we have seen from Fig. 3 that $S11$ did much worse with 50-sec delays than an extrapolation based on Fig. 4 would suggest.

In spite of these reservations, the best performances of pigeons are impressive, and suggest that the passage of time during the delay interval has no inexorable

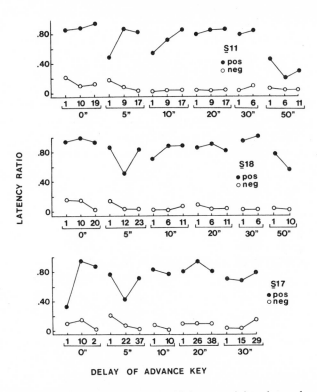

FIG. 3.   Latency ratios obtained from three birds run on the advance key procedure.
Filled circles represent S+ trials; open circles, S− trials. Median values for five consec-
utive sessions are shown. The session number of the first session in each block is indicated.
Data from the first, middle, and last five-session block under each condition are presented.

effects. The data invite an analysis of the factors that underlie such an extended
working memory. Before proceeding to this, further procedures need to be
described.

IV. THE MODIFIED ADVANCE-KEY PROCEDURE

The data presented to this point are somewhat asymmetrical with respect to S+
and S− trials. With longer delays, the latency ratios appropriate to S+ trials decrease more rapidly than the latency ratios for the S− trials increase. This may be
due to the fact that when the bird does not peck at it, the advance key is illuminated throughout the interim condition for a much longer time than when he
does peck the key. This will, of course, provide a much greater opportunity for
such advance responses during S+ trials. There is clearly no symmetrical opportunity to avoid pecking the advance key once the advance response has been
made in an S− trial.

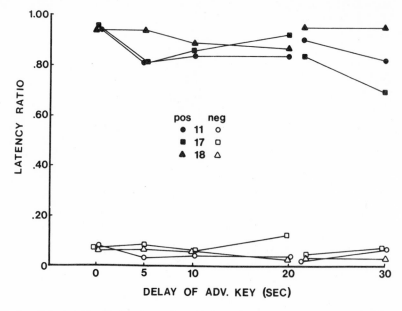

FIG. 4.   Selected "best" data from three birds run on the advance key procedure with increasing delay intervals. Means of blocks of five consecutive sessions are presented. The two sets of points at t = 20 sec represent a replication run under slightly different procedures.

We tried to overcome this asymmetry by limiting the illumination of the advance key to 10 sec following t on every trial. This made the conditions more similar to a discrete trial procedure with respect to the advance response. Thus, in a 30-trial session, the maximum advance key latency was 150 sec for each 15-trial set of S+ and S– trials.

Three new birds were run under this condition after suitable preliminary training procedures. The data from the first, middle, and last block of five sessions under each delay condition are presented in Fig. 5. The data are entirely comparable to those obtained with the previous procedure (see Fig. 3). The latency ratios from S– trials are somewhat greater; this is due to the fact that the maximum latency was 150 sec rather than 900 sec in the other procedure. With similar short latencies for an advance into a terminal S+, the ratios will, of course, be larger with a smaller denominator. Again, we see stable maintenance of good performance through delays up to 30 sec. One bird did well when a 50-sec delay was imposed; a second started in this condition with some promise, but performance then collapsed; the third showed no sign of discrimination with such a long delay.

Selected "best" data from five consecutive sessions are presented in Fig. 6, corresponding to Fig. 4. Again, we see a good replication of points at t = 20 sec. And again, there is little evidence of a deterioration in optimal performance with increasing delay values.

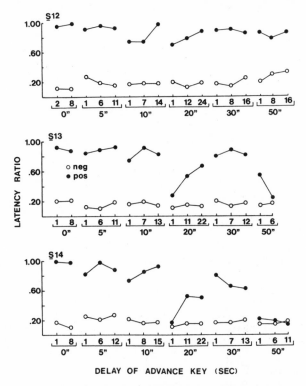

FIG. 5.   Latency ratios obtained from the three birds run on the modified advance key procedure. Filled circles represent S+ trials, open circles, S− trials. Median values from five consecutive sessions are shown. The session number of the first session in each block is indicated. Data from the first, middle, and last five-session block under each condition are presented.

V. THE CONTROL-KEY PROCEDURE

The advance-key procedures described so far do not permit the pigeon a choice between terminal stimuli. The subject can only control the time at which the terminal stimulus appears. In several other working-memory procedures, such as DMTS, the subject determines the terminal stimulus to which he responds. This provides the opportunity for a favorable outcome on every trial. The control-key procedure we now describe permitted the subject a choice of the terminal stimulus on each trial. This involved a conditional discrimination that is in many ways similar to conditional matching to sample.

1. Procedure.   The procedure is diagrammed in Fig. 7. The general parameters, including reinforcement schedules, were the same as those described previously. Each trial began with a 20-sec initial stimulus, which was either a

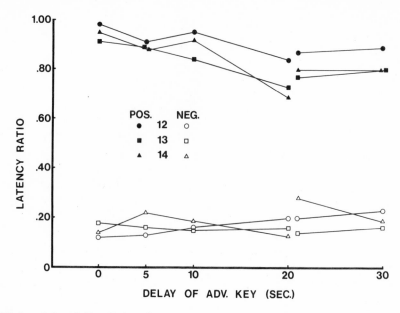

FIG. 6.   Selected "best" data from birds run on the modified advance key procedure with increasing delay intervals. The two sets of points at t = 20 sec represent a replication run under slightly different procedures.

blue S+ or a green S−. The interim stimulus was the white food key. After a delay interval, the left key was illuminated by a red light. This control key was on for 10 sec together with the interim stimulus, unless these stimuli were ended earlier by a peck at the control key. The trial ended with a 60-sec terminal stimulus which was either the vertical white line as S+ or the horizontal line as S−.

The critical aspect of this paradigm is the effect of responses to the control key. If the pigeon pecked it during a trial that began with the green S−, he immediately procured the vertical S+ as the terminal stimulus. If he permitted the control key to stay on for 10 sec without a response, the terminal S− began at that time. Following an initial blue S+, pecking at the control key had just the opposite effects: a response immediately procured the horizontal S−, whereas a failure to respond for 10 sec allowed the trial to end with the vertical S+. Thus, as in the previous procedures, good performance on S− trials is indicated by a low latency ratio, while good performance on S+ trials is indicated by a ratio close to 1.0. It should be clear why the left key is now called the *control key* rather than the *advance key*. A response to it actually controlled the terminal stimulus.

In this procedure, the maximum duration of the interim stimulus was t + 10 sec. The stimulus did not extend for a full minute after t, as it did in the previous procedures. The reason for this is that in the control key procedure, the

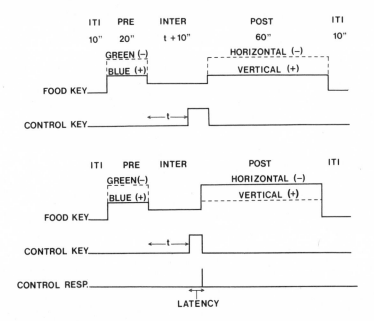

FIG. 7.   Diagram of the control key procedure. The upper panel represents events when the control key is not used, while the lower panel illustrates the effects of using the control key. See text for details.

pigeon could always obtain S+ as the terminal stimulus. In the advance key procedure, he could obtain S+ only on half the trials, and it made some sense to reward the bird for not pecking the advance key on trials ending with S– by providing extended access to the interim stimulus. Sessions generally contained 20 S+ and 20 S– trials.

2. Results.   Preparatory training was long and cumbersome, and the pigeons were subjected to some initial treatments which will not be discussed here. Eventually, three pigeons were run through a series of ascending values of *t*. Their data are presented in Fig. 8 for all sessions, divided into five-session blocks. Note that again, performance is very stable. There is a strong indication that the latency ratios gradually converge as a function of *t*; they increase for S– trials and decrease for S+ trials.

The best data from five consecutive sessions were again selected, and are presented in Fig. 9. It happens that two of the same three birds were run through the same values of *t* in a later stage of research, in preparation for a further experiment to be reported below. This provided a replication. The replicated best data points are shown as unconnected symbols in Fig. 9. Clearly, the optimal performance can be repeated with little variability. Furthermore, there is, as before, little deterioration in that performance as *t* increases.

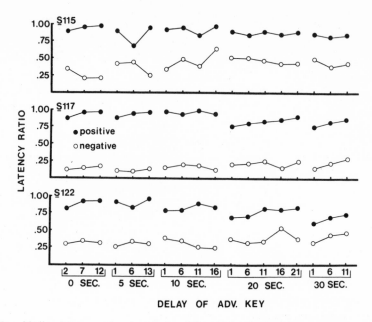

FIG. 8. Median latency ratios for blocks of five trials, obtained from three pigeons run on the control key procedure. The filled circles represent S+ trials; the open circles, S− trials.

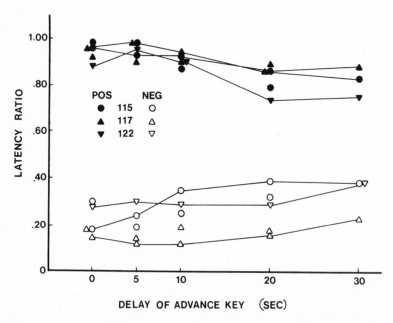

FIG. 9. Selected "best" data from birds run on the control key procedure with increasing delay intervals. Means from blocks of five consecutive sessions are shown. Unconnected points represent replications from a later set of training sessions.

228

3. Discussion. With the advance-key procedure, the terminal stimulus is entirely predictable from the initial stimulus on each trial. The only option for the subject was control over the time that the terminal stimulus appeared. We thought that this relatively simple contingency may have been responsible for the duration of working memory in that situation. The pigeon needs to learn only one set of associations, namely that between initial and terminal stimuli. In the control-key procedure, the associations are more complex: both initial stimuli can be followed by either terminal stimulus, depending on the subject's response to the control key. This procedure is rather more similar to delayed matching, since the occurrence of reinforcement during the terminal phase depends on the subject's behavior. In spite of the greater complexity of the control key procedure, the working memory was not markedly reduced. Furthermore, two subjects trained initially with the advance procedure were eventually shifted to the control key procedure, and transferred their behavior to the control key quite rapidly. They did as well on the latter procedure as on the former with the same delay intervals.

VI. THE FUNCTIONAL CHARACTERISTICS OF THE INITIAL STIMULUS PERIOD

The paradigms that have been described so far indicate that the pigeon can remember an initial stimulus much longer than we had anticipated on the basis of research using DMTS. It would have been tempting to test the limits of this working-memory span, and we intend to undertake studies of this nature. But this would not enhance an understanding of the factors that underlie a relatively extended working memory. Therefore, we have undertaken some experiments and observations of an analytic nature. Those that I will describe here are concerned with two kinds of problems: (1) Analysis of the characteristics of the initial stimulus, and the initial period, which make it memorable for the pigeons. (2) The role of differential feedback for the control key response in the terminal period. Most of the research has been concerned with the first.

Our procedure differs from others in that the prestimuli are differentially associated with reinforcement. The pigeon may remember the associative values of the initial stimuli instead of, or in addition to, their physical characteristics. Furthermore, since the bird pecks only at S+, he may remember his responses, or lack of them, to the initial stimulus. Finally, reinforcement occurs from time to time in the initial period, and this, rather than the discriminative stimulus, may provide a basis for memory.

A. Associative Value of the Initial Stimulus

In the advance procedures the birds were trained to remember either a horizontal or a vertical line as the initial stimulus for correct use of the advance key. If they remember the associative value of the prestimuli, it may be possible to substitute physically different stimuli of the same values and get good transfer of advance—key performance. Transfer of this nature between functionally equivalent stimuli has been demonstrated in the pigeon by Honig and Lindsay (1975). We examined this possibility first with two birds run on the regular advance-key procedure, S11 and S18.

1. Procedure.   These birds had previously been run in a different study (Honig & Lindsay, 1975) with blue as S+ and green as S−, using an advance key to switch out of green into blue. They were retrained on this discrimination in a modified form of the present advance key procedure. On each trial, the pre-stimulus was omitted, and the advance key was never illuminated. The white interim stimulus (associated with VI 120 sec) was illuminated for 60 sec, followed immediately by blue or green (each on half the trials) with their associated reinforcement schedules of VI 30 sec or extinction. When response rates indicated a reliable discrimination among blue, green, and white in accordance with the reinforcement schedules, blue and green were selectively substituted for the vertical S+ and the horizontal S− respectively in the advance key procedure. In blocks of five to eight sessions, they were first presented as the initial stimuli, then as the terminal stimuli, and finally as both initial and terminal stimuli. Aside from the substitution of stimuli, all other training conditions were maintained. The delay interval was 20 sec. These test conditions alternated with blocks of session in which horizontal and vertical were used exclusively as initial and terminal stimuli, in order to reassess baseline performance.

2. Results.   The relevant latency ratios appear in Table 1. The mean values are presented for each block of sessions, together with the values from single sessions bordering the transition from the standard training condition to each of the test conditions. The data from the last session of each block of training sessions and the first of each block of test sessions are underlined. The substitution of colors for lines as prestimuli, as poststimuli, or as both had relatively small effects upon the latency ratios. These birds had never been trained to associate colors as prestimuli with predictable poststimuli. Nor had they been trained to remember either color for the duration of a trial. The good transfer observed here supports the notion that the "value" of the prestimulus or the response rate to it, rather than its visual features, was remembered during each trial, and controlled the performance.

These data also suggest that if the associative values of the initial stimuli are altered, the pigeon's use of the advance key should change appropriately. In the next study, colors were again substituted for lines in an advance-key procedure. Two new birds were used to replicate the study just described; and then they experienced equal reinforcement with colors before they were substituted for lines in further testing.

TABLE 1
Latency Ratios Obtained when Colors were
Substituted for Lines[a]

		S11		S18	
Procedure	Session	Pos.	Neg.	Pos.	Neg.
Standard	Mean	.73	.03	.86	.04
	Last	.81	.05	.83	.01
Color pre-	First	.77	.17	.73	.02
	Mean	.72	.05	.82	.06
Standard	Mean	.86	.02	.91	.04
	Last	.93	.03	.94	.01
Color post-	First	.90	.02	.91	.02
	Mean	.91	.06	.92	.05
Standard	Mean	.83	.06	.86	.02
	Last	.83	.03	.87	.02
Color pre- and post-	First	.80	.17	.82	.02
	Mean	.70	.06	.87	.02
Standard	Mean	.78	.05	.80	.09

[a]Data from the last session of each block of training sessions and the first session of each block of transfer sessions are underlined.

3. Procedure. Subjects 12 and 13 were used; these had been trained, and were run here, on the modified advance key procedure. In this phase of the research, they were first trained in a simple multiple schedule program with blue as S+ and green as S-. When they mastered the discrimination by reaching a ratio of .90, these colors were substituted for lines as prestimuli for a block of five sessions. The delay interval was 20 sec throughout. In further blocks of five sessions, the original procedure with lines only was reinstated, followed by the use of blue and green as pre- and as poststimuli. In this phase, then, we replicated the procedures carried out originally with S11 and S18.

In the next phase, the same birds were equally reinforced for pecking at blue and green, again in a simple multiple–schedule situation. A VI 30-sec schedule was in effect throughout. When the birds stabilized with discrimination ratios around .50, the colors were again substituted for lines as prestimuli for five sessions. There was no point in using them as poststimuli because this would have equalized the consequences of using the advance key.

4. Results. Results from the test sessions are presented in Table 2. The transitional sessions from training to transfer conditions are again underlined. Clearly, when colors with different associative values were substituted for lines,

TABLE 2
Latency Ratios Obtained in Substitution Tests from
S12 and S13[a]

| Procedure | Session | S12 | | S13 | |
		Pos.	Neg.	Pos.	Neg.
Blue positive, green negative					
Standard	Mean	.96	.23	.63	.16
	Last	.91	.23	.85	.13·
Color pre-	First	1.00	.17	.72	.23
	Mean	.81	.21	.76	.30
Standard	Mean	.84	.22	.82	.21
	Last	.79	.23	.87	.18
Color pre-	First	.79	.18	.72	.14
and post-	Mean	.79	.16	.79	.14
Blue positive, green positive					
Standard	Mean	.83	.14	.89	.13
	Last	.99	.11	.84	.15
Color pre-	First	.79	.66	.55	.57
	Mean	.46	.31	.42	.37

[a]Data from the last session of each block of training sessions and the first session of each block of transfer sessions are underlined.

we replicated the previous results. These can be seen in the upper part of Table 2. The latency ratios of bird S12 actually improved slightly both when blue and green were used only as prestimuli, and when they were used both as pre- and as poststimuli. Bird S13 showed a slight reduction in his performance. Following equal positive reinforcement with both colors, the transfer data are quite different (see bottom half of Table 2). The latency ratios with blue dropped for both birds, and increased with green (which was now associated with reinforcement); the increase was particularly marked for S12. Eventually, the ratios for blue and green reached similar intermediate values.

5. *Discussion.*   These two brief experiments support the suggestion that the pigeons do not need to remember the physical attributes of the prestimuli to make correct decisions later in the same trial. They can remember their associative values, or perhaps their differential response to the stimuli. The change in performance that reflects the equalization of the associative values of blue and green is rather convincing evidence of this general point. In this case, the specific values stayed the same while only the associative values were altered. During the 10 transfer sessions in the first part of the study involving birds 12 and 13, these subjects were differentially reinforced for the appropriate response latencies

cued by the blue and green stimuli. If they came under the specific control of blue and green as colors, those latencies should not have changed at the beginning of the transfer sessions following equal reinforcement. Yet the "equalization" of the latency ratios was evident from the first session onwards. The only real problem of interpretation is why the equalized latency ratios were not appropriate to positive trials. They assumed intermediate values. One possible reason is that the equal-reinforcement procedure may have reduced the contrast between the associative values of the two colors, so that blue and green were both less "positive" than was blue following discrimination training.

B. The Role of Differential Responding and of Food Reward in the Initial Stimulus Period

Two factors in our experimental situation are confounded with the associative values of S+ and S- as prestimuli. One of them is the differential rate of responding to the food key. The other is the occasional presentation of the food reward in S+ but not in the presence of S-. The pigeon may remember either or both of these during the interim condition, and base subsequent differential behavior upon them. We undertook two experiments to analyze the importance of these factors. The second, and more comprehensive, will be described now. The results replicate a study in which only the response factor was examined.

First, however, I want to argue that the memory of food presentation can hardly be the *only* cue upon which the working memory is based. In our situation, food was delivered on a VI 30-sec schedule in S+. The initial stimulus periods were 20 sec long; thus food would have been delivered on not more than two-thirds of them. Since rewards were scheduled on an irregular basis, more than one would sometimes be presented during one prestimulus period. Thus, we would expect every session with the advance key procedure to contain at least 5 out of 15 periods with no food reward. If the pigeon were using the occurrence of food reward as the only cue, then he should have done no better on such trials than on S- trials, and the latency ratios for S+ could not exceed .67, even if he were responding perfectly on all of the other trials. Clearly, the pigeons generally did much better than that. Furthermore, we did trial-by-trial analyses from time to time during training sessions, and we never found that the pigeons performed appreciably better on trials in which a reinforcement was presented than on trials in which it was not.

Nonetheless, the presentation of reward may contribute to some degree to the memorability of the initial period. It may be one of several alternative cues for the pigeon to remember. This could become evident in a situation in which other redundant cues are eliminated.

1. Procedure. Two changes in the general control-key procedure were introduced. First, a blue or a green houselight replaced food key lights of the same colors. The blue houselight served as S+ and the green as S–, but the food reward was delivered independently of any responses. In fact, responses to the (unilluminated) food key delayed any scheduled delivery of food for 3 sec. The houselight discrimination was introduced as a multiple schedule with alternating 60-sec periods. Eventually, the houselights were substituted for key lights in transfer tests, where they served as the prestimuli in the control-key procedure.

The second change was that the positive trials were divided into two groups, with food available during the prestimulus on half of them. The VI program did not operate during the remaining prestimuli. The schedule was enriched during the reinforced prestimuli so that the overall density was equivalent to VI 30-sec. This division of S+ trials was instituted both when the key light provided the prestimulus during training, and when the houselight took over that role during testing.

Five pigeons were used for this experiment. Two were veterans from the original advance-key procedure, and they readily transferred their skills to the control-key procedure. The other three had been trained on the latter. All subjects were first retrained on the control-key procedure until they were responding satisfactorily with $t = 20$ sec. At this point, they were trained on the houselight discrimination for 10 sessions which alternated with regular training sessions. In other research using houselight stimuli, we have found that 10 discrimination sessions are sufficient to produce good transfer effects (Honig & Lindsay, 1975). Further "refresher" sessions on this discrimination were given in the course of the experiment, particularly in advance of transfer tests.

After a transfer test which will not be described here, and further stabilization of the baseline condition, the procedure was instituted in which reinforcement was available only during the prestimuli of half the positive trials. Five sessions on this procedure served as the baseline for the first transfer test, in which the houselight was substituted for the key light as the prestimulus. During this phase t was 20 sec except for $S11$, who did not perform as well as the others, and for whom t was 10 sec.

The value of t was then shortened to 10 sec (5 sec for $S11$), and a similar block of baseline training sessions was followed by a transfer test session. Then, t was extended to 30 sec (20 sec for $S11$) and another set of training sessions was followed by a transfer test.

2. Results. Six sets of latency ratios comprise the results of the present study. All of them are shown in Fig. 10. We have ratios from the negative trials of the baseline training sessions and of the transfer sessions. We have ratios from those positive trials from the training and from the transfer sessions in which reinforcement was presented during the prestimulus periods. Finally, we have ratios from those positive trials during training and transfer sessions in which reinforcement was never presented.

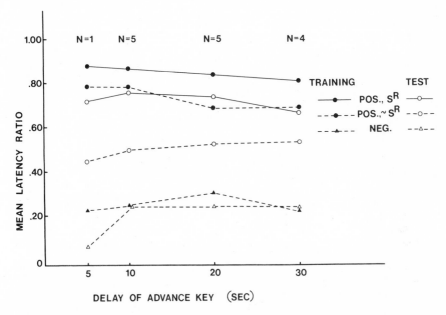

FIG. 10.   Data from training sessions and transfer tests, in which reinforcement in the initial positive periods was presented on half of the S+ trials, and in which house lights were substituted for key lights during tests. Four birds were tested at delays of 10, 20, and 30 sec and one bird at delays of 5, 10, and 20 sec. See text for details.

As one can see from Fig. 10, the latency ratios from negative trials were almost identical whether these were signalled by the green key light or the green houselight. Since the birds did not respond to the key or receive reward in either condition, the only change between training and transfer conditions lay in the nature of the stimulus. Clearly, this change did not affect the behavior of pecking the control key rapidly following the interim period.

There is a relatively small, but consistent, difference between the latency ratios of training trials in which reinforcement occurred and training trials in which it did not. Thus the occurrence of reinforcement seems to contribute to some extent to the memorability of the prestimulus, but its absence is not markedly disruptive. There is a similar difference between training trials in which reinforcement occurred and transfer test trials in which it also occurred. Thus, the behavior of pecking the key again seems to contribute to the memory of the initial period, but it is not an essential cue. However, we note a considerable reduction in the latency ratio on those *transfer* test trials on which reinforcement was omitted. Thus, when neither food reward nor key pecking is available as part of the stimulus complex comprising the initial period, performance falters. But there is still a considerable difference between test ratios of these positive trials and the negative transfer trials, which differed only in the color of the houselight and its associative value.

3. Discussion.   There are two quite different but plausible interpretations of the data from this experiment. One is that a number of cues contribute to the working memory of S+ as a prestimulus. None that we have examined is absolutely necessary, yet none (as far as we can tell) is entirely sufficient. The cues are redundant, and the removal of one, like food reinforcement, still leaves a sufficient number so that performance is maintained at a respectable level. In the absence of cues arising both from food reward and responding to the food key, the value of a stimulus associated with food is still a useful memorial cue, but the memory is "weakened" substantially.

A different interpretation is that the omission of food reward and the elimination of responding to the food key simply decrease the discriminability of the S+ and S- stimuli, and the pigeon is therefore more likely to make errors following the memory interval. Thus discrimination, rather than memory, is affected by the treatments carried out in this study. Two observations particularly support this point: First, the main decrement in performance occurs on S+ trials, in which most of the changes occur, from reinforcement to no reinforcement, and from pecking to no pecking. There is no change in performance in S- trials with the houselight. If we had, say, presented reinforcement during the prestimuli of such trials, we might well have produced errors to increase the S- latency ratios. The second observation is the remarkable lack of any interaction between our experimental conditions and the memory intervals used in this experiment. One would think that if the memory for the prestimulus was weakened by the omission of food and the lack of opportunity to respond to the food key, this would be manifested more strongly at longer than at shorter delay intervals. There is not the least suggestion of this in the data. Either the passage of time does not interact with the "strength" of a cue, or the decrement in performance was due to a reduction in discrimination.

VII. THE ROLE OF DIFFERENTIAL STIMULUS FEEDBACK IN THE TERMINAL PERIOD

In most working-memory situations it is reasonable to suppose that appropriate performance following the memory interval is maintained by differential reinforcement from the terminal stimulus situation. In fact, the differential outcomes are normally an essential aspect of the paradigms involved. In runway alternation studies, for example, the reinforcer (or lack of it) not only "confirms" the rat's rapid or slow running on a particular trial, but it serves as a cue for the next trial. In matching studies and related procedures, two stimuli are generally presented during the terminal period, and the subject has to choose one as an indicator of working memory. The choice of the correct stimulus not only reinforces the proper behavior but in a sense defines the association that the subject is required to master. Our working-memory paradigm provides more flexibility for the presentation of the poststimulus, and thus enables us to study its functional significance for the subject. It does not serve as a cue for the next trial, nor does the pigeon have a choice between more than one poststimulus once the terminal period has begun. Thus, the only function of that stimulus is to reinforce the appropriate criterion response. It may be assumed that the associative values of the poststimuli, together with their associated schedules, differentially maintain this response.

The purpose of the final study to be described in this chapter is to test this assumption. Specifically, we eliminated differential reinforcement in the form of the vertical and the horizontal lines as poststimuli in the control key procedure, although the appropriate reinforcement schedules were maintained during the terminal periods.

1. Procedure.   The aim of the study involves the assumption that the vertical and horizontal lines did indeed serve as S+ and S– with respect to their associative values. This was certainly indicated by the response rates that they controlled during terminal periods. Nevertheless, I thought it wise to verify their effectiveness by using them as prestimuli as well as poststimuli. For three birds used in the study just described, the vertical and horizontal lines replaced blue and green as prestimuli, while the regular VI 30-sec reinforcement schedule was reinstated on the food key during initial S+ periods. These changes produced no disruption in performance. A satisfactory baseline with a 20-sec delay was readily achieved.

The vertical and horizontal lines were then removed from the terminal periods by substituting a plain orange light on all trials. Since a sudden change in conditions might prove disruptive, the following steps were undertaken. First, each subject received three sessions of simple multiple-schedule discrimination training, in which the vertical and horizontal lines were superimposed on an orange background generated by the simultaneous illumination of two colors in the multiple stimulus projector: yellow-green (555 nm) and red (601 nm). A differential response rate was readily achieved, and then these same combinations were introduced as poststimuli: A vertical white line on an orange background served as S+, while a horizontal line on an orange background was S–. (Vertical and horizontal lines on a black background were used as prestimuli.) Fifteen baseline sessions were run in this manner with $t = 20$ sec.

During the next experimental phase the lines were removed altogether during the terminal periods. Orange was the only available poststimulus. However, the appropriate reinforcement schedules were still maintained in accordance with the correctness of the pigeon's control key response. This procedure was carried out for 35 sessions. In a final stage, the vertical and horizontal lines were reinstated and the orange background was removed during the terminal periods for 15 sessions.

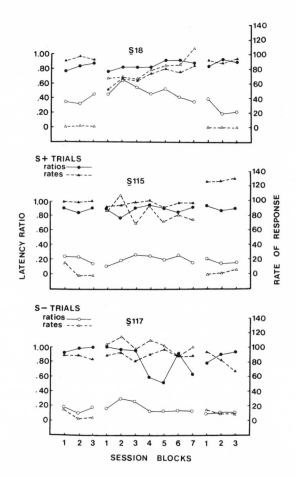

FIG. 11.   Latency ratios and response rates during the poststimulus for three pigeons. During the first and the last three blocks of five sessions, vertical and horizontal lines were presented during the poststimulus periods. During the middle seven blocks of five sessions, only an orange field was presented.

2. Results.   The latency ratios are presented in Fig. 11. The most notable aspect of the data is the very small disruption of appropriate control key responding when the vertical and horizontal lines were removed. *S*18 at first suffers a considerable decline in accuracy, but then recovers to a level of performance quite comparable to the baseline conditions. The performance of *S*115 was practically unaffected. *S*117 shows rather little effect for 15 sessions, then some decline in the latency ratios of positive trials, then a recovery, and then a decline. All birds do very well during the return to the previous training condition with lines alone as poststimuli.

This result was unexpected. Why would performance on the memory task not collapse in the absence of feedback from the poststimuli? One possibility was that the birds "knew" that the trials ended in the reinforcement or extinction conditions even in the absence of differential cues on the key. We determined this by looking at the response rates during "positive" terminal periods following correct behavior toward the control key, and during "negative" terminal periods following an error. These rates are also plotted in Fig. 11. They differ markedly during the baseline and the postexperimental condition, when vertical and horizontal lines were displayed. The difference vanishes when these stimuli are removed, and rates are maintained at a high level. If anything, they are slightly higher for two birds during the extinction condition, presumably because no time is spent consuming the reinforcer.

3. Discussion.   The criterion performance in our working-memory paradigms was established with differential reinforcement of the control key response. It is hard to imagine how it would be achieved otherwise. Why this differential reinforcement was only marginally necessary to maintain the behavior in very well-trained subjects is certainly not obvious. One possible explanation is this: Once the control-key paradigm is mastered, every trial can end with a positive outcome, and a bird that performs well has contact with only one poststimulus (S+) over the course of many training sessions. Thus, the presentation of different stimuli may not be necessary to maintain the behavior. The data do provide some modest support for this notion. S18 made the most errors during baseline training (8.67 per session, on the average), and was most disrupted by the removal of the lines from the poststimuli. S115 made only about four errors per session, and S117 about two, and these subjects were less affected. Nonetheless, S18 improved his performance during the experimental sessions even without differential feedback, and S117 did likewise for a few sessions after a deterioration of his performance.

One empirical approach to testing this interpretation would be to run subjects in a parallel experiment with the advance key rather than the control key procedure. In the former, half the trials end with S+ and half end with S– whether the subject makes the advance response or not. Thus, the subject will continue to have contact with both poststimuli.

Another possible interpretation of the present results is simply that our highly trained subjects failed to process the poststimuli in relation to their own performance. If the stimuli did not functionally serve as "feedback," then the lack of a differential outcome would not be expected to affect the behavior. This notion is compatible with a theoretical account of working memory that follows in the next section.

VIII. GENERAL DISCUSSION

In the current set of experiments, we have established a phenomenon, namely a stable, relatively long-term working memory in the pigeon. The most obvious and important single feature of our data is the relative insensitivity of this memory to the passage of time, at least within the limits of 30 sec. This insensitivity is manifested by the "best data" plots derived from various training conditions, and also by the lack of an interaction between delay intervals and conditions which reduce performance, as observed in the study on the role played by reinforcement delivery and pecking at the food key. This does not, of course, imply that our pigeons never forgot during the delay interval, nor that such forgetting is independent of the passage of time. But forgetting does not seem to be inexorably related to the passage of time, and this affects theoretical interpretations of the data. I shall discuss some interpretations of the data that would be suggested by the theoretical approaches that were reviewed briefly in the introductory section of this chapter.

A. Trace Theory

Perhaps the most traditional interpretation of our results would be that the prestimuli establish particularly strong traces which are well maintained over extensive memory intervals. Extensive data summarized by Roberts and Grant (1976) show that those treatments which are expected to produce "strong" traces also retard the rather rapid forgetting that typically occurs with DMTS in the pigeon. For example, increasing the duration of the sample improves performance. It could be argued that our S+ prestimuli generated particularly strong traces because of their duration, the correlated occurrence of reinforcement, and the high rate of pecking at the food key. The S– prestimuli may have generated weaker traces because some of these cues were not available. A reasonable explanation of our results could be this: The pigeon simply learns not to peck the advance key in the presence of the strong trace generated in S+ trials. Otherwise (in the absence of a trace, or in the presence of a trace of S–) he pecks the key. When components of the positive trace are removed, then the trace is weakened, and performance following S+ will be reduced, as it was in our experiment relevant to this question.

In my view, such an explanation is not adequate to deal with the data presented here. By its very nature, a trace should be sensitive to the passage of time. Forgetting should be orderly. Furthermore, any treatment that strengthens or weakens a trace should enhance or reduce the performance based on memory, but always within the context of an orderly decay function. Data fitting such a model are shown in Fig. 1, where the effects of sample duration upon DMTS are shown. We have no evidence in our results of a clear limitation upon working memory, nor of an orderly decay function, even when the trace of the positive stimulus is presumably weakened by removing food reward and the opportunities to peck at the response key.

A second problem with the trace theory is that it cannot account for our transfer data. A trace is presumably a trace of a physical stimulus. Presumably the trace acts as a cue for the correct response following the interstimulus. In that case, our subjects must have transferred control of responding from traces of line orientations to traces of colors, which had never before been presented within the context of the memory paradigm. Our interpretation of these results was based on the equivalence of the associative values of the stimuli, but in trace theory, to this point, it has not been suggested that associative values generate particular traces.

B. Activation Theory

Lett (in press) has offered a theory of associative memory, according to which the memory of an initial event become "inactive" following the event, and is then reactivated when the subsequent event occurs which is to be associated with the first. Such reactivation normally results from presenting a "retrieval cue," and Lett explains her own long-delay learning in rats on this basis, namely that the memory of the rat's response is "protected" in the home cage while it is inactive, and is then activated when the rat is fed in the training apparatus. It may be possible to extend such a theory to cover working memory as well, and, indeed, where the associative and working memories must be acquired conjointly, as in alternation studies in the runway with long intertrial intervals, this seems like a reasonable approach. In our case, one would have to assume that the memory of the prestimulus becomes inactive when that stimulus is terminated, or shortly thereafter, and is then reactivated when the advance or control key is illuminated.

Such a theory could account for the slow decline of memory as a function of the delay interval. It should have no difficulty with our transfer data on the assumption that the inactive memory need not be restricted to the purely physical aspects of the prestimulus. It is not quite clear, however, why the illumination of the advance key should serve as a retrieval cue. This stimulus is not present during the prestimulus, as retrieval cues usually are. Furthermore, there is no clear mechanism for the termination of the working memory. The theory was designed to account for the establishment of stable associations. If inactive memories are activated through the retrieval cue, such as the illumination of the advance key, why would there not be a lot of interference between the memory laid down on previous trials and the memory from the current trial?

C. Forgetting as Discrimination Failure

Little of our work is directly relevant to the views of D'Amato (1973) and of Worsham (1975) in the sense of providing explicit tests of their hypothesis. But a pragmatic analysis of our findings would not seem to support them. Relevant data for their view are largely provided by proactive interference. In our situation, the same stimuli are generally used as pre- and poststimuli, and appear on the food key. It is thus reasonable to suppose that proactive interference on a given trial would primarily arise from the rather lengthy poststimulus from the previous trial. Now consider two consecutive trials with the advance-key procedure. If these trials begin with the same prestimulus, then the poststimulus of the first must always be opposite in sign from the prestimulus of the second, and this should create interference. Conversely, if they begin with different prestimuli, then the adjacent post- and prestimuli are of the same sign, which should reduce interference. Unfortunately, we have not generally obtained trial-by-trial records, so the appropriate analyses cannot be carried out at this time. But other considerations lend little support to this view. A well-trained bird will make rather few errors, and these tend to be concentrated in the first few trials of a session. We have no evidence that trials within a session "cluster" into good and bad sets, depending on the outcome of the previous trial. In the control-key procedure, a subject that makes few errors can generally obtain S+ as the poststimulus on most trials. This suggests that performance should be poorer on trials starting with S− rather than S+. There is no evidence for this. Furthermore, one would predict that if the pre- and poststimuli are taken from different dimensions (with colors as prestimuli, and lines as poststimuli, for example), performance should be better than if they are from the same dimension. There is no evidence for this either.

Admittedly, these arguments are weak, since the evidence is indirect. Trial-by-trial analyses are indeed crucial, particularly during the earlier training phases, when the subject may not have had the opportunity to learn a discrimination between the prestimulus which follows the intertrial interval, and the previous poststimulus, which precedes it. And yet we should note that the theory of D'Amato and Worsham is a theory of *forgetting*, unlike trace theory and reactivation theory, which are theories of remembering. Since most of our evidence concerns remembering rather than forgetting, I am really more interested in an adequate theory that deals with the former.

D. Memory as an "Instruction"

I want to offer a fourth alternative. This is that the prestimulus establishes an "instruction," which is a state or process that determines the criterion response following the memory interval—whether the pigeon will peck or not peck at the control or advance key. This instruction has the following characteristics: (1) Unless it is forgotten in the course of the memory interval, it is maintained at full strength, possibly with the assistance of "rehearsal" or some form of differential behavior. (2) The instruction is a discrete state; the initial stimulus establishes it at full strength, if at all, and if it is forgotten, it is forgotten completely. (3) Once the criterion response is made, the instruction is terminated, and has no effect upon subsequent behavior. (4) The instruction is established by the initial stimulus, but it is not necessary for the subject to remember the stimulus itself.

This hypothesis has certain clear implications for characteristics of working memory. We can review relevant aspects of our findings, which are, not surprisingly, quite compatible with these implications. Furthermore, we can make predictions about the effects of treatments that have not yet been carried out. First, we should note that forgetting is not an *inherent* characteristic of the instruction, unlike the fading of a trace. The probability of forgetting increases with duration of the memory interval, but the causes of forgetting are probably interference, or a failure to maintain the instruction through rehearsal or some other means (inattentiveness?). Thus, the notion of an instruction is compatible with the relatively long delays that we have observed with little decrement in performance.

Second, the notion is compatible with our transfer data. An instruction could be cued by any of a number of functionally equivalent stimuli, separately or together. If these cues are reduced in number, or weak, then the instruction is less likely to be correctly established, and this is quite compatible with our experiment in which the role of various aspects of the initial period was investigated. In that experiment, there was no interaction between the characteristics of the initial period and the memory interval. It would seem that the probability of establishing the instruction, rather than the forgetting of the stimulus, was affected by the experimental treatments.

Finally, the notion of an instruction may also explain the last experiment described in this chapter. If the pigeon learns to terminate the instruction upon making the criterion response, then the poststimulus as a reinforcer may not enter into the evaluation by the subject of its preceding behavior.

1. Prospective tests of the instructional hypothesis. Certain suggestions for future research emerge from this hypothesis, and fairly clear predictions can be made. Since the instruction is established at full strength, if at all, working memory ought to be relatively insensitive to physical parameters of the initial stimulus. For example, duration should not markedly affect performance, although there would be some limit below which a duration would be ineffective. We actually carried out some work on this question with our very first pilot subjects run on the advance key procedure. Shortening initial periods from 20 to 10 and even to 5 sec, and increasing them to 30 sec, had rather little effect. Latency ratios on S+ trials declined somewhat with the shorter durations, but they were unaffected on S– trials. This change may have been due to the reduced number of initial S+ periods of short duration in which a reinforcer was presented. At the time, we did not realize that reinforcers could provide at least part of the basis of the working memory. The matter of stimulus duration needs to be studied again more systematically, with numbers of reinforcers equated for initial periods of different durations, and with the use of several memory intervals.

Another prediction based on the instructional interpretation is this: Once the criterion response is made, the instruction is terminated; therefore, the subject should respond at a chance level if the memory interval were to be continued. This could be tested with two opportunities for a criterion response within a trial. Pigeons could be trained with memory intervals of, say, 20 and 30 sec on different trials in each session. Then the advance or control key could be illuminated for 5 sec within selected 30-sec trials, but after a 20-sec delay. A response to it would be ineffective, aside from turning off the key. At the end of the 30-sec delay, the key would go on again, the the pigeon could make another criterion response. If the instruction is terminated after the first opportunity, performance on the second opportunity should be poor.

Further, it would be good to determine whether there is any behavior that could be interpreted as accompanying, sustaining, or directing an instruction during the memory interval. This need not be mediating behavior in the usual sense of providing a stimulus that elicits a criterion response, but merely a behavior that facilitates the maintenance of a "set." We have videotaped some of our subjects during the interim periods. While they respond to the food key fairly steadily, they frequently make head movements in the direction of the control key if a peck at it will be the correct response, and they make other head movements — up and down, or in the opposite direction — if such a response should be withheld. However, interruptions of these patterns, occasioned, for example, by delivery of food during the interim period, do not necessarily disrupt the correct response. Nonetheless, a correlation between the occurrence of such behaviors and the accuracy of responding to the control key is worth further study. If differential behavior patterns are seen during the memory intervals of S+ and S− trials, the experimenter could deliberately illuminate the advance or control key either while the pigeon is performing the "appropriate" pattern, or when he switches to the "inappropriate" pattern. This may result in very different probabilities of making the correct response to the control key.

2. Other research that is relevant to the instructional hypothesis.   An informal way of describing the instruction is that the pigeon remembers "what to do" rather than "what it saw." This suggests that the instructional hypothesis is not applicable to those paradigms where the memory of particular physical characteristics of a stimulus is required for the criterion response. In DMTS, it is reasonable to suppose that the choice between comparisons is directed by the relationship between the memory of a particular initial stimulus and the comparison stimuli. In pigeons, performance on this task is characterized by an orderly decline as a function of the duration of the memory interval, even with intervals of 20 to 60 sec (Grant, 1976). It is also sensitive to the parameters of the initial stimulus, particularly duration (Grant, 1976; Roberts & Grant, 1974). It appears to be subject to proactive interference, which we would not expect to find from a "terminated" instruction (Grant, 1975).

In our situation, the pigeon had to remember what to do in the sense of making a particularly well-trained response. An instruction may not be able to encompass a discrimination between two choice stimuli to be presented later in a trial. Thus, if we were to present two different control keys, and the pigeon would have to choose the correct one on the basis of an initial stimulus, we might well obtain results that are close to those typical for DMTS. But possibly other, more advanced species are not limited in this way. Monkeys and dolphins, for example, generally have to choose one of two very familiar stimuli at the end of a trial in a working memory paradigm. Now this choice may be under the control of an instruction established earlier in the trial, e.g., "choose the red panel," or "swim to the high tone." In other words, the subject's capacity may permit him to include a characterization of the correct stimulus in the instruction. The choice would then not be a discriminated response made to the fading trace of a sample stimulus presented earlier. However, we should note that the instructional hypothesis is "stretched" by the study by Herman and Gordon (1974), who used a set of 17 different auditory stimuli to compose their DMTS problems, each of which was unique. We would have to postulate that the instruction could incorporate a representation of a relatively unfamiliar stimulus in such an intelligent species.

Some of the data obtained with monkeys and dolphins conforms more closely to an instructional than to a decay hypothesis of working memory. For example, D'Amato and Worsham (1972) showed that the duration of the sample stimulus had little effect upon DMTS in the monkey, even though durations were reduced to less than .1 sec. In a later paper (D'Amato & Worsham, 1974), they also show that with sufficient preliminary training, monkeys can do as well on conditional delayed matching as they do on DMTS. These findings are not easily handled by a trace theory, nor are they accounted for by the notion that in matching problems the subject depends upon retrieval cues provided by the comparison stimuli. They are more readily explained by the hypothesis that the sample establishes an instruction to choose a particular stimulus which it need not resemble.

Furthermore, in much of the work reported by D'Amato and his colleagues, there is little decline in performance over substantial delay intervals. Typically, intervals up to two minutes are used. At the longer intervals within this range, there is considerable forgetting in many cases, but this is not a universal finding during "baseline" training. It is most often seen under experimental conditions designed to induce forgetting. The "decay" functions are high and flat at lower intervals, and then drop at longer ones; this is in contrast to most data obtained from pigeons, where the memory loss occurs mostly at the shortest intervals. Herman and Gordon (1974) similarly report excellent retention of sounds in a DMTS paradigm by a bottlenosed dolphin for intervals up to two minutes. A loss of memory seems, in general, to be due to retroactive interference, rather than to the passage of time alone. This has been demonstrated systematically by D'Amato and O'Neill (1971) and by Worsham and D'Amato (1973); such a phenomenon is, of course, compatible with the instructional hypothesis. Herman (1975) studied the effects of interpolating sounds during the delay interval in his auditory DMTS task with the dolphin, and obtained interference effects if the sounds filled a large portion of the interval.

If the instruction is canceled when the criterion response is made, then there should be no proactive interference in subsequent trials. But such interference has been observed, and it causes problems for the instructional hypothesis. It has been documented by Worsham (1975) in monkeys, and Herman (1975) also reports that if only two stimuli are used in a delayed matching task, the dolphin is more likely to make an error on the second of two consecutive trials if the sample stimuli are different than if they are the same. Clearly, if the performance of the criterion response cancels the entire memory of the events on that trial, the instructional hypothesis cannot meet the test of such data. The possibility remains that the animal may cancel the instruction as such, but that some memory remains which could influence the establishment of instructions on subsequent trials. This could well be the case when the discrimination requires that the instruction contains particular information on the characteristics of a stimulus that is to be chosen. If the animal has to remember what to do in relation to what it saw or heard, the memory of the latter may persist, although not in the form of an instruction.

The instructional hypothesis does account for much of the data obtained by Olton and Samuelson (1976) and Olton (this volume, Chapter 12) on spatial memory in rats. It will be recalled from the introduction that these subjects could remember within the course of a trial which of eight possible arms they had entered. Olton suggests that the rat stores information on where he has been, and implies that this information is used to instruct itself to avoid returning to the same places throughout the duration of the trial. Furthermore, Olton explicitly incorporates a "reset" mechanism in his model, because the memory of earlier trials does not seem to interfere with performance on later trials. Error analysis based on the sequence of choices within trials does not suggest that earlier choices are forgotten sooner than later ones in the course of a trial, which argues strongly against intratrial interference and against a fading of traces. Instead, it supports my earlier suggestion that some animals, at least, can incorporate representation of specific stimuli — in this case the alleys that the subject has entered within the same trial — into a working memory that directs subsequent behavior. Whether the pigeon has any such capacity we do not know.

Many results, reviewed briefly in this last section, converge upon a hypothesis that suggests a memorial process in which information is held with rather little time-related loss, and which directs subsequent behavior within particular trials. The information may incorporate the representation of a future stimulus that is to be chosen, or the representation of stimuli that have already been sampled. The memorial process is likely to vary in complexity and in the details of its mechanism from species to species and possibly from procedure to procedure. It leads to the conclusion that the control of behavior is not limited to the fading traces of particular physical stimuli, but that behavior can be governed by information which is representative of particular stimuli, and which is stored, used, and forgotten as the occasion requires.

REFERENCES

Blough, D. S. Delayed matching in the pigeon. *Journal of the Experimental Analysis of Behavior,* 1959, *2,* 151–160.

Capaldi, E. J. Partial reinforcement: A hypothesis of sequential effects. *Psychological Review,* 1966, *73,* 459–477.

Capaldi, E. J. A sequential hypothesis of instrumental learning. In K. W. Spence and J. T. Spence (Eds.), *The psychology of learning and motivation* (Vol. 1). New York: Academic Press, 1967, pp. 67–157.

Capaldi, E. J. Memory and learning: A sequential viewpoint. In W. K. Honig and P. H. R. James (Eds.), *Animal memory.* New York: Academic Press, 1971, pp. 111–154.

Capaldi, E. J., & Stanley, L. R. Temporal properties of reinforcement aftereffects. *Journal of Experimental Psychology,* 1963, *65,* 169–175.

Cohen, L. R., Looney, T. A., Brady, J. H., & Aucella, A. F. Differential sample response schedules in the acquisition of conditional discriminations by pigeons. *Journal of the Experimental Analysis of Behavior,* 1976, *26,* 301–314.

D'Amato, M. R. Delayed matching and short-term memory in monkeys. In G. H. Bower (Ed.), *The psychology and learning and motivation: Advances in research and theory* (Vol. 7). New York: Academic Press, 1973, pp. 227–269.

D'Amato, M. R., & O'Neill, W. Effect of delay-interval illumination on matching behavior in the capuchin monkey. *Journal of the Experimental Analysis of Behavior,* 1971, *15,* 327–333.

D'Amato, M. R., & Worsham, R. W. Delayed matching in the capuchin monkey with brief sample durations. *Learning and Motivation,* 1972, *3,* 304–312.

D'Amato, M. R., & Worsham, R. W. Retrieval cues and short-term memory in capuchin monkeys. *Journal of Comparative and Physiological Psychology,* 1974, *86,* 274–282.

Gleitman, H. Forgetting of long-term memories in animals. In W. K. Honig and P. H. R. James (Eds.), *Animal memory.* New York: Academic Press, 1971, pp. 1–44.

Grant, D. S. Proactive inhibition in pigeon short-term memory. *Journal of Experimental Psychology: Animal Behavior Processes,* 1975, *104,* 207–220.

Grant, D. S. Effect of sample presentation time on long-delay matching in the pigeon. *Learning and Motivation,* 1976, *1,* 580–590.

Grice, G. R. The relation of secondary reinforcement to delayed reward in visual discrimination learning. *Journal of Experimental Psychology,* 1948, *38,* 1–18.

Herman, L. M. Interference and auditory short-term memory in the bottlenose dolphin. *Animal Learning and Behavior,* 1975, *3,* 43–48.

Herman, L. M., & Gordon, J. A. Auditory delayed matching in the bottlenose dolphin. *Journal of the Experimental Analysis of Behavior,* 1974, *21,* 19–26.

Hoffman, H. S., Fleshler, M., & Jensen, P. Stimulus aspects of aversive controls: The retention of conditioned suppression. *Journal of the Experimental Analysis of Behavior,* 1963, *6,* 575–583.

Honig, W. K., & Beale, I. L. Stimulus duration as a measure of stimulus generalization. *Journal of the Experimental Analysis of Behavior,* 1976, *25,* 209–217.

Honig, W. K., Beale, I. L., Seraganian, P., Lander, D. G., & Muir, D. Stimulus and response reduction: Two aspects of inhibitory control in learning. In R. A. Boakes and M. S. Halliday (Eds.), *Inhibition and learning.* New York: Academic Press, 1972, pp. 41–71.

Honig, W. K., & Lindsay, H. Transfer of the control of stimulus duration across discrimination problems. *Learning and Motivation,* 1975, *6,* 157–178.

Jarrard, L. E., & Moise, S. L. Short-term memory in the monkey. In L. E. Jarrard (Ed.), *Cognitive processes of nonhuman primates.* New York: Academic Press, 1971, pp. 3–24.

Kamin, L. J. Temporal and intensity characteristics of the conditioned stimulus. In W. F. Prokasy (Ed.), *Classical conditioning: A symposium.* New York: Appleton-Century-Crofts, 1965, pp. 118–147.

Lavin, M. S. The establishment of flavor–flavor associations using a sensory preconditioning training procedure. *Learning and Motivation*, 1976, *7*, 173–183.

Lett, B. T. Delayed reward learning: Disproof of the traditional theory. *Learning and Motivation*, 1973, *4*, 237–246.

Lett, B. T. Long delay learning in the T-maze. *Learning and Motivation*, 1975, *6*, 80–90.

Lett, B. T. Long delay learning: Implications for learning and memory theory. In N. S. Sutherland (Ed.), *Tutorial essays in experimental psychology* (Vol. 2). Hillsdale, New Jersey: Lawrence Erlbaum Associates, in press.

Leyland, C. M., & Honig, W. K. Maintenance of behavior controlling the duration of discriminative stimuli. *Journal of the Experimental Analysis of Behavior*, 1975, *24*, 207–214.

Olton, D. S., & Samuelson, R. J. Remembrance of places passed: Spatial memory in rats. *Journal of Experimental Psychology: Animal Behavior Processes*, 1976, *2*, 97–116.

Revusky, S. The role of interference in association over a delay. In W. K. Honig and P. H. R. James (Eds.), *Animal memory*. New York: Academic Press, 1971, pp. 155–213.

Revusky, S. H., & Garcia, J. Learned associations over long delays. In G. H. Bower (Ed.), *The psychology of learning and motivation* (Vol. 4). New York: Academic Press, 1970, pp. 1–84.

Roberts, W. A. Short-term memory in the pigeon: Effects of repetition and spacing. *Journal of Experimental Psychology*, 1972, *94*, 74–83.

Roberts, W. A. Spaced repetition facilitates short-term retention in the rat. *Journal of Comparative and Physiological Psychology*, 1974, *86*, 164–171.

Roberts, W. A., & Grant, D. S. Some studies of short-term memory in the pigeon with presentation time precisely controlled. *Learning and Motivation*, 1974, *5*, 393–408.

Roberts, W. A., & Grant, D. S. Studies of short-term memory in the pigeon using the delayed matching-to-sample procedure. In D. L. Medin, W. A. Roberts, and R. T. Davis (Eds.), *Processes of animal memory*. Hillsdale, New Jersey: Lawrence Erlbaum Associates, 1976, pp. 79–112.

Spear, N. E. Forgetting as a retrieval failure. In W. K. Honig and P. H. R. James (Eds.), *Animal memory*. New York: Academic Press, 1971, pp. 45–109.

Worsham, R. W. Temporal discrimination factors in the delayed matching-to-sample task in monkeys. *Animal Learning and Behavior*, 1975, *3*, 93–97.

Worsham, R. W., & D'Amato, M. R. Ambient light, white noise, and monkey vocalization as sources of interference in visual short-term memory of monkeys. *Journal of Experimental Psychology*, 1973, *99*, 99–105.

9 Selective Attention and Related Cognitive Processes in Pigeons

Donald A. Riley
H. L. Roitblat
University of California, Berkeley

I. SELECTIVE ATTENTION AND RELATED COGNITIVE PROCESSES IN PIGEONS

It is a common observation that when we notice, think about, or observe some stimulus, it may be difficult to notice, think about, or observe other stimuli. In other words, perception and other cognitive processes are often selective. One explanation for these observations is that in order to notice some stimulus, we must attend to it and we can only attend to a limited number of stimuli at a time. Often, other explanations are available. For example, it may be difficult to notice two things because they are spatially separated, and we can only look in one direction at a time. Such peripheral explanations are usually suggested as alternatives to an attentional explanation. Attention can, then, be viewed as a central adaptation to information overload. There is more information present in the stimulus array than is possible to process so it is necessary to selectively attend to some stimuli at the expense of others.

Selective attention has also been proposed as an explanation for the performance of animals in discrimination problems (e.g., Sutherland and Mackintosh, 1971; Riley and Leith, 1976). Every time a selective attention interpretation has been proposed by some investigator, however, other experimenters have been quick to demonstrate other more peripheral and perhaps simpler mechanisms to account for the apparent attentional effects. After almost 50 years it is still a matter of controversy whether an attentional hypothesis is at all necessary to explain animal discrimination performance (Mackintosh, 1975).

This lack of resolution may be true, in part, because experimenters attempting to investigate attention in animals have usually failed to structure their experiments to provide any *overload* of the animal's ability to take in all the available information within the allowed time. It is our view that when this condition is met, that is, when the animal's information processing ability or capacity is taxed, the likelihood of demonstrating selective attention will increase. The modern study of attention in humans, beginning with Broadbent's book *Perception and Communication* (1958) has been sensitive to this position. Broadbent (1961) also suggested that such a strategy would be useful in studying animal attention.

This chapter presents research that has used two different methods to vary the load placed on the animal's information processing system: Variations in the time available to the animal in which to process the information and variations in the number of stimuli which the animal must process. By manipulating the available time and the number of messages, we can investigate the processes controlling the animal's ability to attend to more than one input at the same time. We have tried to ensure that we are actually taxing the animal's ability by shortening the available time or increasing the number of messages until errors begin to increase.

In the following pages we examine the selective-attention hypothesis and several competing interpretations in the context of the matching-to-sample paradigm in which the number of messages presented and the sample duration are manipulated. An experiment conducted by Maki and Leith (1973) demonstrates the effect of both variations. The procedure is illustrated in Fig. 1.

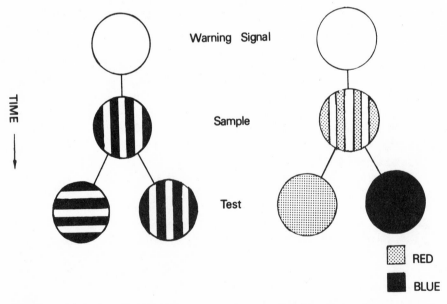

FIG. 1.   Two typical matching-to-sample sequences as used by Maki and Leith (1973). An element trial is depicted on the left; a compound trial, on the right. Warning signals and samples appear on the center key; the two test stimuli appear on the side keys.

First, a white warning signal was projected onto the center key of a three-key pigeon-intelligence panel. In some experiments this warning signal was terminated by a single peck, in others it remained on for a fixed 5 sec. In either case, a single peck to the warning-signal key was necessary for the presentation of the rest of the trial. Failure to peck resulted in the initiation of a dark inter-trial interval and the re-presentation of the entire trial beginning with the warn-ing signal. If the warning-signal key was pecked, it was followed, after a 100-msec delay, by a sample stimulus whose duration was manipulated as a parameter of interest. Sample duration was independent of the number of pecks to the key on which the sample was projected, and none was required. The sample was then followed by the presentation on the side keys of two test stim-uli, one of which matched the sample and was designated correct. A single peck to one of the side keys within 5 sec was necessary to indicate the subject's choice. A random half of the trials on which the subject made a correct response were reinforced with access to a lighted food hopper. Incorrect choices caused the test lights to remain on for 5 sec during which pecks had no effect. Follow-ing the termination of the reinforcer presentation or the test stimuli on those trials on which an incorrect choice or no choice was made, a 5-sec dark intertrial interval occurred. Failure to make a choice resulted in the presentation of an intertrial interval and the re-presentation of the same trial.

As Fig. 1 indicates, the animal was confronted with an element sample on half the trials and a compound sample on the other half. In these experiments, an element was either a solid colored red or blue disk, or three white lines, either horizontal or vertical on a black surround. A compound sample consisted of the pairing of a color element with a line element, and appeared as three white lines on a colored surround. The test stimuli were always two values from the same dimension: The animal was never asked to choose between a color and a line, nor were compound tests presented in this first experiment.

On those trials during which an element sample was presented, the animal had only the information from that single element to process and store for use. On compound trials, however, it had to process the elements from both dimen-sions because it could be tested on either; line and color tests occurred equally often and in random order. Because of this procedure, the information load on compound trials was greater than on element trials.

A summary of Maki and Leith's results appears in the upper two curves of Fig. 2. Several effects are worth noting. First, element performance was consistently superior to compound performance at all sample durations. This was characteristic of both birds and both dimensions. The second important feature is that the birds appear to process information about both dimensions on every trial, even with very short sample durations. The lowest curve in Fig. 2 is the performance that *would occur* if, on compound trials, the bird attended to *only one* dimension per trial, choosing each dimension equally often on a random basis. This simple model assumes that the bird is a perfect selective attender and performs as well on the attended dimension as it does on element

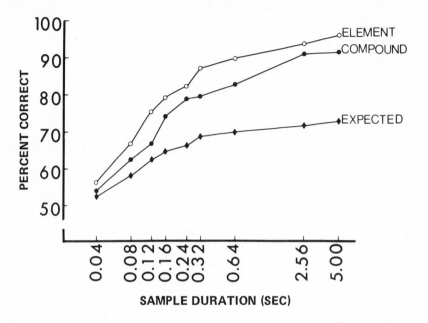

FIG. 2.   Matching-to-sample performance for two birds. The open and closed circles represent respectively performance on element and on compound trials. The diamonds represent performance that would result from a hypothetical bird attending to only one element per compound trial. The resulting curve is a combined average of element performance (perfectly attending to the to-be-tested dimension) and chance (perfectly ignoring the to-be-tested dimension), (Data taken from Maki & Leith, 1973.)

trials. Because it attends to one dimension and ignores the other, if the neglected dimension is tested, performance is dictated by chance. Thus, according to this model, average performance following compound trials will be halfway between chance and element performance. This is true because on half the trials the animal will select the correct dimension, be tested for it, and show element trial performance; while on the other half of the trials it will select the dimension that is not tested and show chance performance. As can be seen in the figure, the model does not come close to mirroring performance following compound samples. We conclude, therefore, that the experimental birds do not behave as predicted by the model and instead appear to attend to both dimensions on most or all trials, sharing their attention between the two dimensions.

The third important feature of Maki and Leith's results is that matching-to-sample performance improves as a function of sample duration over the range of sample durations indicated here and, indeed, may continue to improve even with sample durations longer than 5 sec. These facts are not peculiar to research from this laboratory. Roberts and Grant (1974) have found such improvements following an 8-sec sample as opposed to a 4-sec sample, and Farthing and Opuda (1973) have found improvements as a function of the number of times the bird pecks at the sample. As Roberts and Grant (1974) observed, these facts differ from similar investigations with monkeys. D'Amato and Worsham (1972) found virtually perfect matching-to-sample in monkeys with 40-msec exposure time, and we have made similar observations with humans using our pigeon apparatus. In this chapter, we shall inquire into the reasons for both the element-compound difference and the change in performance with sample duration.

II. THE ANALYSIS OF ELEMENT–COMPOUND DIFFERENCES

The most obvious interpretation of the superiority of element over compound performance is that the bird divides attention and thus capacity between the two elements of the compound during sample processing. This *divided-attention hypothesis* states that when capacity is not adequate to process all information in the brief time available, and when this information is more or less equally divided between two or more incoming messages, each message will suffer relative to performance with a single message. Such a general hypothesis does not state where in the processing system the loss occurs, but it does distinguish between an information processing loss and losses due to other factors.

Maki and Leith (1973) and Maki, Riley, and Leith (1976) have considered two additional classes of explanations to account for element-compound differences that are alternatives to the divided-attention hypothesis. One of these, a *generalization decrement hypothesis*, states that performance following a compound sample is inferior to performance following an element sample because compound samples are always followed by element tests. Consequently, no correct stimulus precisely matches the compound sample. Following an element sample, on the other hand, one of the test stimuli *is* an identical match. The other interpretation attributes element-compound differences to *stimulus degradation* during sample presentation. White lines on a colored field may desaturate the color, making color differences less distinct while the bright colors surrounding the white lines make the lines harder to detect than do black surrounds. This interpretation has also been suggested by Zuckerman (1973) to account for analogous effects in a maintained discrimination.

A. Generalization Decrement

Maki et al. (1976) conducted three tests of the generalization decrement hypothesis and found no support for it. In the first two experiments, element and compound samples were both followed by compound test stimuli that differed from each other on the relevant dimension but were the same on the other dimension. In Experiment 1, the irrelevant dimension was the same as one dimension of the compound sample. For example, if the sample was blue and horizontal, one test stimulus might have been blue and horizontal and be the correct choice while the other was blue and vertical. In Experiment 2, the irrelevant dimension in the two test stimuli had the value that did not appear in the sample. Hence, the blue horizontal sample mentioned above might be followed by a red horizontal and a red vertical test with the former being the correct choice. In both these experiments, the superiority of element relative to compound performance remained undisturbed. In Experiment 1, the correct test choice exactly matched the compound, but never matched the element sample. Thus the experimental arrangements were reversed from those used in Maki and Leith's (1973) experiment. Consequently, according to the generalization decrement hypothesis, matching of the compound sample in this new experiment should have been superior to matching of the element. Nevertheless, no change in the superiority of the element matching over compound matching occurred. In Experiment 2, neither test stimulus exactly matched either the element or the compound sample. Again, however, the superiority of element over compound remained the same. These facts argue strongly against a generalization decrement hypothesis but are consistent with an information overload hypothesis. It is possible to argue, however, that in both experiments the irrelevant dimension interfered with matching performance. In Experiment 1, both tests were at least partially correct in that both keys matched the sample on the irrelevant dimension. In Experiment 2, neither test was completely correct in that both keys mismatched the sample on the irrelevant dimension. Both of these factors may have affected the subject's performance following compound samples.

B. Response Competition and Redundant Relevant Cues

For this reason, Experiment 3 was conducted. In the condition of major interest, all compound sample presentations were followed by test presentations in which one key matched the sample on *both* dimensions and the other test key differed from the sample on *both* dimensions. In this way, both dimensions were redundant and relevant in that they both signaled the correct choice. While the results bear on the generalization decrement hypothesis, the issues raised by them are more far reaching and create new questions for the analysis of element-compound differences. Consequently, we will discuss this experiment in some detail. The experiment compared processing of element and compound samples under two sets of test conditions. For one set of conditions element test stimuli always followed both element (EE) and compound (CE) samples (the first letter refers to the sample, the second to the test). These conditions are identical to the earlier conditions (Maki & Leith, 1973) in which EE trials produced consistently higher performance than CE trials (Fig. 2).

Days with such element tests were alternated with days on which compound tests followed element (EC) and compound (CC) samples. In the compound-test conditions, when a sample was an element, one of the compound-test stimuli was the same as the sample on one dimension and irrelevant on the other; the

other compound-test stimulus differed from the first test stimulus on both
dimensions. For example, if the sample was a red key, the positive test stimulus
might be red and vertical, the negative blue and horizontal. Finally, when a compound sample was presented, the compound-test condition (CC) carried information on both dimensions and so contained one test stimulus that was identical
to the sample stimulus and another test stimulus that differed from the sample
on both dimensions. For example, a red and vertical sample would be followed
by a choice between a red and vertical correct stimulus and a blue and horizontal incorrect stimulus. Thus, with such a sample-test pair, the generalization
decrement hypothesis would predict that performance with compound samples
and compound tests would be identical to performance obtained with element
samples and element tests. In both cases, there is a test stimulus identical to the
sample stimulus and a test stimulus completely different from the sample stimulus. Since the values on both dimensions of the compound sample agree with
the values on both dimensions of the correct compound test, the animal could
base his decision on either or both elements and be correct. Consequently, there
should be no generalization decrement and no possible response competition as
in Experiments 1 and 2. One would expect, according to either of these alterna-

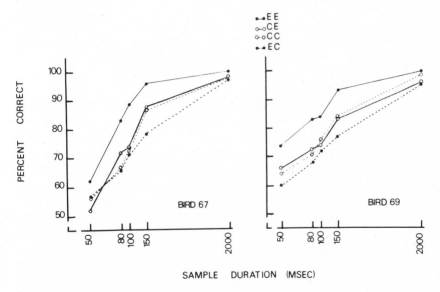

SAMPLE   DURATION   (MSEC)

FIG. 3.   Matching-to-sample performance for two birds under four different combinations
of sample-test conditions. Conditions EE and CE refer to element and compound samples
with an element test condition. Conditions EC and CC employed the same sample conditions
but the tests were always compound tests. Following both element and compound samples,
the test stimuli differed from one another on both dimensions. Thus, following an element
sample, one of the test keys had a stimulus value which matched the sample on only one
dimension. Following a compound sample, one of the test keys matched the sample on
both dimensions, the other on neither dimension. (Data taken from Maki et al., 1976.)

tives to the information overload hypothesis, that performance following compound samples and compound tests would be identical to performance following element samples and element tests.

The results of this experiment, shown in Fig. 3, do not support these predictions. The presence of redundant relevant test pairs did not facilitate performance. In fact, CC trials produced the same level of performance as that produced by CE trials which were both lower than the performance obtained on EE trials. Performance following a compound sample was the same whether the test stimulus was an element or a compound. Thus, neither response competition nor generalization decrement are necessary to account for the obtained difference between performance with element and with compound samples. Response competition does, however, seem to figure into the performance of the other novel condition in this experiment: The EC condition in which compound tests followed element tests. Apparently, in this condition, the birds' performance was partially controlled by the irrelevant dimension. The type of competition found in this condition, however, could not account for the element-compound difference of interest. With compound samples and element tests, there is only the single relevant dimension present on the test keys and thus no competition could occur.

Recall that our impetus for investigating these phenomena was an attempt to understand selective attention in animals in situations in which we were reasonably satisfied that the animals were operating under conditions of information overload. Do the data of the experiments by Maki et al. (1976) come from situations in which the animal is overloaded? Performance in the compound sample conditions of Experiment 3 in which there was no response competition was superior to performance in the compound conditions of Experiment 1 or 2, in which there was both information overload and response competition. Despite the elimination of response competition, however, performance on the compound sample condition CE and CC remained below the performance of the element sample condition in which there was no competition. We feel confident, therefore, in concluding that the superiority of matching performance with an element sample over compound sample is due to the effect of information overload. As persuasive as we find this argument, it does raise the problem of why the birds in Maki et al.'s (1976) CC condition did not utilize the redundancy of compound samples and tests to reduce the information load.

C. Redundant Relevant Cue Facilitation

Because the same values of both dimensions were present in the sample and in the correct test choice, but not in the incorrect test choice, the animal could behave perfectly accurately by attending to only one of the available dimensions and not spending time partially encoding the second. If the animal were to behave in this manner both during sample presentation and during the test, CC performance should equal EE performance. Because the animals in this experiment performed equally in the CC and CE conditions, it follows that there was no reduction in information load.

This is a curious finding. Other experiments have not only found that discriminative performance is as good with compound stimuli as with element stimuli, but actually found that performance improves with compound stimuli above that obtained with element. That is, redundant relevant cues can facilitate discriminative performance.

Zuckerman (1973) found such facilitation when he compared discriminative performance with stimulus elements (hues and line tilts) with performance with redundant relevant compounds of the same stimuli. In the first phase of the experiment, Zuckerman trained the birds to make one response if any of four shorter wavelength hues (shorter than 580 nm) or any of the four smaller angled line tilts (less than 22.5° counterclockwise rotation from vertical) was presented, and to make another response if any of four longer wavelength hues (greater than 580 nm) or any of four larger angled (greater than 22.5°) line tilt stimuli appeared. By testing each dimension separately, he obtained psychometric functions for element discriminative performance.

In a second phase, Zuckerman then presented eight unique pairs of stimuli in which the shortest wavelength hue was always presented in compound with the smallest angle line tilt, the second hue with the second line tilt, etc. Training with these compound stimuli resulted in an improvement in the discriminability of the redundant relevant compounds over the discriminative performance obtained with each dimension individually.

In a third phase, he then presented all possible pairs of hue and line tilt. This means that in addition to the eight pairs of stimuli presented during the second phase, there were also 56 other possible pairs. The eight pairs presented in both Phase II and Phase III were equally redundant, equally relevant, and equally often reinforced in both phases, but the facilitative effect of pairing them disappeared in Phase III.

It is not immediately obvious why redundant relevant cue facilitation should depend on the context in which the pairs are presented, but it seems to depend on just that. When the stimuli were consistently paired, facilitation occurred; when the same pairs were presented among all possible pairs, facilitation disappeared. In the experiment presented by Maki et al. (1976) all possible pairs of stimuli were also presented, and in that experiment, too, no facilitative effect was found. Animals appear to respond differently depending on how the cue pairs are formed. This notion is reminiscent of the work on configural conditioning in which prolonged training with compound stimuli can result in a difference between the signal strength of the compound relative to the signal strengths of its components (Thomas, Berman, Serednesky, and Lyons, 1968; Baker, 1968; Booth and Hammond, 1971; Rescorla, 1972). Perhaps under the consistent pairings situation used by Zuckerman (1973), and perhaps under the conditions used to produce configuring (these may or may not reflect the same phenomena), the animal comes to treat the compound as a new stimulus which is other than a simple combination of its components.

III. STIMULUS COMPOUNDS AND INFORMATION PROCESSING

Another impetus for the view that different kinds of stimulus compounds are processed in different ways comes primarily from the work of Garner (1970, 1974) using human subjects. He and his associates have presented evidence that the nature of the stimulus compound can affect one's ability to process information about it. In particular they have drawn two sets of distinctions that may be of value in the analysis of these two experiments and animal information processing in general.

Garner (1970) distinguishes between two types of compounds, separable and integral, and between two sources of difficulty in a discrimination, state limitations and process limitations. Integral stimulus compounds are those in which the elimination of one dimension in a bidimensional compound necessarily results in the elimination of the other dimension. An archetypical example is a set of cues to be discriminated on the basis of hue and saturation. Elimination of hue necessarily eliminates saturation and vice versa. Separable compounds involve independent dimensions in which the elimination of one dimension does not need to effect the other dimension. An example is a discrimination involving a colored light and a tone.

Discriminability can be limited in either of two ways. A process limitation refers to a discrimination being difficult because the stimuli to be discriminated are so close together that the subject cannot tell them apart very well. A state limitation refers to a discrimination in which the difficulty is caused by the stimuli each being hard to detect alone (e.g., because the illumination is too low or the presentation too brief). If energy were to be added to them, however, the differences between them would be sufficiently large to result in rather good performance. Garner and his associates (e.g., Garner, 1974) have presented evidence regarding the different ways in which these two distinctions interact. Separable stimulus compounds facilitate performance when discriminability is limited by a state limitation but not when discriminability is limtied by a process limitation. Integral compounds, on the other hand, facilitate process-limited discriminations but not state-limited discriminations.

Garner and his associates have also discovered something interesting about the way in which humans rate the similarity and difference between separable and integral stimuli. Scaled differences between integral stimulus compounds obey a Euclidean metric in which the differences along each dimension form the legs of a right triangle and the judged difference corresponds to the hypotenuse of the triangle. Scaled differences between separable compounds, on the other hand, obey a city block metric in which the differences on the two dimensions are added.

A. Garner's Analysis Extended to Animal Research

Garner's analysis seems directly applicable to the understanding of the issues raised in the preceding section. Recall that Zuckerman (1973) found redundant relevant cue facilitation in his maintained discrimination task but that Maki et al. (1976) failed to find such facilitation.

Zuckerman's experiment is an example of process limited discrimination in that the performance was limited by the similarity of the stimuli to one another. Only the values farthest from the criteria could be discriminated with anything near 100% accuracy. Consequently, the fact that the compound cues facilitated discrimination when redundant and perfectly correlated is consistent with the suggestion that this treatment produced integrality of the compounds through the experience of regular and consistent pairing. The abandonment of the regular pairing procedure in the third phase may have reduced the integrality of the cues so that the redundant relevant cues no longer resulted in facilitation of performance.

Chase and Heinemann (1972) also ran pigeons on a bidimensional discrimination task similar to that run by Zuckerman. When the stimuli were redundant, relevant, and consistently paired, the pigeon's choice curves fitted a model consistent with Garner's analysis of integral stimulus compounds. That is, the discriminability of each dimension alone formed the leg of a right triangle, the hypotenuse of which corresponded to the discriminability of the compound.

Further research is necessary to determine whether other features of an integral stimulus also occur as a result of repeated training with consistent correlated pairs. For example, Garner (1970) reported that for humans, redundant relevant integral compounds facilitated discrimination when the difficulty of discrimination was due to a process limitation (as in Zuckerman's experiment), but not when the difficulty was due to a state limitation. At the present time, there are no animal data relating state limitation to integrality and separability.

Consider now the redundant relevant cue experiment by Maki et al. (1976, Experiment 3). There are several differences between their Experiment 3 and Zuckerman's Phase II. Zuckerman used a maintained discrimination in which the difficulty was produced by a process limitation — the stimuli were too similar for perfect discrimination by the subject. Maki et al. (1976), on the other hand, used a matching-to-sample procedure in which the difficulty was produced by a state limitation — the samples were presented too briefly to allow perfect performance. Garner found that redundant relevant integral cues do not facilitate discrimination when the difficulty of discrimination is produced by a state limitation. One would expect, therefore, that even if the birds used by Maki et al. did manage to integrate the compound stimuli presented in Experiment 3, they still would not have shown facilitation because their performance was restricted by a state limitation. We find this to be an unlikely explanation, however. It does not seem reasonable that the matching-to-sample birds formed integral stimulus compounds in the same situations in which it is necessary to assume that Zuckerman's birds failed to preserve integrality, that is in his Phase III. Furthermore, if the birds did treat the samples in a manner similar to that in which humans treat integral compounds, one would expect compound performance to be facilitated to the level of element performance. Humans treat integral compounds as if the compounds varied along a single dimension different from either of the physical dimensions in the compound. If pigeons behaved this way, the memory load would therefore be reduced from two dimensions to one single new dimension: a reduction which should result in the bird treating the compound as a single element. The data from Maki et al. clearly do not support this prediction either, so it is unlikely that they did treat the compounds as integral.

Finally, there is another possible explanation for the lack of facilitation observed in Maki et al.'s third experiment: Matching-to-sample, as opposed to maintained discrimination, requires at least two stages. First, when the sample is presented it must be detected and encoded for later use because it will not be present at the time of choice. Second, a recognition phase occurs during which the subjects are required to match at least one test stimulus against the representation of the sample in working memory (cf. Honig, this volume, Chapter 8) in order to select the correct choice. The two dimensions presented in the sample do not become redundant until the test is presented. Indeed, as we described earlier, on alternate days the two dimensions being followed by element tests were not redundant at all. It may be the case, then, either that the birds in the experiment of Maki et al. never learned to use the redundancy when it was present or that it was not useful at the necessary point in the matching sequence.

To summarize, there is evidence suggesting that pigeons can treat ostensibly separable stimuli as integral. This analysis is consistent with the finding of redundant relevant cue facilitation in the second phase of Zuckerman's experiment, and with the shape of the postdiscrimination gradients Chase and Heinemann (1972) found after redundant relevant compound training. No such effect appeared in the third phase of Zuckerman's experiment or in Experiment 3 of Maki et al. These findings suggest that pigeons may integrate stimuli when two dimensions are consistently and uniquely paired. Such consistent pairings appear to produce facilitation while nonconsistent pairings appear not to produce it. Finally, we have suggested that configural conditioning may reflect the perceptual integration of otherwise separable stimulus compounds.

B. Selective Attention

One consequence of the concept of limited capacity is that an increase in processing of one set of stimuli reduces the capacity for processing another set. If then, an animal could be trained or instructed to attend to one of the dimensions present in a compound task in which its capacity is exceeded, the animal ought to do better on that attended dimension, and at the same time, ought to do worse on the neglected dimension. Presumably, the improvement on the attended dimension ought to be roughly equal to the decrement on the neglected dimension. This has been called the inverse hypothesis (Thomas, 1970).

Employing pigeons in a maintained discrimination task, Blough (1969) found what appear to be selective attention effects which correspond to this description. He trained pigeons to perform in a bidimensional discrimination involving seven similar hues and seven similar auditory frequencies. Of the 49 possible pairs, one pair consisting of an extreme value from each set was designated S+. All other pairs were designated S-. When the task was changed so that discriminations were required on only one dimension (the other dimension being held constant on S+), performance on the varying dimension improved. When tested again with both dimensions varying, Blough found a deterioration on the dimension which had been represented by a single value that corresponded to the improvement on the dimension that had been varying. With further bidimensional training, this difference disappeared and performance returned to its baseline level. As has been pointed out elsewhere (e.g., Leith & Maki, 1975), it is possible to interpret the loss of control on the neglected dimension with mechanisms other than attention: That is, one can apply the laws that govern the strength of association in other situations and still produce a loss of control. The corresponding improvement on the varying dimension and its subsequent loss with further bidimensional training is more difficult to explain however. Blough was careful to ensure that the density of reinforcement to S+ *on the varying dimension* was the same in all three conditions. It therefore seems unlikely that simple changes in habit strength could account for the obtained improvement and subsequent decrement in performance on the varying dimension. Furthermore, the discriminative stimuli were presented for only a brief time — 1.5 sec, during which the bird had to perform a difficult discrimination. The combination of the time pressure from brief stimuli (a state limitation) and the difficulty of the discrimination (a process limitation) probably produced a large load on the bird's system, hence the demonstration of selective attentional effects.

C. Stimulus Degradation

Earlier, in discussing the work of Maki and Leith (1973), we suggested an alternative to the generalization decrement and information load hypotheses. This stimulus degradation hypothesis suggested that element—compound differences found by Maki and Leith were due to a degradation of the quality of each dimension in a compound because of reduced contrast. This hypothesis does not readily apply to Blough's experiment, but for a task with visual stimuli such as Maki and Leith's, it offers an alternative to the selective attention hypothesis. The stimulus degradation hypothesis would be ruled out if matching-to-sample performance were to improve on the attended dimension while deteriorating on the neglected dimension for such a change would demonstrate that the element—

compound difference does not reflect poorer quality stimuli, but divided attention effects. A strong stimulus degradation hypothesis would require that selective attention training have no effect on the element—compound difference. On the other hand, a *failure* to find a selective-attention effect could reflect either less than perfect selective attention or stimulus degradation.

Leith and Maki (1975) conducted an experiment analogous to Blough's but using the matching-to-sample task rather than a maintained discrimination. The task and the stimulus displays were basically the same as those already described in Maki and Leith's (1973) study. Two birds were first tested in the divided attention condition already described, and performance on both element sample trials and compound sample trials was measured. Next, prolonged training occurred during which element samples from only one dimension were used along with compound samples containing both dimensions. First, one dimension was tested for a month, then the other dimension was tested for a month with intervening periods of bidimensional retraining.

During the single dimension training condition compound performance improved relative to element performance. That is, performance on compound trials approached but did not equal performance on element trials. This *reduction* in the element—compound difference for the selected dimension found during single element training was roughly matched by an *increase* in element—compound difference for the neglected dimension upon the return to the two dimension condition. These results show a direct correspondence to Blough's (1969) data. Training intended to produce selective attention to line, caused line performance to improve and color performance to suffer. Training intended to produce selective attention to color, caused color performance to improve, and performance on line to suffer. Because these data are consistent with a selective attention interpretation, they are inconsistent with a strong stimulus degradation hypothesis. Although the failure to completely eliminate the element—compound difference may reflect either stimulus degradation or incomplete selective attention, stimulus degradation is not sufficient to account for element—compound differences.

The data presented by Leith and Maki are of particular interest in that they appear to offer direct support for the inverse hypothesis. Following compound samples, performance on the attended dimension improved and, performance on the neglected dimension deteriorated. Such deterioration is not required by the constraints of the experiment itself; in principle, there is no reason why the animal could not improve in its performance to one set of cues while remaining at the same level of performance on the neglected set of cues.

D. Trial-to-Trial Selective Attention Instructions

The demonstration of an inverse relationship between processing a selected input and processing the other inputs is one aspect of the demonstration of selective attentional effects. Usually, attention is also seen as being flexible

(Kahneman, 1973). It would strengthen the argument that the preceding experiments demonstrated selective attentional effects if it were possible to demonstrate flexibility in the selective performance of pigeons.

In an experiment very similar to that run by Leith and Maki, Leuin (1976) investigated the effect of cueing the to-be-tested dimension on matching-to-sample performance. On every trial, sample presentations on the center key were preceded by one of three stimuli also on the center key. On half of the compound trials on which the bird would be tested for line orientation, the sample was preceded by a white cross on a dark surround. On half of the compound trials on which the bird would be tested for hue, the sample was preceded by a blue and a red spot, one above the other. On the other half of the compound trials with either dimension, the sample was preceded by a plain white disk signalling that either dimension could be tested. These presample stimuli were called line cues, color cues, and warning signals, respectively. They were each presented for a fixed 2.5 sec duration, and a single peck was necessary to initiate

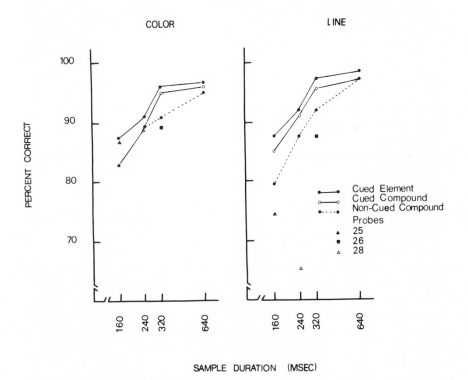

FIG. 4. The effect of pretrial curing on the relevant dimension on matching-to-sample performance averaged over three birds: The three disconnected points in each panel represent the performance on the three birds on catch trials in which performance was tested on the noncued dimension following precued compound-sample presentations. (From Leuin, 1976, used with permission.)

the presentation of the sample. All element samples were preceded by the appropriate cue.

As can be seen in Fig. 4, cueing reduced the difference between elements and compounds relative to elements and noncued compounds. One bird showed a significant effect only for color, a second, only for line and the third bird showed a signifiant effect of cueing on both dimensions.

After completing this part of the experiment, each bird then received an additional three sessions with the stimulus duration which produced the greatest cueing effect for that bird. During each of these three sessions of 432 trials, one-third of the cued compound trials were tested with the incorrectly cued dimension; that is, a line-cued compound was followed by a test on the color differences, and a color-cued compound was followed by a test on the line differences. The results of these "catch" or "probe" trials are also shown in Fig. 4 as three independent points in each panel. Each of the different symbols stands for a bird. Thus one bird was tested at 160, another at 240, and a third at 320 msec. Whereas positive effects of cueing occurred in both dimensions, the effects of the catch probe appeared only in the line dimension. To describe the effect in another way: If the cue instructs "attend to color," the bird does, and it ignores line. If the cue instructs "attend to line," the bird does, but apparently it cannot ignore color.

Leuin's experiment demonstrates selective attention effects in pigeons that are analogous to those found in humans in that attention shifts from trial to trial with the change in instructions. His data are consistent with a view of pigeons as limited capacity information processors. His paradigm has, however, somewhat limited usefulness because his positive effects, while statistically reliable, were necessarily small because the magnitude of a selective attention effect is limited by the magnitude of the uncued element-compound difference. We are currently at work trying to find a paradigm in which there is a greater difference between single element and divided attention conditions. Such a search is well justified because of the additional questions that can then be asked. For example, where in the matching-to-sample sequence do attentional effects occur? If the performance with compound samples is worse than performance with element samples because the subject is constrained in its ability to perceive and encode multiple dimensions, then a cue that allows it to select one dimension and ignore another would improve compound performance. Alternatively, a cue presented after the termination of the sample could have no effect on the actual perception of the sample and so, in this hypothetical situation, no effect on compound performance. If, however, the subjects performance is constrained by rehearsal or response limitations, then a postsample cue as well as a presample cue might improve compound performance (cf. Broadbent, 1970).

We have attempted, albeit with limited success, to increase element—compound differences by increasing the number of dimensions on which the animal must match. The argument was that division of available capacity among three dimensions should reduce performance on all, and thus allow greater opportunity for cued selection to show itself. The third dimension, in addition to color and line tilt, was shape (triangle or circle) placed between two white vertical or horizontal lines. We attempted to teach this new three dimensional problem to two birds that had previously learned the color and line-tilt problems. One bird never reached a comparable level of performance on the third dimension. The other bird did learn, and showed performance comparable to that obtained by Leuin. In addition to the three conditions used by Leuin, this three dimensional experiment also employed a fourth condition that, in some ways, is a better control condition than was used by Leuin. This experiment employed not only cued and noncued compounds with a cued element condition as in Leuin's experiment, but also cued and noncued elements. Even with this more appropriate control procedure cueing effects remained, i.e., the difference between cued elements and compounds on the one hand was less than the difference between noncued elements and compounds on the other. In spite of our expectations to the contrary, performance on three dimensional samples was not worse than performance with two dimensional compounds. The failure to find a difference between two and three element samples may have been due to an insensitivity in the design. If we are correct in our assumptions regarding the pigeon as a limited capacity information processer, then the difference between processing one element and two elements is very large (100% for one element vs. 50% for each of two), while the difference between processing two elements and three is relatively small (50% for two and 33.3% for each of three with a difference of 16.7). Our design may not have been sensitive enough to detect a difference of 16.7% in available capacity. The experiment does serve, however, as a replication of Leuin's experiment with a different bird, some different stimuli, and an appropriate control condition.

The data presented above strongly suggest that the *primary* cause of element compound differences as presented by Blough (1969), Leith & Maki (1975) and by Leuin (1976) is the division of attention between the two dimensions of a compound sample. The effect of this division of attention is to reduce the efficiency of processing information about both members of the compound. Other hypotheses such as response competition, stimulus degradation, and generalization decrement, were, for the most part, eliminated as viable alternatives to a divided attention interpretation.

IV. THE EFFECT OF SAMPLE EXPOSURE TIME ON MATCHING PERFORMANCE

Another of the more intriguing results of matching-to-sample experiments with pigeons in which sample exposure time is manipulated as an experimental variable is the remarkable duration over which performance continues to improve. Examination of Fig. 2 taken from Maki and Leith (1973), shows improvements with samples as long as 5 sec. Even more remarkably, Roberts and Grant (1974) have found that increasing sample duration from 4 to 8 sec still produced an improvement in pigeons' performance. Why these facts strike us as so remarkable is answered in part by the results of directly comparable experiments done with Capuchin monkeys by D'Amato and Worsham (1972) and with humans in our laboratory. Monkeys match perfectly following a 20-msec sample if a 1-sec delay is introduced between sample and test. Performance declines slightly with an immediate test. Humans, in our laboratory, have done equally well on the same apparatus we have used to test our pigeons. Several alternative accounts have been suggested.

A. Readiness

Perhaps the most straightforward explanations might account for some but not all of the sample duration effect. One of these is the hypothesis that the improvement in performance with time is in part a function of when the animal begins to examine the sample stimulus. In our task, the sample is normally preceded by a warning signal and a 100-msec dark interval. We have used two procedures for producing the change from warning to sample stimulus. In one, the sample stimulus was presented 100 msec after the first peck to the warning signal (a white key). In the other, the warning signal stayed on for a fixed period of time. If, within that time, the bird pecked at the warning signal at least once, a sample was presented after a 100-msec delay. In both cases, a failure to peck the warning signal within the requisite time caused the intertrial interval to occur and the re-presentation of the trial. Neither of these manipulations made an obvious difference in our results. It is important to note that in the second procedure, the bird typically pecked at the warning light until the sample stimulus appeared. In these situations the bird pecks vigorously, often shutting its eyes as it strikes the key (Moore, 1973). Consequently, it might miss the first few score milliseconds of the sample stimulus. Examination of any of the previous curves relating sample duration to performance should make it obvious that the major improvement in performance occurs in the first 300 msec. This improvement, then, may reflect fluctuations in the time at which the bird first inspects the stimulus.

In an experiment conducted by Roitblat, Greene, and Riley (1976), we compared performance with a standard 100 msec between sample and test with performance following a 400-msec interval between sample and test. The other parameters of interest were the following: (1) whether the warning signal was presented for a fixed duration or was peck terminated, and (2) whether the sample duration was either 50 msec or 300 msec. Since the data presented by Maki and Leith (1973) indicate that the bird is, for the most part, able to process the information in a 300-msec sample, it must be the case that it can get ready to view the sample within those 300 msec. Consequently, with the 400-msec interval between warning signal and sample, the extra 300 msec ought to

TABLE 1
The Effect of Delay Between Warning Signal and Sample Stimulus[a]

	Delay in msec	Immediate termination of warning signal	Fixed 5-sec warning signal
Bird 67	100	63	78
50-msec sample duration	400	61	71
Bird 67	100	83	87
300-msec sample duration	400	86	87
Bird 13	100	64	67
50-msec sample duration	400	61	66
Bird 13	100	91	85
300-msec sample	400	78	86
Mean	–	73	78

[a]Table data are mean percent correct for each bird for two sample durations and two warning-signal-termination conditons.

provide ample time for the bird to get ready. The longer (300-msec) sample duration provided an internal control condition with which to compare performance. The immediately terminating and fixed-duration warning-signal conditions were included in order to compare the obtained results with both of the previously used warning-signal termination procedures, and to provide a condition, immediate termination, in which we could know unequivocally where the bird's beak was at the start of the interval. With the fixed-duration signal, although the bird tended to peck during the entire duration of the signal, the rate of pecking would vary from trial to trial, and the signal could end anywhere in the progress of a peck. In the immediate—termination condition, since the peck terminated the signal, it was possible to be sure that the bird's beak was in contact with the key at the start of the interval. The results from two birds in this experiment are presented in Table 1.

It is clear that increasing the delay between warning signal and sample does nothing to facilitate the performance. Overall, in fact, performance actually was worse with a longer delay than with a shorter delay. Interestingly, signal termination procedure did not interact with delay duration, but did interact with sample duration. This indicates that simply having time in which to get ready is not sufficient to produce the sample duration effect. Rather, it appears that sample duration per se, and not the interval between the warning signal and sample termination, controls the sample duration effect.

B. Proactive Interference

A second explanation of the sample duration effect is another version of the response–competition hypothesis mentioned during our discussion of the divided–attention experiments. According to the version of the hypothesis relevant now, however, the competition comes from the memory of stimuli presented on the previous trial. The function of increased sample duration, according to this hypothesis, is to increase the time since the last trial, reduce the strength of the memory of the previous stimuli, and thus the amount of interference. One test of this hypothesis would be to vary the intertrial interval to see whether long intervals eliminate the sample duration effect. In previous research we have used, from one experiment to the next, 5- and 10-sec intertrial intervals. No effect of these variations has been detected. In no single experiment, however, have we made a direct comparison of the effect of varying intertrial intervals. In an experiment designed to test this proactive–interference hypothesis, Roitblat, Greene, and Riley (1976) tested three birds with 5-, 10-, and 30-sec intertrial intervals. The results shown in Fig. 5 offer clear evidence against the hypothesis that longer trials achieve their effect on matching-to-sample simply by virtue of increasing the time since the last trial. If anything, increasing intertrial intervals from 5 to 10 to 30 sec decreases the efficiency of performance. This is not to say that variation in the time between trials cannot have other effects.

In another experiment Grant (1975) has shown proactive effects of interfering material within the matching-to-sample task. Furthermore, he has shown that interference effects involving the deliberate manipulation of competing responses decrease as time between the interfering material and the test material

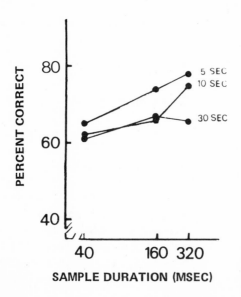

FIG. 5.   Matching-to-sample performance as a function of sample duration and intertrial interval. Performance is averaged over two birds. (From Roitblat, Greene, & Riley, 1976.)

increases. Grant did not find evidence, however, for a decline in matching-to-sample efficiency as intertrial interval was reduced. To the best of our knowledge, there are no data that contradict the present finding. Thus, while the present experiment sheds no particular light on the role of prior interfering effects in immediate or delayed matching to sample, our experiment does rule out the interpretation with which we were concerned. We find no evidence that the increase in efficiency of matching-to-sample duration is in any way related to time since the last trial.

C. The Physical vs. the Functional Duration of the Sample

A third alternative to account for the improvement in performance with increasing sample duration is that pigeons are restricted to extracting information from a stimulus only as long as it is physically present. The data from such paradigms as backward masking and partial report of complex stimuli (See Kahneman, 1968; and Sperling, 1967) indicate that humans are capable of maintaining visual representations of complex stimuli for durations greater than the actual physical duration. Neisser (1967) called this maintained representation of the stimulus an icon. Barring interference, the icon appears to have a minimum duration of about 100 msec. Functionally, this means that humans tend to perceive brief stimuli as having a minimum duration of 100 msec, more or less independent of the actual duration of that stimulus. With the simple stimuli employed in our studies of matching-to-sample, this 100-msec minimum functional duration is sufficient to support perfect or near perfect performance in humans. In other words, the rate of information extraction in humans is high enough to allow complete encoding of the sample before its physical or iconic presence ceases. The duration of the icon and its associated information extraction process can be disrupted by the presentation of appropriate masking stimuli. When presented following the sample, these stimuli are called backward masks (Kahneman, 1973) and by presenting them at different intervals following the termination of the sample, it is possible to interrupt the information extraction or encoding process at different levels of completion.

Actually, there are two separate iconic hypotheses, each with a different potential mechanism to account for the sample duration effect. According to the first, the rate of information extraction in pigeons is the same as the rate in humans, but the pigeons do not maintain icons of the brief samples and thus, information extraction ceases with the offset of the sample. According to the second, pigeons *do* maintain icons of the sample following its physical termination, but the rate at which they can extract or encode the information from the sample is considerably slower than in humans.

According to the first iconic hypothesis, one would expect that a backward mask would have little or no effect on a pigeon's matching-to-sample performance. If pigeons do, however, maintain icons, then a backward mask could be expected to disrupt performance. Furthermore, an immediate mask should be more disruptive than a delayed mask because it should interrupt the processing when it was less complete than a delayed mask would. To examine these alternatives we (Roitblat, Greene and Riley, 1976) conducted an experiment on two birds using line and color, element and compound, and a factorial combination of six sample times and four delay conditions. The delay conditions were: Zero delay between sample and test, and three ½-sec delay conditions — one unfilled, that is, dark, one with the first ¼ sec filled with a visual mask, and one with the last ¼ sec filled with a visual mask.

The study then, enabled us to examine two separate questions: First, what are the effects of a brief delay on matching efficiency with various sample times, and second, what are the effects of masking during this delay?

The effect of delay alone as a function of sample duration is shown in Fig. 6. The data presented show the effects of ½-sec delay on the processing of color in the two upper panels, and the processing of line in the two lower panels. The two birds showed consistent performance in both conditions. For each bird, there was a significant decline in color with a ½-sec delay. Also, for each bird, sample duration by delay interacted significantly for line. For short sample durations, a delay facilitated performance with line samples, while samples of 500 msec or longer, delay produced a deterioration in performance. The impli-

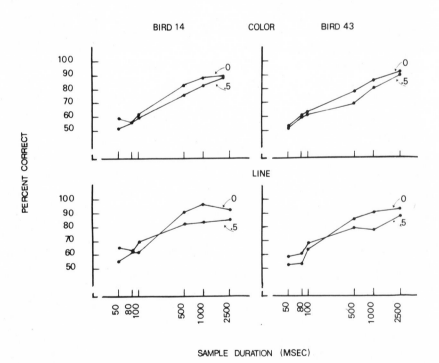

FIG. 6.   Matching-to-sample performance as a function of sample time and immediate versus ½-sec delay between sample and test. (From Roitblat et al. 1976.)

cation of these data is that the pigeon can gain information about lines from an internal representation following brief samples.

What is it that prevented the birds in Maki and Leith's experiment and in the no-delay condition of this experiment from utilizing this extra ability to extract information? Since the test stimulus was on for 5 sec, it should have been to the bird's advantage to hold off making a decision until the representation of the stimulus had reached its maximum, yet they did not. A possible explanation of this is that the test stimuli functioned as backward masks, disrupting the internal representation — image of the stimulus before maximum information could be gleaned. The two masking conditions allowed us to examine this question in part.

If a backward mask could interfere with processing, then one would expect to find such interference in all conditions in which a short delay facilitates performance. This interference can come from at least two sources. Grant and Roberts (1976) showed that simple illumination in the experimental chamber during the sample—test interval was sufficient to disrupt performance. The amount of disruption depended on the duration of the illumination and was independent of the temporal location between the sample and test in the conditions they used. The backward mask in our experiment could also have such an effect, or it could disrupt performance because it somehow confused the bird about, for example, the stimuli to which it was to attend. To control for such effects, and to test only for the maintenance of the representation of the stimulus, both a delayed and an immediate masking condition were employed. Any difference in performance found between the delayed mask and the immediate mask, then, would likely be due to a disruption of the information—encoding and storage process and not to some sort of "rehearsal" disruption, for example. However, since we have no way of knowing a priori for what portion of this ½-sec interval the representation is being maintained, it is also possible that the delayed mask, too, could disrupt the encoding process. Figure 7 shows the results of the two visual masking procedures compared with the nonmasking procedure. In each panel, the test value at 0 delay is shown on the left for comparison purposes. In the three conditions shown on the right in each panel, ½-sec delay occurred between the end of the sample and the beginning of the test stimuli. For one of the masking procedures, the mask was presented during the first ¼ sec of the delay; for the other, it was for the last ¼ sec of the delay.

The results for line-tilt samples are shown in the right panel of Fig. 7 collapsed across the two birds. No consistant difference among the three delay conditions for sample durations of 500 msec or longer was found. For the short sample durations, both immediate and delayed masks disrupt performance, with the immediate mask being more disruptive than the delayed mask. Similarly with color samples, no systematic differences are present among the results for the three delay conditions with long sample durations, but short samples show clear-cut backward-masking effects. Thus, despite the lack of a rise in performance with a simple unfilled delay, the stronger effect of an immediate com-

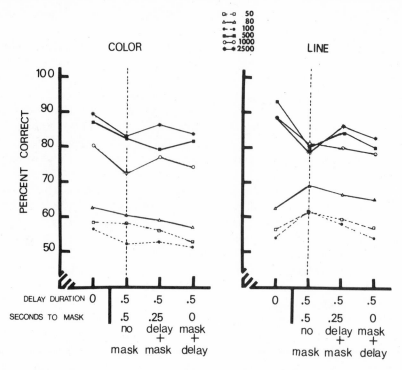

FIG. 7.   The effect of a backward mask on delayed matching-to-sample. The points to the left of the dotted line show 0-delay matching performance. For the three points on and to the right of the dotted line, the ½-sec delay was either unfilled (no mask), filled with a mask during the first ¼-sec (mask plus delay) or with a mask during the second ¼-sec (delay plus mask). The parameters represent different sample times. (From Roitblat et al., 1976.)

pared to a delayed backward mask indicates that processing does continue after stimulus termination for color as well as for lines.

While it is clear from these data that processing can continue following the termination of the stimulus, it is also clear that the net efficiency of this post-stimulus processing is lower than it is during the physical presence of the sample. If it were as efficient, one would expect that performance following a short sample and a short delay would be equal to performance associated with a sample of duration equal to the sum of the short sample plus the delay. Figures 6 and 7 show that this is not the case. An 80-msec sample, for example, with a delay does not produce better performance than a 100-msec sample with no delay. At present, we do not have the data to decide whether the net lower efficiency of encoding during the delay is due to a low rate of encoding throughout the delay or a combination of high rate encoding (that is, at the same rate as occurs during the physical presence of the sample) for an early portion of the delay followed by the decay of the encoded memory trace during late parts of the delay.

To summarize, delays can facilitate matching performance with line samples at short durations, they can disrupt matching performance with both line and color samples at longer durations, and masking effects occur for both lines and colors at short durations. These facts suggest that part of the beneficial effect of increased sample duration is directly related to an increased opportunity to process stimuli. The data also indicate, however, that increased processing duration in the absence of the stimulus does not account for all of the beneficial effect of increased sample duration. Something else also occurs. The "something else" that seems to be going on is an opportunity to benefit from the prolonged presentation of the sample stimulus itself, not from processing time as such. Why should prolonged presentation of a sample aid the animal? Perhaps the presence of the stimulus prevents decay of its internal representation. Alternatively, the increased stimulus exposure might allow the animal to make repeated samplings of the stimulus. If so, continuous presentation of the stimulus may not be necessary for optimal performance. We know from the work of Farthing and Opuda (1973) that number of pecks instead of amount of time can be manipulated as the independent variable determining matching success. Does a peck correspond to a look? Perhaps if we could control the amount of time that the sample stimulus is off following each peck, we would be able to determine whether look time or number of looks is the critical event in determining matching-to-sample efficiency.

V. CONCLUSION

Most animal learning experiments have studied the acquisition of a habit through repeated learning trials. The experiments presented here, on the other hand, stressed the acquisition of information within a single trial. Most recent evidence regarding attention in animals has come from such paradigms as blocking (in this volume, see Chapters 5 and 6 by Fowler and Mackintosh, respectively) and overshadowing. The attentional analysis we suggest here is different from that suggested to interpret data from these other paradigms. The evidence from blocking and overshadowing is consistent with an analysis in which the animal learns to ignore noninformative stimuli. While in some sense this is a form of selective attention, it does not tell us about the limits of the organisms' information processing abilities. Attention is not selective in these situations because the animal *must* select or otherwise exceed its capacity, but rather because the nonattended stimuli provide no information and are, therefore, ignored. The sort of attentional effect involved in blocking and overshadowing in no way depends on any form of inverse hypothesis (Mackintosh, 1975). The data we presented here, however, do seem to support the contention in this chapter that selective attention can best be studied in situations that tax the animal's information-processing capacity. When such a condition is met, the inverse hypothesis and, therefore, a selective attention hypothesis does seem to be supported.

We have presented data indicating that both the time available to the subject as well as the information content of the sample affect the bird's ability to perform adequately in the matching-to-sample task. When the animal's information-processing capacity is exceeded, errors occur. Associative mechanisms, such as generalization decrements, do not, for the most part, account for the data. The result is a view of the pigeon as an information-processing system with a limited channel capacity — a commodity allocated through time. An increase in the load on that capacity can be overcome by an increase in the time available to process information. Conversely, in some situations, reducing the information load by providing redundant relevant cues while keeping the duration constant can facilitate performance. Perhaps the reason Maki et al. (1976) did not find such a facilitatory effect is because pigeons are rather insensitive to redundancy. Perhaps repeated pairings of the redundant stimuli are necessary before the bird can utilize the redundancy. If that is the case, the proper experiment has not yet been run in the matching-to-sample paradigm.

Finally, there are two issues of importance to comparative psychology: (1) comparing the performance of different species on similar tasks (e.g., pigeons and monkeys or humans), and (2) attempting to understand organisms in the context in which they evolved. Certainly, comparing pigeons and other creatures has been fruitful to the study of pigeons. Much of our present analysis has been borrowed from the study of human information processing. We also believe, however, that the study of human information processing can benefit from the study of similar mechanisms in animals. For example, knowing that pigeon performance improves with increases in sample duration while human and monkey performance on matching-to-sample is high even at very brief sample durations renders the human and monkey data more remarkable. What mechanisms not available to the pigeon allow the human to perform so well? Do other organisms improve their performance with increased sample duration or is this peculiar to pigeons, or birds in general? Alternatively, perhaps there is something peculiar about the type of stimuli we have used. Perhaps, by the arbitrary nature of the stimuli, we have failed to discover the true capacity of the pigeon. The use of stimuli such as different kinds of grain — those critical to the bird's health and survival — might produce new insights into the problem of information capacity in the pigeon.

ACKNOWLEDGMENTS

This research was supported by National Institute of Mental Health Grant MH 22153 to Donald A. Riley and by National Institute of General Medical Sciences Grant GM01207-10S1 to The Institute of Human learning, University of California, Berkeley. We thank Charles R. Leith and William S. Maki, Jr., for contributing to many of the ideas discussed in this paper, and Marvin Lamb for his critical reading of the manuscript.

REFERENCES

Baker, T. W. Properties of compound comditioned stimuli and their components. *Psychological Bulletin*, 1968, *70*, 611–625.

Blough, D. S. Attention shifts in a maintained discrimination. *Science*, 1969, *166*, 125–126.

Booth, J. H., & Hammond, L. J. Configural conditioning: greater fear in rats to compound than component through overtraining of the compound. *Journal of Experimental Psychology*, 1971, *87*, 255–272.

Broadbent, D. E. *Perception and communication*. London: Pergamon Press, 1958.

Broadbent, D. E. Human perception and animal learning. In W. H. Thorpe and O. L. Zangwill (Eds.), *Current problems in animal behavior*. London and New York: Cambridge University Press, 1961.

Broadbent, D. E. Stimulus set and response set: Two kinds of selective attention. In D. I. Mostofsky (Ed.), *Attention: Contemporary theories and analysis*. New York: Appleton-Century-Crofts, 1970.

Chase, S., & Heinemann, E. G. Choices based on redundant information. An analysis of two dimensional stimulus control. *Journal of Experimental Psychology*, 1972, *92*, 161–175.

D'Amato, M. R., & Worsham, R. W. Delayed matching in the capuchin monkey with brief sample durations. *Learning and Motivation*, 1972, *3*, 304–312.

Farthing, G. W., & Opuda, M. J. *Selective attention in matching-to-sample in pigeons*. Paper presented at the meeting of the Eastern Psychological Association, Washington, D.C., May 1973.

Garner, W. R. The stimulus in information processing. *American Psychologist*, 1970, *25*, 350–358.

Garner, W. R. *The processing of information and structure*. Hillsdale, New Jersey: Lawrence Erlbaum Associates, 1974.

Grant, D. S. Proactive interference in pigeon short-term memory. *Journal of Experimental Psychology: Animal Behavior Processes*, 1975, *104*, 207–220.

Grant, D. S., & Roberts, W. A. Sources of retroactive inhibition in pigeon short-term memory. *Journal of Experimental Psychology: Animal Behavior Processes* 1976, *2*, 1–16.

Kahneman, D Methods, findings and theory in studies of visual masking. *Psychological Bulletin*, 1968, *69*, 404–425.

Kahneman, D. *Attention and effort*. Englewood Cliffs, N.J.: Prentice Hall, 1973.

Leith, C. R., & Maki, W. S. Jr. Attention shifts during matching-to-sample performance in pigeons. *Animal Learning and Behavior*, 1975, *3*, 85–89.

Leuin, T. C. Selective information processing by pigeons. Unpublished Ph.D. dissertation, University of California, Berkeley, June 1976.

Mackintosh, N. J. A theory of attention: Variations in associability of stimuli with reinforcement. *Psychological Review*, 1975, *82*, 276–279.

Maki, W. S. Jr., & Leith, C. R. Shared attention in piegeons. *Journal of the Experimental Analysis of Behavior*, 1973, *19*, 345–349.

Maki, W. S. Jr., Riley, D. A., & Leith, C. R. The role of test stimuli in matching to compound samples in pigeons. *Animal Learning and Behavior*, 1976, *4* (1A), 13–21.

Moore, B. R. The role of directed Pavlovian reactions in simple instrumental learning in the pigeon. In R. A. Hinde & J. Stevenson-Hinde (Eds.), *Constraints on learning*. New York: Academic Press, 1973.

Neisser, U. *Cognitive Psychology*. New York: Appleton-Century-Crofts, 1967.

Rescorla, R. A. "Configural" conditioning in discrete trial bar pressing. *Journal of Comparative and Physiological Psychology*, 1972, *79*, 307–317.

Riley, D. A., & Leith, C. R. Multidimensional psychophysics and selective attention in animals. *Psychological Bulletin*, 1976, *83*, 138–160.

Roberts, W. A., & Grant, D. S. Short-term memory in the pigeon with presentation time precisely controlled. *Learning and Motivation,* 1974, *5,* 393–408.

Roitblat, H. L., Greene, L. H., & Riley, D. A. *Perception of brief visual stimuli by pigeons.* Paper presented at the meeting of the Western Psychological Association, Los Angeles, April 1976.

Sperling, G. Successive approximations to a model for short term memory. *Acta Psychologica,* 1967, *27,* 285–292.

Sutherland, N. S., Mackintosh, N.J. *Mechanisms of animal discrimination learning.* New York: Academic Press, 1971.

Thomas, D. R. Stimulus selection, attention and related matters. In J. H. Reynierse (Ed.) *Current issues in animal learning.* Lincoln, Nebraska: University of Nebraska Press, 1970.

Thomas, D. R., Berman, D. L., Serednesky, G. E., & Lyons, J. Information value and stimulus configuring as factors in conditioned reinforcement. *Journal of Experimental Psychology,* 1968, *76,* 181–189.

Zuckerman, D. C. Steady state responding based upon simple and compound stimuli. *Journal of the Experimental Analysis of Behavior,* 1973, *20,* 209–218.

10 The Internal Clock

Russell M. Church
Brown University

When a significant event occurs at a predictable time, an animal can learn to adjust its behavior in an appropriate manner. An observer can then use the animal's behavior as a clock to guess quite accurately the time of occurrence of the significant event. What clock did the animal use to predict the event? No external clock was available, so the fact of temporal discrimination suggests that the animal has some sort of internal clock which it can read. Our general question is, what are the properties of this internal clock?

In this chapter, I will briefly review the use of "time" as a stimulus in studies of animal conditioning and learning, describe several types of explanations of temporal discrimination, emphasizing explanations which make use of the concept of an "internal clock." I will then go on to describe some of the properties of the internal clock of a rat, and the types of control that a rat has over its internal clock.

I. TIME AS A STIMULUS

A. Studies of Temporal Discrimination

If we divide events into stimuli (S), responses (R), and outcomes (O), it is possible to consider the following time intervals: The duration of S, R, and O, the interval between S–S, R–R, and O–O, the interval between S–R, S–O and R–O, and the interval between R–S, O–S, and O–R. Most of these time intervals have recognizable names, and an experimental history. In this section, I will briefly refer to some of the studies which suggest that animals may use time as a stimulus.

1. The Duration of a Stimulus.   The duration of a stimulus, like other quantitative properties of a stimulus, can be discriminated by an animal and can influence its behavior. For example, in one study a pigeon was trained to make one response if the stimulus was shorter than a criterion, and a different response if the stimulus was longer than a criterion (Stubbs, 1968). The results were plotted as a standard psychometric function — percentage of responses of one kind as a function of stimulus duration. When duration was scaled in logarithmic units, the psychometric function was approximately a normal ogive.

2. The Duration of a Response.   The duration of a response, like other quantitative properties of a response, can be changed by differential reinforcement. For example, Platt, Kuch, and Bitgood (1973) reported the results of a study in which a rat received food whenever it depressed a lever longer than a criterion duration. The median response duration increased as a power function of the duration of the criterion.

3. The Duration of an Outcome.   The duration of an outcome, like other quantitative properties of a reinforcer, affects the magnitude of reinforcement. For example, in one study, if a pigeon pecked one key it occasionally had access to grain for k_1 sec; if it pecked a second key it equally often had access to grain for k_2 sec. Under such conditions, the relative rate of responding was approximately equal to the relative duration of reinforcement (Catania, 1963).

4. The Interval between Stimulus and Stimulus.   Most of the time intervals investigated by experimental psychologists have been in the order of a few seconds or minutes, but rats discriminate temporal intervals much shorter than a second, and much longer than a few minutes. For example, various clicker frequencies serve as discriminative stimuli, and there is reason to believe that the Kamin effect (Holloway & Wansley, 1973) may be due primarily to generalization decrement, i.e., the level of performance is highest when the test trials occur at the same time (relative to a 12- or 24-hr clock) as the training trials.

5. The Interval between Response and Response.   If reinforcement is made available only if the animal withholds responding longer than a criterion time, the distribution of interresponse times is closely related to the minimum reinforced interresponse time (e.g., Kramer & Rilling, 1970).

6. The Interval between Outcome and Outcome.   For temporal conditioning, a reinforcer (e.g., food powder) is delivered at regular time intervals (e.g., every 30 min). In one experiment (Pavlov, 1927), the rate of salivation of dogs regularly increased as the time of the next reinforcer approached. An aversive event presented at regular intervals can also lead to temporal conditioning (e.g., LaBarbera & Church, 1974). Most recent studies of temporal conditioning have used general activity or a trained instrumental act as the response, and either food or electric shock as the reinforcer. Killeen (1975) has provided a good review of the facts, and some new interpretations.

7. The Interval between Stimulus and Outcome.   When food is delivered at a fixed time after signal onset (inhibition of delay), the response rate increases as the time to next reinforcement approaches (e.g., Pavlov, 1927). Many studies of the relationships between response latency and the interval between warning signal and shock (the CS—UCS interval) in avoidance learning have verified this result and extended its generality.

8. The Interval between Response and Outcome.   In Sidman avoidance a response delays the onset of the next shock by a particular number of seconds. The response rate increases as the time of the next shock approaches (e.g., Anger, 1963; Gibbon, 1972; Libby & Church, 1974).

9. The Interval between Outcome and Response.   In the case of fixed-interval schedules of reinforcement (FI), if the interval of time between the previous reinforcement and the response exceeds a criterion, the animal will be reinforced again. In such situations, animals respond increasingly rapidly as the time of the next reinforcement approaches (e.g., Dews, 1970).

This list of procedures is far from exhaustive, but it illustrates the fact that animals learn to adjust their behavior in a manner appropriate to a time interval. The time interval can begin with a stimulus, a response, or an outcome; it also can end with any of these events. The duration of the interval being timed may be marked by some distinctive cue (filled) or it may not (unfilled). Although the data in this chapter come from only a few procedures, the conclusions about the nature of the internal clock may be quite general. An animal may not be much affected by the nature of the signal that starts, maintains, or stops its timing mechanism.

B. Methods of Investigation

Although, as the last section shows, many different procedures have been used to study animal time perception, in this chapter I will deal only with two general methods: estimation and production. In the method of estimation, the animal is presented with a time interval, and then is required to make a nontemporal choice response. For example, it may hear a 4-sec white-noise signal, and then press the left lever if it is perceived to be shorter than a criterion, or press the right lever if it is perceived to be longer than the criterion. In the method of production, the animal produces a time interval which appears to be within the range of reinforced values. For example, an animal may wait until 30-sec appear to have elapsed, and then make a response. Most of the studies of animal time perception in our laboratory have used only small variations from one of two standard procedures. The general procedures follow:

1. Subjects.   The subjects are male albino Norway rats (Charles River CD). The rats are individually caged throughout the experiment, and each rat receives ad lib water, and a daily 14-g ration of ground Purina chow mixed with about 25 ml of water.

2. Apparatus.   Standard lever boxes (23.2 by 20.3 by 21.9 cm high) are used. Two retractable stainless steel levers project through the front panel. A pellet dispenser delivers 45-mg Noyes Precision food pellets to a food cup mounted on the front wall between the levers. A 6-W houselight attached to the exterior of the transparent acrylic roof of each lever box serves as one signal. White noise, which can be delivered to a speaker mounted behind the front wall of the lever box, provides a second signal. Each lever box is housed in a large insulation board chamber designed to attenuate sounds and block visual stimuli. Each chamber is equipped with a fan for ventilation and an acrylic window to permit the experimenter to observe the rats. A PDP-12 computer is used to control the experimental equipment (light, noise, pellet dispenser, and lever retraction) and to record the time and number of responses (Church, 1973; Dyckman & Church, 1972).

3. An Example of an Estimation Procedure.   In a time-estimation experiment for human subjects, a person might be given instructions to respond "short" when the duration of a signal appears to be shorter than some criterion, and to respond "long" when the signal appears to be longer than the criterion. On each trial the person may be given knowledge of results. An equivalent experiment for rats could be as follows:

On each trial, a signal is presented to the rat, and then the two levers are inserted into the box. The rat is correct if it presses the left lever following a signal shorter than the criterion or the right lever following a signal longer than the criterion. If the rat makes the correct response, it receives a food pellet; if it makes the incorrect response, there is no food pellet and, in some cases, additional stimuli are used to differentiate correct from incorrect decisions. Thus, the two lever responses replace the two verbal responses, short and long; the animal learns the instructions and the criterion through experience; and the food provides knowledge of the results.

Normally, to minimize bias (position habits), we have used a between-trials correction procedure, i.e., if the rat is incorrect on trial *n*, the same stimulus is presented on trial *n* + 1. (The results of these correction trials are not included in the assessment of the level of performance.) Typical results from such a procedure are shown in Fig. 1 (left panel). The data are from a rat that had been

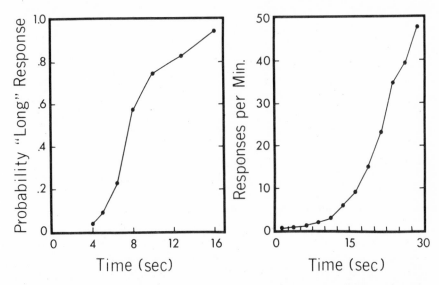

FIG. 1.   Temporal-discrimination data from an estimation method (left panel) and a production method (right panel). The psychometric function in the left panel shows the probability of a "long" response as a function of time; the response gradient in the right panel shows response rate as a function of time.

trained to press one lever following a 4-sec signal and the other lever following a 16-sec signal. This figure shows the mean probability (relative frequency) of a long response for the two extremes and for various intermediate values that were not differentially reinforced during ten 50-min sessions. The probability that the rat estimated a stimulus to be longer than a criterion increased as the signal duration increased from 4 to 16 sec.

4. An Example of a Production Procedure.   In a production experiment for human subjects, a person might be given instructions to respond when the time interval appears to equal a criterion. The instructions could indicate that premature responses were of little importance, but that the person should try to respond as soon as the interval was complete. Knowledge of results (i.e., whether or not the produced time interval is shorter or longer than the criterion) is given following each response. An equivalent experiment for rats could be as follows:

On each trial a single lever is inserted into the box, accompanied by a distinctive signal. Responses during the first 30-sec of the signal have no effect, but the first response after 30-sec results in the delivery of a food pellet, the termination of the signal, and the withdrawal of the lever. After a variable intertrial interval, another trial is begun. This, of course, is simply a discrete-trial fixed-interval schedule. As in the case of the estimation procedure, knowledge of results consists of a pellet of food, and the animal learns the instructions through experience.

Typical results from such a procedure is shown in Fig. 1 (right panel). The response rate of one rat averaged over five 3-hr sessions increased as the 30-sec criterion approached, i.e., the probability that the rat judged the interval to be complete increased as the time approached the criterion.

II. EXPLANATIONS OF TEMPORAL DISCRIMINATION

Studies of temporal discrimination provide ample evidence that there is a relationship between time and behavior. In the estimation procedures, different time intervals lead to qualitatively different responses, e.g., a response on a left or right lever. In the production procedures, different time intervals lead to quantitatively different responses, e.g., more or less rapid responses or responses differing in latency. In this section, I will review some of the alternative explanations for such temporal discriminations. Some of them attempt to account for the behavior without resort to the concept of time as a stimulus. Some of them consider time to be an adequate stimulus for differential behavior, but do not involve the concept of an internal clock. Still others explain temporal discrimination in terms of an internal clock.

A. Explanations Not Involving Time as a Stimulus

One of the major objectives of animal psychologists, especially during the last half century, has been to account for the behavior of animals without violating Lloyd Morgan's canon of parsimony (Morgan, 1894). A second major objective has been to account for behavior of animals without reference to unobserved cognitive or physiological processes (Skinner, 1950). With these objectives, it is easy to see why where would be a serious search for explanations of response gradients that did not involve time discrimination. The ability to keep track of time should not be assumed if a more parsimonious account is available (by Lloyd Morgan's canon). And time, and especially an internal clock, lacks the physical attributes of the standard stimulus and leads to explanations in terms of processes which are not directly observable.

For these reasons there has been a search for explanations of response gradients that do not involve any time discrimination. For example, some behavior that appears to provide evidence for a time discrimination may be based upon reactive responding alone (Church & Getty, 1972). If an animal reacts to the delivery of food by stopping to eat and then responding again at a constantly accelerating rate, the resulting cumulative curve could be characterized as an "FI scallop." Although such a reaction is undoubtedly involved in some response gradients seen under fixed interval schedules (Killeen, 1975), it obviously does not explain all cases. Most simply, it cannot account for the different gradients seen with different fixed intervals between reinforcements, nor the evidence for the discriminative stimulus status of reinforcement (Staddon, 1972).

Another explanation for response gradients involves mediating behavior. The general notion behind the mediating behavior explanation of fixed interval behavior is that the animal does not attend to time per se, (i.e., it does not engage in mental timing), but does attend to its own behavior which is correlated with time. Such mediating behavior might be easy to observe — for example, the animal might slowly turn in a circle and respond on the basis of where it is pointing at the end of the interval. Even if an animal used such mediating behavior, this fact would not be evidence against time discrimination. Instead, it would be a case in which it was possible to identify the hands of the clock.

We have never observed this kind of mediating behavior during a time interval. We have, however, observed animals engaging in repetitive actions, e.g., biting at the front panel, mouthing both paws, rapid head movements in and out of the food cup. Typically during the signal in a time-estimation procedure, a rat engages in some stereotyped rhythmic behavior which is different from its behavior in the intertrial interval (Church, Getty, & Lerner, 1976). Perhaps this is related to an oscillator that causes a clock to advance. Alternatively, the rhythmic behavior might have no relation to the timing performance.

Direct evidence against the mediating response position has been reported by Dews (1962) in a series of articles beginning in 1962. In these "interruption" experiments, a discriminative stimulus was turned on and off in successive segments of a fixed interval. The response rate was much greater in the presence of the discriminative stimulus than in its absence and response rate increased in successive segments of the fixed interval in which the discriminative stimulus was present. Dews (1970, p. 46) concluded that there was "a progressive increase in tendency to respond throughout the interval even when no responding is actually occurring." The interruption experiments have demonstrated that an animal can continue to time an interval independently of its actual responding. Apparently, and these are now my words, the animal has an internal clock which continues to advance whether the animal has the opportunity to respond or not.

The general notion of the "delay of reinforcement" explanation of fixed interval behavior is that responses that occur shortly after a reinforcement are reinforced after a long delay; those which occur long after a reinforcement are reinforced after a short delay. If response strength is related to delay of reinforcement, the latter should be strengthened more than the former. Therefore, a response gradient will emerge (Morse, 1966). This explanation does not dispose of the problem of temporal discrimination. It transfers the problem from the simple relationship between one reinforcement to the next, to the more complex temporal relationship between response and reinforcement conditional upon the time of the response since the last reinforcement. In any case, the attempt to explain the fixed interval gradients without involving the animals' ability to discriminate one time interval from another does not seem to be a worthwhile exercise, since the estimation methods have demonstrated that animals do possess this capacity.

B. Explanations Not Involving a Clock

Of course, it is possible to accept the notion that the time interval serves as a discriminative stimulus without postulating an internal clock. There is a conservative tradition within behaviorism, less fashionable now than 20 years ago, that avoids the use of all intervening variables. If a relationship can be established between time and a response, why introduce the concept of an internal clock? This would require two sets of relationships (between time and the clock, and between the clock and response) to replace the single set of relationships between time and a response.

Although the concept of an internal clock is not required to explain the results of any of the experiments described in this chapter, there are three types of arguments in favor of the concept. First, it is possible that there is a physiological reality to the internal clock, and that we are more likely to find it if we know its properties. Second, there is the argument of theoretical elegance. An intervening variable may simplify the input—output relationships. That is to say, the list of input—clock and clock—output relations may be shorter than the list of input—output relations. Finally, there is the pragmatic argument. It is possible that the concept of the internal clock will lead to the discovery of capacities of animals that otherwise would not have been identified, and that the concept will guide the investigator toward the discovery of general principles of animal cognition and behavior.

C. A Clock Model

When we began research on timing behavior of rats several years ago, the concept of internal clock was, for us, simply a metaphor. As our research progressed, however, we found ourselves searching for the properties of the internal clock. After we discovered some characteristics of the internal clock, our attitude toward it gradually began to change. The concept was no longer a metaphor; we began to believe that the clock actually exists.

Results from both the estimation and the production procedures suggest that animals may have an internal clock. Our assumptions are that the animal has an internal clock which advances as a function of time from (or during) a well-defined event, that the animal adopts a temporal criterion, and that there is a response rule which relates the probability of a particular response to the clock setting and the criterion. In the case of the estimation procedure, the signal starts the clock. When the signal terminates and the levers are inserted into the box, the rat reads the value of the clock and makes a decision to respond on the left (short) or right (long) lever, based upon the relationship between the clock setting and the criterion. If the clock setting is less than the criterion, the rat makes a left response; if the clock setting is greater than the criterion, the rat makes a right response. In the case of the production procedure, the signal starts the clock, and the rat continually makes decisions whether or not to respond based upon the clock setting and the criterion. This type of model contains three basic terms: clock, criterion, and response rule.

1. Clock.   For any given time the clock will have a distribution of settings, and this distribution changes in a regular way with time. If t equals time and $s(t)$ equals the subjective representation of this time (clock setting), then the problem is to specify the relationship between $s(t)$ and t. Of course, the clock may be flexible. That is to say, such factors as the nature of the stimulus and the conditions of reinforcement may affect the relationship between $s(t)$ and t.

2. Criterion.   If there is differential reinforcement of a response as a function of time from an event, the animal will adopt a temporal criterion for the response. The problem is to specify the criterion as a function of the conditions of reinforcement. Of course, it is possible that some of the variability in performance could be a result of variability in the criterion as well as variability in the clock. The source of variability could be in the clock, in the criterion, or both. In many situations, it is impossible to distinguish among these alternatives.

3. Response Rule.   The probability of a response can be predicted on the basis of clock setting, criterion, and conditions of reinforcement. The problem is to specify this rule.

A model for the estimation procedure (Fig. 1, left panel) is as follows: (1) The clock advances as a function of time during the signal of a given trial. (2) The rat gradually adopts a criterion somewhere between a clock setting characteristic of the 4-sec signal and a clock setting characteristic of the 16-sec signal. In the case of a symmetric two-choice situation, the criterion would be halfway between the clock settings characteristic of the two extremes. And (3) if the clock setting on a given trial is greater than the criterion, the rat responds with the long response; otherwise it responds with the short response. If the distribution of clock settings at any time is normal, then a cumulative normal distribution would describe the relationship between clock setting and the probability of a long response.

A model for the production procedure (Fig. 1, right panel) is as follows: (1) The clock advances as a function of time during the signal of a given trial in a manner similar to that described for the estimation procedure. (2) The rat gradually adopts a criterion related to the duration of the fixed interval. Because of the asymmetry in the payoff and the fairly effortless responses typically used, errors for premature responding are probably less serious than errors of waiting beyond the criterion. Thus, the criterion is probably set low. And (3) the response rate, or probability of a response in a short interval of time, is related to the discrepancy between the clock setting and the criterion. The response rate increases as the clock setting approaches the criterion, i.e., there is some monotonic relationship between response rate and time.

If the three terms, clock, criterion, and response rule, have a status as separate concepts, then there should be operations which change one of them while leaving the other two unchanged. That is to say, some operations should change the relationship between time and the clock setting, some should change the criterion, and some should change the response rule. A change in the clock setting, or in the criterion, would displace the curves in Fig. 1 horizontally on the time axis; a change in the response rule would displace the curves vertically on the response axis. For example, consider a drug such as amphetamine at a dose which increases the mean response rate on a temporal discrimination. Does it affect the operation of the clock, the response criterion, or the response rule? One test would be to determine whether the temporal gradient following the drug is displaced in time or in response rate.

Our greatest interest will be in manipulations that change the operation of the internal clock. The first step is to describe the properties of the internal clock, and this requires that the basic terms be firmly connected to stimulus conditions and observable behavior, and that the relationship among concepts be expressed by quantitative rules.

III. SOME PROPERTIES OF THE INTERNAL CLOCK

A. Properties of External Clocks

All clocks, by definition, change with time in a regular way. This is the only property that they all share. A sundial, a digital watch, a capacitor circuit, a stopwatch, and a computer clock all change with time in a regular way, but they differ in many other ways. They operate at different rates; some are more accu-

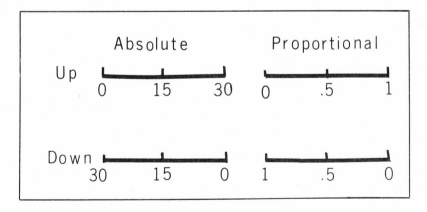

FIG. 2.   Four types of clock. The clocks in the left panels time in absolute units (e.g., seconds); the clocks in the right panels time in proportional units. The clocks in the top row time up; the clocks in the bottom row time down.

rate than others; some are continuous and others are discrete. Some are cyclical, and others change only in one direction. Some are driven by a specific external event, while others depend on internally stored energy. Some time up and others time down.

Figure 2 is a diagram of four types of clocks. An absolute, up timer increases in units related to seconds toward a criterion (upper left panel). An absolute, down timer decreases in units related to seconds (lower left panel). It begins at a criterion and decreases toward a fixed value, conventionally defined as zero. Thus the state of a down timer is specified by its clock setting alone, but the state of an up timer requires the specification of the criterion as well as the clock setting. A proportional timer changes in units related to the duration of the interval to be timed (right panels). Such a timer runs half as fast for an interval of $2c$ sec (say, 60 sec) than for an interval of c sec (say, 30 sec).

In the next section, I will examine some of the properties of the internal clock of the rat to determine which of the properties of various external clocks it possesses. More specifically, I will attempt to answer the following three questions: (1) Does an animal use the same internal clock to time the duration of a light and a sound? (2) Are the units of the internal clock absolute (related to seconds), or are they proportional to the duration of the interval being timed? (3) Does the internal clock time up toward an adjustable criterion value, or does it time down toward a fixed criterion?

B. The Proportionality Result

The shapes of different fixed interval gradients are very similar when the dependent variable is the percentage of the maximum rate, and the independent variable is the percentage of the interval. For example, if an animal on a 30-sec fixed-interval schedule has achieved about 50% of its maximum rate after it is 75% of the way through the interval, the same will be true of an animal on a 60-sec fixed-interval schedule. We refer to this result as "proportionality."

There are many examples of such a proportionality result. One of the more impressive examples was presented by Dews (1970) for fixed-interval behavior of pigeons that was equivalent for intervals varying from 30 sec to 50 min when scaled in proportional units. Some qualifications in the generality of this result are suggested by the data of others (e.g., Catania & Reynolds, 1968 Fig. 1b), but the result has been reported under a wide variety of conditions. Gibbon (1972) has shown that the relative response rate of rats on Sidman avoidance in a lever box is a function of the proportion of the interval completed, and Libby & Church (1974) have replicated this result for Sidman avoidance in a shuttlebox. Many other experiments, including several from our laboratory, support the idea that the response rate, relative to the mean rate, is a function of time expressed as a proportion of the interval, rather than time expressed in seconds. For example, LaBarbera and Church (1974) found this principle to hold for temporal

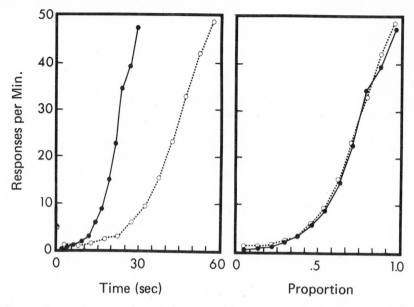

FIG. 3.   Response rate as a function of time (left panel) and proportion of the interval (right panel) of a rat in a 30-sec fixed-interval (solid circles) and a 60-sec fixed-interval (open circles) condition.

conditioning. The psychometric functions of the estimation procedures are also similar with time scaled in proportional units (Stubbs, 1968). The generality of the conclusion is increased by the great differences among the procedures under which it is found.

The proportionality result means that a person could predict the relative response rate much more accurately from a knowledge of the proportion of the interval than from either (1) the number of seconds since the last reinforcement or (2) the number of seconds until the next reinforcement.

Typically, the different treatments in an experiment examining proportionality are given to different animals, or they are given to the same animals in different phases of the experiment. Figure 3 shows a case in which the proportionality result holds even when the different treatments are given to the same animals during the same sessions. In this example, Seth Roberts and I trained rats on two discrete-trial fixed-interval schedules. Specifically, they were given discrete trials of 30-sec fixed-interval reinforcement signaled by a light, and other trials of 60-sec fixed-interval reinforcement signaled by a noise. When an interval was completed, food was primed, and following the next response (1) the food was delivered, (2) the signal was turned off, and (3) the lever was withdrawn. After a variable intertrial interval, another trial was given. The respone rate of one rat is plotted as a function of time (left panel) and as a function of proportion of the interval (right panel). It is clear that the response rate is more closely related to the proportion of the interval that was completed than to the number of seconds since the interval began, or the number of seconds until the next reinforcement was due.

The proportionality result suggests how animals may be timing the interval. They may advance the internal clock at a rate r that is proportional to the duration of the interval to be timed t, i.e., $r = k/t$, where k is a constant. For example, the clock may run twice as fast while timing a 30-sec interval than while timing a 60-sec interval. If each clock setting corresponds to a particular mean relative response rate, then the proportionality result would occur. Of course, the proportionality result does not prove that the units of the internal clock are proportional to the interval being timed, since the assumption that each clock setting corresponds to a particular mean relative response rate may be in error. The next section will show that the units of the clock are absolute, not proportional.

C. Three Properties of the Internal Clock: The Shift Experiment

To determine whether or not rats were timing in proportional units, Seth Roberts and I performed the following experiment (Roberts & Church, 1976; 1978). We trained each rat in a manner similar to that shown for the rat in Fig. 3. By the final day of fixed-interval training, responding increased in a fairly regular manner as the time of food approached under both the signal for the 30-sec and 60-sec fixed intervals.

During the critical part of the experiment, rats continued to receive trials with the 30-sec light signal and with the 60-sec noise signal. In addition, on about one-third of the trials, the 30-sec light signal shifted abruptly to the 60-sec noise signal. Shifts could happen 6, 12, 18, 24, or 30 sec after the trial began. If the rats used the same internal clock to time the light and noise, whether they were timing in absolute or proportional units and whether they were timing up or down could be inferred from their response rate during the trials shifted to the 60-sec noise signal. For example, after 12 sec of light (the 30-sec signal), the light could go off and the noise (the 60-sec signal) could go on. The four possibilities shown in Fig. 2 are as follows: If the animal used an absolute up timer, 12 sec have passed, so performance would be equivalent to an FI-60 after 12 sec. If the animal used an absolute down timer, 18 sec are left, so the performance would be equivalent to an FI-60 when 18 sec are left (i.e., after 42 sec). If the animal used a proportional up timer, 40% of the time has passed, so performance would be equivalent to an FI-60 after 40% of the time has passed (after 24 sec). If the animal used a proportional down timer, 60% of the time is left, so performance would be equivalent to an FI-60 when 60% of the time is left (i.e., 36 sec). Thus the empirical queston is to determine whether the performance of a rat switched from an FI-30 to an FI-60 after 12 sec is equivalent to its performance on an FI-60 after 12, 24, or 42 sec.

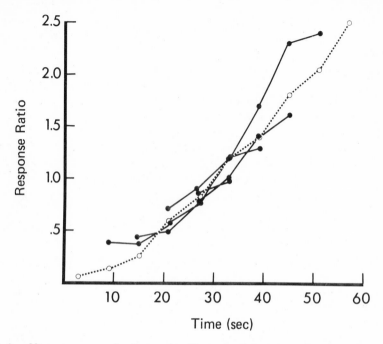

FIG. 4.   Mean response ratio during the 60-sec signal as a function of time since the trial began. Open circles are for trials that began as 60-sec fixed intervals; solid circles are for trials that were shifted to 60-sec fixed intervals. Points from trials that had the shift at the same time are connected.

On shifted trials we primed the food at the time appropriate for an absolute up timer for six rats (absolute group), and primed the food at a time appropriate for a proportional up timer for the remaining six rats (proportional group). The main result on the first day after shifts began is shown in Fig. 4. Since the two treatment groups (absolute and proportional) were not yet distinguishable, we have combined the groups in this figure.

The data are reported as response ratios, defined as the response rate during a 6-sec interval divided by overall response rate. For example, a rat with a response rate of 40 responses per minute during the last 6 sec of a 60-sec interval, and an overall response rate of 20 responses per minute during the entire 60-sec interval has a response ratio of 2.0 in that interval. We used this measure to compensate for the large differences in overall response rate from rat to rat. The open circles show the mean response ratio for trials which began with the 60-sec signal as a function of time since the trial began; the closed circles show the mean response ratio for trials which were shifted to the 60-sec signal at various times (6, 12, 18, and 24 sec after the 30-sec signal began), also as a function of time since the trial began. The major point is that the response ratio in the 60-sec signal was a function of the time since the trial began. It did not matter whether the trial began with a 60-sec signal, or if it was shifted to a 60-sec signal after 6, 12, 18, or 24 sec. To predict the response ratio in the 60-sec signal, one needed to know only the time since the trial began; it did not matter how much of the time consisted of the 30-sec signal and how much of the time consisted of the 60-sec signal.

What do these results tell us about the internal clock? First, they provide evidence that a single clock was used in this task. If the rat used separate clocks to keep track of time during the 30-sec visual signal and the 60-sec auditory signal, then the length of time the animal spent in the visual signal prior to the shift to the auditory signal should have no effect on its behavior. (In Fig. 4 all five functions would begin with the same response ratio.) If, on the other hand, the rat used the same clock to keep track of time during the 30-sec visual signal and the 60-sec auditory signal, the response ratio in the 60-sec signal should be related to the time spent in the 30-sec signal. Figure 4 shows this is the case, so apparently a single clock was used in this task. Since the same clock is used for auditory and visual signals, the clock must centrally located, i.e., more central than the auditory or visual pathways.

Our second conclusion is that the clock advances as a function of absolute, not proportional time. This is clear from the fact that the response ratio was a function of the duration of the combined signal (30 sec and 60 sec). Since it did not matter how much of the combined signal was the 30-sec signal, there is no evidence that the clock timed at a faster rate in the 30-sec signal than in the 60-

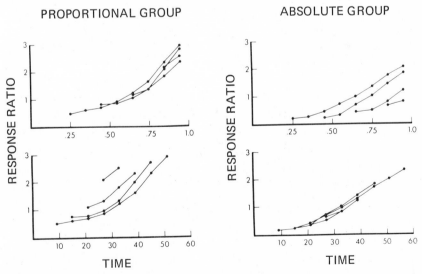

FIG. 5.   Mean response ratio during the 60-sec signal as a function of proportion of the interval (top panels) and time (bottom panel) during the last 30 days for the proportional group (left panels) and the absolute group (right panels).

sec signal. Apparently, the clock advanced at a constant rate, but when the signal was changed from a 30-sec to a 60-sec signal, the criterion was changed to the longer value.

Our third conclusion is that the clock times up, not down. This follows from the similarity of the curves after a shift and the curve without a shift. For example, a rat shifted from an FI-30 signal to an FI-60 signal after 12 sec has a response ratio similar to a rat that has had an FI-60 signal for 12 sec. This means that the rat must advance its clock during the 30-sec signal so it will be in the correct setting when the 60-sec signal shift occurs. If the internal clock were decreasing with time, no simple shift of criterion would account for the similarity of the after-shift and the no-shift curves.

The procedure was continued for 40 3-hr sessions. The means of the last 30 days was used as a measure of the final level of performance of the rats in the two groups. Rats in the absolute group continued to perform in an absolute manner, as shown in the right panel of Fig. 5. Rats in the proportional group, however, changed their behavior. Response ratio was no longer the same regardless of the time of shift when time was scaled in time since a trial began. It became the same only when scaled in proportion of the trial. This result suggests that the rats in the proportional group somehow learned to deal with time in proportional units. Several methods are plausible, and we have no basis for selection among them. They might have learned to change the clock by a constant when a shift occurred, or they might have learned five specific conditional temporal discriminations.

The fact that the rats did not initially time in proportional units suggests that the proportionality result may be less fundamental for the understanding of the mechanism of animal time than had previously been supposed. How is the proportionality result explained? It may be that the clock is timing in absolute units, that the criterion is approximately correct for any given time interval, but that the response rule is proportional. For example, the response ratio may be a function of the clock setting divided by the criterion so a rat with a clock setting of 15 and a criterion of 30 may respond at the same relative rate as a rat with a clock setting of 30 and a criterion of 60.

D. The Internal Clock and Time: The Bisection Experiment

All clocks change in a regular way with time, but the relationship between time and clock setting need not necessarily be linear. The function relating time and clock setting is different for the sundial, the stopwatch, and a discharging capacitor, but all of them can be scaled (transformed) to provide a linear scale. Although the internal clock of the rat seems to be timing in absolute units toward a flexible criterion, the shift experiment did not reveal the scale of the internal clock of a rat. The bisection procedure provides an approach to the problem of determining how the internal clock changes with time, that is to say, how an

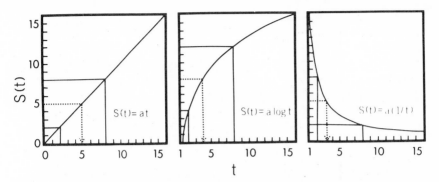

FIG. 6.   The functional relationship between clock setting and time. The three alternatives shown are linear (left panel), logarithmic (center panel) and reciprocal (right panel). (Church & Deluty, 1977. Copyright 1977 by the American Psychological Association. Reprinted by permission.)

internal representation of time changes with physical time. Figure 6 shows three simple alternatives. The clock might advance as a linear function of time, the logarithm of time, or the reciprocal of time.

A bisection procedure for human subjects involves the presentation of two siumuli differing on a dimension, and the person is instructed to judge whether an intermediate stimulus is more similar to one extreme or the other. The point at which the person equally often considers the stimulus too close to the two extremes is a reasonable measure of the "psychological middle." A bisection experiment for animal subjects is much the same. In both cases, knowledge of the results (differential reinforcement) can be given for the responses to the extreme values. Of course, no feedback should be given to the intermediate values since that would presume that the experimenter already knew which stimulus was in the middle of the psychological scale. Let us assume that the model for the response choice experiment is correct. That is to say, the animal adopts a criterion halfway between the clock setting characteristic of the short stimulus and the clock setting characteristic of the long stimulus, and that it responds short if the clock setting is below the criterion and long otherwise. In the example shown in Fig. 6, the rat is trained to make one response to a 2-sec signal and a different response to an 8-sec signal. These two signals can be represented by their respective clock settings, $s(t)$. The time corresponding to a clock setting halfway between these two values is shown by the dashed line. The point of bisection is 5.0, 4.0, and 3.2 sec for the arithmetic, logarithmic, and reciprocal scales. These values are the arithmetic, geometric, and harmonic means of the two values (2 and 8 sec).

This example can be generalized. If clock setting increases as a linear function of time (left panel), then the point of bisection would be at the arithmetic mean. If the clock setting increases as a logarithmic function of time (center panel), then the point of bisection would be at the geometric mean. Finally, if the clock

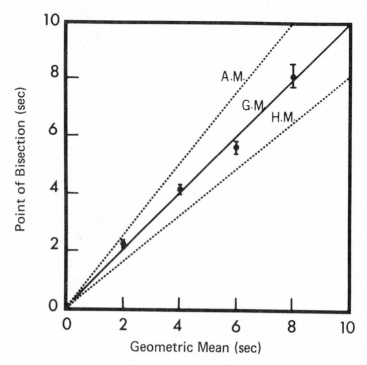

FIG. 7.   Point of bisection as a function of the geometric mean of two intervals. (The vertical lines are plus and minus one standard error of the mean.) (Church & Deluty, 1977. Copyright 1977 by the American Psychological Association. Reprinted by permission.)

setting changes as a reciprocal function of time (right panel), then the point of bisection would be at the harmonic mean.

Church and Deluty (1976; 1977) conducted such a bisection experiment. Twelve rats were trained to press the left lever if the signal was of one duration, and to press the right lever if the signal was of a second duration. On each trial, a signal of one of the two durations was presented, and then the two levers were inserted into the box. For the data described here, the ratios of the two durations were 1:4 (1 vs. 4 sec, 2 vs. 8 sec, 3 vs 12 sec, and 4 vs. 16 sec). A given rat was trained on each of these extremes in different phases of the experiment. After ten sessions at one pair of durations (e.g., if 2-sec signal then left response; if 8-sec signal then right response), the rats were exposed to values intermediate between the two extremes, and distributed at equal logarithmic intervals between them. During this bisection test, half the trials continued to be the extreme values (with differential reinforcement), and the remaining half were intermediate values with no reinforcement. That is to say, there were no correct or incorrect responses for the intermediate values.

The results are shown in Fig. 7. The point of bisection represented the signal duration that was judged half the time to be long and half the time to be short.

The conclusion was that the rats bisected the continuum of duration at the geometric mean, not at the arithmetic or the harmonic mean. The same conclusion followed from experiments that employed a different range of stimuli (2:1 instead of 4:1) and that employed a biased distribution of test stimuli in which none of the stimuli fell below (or, for other subjects, above) the geometric mean. The close correspondence between the point of bisection and the geometric mean is impressive since this quantitative fit did not involve the estimation of any parameters.

These results suggest that the setting of the internal clock increases as a function of the logarithm of time (as shown in the center panel of Fig. 6). This, of course, is Fechner's Law, $s(t) = k \log t$, where $s(t)$ is the clock setting, t is time, and k is a constant.

These data are consistent with the results of Stubbs (1976b), who also reported that the point of bisection is at the geometric mean. Of course, it is possible to introduce various factors to change the point of bisection by adding response bias (Stubbs, 1976a). A greater amount or probability of reinforcement for one extreme than the other, and a greater probability of presentation of one extreme than the other are among the ways in which a criterion shift might be produced that could distort the point of bisection away from the geometric mean.

E. Variability of the Internal Clock

The logarithmic relationship between the clock, $s(t)$, and time, t, is redrawn in Fig. 8. The next problem is to decide how the variability of the clock changes with time. The simplest assumption is that it is constant. This is shown in Fig. 8 by the two parallel lines representing some measure of variability (such as the difference limen). This assumption is consistent with the central assumption of scalar timing (Gibbon, 1972; 1977). Scalar timing implies that Weber's Law holds true for duration discrimination. That is to say, the difference limen is some constant proportion of the standard stimulus: $DL = kt$, where DL is the difference limen, t is the duration of the standard, and k is a constant.

Weber's Law provides a reasonably good description of the way in which the accuracy of time discrimination changes as a function of the length of the interval to be timed. Psychophysical studies of animal time perception have demonstrated that duration discrimination — as measured by the difference limen (DL) — is best for short intervals of time. When the DL is expressed as a ratio of the duration to be judged, however, the ratio (Weber's fraction) is reasonably constant. Typical values of the constant are about .25, but the dolphin has a Weber fraction of about .07 — much lower than human subjects — for tone durations in the range of .3 to 1.2 sec (Yunker & Herman, 1974). The constancy of the Weber fraction was reported by Stubbs (1968) for pigeons within the range of 2 through 40 sec. It was also reported for rats up to 16 sec (Tarpy, 1969).

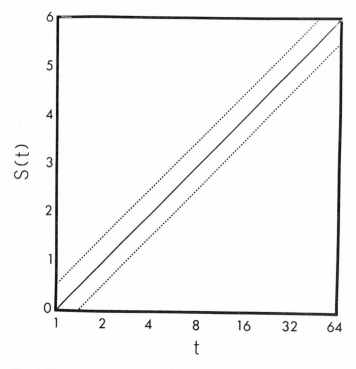

FIG. 8.   Variability of clock setting as a function of time. The dotted lines show some measure of variability (e.g., DL) around a logarithmic relationship between clock setting and time.

Studies in which the animal was differentially reinforced for responses (e.g., holding down a lever longer than a criterion time) have also provided support for Weber's Law. Using the standard deviation as a measure of variability of the latency distribution, Catania (1970) reported that the ratio of the standard deviation to the mean was constant between .6 and 36.4 sec. In the bisection experiment previously described, Church and Deluty (1976; 1977) found that the Weber fraction was approximately constant for the range of time intervals employed. Since in each of these cases Weber's Law continued to apply at the longest intervals examined, there is no known limit to the duration over which Weber's Law holds for animals.

The following is a description of one experiment (Church, Getty, & Lerner, 1976) designed to determine the relationship between the variability of clock setting and time. We used an up-down (staircase) psychophysical method to assess the relationship between the difference limen for duration and time. On each trial a white-noise stimulus was turned on either for a standard duration or for a longer comparison duration. Then the two levers were inserted into the box. The left response was reinforced if the standard duration had been presented; the right response was reinforced if the longer comparison duration had been presented. The duration of the comparison on each trial was determined by an up-down method so the rats were correct about 75% of the time. The difference between the mean setting of the comparison and the standard provides a measure of the difference limen. We tested each rat with standard signal durations which ranged from .5 to 8.0 sec.

The performance of an animal on a timing task can be divided into several independent stages. For example, the animal must first detect the stimulus, begin to time, time during the signal, stop timing at signal termination, and then make a decision. The limitations to an animal's accuracy in estimating temporal duration can be divided into three categories: (1) factors present on some trials, but not on others, e.g., inattention to the task. (2) factors that are present on all trials, but not related to signal duration, e.g., the lag in beginning to time when the signal is turned on and the lag in stopping to time when the signal is turned off; and (3) factors that are present on all trials, and which are related to signal duration. Weber's Law applies to this third category.

According to the Weber model, the growth of the standard deviation of the subjective duration of a signal (linearly related to DL in a normal distribution) is a constant proportion of the duration of the signal t, i.e., $DL = kt$. We assumed that the variance in the subjective duration of a signal (DL) is determined both by factors related to the duration of the signal $(kt)^2$ and by factors unrelated to the duration of the signal V. If these two types of factors are independent, the variances may be added to produce: $(DL)^2 = (kt)^2 + V$. Figure 9

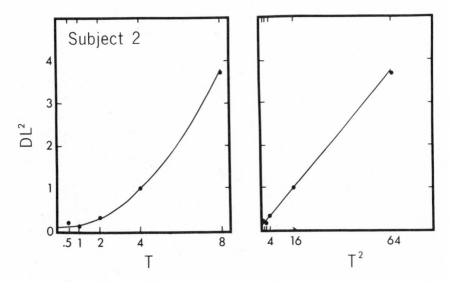

FIG. 9.   The relationship between the squared difference limen and time (left panel) and the square of time (right panel) for one rat.

shows the results for one rat. As predicted by the Weber model with an added source of variance for starting and stopping the clock, $(DL)^2$ is linearly related to t^2, not with t as would be predicted by another popular model (the counter model of Creelman, 1962). The fit was extremely good − it accounted for 99.9% of the variance of the $(DL)^2$ for this subject (the best of three). This fit did involve two parameters estimated from the data, but both of them have clear psychological meaning. The slope serves as a measure of the rate of change in accuracy as a function of increases in duration, and the intercept serves as a measure of the time necessary to start and stop the clock (about 244 msec for this subject). Sternberg's additive factors method provides a way of testing the independence of stages (Sternberg, 1969). Some conditions should change the intercept but not the slope, e.g., a ready signal should decrease the intercept and long or variable intertrial intervals should increase the intercept. Other conditions should change the slope without changing the intercept. It is possible, however, that the functional relationship is fundamental, and cannot be changed by experimental manipulations.

F. Subdivision

In timing an interval, do animals deal with it as a whole, or do they subdivide it into shorter units? Subdivision is the way that people would time in the range we are using if they did not have access to an external timing device. For example, to time 30 sec a person might count rhythmically, "one ... one thousand, two ... one thousand, ..." This is a surprisingly accurate way of dealing with time intervals. Recent historical evidence indicates that Galileo used a similar method to determine the law of falling bodies (Drake, 1975). Perhaps animals also use a related strategy. We have previously noted that rats often engage in some rhythmic behavior during the interval to be timed. Such behavior might serve as an oscillator to drive an internal clock, even though there would be some error in reading the sum of the subdivisions.

The direct approach to the subdivision problem is to instruct a subject to subdivide at a particular rate, or not to subdivide, and to determine the accuracy of timing as a function of the subdivision interval. This approach has been used with considerable success by Getty (1976) with human subjects, and we have tried to employ a similar procedure as follows:

To control a rat's rate of subdivision Marvin Deluty and I used a loud white−noise stimulus that was pulsed during the light signal to be timed. Lerner (1974) found this to be sufficient to drive behavior: Response rate increased in phase with a loud auditory stimulus even though there was no specific relation between the stimulus and reinforcement. Our assumption is that an animal, like a person, would have difficulty maintaining a beat different from (and, especially, out of phase with) the pulse rate.

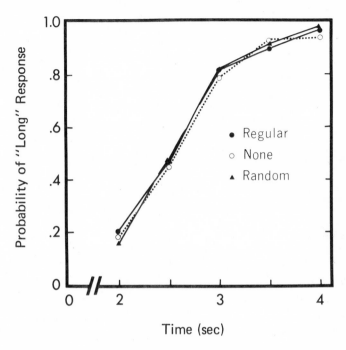

FIG. 10.   Probability of a "long" response as a function of time for groups with regular noise pulses, no noise pulses, and random noise pulses.

We used an estimation procedure as follows: The rats were trained to press the left lever when the duration of a light was at a standard duration of 2 sec, and to press the right lever when the duration of the light was at one of the longer comparison durations (2.5, 3.0, 3.5, or 4.0 sec). Half the stimuli were at the standard duration, and half were at a comparison duration. In different phases of the experiment, noise pulses were given at regular .5-sec intervals, at random intervals averaging .5 sec, or no noise was given. The psychometric functions are shown in Fig. 10. There is no evidence that a regular noise burst improved the accuracy of timing, nor that the random–noise bursts interfered with timing. Similar results occurred when the experiment was repeated with a standard duration of 8.0 sec, and comparison durations were 10, 12, 14, and 16 sec. Our conclusion is that either the rats were not subdividing the interval, or that the noise bursts did not interfere with their subdivision. Although the results of this experiment were negative, the general approach that it represents may be useful. Properties of the clock may be revealed by the differentiation between treatments which interfere with timing from those that do not.

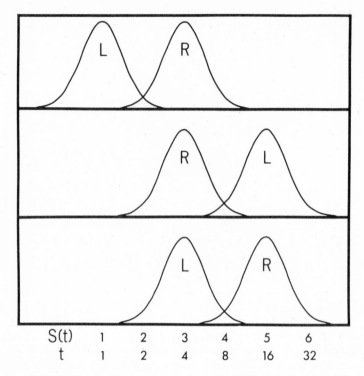

FIG. 11.   Distribution of clock setting for three durations. The top panel shows conditions of training; the middle and bottom panels show two testing conditions: absolute (middle panel) and relative (bottom panel). (Church & Deluty, 1977. Copyright 1977 by the American Psychological Association. Reprinted by permission.)

G. The Decision Rule: Relative or Absolute?

The model of the estimation experiment that we have adopted assumes that the animal recalls one particular duration (the criterion) and compares the current signal to this duration. This is a relative—decision rule. It is also possible that animals use an absolute—decision rule. For example, in the bisection experiment they might recall the probability of reinforcement of the left and right lever response at each clock setting, and then combine these probabilities in some manner (Spencian addition, likelihood ratios, etc.).

Consider the following situation: Rats were reinforced for a left response after a 1-sec signal and for a right response after a 4-sec signal. A signal of a particular duration does not always lead to exactly the same clock setting. Figure 11 shows the frequency distributions of clock settings corresponding to three signal durations (1, 4, and 16 sec), when the distributions are normal with equal variances. The top panel of Fig. 11 shows the distributions of clock settings corresponding to original training. According to the absolute—decision rule, the animal stores in memory the two distributions and their associated outcomes.

When exposed to a new signal, the animal makes a decision regarding which of the two distributions the signal come from, and responds accordingly. According to the relative–decision rule, the animal stores in memory a single criterion duration c that is based upon its experience with the two distributions and their associated outcomes, and a relative response rule (e.g., respond right if $s(t) > c$). When exposed to a new signal, it decides whether the clock setting is greater or less than the criterion, and then responds accordingly.

After the rats acquired the temporal discrimination shown in the top panel of Fig. 11 (left response if 1-sec signal; right response if 4-sec signal), they were retrained under the conditions shown in either the middle or bottom panel of the figure. In both cases, the animals were trained on a discrimination between 4 and 16 sec. Did they find it easier if the 4-sec signal continued to be associated with the right response, as in the middle panel which keeps one of the two absolute decision rules intact? Or did they find it easier if the shorter signal that is now 4-sec continued to be associated with the left response, keeping the relative rule intact? (In this experiment, and most of the others described in this chapter, the response associated with the short signal was counterbalanced. To keep the exposition more concrete, however, I have chosen to speak as if the short signal was always associated with the left response.)

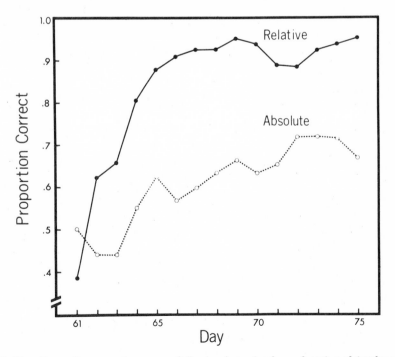

FIG. 12.   Proportion correct responses following 4-sec signal as a function of day for rats with the absolute and relative decision rule. (Church & Deluty, 1977. Copyright 1977 by the American Psychological Association. Reprinted by permission.)

The results of this experiment are shown in Fig. 12 (Church & Deluty, 1977). Previously, a left response was reinforced if a 1-sec signal occurred and a right response was reinforced if a 4-sec signal occurred (as in top panel Fig. 11). Subsequently the rats were trained on a new temporal discrimination — 4 vs. 16 sec. The absolute group had a 4-sec right vs. 16-sec left discrimination (center panel of Fig. 11); the relative group had a 4-sec left vs. 16-sec right discrimination (bottom panel of Fig. 11). The proportion correct on the 4-sec signal is shown in Fig. 12. The rats in the relative group has to reverse the response to the 4-sec signal. Their proportion correct was initially low, but it became high within a few sessions. The rats in the absolute group did not have to reverse their response to the 4-sec signal. Despite this fact, the proportion correct initially decreased on the new temporal discrimination, the rate of learning was much less than for the relative group, and the rats did not regain their former level of proficiency in responding correctly on the right lever for a 4-sec signal. The major result is that rats adjusted more readily to the relative condition in which the response rule remained the same, i.e., the right response continued to correspond to the longer signal, than to the absolute condition in which one of the S—R associations remained the same, i.e., the right response continued to correspond to the 4-sec signal.

Although, as in other cases of transposition, it may be possible to construct an absolute theory, my present conclusion is that the animals were using a relative-decision rule: The rats in the relative group merely had to change the criterion (from a value intermediate between 1 and 4 sec to a value intermediate between 4 and 16 sec); the rats in the absolute group had to change the criterion and also the response rule.

IV. CONTROL OF THE INTERNAL CLOCK

External clocks differ in the extent to which they can be controlled. Sundials are at the one extreme. They change regularly with time, but they cannot be stopped or otherwise controlled. In contrast to this lack of flexibility of a sundial, consider the properties of a stopwatch:

1. it can be initialized;
2. it can be started timing at a constant rate;
3. it can be stopped and then holds a constant value indefinitely;
4. it can be restarted from this constant value; or
5. it can be restarted from the initial value; and
6. it can be read while it is timing or when it is stopped.

Of course, the stopwatch can be controlled in only a limited manner. The rate cannot be changed; it cannot time in reverse; and constant values cannot be arithmetically combined with the time. A standard clock on a computer has these properties and others.

Does the internal clock of the rat run continuously, or can it be stopped? It is possible for a person to time an interval with an external clock that runs continuously. One simply reads the clock at the beginning and the end of the interval and performs a subtraction. Alternatively, if the external clock can be stopped (like a stopwatch), one can advance the clock only during the interval to be timed and, if the clock began at zero, its reading is the desired time interval. Dews (1962) demonstrated that the internal clock of a rat could continue to run during an interval when the animal was not responding. Seth Roberts and I performed an experiment to determine whether the internal clock of a rat could be stopped (Church & Roberts, 1975; Roberts & Church, 1978).

A. Stopping the Internal Clock: The Gap Experiment with a Production Procedure

We trained rats to press a lever on a discrete-trial 1-min fixed-interval schedule of reinforcement. At the beginning of a trial a lever was inserted in the box; 1 min later a pellet of food was primed such that the animal would receive the food immediately following the first response after it was primed; then the lever was

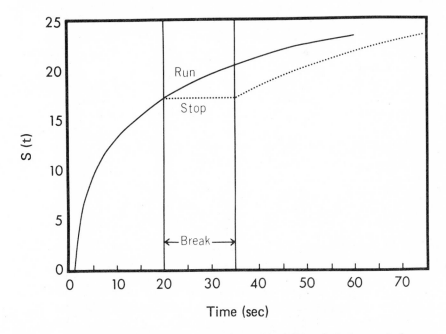

FIG. 13.   Clock setting as a function of time for a subject with a clock that ran during a break (solid line) and a subject with a clock that stopped during the break (dashed line).

withdrawn for the intertrial interval. By the end of training on this fixed-interval schedule of reinforcement, there was a steep temporal gradient, i.e., the response rate increased as the time of the next reinforcement approached. We assumed that there was some monotonic relationship between time and the setting of the clock and between the setting of the clock and response rate. The increase in response rate was an indication that the clock setting was approaching the criterion.

The next phase of the experiment provided the test of whether or not the clock could stop. During the next 50 days the rats were given fixed-interval training as before, but now the fixed intervals were occasionally interrupted by a 15-sec break. During a break the lever was withdrawn and white noise was turned on. The problem was to determine what the clock does during the break. Figure 13 shows two possibilities. If the clock ran during the 15-sec break, the clock setting would continue to increase during that time (solid line); if the clock stopped during the break, the clock setting would remain constant for that period of time, and then continue to increase after that time (dashed line). If there is a

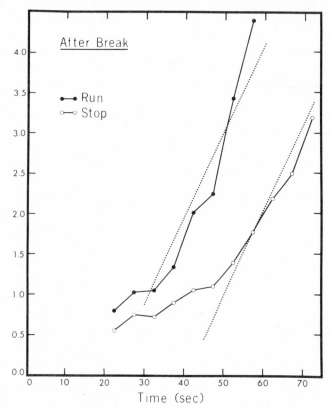

FIG. 14.   Mean response ratio after a break as a function of time since a trial began for the Run and Stop groups.

monotonic relationship between clock setting and response rate, after a break the response rate of rats that stopped their clocks at time t should be the same as the response rate of rats that ran their clocks at time $t - 15$ sec.

Breaks were scheduled to occur at one of eight different times during the interval, and about one out of four intervals included a break. What happened to the time until the next priming depended on the group. There were two groups: a run group and a stop group. For rats in the run group, time ran during the break. If there were 40 sec to priming when the break began (i.e., the break occurred 20 sec after the trial began), there were 25 sec to the next priming when the break ended. For rats in the stop group, time stopped during the break. If there were 40 sec to priming when the break began, there were still 40 sec to priming when the break ended.

During the last 20 days, the two groups (run and stop) were indistinguishable before a break, but differed after a break. Figure 14 shows the response rate after breaks as a function of time since the trial began. The response rate of rats in the stop group was approximately the same as that of rats in the run group, 15 sec previously. It appears that the clock of the rats in the stop group did, in fact, stop during the 15-sec break, while the clock of the rats in the run group did run during the break. The best estimate of the horizontal difference between the two straight lines, fitted with equal slopes to the last six points of each group, was 18.5 sec, a value significantly different from 0, but not from 15 sec. This experimental result is particularly meaningful since the theoretical prediction was quantitative: if one group was accurately running the clock and the other was stopping the clock, the horizontal difference between the response rates of the two groups would have been exactly 15 sec.

These data suggest either that rats in the run group learned to run the clock or that rats in the stop group learned to stop their clocks. What did the animals do initially? A comparison of the performance at the beginning of training (the first two sessions) and the end of training (last 20 sessions) showed that the temporal gradient of the stop group on the final sessions was indistinguishable from that of both groups initially, but that the final level of the run group was displaced from these three groups by about 15 sec. Apparently, all subjects stopped their clocks initially during the break, but the subjects in the run group learned to run their clocks during the interval.

B. Stopping the Internal Clock: The Gap Experiment with an
   Estimation Procedure.

Although we have assumed that an animal deals with the production and estimations tasks with the same internal clock, can the same properties of the internal clock be inferred from the two types of tasks? The previous experiment employed a production procedure (fixed-interval reinforcement); the next experiment employed an estimation procedure. The major question was the same: Can the clock stop?

Four rats were trained to press the left lever following a short signal (8 sec) and the right lever following a long signal (14.7 sec). All sessions were 50 min. The signal in this study was the houselight being off, although similar results occurred in other studies in which the signal was the presence of a houselight (Roberts & Church, 1978). After five sessions of this training, the rats were given 25 additional sessions in which there were eight signal durations spaced at equal logarithmic intervals between 8 and 14.7 sec. A left response was rewarded if the signal was 10.4 sec or less; a right response was rewarded if the signal was 11.3 sec or more. In the third phase of this experiment (the next 15 sessions), the conditions of the previous phase were continued and, in addition, there was a single 2-sec break on half the trials, equally likely to occur at each instant of a signal (prior to the last 2 sec). The experimenter's clock ran during the break for two of the rats (run group) and it stopped during the break for the other two rats. What did the rat's clock do during the break? Let us consider a specific case, e.g., a signal on for 8 sec, off for 2 sec, and on again for 2.4 sec. If the rat's internal clock ran during the break, the animal would time it as 12.4 sec and usually make the long response; if the rat's internal clock stopped during the break, the animal would time it as 10.4 sec and usually make the short response. The results during the 15 sessions with breaks are shown in Fig. 15. The psychometric function with breaks was displayed about 1.5 sec (s_m = 0.36) to the right of the function without breaks. (This is the mean horizontal distance at y = .5 between straight lines fitted to the two functions for each individual.) This was significantly different from the 0-sec displacement that would occur if the rats ran their internal clocks during the break, but not significantly different from the 2-sec displacement that would occur if the rats stopped their internal clocks during the break. As in the previous production experiment, all rats in this estimation experiment stopped their clocks during the break; unlike the

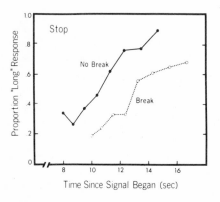 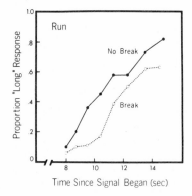

FIG. 15.   The probability of a "long" response as a function of time since signal began for trials with 2-sec break (dotted line) and trials without breaks (solid line). The stop group is shown in the left panel; the run group is shown in the right panel.

previous experiment, rats in the run group did not learn to run their clocks during the break. We were primarily interested in the initial behavior of the animals — in the way in which their clocks normally operated. In the present study this initial behavior remained stable for many days. Presumably, the rats in the run group maintained their initial behavior because they lost only a small percentage of the possible reinforcements by continuing to stop their internal clocks during the breaks.

C. Flexibility of the Internal Clock

The previous experiments have shown that the clock can operate in at least two modes: run or stop. With the production procedure we found that the clock is more flexible than one might have supposed. Like a stopwatch, it can either be run or stopped. How this flexibility is achieved has not been determined. For example, the rat may have acquired (1) a rule to run the clock during the interval, or (2) a rule to stop the clock during the interval and then jump ahead 15 sec at the end of the interval. In other situations, it is possible that the rat would have initially run its clock, although we have no knowledge of the conditions under which that would happen. One might speculate that if the conditions of the break are similar to the conditions of the intertrial interval, or if the conditions of the break are very different from those of the timing stimulus, then the animal will stop its clock. Although it is still possible that the clock is always running during the intertrial interval and resets at the start of a trial, the fact that it appears to stop during a break suggests that it is probably also stopped when it is not needed, e.g., during the intertrial interval.

The results of this experiment rule out certain types of clocks. For example, it makes it difficult to believe that the animal is dealing with time only retrospectively, i.e., that it estimates how long it has been since a signal onset. It also rules out clocks based upon passive decay of some process. Apparently, the clock is based upon some active counting up or down, and, as we have determined in a previous experiment, the counting is undoubtedly upward.

Of course, the animal may not have learned any general rule, but rather eight specific instances. There are several approaches to trying to decide whether the animal is learning a rule or a set of independent instances: (1) greatly increase the number of instances; (2) train according to some instances, and test on instances that have not yet been used; or (3) train according to instances with a consistent rule, and compare the performance to training with an inconsistent rule. Such experiments should discredit the notion that animals are learning instances independently of each other. Their behavior could be described either as rule learning or the learning of specific instances that generalize very broadly. The latter distinction is more subtle. Since rule learning depends primarily upon the variety of instances, and generalization depends primarily upon the similarity of a test case to a previous instance, the distinction is meaningful. It is possible that a group with the greatest training on the most similar instance (generalization) will do less well than a group with training on the greatest variety of instances (rule learning).

Some of the properties of the internal clock that we have described are natural, in the sense that they appear in the absence of explicit training. For example, in the shift experiment, rats initially showed that they kept track of how far along in the interval they were in terms of absolute time units (e.g., seconds), rather than in terms of percentage of the interval; in the gap experiment, rats showed they stopped timing during a break in the signal. These natural properties reveal the characteristics of the internal clock most certainly. We have found, however, that a rat can be trained to perform as if its clock had other properties. When a rat can be trained to behave as if its clock had a given property, there is the possibility that the operation of the clock has been modified, but it is necessary to consider other alternative strategies. If a rat cannot be trained to behave as if its clock had a particular property (e.g., running backward), this is evidence that the internal clock does not have the property in question.

The idea underlying most of the previous research on animal time perception is that the animal is a simple transformational machine. The relation between stimulus input and response output may be regarded as fixed by quantitative laws (e.g., Weber's Law, scalar timing, proportionality, or the power law). The present findings, e.g., the rats initially stopped their clocks, but with training could learn to run them during the break, suggest that the signal is actively processed before it is manifested in overt behavior. We now believe that the stages between input and output involve active processing, and that the animal may be trained to adopt different timing strategies.

V. CONCLUSIONS

The objectives of this chapter were to describe the ability of animals to process temporal cues, and to identify the minimum characteristics of an internal clock necessary to account for the facts of animal time perception. Many facts of temporal discrimination are consistent with the simple notion that an animal advances an internal or biological clock at a fixed rate, and reads the clock when necessary. Recent data suggest that animal time perception requires more than a passive reader of an ongoing biological process. In addition to maintaining an accurate internal representation of time that they can read, there is some evidence than animals are able to control the operation of the internal clock − to vary the relationship between real time and its internal representation. The results of our experiments have led to the following conclusions: (1) The facts of temporal discrimination by animals are best explained by a model which includes an internal clock, a criterion, and a relative response rule. (2) There is a single internal clock, centrally located, that times up at a fixed rate. The mean setting of the clock is proportional to the logarithm of time, and its standard deviation is constant. (3) The clock can be controlled. It can stop or run on command and, with training, it can keep track of the proportion of an interval.

ACKNOWLEDGEMENT

This chapter is based upon research supported by NSF Grant GB-43208 and PHS Grant GM-23247. Many of the ideas were developed in collaboration with Marvin Z. Deluty and Seth Roberts.

REFERENCES

Anger, D. The role of temporal discriminations in the reinforcement of Sidman avoidance behavior. *Journal of the Experimental Analysis of Behavior*, 1963, *6*, 477–506.

Catania, A. C. Concurrent performance: A baseline for the study of reinforcement magnitude. *Journal of the Experimental Analysis of Behavior*, 1963, *6*, 299–300.

Catania, A. C. Reinforcement schedules and psychophysical judgments: A study of some temporal properties of behavior. In W. N. Schoenfeld (Ed.), *The theory of reinforcement schedules*. New York: Appleton-Century-Crofts, 1970, pp. 1–42.

Catania, A. C., & Reynolds, G. S. A quantitative analysis of responding maintained by interval schedules of reinforcement. *Journal of the Experimental Analysis of Behavior*, 1968, *11*, 327–383.

Church, R. M. Seven types of data from computer-controlled experiments. *Behavior Research Methods and Instrumentation*, 1973, *5*, 122–124.

Church, R. M., & Deluty, M. Z. The bisection of temporal intervals. *Journal of Experimental Psychology: Animal Behavior Processes*, 1977, *3*, 216–228.

Church, R. M., & Deluty, M. Z. *Scaling of time by rats*. Paper read at meeting of Psychonomic Society, St. Louis, Missouri, November 1976.

Church, R. M., & Getty, D. J. Some consequences of the reaction to an aversive event. *Psychological Bulletin*, 1972, *78*, 21–27.

Church, R. M., Getty, D. J., & Lerner, N. D. Duration discrimination by rats. *Journal of Experimental Psychology: Animal Behavior Processes*, 1976, *2*, 303–312.

Church, R. M., & Roberts, S. *Control of an internal clock*. Paper read at meeting of Psychonomic Society, Denver, Colorado, 1975.

Creelman, C. D. Human discrimination of auditory duration. *The Journal of the Acoustical Society of America*, 1962, *34*, 582–593.

Dews, P. B. The effect of multiple S^Δ periods on responding on a fixed-interval schedule. *Journal of the Experimental Analysis of Behavior*, 1962, *5*, 369–374.

Dews. P. B. The theory of fixed-interval responding. In W. N. Schoenfeld (Ed.), *The theory of reinforcement schedules*. New York: Appleton-Century-Crofts, 1970, pp. 43–61.

Drake, S. The role of music in Galileo's experiments. *Scientific American*, 1975, *232*, 98–104.

Dyckman, H. L., & Church, R. M. The TIICIE system for interactive control of independent experiments. *Computers in the Psychology Laboratory*, 1972, *2*, 27–34.

Getty, D. J. Counting processes in human timing. *Perception and Psychophysics*, 1976, *20*, 191–197.

Gibbon, J. Scalar expectancy theory and Weber's Law in animal timing. *Psychological Review*, 1977, *84*, 279–325.

Gibbon, J. Timing and discrimination of shock density in avoidance. *Psychological Review*, 1972, *79*, 68–92.

Holloway, F. A., & Wansley, R. A. Multiphasic retention deficits at periodic intervals after passive avoidance learning. *Science*, 1973, *180*, 208–210.

Killeen, P. On the temporal control of behavior. *Psychological Review*, 1975, *82*, 89–115.

Kramer, T. J., & Rilling, M. Differential reinforcement of low rates: A selective critique. *Psychological Bulletin*, 1970, *74*, 224–254.

LaBarbera, J. D., & Church, R M. Magnitude of fear as a function of expected time to an aversive event. *Animal Learning & Behavior*, 1974, *2*, 199–202.

Lerner, N. C. *An analysis of reactive responding in response to shock.* Unpublished Ph.D. dissertation, Brown University, 1974.

Libby, M. E., & Church, R. M. Timing of avoidance responses by rats. *Journal of the Experimental Analysis of Behavior*, 1974, *22*, 513–517.

Morgan, C. L. *Introduction to comparative psychology.* London: Scott, 1894.

Morse, W. H. Intermittent reinforcement. In W. K. Honig (Ed.), *Operant behavior: Areas of research and application.* New York: Appleton-Century-Crofts, 1966, pp. 160–212.

Pavlov, I. P. *Conditioned reflexes* (trans. by G. V. Anrep). London and New York. Oxford University Press, 1927.

Platt, J. R., Kuch, D. O., & Bitgood, S. C. Rats' lever-press duration as psychophysical judgments of time. *Journal of the Experimental Analysis of Behavior*, 1973, *19*, 239–250.

Roberts, S., & Church, R. M. *Control of the rate of an internal clock.* Paper read at meeting of Eastern Psychological Association, New York, April 1976.

Roberts, S., & Church, R. M. *Control of an internal clock.* Manuscript submitted for publication, 1978.

Skinner, B. F. Are theories of learning necessary? *Psychological Review*, 1950, *57*, 193–216.

Staddon, J. E. R. Temporal control and the theory of reinforcement schedules. In R. M. Gilbert and J. R. Millenson (Eds.), *Reinforcement: Behavioral analyses.* New York: Academic Press, 1972.

Sternberg, S. The discovery of processing stages: Extensions of Donders' method. *Acta Psychologica*, 1969, *30*, 276–315.

Stubbs, A. The discrimination of stimulus duration by pigeons. *Journal of the Experimental Analysis of Behavior*, 1968, *11*, 223–238.

Stubbs, D. A. Response bias and the discrimination of stimulus duration. *Journal of the Experimental Analysis of Behavior*, 1976, *25*, 243–250. (a)

Stubbs, D. A. Scaling of stimulus duration by pigeons. *Journal of the Experimental Analysis of Behavior*, 1976, *26*, 15–25. (b)

Tarpy, R. M. Reinforcement difference limen (RDL) for delay in shock escape. *Journal of Experimental Psychology*, 1969, *79*, 116–121.

Yunker, M. P., & Herman, L. M. Discrimination of auditory temporal differences by the bottlenose dolphin and the human. *Journal of the Acoustical Society of America*, 1974, *56*, 1870–1875.

11 Cognitive Structure and Serial Pattern Learning by Animals

Stewart H. Hulse
The Johns Hopkins University

I. INTRODUCTION

In one of his more celebrated phrases, Guthrie once accused Tolman of leaving rats "buried in thought" as the creatures struggled to select among alternative paths to a goal in a multiple-choice-point maze (Guthrie, 1952, p. 143). Guthrie was, of course, referring to the question of how rats turned thought into action, a problem which is but one of many that have had their initial development in data that have come from the display of behavior in spatial mazes. The questions of place vs. response learning, and spatial memory [to which Chapters 12 (Olton) and 13 (Menzel) in this volume speak directly] are other cases in point, and so is the puzzle of how creatures manage to put things into some proper serial order. It is to the latter problem that this chapter is directed.

The problem of serial order is inherent in the fundamental assumptions of Aristotelian thought and in the tenets of associationism from which so much of 20th-century thinking about the learning process has derived. But Hull (1931) and Skinner (1934) saw the problem of serial order as a matter of considerable theoretical interest, taking as their point of departure the problem of how *responses* became chained to form complex serial habits. Each provided descriptions of this process that were quite similar in several respects. Both postulated the development of associations between neighboring pairs of stimuli and responses occurring in some temporal-spatial order. Both emphasized (Hull especially) the importance of response-produced cues in providing discriminative stimuli for successive responses in the chain. Hull added the concept of drive stimulus as a mediator for the response elements of an entire chain and gave to psychology the r_g–s_g mechanism — a "fractional" stimulus–response representation of the goal — as a theoretical model not only for the behavior of rats in mazes, but also for directed thinking itself. And there, within the domain of animal learning, the problem of how responses are put together in serial order has rested to this day. Quite literally, there appear to have been no major new developments either empirically or theoretically since the early 1930s.

Similar comments can be made about the development of our understanding of how *stimulus events that occur in temporal succession* influence some aspect of the behavior of animals. Clearly, there has been some attention to the effects upon a response of the order in which stimuli are put together in time. Many of the chapters in this book testify to that fact. Stimulus order is characteristic of problems that are of current interest not only in Pavlovian conditioning, but also in the broader fields of generalization and discrimination. However, the primary focus of attention has been upon the organism's reaction to the attributes of given stimuli considered singly, not upon any effects that may appear because stimuli occur in some temporal order. In few cases, in other words, have broad new theories emerged that are addressed directly to the problem of serial order per se among multiple sets of stimuli.

One possible exception, important for the large amount of research that has resulted over the past 30 to 40 years, lies in the realm of intermittent reinforcement. Here, events of interest are derived from the arrangement of two simulus events — reinforcement and nonreinforcement — in orders that are either temporally based or response based, the latter, of course, reducing to temporal order as well. Once again, however, attention has centered on the rather gross aspects of behavior resulting from the use of one schedule or percentage of reinforcement as compared with another, e.g., relative rates or distributions of response rates, relative resistance to extinction, and so on. Furthermore, theoretical developments within the domain of intermittent reinforcement generally stress the emotional (Amsel) or associative (Capaldi) effects of reinforcement as compared with nonreinforcement — granting that Capaldi does make important theoretical use of the temporal order and distribution of the two. However, the general point I wish to make — to draw things together — is that where there has been some theoretical nod to serial order, there seems to have been relatively little interest in the amount of information to be obtained from temporally constructed *patterns* of stimuli, patterns viewed as information—carrying *formal structures*.

If the problems of serial order and the study of formal structure among stimulus events have been neglected in animal learning, such is not the case in that realm of experimental psychology devoted to human learning and cognition. From today's vantage point, Lashley (1951) was perhaps the first to open the problem to fresh scrutiny, and his landmark paper — together with the advent of the computer as a model for behavior and the development of learning theories based on stochastic processes — quickly stimulated a number of theoretical and empirical developments, a flurry of activity that continues until the present time.

Much of the activity centers about how people learn to organize and remember various serially ordered patterns, of which language, music, and speech are important examples. Serially ordered patterns occur along a continuum which ranges from patterns that afford little or no opportunity for description in abstract, formal terms, to patterns amenable to a complete formal system for conveniently describing the sequence. If a formal system is available for use and can be sensibly applied, then its coded description of some pattern is shorter and more compact than the pattern itself. For example, the serial pattern *NRRNNNRNRR* has little formal structure. It can best be described (or regenerated) by simple enumeration of each successive element. The structure *NRNRNRNRNR*, on the other hand, has a great deal of formal structure; it can be entirely described and coded by the simple rule that N and R alternate five times.

The structural specification of serial orders, together with study of the psychological properties that serial patterns possess, have occupied cognitive psychologists for some time. Interest has ranged from relatively simple patterns based on strings of numbers, letters, or the like (e.g., Jones, 1971; Restle, 1970; Simon & Kotovsky, 1963; Vitz & Todd, 1969), to patterns based on structures associated with time and with time intervals (e.g., Garner & Gottwald, 1968; Jones, 1976), to the complex hierarchical structures associated with western music (Jones, 1974; Restle, 1970; Simon & Sumner, 1968). Let us examine some of the fundamental characteristics of modern concepts of serial structure, and then see how they might be meaningfully applied to the study of animal learning and behavior. This will help to set the stage for some research to be described in due course.

II. COGNITIVE STRUCTURES AND SERIAL PATTERN LEARNING

Virtually all cognitively oriented theoretical speculations about serial order share common features. First, some formal system is established for specifying the structure of any given serial pattern. Such formal structures are based on certain fundamental assumptions. For an early example, paraphrasing Simon & Kotovsky (1963), we assume that, as people approach a problem requiring the learning of a serial pattern, they (1) come with a *set* of primitive *elements*, a list of familiar items such as numbers or letters, (2) know the element set frontward and backward, (3) have a concept of "same" or "equal," (4) have a concept of "next" on an ordered list, (5) can identify and produce a cyclical pattern (i.e., have some notion about the concept of periodicity), and (6) can keep track of a small number of symbols in immediate memory. From the foregoing assumptions or something closely akin to them, today's formal systems have then emerged. Interestingly enough, because many modern systems share the same fundamental assumptions, the predictions they make about, say, the relative difficulty of one as compared with another pattern often differ very little even though their schemes for formal coding of structure may vary substantially (Simon, 1972).

Once some system for developing and formally describing structure has been established, a second fundamental proposition is that from the rules of the system come methods for distinguishing simple from complex structures. A third is that people can and will *induce* the structure of the pattern, encoding it internally in a manner that is related to the formal coded structure of the pattern. This is not to say that a true isomorphism necessarily exists between a pattern's formal structure and the structure imposed on the pattern by the learner (although that is often a common assumption). Instead, a pattern's formal structure and the learner's internal representation may parallel each other only in the functional sense that the more complex the formal structure, the more complex the internal representation of that structure. Finally, all models assume that the more complicated the internal representation of the structure, the more difficult the structure must be to learn and to remember.

To illustrate some of the foregoing principles, consider two serial patterns constructed from the digits 1, 2, 3, 4, 5, 6, and 7: 123345567 and 163435527. Both are of the same length and both contain the same digits with the same frequencies. Examine the first pattern. While the procedures used to specify formal structure vary somewhat from theorist to theorist, all systems would specify rules for dividing the larger pattern into a periodic set of three subpatterns of three elements each (123–345–567). Then, some system would be invoked to code the fact that within each subpattern all successive elements increase by one. Broadly speaking, two classes of rule are required to describe the pattern: a rule specifying the pattern's periodicity, and a rule describing how elements are ordered within each period. For the second pattern, matters are clearly more complicated. First, there is no simple periodicity to the pattern. Next, there are few rules specifying the relationship between more than two successive elements in the pattern. The sequence 343 could be encoded internally as a "trill" in Restle's (1970) system, while the pair of 5s could be encoded by an *equals* rule. But compared with the first pattern, anyone faced with the task of learning the second would be hard-pressed to discover principles that would reduce pattern complexity, make the pattern easy to represent internally, and render the pattern easier to learn and remember. The learner might well be forced to resort to an encoding strategy no more efficient than simple memorization of pairwise relationships among neighboring elements in the series, and that would require learning six "rules" as compared with two. A wealth of research over the past 10 or 15 years has shown that such analyses of the formal complexity of pattern structure lead to very accurate predictions about the facility with which patterns will be learned.

III. APPLICATION OF COGNITIVE STRUCTURES TO SERIAL PATTERNS IN ANIMAL LEARNING

It is entirely an open question whether the techniques that have been used fruit-fully to explore people's management of serial patterns can also be meaningfully applied to the behavior of nonhuman species. Nevertheless, the question seems an eminently sensible one to ask given the current resurgence of interest in the comparability of humans and nonhumans with respect to intellectual achievement and capacity.

A. Element Sets and Symbols

One reason questions pertaining to serial learning may not have been asked of animals using the new and modern techniques of cognitive psychology may stem from the lack of an appropriate element set to use in animal experimentation. As we have seen, all modern theories of human pattern learning make the tacit assumption that tests of their validity are appropriately made with sets of items that are already highly familiar to the learning organism. Thus, serial patterns are developed from element sets such as numbers, letters, or sounds which the typical human participant in a pattern-learning experiment has spent many years coming to know quite well. Parallel element sets have not been developed for explicit use with animal subjects, however, and it could be that the lack of an appropriate element set — together with a reluctance to attribute complex cognitive capabilities to animals other than man — may have led to almost 40 years of neglect of the problem of serial order in nonhuman species.

Many potential element sets exist for animals, however. For chimpanzees, one might be developed based on arbitrary symbols that would be comparable in every respect to those used for human subjects. Premack is clearly close to this idea for serial pattern learning in his work on concept formation in this species (see Chapter 14 in this volume). For rats, the problem may be somewhat more difficult because the class of potential element sets seems smaller. Certainly olfactory cues would be likely candidates, however, tactile cues seem equally feasible, and Olton's work described in this volume suggests that spatial location of food may also be worth considering. Another likely class — that which will be the focus of the remainder of this article — consists of those stimuli that are typically used as appetitive reinforcers in animal learning experiments, namely, pieces of food. Food for a hungry animal, for example, possesses the desired characteristic that it is already highly familiar, even to a young animal. Furthermore, if food varies in quantity, there are certain correlated changes in behavior to be expected: Animals typically respond with greater alacrity to a large as compared with a small quantity of food, and given a choice, animals select large over small quantities of some palatable substance. Without doubt, it is highly unlikely that animals already know an element set based on food quantities in the sense that they can "count" it, and "know it frontward and backward" as Simon and Kotovsky postulated for their theory of human serial pattern learning. But at an empirical level, at least, a convenient working hypothesis is that animals do (or can rapidly learn) to appreciate *order* among different quantities of food. All that remains is to specify some formal system that establishes the rules by which elements from a given set of food quantities are to be combined to form a serial pattern.

B. Reinforcers Are Stimuli

At this point I reemphasize that I intend to treat reinforcing events as *stimuli* with *multidimensional properties*. Furthermore, I wish to stress their properties as information-carrying events when they are combined into temporal and spatio temporal *structures*. Both points are already obvious, perhaps, but they bear repeating.

I also wish to draw specific attention to the fact that food for hungry animals has many properties other than those normally associated with other classes of stimuli, like numbers, letters, lights, and sounds, from which serial patterns have typically been constructed for study with both human and nonhuman species. Food has many affective and nutritive properties which assure that hunger is managed and the organism survives. Furthermore, the absence of food in a context in which food normally occurs generates frustration, and that creates affect of yet another sort. To generate patterns from different quantities of food is not to deny, therefore, that changes in affect, need, or drive may covary with the several elements comprising a pattern. But I shall pursue the view that information contained in serial structures of food quantity can be treated as conceptually independent of the very real and important emotional-motivational properties of nutritive substances.

Of course, emotion, excitation, inhibition, frustration, and the like, may be crucial factors underlying the manner in which an animal is able to learn and remember a serial pattern with some given formal structure. But that underlying process, whatever it may be, then becomes a matter for independent empirical investigation and is entirely ancillary to the question of the utility of the concept of formal structure for describing serial learning in animals.

IV. PATTERNS OF REINFORCEMENT

My initial approach to the problem of structure in serial patterns was undertaken in 1973 (Hulse, 1973). At that time, I was interested in reinforcement in general, and the notion of reinforcers as information-carrying stimuli in particular — information that depended upon the context in which reinforcing events occurred. All this led to the concept of a *pattern of reinforcement*, a relatively primitive concept that led, as things turned out, to the question of how reinforcing stimuli can be put together according to the principles developed by psychologists interested in human cognition and human pattern learning.

To summarize that earlier work, we noted that in any learning situation reinforcing events, or *elements, vary* from one occasion of a response to the next. This will happen in some small way no matter how hard an experimenter attempts to keep his reward or punisher constant in some physical sense, and often, of course, variations in some feature of the reinforcing elements in a learning situation are deliberately introduced — as in partial or varied reinforcement. More generally, however, reinforcing elements are by nature multidimensional in that they can be assigned *attributes* such as quantity, intensity, delay, probability, and so on, attributes that can change alone or together in *value* from one response to the next. If the formal structure of a pattern is such that the value of one or more attributes changes haphazardly from one response occasion to the next, an *averaged* pattern of reinforcement results. Strictly speaking, an averaged pattern has no consistent element-to-element formal structure (since none is defined), and animals as well as people can only abstract certain of the general features of averaged patterns — such as the central tendency and variance of their elements — going on to respond to some collective property or set of properties characteristic of or derived from the pattern as a whole. From the 1930s to the present, averaged patterns have been used to study such phenomena as reinforcement contrast, behavioral contrast, the effects of partial and varied reinforcement on resistance to extinction, and so on. Work somewhat relevant to the present view has been done by Bevan (e.g., Bevan, 1968; Bevan & Adamson, 1960) in the context of adaptation-level theory.

If, in contrast to the arrangements of elements in averaged patterns, the formal structure of the pattern calls for the values of some attribute to be *ordered* in series from element to element, then a *serial* (or sequential) pattern of reinforcement results. Outside the domain of reinforcement, serial patterns so defined contain the germ of the more general serial patterns developed within human cognitive psychology, and one must only add formal operator rules (such as a *next* or *complement* rule) to some set of reinforcing elements to achieve a pattern with a complete formal rule structure. Within the domain of reinforcement however, such patterns — formally defined or not — have received virtually no attention at all. The only possible exceptions are patterns afforded by operant schedules of reinforcement that are built from a binary element set consisting of a finite quantity of reinforcement and no reinforcement arranged (usually) according to counting or timing contingencies, or to some combination of the two. Bitterman's early work comparing single-alternation with random arrangements of reinforcement and nonreinforcement (e.g., Tyler, Wortz, & Bitterman, 1953) provides another early example, an example which treats the problem in a manner that bears at least a family resemblance to that proposed here.

In any event, it was within the context of simple serial patterns of reinforcement that experimentation began on the behavioral properties of patterned strings of elements with multidimensional features. The first of that research was reported in Hulse (1973). The initial experiment most relevant to the points under discussion in this chapter was undertaken later, however, and we turn to its description now to underline the utility of some of the points made thus far.

A. An Initial Experiment

Hulse and Campbell (1975) studied the properties of patterns of reinforcement constructed from an element set of five quantities of food: 0, 1, 3, 7, and 14 food pellets. For one group of animals (the Seq-D group), the structure of the pattern was based on a simple *next* rule in a set ordered monotonically from the largest to the smallest element, that is, the rule defining the quantity of each successive element, $E(i)$, was of the form $E(i) > E(i + 1)$. For a second group (the Seq-I group), the order of the set was reversed such that the elements became progressively larger with application of the *next* rule defining the size of each successive element. Here, $E(i) < E(i + 1)$. For three other groups, patterns were used in which the values of the successive five elements varied from one presentation of the pattern to the next. For one group, a different random order of all five food quantities was used each time a subject was exposed to the pattern. For a second group, the order of the first four elements in the series varied on each occasion, but the final element was always 0 pellets. For a third group, the order of the first four elements also varied with each presentation of the pattern, but the final element was always 14 pellets.

Given these structures, rats learned a brightness discrimination in a T maze under conditions where a correct initial choice of S+ was reinforced with an *entire pattern* of reinforcement. Thus, rats at 80% of normal body weight were trained to choose the bright or dark arm of a T maze. Each *trial* of the experiment consisted of five *runs*. On the first run of a trial, the rat was free to choose either the S+ or S− arm of the T. Given a choice of S+ for rats in the Seq-D group, for example, the initial free-choice run was rewarded with 14 pellets of food. Then, however, the door to the S− arm was locked and the animal was forced to return to the S+ arm for 4 additional runs to sample the remaining four elements in the pattern: 7, 3, 1, and 0 pellets. Similarly, a correct choice of S+ for rats in the Seq-I group was reinforced initially with 0 pellets of food, but the rat then sampled 1, 3, 7, and 14 pellets on the remaining 4 runs of the trial. Parallel procedures were used for the random groups.

If the rats in any condition made an incorrect free choice of S−, they received no reward on that run nor on a second run of that trial forced to the S− arm. Thus S− trials were limited to two runs per trial (the animals proved utterly intractable when an attempt was made to balance S+ and S− experience with five runs to nonreinforcement in S−).

We were interested in two major features of the data of the experiment. First, would the rats learn the discrimination? This was not a trivial consideration for the Seq-I condition at any rate, because a correct initial choice of S+ was reinforced with 0 pellets, and there was considerable delay before primary reinforcement could be obtained on the second run of a trial. Second, how might the rats respond to the changing food quantities in the several patterns? For one possibility, if the rats were sensitive to the serially changing quantities in the Seq-I and Seq-D conditions, progressively faster running might be predicted across the elements of the former, and progressively slower running across the elements of the latter.

Results.   The results of the experiment showed, first of all, that all the rats did indeed learn the brightness discrimination, although learning was somewhat slower in the Seq-I condition. Second, as Fig. 1 shows, the animals in the Seq-I and Seq-D conditions learned to *track* the patterns of reinforcement in that, at

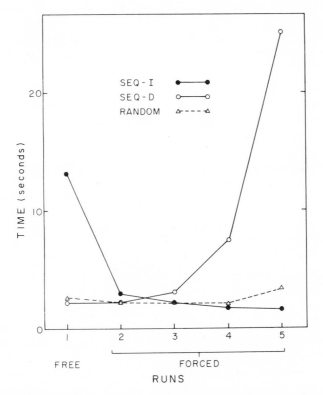

FIG. 1.   Mean asymptotic running times to increasing (Seq. I), decreasing (Seq-D), or random sequences of reward quantities in the Hulse and Campbell experiment. (From Hulse and Campbell, 1975. Copyright 1975 by the Psychomomic Society. Reprinted by permission.)

asymptote, their running times mapped directly onto the changing quantities of food, decreasing across the runs of a trial if food quantities increased, while increasing if food quantities decreased. The 0-pellet element was by far the most salient in this regard; under both conditions the difference in running time between the 0-pellet element and any other element was by far the largest. Although the last element in a pattern was always constant for two of the random groups, none of the rats in any of the random conditions learned to locate any element in the pattern. They all ran with approximately equal speed to all elements, so their data are pooled for purposes of presentation in Fig. 1.

Implications abound for the results of the experiment. The set of results on which I wish to focus in the remainder of this chapter, however, are those associated with the rats' ability to track the increasing and decreasing serial patterns with accuracy. What factor or set of factors might lead the animals to impose such ordered responding upon a serially-arranged pattern of reinforcing elements, and what might this have to do with more general considerations regarding serial pattern learning per se?

V. MECHANISMS FOR SERIAL ORDERING

There are many possible characteristics of an ordered series of food quantities that could be used by rats to track the series under the Seq-I and Seq-D conditions where they successfully did so. In this section, we shall list those that seem most pertinent, develop them briefly, and set the stage for some further experimentation.

1. Hunger. Rats run to a series of decreasing food quantities could conceivably have slowed their response latencies because of progressively decreasing hunger through the runs of a trial. The Hulse and Campbell data showed no latency changes to the several elements across *trials* of a day, however, nor were trial-to-trial changes characteristic of animals run to a series of decreasing (or increasing) food quantities. The failure of the random conditions to show progressive changes in running times within the runs of a trial also speaks to the inadequacy of changes in hunger as an account for the data.

2. Temporal anticipation. Animals might well slow their running times across the runs of a decreasing series of food quantities in simple temporal anticipation of a final, zero quantity, or increase speeds in corresponding anticipation of a final, large quantity. Temporal anticipation would require relatively fixed intervals between runs to successive elements, enabling the animal to use time as an approximately fixed frame of reference — conditions which prevailed in the Hulse and Campbell experiment. While temporal anticipation should depend on the number of elements in the pattern, it ought, however, to be independent of the *order* of the magnitudes of the elements preceding 0 pellets in the decreasing sequence and 14 pellets in the increasing sequence. The Hulse and Campbell experiment showed that animals could not systematically order their responding when the elements preceding the final element of a pattern were not fixed in quantity and serial location from trial to trial. Tracking, in other words, was dependent upon a *consistent* internal *structure* of the pattern. Consequently, temporal anticipation per se is not a likely explanatory principle for the animals' behavior.

3. Counting.   The same reasons that rule out temporal anticipation of zero reinforcement as an explanation for tracking also dispose of literal counting of the number of successive elements as a factor helping to generate the data in the Seq-I and Seq-D conditions. If the rats could count elements, they should have been able to locate the final, fixed element in the pattern independently of any fixed order of the quantities preceding the final element. In particular, the 14-pellet element and the 0-pellet element should have differentiated themselves in the two groups in which the order of the preceding quantities was randomized from trial to trial; differentiation of the 0-pellet element might have been especially sharp given its apparent salience in the Seq-D condition. Because the animals in the randomized groups failed to differentiate the final 14 and 0-pellet elements, counting − independent of a fixed order of elements − was not sufficient for generating accurate location of the final elements in the Seq-I and Seq-D conditions.

4. Frustration.   As Hulse and Campbell noted, frustrative effects that change through the course of runs to a series of elements do not adequately account for the data. On the assumption, for example, that graded reductions in reward are sufficient to generate conditioned frustration (Bower, 1962), then rats run to a series of decreasing quantities ought to be progressively more frustrated and so run faster and faster to each successive element. This prediction is counter to the data.

While frustrative effects can be ruled out, this is not to say that other, generalized emotional-motivational effects might not have been at work. If a series of increasing food quantities were to produce a generalized excitatory state, for example, progressive increases in running speed would be predicted across the runs of a trial. Similarly, generalized inhibition from a series of decreasing food quantities would produce progressive slowing across runs leading to smaller and smaller quantities of food. At the very least, however, we can say that such effects − if they existed − were dependent upon the order in which elements were put together, because the data showed no indication of progressive changes in running times either within or across trials when the several elements occurred in random orders from trial to trial.

5. Serial associative chains. While excitation, inhibition, motivational changes, and temporal anticipation are not likely factors accounting for the rats' behavior, the possibility cannot be discounted that the animals learned a series of S—S or S—R associations between successive elements (Hull, 1931; Skinner, 1934; Capaldi, 1967, 1971). Given the set of ordered elements, 14—7—3—1—0 food pellets, then 14 pellets could become directly associated with 7 pellets, 7 pellets with 3 pellets, and so on, through any simple learning process (Pavlovian conditioning would do). The same line of reasoning could also postulate the development of remote associations, which would further add to the associative chain. The only additional assumption that would then be required would be the assumption that the several food quantities represented by the set $\{14 \ldots 0\}$ map in some direct monotonic fashion onto response strengths measured, for example, by running times. This is certainly not an illogical supposition as we have seen. Nor is it beyond the realm of possibility that different elements might become associated with different response strengths after the micromolar theory of Logan (1960). In either case the S—R events of one trial tell the organism precisely what to do on the next, and the animal runs through the sequence of elements in rather mechanical fashion — generating appropriate running times in the process. A hypothesis based on the premise of associative chaining easily accounts for the Hulse and Campbell data.

6. Inducing or encoding the pattern's structure. While associative chaining fares well, an equally useful account can be postulated in the terms associated with the formation of cognitive structures in human serial pattern learning. Based on our earlier discussion, this account calls for the internalization of some functional parallel of a serially ordered pattern as that pattern is formally defined by the experimenter. As we have seen, the formal definition of the structure of the simple monotonic pattern of 14—7—3—1—0 food pellets is based on the concepts of an ordered element set and the application of a *next* rule to arrive at the value of successive elements in the pattern. Again, this is *not* to say that the rat will (or can) internalize the experimenter's formal rule, per se — an assumption that is often made for human serial pattern learning.

The primary question, the simplest and most basic question, is whether the rat might encode or induce any internal representation that would depend upon some property or structural feature of the larger formally defined serial pattern, in contrast to learning something about simple pairwise associations between neighboring elements in the pattern. If this were so, then there would be a kernel of evidence for serial pattern learning that would be truly analogous to some of the features of human serial pattern learning. It would then follow that other analogies might exist between the processing of serial patterns in man and in the rat (and in other nonhuman animals). This could be true even though the characteristics of the relevant mechanisms might be not only quantitatively but also qualitatively different.

VI. EMPIRICAL ASSESSMENT OF ENCODING

The rationale behind the experiments to be reported now, then, grew from the assumption that rats would respond to some characteristic of a serial pattern that would necessarily depend upon incorporating something more of the patterns' structure than simple element—to—element associations. Some of this work has been described in part elsewhere (Hulse & Dorsky, 1977), while some of it is new. (At this point I also wish to explicitly acknowledge the contribution of Noah Dorsky not only to the development of the empirical work, but also to the thinking that suggested certain experiments over others and led to the conclusion that one interpretation of the data was to be preferred to others that seemed reasonable at the time.)

The empirical strategy of the research hinged upon one fundamental principle. In the first two experiments, various alterations were made in the internal structure of the ordered five—element pattern (14—7—3—1—0 pellets) used in the Hulse and Campbell (1975) experiment. Each structural change was designed to illuminate the contribution of one possible mechanism to the rat's ability to track the pattern. The first experiment compared monotonic with nonmonotonic patterns built from the five-element set while a second compared strong monotonic patterns with weak monotonic patterns. A third experiment tested the effects of initial training with a series of relatively short two-, three, and four-element monotonic and random patterns upon the rats' subsequent ability to respond to a longer, five-element pattern. A fourth experiment provided some preliminary data concerning the possible role of "chunking" or periodicity in learning about pattern structure. A final experiment showed, among other things, that elements drawn from the range of quantities used in the first four were discriminable from one another — and could generate differential responding.

In most cases, while we were interested in the animals' reaction to all elements, we were especially interested in the animals' behavior with respect to the motivationally significant 0-pellet element. This element generated large latency differences with respect to all other elements in the Hulse and Campbell experiment, especially if it were incorporated in a pattern in which quantities decreased. Not surprisingly, perhaps, it appeared to be very salient with respect to the other quantities. These facts led us to surmise that we should test our ideas about structure using patterns that began with large quantities and ended with small ones, and that we should use the animals' response to 0 pellets as an important index of their ability to master the several patterns. Accordingly, we emphasized data analyses which determined not only how much the animals differentiated responding to 0 pellets, but also when in the course of an experiment differentiaion of responding to 0 pellets began to appear.

A. Monotonic and Nonmonotonic Patterns (Experiment 1)

First, we compared the rat's reaction to the monotonic 14—7—3—1—0 pattern with a nonmonotonic pattern consisting of elements arranged in the order

14–1–3–7–0 food pellets. The sequences are identical in that both contain five elements, both share a common first and last element (14 and 0 pellets), both contain equivalent amounts of food (assuring equivalent changes in hunger), and – given a constant interrun interval during the course of a trial – both assure an equal opportunity for temporal anticipation of the final 0-pellet element. Also, each pattern calls potentially for an identical number of one-to-one associative links between successive elements. Therefore, differential responding to 0 pellets should appear with equal facility in both patterns.

The apparatus used to test the foregoing prediction was a straight enclosed runway 92 cm long and 10 cm wide with a 30-cm start box and a 30-cm goal box each separated from the runway by a guillotine door. Inside height throughout was 14 cm. Removable food cups could be placed in a short, 11-cm niche located at a right angle to the end of the goal box. The start box was wood color, while the remainder of the apparatus was painted flat black. The apparatus was covered with hinged pieces of Plexiglas and hardware cloth. Timing circuits measured running time from the moment the guillotine door at the start box went up until the animal bridged a contact-relay circuit 20 cm into the goal box.

Animals were reduced to 85% of their normal body weight, tamed, and permitted to explore the apparatus according to standard procedures. When the experiment proper began, one group of rats (n = 10) was exposed to the monotonic decreasing pattern of reinforcement (14–3–7–1–0 pellets) while the other (n = 10) was exposed to the nonmonotonic pattern (14–1–3–7–0 pellets). Over each of 17 days of testing, the animals received four *trials* each consisting of five *runs* to the successive elements of the respective patterns. Animals were confined in the goal box until the food was consumed or for 10 sec in the case of 0 reinforcement. If a rat failed to complete a run within 30 sec, the run was terminated by removing the rat from the apparatus. Interrun intervals were approximately 10 to 15 sec, while intertrial intervals were approximately 10 to 15 min.

1. Results. As in the Hulse and Campbell (1975) experiment, rats responded rationally to the broader features of both patterns of reinforcement. For example, as Fig. 2 shows, large rewards led to shorter mean running times at the end of training than did small rewards. However, the monotonic and nonmonotonic conditions differentiated themselves most sharply in terms of responding to the final, 0-pellet element. Responding to the 0-pellet as compared with the 14-pellet element in the monotonic condition was reliably slower on Day 1 (but not on Trial 1) of the experiment, while a parallel difference between the two elements did not appear until Day 10 in the nonmonotonic condition. Furthermore, as Fig. 2 shows, there was substantially slower asymptotic responding

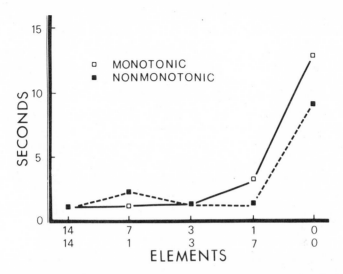

FIG. 2.   Mean asymptotic running times to monotonic (14−7−3−1−0 pellets) and non-monotonic (14−1−3−7−0 pellets) serial patterns of reinforcement quantity.

to the 0-pellet element in the monotonic as compared with the nonmonotonic condition.

In the monotonic condition, a nonparametric test for trend showed a highly reliable effect ($p < .01$) for monotonic ordering of the means, and the asymptotic mean data shown in Fig. 2 are quite typical of data for individual animals. Animals in the nonmonotonic condition showed sensitivity to differences in quantity among the initial three elements of their pattern in addition to terminal slowing to the final 0-pellet element. Nine of 10 rats slowed responding to the 1-pellet element following the initial 14-pellet element, and the same animals speeded their responding to the larger 3-element pellet that immediately followed (both $ps < .01$).

   2. Discussion.   The data showing earlier and more sensitive responding to the 0-pellet element in the monotonic versus nonmonotonic condition, like those of the Hulse and Campbell experiment, cannot be accounted for on the basis of differences in hunger or temporal anticipation of reinforcement. Nor can they be attributed to negative contrast effects associated with differences in quantity between neighboring elements. Thus, if larger contrasts predict greater tracking facility, contrasts are always larger in the nonmonotonic condition than in the monotonic condition (e.g., 7 pellets precedes 0 pellets in the former, but 1 pellet precedes 0 pellets in the latter). Furthermore, while there was evidence showing that animals were sensitive to element-to-element features of both patterns, pairwise chaining between successive elements cannot account for differential responsiveness to the 0-pellet element because each pattern incorporated identical numbers of pairwise, element-to-element associations.

Instead, the data are in accord with two propositions: (1) the rats were sensitive to some feature or features associated with a larger portion of the structure of the patterns than element-to-element associations; and (2) patterns with simpler formal rule structures were encoded by the rats with simpler internal representations — these leading, in turn, to more accurate location of the 0-pellet element within the pattern structure.

B. Strong Monotonic and Weak Monotonic Patterns (Experiment 2)

The second experiment was designed to provide a further, more rigorous test of the conclusions reached in the last experiment. Here, we compared the rat's ability to track the strong monotonic pattern of the last experiment (14—7—3—1—0) pellets with the weak monotonic pattern of 14—5—5—1—0 pellets. Again, both patterns share common total quantities, common numbers of elements, common opportunities for temporal anticipation of the 0-pellet element, and so on. Both patterns also have identical final pairs of elements, 1 and 0 pellets. The two patterns differ, however, in that the structure of the weak monotonic pattern is somewhat more complex than the structure of the strong monotonic patterns. Each successive element of the strong monotonic pattern is generated by repeated application of the rule $E(i) > E(i + 1)$. For the weak monotonic pattern, repeated application of the same rule generates all but the third element; this element is identical to the second element and follows an *equals* rule.

If rats find serial patterns generated by simple consistent rules easier to learn than patterns generated by more complex rules, as Experiment 1 shows, then the strong monotonic pattern ought to be easier to learn than the weak monotonic pattern. Again, the strongest evidence bearing on this prediction would be earlier slowing of the run to the 0-pellet element in the strong monotonic pattern combined, perhaps, with greater overall differentiation of response times among the several reinforcing elements in the pattern. The fact that both patterns end with a 1—0 pair of elements is particularly useful. If the animals did respond differentially to the 0-pellet element, it could not be because 0 pellets was predicted by two different quantities of food on the run just preceding the run to 0 pellets. Instead, differential performance would have to be ascribed, once again, to some feature or set of features inherent in larger portions of the pattern.

The strain and sex of rat, the apparatus, and the basic procedures of the experiment were virtually identical to those used in the experiment just described. Following initial deprivation, taming and exploration of the apparatus, the animals were run in the straight runway four trials per day, each trial consisting of five runs to the several elements of the two patterns. An interrun interval of 15 sec was used, while approximately 10 min elapsed between successive trials. Testing continued for 11 days.

1. Results.   Once again, the general features of the data were in line with results to be expected concerning the rats' reaction to major features of the element set. As Fig. 3 shows, large rewards generated fast mean running times, while small rewards generated slow mean running times at the end of the experiment. In the strong monotonic condition, the animals at asymptote ordered their running times across the successively decreasing quantities of food ($p < .01$), but the animals in the weak monotonic condition differentiated only the fourth and fifth elements.

As before, the sharpest distinction in the behavior generated by the two patterns was that associated with the 0-pellet element. Rats in the strong monotonic condition differentiated the 0-pellet element from the others on Day 1 of testing (as they had in the previous experiment), whereas rats in the weak monotonic condition did not do so reliably until Day 4. Furthermore, as Fig. 3 amply testifies, responding to the 0-pellet element at the end of the experiment was reliably slower in the strong monotonic condition than in the weak monotonic condition.

Like the earlier work we have discussed, the discrepancy in accurate tracking between the two patterns cannot be accounted for on the basis of differences in hunger, temporal discrimination, and so on. Possibly, the middle elements of the weak monotonic condition were relatively difficult to locate because of the branch of the pattern's structure at that point: Five pellets predicts first an addi-

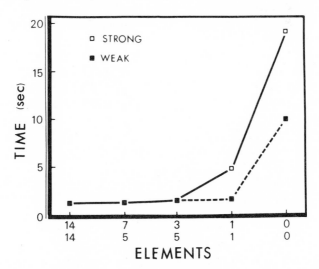

FIG. 3.   Mean asymptotic running times to strong monotonic (14–7–3–1–0 pellets) and weak monotonic (14–5–5–1–0 pellets) serial patterns of reinforcement quantity.

tional 5-pellet element, and then a 1-pellet element. An associative-chaining hypothesis would predict that this should lead to generalization and to some associative confusion between the outcomes predicted by the 5-pellet element, and the data are consistent with that interpretation. A pair-wise chaining hypothesis would also predict, however, that the fourth 1-pellet element should lead to equal differentiation of the 0-pellet element in both the strong and weak monotonic patterns, and the data are clearly *not* consistent with that prediction. Once again, simplicity of pattern structure seems to have been correlated with ease of tracking the elements of the pattern.

2. A cross-study comparison. It is interesting to note briefly that the trials on which responding to the 0-pellet element first differentiated itself reliably in the two experiments just described were perfectly correlated with the objectively defined structural complexity of the three patterns involved. For the strong and weak monotonic patterns, and for the nonmonotonic pattern, the rats began to respond reliably slower to the 0-pellet element than to the 14-pellet element on Days 1, 4, and 10, respectively, that is, after approximately 4, 16, and 40 trials ($p < .01$).

This comparison must be hedged, of course, because the experiments incorporated different subjects run at different times, and so on, but the apparatus and general features of procedure were identical and the comparison, though tentative, seems justified.

Summarizing to this point, the foregoing research suggests that rats do indeed encode some internal representation of a formally defined serial pattern, and that their performance with respect to the pattern is well correlated with the structure of the pattern. Simple formal structures are easy to learn, while complex formal structures are more difficult to master.

We hasten to repeat that we have no idea in what form the rat encodes a formal structure such that it is rendered easy to learn. Many theories of human serial pattern learning assume that people encode patterns using rules that are much the same as the rules used to generate the formal structure of the patterns (e.g., Simon, 1972). We have no data to suggest that rats do anything remotely resembling the things that people do in this particular regard. The data do argue, however for *some* kind of functional parallel between processes used by people and by animals to master serial patterns. But the properties of those processes, both quantitatively and qualitatively, remain to be discovered. The next experiment provided an initial, tentative step in that direction.

C. The Extrapolation of Serial Patterns (Experiment 3)

In developing one of the original models for the processing of serial structures and for the learning of serial patterns, Simon and Kotovsky (1963) took as one of their starting points the fact that people are adept at extrapolating or adding the next element to a structured pattern based on a familiar set of elements.

Given the simple structure of letters *ababab* and told to supply the element that would occur next were the pattern to be extended, they point out that people have a predilection for supplying the letter *a*. This fact suggests that people induce the periodic repetition of the *a* and *b* elements and extrapolate the pattern accordingly. Extrapolation of this type appears to occur naturally even though there is nothing in the *formal* structure of the pattern as defined which requires that the supplied element be *a*; it could just as easily be *c* (and then, say *dcdc*) or any other element from the set in question. The same consideration would presumably hold for a serial pattern *abcde* which implies application of the operator rule *next* and would lead people to supply the letter *f*, were they called upon to generate another letter to "fill in a blank" at the end of the series. Simon (1972) goes on to show that most theories of serial pattern learning (e.g., Jones, 1971; Restle, 1970) are similar in that they are based on rules such as *same, next, immediate precedessor*, and *complement*, and he summarizes how such theories generate patterns that vary in complexity and hierarchical structure.

In the same vein, Restle and Brown (1970) have shown that people can be *biased* to induce certain structures from a pattern containing an ambiguous structure by giving them initial experience with one as opposed to another form of rule. One pretraining pattern emphasized *trills* of numbers (565343323121), while a second emphasized *runs* of numbers (654354324321). The test sequence was ambiguous with respect to both trills and runs (2123434565). The experimental question was whether subjects pretrained on the trill or the run pattern would make errors as they learned the test pattern characteristic of those to be expected if they were applying the rule they had been biased to apply. In general, that proved to be the case. For example, subjects pretrained with the trill pattern tended to make more errors at the fourth position in the test pattern than those subjects pretrained with the run pattern; they tended to say "1" instead of "3."

All of these considerations lead to two simple questions that can be asked of rats using the general techniques of the experiments described thus far. First, given experience with a series of monotonically decreasing patterns of food quantities such that accurate tracking of the patterns has emerged, can rats extrapolate a decreasing series by running yet slower to a new, smaller ("blank") element added to the end of the series? Second, can rats be biased by experience with monotonic as compared with random patterns such that the animals are relatively quick to learn a new monotonic series containing elements they have never before experienced? In a related sense, might experience with random or monotonic series actually interfere with and so retard the acquisition of accurate tracking of new ordered series? The following experiment was designed to seek some initial answers to these questions.

Two groups of rats were given preliminary training in the same straight runway used in earlier research. They ran to serial patterns of elements drawn from an element set of 10, 5, 3, 1, or 0 food pellets. The patterns varied in length across the seven trials of a day. Within a day, three two-element, three three-element and one four-element patterns were used. For one group of rats (the M group) all patterns in which the occurrence of a given element necessarily predicted the value of the next were avoided. For example, a 1—0 sequence was avoided because 1 pellet would necessarily be followed by 0 pellets given the constraint that any pattern had to be at least two elements in length. For the rats in the M group, then, the only feature of the patterns that was consistent across trials was the fact that if $E(i)$ represents the quantity of an element E on same run, i, then $E(i) > E(i + 1)$. The values of the beginning and ending elements were never consistent, and the length of the patterns varied unpredictably.

For rats in the second group (the R group), the same elements were used — trial for trial — as those used in the M group, but their values were arranged in random order from trial to trial, sometimes decreasing or increasing over all elements, sometimes occurring in nonmonotonic order. For the R group, then, nothing at all was consistent about the structure of patterns except that the elements were drawn from the same set used for the M group, and the animals received seven trials identical in length to those of the M group.

Preliminary training for both groups continued for 10 days (70 trials). On Day 11 of the experiment, the groups were split. Half the rats in the M group (the MM condition) learned a new monotonic pattern consisting of five elements: 16—9—3—1—0 food pellets. The other half (the MNM condition) learned a nonmonotonic pattern consisting of 16—1—3—9—0 food pellets. Similarly, half the rats in the R group (the RM condition) learned the monotonic pattern, while the other half (the RNM condition) learned the nonmonotonic pattern. Note that the new patterns were longer by one element than any of the patterns used in preliminary training, and note that they both began with an element (16 pellets) that was larger by more than half than any used in preliminary training, and thus quite different from any with which the rats had experience. Finally, both patterns share the properties discussed in connection with earlier experiments, e.g., both contain equivalent amounts of food, equivalent numbers of pairwise association, and so on. Testing in the transfer phase of the experiment continued for five days, five trials per day.

1. Initial learning and extrapolation. The best characterization of the behavior generated in both the random and monotonic conditions of the first phase of the experiment is that all rats learned to run at just about the same rapid response speeds to all elements. However, by the 10th day, the end of the preliminary phase, there was a reliable tendency for the second element to generate running times that were longer than those to the first element in the monotonic condition but not in the random condition. The slowing to the second element held true for the two-, three-, and four-element trials taken together and for the two-element trials taken alone ($ps < .05$), but not for the three- and four-element trials taken alone ($ps > .05$). The means were on the order of 1.0 sec for the first element and 1.2 to 1.3 sec for the second element, and so although reliable and in the direction to be expected on the basis of the extrapolation of a decreasing series, the absolute value of the differences was not large and impressive. The same pattern of results was true for the very first five-element trial of the transfer phase. Mean running times ranged from .9 to 1.5 sec to all elements (including 0 pellets) and showed no particular order effects in any condition ($ps > .05$). By and large, the rats' responding seemed undisturbed by the addition of a fifth element to the longest pattern experienced earlier, however, and similarly, exposure to a new, very large element failed to disrupt running behavior.

The foregoing data provide little direct evidence that the animals in the M condition learned to track the several patterns in any fashion that suggests marked extrapolation of a decreasing series of elements. Perhaps, after all is said and done, the task demands of preliminary training were simply unsuited for direct demonstration of extrapolation; there are any number of reasons that could be summoned post hoc why rats might have settled for the strategy of running as fast as they could regardless of pattern length. The important question remains, however, whether preliminary M or R training biased animals (after the fashion of Restle & Brown, 1970) such that the task demands of the transfer tests would generate performance for the M condition that would differ appropriately from the NM condition. Such, in fact, turned out to be the case.

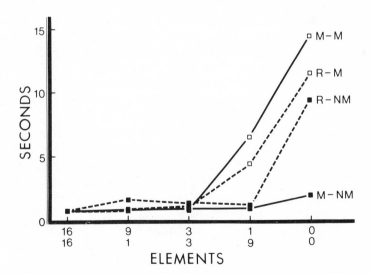

FIG. 4. Mean running times on the last day of a transfer test to a monotonic (M) serial pattern (16−9−3−1−0 pellets) and to a nonmonotonic (NM) serial pattern (16−1−3−9−0 pellets) following initial training with a different monotonic (M) or random (R) serial pattern of reinforcement quantity.

TABLE 1
Mean Running Times (Seconds) to the Fourth and Fifth Elements
During the Transfer Phase of the Extrapolation Experiment[a]

	Group							
	RNM		RM		MNM		MM	
Element	9	0	1	0	9	0	1	0
Day 1	1.3	3.2	1.6	1.6	1.5	2.0	1.8	3.7
Day 2	1.2	3.3	1.7	1.8	1.3	2.0	3.7	8.1
Day 3	1.2	4.0	1.8	5.3	1.2	1.7	5.0	10.1
Day 4	1.2	5.5	2.1	9.5	1.3	2.2	6.4	14.8
Day 5	1.4	9.2	4.3	12.0	1.1	2.5	6.7	14.3

[a]Based on the appropriate error term from the analysis of variance of these data, any mean difference larger than 2.39 sec and 3.12 sec is reliable at $p < .05$ and $p < .01$, respectively.

2. Transfer test.   Figure 4 shows mean running times to the monotonic (M) and the nonmonotonic (NM) patterns during the last day of the transfer test. Table 1 shows the development of differences in daily mean running times to the last two elements of each pattern over the entire five days of transfer. Both sets of data show that responding to the M and NM patterns turned out to be quite different following preliminary training with the M as compared with the R pattern sequences.

As one would expect on the basis of direct positive transfer of a bias to detect and respond to monotonic arrangements of elements, the MM condition generated sharpest differentiation of the 0-pellet element by the end of the transfer phase of the experiment. This was true relative not only to the RM condition, which seems the most direct and appropriate control, but also to any other condition in transfer.

Preliminary training with the set of monotonic patterns also seems to have generated *negative* transfer to the acquisition of any pattern responding at all to elements of the new NM pattern. Relative to the RNM condition (which seems, once again, the most appropriate control), to the MM condition, or to any other condition in the experiment, the MNM condition shows much less indication of tracking during the transfer phase. As a matter of fact, there is only marginal suggestion of any tracking whatsoever, a slight (and nonsignificant) slowing of responding to the final, 0-pellet element relative to the fourth, 9-pellet element.

Behavior during transfer following preliminary training with the random patterns indicated most generally that tracking of the new patterns was much like that seen in earlier experiments when rats came upon monotonic and nonmonotonic patterns for the first time. The RM as compared with the RNM condition led to earlier differentiation of the 0-pellet element and more marked differentiation among the last elements in the pattern. The basic thrust of the data indicates that preliminary training with randomly ordered sets of elements failed to bias the rats either for or against learning the new monotonic and nonmonotonic patterns.

D. Periodicity of Structures (Experiment 4)

Simon and Kotovsky (1963) take as a given that, as people induce structural patterns, one of the first things they do is to divide any given pattern into substructures that recur periodically. Indeed, this and the additional concept of hierarchical structures (to which repeated periodic patterns naturally lead) have provided one of the starting points from which various coding schemes for serial patterns then depart. It is natural to ask, again, if animals do anything that parallels human performance with respect to periodic structure.

Some initial evidence shows that rats do indeed respond to periodicity. The task was once again the familiar one of learning to track the decreasing monotonic pattern of 14–7–3–1–0 food pellets in a straight runway. The experimental variable was whether or not an *intertrial* interval was used during the course of acquisition that was different from the *interrun* interval between successive elements of the pattern. It will be recalled that in all of the research reported thus far, inter*trial* intervals on the order of 10 to 15 min were used routinely, while inter*run* intervals were on the order of 10 to 15 to 20 sec. The earlier experiments thus afforded the animals an opportunity to "chunk" the patterns across the trials of a day into five-element structures, with a temporal interval serving to mark successive chunks. By eliminating the difference between the intertrial and interrun intervals, the new experiment eliminated the opportunity for the animals to "chunk" on the basis of a temporal marker. The consequent pattern was a "sawtooth" pattern which over four repetitions per day took the form 14–7–3–1–0–14–7–3–1–0–14–7–3–1–0–14–7–3–1–0.

People would probably induce the periodic structure of the pattern without the aid of a temporal interval to mark repetitions of the five-element substructure. They would use other markers based most likely on characteristics of the successive elements themselves. But rats had a relatively difficult time managing the patterns. As we have seen, rats tested with a 10- to 15-min intertrial interval will normally begin differentiating the elements of the pattern (at least, say, the 14-pellet element from the 0-pellet element) within the first four or five repetitions of the structure. Without the temporal marker, however, the animals just began to differentiate the 0-pellet element from the others after some 20-odd *days* of training (roughly 80 repetitions of the five-element structure, four repetitions per day).

Clearly, this experiment raises many questions. Zero reinforcement, which has shown itself to be such a salient stimulus in all the research under discussion, apparently failed to provide an easily usable marker to differentiate subsections of the pattern. The 14-pellet element likewise appears to have been of little utility, and so does the contrast between the 1- and 0-pellet elements. It would be premature to speculate further on the matter, except to point out that the elimination of an intertrial interval may not have modulated the rat's reaction to a serial pattern of food quantities so much as the omission may simply have changed the task demands with which the animal was faced. A situation in which 0 food pellets is followed by a long, empty interval in another "neutral" location away from the experimental apparatus may suggest a different problem (or strategy) to the rat, than the case in which 0 food pellets quickly leads to a fresh insertion into the start box and to an opportunity to run rapidly to 14 food pellets. Once again, much further research is obviously called for, but in any case the problems encompassed by the the concept of periodicity in serial structure seem an interesting locus for comparing the cognitive capacities of people with those of other animals.

E. Free Choice of Food Quantities Correlated with Spatial Location (Experiment 5)

In much of the data produced thus far, our interest has centered on the differential performance associated with 14 as compared with 0 food pellets. While we have not ignored other quantities in the patterns, and while the manner in which the animals tracked them has been in line with predictions based on formal structure, we have provided no independent, converging evidence that the rats could really distinguish all the quantities in a pattern. In fact, one is often struck more by the similar running times generated by 14, 7, and 3 food pellets than by the differences among them.

In order to provide some independent evidence that quantities in the range used in the earlier experiments were indeed discriminable from one another, we ran the following experiment. Basically, the strategy was to locate a given quantity of food at the end of an arm in one of Olton's radial arm mazes (cf. Chapter 12), turn the rats loose to choose freely among the arms, and see (1) whether the rats would adopt some consistent pattern of choice and (2) whether the pattern of choice would correspond to the order of running times we had obtained in the work with runways.

To this end, we used an elevated four-arm radial maze and located 18, 6, 1, and 0 pellets at the end of the arms, each quantity always associated from trial to trial with its own arm. The arms were separated from the central platform by guillotine doors.

Thirteen rats were trained, five trials per day. At the beginning of a trial, all four guillotine doors were raised simultaneously, and the rat was free to select one of the arms. A rat was considered to have made a choice when it moved at least 15 cm onto the arm from the central platform. After retrieving the food (if any) from the end of the arm, the rat was permitted to return to the central platform, and the guillotine door to that arm was closed. The rat was then free to select a second, a third, and finally, a fourth arm. If a rat failed to make a choice within 60 sec, the run of the trial ended. In effect, then, the animals sampled the elements without replacement.

Twelve of the thirteen rats met a choice criterion of selecting the arms in the order 18–6–1–0 food pellets, learning to choose the quantities in the decreasing order on 8 of 10 successive trials. A mean of 36.2 trials was required to reach the criterion (range 20 to 70 trials). We also examined the animals' choice structures as a function of whether a given choice was "correct" with respect to the optimal choice structure defined by obtaining the maximum amount of reinforcement with the minimum delay, i.e., the order of choice for which the animals actually settled, 18–6–1–0 food pellets. For the optimal choice structure, $p = .25$ of selecting 18 pellets on the first choice, $p = .33$ of selecting 6 pellets on the second choice, $p = .50$ of selecting 1 pellet on the third choice, and $p = 1.0$ of selecting 0 pellets on the fourth choice. Put simply, all 13 rats showed an essentially random distribution of choices on the first day of the experiment, but virtually perfect optimization on the last day of the experiment. If, on the last day, an animal did misorder and select 6 pellets on the first choice, the "error" was corrected on the second choice by going to 18 pellets. The animals never misordered the final 1- and 0-pellet elements.

Latency-to-choose data were obtained on the last 6 of the 13 animals run in the experiment. Over the last four of the criterion trials, the means for the 18-, 6-, 1-, and 0-pellet quantities were 2.8 sec, 5.1 sec, 13.4 sec, and 31.2 sec, respectively ($p < .01$). The latency data thus match the choice data perfectly.

Although the data of the experiment were obtained with quantities that were not altogether identical to those used in earlier work, we conclude that animals were able to discriminate among food quantities that, in general, were drawn from the same range of quantities as those used earlier — especially among those quantities close to 0 pellets. Of greatest importance, the rats' order of preference for the food quantities at asymptote was perfectly correlated with latencies of choice to larger as compared with smaller quantities of food. Taken together then the data lead to two important conclusions. First, latency data and choice data, while independent, are highly correlated and therefore converge on some common measure that can provide a meaningful index of pattern complexity. Second, conditions were sufficient in *all* the experiments described in this section for rats to be sensitive to structures based on more than two (or three) quantities of food. The latter point is especially crucial given our postulate that behavior with respect to given elements in a pattern is potentially a function not only of relationships among neighboring elements but also of relationships defined by larger multielement structures of a serial pattern.

VII. THE SENSITIVITY OF ANIMALS TO STRUCTURE

We have known for some time that animals like rats and pigeons are sensitive to structures based upon binary element sets of food and no food. The plethora of work with schedules of reinforcement within the tradition of the experimental analysis of behavior is ample testimony to that fact, and so is work emanating from the Neo-Hullian tradition. In the latter case, for example, Amsel and Capaldi have suggested in rich theoretical detail how rats master simple binary structures based on the alternation, systematic distribution, or random allocation of reinforcement and nonreinforcement from one response to the next. Furthermore, as we noted earlier in this paper, Tyler, Wortz, and Bitterman (1953) drew early attention to the fact that *consistency* of a pattern of reinforcement, a single-alternation as opposed to a random pattern in particular, makes a substantial difference in rats' reaction to the pattern, specifically in resistance to extinction in particular. Tyler et al. were developing a theory stressing the relative discriminability of acquisition from extinction given single alternation as compared with random patterns. We would simply urge that the concept of the *formal structure* of a pattern, as we have discussed the concept in this chapter, may provide a theoretical umbrella covering much of this earlier work.

The empirical work we have described suggests that rats are sensitive to structures which are more complex than those studied earlier by others. Furthermore, the evidence suggests that useful theoretical models for the formal description of such structures can come from those developed for human pattern learning. We have shown specifically in this regard that rats are sensitive especially to patterns that vary in the formal complexity of their structures, and that rats, like people, find complex structures more difficult to learn than structures that are formally simple. We have also shown that rats, again like people, can be biased to respond predictably to structure depending upon the features of certain structures to which we preexpose them.

One logical conclusion is that there may be many functional parallels between the behavior of people and nonhuman animals. The developing climate in animal psychology nurtures the idea that nonhuman animals may possess capacities far beyond those we have been willing to ascribe to them in the past (see Herrnstein, Loveland, & Cable, 1976, for a recent example in another domain of psychology). If this is so, then theoretical descriptions of those capacities will necessarily have to become more sophisticated, not unlike an earlier state of affairs in language learning and rule-governed behavior in humans.

A. Internal Mechanisms

In human pattern learning, the explicit assumption is usually made that given a formal rule structure for the description of a pattern, people in fact induce and encode in memory a structure that is a direct representational parallel to that formal rule structure. For the pattern *abab*, for example, the assumption is made that people induce the periodicity of the pattern, and that some form of a *next* rule and a *repeat* rule is then encoded and used, literally, to reconstruct the pattern in recall. These are exactly the rules that are necessary to write the pattern in the first place. We have, of course, made this point before.

The point that also needs additional reemphasis is that we can, at this juncture, only speculate about the characteristics of whatever mechanisms a rat may actually utilize to induce, internalize, and encode the formal structure of a pattern. We have worked with an element set of food quantities, and we stated at the very outset that food (like any other "reinforcer") is a multidimensional stimulus. We do not know for sure which dimension or set of dimensions the rat may, in fact, respond to. Since much of the data suggest that the animals were especially sensitive to zero reward, and since there is an abundance of evidence suggesting that zero reward in the context of finite quantities of reward generates an emotional–motivational state, the animals might have been responding to some form of a motivational dimension correlated possibly with changes in food quantity. Other possible dimensions, including the dimension of numerosity itself, are not hard to conjure. Whatever the internal mechanisms or processes by which the rat manages serial patterns, however, it is important to remember that we do know they must encompass the animal's differential sensitivity to patterns that are at least as different in rule structure as the several patterns studied in the research reported in this article. Whether unravelling the rat's internal mechanism or mechanisms for managing serial pattern learning will lead to parallels or to discontinuities between animals and people remains to be seen.

Of course, it is also well to remember that the assumption that *people* actually internalize and use the formal rules required to generate patterns in recalling or extrapolating patterns is just that, an assumption. For example, Simon (1972) notes in the context of discussing the adequacy of one formal rule structure as opposed to another in accounting for pattern complexity and difficulty, that we would be best off trying to discover the "sociological and psychological" conditions which determine the adoption of one as opposed to some other coding strategy. He says this because the internalizations that people actually use will depend upon a great many things ranging from task demands to previous experience with pattern learning.

VIII. CONCLUSION

In this chapter, I have tried to show that cognitive models for human serial pattern learning provide a promising path for the study of comparable problems in animal behavior. Clearly, the surface has been but barely scratched. Hopefully, however, the concepts involved in the idea of structure in pattern learning can lead to some new understanding of problems as old as those encompassed by partial reinforcement, and as natural and ethologically oriented as the manner in which animals react to changes in location, distribution, and quantity of food supplies. In the more abstract it ought to be fun just to discover in general how well nonhuman animals can manage problems couched in the cognitive terms of formally defined serial structures.

I close on a point of pure speculation, speculation which nevertheless seems to be attracting a respectable body of bedfellows. Griffin remarks in his recent book, *The Question of Animal Awareness* (1976), that a viewpoint which avoids anthropomorphism, embraces Lloyd Morgan's canon, and limits itself to descriptions of behavior in terms "that would be equally applicable to a living animal or an appropriately contrived machine" has served science well for "more than 50 years." He adds that the method of researchers operating within this tradition has been "to assume no mental states or subjective experiences, and see how much of animal behavior can be accounted for on this parsimonious basis. This has now been done on a large scale, and some of the results suggest that it is time to review our perspectives and strategies in the light of new discoveries (Griffin, 1976, p. 55).

The results to which Griffin refers include, among others, those of von Frisch on the communication dances of bees and the Gardners on the acquisition of sign language in chimpanzees. His review of these discoveries leads him to the important question of continuity in the cognitive or mental capacities of species, a question to which some contributors to this volume have been devoting considerable energy. He espouses in the process, however, a study of problems such as mental awareness and experience, offering the development of language in animals as a tool to probe directly for such things. This general strategy may be unfortunate insofar as it is aimed at a study of mental awareness and consciousness per se, because it could lead to problems in the study of nonhuman animals that in earlier times led ultimately to the invalidation of introspection as a tool and the corresponding collapse of the structuralist approach to the study of mind and mental action. Perhaps it would be well to benefit from the past and turn, instead, to the tools and techniques afforded by modern concepts of cognition and information processing. These, or other methods yet to be developed, may prove more useful in the long run.

But if one can argue with Griffin's proposals toward specific courses of action, one cannot argue with the proposition that a reevaluation of our approaches to the question of the cognitive capacities of nonhuman species is long overdue. For too long, we have adopted a homocentric view with regard to this question, assuming that nonhuman animals *by definition* fall far short in both quantitative and qualitative terms when it comes to things that we would place under the rubric of thinking, imaging, and the like. As a matter of fact, the English language contains no parallel to the word *homocentric* that would place animals, comparably, at the center of anything at all. What would be lost if we were to drop our homocentric view of thought and cognition and adopt the working proposition that other species were *at least* as smart and thoughtful as we are? We could then go on to use new methods of research to test this working hypothesis, bearing in mind the facts of species-specific modes of action, constraints on learning, the importance of the relevance of certain cues to certain consequences, and so on — facts that have already emerged and are continuing to appear at such a rapid pace. No doubt differences — and sharp discontinuities — of both a quantitative and qualitative nature would emerge between man and other animals soon enough. But would an approach that would permit nonhuman animals to indicate for themselves when we have asked too much of them be any less parsimonious than an approach that simply denies them capacity in the first place? We must be clever as we phrase the questions we wish to put, but perhaps we should not be surprised or awed at the answers we obtain.

ACKNOWLEDGEMENTS

The preparation of this chapter and the research it reports were supported by National Science Foundation Research Grant BMS 73-01400-A02. I thank many people for their help in various aspects of the work, but especially Carlos Barrera, Diane Debs, Larry Durban, and Christine Stutz. Many of the ideas were worked out with Noah Dorsky, and he deserves my special appreciation.

REFERENCES

Bevan, W. The contextual basis of behavior. *American Psychologist*, 1968, *23*, 701–714.
Bevan, W., & Adamson, R. Reinforcers and reinforcement: Their relation to maze performance. *Journal of Experimental Psychology*, 1960, *59*, 226–232.
Bower, G. H. The influence of graded reductions in reward and prior frustrating events upon the magnitude of the frustration effect. *Journal of Comparative and Physiological Psychology*, 1962, *55*, 582–587.
Capaldi, E. J. A sequential hypothesis of instrumental learning. In K. W. Spence and J. T. Spence (Eds.), *The psychology of learning and motivation: Advances in research and theory* (Vol. 1). New York: Academic Press, 1967.
Capaldi, E. J. Memory and learning: A sequential viewpoint. In W. K. Honig and P. H. R. James (Eds.), *Animal Memory*. New York: Academic Press, 1971.
Garner, W. R., & Gottwald, R. L. The perception and learning of temporal patterns. *Quarterly Journal of Experimental Psychology*, 1968, *20*, 97–109.
Griffin, D. R. *The question of animal awareness*. New York: Rockefeller University Press, 1976.
Guthrie, E. R. *The psychology of learning* (Rev. ed.). New York: Harper & Row, 1952.
Herrnstein, R. J., Loveland, D. H., & Cable, C. Natural concepts in pigeons. *Journal of Experimental Psychology: Animal Behavior Processes*, 1976, *2*, 285–302.
Hull, C. L. Goal attraction and directing ideas conceived as habit phenomena. *Psychological Review*, 1931, *38*, 487–506.
Hulse, S. H. Patterned reinforcement. In G. H. Bower (Ed.), *The psychology of learning and motivation* (Vol. 7). New York: Academic Press, 1973.

Hulse, S. H., & Campbell, C. E. "Thinking ahead" in rat discrimination learning. *Animal Learning and Behavior*, 1975, *3*, 305–311.

Hulse, S. H., & Dorsky, N P. Structural complexity as a determinant of serial pattern learning. *Learning and Motivation*, 1977, *8*, 488–506.

Jones, M. R. From probability learning to sequential processing: A critical review. *Psychological Bulletin*, 1971, *76*, 153–185.

Jones, M. R. Cognitive representation of serial patterns. In B. Kantowitz (Ed.), *Human information processing: Tutorials in performance and cognition*. Hillsdale, New Jersey: Lawrence Erlbaum Associates, 1974.

Jones, M. R. Levels of structure in the reconstruction of temporal and spatial serial patterns. *Journal of Experimental Psychology: Human Learning and Memory*, 1976, *2*, 475–488.

Lashley, K. S. The problem of serial order in behavior. In L. A. Jeffress (Ed.), *Cerebral mechanisms in behavior*. New York: Wiley, 1951.

Logan, F. A. *Incentive*. New Haven: Yale University Press, 1960.

Restle, F. Theory of serial pattern learning: Structural trees. *Psychological Review*, 1970, *77*, 481–495.

Restle, F., & Brown, E. R. Serial pattern learning. *Journal of Experimental Psychology*, 1970, *83*, 120–125.

Simon, H. A. Complexity and the representation of patterned sequences of symbols. *Psychological Review*, 1972, *79*, 369–382.

Simon, H. A., & Kotovsky, K. Human acquisition of concepts for sequential patterns. *Psychological Review*, 1963, *70*, 534–546.

Simon, H. A., & Sumner, R. K. Pattern in music. In B. Kleinmuntz (Ed.), *Formal representation of human judgment*. New York: Wiley, 1968.

Skinner, B. F. The extinction of chained reflexes. *Proceedings of the National Academy of Sciences*, 1934, *20*, 234–237.

Tyler, D. W., Wortz, E. C., & Bitterman, M. E. The effect of random and alternating partial reinforcement on resistance to extinction in the rat. *American Journal of Psychology*, 1953, *66*, 57–65.

Vitz, P. C., & Todd, R. C. A coded element model of the perceptual processing of sequential stimuli. *Psychological Review*, 1969, *76*, 433–449.

12

Characteristics of Spatial Memory

David S. Olton
The Johns Hopkins University

I. INTRODUCTION

The focus of the experiments to be discussed here is working memory, particularly the manner in which working memory processes lists of items. This emphasis on multiple items is unusual (see Thompson and Herman, 1977). As indicated elsewhere in this volume by Honig (Chapter 1), most previous working memory experiments have used a delayed-matching-to-sample (DMTS) procedure in which only a single stimulus is presented as the sample. We wanted to extend the investigation of the characteristics of working memory to the representation of multiple events in working memory. Because of the difficulty animals have learning nonspatial DMTS tasks, we used a spatial maze procedure.

The importance of spatial location in animal discrimination has been well documented. (See Olton, 1973; Olton & Isaacson, 1968, for a discussion of aversively motivated tasks. See Olton & Samuelson, 1976; Sutherland & Mackintosh, 1971, particularly Chapters 3, 4, and 13, for a discussion of appetitively motivated ones.) Nonetheless the vast majority of current experimental procedures have made spatial learning impossible. Either spatial cues are minimized as in an operant box, or spatial cues are explicitly made irrelevant, as in a visual discrimination task in a T maze. This situation is paradoxical. On the one hand, rats consistently demonstrate a preference for solving discrimination tasks on the basis of spatial cues; on the other hand, experimenters just as consistently prevent the rats from effectively exploiting this preference. The radial-arm-maze experiments described here were designed to eliminate this paradox. Our hope was that if rats were allowed to solve complex discrimination problems on the basis of spatial location (i.e., space was made a relevant stimulus dimension), they might exhibit a substantially greater ability than in the more usual types of discrimination procedures which force them to use nonspatial cues. If such were the case, questions about memory processes, which have not been addressed with nonspatial procedures because of the animals' poor performance, might be asked in a spatial one. Our strategy was threefold: first, provide the animal with an abundance of spatial cues; second, explicitly associate these cues with reward, making space a relevant stimulus dimension; third, test the animals in such a way to be certain they were using spatial stimuli to perform the discrimination.

II. EIGHT-ARM MAZE

A. Procedure

An elevated eight-arm radial maze as portrayed in Fig. 1 was the apparatus. One pellet of food was placed in a hole at the end of each arm. Food-deprived rats were placed in the center of the apparatus and allowed to choose freely among

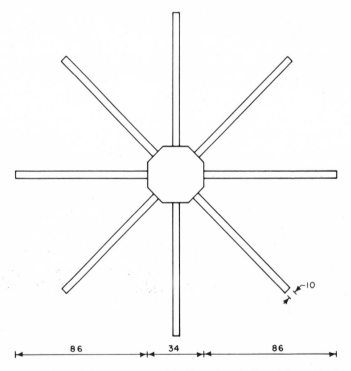

FIG. 1.   A top view of the apparatus, with dimensions indicated in centimeters. (From Olton & Samuelson, 1976. Copyright 1976 by the American Psychological Association. Reprinted by permission.)

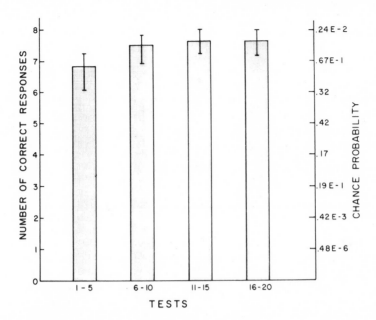

FIG. 2.   The left-hand ordinate indicates the mean number of correct responses within the first eight choices, the right-hand ordinate the chance probability or each of the values on the left hand ordinate. The abcissa presents blocks of test days. The vertical line on each histogram indicates the range of the scores.

all arms until they had obtained all eight pieces of food. The optimal strategy under these conditions is to choose each arm once and not repeat choices to any arms. We found that animals performed very well in this task which for brevity's sake will be referred to as C8, indicating that the optimal strategy for the animal is to choose each of the eight arms once. Figure 2 presents data from a group of animals that were first shaped to run on the apparatus by placing pellets of food at different distances down the arms and then tested for 20 consecutive days. (The first day of data analysis was the first day on which the animal completed eight choices.) The left-hand ordinate is the number of correct responses within the first eight choices. The right-hand ordinate is the chance probability for each number of correct responses within the first eight choices. An important point to remember about the procedure is that all arms are available to the animal at every choice. Thanks to the help of Bert Green (personal communication), I am able to say that the C8 paradigm is an example of a classic "occupancy problem," i.e., in how many ways can a set of objects be placed in a set of positions with a given number of positions left vacant (Feller, 1950, page 69). The probability of eight correct responses within the first eight choices is .0024, the probability of seven correct responses is .067, the probability of seven or eight correct responses is .069, etc. The value expected on the basis of chance performance (assuming random choices) is 5.3 correct responses in the first eight choices. Thus a slight increase in the number of correct responses represents a substantial improvement in the accuracy of performance.

Two results are obvious from Fig. 2. First, even on the first few days of testing animals made more correct choices than expected by chance. Second, choice accuracy improved during subsequent testing; every animal performed better during the last five days of testing than during the first five days. Thus after shaping animals were already predisposed to perform appropriately in the C8 procedure, but training enhanced this predisposition.

B. Strategies

A number of different strategies could be used to solve the radial-arm-maze problem, each of which would markedly reduce the load on working memory and make the task relatively uninteresting. We were particularly concerned about three possible strategies — response chains, general algorithms, and intramaze marking — and wished to determine if they were major factors contributing to the accuracy of performance.

Response chains were considered important because a number of experiments have demonstrated that rats can form very complex behavior sequences through the use of chains (Hulse, Deese, & Egeth, 1975, page 56). In the present case, a rat might solve the task by learning to choose the arms in the same order every day, say, 14726385. If the animal had this sequence stored in long-term memory (LTM), successful performance would require holding in working memory only the arm which had just been chosen and the arm which followed that choice; the other six choices could all be ignored. General algorithms were considered important because they are another way of making the task easier. For example, the rat might learn to choose adjacent arms in a clockwise order. The animal would have to store this strategy in LTM but during performance of the task would need recall only the strategy and the immediately preceding choice to respond perfectly.

The daily choice behavior of each rat was examined to determine if there were any consistent response chains or algorithms present. The qualifier "consistent" is important here. As anyone who has worked through a table of random numbers knows, many apparently nonrandom sequences appear. There are a limited number of ways in which eight different choices can be ordered. The critical issue is consistency across days. As Russell Church (personal communication) has pointed out, the raw data presented in Olton and Samuelson (1976) certainly do not meet the criteria for true randomness (see Bryant & Church, 1974), largely due to two tendencies on the part of the rats. First, they preferentially turned in a clockwise or counterclockwise manner when leaving an arm. Second, they usually skipped at least one and not more than three arms before making the next choice. But even these two tendencies were not always exhibited, and most important, choice accuracy was routinely high irrespective of choice order. Thus neither response chains nor general algorithms were necessary for accurate performance, a point which we have subsequently tested in a more direct manner, as will be discussed later (see Section IV, B.2).

The third possible strategy we considered was the use of an intramaze marking system. For example, the animal might leave the rodent equivalent of a check mark on each arm as it was chosen. If such were the case, the animal would need only investigate each arm, determine whether the check mark was present, and then respond appropriately. During performance of the task, the marking system would have to be recalled from LTM and the appropriate sign left on each arm; once a choice was made, there would be no need to hold that choice in working memory because the mark left on the arm would serve the same function.

The likelihood of such a marking system's being used by rats in mazes (Woodworth, 1938) or in naturalistic conditions (Calhoun, 1963, page 71) is very small. Nonetheless, some studies (see Means, Hardy, Gabriel, & Uphold, 1971, for a review) have argued for the presence of an "odor trail" left by rats while traversing a maze. The basic procedure of these experiments is to run animals through the apparatus, alter the floor in some manner, and determine if this alteration has some effect upon subsequent behavior. The assumption is that the effective stimulus for any behavioral change must be an olfactory one, deposited by the rats as they moved over the floor. As Means et al. (1971) point out, there are several important points which need to be emphasized but which are often overlooked. First, any influence of "odor trails" on behavior (especially choice behavior as contrasted to go—no go behavior) is a minor one. Second, the effect occurs in most cases only after nonrewarded trials. Third, the effect is highly dependent on the characteristics of the testing situation and appears only when there is a single trail left on an otherwise clean floor or when there are multiple trails from animals tested under identical conditions. Thus the likelihood of choice behavior in the present paradigm being influenced by some kind of intramaze marking system is very remote. Nonetheless, this strategy is a logical solution of the C8 problem and for that reason needs to be examined.

Our approach to this question was to treat the intramaze marking system as a possible relevant redundant cue (see discussion by Riley, this volume; Chapter 9). Evaluation of the role of relevant redundant cues is made by separating the redundancy and comparing the effectiveness of each cue individually. On test days, each rat was confined to the center compartment after the third choice. The arm assembly was rotated 45° and food replaced on the three arms already chosen so that all arms contained food. The animal was then released from the center compartment, and while it was on the arm making its fourth choice the center compartment was rotated 45° to match the arms. Five correct choices were allowed following rotation so that a total of eight correct choices were made on each day.

In the following discussion, "chosen arm" refers to an arm which had been chosen prior to maze rotation while "unchosen arm"designates an arm which had not been chosen prior to maze rotation. Likewise, "chosen spatial location" refers to the position in the testing room of an arm which had been chosen prior to maze rotation while "unchosen spatial location" indicates the position in the testing room of an arm which had not been chosen prior to maze rotation. The result of maze rotation was to dissociate the relevant redundant cues of arms and spatial location; unchosen arms were placed in chosen spatial locations and chosen arms were placed in unchosen spatial locations. To the extent that intra-maze cues (such as odor trails, etc.) direct choice behavior, rats should go to unchosen arms while repeating chosen spatial locations. To the extent that spatial location cues direct choice behavior, rats should go to unchosen spatial locations while repeating chosen arms.

Three quantitative measures of the relative importance of two sets of redundant relevant cues were calculated, each of which has been fully discussed elsewhere (Olton, Collison, & Werz, 1977). Only two will be reported here because the third is a relatively biased measure. Scores on both measures have the following characteristics: A score of 0 indicates complete discriminative control by spatial-location cues; a score of 1.0, complete control by intramaze cues; a score of .50, equal control by spatial-location and intramaze cues. The scores are sensitive to two different characteristics of choice behavior. The first one measures changes in choice behavior only at the altered spatial locations, i.e., chosen spatial locations that contain unchosen arms following rotation. The second one measures changes in choice behavior at all spatial locations.

1. Number of repetitions of chosen spatial locations.   To the extent that animals choose on the basis of spatial-location cues, following rotation they ought to respond to the chosen spatial locations as usual and the number of repetitions of the first three spatial locations should not change from that observed on control days when the maze was not rotated. To the extent that animals choose on the basis of arm cues, following rotation they ought to repeat chosen spatial locations in order to respond to unchosen arms and the number of repetitions of the altered spatial locations should be greater on test days as compared to control days. The left half of Fig. 3 presents the mean and range of the number of repetitions of the first three spatial locations on control and test days. As can be seen from the figure, there is virtually no change following maze rotation on test days and the mean score in the upper part of the figure is .04, indicating that the animals' choice behavior was guided almost exclusively on the basis of spatial-location cues.

2. Number of different spatial locations chosen.   To the extent that animals choose on the basis of spatial location, following rotation they ought to respond to all spatial locations as usual and there should be no difference in the number

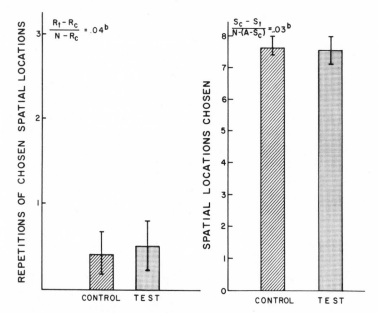

FIG. 3.   Results of the test for relative importance of an intramaze marking system and extramaze cues. For further explanation, see text.

of different spatial locations chosen on test days as compared to control days. The right half of Fig. 3 presents the mean and range of the total number of different spatial locations chosen within the first eight choices on control days and test days. Again there was virtually no change in performance following rotation on test days and the mean score in the upper part of the figure is .03 indicating that the animals' choice behavior was guided almost exclusively on the basis of spatial-location cues.

In summary, the data consistently demonstrate that in the C8 task rats do not depend upon response chains, algorithms, or intramaze marking. The implication of these results is that the rats must have been able to identify each of the eight spatial locations individually and hold in working memory the information whether or not a particular arm had been chosen on that day. Our next step, then, was to determine some of the characteristics of the memory storage.

C. Characteristics of Spatial Working Memory

1. Interference.   Our first question was whether the accuracy of choice behavior would be altered as the number of choices increased. Experiments with humans (see Hulse, Deese, & Egeth, 1975) indicate that as the number of items to be remembered increases, the accuracy of recall decreases. If a similar principle holds for rats in the C8 task, choice accuracy ought to decrease as the number of previous choices increases. This prediction assumes the rats remember which places have been chosen and ought not to be repeated, an assumption that has had considerable support (Olton, 1972; Olton, Walker, Gage, & Johnson, 1977).

To answer this question, we determined the probability of a correct response on each choice, corrected it for the expected chance probability, and expressed the result as a percent maximum performance score. (The details of this procedure are given in Olton and Samuelson, 1976.) The resulting scores can range from +1.0 indicating perfect performance, through 0 indicating chance performance, to -1.0 indicating errors on all choices. (In signal-detection terms, a positive score would be equivalent to a positive d' indicating accurate discrimination and responding; a 0 score, a 0 d' indicating a failure of discrimination; and a negative score, a negative d' indicating accurate discrimination among arms but inaccurate responding.)

The results of this analysis are presented in Fig. 4. There are three important points. First, the probability of a correct response gradually declined across choices indicating that as the number of arms to be remembered (i.e., not repeated) increased, choice accuracy decreased. Second, even on the eighth choice all animals performed substantially better than expected by chance.

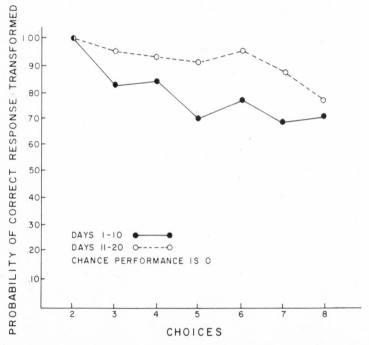

FIG. 4.   The mean probability of a correct response corrected for chance and expressed as a percentage maximum performance score for choices two through eight.

Third, choice accuracy increased from the first ten days of testing to the second ten days of testing, a finding corroborating that previously reported in Fig. 2. The implication of these data is that the accuracy with which information could be processed in working memory decreased with each additional choice the rats made.

The above analysis, of course, leaves unresolved the issue of whether the observed performance decrement was due to the number of choices or the passage of time because the two were inextricably interrelated in the basic C8 experiment. The obvious procedure to distinguish between these two alternatives is to separate time and choices. We did this by allowing the animal to make four choices and then confining him to the center of the apparatus for a delay period of two minutes, more than the amount of time usually required to complete the last four choices. Following confinement the animal was allowed to choose freely among all arms until the remaining four unchosen arms were selected. To the extent that the performance decrement observed in Fig. 4 was directly due to the increased number of choices, performance with the confinement delay ought to be no different from performance without confinement because no choices were made during the confinement period. To the extent that the performance decrement was due to the passage of time, performance with confinement ought to be worse than performance without confinement.

The results of the experiment are presented in Fig. 5, which illustrates the mean and range and of the number of different spatial locations chosen during control days without confinement and during test days with confinement. There was virtually no effect of the confinement on choice accuracy indicating the performance decrement during each day's test occurred from the increased number of choices and not because of the passage of time. These data are consistent with "interference" theories of forgetting (see Hulse, Deese & Egeth, 1975), which propose that information is lost because of new information that interferes with the storage and/or retrieval of previous information. Such a statement is not meant to imply that there is no decay process in rodent spatial memory, because there probably is, but the time course is over hours rather than minutes (Olton, 1972; Walker, 1956). Within the parameters used here, time is a relatively unimportant factor.

2. Serial Order. The analysis of the probability of a correct response (Fig. 4) provides information about the likelihood of an error but not about the original sequential position of the arm to which the error was made. Experiments with humans (see Hulse, Deese, & Egeth, 1975) have generally demonstrated both a "primacy" and a "recency" effect; items at the beginning of a list are generally remembered better than those in the middle (primacy) as are items at the end of a list (recency). In the C8 task, primacy would appear as a decreased probability of making an error by repeating a choice made early during the day's test, recency would appear as a decreased probability of making an

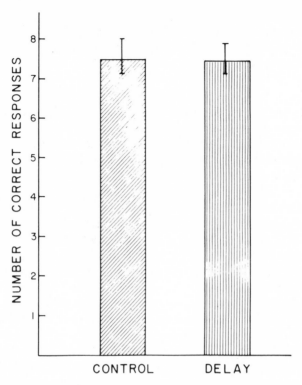

FIG. 5.   The effects of delay produced by confinement in the center platform on choice accuracy as indicated by the mean (histogram) and range (bar) of the number of correct responses in the first eight choices.

error by repeating a choice made late during each day's test. To obtain evidence about primacy and recency, we determined for each correct choice the relative probability of an error by repeating that choice, divided by the number of opportunities to make an error by repeating that choice. Scores can range from 0, indicating that no errors were made to the choice in question, to some positive number, indicating that some errors were made to that choice. The more positive the score, the greater the relative probability of an error to that choice. (Further details are given in Olton & Samuelson, 1976).

The results of this analysis are presented in Fig. 6. For both Days 1 to 10 and Days 11 to 20, the relative probability of making an error by repeating a previous choice declined slightly as a function of the sequential position of the correct choice. These data indicate that when an error was made it was least likely to be made to the just previous choice. This type of result is usually interpreted as evidence for a "recency" effect; i.e., the items placed in memory most recently are remembered best and thus fewer errors are made to them. The figure provides no evidence for a primacy effect, i.e., a decrease in the probability of an error to the first choice of the day. Thus memory processing in the C8 procedure is characterized by a small recency effect but no primacy effect suggesting that the items most recently entered into the memory store are remembered best.

3. Confusion Among Items.   The analysis of the probability of a correct response (see Section C.1) describes the likelihood that any given response will be an error and the analysis of the probability of repetition (see page 350) describes the sequential distribution of these errors among previous choices. The question remains as to the spatial distribution of errors. In particular, when errors occurred, did they tend to be made by repeating arms close to ones which still contained food, suggesting that there was some generalization or confusion between chosen and unchosen arms? We calculated an error-location score (see Olton & Samuelson, 1976 for details), which reflected the spatial distribution of the remaining correct arms with respect to each arm on which an error was made, and then compared this score to the value expected by chance. In every case, the error-location scores closely approximated the chance value, demonstrating that when errors occurred there was no tendency for them to be made to arms close to correct ones, and suggesting that these errors did not arise because of generalization or confusion among arms.

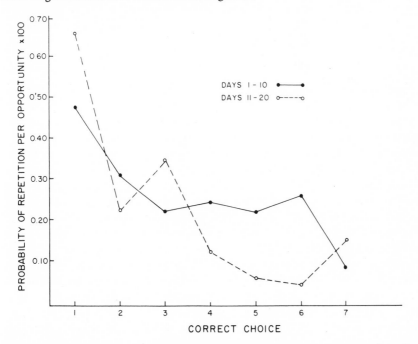

FIG. 6.   The mean relative probability of making an error by repeating each of the first seven correct choices corrected for the number of opportunities to repeat that choice.

4. Resetting.   One final question we considered was how rapidly rats could "forget" or at least isolate the memory of previous choices. If there is limited working-memory capacity, being able to forget is often as important as being able to remember because the memory process will be more effective the fewer the items that are already in storage. One of the reasons for testing animals only once a day had been to minimize any proactive interference from one test to the next. Since the rats performed so well with a 24-hr interest interval, we decided to shorten the interval as much as possible – to approximately 1 min. The analysis of the probability of a correct response (see Section C.1) demonstrated that as the number of choices increased, accuracy decreased, at least within each day's test. If the processes underlying this performance decrement were to continue between tests as well, performance accuracy ought to decline across tests. If, on the other hand, the animal was able to clear working memory of the items from one test before beginning a second, performance on the second test might be just as accurate as on the first.

We addressed this issue in the following manner. The animal was allowed to choose freely until all eight arms had been chosen. After the last choice, the guillotine doors were lowered confining the animal to the center of the apparatus. The experimenter rebaited for all eight arms, a process which took about 1 min, raised the guillotine doors and allowed the animal to choose freely until all eight arms were chosen again. The confinement, rebaiting, retesting process took place daily for a series of four consecutive tests, followed subsequently by a daily series of eight consecutive tests.

To our surprise, the animals found the consecutive test procedure only slightly more difficult than the usual daily procedure; choice accuracy remained consistently high throughout all tests although errors on the last few choices of each test did become more frequent. The data from four animals each given eight consecutive tests with a one minute interest interval on four separate occasions are presented in Fig. 7. Performance on the initial test was almost perfect, probably due to the extended testing experience of these animals. Within each test, the usual decrement in choice accuracy on the last few choices of the test occurred. Between tests, however, there was a consistent and substantial recovery of choice accuracy so that performance on the first few choices of any given test was substantially greater than that expected by extrapolating the curve from the last few choices of the previous test. Indeed, with only two exceptions (two rats, one choice each on one of the eight tests), performance on choices two, three and four was perfect; the deleterious effects of the sequential testing procedure did not consistently appear until choices seven and eight. These data suggest that the animals must have had some means of isolating information from any given test so that it caused minimal disruption of the memory required for performance on subsequent tests. In many respects, the phenomenon is similar to the release from proactive interference in human associative learning (Wickens, Born, & Allen, 1963). The mechanism of resetting is at present unspecified. Its effectiveness, however, is clearly demonstrated.

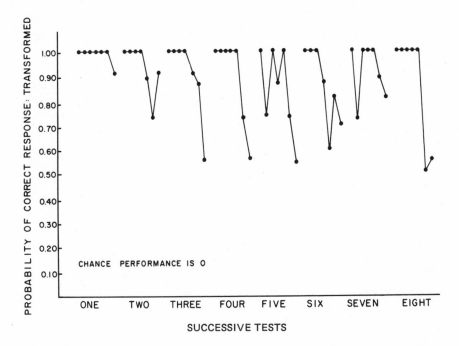

FIG. 7.   The mean probability of a correct response corrected for chance and expressed as a percentage maximum performance score for choices two through eight on eight successive tests. The improvement in choice accuracy from the end of one test to the beginning of the next is an indication of "resetting."

5. Summary.   Before proceeding further, let me summarize the conclusions I think are appropriate at this time. The cognitive requirements of the C8 procedure are straightforward; the animal must be able to locate each of the eight arms and determine whether it has been chosen. Numerous strategies are possible, many of which substantially decrease the amount of information which has to be stored in working memory. But the data indicate that none of the obvious strategies were used by the rats. Since the testing procedure provided the animal with all eight alternatives at every choice, the results suggest that the rats must have been able to identify each of the eight arms and remember over a period of several minutes which arms had been chosen and which had not.

The data analyses provide the following description of the animals' behavior. First, choice accuracy was very good even on the eighth choice. Second, choice accuracy declined slightly but consistently as a function of choices within a test. Third, the probability of making an error by repeating a previous choice was a declining function of the sequential position of that choice. Fourth, errors were distributed randomly in space with respect to correct arms. Fifth, the decrement in choice accuracy as a function of choices that occurred within a test was markedly suppressed between tests.

These results suggest the following conclusions about the memory underlying spatial discrimination. First, memory is accurate and substantial and can easily handle eight different items. Second, there is interference among the items to be remembered within each test. Third, there is a slight recency but no primacy effect. Fourth, errors do not result from generalization or confusion among the arms. Fifth, the memory of choices on one test can be effectively isolated from the memory of choices on previous tests.

III. COMPARISON TO OTHER TESTING PROCEDURES

How does the C8 procedure compare with other types of tasks which have been used to assess animal memory? First, a few similarities. The C8 procedure can be considered as a variant of the delayed-matching-to-sample (DMTS) procedure (see Honig, Chapter 8). In DMTS, a stimulus is presented, removed, and followed by a set of stimuli, one of which matches some characteristic of the original stimulus. The animal is usually rewarded for responding to the stimulus in the comparison set that matches the sample presented previously although this doesn't have to be the case. The C8 task is similar in that the animal makes a choice (is given a sample), returns to the center platform, is presented with a comparison set of all arms including the one just chosen, and directs the next response to one of these arms on the basis of whether it has been a previous sample. There are specific differences, of course, because: (1) the number of stimuli in the sample gradually increases during each day's test; (2) the animal (rather than the experimenter) chooses the sample; and (3) when the comparison set is presented, the animal is rewarded for choosing an arm different from one that has been a sample. Nonetheless, the general parallel between C8 and DMTS is striking, and if the comparison is valid it raises the question as to why animals perform the C8 task so well and other DMTS tasks so poorly. An answer would provide considerable information about the important characteristics of both radial-arm-maze tasks and delayed matching to sample ones.

The radial-arm-maze procedure can also be considered as a type of alternation problem because animals are rewarded for choosing an arm different from the ones previously chosen. Rats "spontaneously" (i.e., without training or differential reinforcement) demonstrate a tendency to alternate among spatially different alternatives, a phenomenon which has been known for some time (Dennis, 1939; see Douglas, 1966) even with delays of many minutes between choices (Walker, 1956). More recently, a series of experiments by Lachman (Lachman & Brown, 1957; Lachman, 1965; 1966, 1969) based on a procedure described by Crannel (1942) has used an apparatus with three, four, or five arms radiating from a central start arm. Rats, rewarded for the first choice of each arm, learned rapidly and performed well. Analysis of choice patterns indicated that the rats did not exhibit stereotyped response patterns and tended to choose a correct arm that was maximally distant from the arm just previously chosen. Thus the basic behavioral tendencies exhibited by animals in the radial-arm maze (choice alternation, choice accuracy, lack of response stereotype, ability to span long periods of time between choices) have been well documented over a number of years.

Other experiments, although slightly different from the present one, have used a procedure in which the optimal strategy is to choose each item from a known set of items until the entire set is chosen. An example is the "traveling salesman problem" of Menzel (1973). Chimps first observed 18 food items being distributed around a large enclosed compound and were then released to search for the food. They obtained an average of 12.5 food items and did so in a manner which tended to minimize the distance which had to be traveled. Another example is the "missing scan" technique of Buschke (1963). Subjects were successively presented with all but one item from a known list and then asked to identify the item that was missing. They had no difficulty in performing accurately with lists of up to 12 items.

Now, a few differences. Although the apparatus is reminiscent of the "sunburst" maze used by Tolman, Ritchie, and Kalish (1947), the procedure is very different. In Tolman's experiment, animals were first trained on an elevated maze to follow a runway from a start location to a goal location. An additional 18 runways were then placed around the start area radiating away from it in different directions. The runway usually used to go to the goal area was blocked, forcing the animals to return to the starting area and enter a new runway. The question was whether rats would choose a runway oriented towards the goal area, suggesting the development of an "expectancy" during the original training. Although the results were far from clear cut, the two runways oriented toward the goal area were chosen more frequently than any others.

Several points should be made about the Tolman experiment. First, Tolman's animal had to remember only a single goal area (instead of eight) to perform appropriately. Thus although the sunburst apparatus was similar to the C8 one, the testing procedure was markedly different. Second, the specific results of the Tolman experiment have not been replicated (e.g., Gentry, Brown, & Kaplan, 1947; Gentry, Brown, & Lee, 1948) which is ironic because the experiment is often cited as a "classic" in support of the spatial learning hypothesis. Third, there is a problem even with the logic of the experiment. Certainly the animal ought to choose an arm radiating to the goal area if there is reason to believe that reward lies in that direction *and* that the runway is straight. But the rats' previous experience on the apparatus had always been with a runway that had a series of right angle turns in it. If there is no reason to assume that the runway oriented in the direction of the goal actually leads directly to the goal, then an equally "intelligent" response might be to try to pick an alleyway that leads just beyond the block in the original one (as was the case in the experiment of Gentry et al., 1948). In short, Tolman's experiment was by no means definitive, even though the conclusions drawn from it are correct.

The C8 procedure is also not equivalent to a serial T or Y maze with an equal number of choices. In the serial-maze task each choice can be made solely on the basis of the information present at each choice point and there are only two options available to the animal at any given time (assuming the experimenter has prevented retracing). In the C8 task, however, all eight alternatives are present on every choice and the animal must remember all of its previous choices in order to perform correctly. The C8 procedure is not a response-chain test either; the problem doesn't have to be solved in that way, and rats don't perform in this manner. Nor is it a test of "cognitive maps" (Menzel, 1973; see also Chapter 13, this volume) or complex reasoning (Premack, Chapter 14, this volume). The rats may learn about the relationships among all the arms and be able to deduce that a rapid way of going from one arm to the adjacent arm would be taking the straight line between them, but they don't have to do so because the task can be successfully performed by treating each arm as an isolated stimulus, completely independent of each of the others.

IV. REPLICATIONS AND EXTENSIONS

The radial-arm-maze procedure is a relatively new one and our first concern was determining the generality of the results. In particular, we wanted to be certain that we weren't dealing with some idiosyncratic combination of animals, apparatus, and training that would have limited application to any other set of circumstances. Consequently, we extended our testing to other rodents and introduced some variations of the original procedure.

A. Other Animals

In addition to rats, we have tested gerbils (*Meriones ungulatus*), first-generation offspring of wild rats, and weanling albino rats. The gerbils were chosen because of their characteristic "ventral rubbing" (see Glickman, 1973). By pressing their ventral surface onto a protruding object, gerbils deposit a secretion from a gland located on their ventral surface. This secretion is commonly used to mark territories. Gerbils are of interest because ventral-gland secretions could easily be adapted to an intramaze marking system. First-generation offspring of wild rats were used to be certain that the behavior we observed in the radial-arm-maze task wasn't some fluke of the extensive inbreeding of laboratory rats. We found that wild-caught adult rats were very difficult to handle and to test. For this reason, we bred them in the laboratory and handled the offspring daily. The offspring were sufficiently tractable as adults to be tested without undue difficulty, while still maintaining most of the characteristic behaviors of wild rats. Weanling rats were tested to determine if they could perform as well as adults. Accurate choice behavior on the radial-arm maze requires a relatively complex cognitive apparatus, one which might not be fully developed in the young rat.

We tested groups of these animals for 30 days in the C8 procedure. Reward was a 190-mg Noyes food pellet for the wild rats, a 45-mg Noyes pellet for the gerbils and infant rats. Animals were often tested twice a day instead of just once. All other details of the procedure were the same as described for the original study. The gerbils, first-generation offspring of wild rats, and infant lab rats performed essentially the same as the adult lab rats described previously. These results suggest that the conclusions drawn from the original experiments with lab rats can be generalized at least to several other rodents.

Kamil (1975) has reported data on the foraging activity of amakihi (*Loxops virens*), a species of Hawaiian honeycreeper. These animals systematically visit nectar-producing flowers in a pattern which suggests strong avoidance of recently visited flowers. This behavior is a clear analog of that observed on the radial-arm maze, and a comparison of the mechanisms might help elaborate the similarities and differences in the behavior of the two species.

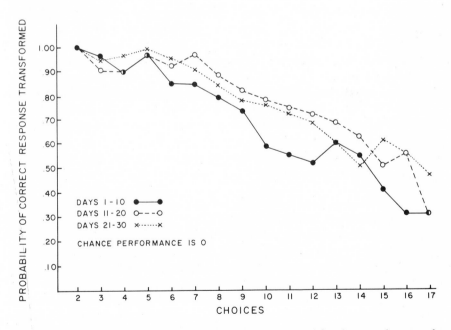

FIG. 8.   The mean probability of a correct response corrected for chance and expressed as a percentage maximum performance score for choices 2 to 17 on the 17-arm maze. (From Olton, Collison, & Werz, 1977.)

B. Procedural Variations

1. Task Difficulty.   A second series of experiments was designed around an elevated 17-arm radial maze, chosen to make the task more difficult (Olton, Collison and Werz, 1977). Laboratory rats were trained in the usual fashion in a C17 paradigm: One pellet was placed at the end of each arm, and the animal allowed to choose freely until all pellets were obtained or until 20 min had passed. The rats performed well, making more than 14 correct responses in the first 17 choices ($p < .02$ for any single day; chance performance is 10.9 correct in the first 17 choices). As indicated in Fig. 8, choice accuracy declined as the number of choices increased but even on the 17th choice the performance of all animals was better than chance. There was only a slight indication of serial ordering with a very small recency effect restricted to the last few choices. Two strong response tendencies were observed; consistent turning either clockwise or counterclockwise when leaving an arm and making the next response to one of the closest four arms. These two tendencies resulted in more than 90% of the responses being made to the four arms on either side of the arm just chosen.

2. Confinement Between Choices.   The two response tendencies just described confound the interpretation of the data because the observed performance characteristics could be due to response processes rather than memory processes. To help clarify the situation, we placed a circular barrier around the center platform with a guillotine door at the entrance to each of the 17 arms. Animals were confined to the center platform for 20 sec, each time they returned from an arm. During this confinement, they moved about the center platform, usually poking at the doors. To assess the effectiveness of confinement in disrupting the response tendencies seen in the free-choice situation, conditional probabilities were calculated between the location of each choice and the location of the subsequent choice. For this analysis, the arm just chosen was numbered 0. The arm immediately adjacent to it in a clockwise fashion was numbered +1, the next one +2, etc., to +8. The arms in the opposite direction were numbered -1, -2, etc., to -8. The results of this analysis, both for the free-choice procedure and the guillotine-door procedure are presented in Fig. 9. With the free-choice procedure, the distribution of choices was highly skewed with the vast majority of choices being to arms near the one just chosen. With the confinement procedure, the distribution was almost flat; except for a low probability of returning to the arm just chosen, animals distributed their choices almost equally around the apparatus.

What was the effect of confinement on choice performance? First, animals performed just as accurately as in the free choice task, making more than 15 correct responses in the first 17 choices. Second, there was the usual decline in choice accuracy as the number of choices increased. Third, there was absolutely no evidence of serial ordering. These data demonstrate that the high level of choice accuracy in general and the decline in choice accuracy over choices are

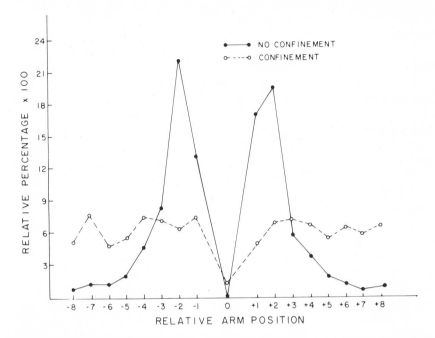

FIG. 9. An indication of the relative spatial locations of consecutive choices determined by conditional probabilities for the free choice procedure (solid line) and the confinement procedure (dotted line). (From Olton, Collison, & Werz, 1977.)

both independent of the response tendencies observed in the free-choice task; the decline in the probability of repeating a choice across choices is not. The conclusions drawn previously about choice accuracy and interference among choices as memory characteristics are supported, but the suggestion of a recency effect is not. The appropriate conclusion seems to be that there is no serial ordering of items in working memory.

3. *Learning.* Another experiment with the 17-arm apparatus had to do with the role of learning in performance. In all the other procedures, we first shaped animals extensively on the apparatus before the first day of data analysis. Performance on the first day of data analysis was substantially more accurate than expected by chance. To what extent did the shaping procedure train the animals to perform in the correct manner? To address this question, we constructed a 17-arm radial maze of hardware cloth that was exactly the same dimensions as the elevated variety. The hardware cloth was bent so as to form a tunnel down which the animal could run and the maze was placed on the floor. With this apparatus animals were no longer hesitant to enter the arms; we could obtain 17 choices from each animal even on the very first day of testing. The animals were tested in the usual C17 procedure with one pellet at the end of each arm. But

the data analysis was taken from the very first day of testing — the first time the animals were even placed in the apparatus or entered the testing room. The results of this procedure are indicated in Fig. 10. Performance on the first few days was essentially chance (12 correct out of the first 17 choices). Performance gradually improved over days until it reached asymptote at about 15 correct in the first 17 choices.

These results suggest that substantial learning takes place during the shaping procedure on the elevated apparatus. The nature of the leaning is as yet unclear. One possibility is that the animals are learning the stimuli that define each of the arms. Another is that they are learning the reward contingencies. A failure to accurately identify the arms or to appreciate the reward contingencies would lead to poor performance on the first few days of testing. Experiments are under way to distinguish between these two possibilities.

V. ETHOLOGICAL CONSIDERATIONS

A fundamental discrimination problem for any animal is finding food. In particular, consider an animal's reaction to finding some food, but not in sufficient quantity to provide a complete meal. Where should subsequent food searching behavior be directed? One alternative is to stay in the immediate vicinity of the first food source. Such a "win—stay" strategy is appropriate, if food sources tend to congregate so that finding one source increases the probability of finding additional sources nearby. Another alternative is to leave the

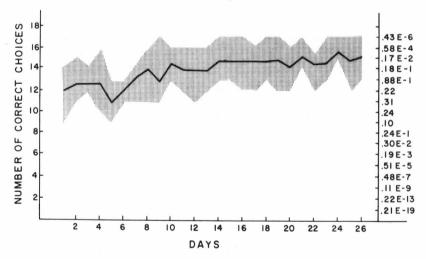

FIG. 10.   The mean and range of the number of correct responses in the first 17 choices for each day of testing in the 17-arm maze on the floor. Day 1 was the first day the animal was in the apparatus. (From Olton, Collison, & Werz, 1977.)

site of the initial find and search elsewhere. This "win–shift" strategy is appropriate if food sources are dispersed in space, or if a source, once emptied, requires time to be replenished.

An example of the win–shift strategy has been nicely documented by Kamil (1975, in press), who studied the systematic foraging patterns of amakihi (*Loxops virens*), a species of the Hawaiian honeycreeper. These birds have a home territory and feed on the nectar of mamane flowers in that territory. Kamil set up observation sites so that he could identify individual clusters of mamane flowers, and recorded the pattern of visits to these sites by the honeycreepers. On any given day, resident birds (birds whose home territory included the marked mamane flowers) were unlikely to return to a cluster of flowers that they had visited previously on that day. Thus the resident birds had some means of determining which flowers had already been chosen and avoiding those clusters. In contrast, intruding birds (birds whose home territory did not include the marked flowers) often chose a previously visited cluster. Because intruding birds were unable to identify which flowers had already been visited by the resident bird, the flowers themselves were apparently unable to act as a useful discriminative stimulus. Together these data suggest that the resident birds adopted a win–shift strategy and did so by remembering the location of the flower clusters that had been visited that day.

Kamil points out three important conclusions from his experiment. First, the honeycreepers developed a search strategy that was appropriate to their food source. A flower once emptied of nectar requires time to replenish that nectar. Avoiding just-chosen flowers should increase the amount of nectar obtained on each visit. Second, this systematic foraging among the flowers was directed by memory, which in the current context would be described as spatial working memory. Third, selection pressures in the natural environment may predispose an animal to certain types of food-searching strategies and influence behavior in laboratory discrimination-learning tasks.

This latter point is of particular interest in considering the ease with which rats seemed to learn the radial-arm-maze procedure. Clearly the response requirements favor a win–shift strategy; having found food in one location the animal ought to search elsewhere because food will not be replaced in the original location until the test has been completed. The question is: Are rats naturally predisposed to follow a win–shift strategy in food searching tasks?

We approached this question in two ways. One was to use the 8-arm radial maze but change the procedure so that it favored a win–stay strategy (Olton & Schlosberg, in press). All rats were allowed to make four choices and then confined to the center platform by guillotine doors. After confinement, one group was rewarded for choosing the four arms not chosen prior to confinement, the usual win–shift procedure. A second group was rewarded for choosing the four arms chosen prior to confinement, a win–stay procedure. The difference in choice accuracy between the two groups was striking. The win–

shift group learned rapidly and within 30 tests was making an average of more than 3.5 correct responses in the four choices following confinement. The win—stay group showed no signs of learning the task; even after 50 trials they were responding only slightly above chance.

In a second approach to the win—shift vs. win—stay question, we tested individual rats in a small seminaturalistic observation area (Olton, Walker, Gage and Johnson, 1977). The apparatus was a pen, 2 by 3 m, filled with small compartments, tunnels, and three towers on which food could be placed. (Towers were chosen to make the response of gathering food readily observable and quantifiable. Although rats are usually considered to be burrowing animals, they had no difficulty climbing the towers and bringing the food down. In subsequent experiments, we found that wild rats often leaped from tower to tower, crossing spaces of .5 m, with no apparent difficulty.) Rats were deprived of food and water for about 21 hr each day and then released into the observation area to obtain food. During the first 45 min of this time, we recorded the behavior of each animal, noting particularly the order in which the rat visited each of the possible food locations.

In one procedure, there was a pile of food on each of the three towers. Here rats alternated choices among the towers. Having obtained food from one tower, they were most likely to make their next choice to a different food tower (even though all towers still had food on them). In another procedure, only one tower had a pile of food on it, but the tower which contained food changed each day. Here, finding food and not finding food had different consequences on subsequent choice behavior. After responding to a tower that did not have food, the rat almost never returned to that tower for the rest of that day. After responding to a tower that did have food, the rat was as likely to go to a different tower (providing that it had not already been chosen) as to repeat the food tower. These two patterns of behavior indicate a strong win—shift preference. In the first procedure, when food could be obtained on any tower, the rats switched from one tower to the next, obtaining some food from each rather than responding to a single tower and removing all the food from it before going on to the next. In the second procedure, when food was on only one tower, the rats went to all the towers even if they found the single source of food on their first choice.

Other experiments support this picture of rats as win—shift animals. For example, Barnett and his colleagues have studied both wild and laboratory rats in a "residential" plus maze (Barnett & Cowan, 1976; Barnett, Dickson, Marples, & Radha, 1978). Three of the arms contained different kinds of food, while the fourth was empty. The rats lived in the maze all the time but were confined to the center area for 21 hr per day. The other 3 hr they were free to explore the entire apparatus. Barnett demonstrated that the rats went on very regular "patrols" of the environment, responding to each of the arms in a systematic way. These patrols usually came when the animal was first released from confinement, and also after meals. The exploratory tendency reflected in these patrols is again compatible with the type of shifting behavior seen in the radial arm maze procedure.

Another extensive analysis of exploratory behavior has been carried out by Bättig and his colleagues with an ingenious hexagonal maze (Bättig, Driscoll, Schlatter, & Uster, 1976; Uster, 1977; Uster, Bättig, & Nageli, 1976). The maze was constructed with inserts that could be moved to make many different patterns, and with photocells in each of the alleys to record the animals' movements. The entire apparatus was connected on line to a small computer system, which was programmed to obtain several different indices of exploration. The animals were placed in the maze for a 6-min period and their patterns of movement through the apparatus noted. Of most importance to the spatial memory experiments described here is Bättig's finding that the animals quickly adopted a very efficient pattern of movement through the apparatus so that they covered all alleys in a brief period of time and with a minimum of return visits to already visited alleys. The behavior looks much like the patrols described by Barnett — a tour through the environment designed to include a visit to each spatial location.

In short, the win—shift propensity of rats has appeared in a variety of situations ranging from standard laboratory tasks to seminaturalistic settings. Many studies (Bolles, 1970; Kamil, 1975, in press; Herman & Albeit, 1973) have emphasized the influence of species-specific predispositions on performance in laboratory tasks. In light of these considerations, an important factor in the success of the radial-arm-maze task in assessing spatial working memory seems to be its compatability with the natural win—shift tendencies the rats bring to the task (see also Olton, 1972).

VI. A MODEL FOR SPATIAL WORKING MEMORY

As a means of summarizing the work completed and highlighting questions that future research must consider, I present a simplified working model. The radial-arm-maze experiments were not designed to prove the model, and it was developed post hoc to fit the results obtained. Thus, I offer it not as an explanation, nor as a theory, but rather as a useful heuristic. I will first describe its general characteristics and then discuss each of its more important components.

A. General Organization

Figure 11 presents the model. The system begins with sensory input that enters into a temporary register. A comparison process attempts to match the contents of the temporary register with each of the items in working memory. A match indicates that the choice in question has already been made and should not be repeated; information in the temporary register is deleted, a decision made as

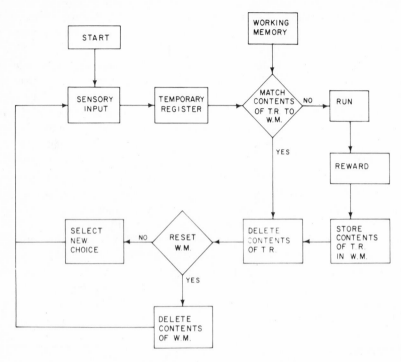

FIG. 11.   A model of the memory processes underlying performance on the radial-arm-maze paradigm. For explanation, see text.

to whether to reset working memory, a search is initiated for a new choice, and new sensory input is obtained. A failure to match the contents of the temporary register and some item in working memory indicates that the choice in question has not been made previously and ought to be made now. Running down the arm produces reward. The information defining the choice which was in the temporary register is stored in working memory so that the choice will not be repeated, the temporary register is cleared, the reset decision made, a search for another choice is initiated, and new sensory input is obtained. This continuous recycling process is terminated by the experimenter after a criterion of time or choices is reached.

Clearly the model is a very simplistic one. It does not consider many important issues such as the role of long-term memory, the fate of the information in working memory when resetting occurs, etc. It also makes a number of assumptions; an item is stored in working memory as a choice only after the animal runs down an arm and reward is obtained, the reset mechanism is activated just prior to obtaining new sensory input, etc. No data are directly available to evaluate these assumptions.

B. Comparison of Temporary Register and Contents of Working Memory

The comparison process which compares the contents of the temporary register with those of working memory encodes a choice on the basis of specific stimuli. Current evidence demonstrates that these stimuli are not intramaze markings, response chains, or general algorithms, and the suggestion has been made that the most likely stimuli are extramaze ones. Such a conclusion is based on reasoning by elimination, a hazardous procedure at best. Future research must obtain direct positive evidence on this point by investigating the role of explicit extramaze stimuli in guiding choice behavior. The results should indicate the amount of discriminative control exerted by extramaze cues as a general class and also provide information about the importance of the specific relationships among each of the available extramaze cues.

C. Working Memory

The characteristics of working memory described so far are: limited capacity, interference among contents, lack of decay for periods of up to several minutes, little if any serial ordering, and no generalization or confusion among items. These characteristics were found with the original 8-arm maze and a more difficult 17-arm version, with possible confounding factors such as response tendencies and intramaze marking strategies controlled, and with several different kinds of rodents. A number of additional characteristics need to be specified. To name a few: What is the capacity of working memory? What are the factors that influence the amount of interference among any set of choices? How does the interference produce loss of information — by displacing individual items in an all-or-none fashion, or by leading to gradual degradation of all items?

D. Selection of New Choice

The factors that influence the selection of a new choice are relatively unknown at the present time. A number of response dispositions (thigmotaxis, centrifugal swing, etc.) bias the selection mechanism in the free choice procedure so that arms near the one just chosen are more likely to be entered than arms farther away. But our experimental evidence indicates that these response tendencies are primarily a matter of convenience in moving about the apparatus rather than a strategy for performing correctly because interference with them does not affect choice accuracy. The question remains as to whether rats can adopt a strategy in choosing among arms. Can they learn to group choices together in such a way to decrease the amount of information that has to be stored in working memory, or is the next choice always just a random selection? This issue really goes beyond the question of memory into the area of problem solving and hypothesis testing, but it is one that ought to be addressed and one for which the radial arm maze procedure is well suited.

E. Resetting

The resetting mechanism is an important and effective means of making choice behavior on subsequent tests more accurate, presumably by eliminating items no longer relevant from working memory. Current evidence indicates that resetting takes place at the end of a test. Can resetting be placed under discriminative control so that it can take place at any point in a test? How does resetting address the contents of working memory, in "batch" processing so all items are eliminated in parallel or by single item processing? If the latter, what variables influence the order in which items are handled? Release from proactive inhibition (Wickens et al., 1963) has become an important tool for examining the characteristics of human associative memory. If the mechanism of resetting is similar to that of release from proactive inhibition and can be accurately specified, it may provide a similar tool for the study of animal associative memory.

VII. COMPARISON WITH OTHER MODELS

Now that the processes thought to underlie performance in the radial arm maze have been presented formally, the model presented here can be compared to those suggested by other contributors to this volume. The model proposed by Honig (Chapter 8) is most similar to the one here, which is not surprising since we have both addressed similar issues. Our models agree that working memory can be very accurate, can hold information for relatively long periods of time, and is unaffected by decay. One issue addressed by Honig, but not included in the model proposed here, is the characteristics of the to-be-remembered stimulus (the "prestimulus" in Honig's terms) that are actually stored in working memory. In developing his "instruction" model of working memory, Honig provides evidence that the response to the prestimulus is relatively unimportant; pigeons perform just as accurately in his procedure with and without differential responding to the prestimulus (see Chapter 8, this volume).

The role of the response in maze learning has had a long and tortuous history that need not be reviewed here (see, for example, Blodgett & McCutchen, 1947; Restle, 1957; Tolman, 1933). In the radial-arm-maze experiments, the issue is the extent to which actually running down the arm of the maze is important for correct performance. John Walker, a graduate student at Hopkins, has provided convincing data that in our procedure the response itself is unnecessary for information to be accurately stored in working memory. He trained animals in a four arm radial maze with the usual free choice procedure to a criterion of 20 successive tests of perfect accuracy (four correct responses in the first four choices). Then followed a series of tests in which the rats were first placed at the end of an arm (and allowed to eat the food there) prior to being put on the center platform for the usual free choice procedure. The question is whether the animal can remember the arm on which he has been placed even though the response of running to the end and back has been eliminated. Accurate memory is demonstrated by the rat choosing all the arms on which he has not been placed before going to the arm on which he has been placed. The experiment was carefully conducted; rats were placed on one, two, or three arms before being returned to the center for the free-choice procedure, they were carried to each of these arms over a variety of different spatial routes, and the placement tests were given in counterbalanced order along with the usual free-choice procedure. The first time the rats were placed at the end of an arm before being put in the center they performed better than chance but not perfectly. After about a week of training in the placement procedure, the rats' performance with placements was indistinguishable from that in the usual free-choice procedure.

These data are consistent with Honig's suggestion that an instruction may be stored in working memory. Certainly, in our procedure the actual response of running down the arm is not necessary for the rat to identify or remember the arm. Thus either the stimulus characteristics at the end of the arm, or an instruction associated with these stimulus characteristics, must be stored in working memory. The data are also relevant to the possible use of an intramaze marking strategy (see Chapter 8, this volume). In Walker's procedure, of course, no opportunity was given to mark the entrance to the arm on which the rat was placed because the experimenter carried him to the arm and back to center platform. The fact that the rats subsequently chose without difficulty indicates the unimportance of intramaze marks in our procedure.

In his discussion of Pavlovian conditioning, Rescorla (Chapter 2, this volume) emphasizes a "cognitive perspective" in which the animal is perceived as reacting to the predictive relationships between pairs of stimuli. Maze learning, especially in the descriptions offered by Tolman (1932), has traditionally been considered in this fashion. As Rescorla indicates (Chapter 2), little information is available about spatial relationships studied with a Pavlovian procedure. An important question is whether the concepts about stimulus relationship developed by Rescorla in his temporal procedure can be applied to a spatial procedure, providing a direct test of similarity of relational learning in these two situations. The Walker experiment just described is relevant here as a crude, but potentially useful, prototype. Logically, the stimuli associated with the entrance to an arm may be thought of as a CS while the stimuli associated with the end of an arm may be thought of as a US. There are procedural differences from Pavlovian procedures; the rat presents the stimuli to himself in the maze while the experimenter has control of stimulus presentation in the Pavlovian procedure, but the logical predictive relation still holds. From this viewpoint, the Walker procedure may be thought of as successful backward conditioning. The US (end of the arm) is presented to the animal during placement on that arm. This US must evoke the CS (the start of the arm) because when subsequently presented with the CS in the center of the apparatus the rat reacts as if the CS–US combination has already been experienced. To be completely analogous to the Pavlovian procedure, some changes would have to be made to temporally separate the CS and US (perhaps by a tunnel), to prevent the pairing of US and CS (by removing the animal from the end of the arm after each choice and carrying him back to the center), and to control the stimulus presentation (by opaque guillotine doors). With these changes and appropriate manipulation of the predictive relationships between the stimuli at the start of the arm and the stimuli at the end of the arm, a series of spatial experiments could be initiated which would be analogous to the temporal experiments of Rescorla. The focus of the experiments would, of course, be the reaction of the animal to the predictive relationships among the pairs of stimuli. Since rats in mazes seem to be very good at understanding predictive relationships, this technique might be a particularly powerful means of addressing this issue.

Menzel (1973; see also Chapter 13, this volume) has presented persuasive evidence that chimpanzees not only store information about many spatial locations but also determine the spatial relationships among these locations. When presented with a "traveling-salesman" type of problem in which food was hidden in up to 18 different locations, the chimpanzees retrieved most of the food and did so with the notion of a "cognitive map," a device that stores information about spatial locations and determines the relationships among them. In our procedure, we find no evidence of such a map. Indeed, analysis of choice patterns in the 17-arm-maze confinement procedure indicates that both correct choices and incorrect choices appear to be randomly distributed among the arms (Olton et al., 1977). Given the spatial location of any choice N, the location of choice $N + 1$ is unpredictable (with the restriction that $N + 1$ is more likely to be a correct arm than an incorrect arm). Of course, our procedure did not provide any differential reinforcement for correct mapping as did Menzel's; the failure to find mapping in the radial arm maze experiments cannot be taken as evidence that rats cannot demonstrate this ability. An important question is whether rats, tested in a procedure similar to that of Menzel, could demonstrate through their response patterns the shortest possible path that encompasses all food locations.

Riley (Chapter 9, this volume) has discussed the facilitation of memory by redundant relevant cues and summarizes his discussion by suggesting that pigeons can treat independent stimuli as integral. One question we have not addressed is why working memory in the radial arm maze procedure is able to process so much more information than working memory in operant-box procedures. The answer may lie in the number of relevant redundant cues available to the animal. In most operant working-memory procedures, only one or two relevant redundant cues are available in the sample stimulus. In the radial-arm-maze task, there are many relevant redundant cues and these include several different sensory modalities. Indeed, a place learning procedure like the radial arm maze task might be thought of as the logical extreme in relevant redundant cues; all the stimuli associated with each place are both relevant and redundant. Riley has shown that performance is facilitated when just a single relevant redundant cue is added to the sample stimulus. If the conceptualization of "place" as the conjunction of many relevant redundant cues is correct, then accurate performance in the radial-arm maze may be a simple extension of the relevant redundant facilitation described by Riley. Such an idea is testable, of course, by reducing the number of relevant redundant cues in the radial-arm-maze task and determining if the accuracy of performance decreases as expected. Some evidence supporting this view has already been obtained (Blodgett, McCutchen, & Mathews, 1949).

VIII. CONCLUSION

The radial-arm-maze task has been markedly successful in examining the characteristics of animal working memory — particularly the memory for multiple items. In summarizing our work, I should like to address two questions. First, what characteristics of the testing procedure were responsible for its effectiveness in examining working memory? Second, how can working memory best be described?

I think there are three aspects of the testing procedure which were largely responsible for its success. First, the apparatus was a maze. Given our current sophisticated operant technology, use of a maze might appear as nostalgic anachronism. But in contrast to the "misbehavior" that is often seen in operant boxes, behavior in mazes is almost always adaptive, flexible, and responsive to the reinforcement contingencies arranged by the experimenter. Tolman (1948, p. 198) commented: "The major part of rats' learning in most situations seems to consist in their discovering the instructions. Rats in mazes don't have to be told. The explanation (for rapid learning and good performance in mazes), as I see it, is that in the case of mazes, rats know their instructions." The instructions in working-memory procedures are complex. The maze is particularly appropriate for investigating working memory because it is an effective means of making these instructions clear (see also Gleitman, 1974).

Second, reinforcement was consistently paired with spatial location, making space a relevant stimulus dimension. The importance of spatial location in directing animal discrimination behavior has been amply documented (see Section I). All of the evidence suggests that rats, like many other animals, have a strong preference to solve discrimination problems on the basis of their spatial characteristics. In making space a relevant dimension, we catered to this preference and increased the likelihood that the rats would focus on the appropriate stimulus dimension.

Third, we arranged the reward contingencies to be compatible with the rats' normal food searching strategy. In a previous series of experiments (Olton et al., 1977), we investigated the choice behavior of rats searching for food in semi-natural conditions. With many possible food locations, the rats consistently demonstrated a win–shift strategy; after finding food in one location they went on to investigate each of the other possible locations rather than continuing to remove food from the cache they had just found. The optimal strategy in the radial arm maze is consistent with his win—shift strategy because after finding food in an arm the animal ought to go to other arms rather than returning to the one just chosen. Other data (unpublished observations) indicate that win—shift behavior on the radial arm maze is much easier to learn than win—stay, presumably due to the compatibility of this strategy with rats' natural predispositions.

In short, all three of these procedural details were designed to make the radial-arm-maze task easy for the rats. Since we were interested in memory, rather than learning, we wished to make the training stages of the experiment as brief as possible. The rapidity with which the rats developed their high level of choice accuracy suggests that they had no difficulty in understanding the instructions, focusing on the relevant stimulus dimension, and developing the appropriate choice strategy.

The spatial tests used here indicate that rats have a substantial capacity for processing information in working memory, and spatial tests used elsewhere have provided clear evidence of the formation of a learning set by rats (Olton et al., 1977). The fact that rats perform so well in spatial tasks is often greeted with surprise. This reaction is important because it tells us that we have been consistently underestimating the true cognitive capacity of rats with nonspatial testing procedures. Herman and Arbeit (1973) point out that an important component of any comparative study is adapting the experimental procedure to the idiosyncratic preferences of the species being tested. A comparative analysis was not the major focus of the present studies. Nonetheless, the results reported here provide a substantially increased estimate of rats' cognitive abilities and should be useful in any comparative estimate of memory abilities across species.

These experiments also provide specific information about the characteristics of working memory. These characteristics have been formalized in our model, and can be summarized here: (1) capacity for at least 17 items and probably about 25; (2) no decay of the memory trace during the time required to complete the test; (3) no serial order (primacy or recency) effect; (4) proactive interference among items within a test; (5) release from proactive interference between tests; (6) no generalization between correct and incorrect arms; (7) no strategy in the selection order of items to be remembered.

In conclusion, the past 50 years have seen a marked change in the technology associated with animal learning. At the beginning of the 20th century the apparatus of choice was inevitably the spatial maze, ranging in design from an unpretentious T to elaborate miniature versions of the one at Hampton Court. The current apparatus of choice is almost inevitably the operant box, especially when interfaced with solid-state circuitry or minicomputers. Implicit in this technological change has been the assumption that the questions originally asked in spatial mazes could just as readily be asked in nonspatial operant procedures.

I think this assumption is open to question. Certainly the argument is not that operant procedures should be discarded; they have more than proved their usefulness for some types of questions. But spatial procedures may be uniquely adapted to addressing certain issues, especially those more cognitively oriented ones typical of the papers presented in this volume. The radial-arm-maze experiments reported here provide preliminary support for this viewpoint. Future experiments, applying spatial procedures to other types of questions, will ultimately determine the validity of this position.

ACKNOWLEDGMENTS

This research was supported in part by National Institute of Mental Health Research Grant 1-R01-MH-23213 to David S. Olton. I thank N. Dorsky, H. Egeth, S. Hulse, S. Kosslyn, L. Herman, and W. Honig for their help in preparing the manuscript, C. Collison, B. Pappas, J. Walker, M. Werz, and W. Wolf for assistance in data collection and analysis, and P. Best, A. Black, A. Kamil and J. O'Keefe for encouragement and insights throughout.

REFERENCES

Barnett, S. A., & Cowan, P. E. Activity, exploration, curiosity, and fear: an ethological study. *Interdisciplinary Science Reviews,* 1976, *1,* 43–62.

Barnett, S. A., Dickson, R. G., Marples, T. G., & Radha, E. Sequences of feeding, sampling, and exploration by wild and laboratory rats. *Behavioral Processes,* in press.

Bättig, K., Driscoll, P., Schlatter, J., & Uster, J. J. Effects of nicotine on the exploratory locomotion patterns of female Roman high- and low-avoidance rats. *Pharmacology, Biochemistry, and Behavior,* 1976, *4,* 435–439.

Blodgett, J. C., & McCutchen, K. Place versus response-learning in the simple T-maze. *Journal of Experimental Psychology,* 1947, *37,* 412–422.

Blodgett, H. C., McCutchen, K., & Mathews, R. Spatial learning in the T-maze: The influence of direction, turn, and food location. *Journal of Experimental Psychology,* 1949, *39,* 800–809.

Bolles, R. C. Species-specific defense reactions and avoidance learning. *Psychological Review,* 1970, *77,* 32–48.

Bryant, D., & Church, R. M. The determinants of random choice. *Animal Learning and Behavior,* 1974, *2,* 245–248.

Buschke, H. Retention in immediate memory estimated without retrieval. *Science,* 1963, *140,* 56–57.

Calhoun, J. B. *The Ecology and Sociology of the Norway Rat.* Washington, D.C.: Public Health Service Publication No. 1008, 1963.

Crannel, C. W. The choice point behavior of rats in a multiple path elimination problem. *Journal of Psychology,* 1942, *13,* 201–222.

Dennis, W. Spontaneous alternation in rats as an indicator of the persistence of stimulus effects. *Journal of Comparative Psychology,* 1939, *28,* 305–312.

Douglas, R. J. Cues for spontaneous alternation. *Journal of Comparative and Physiological Psychology,* 1966, *62,* 171–183.

Feller, W. *Probability theory and its applications* (Vol. 1.) New York: Wiley, 1950.

Gentry, G., Brown, W. L., & Kaplan, S. An experimental analysis of the spatial location hypothesis in learning. *Journal of Comparative and Physiological Psychology*, 1947, *40*, 309–322.

Gentry, G., Brown, W. L., & Lee, H. Spatial location in the learning of a multiple T-maze. *Journal of Comparative and Physiological Psychology*, 1948, *41*, 312–318.

Gleitman, H. Getting animals to understand the experimenter's instructions. *Animal Learning and Behavior*, 1974, *2*, 1–5.

Glickman, S. E. Responses and reinforcement. In G. H. Bower (Ed.), *The psychology of learning and memory* (Vol. 7). New York: Academic Press, 1973, pp. 207–242.

Herman, L. M., & Arbeit, W. R. Stimulus control and auditory discrimination learning sets in the bottlenose dolphin. *Journal of the Experimental Analysis of Behavior*, 1973, *19*, 379–397.

Hulse, S. H., Deese, J., & Egeth, H. *The Psychology of Learning*. New York: McGraw-Hill, 1975.

Kamil, A. C. Systematic nectar foraging, or learning can be important to an animal in its natural habitat. Paper present at the meeting of *Psychonomic Society*, Denver, Colorado, November 6, 1975.

Kamil, A. D. Learning and memory in the wild: Systematic foraging for nectar by amakihi (*Loxops virens*). *Journal of Comparative and Physiological Psychology*, in press.

Lachman, S. J. Behavior in a multiple-choice elimination problem involving five paths. *Journal of Psychology*, 1965, *61*, 193–202.

Lachman, S. J. Stereotype and variability of behavior in a complex learning situation. *Psychological Reports*, 1966, *18*, 223–230.

Lachman, S. J. Behavior in a complex learning situation involving five stimulus differentiated paths. *Psychonomic Science*, 1969, *17*, 36–37.

Lachman, S. J., and Brown, C. R. Behavior in a free choice multiple path elimination problem. *Journal of Psychology*, 1957, *43*, 27–40.

Means, L. W., Hardy, W. T. Gabriel, M., & Uphold, J. D. Utilization of odor trails by rats in maze learning. *Journal of Comparative and Physiological Psychology*, 1971, *76*, 160–164.

Menzel, E. W. Chimpanzee spatial memory organization. *Science*, 1973, *182*, 943–945.

Olton, D. S. Discrimination behavior in the rat: Differential effects of reinforcement and nonreinforcement. *Journal of Comparative and Physiological Psychology*, 1972, *70*, 284–290.

Olton, D. S. Shock motivated avoidance and behavior. *Psychological Bulletin*, 1973, *54*, 313–326.

Olton, D. S., Collison, C., & Werz, M. Spatial memory and radial arm maze performance of rats. *Learning and Motivation*, 1977, *8*, 289–314.

Olton, D. S., & Isaacson, R. L. Importance of spatial location in active avoidance tasks. *Journal of Comparative and Physiological Psychology*, 1968, *13*, 719–724.

Olton, D. S., & Samuelson, R. J. Remembrance of places passed: Spatial memory in rats. *Journal of Experimental Psychology: Animal Behavior Processes*, 1976, *2*, 97–116.

Olton, D. S., and Schlosberg, P. E. Food searching strategies in young rats: Win–shift predominates over win–stay. *Journal of Comparative and Physiological Psychology*, in press.

Olton, D. S., Walker, J. A., Gage, F. H., & Johnson, C. T. Choice behavior of rats searching for food. *Learning and Motivation*, 1977, *8*, 315–331.

Restle, F. Discrimination of cues in mazes: A resolution of the "place-vs-response" question. *Psychological Review*, 1957, *64*, 217–228.

Sutherland, N. S., & Mackintosh, N. H. *Mechanisms of Animal Discrimination Learning*. New York: Academic Press, 1971.

Thompson, R. K. R., & Herman, L. M. Memory for lists of sounds by the bottle-nosed dolphin: Convergence of memory processes with humans? *Science*, 1977, *195*, 501–503.

Tolman, E. C. *Purposive Behavior in Animals and Men.* New York: Appleton-Century, 1932.
Tolman, E. C. Sign-Gestalt or conditioned reflex? *Psychological Review,* 1933, *40,* 246–255.
Tolman, E. C. Cognitive maps in rats and men. *Psychological Review,* 1948, *55,* 189–208.
Tolman, E. C., Ritchie, B. G., & Kalish, D. Studies in spatial learning. I. Orientation and short-cut. *Journal of Experimental Psychology,* 1946, *36,* 13–25.
Uster, H. J., Analyse des esplorationsverhaltens von ratten in labyrinthen unterschiedlicher komplexitaet. Doctoral Dissertation, Eidgeonoessichen Technischen Hochscule, Zürich, Switzerland, 1977.
Uster, H. J., Bättig, K., & Nägeli, H. H. Effects of maze geometry and experience on exploratory behavior in the rat. *Animal Learning and Behavior,* 1976, *4,* 84–88.
Walker, E. L. The duration and course of the reaction decrement and the influence of reward. *Journal of Comparative and Physiological Psychology,* 1956, *49,* 167–176.
Wickens, D. D., Born, D. G., & Allen, C. K. Proactive inhibition and item similarity in short-term memory. *Journal of Verbal Learning and Verbal Behavior,* 1963, *2,* 440–445.
Woodworth, R. S. *Experimental psychology.* New York: Holt, 1938.

13 Cognitive Mapping in Chimpanzees

Emil W. Menzel
State University of New York at Stony Brook

I. INTRODUCTION

Biologists are drawn to study events which *seem* to contradict what we have been taught to expect on the basis of our knowledge of non-living things . . . Like a stone released in mid-air, a bird ought to fall; yet it flies away. An animal resists, evades, utilizes its environment instead of meekly submitting to its influences; rather than move toward increasing probability, it survives, reproduces, grows and evolves. Yet we do not *believe* that it does all this against all the 'laws' of physics — our *faith* is that upon closer investigation it will turn out to be a special case . . . . (Tinbergen, 1972, p. 20)

> All science necessarily presents, it seems to us, but a map and picture of reality. . . .
> Our account of mind is, we hold, a map account. And so is the physicists's account of
> matter. . . . (Tolman, 1932, pp. 424–425)

This paper examines how chimpanzees move about with respect to one another and various test objects in outdoor situations, how they sometimes cause one object to move with respect to others, and what such facts might signify about their cognitive organization. Of particular interest is this question: At what point are we forced to assume that the animals' movements imply that they have "mapped out" the environment, or that they possess an internal model representing current events in space and time (Pantin, 1965)?

Cognitive mapping has been the subject of considerable research in the past few years (for reviews, see Jerison, 1973; O'Keefe & Nadel, 1978; Siegel & White, 1975; and the volume edited by Downs & Stea, 1973). In its most general sense, it is the process of collecting and organizing information regarding a particular "space" or "space-time structure." And from a purely geometrical point of view (as well as from a psychological point of view), "Space is the set of all possible relative positions of bodies. . . . Moving from positions to trajectories we may obtain a characterization of space-time as the set of all possible trajectories of bodies" (Suppes, 1973, pp. 394–395). To have mapped out a given area is thus (at a minimum) to know: (1) selected objects and features in that area – or at least their general attributes – and (2) their positions relative to one another. To have mapped out the area cognitively rather than literally is to have stored the information somewhere other than "out there" (for example, on a piece of paper), and presumably to have stored it internally.[1]

No mapping, of course, is completely detailed or completely accurate. It can be "complete" only from the standpoint of a particular observer with a particular set of interests. Further, unless one uses the term "cognitive map" as a noun, it is not necessarily implied that the animal actually possesses some particular form of entity – hypothetical or neural – in the head. Cognitive mapping implies only that the subject has the necessary information and *could* conceivably construct a map, assuming that he knew how to do this and cared to do it.

As the concept of cognitive mapping is ordinarily used in psychology, it also implies at least the following. First, the prime function of exploration and perceptual surveys is to cope with the environment, rather than merely to have sensations or make responses. As animals look around, locomote, and manipulate objects in their environment, their attention tends to be focused on discovering and exploiting "what is out there," and only secondarily, coincidentally, or in specially contrived situations with less than normal stimulus input do they focus their attention on what internal sensations were produced in them by the environment, or what responses they made or what motor patterns they employed.

Second, information about external objects and events is not merely picked up and retained; it is also filtered, reordered, organized, and structured by the animal. Information regarding particular pairs or groupings of objects (i.e., particular S–S relations) is, in short, integrated in such a way that the animal may be said to have an overview of the entire environmental structure as well as a knowledge of the multitude of smaller meanings that constitute it. (Thus the animal should in principle be capable of deriving new information that would not necessarily be available from other forms of spatial orientation. For example, he should be capable of comparing the relative efficiency of several longer itineraries "at a glance," and, given the position of a new object relative to any one known static object, he should in principle also be able to determine its position

---

[1] In their recent volume on the philosophy of geography, which became available after this chapter was written, Robinson and Petchenick (1976) take a similar position when they state that the minimum operations involved in any form of mapping are judgments of "like vs. unlike" and "proximate vs. separate."

relative to all possible other known static objects.) Although in many cases — particularly in a laboratory apparatus where only a small portion of the field can be surveyed at a time — the animal must perforce build up his "overview" by integrating various "elemental" S–S relations with each other, there is no necessity for this procedure. In other cases (for example, when an animal looks down from a hilltop before descending into a valley) it is most likely that the overview is achieved first, and that only after this does the animal differentiate specific details. For a free-living animal in the outdoors, and especially for arboreal animals or those capable of flight, the "objects" of perception are, in other words, of no fixed size. The identical object can alternately be viewed as an element, an object, or a larger structure, according to the animal's momentary position with respect to that object and the vagaries of his attention (Menzel, 1969a).

Third, if animals have had occasion to become disoriented, to forget some detail, or to suspect that something might be new or out of place, they will tend to explore the environment in such a way as to reorient themselves, to update their knowledge, or to put the new information into the old frame of reference.

Cognitive mapping is by no means a complete explanation of how animals are able to get around in the world. It is largely a metaphorical statement about what sorts of information they collect and how they organize it. That is, it is a (psychological) structural concept, rather than a developmental, functional or evolutionary concept (Catania, 1973); and as such it does not answer but rather poses further questions such as the following: What motor patterns will an animal use to get where it is going (Guthrie, 1952)? What sensory channels and what perceptual cues did the animal initially use to pick up his information (Restle, 1957)? How much prior experience, and of what type, is required before information is organized in maplike form (Hull, 1952)? Does the process of mapping (verb) actually involve the construction of a map (noun, physical entity), image, picture or particular neural counterpart thereof in the brain (O'Keefe & Nadel, 1978; Pylyshyn, 1973)? Are these maps completely veridical, or are there "broad maps," "narrow, strip maps," etc. (Tolman, 1951)? Can information about the relative positions of objects be transmitted or "handed over" from one animal to another? Are all species or only some of them capable of cognitive mapping or central representation of space (Pantin, 1965)? How did the ability for such central representation evolve (Jerison, 1973; Lorenz, 1971; Pantin, 1965)?

In my opinion, most of the old controversies that once surrounded the concept of cognitive mapping would not have arisen if psychologists had been more careful to distinguish between these questions. Structural, functional, developmental, and evolutionary questions are all essential to a complete psychology, but they are logically independent of each other. Thus, for example, even a complete specification of what an animal knows (a structural and cognitive problem) tells one little if anything about what motor patterns he will use in getting to where he is going – or vice versa. Guthrie (1952) was quite correct when he said that Tolman's theory left the animal "buried in thought" and did not predict its actual movements; but Guthrie failed to recognize that the converse was equally true, namely, that any theory that restricts its goals to predicting an animal's movements as such leaves the animal "lost in action" and says little if anything of direct interest to cognitive theory (Miller, Galanter, & Pribram, 1960). Guthrie was simply not interested in cognition, whereas Tolman, at least in his earlier formulations, was not particularly interested in animals' movements as such.

II. SOME OBSERVATIONS AND EXPERIMENTS

The longer one watches chimpanzees, especially in naturalistic settings, the more one is impressed with their incredible alertness, acuity, and general ability to take into account a large number of details simultaneously before responding (van Lawick-Goodall, 1968, 1971, 1973; Nissen, 1931; Reynolds, 1965; Teleki, 1974; Wrangham, 1975). Adults at least are probably constantly cognizant of where they are in their home range, the general line of march of the group, the individual identities and moment-to-moment locations of other chimpanzees (especially preferred companions, those more dominant than they, and whoever is closest to them), the availability of potential cover in which they (or a predator) might hide, the relative efficiency of various potential routes that they might take from their present position to various goals, the odds of beating other animals, who must take different routes to the same goals, and so on. If they appear to be unemotional and nonanxious, it is probably only because they can ordinarily anticipate long ahead of time the sorts of situations that are likely to become dangerous or distressing to them, and can adjust their position accordingly to keep out of such situations (Menzel, 1975).

Where might the animal be getting his information for such performances? Following Tolman (1932) we may say that at a minimum the animal might be getting his information from: (1) direct perception of the immediate features and general layout of the environment; (2) having perceived the same or similar environmental conditions on previous occasions, (which topic may be subdivided into the topics of early experience, learning, memory and inference); and (3) the performances of other chimpanzees (communication). Although some theorists, for example, Gibson (1966), would argue that the latter two modes of information getting can be reduced to the first one, and although I myself am not particularly attached to the above classification, I shall for purposes of convenience use it as the basis for organizing the rest of this chapter. That is, I shall work up from some very simple problems regarding direct perception to more complicated problems of memory and social communication. Then, in the final section of the chapter, I shall describe where we or at least I might go from here.

A. Direct Perception of "Field Relations" in Normal Chimpanzees

Our problem here is essentially the same one that Köhler (1925) posed in the first few pages of his classic monograph. Presumably, all details of the test situation can be surveyed at a glance by the subject.

1. Performance in "Unobstructed" Spaces

Say that a chimpanzee is at one position in three-dimensional space and an object is visibly present at another position in this space, and the intervening space is unobstructed. How will the chimpanzee proceed to get the object, and what does this tell us about his ability to take into account the relative positions of objects and his own position with respect to those objects?

Assuming that the object is an attractive one such as a toy or a piece of food or another chimpanzee, and that our subject sees it, the most likely route for our subject to take will of course be a straight line. And in such a case one would not call the chimpanzee's behavior "intelligent," as one would not call the straight movement of an apple dropping from a tree intelligent. However, there is more going on than one might imagine: The only invariant property of the chimpanzee's behavior is that it takes him to the goal object; there is no necessary invariance in his *travel path*, and he does not merely act in such a way as to produce an "optical magnification" of the retinal image of the object.

Consider, for example, the possibility that the chimpanzee and the test object are in two different trees at a height of about 3 m and the intervening space is empty space. Obviously the chimpanzee's approach route will no longer be along the line of Euclidean least distance — unless he is a "superchimp" who can actually leap this far, and unless he has strong incentive for so doing — for the chimpanzee knows his inability to fly and the consequences of not very accurately assessing one's leaping capacity. How will he proceed? He will of course visually check out the various routes that are available via the network of trees and branches. For example, if there is no way to get directly from his tree to others, he might descend to the ground, proceed to the tree containing the test object, and then ascend that tree. (It is not necessary for him to keep the test object in sight all the time, either.) Alternatively, if the branches of the two trees touch each other or a third tree at some greater height, he might climb higher and use this network of branches to proceed to his goal (Nissen, 1931). Ordinarily the fastest route via this "city-block metric" can be selected even if the chimpanzee has not had any previous experience with the particular trees in question and even if he has not travelled that exact route before. Moreover, chimpanzees can ordinarily discriminate from a distance which branches are strong enough to bear their weight without breaking and which can be bent over (either manually or by being rocked back and forth) to form a bridge to the next tree. There is even some suggestion that they know the routes along which *other* animals might proceed, for small chimpanzees will sometimes escape larger ones by climbing out to very thin branches, rather than using some other route. And in preying on small monkeys, adult male chimpanzees seem to be very acute in assessing and blocking off their prey's potential escape routes (van Lawick-Goodall, 1971; Teleki, 1974; Wrangham, 1975).

Another aspect of behavior in trees deserves mention. If the goal object is something of which the chimpanzee might be cautious (for instance, a bigger chimpanzee) he will most often approach it from overhead rather than coming up from beneath it, even if this involves taking a longer route.

Another instance in which a chimpanzee would seldom take the Euclidean shortest line to an object is when the space is relatively large and devoid of vertical structures. Chimpanzees, like most vertebrates, seem to be cautious of open places. This is particularly true of young animals, especially those that have been raised in the laboratory. It is most obvious when the situation is an unfamiliar one. Thus, if a young chimpanzee is at point A in a large cage and a banana is thrown over to point B (see Fig. 1a), he will very often not take the shortest path to the banana if in so doing he has to get more than a few feet from the cage wire. Put a vertical structure or two (a 1-m stake or another animal will do) along the line, however, and this behavior is easily corrected (see Fig. 1b).

Still another instance in which a roundabout route would be taken across physically unobstructed space is when a dominant animal or a stranger is present in the situation. Say that B is a banana and A2 is another chimpanzee who happens to be dominant to A1, but who has not seen the banana. What will A1 do? Most likely he will do nothing at all with respect to the banana until A2 leaves the scene; he will in effect act like it is not even there, for A2 obviously constitutes a psychological obstacle to his getting the food for himself. Van Lawick-Goodall (1971) reports that she has seen chimpanzees wait a half hour or more in cases such as this, and then race over as soon as their potential competition leaves. Even more interestingly, if A2 remains in the situation but shows no indication of spotting the food, and becomes engrossed in some other activity (or lies down and closes his eyes), A1 might circle around until he is out of A2's

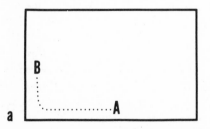 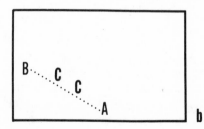

FIG. 1.   Travel paths of an animal going across a cage to a goal object when vertical structures other than the cage fence are absent (a) or present (b).

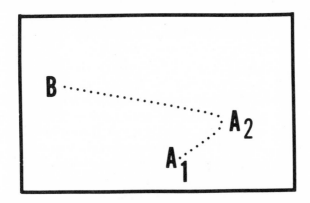

FIG. 2.   Travel path of a group-living animal going to a distant goal object.

angle of vision, and then sneak in for the food. In other words, A1 knows that A2 constitutes an obstacle only if A2 knows what he is up to. In some cases, indeed, subordinate chimpanzees might actually lead their potential competitors away and proceed in the opposite direction from the food, and then circle back after they have shaken off the other animal (van Lawick-Goodall, 1971; Menzel, 1974). In other cases, they might distract the dominant animal by playing with him for a while, or groom him until he lies down and dozes off, and then go for the food.

One more instance in which the chimpanzee will not proceed forthwith to an attractive object is when to do so would take him too far from his companions, or force him to travel in the opposite direction from the one in which they are proceeding. Here chimpanzees (in particular mothers and infants) would be most likely to go over to their companions first and then to the object (see Fig. 2). This behavior is most common when the incentive is something other than food, but it does in many cases occur even with food. A1 would not, of course, necessarily have to travel over to A2 to recruit his company in going over to B. Older animals in particular might simply glance back and forth between A2 and B, and then (when A2 is attending) get up and take a step or two in the direction of B, and wait for A2 to join them. Or, if this does not suffice, they might beckon to A2 or purse their lips in a "pout face" and then start very slowly toward B.

As the foregoing suggests, there is probably no situation that consists *merely* of the test animal and a single test object. Such a situation is a conceptual tour de force on the part of the experimenter. Nor can we solve this problem by removing all objects and animals other than the ones in which we are interested. Put by himself without companions in a bare open space whose location relative to other features of the environment is totally unknown to him, the normal chimpanzee would respond even more strongly and with greater emotionality than before, and try his best to get back to a familiar setting. In other words, he is if anything more distracted by the absence of familiar stimuli than by their presence; and in this sense he is always taking them into account.

2. Performance in Obstructed Spaces

The term "obstruction" or "barrier" is always to some degree a psychological one in the sense that it cannot be defined solely on the basis of physical objects and without taking into account the capabilities of the subject. Here we are concerned with how chimpanzees might perform when they are on the ground and some large inanimate object or structure lies between them and their presumed goal, and they cannot proceed directly through it.

To my knowledge, no formal experiments on this topic have been reported since the days of Köhler. Practically all learning tests that have been conducted on primates in the last several decades involve manual rather than locomotor performances, and test apparatus several hundred times smaller than the barrier situations and spatial problems that primates face "naturally." (For a review, see Rumbaugh, 1970.)

No one who has worked with normal chimpanzees above the age of 2 or 3 years would, however, doubt Köhler's claim that these animals are better, say, than chickens or dogs in circumventing barriers or detours. In other words, as long as a barrier can be perceived at a distance, chimpanzees rarely run headlong into it; rather, they seem to anticipate it and start to circumvent it before actually getting to it. The principal difficulty I encountered in testing detour performance of this type with truly novel situations is that the typical chimpanzee faced with a novel barrier will be more interested in it than in the presumed goal object, and it is only after investigating it, climbing all over it, and possibly trying to dismantle it, that he will view the "problem" in the same terms that his human observer does.

Another interesting but formally unstudied aspect of barrier performance is the apparent ability of animals to learn what physical objects constitute a barrier *for some other animal.* The simplest examples of this are probably the tendency to interpose one's mother (or a tree or a rock) between oneself and a pursuer; and I would guess that normal chimpanzees learn to do this even before they can locomote independently of the mother. (Consider, for example, the tendency of a several-month-old infant to move to that side of the mother which is opposite to whomever or whatever it is that he is trying to avoid.) Another simple example has been noted by Hediger (1955): not only chimpanzees but many animals in captivity seem to learn that their cage wire protects them from an advancing human, and very quickly come to tolerate a much closer approach when the cage door is closed than when the cage door is open. An anecdote of my own is the following case.

In trying to tame a group of five infant chimpanzees that had just arrived at the lab from the jungle, I went into their cage daily to feed them. Whereas they

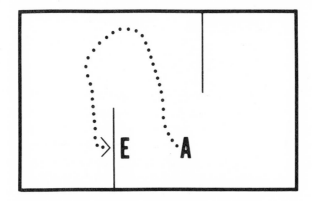

FIG. 3.   Reverse detour performance: Travel path of an animal who is too timid to take food from the hand of a person (E) except when there is a locomotor barrier (cage fence) between them.

would already take food from my hand when I was outside the cage, they would not come close enough to take it once I was inside the cage. However, the most timid animal soon hit on a very neat strategy. As Fig. 3 shows, the cage contained a number of partial walls made of wire mesh, and I (E) happened to be sitting near one of them. The timid animal, A1, made a very neat detour which was precisely the opposite of what one would expect in a Köhler-type problem; and once he was on the opposite side of the wire from me he oriented toward the food in my hand, put his lips to the wire, and made a "food bark." I gave him some food and then, as there were several other partial walls in the cage, I shifted my position to see if he would follow the same strategy using different routes. He did so with no hesitation. This behavior persisted for several days, until he was bold enough to permit me to touch him. Then, instead of only detouring so as to keep the wire between us, he came to also detour in either direction, according to whether I raised a hand as if to slap him for making a direct approach, or acted more friendly.

3. Tool Using and Active Modification of the Relative Positions of Objects

Many if not most animal tool-using performances may be viewed as special cases of detour behavior and the perception of the relative positions of objects; they differ from the types of behavior that have been described above principally in that obstacles are overcome by manipulative rather than locomotor means (Köhler, 1925; Tolman, 1932). Figure 4 shows a particularly clear-cut case in point. It is apparent that in using branches as ladders, the chimpanzees are actively modifying the positions of objects in such a way as to create new pathways to various points in space. I should add that these performances were acquired "spontaneously," without any intentional reinforcement on our part;

FIG. 4. A group of chimpanzees uses branches as ladders to peek into an observation house, avert electric shock wires on trees, and escape from their enclosure. In some of the first instances in which they set up their ladder on the 6-inch-wide (15-cm-wide) elevated runway (about 8 feet (2.5 m) above ground level) to get into the trees, one animal (Rock) held the base of the ladder and solicited another one (Gigi) to position the top. From Menzel 1972, 1973a.

and once a single member of the social group instituted a new variation on branch-use, the others quickly picked it up too. Eventually the animals learned to use long branches to escape from the enclosure and when these were confiscated they started to pull poles out of the ground for this purpose. It took several years for the social group to progress from their first efforts at simple pole vaulting to this final variation on the use of branches as "climbing tools" (Menzel, 1972, 1973a; McGrew, Tutin, & Midgett, 1975). The use of portable branches as ladders or bridges has, incidentally, never been reported in wild chimpanzees or even in other groups of captive animals.

Needless to say, there have been many dozens of other studies of tool-using performance in chimpanzees (for reviews, see Beck, 1975; Rumbaugh, 1970; van Lawick-Goodall, 1970), and there is no question that not only in the laboratory but also under natural conditions the chimpanzee is second only to man in the variety and seeming complexity of his performances. I shall make no attempt to review those studies here, but shall make a few rather sweeping and dogmatic pronouncements on the topic of tool using.

First, just as locomotor detouring around obstacles is defined by the *directionality* of an animal's travel path with respect to objects (rather than by the "walking movements" or "climbing movements" which merely furnish the energy for such performances), so also the central problem of tool using is not to account for the animal's movements as such, but to account for the consequent relative positions of *objects* and how each object comes to produce a given effect upon others. Schiller (1952) and Hall (1963) argued that animal tool use involves no apparent intelligence, goal direction, or perceptual problems because it appears almost as soon as the animal is capable of performing the requisite "innate motor patterns" and is provided with the appropriate objects. This in effect takes for granted the very phenomenon to be explained.

Second, I believe that the analysis of tool using has been held back unnecessarily for many years simply because most psychologists still tend to equate such analyses with old theoretical controversies — such as insight vs. association learning or instinct vs. learning — and with the question of whether or not some aspect of tool using can be used as a defining characteristic of man. There is no more reason to identify an analysis of animal tool using with "insight" theory, for example, than to identify every study that is conducted in a Skinner box with "trial and error" or S–R theories of the 1930s. The phenomena of animal tool using exist independently of any of the theories that have been built up around them, and they are at least as interesting and deserving of experimental attention as other behavioral phenomena. This is particularly true in the case of species such as chimpanzees, which are known to engage in a variety of tool-using behaviors under natural conditions.

Third, although tool using is best viewed as an example of the general perception of object relations, it is undoubtedly a rather special case. Most of the tool-using performances of wild chimpanzees seem to occur in connection with feeding and agonistic activities and otherwise chimpanzees, like all other nonhumans, seem to take the world largely "as it comes." Performances such as those shown in Fig. 4 are the exception rather than the rule for wild animals. In my opinion, the fundamental limits to chimpanzees' abilities lie less in their *general* visual perceptual abilities or so-called general intelligence (as Köhler maintained) or in their repertoire of innate motor patterns (as Schiller and Hall maintained) than in more specific motivational factors and perceptual-motor coordinations, and these in turn are heavily influenced by social facilitation and early social experience (Menzel, 1972; 1973a; Menzel, Davenport, & Rogers, 1970; van Lawick-Goodall, 1973). Given their considerable ability to take into account the relative positions of each other and of static inanimate objects, to recognize each other as the same individuals despite variations in location and orientation, and to modify each other's locations and behaviors through manipulation, I for one would expect them to be far better tool users than they are. The major reason for further research in this area is not to show how smart and "almost human" chimpanzees are, but to determine more precisely what factors *limit* or constrain their performance.

4. Predictive Behavior, and Performances of Multiple Animals with Multiple Goals

An infant chimpanzee following its mother by vision can ordinarily get to the object it is pursuing by attending to a single piece of information: spatial distance, as indicated by the magnitude of the retinal stimulus. Other goal-directed activities are not, however, so easily accomplished, for they require the orientation of at least two coordinates, a temporal and at least one spatial axis. Following Rosenblueth, Wiener, and Bigelow (1943) and Krushinskii (1960), these activities are sometimes called "predictive or "extrapolative" behaviors. The greater the number of independent pieces of information that are required for the performance, the higher the order of predictive ability that is called for.

For example, if one chimpanzee (A1) is trying to catch up with another one (A2) that is moving at a constant velocity, and at each instant merely aims directly at A2's momentary position, as if to maximize the momentary magnitude of the retinal stimulus received from A2 (as in Fig. 5a), one would not ordinarily speak of the behavior as predictive. If A1 takes a course such as the ones shown in Fig. 5b or 5c (where B is a barrier), which will bring him and A2 into contact at some future time and which seem to require orientation of both spatial and temporal coordinates, at least "first order" predictive ability seems to be operating. If A1 can accurately cast a stone at a moving target, or if (as in Fig. 5d) he can anticipate that A2 is going to a *particular* goal object ($B1$) and can either compete or not compete according to his dominance status with respect to A2 and the relative lead that A2 has over him, this would seem to

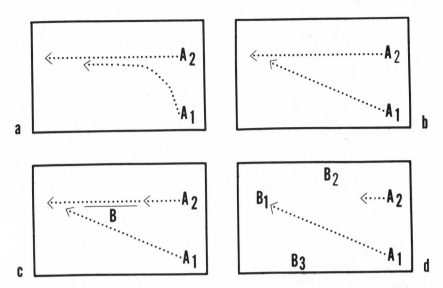

FIG. 5.   Various types of travel paths, some of which presumably involve prediction or extrapolation of the path of a stimulus animal (A2). Assume A1 and A2 are travelling at equal speeds. B is a goal object or a barrier.

require at least second-order predictive ability. Rosenblueth et al. (1943) proposed, and Krushinskii (1960) and others have demonstrated, that one of the features of discontinuity observable when comparing "higher" animals with "lower" ones lies in the fact that lower animals are limited to predictive behaviors of a low order, whereas higher animals are capable potentially of higher orders of prediction.

Chimpanzees and in fact all species of primates that I have observed seem easily capable of the forms of predictive behavior shown in Fig. 5. Indeed, in watching the travel behavior of primate groups, one of the most ubiquitous features seems to be that once a "leader" initiates travel, others very frequently take over from there and range some distance ahead of him, occasionally glancing back at him and correcting their direction to match his (for an experimental demonstration, see Menzel, in press). Similarly, in competing for food it is quite rare to see several animals racing for the same piece of food (unless it is confronted suddenly, as when a human observer throws it directly between several animals who sit a few meters apart). Most often there is no contest at all. As soon as the animals see who has the clear lead or who is most dominant, all but one usually quit.[2] And once the winner has the food he is very rarely molested; indeed, even a more dominant animal will generally beg for a share,

---

[2]This example assumes that only a single small piece of food is involved. If the objective is a larger food supply there might of course be more severe competition.

rather than try to take it by force (van Lawick-Goodall, 1971; Wrangham, 1975). Distal signals of threat or aggression seem to occur mostly when the outcome of a contest for an objective is still unpredictable, and overt fighting is most common if the contest was a close one or the winner won by a narrow margin.

Let me give one example of actual experimental data (Menzel, 1974, 1975). The situation is a highly complicated one by laboratory standards, for it involves multiple animals and multiple goal objects; but by the standards of everyday primate behavior it is undoubtedly very simple.

A group of six juvenile chimpanzees is locked into a small cage that borders on a 1-acre (about .4 hectare) enclosure. Prior to this test they have lived together for many months, and they are thoroughly familiar with the enclosure and with the general experimental procedures. An experimenter enters the enclosure and positions six stakes, each containing a single piece of fruit, at least 10 feet (3 m) apart from each other and about 100 feet (30 m) from the release cage door. (The chimpanzees cannot observe this procedure but all of the stakes are clearly visible from the release cage door.) Then the experimenter leaves the enclosure, ascends an observation tower, and opens the release cage door by means of an overhead cable. All of the animals are released simultaneously and are free to go wherever they choose. The experimenters record by mapping or by photography where the animals go, where each and every animal is located precisely as a timer sounds a click every 30 sec, who gets which piece of food, and their general social interactions. About 2½ min later (by which time the food is invariably gone), the experimenters clap their hands, whereupon the animals usually run back to the release cage and the procedures for the next trials are begun. (If not, the animals are rounded up.)

Eight such trials are conducted each day. On two trials three food stakes lie on the left half of the enclosure and three lie on the right half. On the remaining trials the left-right distributions of the food stakes are 0–6, 1–5, 2–4, 4–2, 5–1, or 6–0. The various conditions are presented in random, balanced orders, and the entire experiment lasts 10 days.

From the performance of individual chimpanzees in laboratory conditions, one would expect that the animals would have no difficulty in perceiving which half of the enclosure holds the greater food supply on any one trial, and that they would almost always go in this direction. These are, indeed, precisely the results that are obtained if one looks at the performance of the group majority, or treats the group as a whole as if it were a single individual. On 93% of the 60 trials involving a difference in food supply, more animals went in the direction of the larger food supply than went to the smaller food supply. Individual animals, however, were far more variable than one would expect from laboratory studies, and for good reason. If every individual had followed his tendency to go to the larger food supply and *without regard for what others were doing*, then, because of social factors, someone would go without food. Optimum performance for the group as a whole would in short consist of matching the number of individuals going left or right to the number of food units in each direction and directing each individual to a particular food stake. This in turn is not possible unless each individual can in effect take into account ahead of time where other individuals are going.

Figure 6 shows the ability of the group as a whole to match the number of individuals going left or right to the number of food stakes. Other data revealed that on 88% of the trials at least four of the six chimpanzees were successful in obtaining food and, on 54% of the trials, five or more obtained food and this despite the fact that the smallest animal almost never competed in the races, and others frequently quit if they found themselves outdistanced. (A subsequent test in which only the smallest animal was shown a hidden supply of food indicated that his failure to run was not due to any lack of food awareness, but rather to the social competition per se.)

Observation of the animals strongly suggested that each individual, on coming out of the release cage, watched carefully where his preferred companions and more dominant individuals were going, who had the biggest lead, and so on, and then chose his direction accordingly. Occasionally, the whole group started in the direction of the larger food supply but then milled about and pulled each other this way and that, until finally a smaller party split off and headed toward the smaller food supply.

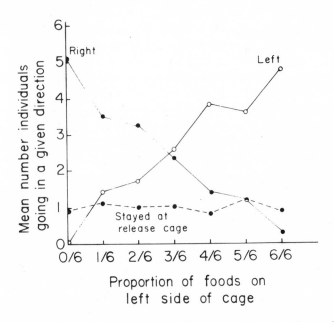

FIG. 6. Effects of dispersion of the food supply on group dispersion. Except for failures to run (most of which were attributable to the smallest animal in the group), there is a close match of the number of animals going in a given direction and the number of foods in that direction. (From Menzel, 1974.)

B. Early Experience, Development, Learning, and Memory

Köhler's (1925) monograph and current field studies are apt to convey the impression that a primate's performances with respect to objects in space are largely independent of prior experience, that they are principally determined by the animal's direct optical apprehension of the situation, and that things not perceptibly present but "merely thought about" occupy chimpanzees little if at all. In this section, I shall correct or at least amend this impression by examining the ontogenesis of behavior, and performance in delayed reaction situations. It should, however, be noted that the problem actually breaks down into two logically distinct questions, which some psychologists have tended to confuse with each other: (1) Is experience necessary? (2) How are experiences organized and utilized? The second of these questions is far more important in any discussion of cognitive mapping.

1. Early Experience

If one's criterion of innateness is that a behavior must appear in full-blown form the very first time that a chimpanzee is exposed to the appropriate situation (despite having been reared, up to the time of testing, in total social isolation in a bare grey cubicle), probably no behavior that is described in this paper can be called innate. At the Yerkes Primate Center, 16 chimpanzees were separated from their mothers on the day of birth and maintained for the first 2 years of life in small cubicles, never seeing anything outside their cubicles. Following this rearing period they were compared with each other and with wild-born controls on an enormous number of different tests. (For a review, see Davenport & Rogers, 1970a.) The entire experiment continued for more than 15 years, and most individuals were observed and tested almost daily until they were fully adult (12 years or older). The restriction-reared animals and wild-born controls were treated differentially only for the first 2 years of life, and after that time they lived in the same laboratory environments and were all given the same sorts of formal tests; thus the behavioral differences between them are presumably traceable to the differences in their *early* experiences.

Of major interest here is the fact that on their first exposure to novel test situations, the restriction-reared chimpanzees rarely if ever showed a normal chimpanzee's ability to cope with objects in space. At 2 years of age, they showed little propensity to explore novel areas or to even touch bananas, sticks, or indeed any novel object, let alone put two objects together via manipulation, or use one object as a tool to affect another in some fashion deemed appropriate by an experimenter (Menzel, Davenport, & Rogers, 1963a, 1963b, 1970; Menzel, 1964). Initially their fear of novelty seemed to be the major factor limiting their performances. But even after they had been exposed to many objects and had reached the point at which they would grasp new objects immediately and manipulate them persistently, they showed relatively few instances of spontaneous instrumental play. And when they were tested at the age of 6 to 8 years on Köhler-type problems where food was presented outside of the cage wire and a straight stick was available for raking in the food, only one of the eight restricted animals as opposed to nine of the ten wild-born animals solved the problem on the first 15-min trial, and the differences between the average performance of the groups persisted throughout the 14 days of testing. Their ability to cope with more clearly spatial types of problems was also grossly different from that of wild-born animals. At 2 years of age, even those restriction-reared animals that were not afraid of novel vertical structures essentially never climbed on them in many hours of testing, whereas wild-born controls spent about 30% of their time in climbing. Many of the restricted animals failed to circumvent or even climb over simple barriers (Menzel, 1964; Menzel et al., 1963b). When placed on a table or a bedboard, they frequently stepped off into space and landed on their head, and from detailed observations and films of their behavior we had the strong impression that they were incapable of perceiving the dropoff. When we rolled a ball at them from across the test room, they initially seemed incapable of predicting the path of the ball. Animals that were still cautious of the ball might tremble, whimper, and then scream as the ball got closer and closer to them, and finally collapse when the ball touched them. Only after considerable practice did they simply step aside so that the ball would miss them. Similar behaviors were seen when the approaching object was a human being or another chimpanzee.

A few months of exposure to more "enriched" environments produced a marked recovery in these behaviors. But even as adults the restriction-reared animals seemed to be far less skilled than wild-born animals. Unfortunately no formal tests were made in adulthood of their performance on complex barrier tasks or spatial memory and performance in outdoor situations. But in view of the fact that extensive data were collected on "standard" laboratory tests and substantial long-term deficits were found even there (Davenport & Rogers, 1970a), such complex tests seem almost superfluous.

2. Maturation of Patterns of Exploratory Behavior in Wild-Born Chimpanzees

In contrast to many other species of primates, chimpanzees have relatively "open" social groups, and males are not necessarily the leaders of travel. Adult females often travel long distances by themselves, and frequently leave their usual home range to enter new areas. For the first 3 to 4 years of life, all animals are almost totally dependent on their mothers and close relatives for knowing where to go, and it is rare to see chimpanzees younger than about 6 years of age travelling alone; but after that time males and females alike become highly skilled long-distance travellers and explorers. Since their home range might be 20 km² in size and resources might be quite thinly distributed and widely scattered throughout the year, there is every reason to suspect that individual chimpanzees must know their environment very well (van Lawick-Goodall, 1968, 1971, 1973; Teleki, 1974; Wrangham, 1975).

Unfortunately there are, at least to my knowledge, no field data available on how chimpanzees go about exploring a new area or how these patterns of exploration change as the animals gain maturity and experience. The following experiment (Menzel, 1969b) is suggestive.[3]

A total of 12 male and 9 female captive wild-born chimpanzees were released (one at a time) into an unfamiliar 1-acre (.4 hectare) outdoor enclosure, which was located about a quarter mile (.4 km) from the area in which they were usually housed. I sought to discover where the animals would go, how systematic their coverage of the area would be, what reference points they would use in "spatial" selections, and how these behaviors would vary with the sex and estimated age of the animal. Each chimpanzee was carried from his home cage to the test enclosure in a small transport cage. The transport cage was placed just inside the enclosure fence. The experimenters left the enclosure, ascended the observation tower, and then opened the door of the transport cage. The animal was free to roam for 36 hr. The basic data consisted of maps showing where the animal had gone, and checklist observations and written descriptions of what the animal did in each location at any given time. For purposes of comparing the chimpanzees' initial reactions to the test area with the reactions of other species, we also tested 30 macaques of three different species, but left them in the enclosure for only 1 hr each.

No sex differences were noted in the animals' immediate reaction to the situation, but species differences were obvious even within the first few seconds of testing and age differences among chimpanzees were next apparent. All animals other than one or two infant chimpanzees immediately ran out of the transport cage and appeared highly excited or disturbed. However, the stump-tail macaques climbed up the nearest available cage wire and hung there for a time, screeching; the irus macaques for the most part ran rapidly and silently to the farthest part of the compound, and the rhesus either climbed the wire or ran. The initial reactions of the infant and juvenile chimpanzees were very much like those of wild-born members of this species tested alone in a small indoor room: their behavior consisted of running, screaming, orienting toward any signs of an observer, climbing the walls and trying to open the cage doors. However, the present animals did not pace around the periphery of the entire area as in more confined circumstances. Instead, they at first ran back and forth along a 20- or 30-foot (6-m or 9-m) sector of the fence, returning repeatedly to the area of the transport cage. Older chimpanzees usually gave a single bark or hoot, and took off at a slow trot, covering far more area per linear distance traveled than the youngsters. Seven of the 9 chimpanzees who weighed less than 25 kg, and only

---

[3]The remainder of this section and Fig. 7 are from Menzel 1969b. Copyright 1969 by S. Karger A.G., Basel.

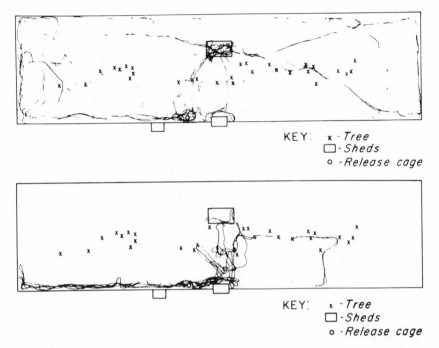

KEY: x -*Tree*
      □ -*Sheds*
      o -*Release cage*

KEY: x -*Tree*
      □ -*Sheds*
      o -*Release cage*

FIG. 7.   Travel routes in the first hour of testing of (a) an adult male, Jose, and (b) a 2-year-old female, Gigi. Gigi first used the transport cage as her "home base," and then shifted gradually to a fallen tree branch and finally to a nearby tree by the central shed.

1 of the 12 larger chimpanzees were within 20 ft (6 m) of the release point at the end of 60 sec. The four species differed significantly in location, in average distance from the starting point, and in dispersion; that is, they differed in where they went, how far they went, and in interindividual variability of travel. Also, while there were no species differences in the amount of area covered in the first hour, chimpanzees spent significantly more time in the center of the area than did the macaques, and their coverage of the area, at least by adults, was more systematic.

A complete record was taken on 15 chimpanzees to determine the number of different geographical sectors, of 205-square-foot (19-m^2) size entered in 8 hr time and 4 hr per day. The total amount of area explored varied as a direct function of the size or weight of the animals (Spearman's rank correlation = .88 for the 9 males .94 for the 6 females, and .87 for all 15 chimpanzees).[4] The data

_____

[4]Even though the macaque samples were quite restricted in range of sizes and ages (weights ranged from 3 to 7.5 kg) the correlation between body weight and the amount of area covered in the first hour was statistically significant for the males (Kendall's rank order partial $\tau = .80, p < .01$, partialing out species factors). No significant relation was detectable in the female data (partial $\tau = .07$). As in chimpanzees, the amount of area covered bore little relationship to the amount of running per se.

from the other 6 chimpanzees, who were tested first and whose activity was charted on a shorter schedule are consistent with this picture but not so striking, probably because the short time samples are biased by the different temporal distribution of travel behavior in some animals. For the total 21 animals and 15 min of mapping on each of 8 hr, Spearman's rho p = .58, $p < .01$. Insofar as it is possible to judge the matter, sex differences in weight tended to lower the correlation between bodily size and travel; that is, some females covered more area than males of equal size. The exact ages of these wild-born animals were unknown, of course, but as age would be judged from weight and from other morphological criteria, it is apparent that the age differences in behavior were substantial.

Figure 7 shows the travel routes of an adult male (panel a) and a representative but active 2-year-old female (panel b) in the first hour of testing. It might be noted parenthetically that 2 of the 3 adult males covered more ground in the first 15 min than any infant or juvenile did in 2 days. As a comparison of these figures suggests, adults in general, and the adult males in particular, ranged farther, traveled in much longer single moves, rather than going back and forth in small circles, used the tree line as well as the fence line as a major route, and spent more time in the center of the area. When the adult animals traveled, they tended to explore areas in which they had not previously been, even if they had been inactive for a long period. All the above phenomena emerged in the juveniles, too, but in lesser degree, and only after much longer exposure to the situation.

The temporal distribution of activity was quite different in the various age-sex clases. The typical reaction of the older animals, especially males, was to move within several minutes to a lookout point or home base other than the transport cage and usually near the shelter. There they would sit and scan the area for many minutes. We could usually predict from the direction of their scanning where they would go on their next run. The amount of time that they locomoted was not particularly large. Especially on the second day of testing, they spent less time than did juveniles in overt locomotor activity, and they moved more deliberately. By contrast, both initial disturbance and later exploratory behavior in juveniles and infants showed slower habituation. Exploration in juveniles was also more easily distractable by whatever objects lay in the immediate path and was generally less efficient in covering the area systematically. After whimpering and other signs of disturbance had habituated, the youngsters simply made short forays from a home base (invariably by the concrete shelter, a tree, a large fallen tree limb, or some other vertical structure such as the cage fence), climbed, rolled in the grass, or collected objects for manipulation. In general, the behavior of all the chimpanzees was characterized by (1) establishing a base point, (2) moving out to explore new features gradually, with frequent returns to a base, and (3) perhaps occasional shifts in the base of operations. Only after general exploration declined, and only in a resting place, did finer activities such as manipulation become prominent. Objects were usually transported to a favored area before being investigated extensively. On the second day, most of the adults and adolescents spent the majority of their time within a 100-square-foot (9.3-m^2) area, digging in the ground with sticks, building small ground nests, eating grasses or the bark from the tops of the tall pine trees, or sleeping; in contrast, the juveniles roamed. The variety of objects manipulated and the variety and skill of the chimpanzee, even in most infants, far exceeded that seen in the macaques, and adult chimpanzees showed more skilled manipulations than did youngsters.

Most of the chimpanzees' sleeping locations at night time were predicted within an hour or so from the start of the test, from a given animal's daytime home base, or from his visual checking out of a particular tree. All animals slept on, in, or alongside a vertical structure. Only juveniles stayed near the fence. Probably because of the lack of suitable vegetation only one adult and four juveniles built tree nests.Most adults explored the top of at least one tree, but then abandoned it. A majority of the animals slept on or beneath the concrete shelter, and of these all slept directly on the edge or corner of the floor or of the 3-m-high roof. It is noteworthy that the edges of the artificial structures or rooms are preferred resting places not only for chimpanzees, rhesus, gelada, and in fact most primates in laboratory situations, but also for at least rhesus in the free-ranging state (Menzel, 1969a). Chimpanzees or rhesus are probably not as concerned with artificiality and naturalness as are investigators. In primates' use of the shelters and fences, it is probably the visual prominence, verticals, edges, and shade as such which are critical.

In general, most activity in the field enclosure was centered about objects of some kind. A three-dimensional *behavioral* map of the compound in which frequency of entry formed the vertical dimension and the axes of the compound formed the other two dimensions would in fact correspond very closely to an ordinary three-dimensional geographical map: Chimpanzees traveled from one structure or object to the next, apportioning their time at each place roughly in accordance with the prominence of that feature. There was considerable focus on the edges of a feature. In this respect, the data are analogous to data from human studies of eye fixations of a picture. From the standpoint of information gathering, a prime difference in the present sort of situation is that here the animals are actually inside the "stimulus" and they must move themselves about bodily to cover the stimulus.

In sum, the data suggest the following: (1) There is no such thing as free space for an animal. The spatial world is structured by the animal's species characteristics, physical maturity, early experience, and experience in a defined situation. (2) Space is always structured in terms of prominent objects, and so perhaps a more basic question than empty space is: What is a prominent object for the animal, and how do objects come to be prominent in particular fashions? It is most likely, for example, that with a greater variety of suitable trees, fence following and fence climbing would have been negligible. The cage fence was simply the most accessible and prominent vertical surface. (3) Presumably a major function of curiosity, exploration, or responsiveness is to learn what is there. The seeming lack of responsiveness on the part of older animals to simple stimuli or under routine circumstances might in large part reflect their greater rapidity and efficiency in extracting information from the environment, their greater ability to assess the relevant information at a distance, and their "acquired need" for greater levels of complexity (cf. Fowler, 1971; Dember and Earl, 1957). This factor would eliminate some of the necessity for exploratory activity (Menzel, 1966). (4) The slowness with which exploratory efficiency develops in the chimpanzee is further related to the slowness of physical maturation in this species (e.g., because of their sheer size and strength, adult chimpanzees can move out farther than an infant and still return to a secure base in the same amount of time), and to the fact that chimpanzees learn to use and exploit their world in a far more detailed fashion than do macaques. In other words, the amount of information out there to extract is in great part a function of a species' genetic potential, and species with greater perceptual capacities generally require longer to fulfill their potential.

3. Exploratory Behavior as a Problem in Learning

A vast majority of the hundreds of studies that have been conducted on the exploratory behavior of animals focus attention on the motivational (or acquired-motivational, incentive) aspects of this behavior, and largely ignore the fact that the animals might also be learning the nature and relative positions of objects. Thus, I have been able to find only a handful of studies in which the investigation analyzed *where* the animals were going; customarily, the dependent variable is the number of times the animal moves from one sector to another, or the frequency of various sorts of behaviors — irrespective of location. Obviously the temporal course of "amount of activity" and the motivational aspects of performance are interesting in their own right, and there is nothing wrong with such analyses. What, however, is the function of a given level of activity? Why do animals eventually "satiate"? Why do they satiate at different rates? Surely motivational factors are only part of the answer. One explanation, which dates back to Tolman (1932) and Woodworth (1958) is that the animals are trying to learn what is "out there," and thus they ordinarily tend to persist until they have learned enough to satisfy themselves. Older animals engage in less overt locomotion and manipulation because they are more skilled in extracting the necessary information from the environment and because they are more apt to rely on visual scanning and other forms of distal perception, rather than on peripheral stimulation.

The fact that travel behavior is highly orderly and systematic with respect to the various features of the environment is, of course, evidence for a cognitive

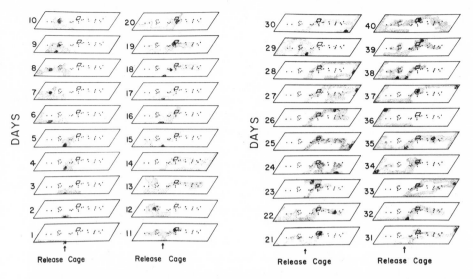

FIG. 8.   A day-by-day time series of maps showing the gradual process of exploration and the increase in the size of daily ranges and day-to-day variability. Frequencies of entry into a given sector are ignored. Stippled sectors were entered by at least one of the four animals on a given day, and striped areas show the places in which the animals were observed on the largest number of observation intervals. Heavy dots are trees and the outline in the center of the enclosure is a concrete shelter. (From Menzel, 1974.)

interpretation. To study the patterning of travel behavior in more detailed fashion, I conducted a series of tests in which juvenile chimpanzees were given 30 min a day to explore the one-acre enclosure, and then were removed from the enclosure. Testing continued for at least 40 days. In most of these tests, we worked with small social groups rather than with single individuals, largely because by this time I was equally interested in the social aspects of travel behavior.[5]

Figure 8 shows the day-by-day exploratory patterns of one social group of four 3-year-old juveniles. At first, when the animals appeared very cautious of the novel environment, they stayed very close to the release cage and the walls

---

[5]In this discussion I shall focus attention only on the reactions of the group as a whole. This is actually a sufficient basis for predicting more than 90% of the variance of each individual's locational data, for these juveniles were very dependent upon each other. They rarely went more than 50 feet (15 m) from their nearest neighbor and were most often all within a 20-foot circle. With repeated tests there was considerable loosening up and the animals less often clung to each other or engaged in direct physical contact; but nevertheless they still traveled as a highly coordinated unit. Even several years later, after the animals reached adolescence and had lived in the enclosure for an extended period of time and occasionally spread out long distances from each other, I suspect (with some backing from actual data) that each animal was almost continuously aware of where every other animal was located at any given time.

of the enclosure, and they usually started the session by going back to places where they had been the previous day, and then expanding out a little from there. As the days passed, however, they came to cover more and more ground on a given session, and to alternate areas from day to day. On all sessions, the particular area where the animals spent the most time contained some large vertical structure such as a tree, which was usually used for climbing and swinging. The tree line as well as the fence lines came to be used as the major routes of travel. Open areas, especially those containing no objects other than grass, were rarely entered, except when the animals passed through them quickly en route to some other place. Behaviorally speaking, space was always structured in terms of objects. If there were such a thing as empty, homogeneous Euclidean space, probably no chimpanzee would enter it. Three-dimensional behavioral maps in which the XY coordinates of space form two dimensions and "time of occupation" forms the third dimension would in fact show a high correlation with ordinary topographical maps showing the amount and kind of environmental structures in a given area.

It can be seen from Fig. 8 that as the chimpanzees gained experience in the situation their patterns of travel on a given day came increasingly to look like the patterns that an adult might show on its *first* encounter with the same situation (see Fig. 7a). There was, however, no evidence for an eventual intersession decrement in exploration (satiation), as one might expect of adults. A decrement did not occur until several months later, when we housed the chimpanzees permanently in the enclosure. Both within a day and across days the animals seemed to temporarily satiate on *specific* objects and areas (as evidenced by their frequent changes in the places they went and the types of objects they played with); but they did not stop travelling or manipulating in general.

One of the best ways to inductively study the systematic nature of the animals' patterns of exploration is to make travel maps similar to those shown in Fig. 8 on sheets of clear plastic, and then superimpose these sheets one on top of the other, or all on top of a detailed topographical map. What emerges from such a study is that the animals invariably seem to be gradually and systematically covering most of the unexplored "gaps" in the situation. For the present group, I constructed Fig. 9 directly from the data of Fig. 8; what emerges in Fig. 9 is a steady increase in the (cumulative) percentage of the total area covered. Had the enclosure been of infinite size, however, there is little doubt that exploration would have permanently stopped at some point far short of 100%; for no species of animal is completely nomadic. The size of a given social group's home range is finite, and is presumably determined in part by how much spatial and object information can be assimilated.

Finer analyses of such data would show further that the specific types of behavior that emerge in a given sector of the cage ordinarily change to some degree after the animals have been in that sector on one or more sessions. In other words, the animals seemed to be learning not merely what is out there but

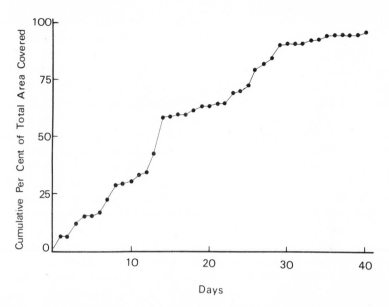

FIG. 9.   Exploratory behavior as the gradual process of covering the whole field. Here the group was given 1 point each time any animal entered a sector in which none had been before; the maximum possible score was 351. (From Menzel, 1974.)

also the detailed characteristics of each specific sector of the field. The fact that the process of covering new areas speeds up at some point (see in particular Day 13 in Figs. 8 & 9) also suggests that there was considerable transfer from the left half of the enclosure to the right half. In making such statements, I am of course going well beyond what can be experimentally verified; but tests in which we introduced changes in the situation after the animals had explored most of the area (see the following section; also Menzel, 1974) to test what they had learned would support such speculations.

4. Memory

Perhaps the simplest way to assess the extent to which animals know the nature and relative positions of objects in a familiar environment is to make selected changes in the environment once it has been explored. If the animals immediately investigate the detail that has been changed or otherwise react to it in some fashion that one would not expect by chance, obviously they must discriminate the difference between the present state of the environment and the past state, and hence they must have had some notion of the past state. A lack of differential response, on the other hand, proves nothing other than that one cannot reject the null hypothesis.

a. Detection of novelty.   A large number of such tests were conducted on the same social group of four juveniles whose initial exploratory behavior has been described above. After the animals had explored most of the enclosure, we tested them alternately under standard "baseline" conditions or under conditions where a single new object was introduced into the field, or a single old object was removed from the field, or a single old object was moved from one place in the field to another. Between tests the animals were housed in their home cage, about 100 yards (or 90 m) from the enclosure, and there was an interval of at least 24 hr between each test; thus, to detect the change, the animals had to remember the layout of the field for at least one day.

Under these conditions, the chimpanzees' memory seemed at least as acute as our own. Not surprisingly, the animals were most responsive to new objects that were introduced into the field, only moderately responsive to old objects that were simply moved from one place to another, and least responsive (often showing no differential response) to a location from which an already-present object was removed without leaving any trace. It was, however, principally *visual* changes to which the animals responded. Objects that were hidden from sight were essentially never detected, and sometimes the chimpanzees actually stepped on them on their way to some other goal. To illustrate the acuity of the chimpanzees, consider the following test (Menzel, 1971).

In addition to the uncountable number of objects (e.g., trees, sticks) that were already in the 1-acre (.4 hectare) area, we introduced 20 toys and household articles and located them at random. The chimpanzees were given 10 half-hour sessions, one every other day, to learn the nature and location of these test objects. (Intervening sessions were conducted with none of these objects present.) Then, on a series of 10 critical test days, one more object was added to this collection every other day. Thus on Day 1 of the critical tests there were 21 objects (20 old ones plus 1 new one), on Day 2 there were 22 objects, and so on until on Day 10 there were 30 objects. For the first 5 days each brand-new object of the day was placed in a new area, and on Days 6–10 the brand-new object was placed in the location where one of the 20 old objects had been, and the displaced old object was placed in a new location so that now the animals had to choose between "object novelty" and "novelty of place."

The results of each of the 10 critical test days is shown in Fig. 10. The chimpanzees invariably spotted the brand-new object within about 15 sec of their emergence from the release cage, and they marched as a group in a direct line to that object. Sometimes they made contact with old objects while en route to the new ones; but such contacts were relatively brief. Furthermore, over the 10 days, the correlation between the location of the new object and the chimpanzees' direction of travel is about .90. Object novelty was a much more effective variable than novelty of place.

I have recently conducted more elaborate tests of this sort on a family group of marmosets (*Saguinus fuscicollis*), which are of course a considerably more

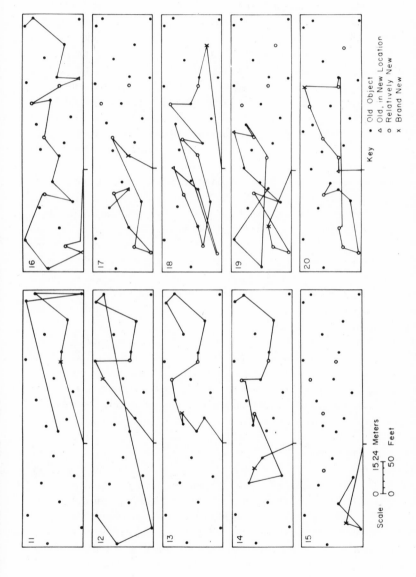

Key   • Old Object
      ▲ Old, in New Location
      o Relatively New
      x Brand New

Scale 0   15.24 Meters
       ⊢————⊣
       0   50   Feet

FIG. 10.   Maps of each critical test day (Days 11 to 20), showing the sequence in which various objects were touched by the group of four chimpanzees. Note the tendency for the group to go in a straight line toward the brand new object (Xs). (From Menzel, 1976.)

"primitive" primate than chimpanzees. Testing was conducted in a 4- by 10-m greenhouse, which was heavily loaded with natural vegetation. The test objects were presented in such a way that we could assess the animals' ability to detect changes in the object per se, its location in the greenhouse, its orientation (i.e., whether an elongated object was changed from an originally vertical to a horizontal orientation or vice versa), and the various combinations of these changes. The results showed that the animals were responsive to each and every one of these types of change, that a change in two or more dimensions produced a greater increase in investigation (of the changed object) than a change in only one dimension, and that (even though marmosets possess a highly developed olfactory system) it was the visual aspect of the change that was critical. Delays of 24 hr between initial exposure to an object and the subsequent critical test produced no decrement in performance; and the object that was changed could be picked out from up to 30 others objects (not including the uncountable number of objects that were present already).

Novelty-detection tests of this sort are, in my opinion, probably the simplest and most straightforward way of testing an animal's knowledge of its familiar environment, and they would also be the most relevant to the real-life problems that animals face outside of the laboratory. I should not be surprised if chimpanzees in the wild could detect changes in the familiar portions of their home ranges even after not having been in that particular location for weeks. I would also bet that their memory for the locations of favorite fig trees, termite-nest mounds, and placed where they have narrowly escaped predators goes well beyond this. The recent field studies of Wrangham (1975) and Teleki (1974) provide some support for this possibility.

b. Delayed-response tests.   In a Wisconsin-type test apparatus where the locations of food rewards are less than .3 m apart and where 50 or more trials are given in rapid succession using the same locations, chimpanzees' memory for locations is not very impressive. Tested on a scale that more closely approximates the conditions under which the animals actually live, however, and tested with procedures which minimize trial-to-trial interference factors, the story is quite different (e.g., Tinklepaugh, 1932; Köhler, 1925). From the several thousand test trials I conducted in outdoor situations over a period of several years, I am of the opinion that chimpanzees' spatial memory (at least on the scale tested, and in situations familiar to them) is probably better than our own would be in the same situation. Indeed, their performance in many cases seems to be a good first approximation of the performance which we would exhibit, had we an actual map of the area, showing the locations of a number of hidden objects. I shall first describe the results of some of the more complex tests that we have administered (Menzel, 1973b) and then some of the details of the chimpanzees' search strategies.

(1) *The "traveling-salesman" problem.*   The procedure was a delayed response variation on the traveling-salesman combinatorial problem. A chimpanzee was

shown the location of a number of hidden goals in a field, and the basic question was whether he could organize his subsequent search in such a way as to get the best possible reward in the shortest possible time or with the shortest possible overall mileage.[6]

The subjects for these experiments were six wild-born chimpanzees (including those whose performance has been described in earlier sections of this paper). At the time of these experiments they were 5 to 7 years old, and had lived as a group in the 1-acre (4,047-m^2) enclosure for more than a year, and had received extensive formal test experience. Their formal test experience included delayed response tests with single, but not multiple, hidden goals, and one animal (Bido) had received fewer than 10 prior formal trials with single hidden goals.

Before a trial began, all six animals were locked in a release cage on the periphery of the field. Then one experimenter took out a previously selected test animal and carried him about the field, accompanying a second experimenter who (in Experiment 1) hid one piece of fruit in each of 18 randomly selected sectors of the field. Throughout this 10-min process, the animal was not permitted to do anything other than cling to his carrier and watch the baiter; thus, primary reinforcement and locomotor practice during the information-gathering phase of a trial were eliminated.

After being shown the foods, the chimpanzee was returned to the group. The experimenters left the field, ascended an observation tower and, within 2 min, pulled a cable that opened the release cage door. All six animals were released simultaneously and were free to roam. The five animals that had not been shown the food on a particular trial had no way to find the food other than through guesswork or cues such as odor, the behavior of the test animal, and inadvertent cues from the experimenters; thus, they served as controls for factors other than visual memory. (The emotional dependence of the animals on each other precluded the possibility of testing each animal alone.)

On a map that showed the location of each piece of food, the experimenters recorded the time at which each food pile was found or rechecked and the identity of the animal involved. In addition, qualitative notes were made on behavior related to the search. Observation continued for at least 1 hr.

One trial was given each day for 16 days. Belle, Bandit, Bido, and Gigi each served as test animals on 4 trials and as control animals on the remaining 12 trials. Shadow and Polly were controls on all trials. On each trial the experimenters followed a different path and used a different set of 18 hiding places. To choose paths completely at random in this experiment and the next one would have meant carrying a heavy animal many hundreds of meters. Therefore we initially used routes of the sort shown in Fig. 11 and deferred complete randomization until later experiments that used fewer pieces of food. The food locations

---

[6]The remainder of this section and Fig. 11 and 12 are from Menzel, 1973b. Copyright 1973 by the American Association for the Advancement of Science.

for a particular trial were determined by a table of random permutations of 9 sectors along the Y axis and 39 along the X axis of the enclosure. Within any one of these 351 sectors, we selected the exact hiding place on the basis of available natural cover and, if possible, avoided using the same type of cover (for instance, grass clumps) more than a few times in one trial or the same exact place more than once in an experiment.

Overall, the test animals found a total of 200 pieces (12.5 per trial); the animals serving as controls found a total of 17 (.21 per animal per trial). Usually, the test animal ran unerringly and in a direct line to the exact clump of grass or leaves, tree stump, or hole in the ground where a hidden food lay, grabbed the food, stopped briefly to eat, and then ran directly to the next place, no matter how distant or obscured by visual barriers that place was. His pace slowed as more and more food was obtained, and eventually he lay down for long rests; but he never seemed to wander around the field as if conducting a general search. Control animals obtained food principally by searching around the test animal or begging from him directly. Only in four instances did a test animal search the ground more than 2 m from a food pile, as controls did on an uncountable number of occasions. It would seem that the major cue of food location was visual memory, and that the test animal did not merely recognize each hiding place on the basis of local cues once he chanced to pass by that place.

Figure 11 shows each test animal's performance on the trial on which he found the largest number of foods. (These trials were not necessarily the best in terms of how the animal organized his travel route.) Each animal proceeded more or less in accord with a least-distance principle (Tolman, 1932) and on no trial did his path bear any systematic relation to the path that he had originally experienced when he was being carried by the experimenter. On the average, the itinerary of a given trial was 64% as long as the mean of all possible ($N!$) itineraries on that trial, and none of the 16 trials exceeded this chance-expected value. Extensive baseline data on the animals under routine (nontest) conditions indicated that the routes shown in Fig. 11 were unlikely when the animal had not been shown the food.

A second experiment tested whether the chimpanzees could remember the type of hidden food as well as its location. The same test procedure and animals were used, but now 9 of the 18 food piles contained a piece of nonpreferred food (vegetable) and 9 contained a piece of preferred food (fruit). The four test animals received three trials each.

The results were similar to those of the first experiment, except that on most trials the preference for fruit and the least-distance strategy were additive determiners of choice. For example, in the first 9 responses of her first trial, Belle took 9 fruits to 0 vegetables; Bandit, 7 fruits to 2 vegetables; Bido, 7 fruits to 2 vegetables; and Gigi, 4 fruits to 5 vegetables; most of the remaining foods were taken later. (Only Gigi's preference for fruit on Trial 1 was not significant by median test; and on subsequent trials she "corrected" this.) If the itinerary to

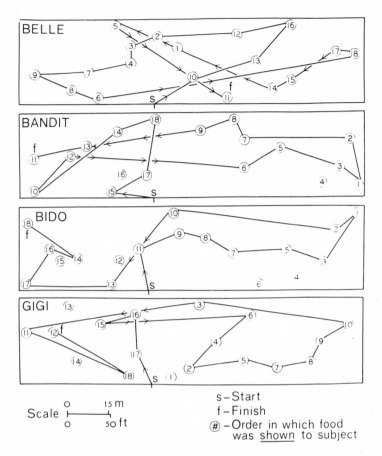

Scale

s – Start
f – Finish
– Order in which food
was <u>shown</u> to subject

FIG. 11.   Maps showing each test animal's performance on the trial (out of four) on which it found the largest number of foods. The connecting lines give an exact picture of the order in which the various places were searched and a rough idea of the animal's general travel routes. Where the line touches a point, that place was searched.

fruits and the itinerary to vegetables are considered separately, each showed a reasonable least-distance pattern.

It is unlikely that all 18 places were taken into account simultaneously at all times throughout a trial in these two experiments. On several occasions, a test animal actually stepped on one pile of food on his way to another, and then, sometimes 10 min later, returned to it. Also, on several trials, a striking example of sudden recall occurred while an animal was apparently asleep. After having eaten many pieces of food and lain supine with his eyes closed for up to 30 min, the test animal suddenly jumped to his feet and ran 10 to 30 m straight to a hidden piece of food.

In only 11 instances (range 0 to 5 per animal) in these two experiments did a chimpanzee recheck a place that it had already emptied of food. Places that had already been emptied by another animal were, however, often rechecked — as were places that had been searched without actually finding the food.

A third experiment examined with a less complicated procedure the relative importance of "place" vs. "response" and route cues (cf. Restle, 1957). The same test procedure and animals were used, but now only four food piles were shown on a particular trial, two on the left third of the field l, and two on the right third, r. The exact locations varied from trial to trial, as did the order in which the four piles (l_1, l_2, r_1, r_2) were shown. In this and subsequent experiments, the animals were tested in two independent trios (Shadow, Bandit, and Belle; Polly, Bido, and Gigi) rather than all together.

On none of 28 trials (7 per test animal) did a chimpanzee go to the four foods in the same order we had shown them, or the reverse of that order. However, the results again indicated an acute memory of places and perception of relative distances. On all but two trials, the animals cleaned out both piles on one side of the area, then went to the other two piles on the other side, *and then quit*. They followed an $l–l–r–r$ sequence 14 times and a $r–r–l–l$ sequence 12 times, and often used the shortest of all 24 possible itineraries.

A fourth experiment essentially replicated these last results on travel organization when the use of cues other than distant vision were restricted almost completely. All procedures were the same as in the prior experiment except that, instead of carrying the chimpanzee about the field, one experimenter held the animal directly in front of the release cage door while a second experimenter walked from one predesignated place to the next, held a piece of fruit aloft at each place, and then dropped it in the grass. (It was not covered up further and was ordinarily visible from a few meters.) On the 13 trials in which the animals went to all four places, there were only three times that they failed to follow an $l–l–r–r$, or $r–r–l–l$ sequence of travel. (The remaining 11 trials on which one or more foods was missed indicate some loss of information by comparison with the prior experiments; but these trials tell one nothing about the principal question of how an itinerary between four points is organized.)

It is possible that in the preceding tests the chimpanzees failed to take into account all food places at the start of a trial, and instead recognized one of the nearest available places, went to it, looked about, recognized another goal location that was close to their present position, went to it; and so on. Therefore, we conducted a further experiment. It differed from the preceding experiments in only one detail: Two pieces of food were hidden on one third of the field, and three pieces were hidden on the opposite third of the field. On the foregoing hypothesis, one would not expect a preference for going first to the side with three pieces.

Figure 12 shows the results of each animal's first four trials. On 13 of 16 trials the chimpanzees went first to the side with the larger clustering of food.

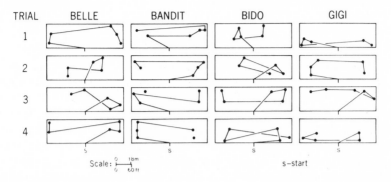

FIG. 12. Maps showing each test animal's first four trials. Since the release cage was not in the center of the field and we wished to avoid biasing right and left positions, no food was hidden on the extreme right section of the field. This portion of the enclosure is not shown on the maps.

Thus, in addition to following a least-distance strategy, they maximized the rate of food acquisition. In subsequent trials, the first-choice selection of the side with three foods declined slightly; but the overall results remain better than chance.

In sum, the chimpanzees appeared to perceive directly the relative positions of selected classes of objects and their own position in this scaled frame of reference. They proceeded on the strategy "Do as well as you can from wherever you are," taking into account the relative preference values and spatial clumpings of the foods as well as distances. If locomotor practice or primary reinforcement were necessary at all, it was before the experiments began — which renders these variables of greater developmental than structural interest. Although it would be physically impossible for animals to sort over all $N!$ possible routes in the length of time allowed, and although it is unlikely that space as they perceived it can be compared literally to a picture on a piece of paper, their achievements are a good first approximation of those at which an applied scientist would arrive from his real maps, algorithms, and a priori criteria of efficiency. "Cognitive mapping" is not the only possible explanation of the above facts, but it describes the facts more accurately and succinctly than any alternative term of which I am aware.

(2) *Further details of search strategy.* The major reason that we took extreme care in hiding the goal objects amid the natural cover already available before the time of the particular test trial was that the chimpanzees seemed to be very acute in knowing what constituted a likely looking hiding place and in detecting any change in the enclosure or any hiding place that looked as if it had been "rigged." If, for example, we placed food in one of the barrels or other large movable objects that were left in the enclosure to serve as playthings, but moved

that object about 10 feet (3 m) from its previous location, or moved it from a horizontal to a vertical orientation, even chimpanzees that had been given no cue seemed to spot the change almost immediately; and they raced straight to it and searched it as if looking for food. (The fact that food, rather than a snake or some other object or no extrinsic reward was involved could of course be guessed from the context of the test. If we randomly varied the nature of the hidden object, the chimpanzees were much more circumspect in how they responded to an object that had been moved and that could conceivably contain food — in some cases investigating it with a stick rather than by hand.) Or, to take another example, if we plucked several handfuls of grass and placed this grass in a lump (instead of spreading it out to look "natural"), or if we arranged a pile of tree bark too neatly or even placed it a considerable distance from any tree, the chimpanzees almost always investigated it if they came within sighting distance of it.

Even more interesting, it was hazardous to hide food too often in the same general class of hiding place — even on a single trial. For example, if on a single trial we had hidden food at the base of several adjacent trees (or several adjacent fence posts, or fallen logs, or in several ant hills, etc.), and if the test animal had uncovered three or more of these rewards in close succession, the control animals seemed to immediately spot this regularity, and they would race ahead of the test animal and start checking other hiding places of *the same class*, especially any toward which the test animal started to orient. In the case of some objects (e.g., fence posts) the potential hiding places were 10 feet (3 m) or more apart, and the chimpanzees ran directly from one to the next, not searching any of the intervening points manually.

It was curious to us that after their first trial or two the chimpanzees that were being shown the food as it was being hidden seldom if ever tried to take some. More often than not they gave one the impression that they were not even looking at the food, and to catch their attention we had to hold it almost in front of their face or sometimes even touch it to their lips. Their attention seemed to be directed far more toward the hiding place per se. Thus, they glanced only momentarily at the food, then at the hiding place as we were arranging it, and then seemed to orient toward the nearest large vertical structure or (if none was within a few yards) squirmed around in our arms and oriented around the field in general. Although it is notoriously difficult to tell precisely what a chimpanzee is attending to from such behavior alone (for one thing these animals seem to have an extremely broad field of vision, and for another they often avert their gaze away from that which interests them the most, especially in social situations), all observers had the distinct impression that the animals were engaged in first locating the position of food relative to the local cues of the hiding places, and then locating that place relative to the nearest prominent landmark or (if none was available in the immediate vicinity) the field in general.

Their subsequent travel and search behavior tended to corroborate these impressions. If food was located on or at the base of some tall vertical structure, they usually ran without hesitation straight for it; and if that structure was in the middle of an open area devoid of other structures, a control animal often took the cue from the test animal, raced ahead of him, and beat him to the structure. If, on the other hand, the food was hidden in an area relatively devoid of landmarks or of distinctive smaller objects which could conceivably serve as hiding places, the test animal usually slowed up when he got within 5 yards (4.5 m) or less, and carefully scanned the ground, as if looking for the "local cue." Over any series of 10 or so trials, the correlation between the test animal's travel angle and the straight-line path to the goal was typically .90 or higher, and what varied most was the probability that the animal would run to "his" goal rather than drift after another animal. (Occasionally the chimpanzees took an indirect route to their goal because they were circling a flooded area of the field, or utilizing a preferred trail, or apparently avoiding an area in which they had encountered a snake in the previous several days, or shaking off a more dominant animal who was following them too closely.) In short, the *general* locus of the food was no problem at all. By far the most frequent "error" was going to a grass clump, hole in the ground, etc., that looked (to us) almost precisely like the "correct" one but was located very close to it. The only time that the chimpanzees missed the hiding place by 10 feet (3 m) or more was when we hid the food at the base of one fence post, and they went to the immediately adjacent fence post.

The chimpanzees were also very quick in learning any nonrandomness in our pattern of baiting the field. For example, in many experiments we hid no food closer than about 10 yards (9 m) from the release cage and within half a dozen trials control animals abandoned their practice (carried over from the immediately prior experiment) of searching within that zone. In other experiments we hid no food farther than about 50 yards (45 m) from the release cage on the right half of the field, and the animals soon stopped searching outside of these limits. In still other experiments, we did not hide food in the center third of the enclosure, and again the animals learned this quite readily. Still further, in some experiments where we did not cover the food completely but left it in a position from which it could be seen from about 5 yards (4.5 m) away (i.e., from a chimp-level viewing position on the ground) one animal, when she was tested as a control, soon came to race ahead of the test animal and then climb a tree and scan the field from a height.

Perhaps the most impressive behavior, however, occurred in an experiment in which two piles of food were hidden on a given trial and were located at precisely contralateral angles and equal distances from the release cage — one pile on the right half of the field and the other on the left. Even though these angles and distances were varied at random from one trial to the next, the control animals (who had no cues to the exact location of the food other than the above nonrandomness and the behavior of the test animal who had been shown the food) started to race over to the second location almost as soon as the test animal had found the first pile of food. In some cases the test animal did not accompany them (since he was busy eating his food), and yet they commenced their manual search only when within 5 yards (4.5 m) or so of the correct location, and they searched up and down the correct imaginary directional line, with an error of less than 20° in angle and perhaps 5 yards (4.5 m) in distance. The animals were definitely not using olfactory cues or attending to visual traces of the path we had used in hiding the food, since we could vary these without affecting their performance. I cannot conceive of any explanation of their acuity in knowing the correct angle or distance with respect to the release cage, which does not assume an ability for "mapping" that is independent of any *particular* local cues. I say this because the chimpanzees might take any conceivable path in getting to the correct zone, and they showed no evidence of sighting on any specific feature (including the release cage).

C. Social Communication of Object Locations

Humans know the nature and relative positions of objects not merely by direct perception of the immediate environment and by memory of and inferences from their past experiences in that environment, but also by having been told or given a written message or map or picture or some other representation of the environment by another human. How far can chimpanzees go in the latter directions? From recent studies of chimpanzees' ability for cross-modal transfer, perception of pictures (Davenport & Rogers, 1970b, 1971) and learning of humanoid language (Fouts, 1975; Gardner & Gardner, 1969; Premack, 1971), one might expect them to go as far as many preschool children. Using sign language it should not be difficult to "tell" a language-trained chimpanzee that food (or some other object) is hidden in one location rather than another, that object A is inside (rather than behind, or on top of) object B, and so on.

My own experiments on this score (Menzel, 1974, in press) made no attempt to test the upper limits of capacity. I was not concerned with training chimpanzees on human-type tasks but rather with discovering what wild-born group-living animals are *already* capable of doing, and what they communicate to each other using their own spontaneously developed signal system. Thus the only reason that we as experimenters sometimes entered into the chimpanzees' communication system was to gain a more precise control over the behavior of the signaller (i.e., we used ourselves as ethological dummies or models of chimpanzees); and the major social cues we utilized were modelled after those we had already observed the chimpanzees using in their own social interactions. Cues such as manual pointing, which are used very rarely by chimpanzees, were included largely to compare their effectiveness with more natural cues.

The procedure used in our tests of social communication of object location was an elementary variation on the delayed-response procedures that have been described in previous sections of this paper. Instead of carrying the test chimpanzee all the way over to the hidden goal and showing it to him directly, we gave him some more indirect cue. Then we returned him to the release cage, removed ourselves from the situation, ascended the observation tower, and pulled a cable that opened the release cage door. If the test chimpanzee can get to the approximate location of the food more efficiently than one would expect by chance, then obviously.we can be said to have communicated something to him. And if, in addition, the control animals are the ones to find the food, it is obvious that they are not simply following the leader but are extrapolating ahead of him.

Over a series of several experiments a variety of conditions were tested, and there was unequivocal evidence for communication. Consider the results of an experiment in which one experimenter held the test animal just outside the door of the release cage while another experimenter stood about 1 yard (1 m) away and performed one of the following sets of actions: (1) He glanced at the chimpanzee, turned to face the direction in which food had previously been hidden [the food was not covered up completely but left partially visible so that it could be spotted once the animals got within about 5 yards (4.5 m)] and walked 10 paces holding his hands behind his back. Then he stopped, leaned forward as if orienting "out there," and then turned and walked back to his original position. This was the Walking condition. (2) He glanced at the chimpanzee, then turned to face in the direction of food, pointed an arm toward the food several times, glanced again at chimpanzee and back toward the food, and then turned to face in his original direction (Pointing condition). (3) He first walked as in the walking condition and then pointed as in the pointing condition – to give a composite cue. (4) He neither walked nor pointed but instead glanced at the chimpanzee and then turned slowly in place in a complete circle, orienting all around the field and giving no special attention to any one direction, as if uncertain as to where the food was located. This is of course a control condition which would be expected to lead to random travel with respect to food – unless the animals utilized cues of which we were unaware. These four conditions were administered in random balanced orders to each of the four test animals.

One of the four test animals (Bandit) stopped running after a few days, probably because under these conditions where he did not know the precise location of the food, the control animals picked up the cue of direction from him, raced ahead of him, searched the field, and almost invariably found the food and left him none. The results for the other three test animals (10 trials per condition per test animal) are shown in Fig. 13. It may be seen that the test animals' travel direction in the control condition was completely random with respect to the food, that either walking, manual pointing, or a combination of these cues is a very effective (social) cue of the direction of food, and that there is no difference in their relative effectiveness.

Another experiment was conducted in which two food piles were hidden at random in the field and varied in size. The (human) cue giver gave a walking-plus-pointing cue in *each* of these directions, successively (starting at random with the left or right and the large or small food pile). However, he walked 5

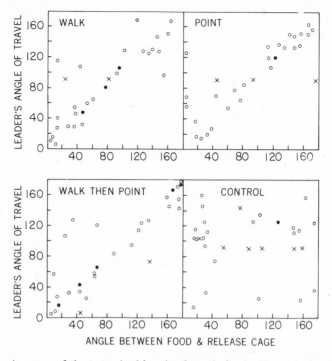

FIG. 13.   Accuracy of the test animals' angle of travel after having received various social cues from a human informant. Each point shows the results of a single trial. Filled circles are trials on which the food was found in less than 30 sec; X's are trials in which the test animal travelled less than 3 m in the first 30 sec.

paces in the direction of the small food pile and 15 paces in the direction of the large food pile. It should be emphasized that neither the test animal nor the controls actually saw the food. Following the administering of these cues, the chimpanzee was returned to the release cage and the experimenters left the scene as usual. On the basis of earlier experiments, in which we had observed that test animals going in the direction of food walked farther and faster before stopping to wait for followers if they had seen a large vs a small pile of food, we predicted that the animals should almost immediately discriminate between these two cues.

Each of the four test animals received 10 trials. On 32 of these 40 trials, the group majority first searched in whichever direction we had earlier walked the farthest; and the last 4 sessions (16 trials) were errorless. Moreover, the test animals remembered *both* cues, for after the first pile of food was found they did not just sit around or return to the release cage (as in the last experiment described), but commenced to search the other half of the field. In this experiment as in the last one, where the test animals did not know the exact location of the food, the control animals were usually the finders. One test animal (Bido) took to reversing herself and going in the direction of the smaller food pile if she was overtaken by the control animals; and in this case the control animals continued on the originally set course and found their pile of food before Bido found hers. Since none of the animals had actually seen the food and yet all animals seemed to know where to search, it seemed clear that the test animal had gotten a social cue from us, and the control animals had gotten a social cue from the test animal.

As Figure 13 shows, on most trials the animals' travel direction was usually within 10° of a straight-line path to the goal. Some of the trials on which the test animals originally went off course, however, are perhaps the most convincing evidence of all that they actually knew the direction of the food on the basis of social cues alone. Figure 14 is based on the data of an experiment in which we varied how far we walked toward the goal before giving a pointing cue; and it shows the results of several trials in which, for reasons unknown to us, the test animal wandered after some other animal or otherwise went in the "wrong" direction initially. It may be seen from Fig. 14 that the animals' cue of direction was not any one particular object, but could seemingly be almost any object or stimulus relationship lying along a given imaginary line or region of space

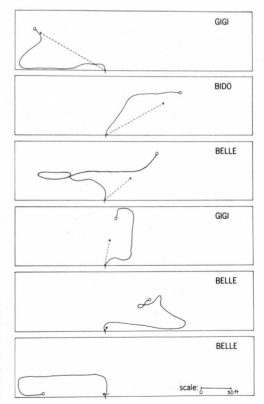

FIG. 14.   Maps showing the test animals' travel routes on some of the trials on which they initially started out at an angle much different from the "correct" one. Slashed lines show how far the experimenter had carried the test animal before giving it a manual pointing cue and then returning it to the release cage. On no trial did a test animal manually search the field until it corrected the initial move and passed the point at which it was given the cue.

pointed out by the signaller. Moreover, the animals seemed to know something about the distance of the food as well as its direction, for they did not search any point in the field except those beyond the last position occupied by the signaller.

Many authors have wondered why wild chimpanzees have not developed a rudimentary language or set of manual gestures for indicating the nature and location of distant, hidden objects. The answer seems rather obvious. Chimpanzees are largely quadrupedal animals rather than bipedal animals like man, and anyone who watches them from a height or even from the ground can already gauge the direction in which they are pointing with very good accuracy; and manual pointing is probably less, rather than more, accurate than bodily pointing. Its principal advantage is economy. The same is true for bodily vs. manual gestural ways of specifying the nature or relative desirability of goal objects. To equate communicative ability with propensity for the use of a gestural or vocal response system is, in my opinion, anthropocentric.

D. Planned Future Extensions of the Research

Using the term "we" in the editorial sense to refer principally to myself and others whose arms or minds I can twist, it is crystal clear where we should go next. The sorts of observations and experiments I have described in this chapter are rather like snapshots of the everyday behavior of captive chimpanzees taken with a normal camera lens; to achieve a more satisfactory "big picture" of chimpanzee behavior we must go in at least two directions in subsequent research. First we must zoom out still farther and examine problems such as group foraging strategies, social communication, and geographical orientation in conditions that increasingly approximate those in which free-ranging primates actually live. In this respect my own experiments are at best restricted, miniature models of what *might* be occurring in the field, and there is no way to know precisely how representative they are until we test the matter directly.

I am not merely arguing for field research here, and I am certainly not arguing for old-time ethology. Most current primate research that is based on such models is no more relevant than any other, for relevance lies first of all in theoretical and methodological concerns and only secondarily in the setting per se. The problem, then, is to discover how well the principles of performance that may be derived from relativelycontrolled situations actually hold up in relatively uncontrolled, or real-life, situations; and, equally important, to discover what we have thus far left out of the account. Some hard-headed learning theorists will no doubt see this sort of work as a flight from the laboratory and an abandonment of controls, but I prefer to look at it as an *expansion* of the laboratory to include more and more of the nearby surround, and a *refinement* of controls to the point where our old strong-arm methods might no longer be necessary.

Secondly, we must zoom in still closer with our seminaturalistic analyses to make more direct contact with the sorts of problems on which more hard-headed experimentalists have been working, and to discover the actual perceptual and cognitive mechanisms which underlie various modes of mapping. Is it possible, for example, that for chimpanzee, as for man, information about the nature and relative positions of objects can be picked up, integrated, and stored in either analog, picture-like, form or in digital, language-like, form, and that these forms of representation are interchangable and reversible in the sense that cognitive maps can be reconstructed from language-like descriptions, and vice versa (cf. Attneave, 1974)? Let me briefly describe a project that David Premack and I are currently undertaking to get at this question.

In the course of the studies described in the last section of this chapter, we discovered by accident that if the chimpanzees had access to even a ¼-inch (.6-cm) peephole in the wall of the release cage and saw the experimenter hiding the goal object in the field, or even giving another animal a pointing cue of location, they could respond almost as effectively as an animal who was carried out into the field and directly shown the nature and location of the goal object. What is the difference between such a monocular view of the world from a fixed position and looking at a color movie or videotape or a photographic slide or a line drawing of the same scene through the same peephole? In principle it would not be difficult — at least with human subjects, and most likely with chimpanzees (cf. Davenport & Rogers, 1971) — to substitute in place of the real world out there a movie or a picture that would, psychologically speaking, contain all of the same visual information. In other words, "When it is carefully arranged that [a] picture is seen through an aperture so that the frame is invisible, the head is motionless, and only one eye is used, *the resulting perception may lose its representational character*" (J. J. Gibson, cited by Hagen, 1974) and be indistinguishable from the actual scene.

The question of what visual information a chimpanzee obtains from a direct look at the real world containing trees, bananas, hiding places, and his companions in the flesh can, then, be analyzed by comparing his behavior after a direct look with his behavior after he has seen a picture, map, or other still more symbolic representation of that same scene. Or, conversely, we may by the same procedures analyze the limits of the animals' ability for using pictures, maps, or other visual material as representations of the real world, or of their ability to use these various types of representations interchangably.

It is not our intention to mechanically run through all the parameters along which perception of pictures or abstract symbols (e.g., those used in Premack's studies of language employing visual token objects) may be distinguished from direct vision (Hagen, 1974), but rather to focus attention on parameters that are of particular interest to problems of everyday foraging behavior, space perception, and social communication. For example, varying the vantage point from which a picture is taken and rendering a picture into a progressively more cartoon-like abstractions will permit us to assess a chimpanzee's ability to use pictures as actual representations, or maps, of his familiar environment; varying the rate of playback of a cue movie will permit us to assess whether the apparent velocity of a leader's locomotion is a sufficient cue of the incentive value of the goal; and playing a cue movie backward or with its various scenes presented in scrambled rather than normal order will permit us to determine whether the "syntax" as well as specific "elements" of a leader's behavior function as effective cues.

III. GENERAL CONCLUSIONS

In formulating this chapter and the research that it describes, I have tried to focus attention on a particular class of phenomena in a particular class of animal and to let theoretical problems and textbook topics of psychology emerge as they will from the analysis. Why do chimpanzees move about as they do? Where will they go next? How is it possible for them to do so? If it were indeed possible to answer these simple-minded questions in full detail, especially in natural or everyday conditions as opposed to artificial or highly restricted conditions, we would have solved most of the problems of chimpanzee psychobiology.

The ultimate biological answer to these questions no doubt lies in the fact that the resources necessary for the survival and reproduction of the genotype are not all found in the same locus. Thus: (1) Those chimpanzees who are to survive and reproduce must distribute themselves in space and locomote from one place to the next over time in accordance with the spatiotemporal distribution of the resources and their own metabolic and other general biological requirements. (2) To succeed in this endeavor, they must perforce have some mechanisms for so doing. (3) These mechanisms are different from those of other organisms that have specialized in exploiting different niches and have been subjected to different selection pressures and learning experiences.

The concept of cognitive mapping is an attempt to answer the third of our naive questions, namely *how* animals are capable of getting around as they do. It is not, of course, a complete answer. It merely points to one rather specialized mechanism (namely the ability to perceive the nature and relative positions of objects, including oneself) and there are obviously other specialized mechanisms (for example, the chimpanzee's sensory and locomotor equipment) that are also necessary. How these various mechanisms are coordinated with each other is one of the basic problems in neurophysiology.

Thoroughgoing behaviorists might object that we are not warranted in positing any process internal to animals, let alone assuming that this process is a cause of behavior, when all that we have demonstrated is that behavior is organized with respect to objects in the environment. In other words, "cognition *is* the organization of behavior per se, rather than some other organized process that determines the behavioral one" (Rachlin, in press).

This argument seems to me to dodge or displace the problem rather than to solve it. If the organization of a normal chimpanzee's behavior is not predictable solely from our observation of inanimate objects, or of other species of animals, or even of other chimpanzees with dissimilar experiences that are subjected to the same immediate environmental variables, and if moreover this behavioral organization is also presumably dependent upon the chimpanzee having his eyes open and his brain left reasonably intact and unfogged, then obviously the *source* of organization is not entirely outside the skin. There must be something going on under the skin, either in the chimpanzee or in the human observer or (more likely) in both.

The question is the following: What is going on in the animal and where? Gibson (1966) might claim that what is going on is nothing like the real constructing of maps and that to locate this process in the deep, dark recesses of the brain (e.g., Jerison, 1973; O'Keefe & Nadel, 1978) is to go too far inside the skin. All that is required is that the animal directly perceive the structure of events — and this in turn requires no central integration or elaboration or reworking of the input but only the ability to pick up and respond to higher order peripheral stimulation.

I am an ardent admirer of Gibson, and I don't doubt that his theory could explain much of the data cited in this chapter; but when he starts talking about how animals can "see" things that are hidden from sight or even located in a different room he loses me. Direct perception of structure might be able to account for "correct" performance and veridical perception under normal circumstances where the animal has been exposed to continuous transformations of the visual input and to the whole geographical area in question, but Gibson's theory leaves me wondering why *all* performance isn't correct, and why certain very systematic types of errors and nonveridical perceptions occur (see also Hochberg, 1975). There is no solvable problem for which all of the necessary information has not been available out there (somehow and somewhere) for many years. To say, "All the animal has to do is to pick up the available information," explains nothing until we also know whether he can and does pick it up. X-ray vision (for example) would be an even simpler and more direct method of seeing hidden objects than the methods Gibson discusses; but so far as we know no species exploits it. Some species, moreover, can obviously pick up higher order information that other species might have to acquire by more indirect means. (Consider, for example, a bird that can perceive at a glance, from the air, the entire layout of an environment that a terrestrial animal might take weeks to cover.)

In a recent article, Gregory (1975) very cogently reviews the modern criteria and evidence for believing that cognitive concepts are necessary. The present chapter, (which was, incidentally, completed just the day before I received

Gregory's article), has presented almost all of the same arguments, albeit in somewhat more old-fashioned terms, and has marshaled the same sorts of evidence. However, probably the strongest single argument for the concept of cognitive mapping is parsimony. There is simply no other term that comes so close to the truth and summarizes so many aspects of behavioral and perceptual organization and does so in two words or less.

Hull (1952) tried to account for behavior in space without making any assumptions about cognitive organization, but these assumptions crept back into his theory in concepts such as stimulus generalization (cf. Guttman, 1963) and even then it took half a dozen more principles to say as much as is encompassed by the map principle. Skinner's (1969) attempt to account for how animals get around the world amounts principally to saying that they will approach those objects or areas which have in the past led to reinforcement. But except in those cases in which direct sensory information regarding the locations of "reinforcers" is available in the environment at the time of the response (for example, from olfaction or sight of a trail in the snow), it is not at all clear from Skinner's account how this is possible unless the animal knows the relative positions of objects and his own position relative to them. Such knowledge is not explained; it is assumed.

It is quite true, as Skinner says, that map concepts are useful largely for those varieties of learning problems that can be conceptualized in spatial terms. But I am hard put to think of any problem that could *not* be so conceptualized if one so chose (see, e.g., Lorenz, 1971, p. 223; Luria, 1968; Siegel & White, 1975). As Einstein (1961, p. 141) once commented, "It is characteristic of thought in physics, as in the natural sciences generally, that it attempts to make do in principle with "space-like" concepts *alone*, and to express with their aid all functional relationships having the status of laws." (Einstein was not ignoring time here; "space-like concepts" may include space-time.) The difficulty with the older spatial theories such as those of Tolman and Lewin was not that they went too far in emulating the more mature sciences, but that they did not go far enough.

If a general theory of animal behavior is possible — and Seligman and Hager (1972) and Hinde and Stevenson-Hinde (1973) notwithstanding, I believe that the time is ripe for reconsidering such a possibility — its roots will undoubtedly lie not in old-time learning theory or ethology or some reincarnation thereof but in the modernized theory of natural selection (Simpson, 1958; Alexander, 1975; Williams, 1966; Wilson, 1975; Wyers, 1976). At the same time, unless these new pretenders to general theory can actually derive and explain the full range of primate cognitive and social phenomena — and I share Campbell's (1975) opinion that at present they cannot — they are only approximations to the real article. Biologists are on the verge of moving in to shore up these gaps. If we psychologists don't lead them now, we will have to follow them a few years hence.

Just how important will concepts such as cognitive mapping be in such a general theory? In my opinion, cognitive mapping will be superseded by more molecular behavioral concepts only when the latter concepts have themselves gone cognitive or otherwise incorporated map-like principles. The description that I have given of cognitive mapping here is, for example, quite compatible with Rescorla's description, Chapter 2, of classical conditioning: The essential feature in either case is "the learning of relations among environmental events, [some of] which occur outside the organism's control"; and the essential difference is that mapping involves the set of all possible such relations, rather than a single relation (cf. Suppes, 1973, and Section I of this chapter). From a developmental point of view, cognitive mapping might in some instances be a special case of classical conditioning (i.e., a map may be built up from specific pieces of information); but from a structural point of view it is more likely that classical conditioning is a special case of cognitive mapping.

The final question remains whether cognitive concepts and the knowledge-performance distinction cannot be expected to *eventually* vanish from psychology (just as mentalistic and dualistic concepts have vanished from psysics), if only we can achieve better prediction and control of behavior. I shall not answer this question but propose a riddle. Suppose that a man, a coconut, a coconut crab, and a rock are poised on the top of a tall tree. Given the laws of behavior that pertain to all of them, we could undoubtedly predict and control close to 100% of the variance of their travel routes. Have we thereby learned all we care to know about where they are going, biologically and psychologically speaking? Is our account equally adequate for each subject? Would a similar degree of prediction and control necessarily tell us more in any other test situation — and if so, why?

ACKNOWLEDGMENTS

Preparation of this chapter was supported in part by Grant BMF 75–19748 from the National Science Foundation. I thank Palmer Midgett, who helped collect much of the data, and Everett Wyers, Marcia Johnson, Marvin Levine, and the editors of this volume, who provided helpful critical commentary. Parts of this chapter have already appeared in earlier papers (Menzel, 1969b, 1973b).

REFERENCES

Alexander, R. D. The search for a general theory of behavior. *Behavioral Science,* 1975, *20,* 77–100.

Attneave, F. How do we know? *American Psychologist,* 1974, *29,* 493–499.

Beck, B. B. Primate tool behavior. In R. H. Tuttle (Ed.), *Socioecology and psychology of primates.* The Hague: Mouton, 1975, p. 413–448.

Campbell, D. T. On the conflicts between biological and social evolution and between psychology and moral tradition. *American Psychologist, 1975, 30,* 1103–1126.

Catania, A. C. The psychologies of structure, function and development. *American Psychologist, 1973, 28,* 434–444.

Davenport, R. K., & Rogers, C. M. Differential rearing of the chimpanzee. In G. Bourne (Ed.), *The chimpanzee* (Vol. 3) Basel: Karger, 1970, p. 337–360. (a)

Davenport, R. K., & Rogers, C. M. Intermodal equivalence of stimuli in apes, *Science, 1970, 168,* 279–280. (b)

Davenport, R. K., & Rogers, C. M. Perception of photographs by apes. *Behaviour, 1971, 39,* 318–320.

Dember, W. N., & Earl, R. W. Analysis of exploratory, manipulatory and curiosity behaviors. *Psychological Review, 1957, 64,* 91–96.

Downs, R. M., & Stea, D. (Eds.), *Image and environment.* Chicago: Aldine, 1973.

Einstein, A. *Relativity.* New York: Crown, 1961.

Fouts, R. Capacities for language in great apes. In R. H. Tuttle (Ed.), *Socioecology and psychology of primates.* The Hague: Mouton, 1975, p. 371–390.

Fowler, H. Implications of sensory reinforcement. In R. Glazer (Ed.), *The nature of reinforcement.* New York: Academic Press, 1971, p. 151–195.

Gardner, R. A., & Gardner, B. T., Teaching sign language to a chimpanzee. *Science, 1969, 165,* 664–672.

Gibson, J. J. *The senses considered as perceptual systems.* New York: Houghton-Mifflin, 1966.

Gregory, R. D. Do we need cognitive concepts? In M. Gazzaniga and C. Blakemore (Eds.), *Handbook of psychobiology.* New York: Academic Press, 1975, p. 607–628.

Guthrie, E. R. *The psychology of learning.* New York: Harper & Row, 1952.

Guttman, N. Laws of behavior and facts of perception. In S. Koch (Ed.), Psychology: *A study of a science* (Vol. 5). New York: McGraw-Hill, 1963, p. 114–178.

Hagen, M. A. Picture perception: Toward a theoretical model. *Psychological Bulletin, 1974, 81,* 471–497.

Hall, K. R. L. Tool-using performances as indicators of behavioral adaptability. *Current Anthropology, 1963, 4,* 479–494.

Hull, L. L. *A behavior system.* New Haven: Yale University Press, 1952.

Hediger, H. *Studies of the psychology and behavior of captive animals in zoos and circuses.* New York: Criterion, 1955.

Hinde, R. A., & Stevenson-Hinde, J. (Eds.), *Constraints on learning: Limitations and predispositions.* New York: Academic Press, 1973.

Hochberg, J. Motion pictures, eye movements and mental maps: Perception as purposive behavior. Paper presented at the annual convention of the American Psychological Association, 1975.

Jerison, H. *Evolution of the brain and intelligence.* New York: Academic Press, 1973.

Kohler, W. *The mentality of apes.* New York: Harcourt, 1925.

Krushinskii, L. V. *Animal behavior: Its normal and abnormal development.* New York: Consultants Bureau Press, 1960.

Lorenz, K. Z. *Studies in animal and human behavior* (Vol. 2). Cambridge, Massachusetts: Harvard University Press, 1971.

Luria, A. R. *The mind of a mnemonist.* New York: Basic Books, 1968.

McGrew, W. C., Tutin, C. E. G., & Midgett, P. S. Tool use in a group of captive chimpanzees. *Zeitschrift für Tierpsychologie, 1975, 37,* 145–162.

Menzel, E. W. Patterns of responsiveness in chimpanzees reared through infancy under conditions of environmental restriction. *Psychologische Forschung, 1964, 27,* 337–365.

Menzel, E. W. Responsiveness to objects in free-ranging Japanese monkeys. *Behaviour, 1966, 26,* 130–150.

Menzel, E. W. Naturalistic and experimental approaches to primate behavior. In E. Willems and H. Raush (Eds.), *Naturalistic viewpoints in psychological research.* New York: Holt, Rinehart & Winston, 1969, p. 78–121. (a)

Menzel, E. W. Chimpanzee utilization of space and responsiveness to objects: Age differences and comparison with macaques. *Proceedings of the International Congress of Primatology,* 1969, *1,* 72–80. (b)

Menzel, E. W. Group behavior in young chimpanzees: Responsiveness to cumulative novel changes in a large outdoor enclosure. *Journal of Comparative and Physiological Psychology,* 1971, *74,* 46–51.

Menzel, E. W. Spontaneous invention of ladders in a group of young chimpanzees. *Folia Primatologica,* 1972, *17,* 87–106.

Menzel, E. W. Further observations on the use of ladders in a group of young chimpanzees. *Folia Primatologica,* 1973, *19,* 450–457. (a)

Menzel, E. W. Chimpanzee spatial memory organization. *Science,* 1973, *182,* 943–945. (b)

Menzel, E. W. A group of young chimpanzees in a one-acre field, In A. M. Schrier and F. Stollnitz (Eds.), *Behavior of nonhuman primates* (Vol. 5). New York: Academic Press, 1974, p. 83–153.

Menzel, E. W. Communication and agression in a group of young chimpanzees. In P. Pliner, L. Krames, and T. Alloway (Eds.), *Nonverbal communication of agression.* New York: Plenum, 1975, p. 103–133.

Menzel, E. W. Communication of object-locations in a group of young chimpanzees. In D. Hamburg and J. Goodall (Eds.), *Perspectives on human evolution* (Vol. 5). New York: Staples Press, (in press).

Menzel, E. W., Davenport, R. K., & Rogers, C. M. The effects of environmental restriction upon the chimpanzee's responsiveness to objects. *Journal of Comparative and Physiological Psychology,* 1963, *56,* 78–85. (a)

Menzel, E. W., Davenport, R. K., & Rogers, C. M. Effects of environmental restriction upon the chimpanzee's responsiveness in novel situations. *Journal of Comparative and Physiological Psychology,* 1963, *56,* 329–334. (b)

Menzel, E. W., Davenport, R. K., & Rogers, C. M. The development of tool using in wild-born and restriction-reared chimpanzees. *Folia Primatologica,* 1970, *12,* 273–283.

Miller, G. A., Galanter, E., & Primbram, K. H. *Plans and the structure of behavior.* New York: Holt, 1960.

Nissen, H. W. A field study of the chimpanzee. *Comparative Psychology Monographs,* 1931, *8,* 1–122.

O'Keefe, J., & Nadel, L. *The hippocampus as a cognitive map.* London and New York: Oxford University Press, 1978.

Pantin, C. F. A. Learning, world-models and pre-adaption. *Animal Behaviour Supplements,* 1965, *1,* 1–8.

Pylyshyn, Z. W. What the mind's eye tells the mind's brain: A critique of mental imagery. *Psychological Bulletin,* 1973, *80,* 1–24.

Premack, D. On the assessment of language competence in the chimpanzee. In A. M. Schrier and F. Stollnitz (Eds.), *Behavior of nonhuman primates* (Vol. 4). New York: Academic Press, 1971, p. 185–228.

Rachlin, H. Reinforcing and punishing thoughts. *Behavior Therapy,* (in press).

Restle, F. Discrimination of cues in mazes: A resolution of the "place vs. response" question. *Psychological Review,* 1957, *64,* 217–228.

Reynolds, V. *Budongo: An African forest and its chimpanzees.* Garden City, New York: Natural History Press, 1965.

Robinson, A. H., & Petchenik, B. B. *The nature of maps.* Chicago: University of Chicago Press, 1976.

Rosenblueth, A., Wiener, N., & Bigelow, J. Behavior, purpose and teleology. *Philosophy of Science,* 1943, *10,* 18–24.

Rumbaugh, D. Learning skills of anthropoids. In L. Rosenblum (Ed.), *Primate behavior: Developments in field and laboratory research.* New York: Academic Press, 1970, p. 2–70.

Seligman, M. E. P., & Hager, J. L. (Eds.), *Biological boundaries of learning.* New York: Appleton-Century-Crofts, 1972.

Schiller, P. Innate constituents of complex responses in primates. *Psychological Review,* 1952, *59,* 177–191.

Siegel, A. W., & White, S. H. The development of spatial representations of large-scale environments. In H. W. Reese (Ed.), *Advances in child development and behavior* (Vol. 10). New York: Academic Press, 1975, p. 10–56.

Simpson, G. G. The study of evolution: Methods and present status of theory. In A. Roe and G. G. Simpson (Eds.), *Behavior and evolution.* New Haven: Yale University Press, 1958, p. 7–26.

Skinner, B. F. *Contingencies of reinforcement.* New York: Appleton-Century-Crofts, 1969.

Suppes, P. Some problems in the philosophy of space and time. In P. Suppes (Ed.), *Space, time and geometry.* Dordrecht, Netherlands: Reidel, 1973, p. 383–401.

Teleki, G. Chimpanzee subsistence technology: Materials and skills. *Journal of Human Evolution,* 1974, *3,* 575–594.

Tinbergen, N. *The animal in its world* (Vol. 1). Cambridge, Massachusetts: Harvard University Press, 1972.

Tinklepaugh, O. L. Multiple delayed reaction with chimpanzees and monkeys. *Journal of Comparative Psychology,* 1932, *13,* 207–243.

Tolman, E. C. *Purposive behavior in animals and men.* New York: Appleton-Century-Crofts, 1932.

Tolman, E. C. *Behavior and psychological man.* Berkeley: University of California Press, 1951.

Van Lawick-Goodall, J. The behaviour of free-living chimpanzees in the Gombe Stream Reserve. *Animal Behaviour Monographs,* 1968, *1,* 161–311.

Van Lawick-Goodall, J. Tool-using in primates and other vertebrates. In D. Lehrman, R. A. Hinde, and E. Shaw (Eds.), *Advances in the study of behavior* (Vol. 3). New York: Academic Press, 1970, p. 195–249.

Van Lawick-Goodall, J. *In the shadow of man.* Boston: Houghton-Mifflin, 1971.

Van Lawick-Goodall, J. Cultural elements in a chimpanzee community. In E. W. Menzel (Ed.), *Symposia of the Fourth International Congress of Primatology* (Vol. 1). Basel: Karger, 1973, p. 144–184.

Williams, G. C. *Adaptation and natural selection.* Princeton, New Jersey: Princeton University Press, 1966.

Wilson, E. O. *Sociobiology.* Cambridge, Massachusetts: Harvard University Press, 1975.

Woodworth, R. S. *Dynamics of behavior.* New York: Holt, 1958.

Wrangham, R. The behavioural ecology of chimpanzees in Gombe National Park, Tanzania. Ph.D. thesis, Cambridge University, 1975.

Wyers, E. J. Learning and evolution. In L. Petrinovitch and J. L. McGaugh (Eds.), *Knowing, thinking, and believing: Festschrift for Professor David Krech.* New York: Academic Press, 1976, p. 29–70.

14 On the Abstractness of Human Concepts: Why It Would be Difficult to Talk to a Pigeon

David Premack
University of Pennsylvania

"If a lion could talk we could not understand him," is one of Wittgenstein's (1953) better known aphorisms, one which he did not explicate, thus assuring it a long and richly implicational life. Men were not talking to apes in Wittgenstein's day, however, as they are now to some extent, and it is therefore of interest to ask what bearing this fact has on the aphorism. Some would insist that the chimpanzee data visibly refute the aphorism's claim, therefore, we need not trouble ourselves further with its possible meanings. I do not think, however, that the chimpanzee data at all refute the aphorism. On the contrary, when those data are added to data from other species, the combination is notably helpful in assigning a specific interpretation to the aphorism; my objective here is to clarify the interpretation and show how it will help explain the difficulties one might have in talking to a lion. I will show why it is possible to talk to apes, and why, in contrast, it would be difficult to talk to lions. Regrettably I will have to diminish the elegance of the aphorism. I will have to give up lions, a species for which we have no data and substitute pigeons, a species for which we have some data, less than we need, but far more than for lions. Hopefully, I will be forgiven for deposing the king of beasts for a mere bird.

In contrasting ape and pigeon, rather than man and lion, I depart from a tradition in which the world is coarsely divided into man vs. all other animals; we are today in a position to produce a finer division, and with it to move closer to a theory of human intelligence. Although we are not yet able to enumerate the elements of which human intelligence consists, we have made some progress toward this end. For instance, if in considering intelligence we focus only on language we will find, very likely, that no infrahuman species, chimpanzee or otherwise, can reproduce human syntax. But if we reject this rather narrow approach and instead analyze intelligence into the several capacities that it encompasses, such as semantic memory, representational capacity, causal inference, intentionality, and concept of self, we will find that the ape, though unable to reproduce human syntax, has many of the other capacities. In contrast, lesser species not only cannot reproduce human syntax but lack other capacities as well.

I. CONCEPTUAL ABSTRACTNESS

I will focus, in this chapter, on conceptual abstractness, a key aspect of intelligence helpful both in characterizing the human case and in clarifying the difficulty we would have in trying to talk to a pigeon. Much of the success we have in talking to one another comes from the abstractness of our concepts. A species whose concepts were less abstract would be insuperably more difficult to talk to, and in what follows we will see why.

How shall we define abstractness? The concept of transfer will provide both a measure and an operational definition. Transfer is not a specific condition, of course, but a contrast between two conditions — one in which an individual is trained and another in which it is tested. In training, the individual learns to respond differently to different items, for example, to turn left when shown A-A, and right when shown A-B. In the transfer condition, new items will be substituted for A and B, for example, the individual will be given C-C and C-D. If, for all possible substitutions on A and B, the individual continues to turn left when the items are like, and right when they are different, we would consider its concept of same-different to be maximally abstract. If, on the other hand, the individual responds differentially for some substitutions, but not for others, this would indicate limitations on the abstractness of its concepts.

It is not only same-different, of course, that could be used to illustrate degrees of abstractness. Consider *problem* as in problem-solving. A species could have a very limited concept of *problem*, one in which, for example, *problem* referred exclusively to unobtainable physical items, even to those unobtainable specifically on the vertical axis. Conversely, the concept could be as abstract as it is in the human adult, where the conditions that exemplify *problem* are indeterminately large, including not only inaccessible apples, but also cars that will not start, as well as intractable mathematical problems.

In illustrating abstractness, we could use decidedly less traditional examples such as jump, give, scratch, and the like — all actions in which species engage. Actions, we will agree, are not typically evaluated for their abstractness, yet it might be clarifying to see them in this light. There is reason to believe that motor action is not an equally abstract concept in all species; some species are better than others in both producing and recognizing diverse instances of an act. The considerable advantage of examining action as abstract is to show that abstractness is *not* a special property, applicable only to *certain* concepts; but a general property, applicable to *all* of a species' concepts.

Species seem to demonstrate three main forms of limitations on transfer, and consequently on abstraction. First, there appear to be species which cannot transfer to values outside the particular range on which they were originally trained. These species may be able to interpolate (i.e., transfer to new values within the training range), but they are unable to extrapolate. This is clearly a severe limitation. A species suffering from such a limitation for all possible dimensions would be a victim of training — bound to it and unable to perform beyond its immediate values.

Second, a species might escape the first constraint but prove unable to transfer to values that lie on dimensions different from training. Examples of this kind appear to be commonplace, and we will describe several later on.

Third, a species might escape both of the above constraints, and yet prove incapable of making a true same-different judgment under any transfer conditions. For instance, when given a pair of different stimuli, even though all differences were unquestionably suprathreshold, members of this species may be incapable of responding "different." Instead, the probability of their responding "different" may increase with the magnitude of the difference between the stimuli. Hence a judgment that we (and certain other primates) would treat as digital or categorical, they treat as analogue. In the limiting case, a species might suffer this constraint not only in same-different judgments, but generally, and thus be totally lacking in categories.[1]

II. GENESIS OF ABSTRACTION

The very possibility of abstraction derives from a basic property of our experience: successive experiences are related, and/or we find ways to relate them. We need only experience a set of related items to consider the possibility of constructing or finding a single item that will represent the set. For instance, after experiencing a series of visual events, human subjects represent the series by constructing another visual event, a prototype that minimizes the difference between itself and the other events.

---

[1]It is evident that these three factors alone will not account for the difference between human and animal concepts; richer principles are needed. In the human adult, probably the most impressive cases of transfer and thus of abstraction involve metaphor: a relation that is observed in one "problem space" is transferred to quite a different "problem space", sometimes with a surprising degree of illumination. That such cases could be reduced to interdimensional transfer is highly improbable; in general, the analysis of metaphor has not proceeded to a point where reductions of this kind even seem sensible. I present only the three factors here because we will be concerned with only simple cases.

Impressive laboratory examples can be found in the work of Posner, K. Smith, Rosch, and their associates. For example, in the landmark experiment by Posner and Keele (1968), subjects were first shown grids with varying amount of fill, then presented with three kinds of stimuli: grids they had seen before, grids they had not seen before, and grids which, while new, minimized the difference between themselves and the grids actually seen. The first and last sets of grids were best recognized. Although the representative or prototype grids had never actually been seen, they were judged to be as familiar as those that had been seen, and like them were recognized in the shortest time. These results can be understood by assuming that human subjects do not simply memorize individual grids, but construct a representation analogous to a measure of central tendency — a grid representative of those that were actually seen.

Similar tests by K. Smith (1966) with pairs of letters, support a similar interpretation. Smith generated lists of letter pairs by using matrices that have one list of letters on the horizontal and a different list on the vertical. All letter pairs laying along the diagonal of the matrix were discarded, the rest of the content of the matrix was combined in a random list and read to subjects who were then asked to recall as many of the letter pairs as possible. The most common error was the so-called grammatical intrusion — letter pairs from the diagonal which, of course, belonged to the matrix, but which the subjects had never heard. One way in which to explain this outcome is to assume that subjects induce the structure underlying the list, memorize the content of the vertical and horizontal lists, and generate their output on the basis of the grammar $S \rightarrow V + H$; that is, any member of the vertical (or first position) can go with any member of the horizontal (or second position).

Recently, Rosch (1973) presented evidence that natural categories such as furniture, dogs, fruit, and the like are not defined by criterial features, but have an internal structure based on a prototypic member, maximally representative of the class, and from which other members deviate more or less. The relation between Rosch's work and that by Posner, Smith, and their associates is evident.

III. ABSTRACTION IN ANIMALS

The events for which a particular species will construct abstractions must depend on both its perceptual and conative predilections: insectivores will not attend to speech, while children are unlikely to attend to brightness gradients enveloping forest rocks. Despite profound differences in the nature of the events that concern different species, all species may connect *relatable* experiences and construct abstractions for the resulting set.

The kinds of devices needed to construct abstractions are usually thought to be of two classes. Visual or sensory events such as grids, furniture, vegetables, etc., could be represented by visual or sensory prototypes. Speech could not be represented in this way, but would require rules, a simple example was found in the grammatical rule proposed for the results of the Smith experiment. Although prototypes could not serve universally, the converse is not true; in principle, rules could be used to generate both pictures and sentences.[2]

Suppose a forest animal encounters a series of brightness discriminations in the form of natural objects, all of which are darker on one side than the other. The objects and the light enveloping them both vary widely, yet in every case it is on the darker side that the animal finds its prey. On every return visit, the animal can find its prey by having memorized the correct brightness associated with each object; alternatively, it can deal with the whole series by learning to approach the darker side of every object. Although we are inclined to reserve abstraction for more complex relations, *darker than* and other comparably simple relations are already abstractions, as the transfer measure will show. Animals that have learned to approach the darker side can find insects not only in the vicinity of objects they have already explored but in the vicinity of indeterminately many others as well.

In one important sense, however, *darker than* and other such relations differ from speech rules and prototypes. Both a speech rule and a prototype are forms of abstraction that rely on many exemplars: an individual is not likely to induce even the simple rule, $S \rightarrow V + H$, on the basis of one letter pair, or to construct the category furniture after experiencing, say, a chair. However, one could learn to approach the darker side of an object on the basis of one exemplar.

Another way of making the same distinction is to observe that whereas rules or prototypes are induced, relations such as *darker than* are not induced but are merely used. Relational concepts such as *darker than, larger than*, etc., as well as absolute concepts such as *red, round, vertical*, etc., are primitives, the elements that species use in solving problems. For instance, in learning which concepts an experimenter has arbitrarily designated as correct, the individual may test the hypothesis that it is the darker one, the vertical one, the one with the red dot, etc. These hypotheses do not generate *darker than, red*, and *vertical* but presuppose them as primitive elements. The hypotheses require these elements in order to be formulated in the first place. *Darker than, red, vertical*, and the like are the building blocks from which associations are formed, rules are induced, and prototypes constructed.

Many of us can recall that the question of relational learning in animals originated in the transposition experiments. Animals trained to choose grey when given grey and white, subsequently chose black when given grey and black;

---

[2]The necessity to represent speech with rules presents an interesting paradox, (e.g., Fodor, 1975). A child induces the rules underlying the structure of the speech he experiences. But the rules the child induces are themselves linguistic. How does a child who does not yet know language induce rules that are linguistic? Fodor's answer that one must know (mental) language in order to learn (public) language is not one we need pursue here.

Köhler (1929) explained this by maintaining that the animals were responding on the basis of "darker than." Spence (1937) rejected this explanation, maintaining that it was unnecessary to grant the animals a capacity for relations, and that the results could be derived from his absolute theory of discrimination learning. All of this is well known, and I return to it because, as in most controversies, the two positions ended up being mutually exclusive – either the animal learns relations or it learns absolute values. Logically, of course, the two positions are not mutually exclusive and we will show that both are correct. Vertebrate species appear to form associations on both levels, presumably more or less concurrently. That is, on one level they learn (to use) the underlying relation, and on another, to use the actual stimulus values in which the relation was experienced. As we will see, species differ, not in their ability to learn to use relations, but in the weight they assign to the relational and absolute factors.

IV. MATCH-TO-SAMPLE

The tests that have been most widely used to study abstraction or relational learning in animals are match-to-sample, oddity, or their combination. In a typical matching problem the subject is presented with three items, A, the sample, and two alternatives, A and B. The subject is taught to put the like items together (the number of items is irrelevant; four alternatives could be given, with three of them like the sample, and the subject could be required to put all three with the sample). In the oddity problem the stimulus configurations are the same, only the subject is taught to put the unlike items together. In one of several composite approaches (e.g., McClure, 1975) the subject is taught both procedures at the same time, being required to put like items in one location, unlike items in another. Some species learn these first steps much faster than others. Three-year-old children may require no more than two or three trials, in contrast to pigeons, which may require hundreds of trials; but probably all vertebrate species can be taught the first step in some number of trials. The point of interest does not arise until we ask, what is it that the species has learned? Simply to put the A's and B's together, or something substantially more abstract?

The question is answered by the transfer test, by substituting new items for those used in training and then repeating the test. There is now good reason to believe that not all vertebrate species will pass, where by "pass" is meant, in the weaker case: *show savings in learning the new problem*; or, in the stronger case: *perform as accurately on the new problems as on the training ones.* Generalizing from the data available, incomplete as they are, there is little reason to believe that, except for the dolphin, any nonprimate will pass.

Although the pigeon literature on generalized match-to-sample is uniformly negative (see Cumming & Berryman, 1965, and Farthing & Opuda, 1974, for recent summaries), there are three notable exceptions based on modifications of the standard paradigm, and I will examine them here.

1. Zentall and Hogan.   A paradigm recently introduced by Zentall and Hogan (1974) is recommended as showing abstract concept learning in pigeons, and while I think it does not, the paradigm does demonstrate a kind of transfer that is puzzling. In the first of two steps some pigeons were trained to peck a key that matched the sample in hue, and others to peck one that did not match the sample (oddity). Then all the birds were shown new colors, and were trained either to match or mismatch (oddity) the colors. For half the birds, the second task was the same as the first (matching after matching, or oddity after oddity), whereas for the other half, the second problem was different from the first (matching after oddity, or oddity after matching). They found that the non-shifted group, in which the second problem was of the same kind as the first, did better than the shifted group. They repeated the study, adding a change in dimension to the paradigm shift; birds were trained (on either matching or oddity) on brightness values, and then changed to color, some with and some without a shift in paradigm. Here too they found that the non-shifted groups did better than the shifted group. In both cases they interpreted this to mean the birds are capable of "learning the concepts of same and/or different." (Zentall & Hogan, 1974.)

At least two points are incompatible with this interpretation. First, the birds showed no savings in the learning of the second problem. For instance, birds taught to match red and red (and green and green) showed no savings when required to match yellow and yellow (and blue and blue). Similarly, birds taught to mismatch red and green showed no savings when required to mismatch yellow and blue. Given the failure to show intradimensional savings, it is no surprise that the birds also failed to show interdimensional savings, that is, after being taught to match (or mismatch) brightness to show savings when required to match (or mismatch) hue.

But how shall we explain the transfer data that the writers do report? The difference they find does not arise from an advantage to the nonshifted birds, but from a disadvantage to the shifted ones. That is, a bird shifted to a problem like the original one does no better on the second one than on the first; it is only that a bird shifted to a problem different from the original one does worse on the second one than on the first. There is no facilitation, therefore, as there is when a concept is abstract and the subject can recognize the concept even though it is instanced by new values. Instead, there is inhibition and an inhibition that is the more surprising because it apparently occurs on an interdimensional basis. For instance, birds shifted from oddity on brightness to matching on color — an interdimensional change — appear to show almost as much disadvantage as birds shifted from oddity on color to matching on color — an intradimensional change.[3]

If data of this kind were reported for primates we would interpret them as evidence for the abstractness of the underlying concepts, but we cannot make the same interpretation in the case of the pigeon, for it would be incompatible with the rest of the pigeon data. Surely if the interdimensional inhibition indicated an abstract concept of same and different, the birds would at least show transfer from one matching problem to another or from one oddity problem to another. Since they do not, I suspect the inhibition they show when transferred from oddity to matching needs to be interpreted in a different fashion — one that does not attribute abstract concepts of same/different to the bird.

   2. Honig.   In an extensive series of studies reported in 1965 Honig trained pigeons to peck one key when the colors matched (A-A), and a different key when they did not (A-B). He then gave the birds an unusual generalization test, using differences between pairs of hues, rather than individual hues as the generalization scale. In one test, the pairs of hues were made up of those used in training, while in the second test the hues lay between those used in training. The results were the same. When tested on differences varying from zero to 70 mu, the birds showed generalization for the dimension of difference in hue, pecking the so-called identity key most when the stimuli were identical and progressively less as the difference in hue increased. Indeed, they pecked the identity key least when the hue difference was maximum, 70 mu, a difference greater than the 40 mu Honig had used in training.

   What did the birds do when tested on differences made up of hues that lay outside the training range? Unfortunately, tests for this case are incomplete, but the few that are available suggest failure of an interesting kind. When birds trained on the range 560–600 mu were presented differences made up from stimuli in the range 590–630 mu, they ". . .demonstrated a consistent preference for the values closer to the original training range. . .this result overrode any transfer. . . ." (Honig, 1965). In other words, when tested on differences made up of values outside the training range, they responded not to the difference as much as to the absolute values.

   On the other hand, when the birds were tested on pairs of *like* stimuli from the new range 590–630 mu, they responded correctly, pecking the identity

[3]The comparison between the intra-and inter-dimensional effect is not as easily extracted from the data as one would like, nor is it an entirely legitimate comparison for the difference was not treated as a variable in either experiment. Far more disturbing is the suggestion that the whole paradigm shift effect is owed to one group, viz., the group shifted from oddity to matching. The curves given suggest that three of the four groups perform at about the same level, and that only the oddity-matching group performs below this level.

key. Thus they could be said to have failed the transfer test on unlike pairs, while passing it on like pairs.

These data can be explained by considering that the pigeon does not form associations exclusively on either a relational or absolute basis, but forms them on both levels more or less concurrently. However, to show that the bird forms associations on both levels requires special tests, one of which is to put the two levels of learning into opposition, and this is exactly what has been done, however inadvertently, in the test above.

Whenever the bird is given pairs of *unlike* values its tendency to respond on a relational basis will be opposed by its tendency to respond on an absolute basis. The relational factor requires that the bird peck the nonidentity key, the absolute factor that it peck the key with the hue that is most like the one it has been trained to peck. This competition will not arise if the hues composing the pair are ones on which the bird has already been trained, for then its tendency to peck both will be about equally strong. But when, as in a transfer test, the hues are new, the tendency to peck both need not be equally strong. If one hue is closer to a training hue than the other, the bird will be more inclined to peck it, and this differential tendency to respond to a particular hue will compete with the relational factor. What the bird does will depend on which factor is stronger. If the absolute factor is stronger, the bird will not respond on a relational basis but will simply peck the key with the hue most like those it has been trained to peck — apparently the case with Honig's pigeons.

This problem did not arise when the bird was given pairs of unlike stimuli on which it had been trained to respond equally (i.e., pairs of old stimuli), and, of course, it could not arise when it was given pairs of *like* stimuli (when the stimuli are the same, the bird cannot have a differential tendency to respond to one or the other). Thus in the case of like pairs, no absolute factor can interfere with the relational one and, provided the organism has actually formed associations on a relational level, it should pass transfer tests no matter how removed the transfer stimuli may be from the training ones.

This is quite what the birds in Honig's study did, succeeding on like pairs, failing on unlike ones. Moreover, their failure on the unlike pairs also indicates how relatively weak the relational learning was compared with the absolute. As we will see, this weight appears to differ phylogenetically, the relative factor being stronger in primates.

Having trained pigeons to respond differentially to pairs of like and unlike hues, Honig raised the important question, How would the birds respond to pairs of like and unlike brightnesses? In a properly executed test of this kind there could be no similarity between the hues and brightnesses; therefore, if a species passed a test of this kind we could attribute to it an abstract concept of same-different. It is therefore an important question.

Did the birds pass the transfer test? Unfortunately, in many of the test cases no answer was possible, for rates of responding fell to an unreliably low level, making judgment in these cases impossible. However, for those cases where a judgment could be made, the birds responded correctly to the pairs of like brightnesses but incorrectly to the pairs of unlike ones. By and large they over-responded to the identity key, in effect treating pairs of unlike brightnesses as pairs of like ones.

Perhaps the birds' performance can be understood on these grounds. The transfer test was actually not the first time the birds had confronted pairs of like brightnesses. Honig tells us that in this long series of tests all hues were equated for brightness from the very beginning. Therefore, when the birds were reinforced for pecking the identity key in the presence of like hues, they were necessarily also reinforced for responding in the presence of like brightnesses. It is true that when they responded to the nonidentity key they were also reinforced for responding in the presence of like brightnesses. Is it possible that the birds used both hue and brightness when members of both pairs were alike, but only hue when the members of both pairs were not alike? Unfortunately we do not really know what use of brightness the birds made throughout the series concerned with hue. But, in any case, they did not pass the brightness series. Moreover, I see nothing in their previous training that should have prevented them from responding correctly to the pairs of unlike brightnesses. On the one hand, the birds' success on pairs of like brightnesses could be attributed to previous training – and does not require invoking an abstract concept of same-different – and on the other, if they had such a concept they should not then have failed on pairs of unlike brightnesses.

These results suggest that unlike the primate, the behavior of the pigeon is preponderantly controlled by absolute rather than relational factors, and that it does not always transfer concepts from one dimension to another. While pigeons fail to transfer hue to brightness, the chimpanzee Sarah, trained to apply the quantifiers "all," "none," "one," "several," to sets of items varying only in *shape*, correctly applied the quantifiers to sets varying in *color* in one case and *size* in another (Premack, 1971, 1976). "All," "none," "one," "several," were, to that extent at least, abstract words in the ape even as they are in man, applicable not only to the training dimension but to other dimensions as well.

3. Urcuioli and Nevin. Recent studies by Urcuioli and Nevin (1975), and by Urcuioli (1977) purport to show transfer of matching and oddity in the pigeon. These authors argue that the pigeon fails transfer tests on the standard matching paradigm because when trained with that paradigm the bird may learn "to peck only the matching alternative" and not learn "not to peck" the nonmatching one. They, therefore, separated the two tasks, training the birds to peck a lighted side key when it matched the sample key in hue, and not to peck for a criterion duration when the two keys did not match. In a second procedure, the training rule was reversed, and the birds were taught to peck when the keys did not match, and not to peck when they did.

In the transfer test following the first procedure (peck when the keys match) the birds responded at the same latency to the new matching cases as to the training ones. But they did not suppress responding to the nonmatching cases in the same degree as they did to the training cases. Instead, they showed generalization, suppressing most successfully when the difference between hues was large, least successfully when it was small. Thus, although they responded categorically to the new instances of same, they did not treat the new instances of different in this manner. That is, they did not treat the pairs of hues as being same or different, but responded to degrees of difference, suppressing more for larger differences than for smaller ones.

The birds' success in responding categorically to the new matching cases must be viewed with reservation. First, data for the birds' initial responses to the new cases are not reported; only data averaged over the session are reported, leaving open the possibility of learning over the course of the session. Second, and more important, the birds' prepotent disposition in this situation was to peck — as usual, all pretraining was devoted to pecking — rather than to suppress pecking and, strictly speaking, it was not shown that the disposition to peck was well controlled by the relation between hues or any other stimuli. Suppose, that if given pairs of achromatic stimuli, for example, two blacks or two whites, they had responded as quickly as they did to the chromatic pairs. Should we then conclude that the birds' responding was controlled by an abstract concept of same? This conclusion would be incompatible with other pigeon data (e.g., Farthing and Opuda, 1974; Honig, 1965); an alternative conclusion would be that pecking (in contrast to not-pecking) was not well controlled by any stimulus.

This interpretation is given some support by the results for the second procedure, where the training rule was reversed and the birds were taught "to peck" non-matching hues, and "not to peck" matching ones. In the transfer test following this procedure, the birds no longer showed generalization on the color difference, but responded categorically, pecking new non-matching pairs as quickly as old ones. However, they now failed on the new matching cases; they did not suppress responding to the new matching cases as well as they did to the old ones. The results from the two procedures are therefore inconsistent and give different pictures of the birds' ability to deal with same-different. In the first procedure, the birds responded categorically to same but in an analogue fashion to different; whereas in the second procedure they responded categorically to different but in a more or less analogue fashion to same. The explanation for this inconsistency would appear to lie in the response measure.

With pecking as a measure, the birds were totally successful, treating all new cases — whether of same or different — like old ones; but with not-pecking as the measure they were decidedly less successful, showing generalization (rather than categorical responding) on difference in one case, and partial failure to suppress to the new cases of same in another. Although go no-go discrimination

may be recommended on some grounds, it appears to have the drawback of providing two response measures of unequal sensitivity, for example, one measure
suggesting that pigeons treat hue-difference in an analogue fashion, the other
measure that they treat it categorically. In requiring differential responding
rather than mixing responding with no responding, the Honig procedure avoids
this problem.

The logic of the argument that led Urcuioli and Nevin to use a go no-go discrimination in the first place is not entirely clear. Does transfer in match-to-
sample really require that the bird learn both to peck like hues and not to peck
unlike ones? Suppose the bird learned only to peck like hues. If this disposition
were stronger than the one to peck unlike hues, this alone should assure successful transfer. Moreover, the standard match-to-sample paradigm does provide
negative information: pecks to the non-matching alternative are not rewarded,
and this should serve to weaken the disposition.

The bird's failure to show transfer on standard matching is better explained,
I think, by the account given earlier. In a standard matching paradigm the
absolute and relational factors are pitted against one another and the relational
factor is obscured. The two factors are not opposed in either the Urcuioli-Nevin
procedure or in the Honig procedure, and in both cases we obtain at least some
evidence of relational learning in the bird.

Notice that in both the Honig and Urcuioli-Nevin procedures the birds do not
give evidence for a categorical concept of same and different such as we find in
both people and chimpanzees. Instead, the birds gradually shifted – as the
difference between the hues increased – from the identity to the non-identity
key, the change being continuous rather than categorical. I would expect
humans and apes to show a discontinuous change, judging the pairs of stimuli
to be either same or different, not more or less different, and I have depicted
this supposed difference between the species in Fig. 1, superimposing a curve
for same-different judgments on the generalization gradient produced by the
birds in Honig's experiments. Of course, we do not know how either people
or apes would actually respond if trained as the birds were. It seems quite
possible that their reaction time for the judgment of difference would vary with
the magnitude of the difference; but it does not seem likely that, even if trained
like pigeons, they would treat same-different as an analogue distinction. While
we do not know how people would respond to the pigeon procedure, we do
know this much. In the case of people and apes there is no difficulty in finding
procedures that give rise to categorical same-different judgments; so far we are
unable to find any such procedure for the bird.

There is a second reason for doubting the same-different character of the
pigeon's differential response to A-A versus A-B. If children and chimpanzees
are not first taught to use the pieces of plastic as names for objects and/or
actions, they seldom if ever learn to use them as names for "same" and "different" (Woodruff & Premack, unpublished data). This fact, of considerable inter-

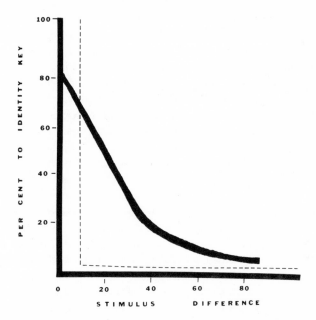

FIG. 1.   A schematic contrast between the pigeon's analogue response to stimulus difference (based on Honig, 1965) and digital response found in man and ape.

est in its own right, further differentiates the higher primate from the pigeon; for the pigeon learns to respond differentially to A-A versus A-B without first learning to peck keys that have been differentially associated with either objects or actions.

The impression that same-different judgments are more demanding than either matching or oddity is supported by other evidence. First, while children and chimpanzees do not acquire "same-different" without pretraining of the kind described above, they acquire generalized match-to-sample or oddity directly, without pretraining on other semantic functions. Moreover, the difference is not that between having to learn two judgments in the case of "same" and "different" versus only one in the case of either matching or oddity, for the procedure in which matching and oddity are combined (e.g., McClure, 1975) has no more preconditions than either matching or oddity alone. Second, when judgments are difficult, an animal may succeed with match-to-sample but fail with same-different. For instance, numerosity judgments are more demanding for chimpanzees than most other kinds of judgments (e.g., Premack, 1976), and Sarah was appreciably better at matching numerosities than at making same-different judgments about them (Woodruff, Kennel, & Premack, unpublished data). Perhaps the difference can be understood by considering that in making a same-different judgment one must first match, or mismatch, perceptually if not actually, and then comment on the outcome, saying either "same" or "different," so that the latter adds at least one step to the former.

The bird's failure to treat same-different as a categorical distinction suggests that it might fail in a similar fashion with the human distinction between colored and not colored (chromatic and achromatic). That an individual has the concept of a dimension such as *color* is not shown either by the fact that it generalizes on the dimension, such as the pigeon does on hue, or responds discriminatively to values of the dimension, such as the pigeon also does. Responding discriminatively to values on a dimension shows only that the subject might be taught something roughly comparable to labels for the values (e.g., "red," "green," etc.), but not that it could be taught a name for the dimension itself (e.g., "color," "brightness," etc.).

Perhaps the simplest way to show that the pigeon does not have the human concept of color would be to train it to peck the left key in the presence of certain chromatic values and right key in the presence of certain achromatic ones. To say that the bird makes the human distinction, in effect, "knows what kind of thing a color is" — and therefore accepts blue, red or green as instances of color no less than the yellow on which it was trained — requires that the bird peck the left key to all chromatic values and the right key to all achromatic ones. But will the bird respond in the categorical manner required by the human distinction between colored and not colored? Or will it simply generate gradients around the training stimuli?

The same point could be expanded upon by a slightly different test. After training the bird in the manner described we could offer not only the left and right keys used in training but an array of keys, several on each side of the original ones. Subjects with an abstract concept of color would seem likely to treat the chromatic and achromatic values as being mutually exclusive, exhibiting the categorical nature of the distinction by selecting only the left-most key for all chromatic values, only the right-most for all achromatic ones. In contrast, an individual that did not have an abstract concept of color would distribute its responses over all the keys, perhaps in a manner described by a gradient with three peaks: one centered about the chromatic training values; another about the achromatic training values; and a third, more or less central peak, for the values that did not fall on either generalization gradient.

V. ABSOLUTE VERSUS RELATIONAL LEARNING

The assumption that in pigeons the absolute factor is stronger than the relational one will explain the birds' consistent failure on generalized match-to-sample. After being trained to select, for example, red when the sample is red and the alternatives are red and green, and green when the sample is green and the alternatives are green and red, birds are tested on new values, as by being given a

X_1 X_2 X_N A_1 A_2 A_3 B_3 B_2 B_1

Training   Stimuli

FIG. 2. The stimulus arrangements needed to reduce interference from the absolute factor and thus show learning for the relational factor. The pairs A_1-B_1, A_2-B_2, etc., are ideal alternatives, being equally distant from the training stimuli. The pairs X_1-X_N are more or less satisfactory, since they are distant from the training stimuli. See text.

yellow sample along with red and yellow alternatives. When tested in this fashion individual birds either perform at chance, or more often, select the old stimulus values, red and green in the present example.

The transfer test puts the absolute and relational factors into opposition, for though the bird may have learned to peck the matching alternative, it will at the same time have learned to peck red and green, the hues used in training. Moreover, its tendency to peck these values will be maximal just before the transfer test. In the early part of training the bird will err and go unrewarded, but during the terminal part of training it will rarely make a mistake, and thus will be repeatedly fed for pecking red and green. Hence, it will come to the transfer test with its tendency to peck the training hues at maximum strength.

In the transfer test with, say, yellow as the sample and yellow and red as alternatives, the relational factor will require that it peck yellow, the absolute factor that it peck red. If the factors are about equally strong, the bird will respond at chance; if the absolute factor is stronger, the bird will peck red. Only if the relational factor is stronger than the absolute one will the bird pass the transfer test. Pigeons consistently fail, in contrast to children and apes, who consistently pass transfer tests of this kind. I conclude that pigeons and primates differ in the weight they assign the two factors; the primate assigning greater weight to the relational factor, the pigeon to the absolute factor.

A simple test of this account can be made by modifying the transfer test in a way that would reduce the strength of the absolute factor. For instance, after training on red and green, do not pit yellow, the new value, against red, the old value; rather present two new colors at the same time. With yellow as the sample, and yellow and blue as alternatives, the bird should have either no tendency to peck these new hues or an equal tendency, and if so there should be no interference with the tendency to peck the matching alternative. In general, we must use alternatives for which the bird's tendency to respond is about equal. We can realize this objective in either of two ways: elegantly, by using as alternatives pairs of stimuli that are equally distant from the training ones, for example, the pairs A_1-B_1, A_2-B_2, etc. (see Figure 2); or somewhat less elegantly by using pairs of stimuli, all of which are distant from the training ones, for example, the pairs X_1-X_2, etc.

Of course, opposing the relational and absolute factors is not the only way to demonstrate the two levels of learning. In fact, it is not a universally applicable procedure, but one that depends on the special set of circumstances that we have discussed, viz., that the absolute factor be stronger than the relational one. Although pigeons apparently come naturally to this special state of affairs, higher primates do not, and therefore if we had no other procedure for demonstrating the two levels of learning, we might be unable to show the absolute factor in the ape or child, even as we have difficulty showing the relational factor with the bird.

1. A General Test for the Two Factors

In a more widely applicable procedure we do not pit one factor against another, but use two different measures of behavior, one that reflects the relational factor and another that reflects the absolute factor. The test can be done with any relation, not only the one used in the example, and it goes as follows. We teach a chimpanzee the name of the relation "color of," using as exemplars red and apple, yellow and banana. The animal is given the incomplete sentences "red? apple" (What is the relation between red and apple?) and "yellow? banana," along with the new word "color of," which it substitutes for the interrogative marker, forming the strings "red color of apple" and "yellow color of banana." (It is also trained in an identical fashion on the negative exemplars "red not color of banana" and "yellow not color of apple.") Choice tests are then used to establish that the desired associations have formed. For example, the animal is given the same questions as before — "red? apple," "yellow? banana," "red? banana," "yellow? apple" — with the greatly expanded alternatives consisting not only of "color of" and "not color of," but also "shape of," "not shape of," "name of" "not name of," and whatever other relevant alternatives may be in its repertoire, along with some irrelevant ones (e.g., "tomato" "brown" "horse," etc.). Consider that the animal passes the choice test, as indeed it does (Premack, 1976), making it possible to turn to the transfer test which is of major interest.

In the transfer test we give the animal these questions: "pink? tomato" (What is the relationship between pink and tomato?), "orange? tangerine," "purple? plum," while offering the same alternatives as before. The successful chimpanzee will answer all three correctly, showing that it has learned a general marker for the relation between a color and an object that instances the color. In addition, we include a second measure, specifically the latency of the animal's choice. It seems reasonable to anticipate the following outcome. Although the animal will answer correctly in all three cases, it will answer most quickly in the case of pink and tomato, least quickly in the case of purple and plum, and at an intermediate speed in the case of orange and tangerine. This order of reaction times would be predicted from the relation between the training and transfer hues. Pink is closest to red and yellow, purple the farthest, and orange intermediate.

On the one hand, the animal forms an association between the use of a particular piece of plastic and the abstract relation "color of." On the other hand, it also forms an association between the use of that piece of plastic and the specific relation between red and apple in one case, and yellow and banana in the other. The piece of plastic is thus associated with the general relation *color of*, and also with the specific instances red–apple and yellow–banana, in terms of which it experienced the abstract relation. The first level of learning makes it possible for the animal to pass the transfer test, to recognize the relation between purple and plum, orange and tangerine, etc., as instances of the general relation. But the second level of learning also enters, affecting the animal's speed of processing; cases similar to the training ones are matched or recognized faster. Percent-correct should reflect the relational factor, latency the absolute one.

2. Evidence for the Absolute Factor in the Chimpanzee

The relational factor in the primate so outweighs the absolute one that we only find evidence for the latter in special circumstances and even then it comes as a surprise. A recent outcome with four young chimpanzees illustrates this point. All four animals were trained to do match-to-sample in a laboratory setting with toys as objects. For reasons independent of the present discussion, G. Woodruff decided to test the animals outdoors, using not only toys but natural objects such as sticks, plants, and the many flowers that were then in bloom in the compound. The procedure used in the compound was the same as the one used in the laboratory, except for the change in objects. Only toys had been used in the laboratory, but in the compound toys were used on half the trials and natural objects on the other half.

All four animals failed to transfer; they consistently chose the toy whether the sample was a toy or a natural object. Differential feedback, given on all trials, did not deter their incorrect choice of toys; they persisted in this error throughout the first session. In the next session, all toys were removed and the animals were tested on natural objects alone. They immediately performed correctly at about the 85% correct level, their usual level of performance. In the third and final session, the toys were restored, being used as the sample on half the trials as in the first session, and now all four animals performed correctly, choosing both toys and natural objects on appropriate occasions, at about the 87% level (Woodruff & Premack, unpublished data).

Their initial choice of toys could not have been simply avoidance of the natural objects, based on unfamiliarity or novelty, for the natural objects were highly familiar. Indeed, while foraging in the compound all of the animals routinely ate many of the plants and flowers that were used in the test.

The exclusive choice of toys in the first session is evidence for the absolute factor, and reflects the original training. The animals had learned not only (1) to select matching objects, but also (2) to select objects with certain class properties. The original transfer tests, based exclusively on toys, gave evidence only for the relational rule, obscuring the fact that there was a second level to the learning. With the change in procedure, however, the animal was required to choose items that were not toys, putting the relational and absolute dispositions into opposition, and initially at least, the absolute factor outweighed the relational one.

This outcome may be considered the more surprising because the test was not done in the lab, where the disposition to select toys would presumably be strongest. Instead, the toys were taken to the compound (as opposed to the flowers having been taken to the laboratory), and nevertheless the animals chose toys. However, context may be no less important for the relational factor than for the absolute one. If so, the change in context would have disadvantaged both factors equally, and one would predict the same results whether the toys were taken to the compound or the flowers to the lab.

VI. ARE ABSTRACTIONS THE PRODUCT OF A BURDENED MEMORY?

When trained on match-to-sample, pigeons are often given no more than three problems before being tested for transfer, whereas monkeys may be given a hundred or more problems (e.g., Moon and Harlow, 1949). Inequities of this kind make comparing the species problematic, and of course this is not the only difference distinguishing the treatments given these species. Monkeys are almost always tested on objects, objects that differ multi-dimensionally, whereas birds are tested on two-dimensional colors or brightnesses and colors or brightnesses that differ in only one dimension. Although these differences are the coincidental by-product of the apparatus to which experimenters of different stripe are committed, they could themselves account for the differences between the species.

Nevertheless, most of the above differences are ignored, except for one — the number of problems that precede the transfer test (e.g., Premack, 1976). This difference is seized upon because it fits in with the theory that attributes abstraction to a burdened memory. The question is asked, "Why should the individual induce the matching principle in the first place, why not simply memorize the individual problems?" And a favorite answer given is that, in fact, the individual does memorize the individual problems, but abandons this approach once the number of problems becomes too great. On this view, if the individual is given only a few problems, it will not induce the matching principle, for abstraction is seen as a strategy such as semantic clustering and other such devices, adopted primarily to accommodate an overburdened memory.

Even if abstraction, semantic clustering, and the like are affected by memory load, this would not explain the genesis of these devices. Should we assume that these devices are always at hand but in a dormant status, and only called into play the first time memory is burdened? Or are these devices learned, so that if a child were perfectly sheltered, never once experiencing any memory strain, it would rely completely on rote memory, never forming classes or inducing rules?

Engaged by these questions, we gave four approximately three-year-old African-born chimpanzees, one male and three females, three match-to-sample problems in a standard format, either one sample and two alternatives or one sample and three alternatives, all items consisting of toys. After the subjects reached a criterion of from 80 to 90% correct on the three training problems, we gave them a transfer test, also using toys. All four subjects passed the transfer test, responding correctly on the first trial of each new problem, and at the 90% level on the first five trials of each of the first four transfer tests given, a level of accuracy that compares favorably with the asymptotic level on the training series (Woodruff & Premack, unpublished data). Was it necessary to have given even three problems? Probably not, we simply gave three for good measure, but, in any case, it would be difficult to maintain that three problems burdened chimpanzee memory, forcing them to adopt an abstraction strategy.

These results are reminiscent of data obtained earlier on the question of whether chimpanzees are capable of semantic clustering. To answer this question, we modified the test for the chimpanzee, using recognition rather than recall. We gave the animal nine items, then removed them, and required it to select the nine-item sample from a set of up to 18 items, a form of delayed match-to-sample. The nine items in the sample always consisted of three each of food, toys, and doll's clothing, and semantic clustering was measured by the degree to which the animal selected the items in clusters. The animal did indeed show runs of this kind, but it showed even more clustering when simply required to hand back the nine items in the sample one at a time (as a means of assuring us that it had attended to all the items in the sample) (Premack, 1976). Thus, the animal showed semantic clustering both with and without the pressure of memory, more without such pressure than with. Chimpanzees spontaneously judge the items around them to be same or different, and give evidence of these judgments by sorting, that is, by grouping together, either in time or space, those items they consider to be the same (Hays and Nissen, 1971; Premack, 1976). In the same manner, chimpanzees spontaneously learn relations and form abstractions.

Indeed, the chimpanzee almost certainly does not learn to select the matching alternative in the context of the match-to-sample training. The disposition to put like items together or to contact them in the same interval of time can be seen in the chimpanzee's daily behavior, long before it has been trained on match-to-sample. For instance, the following entries are from a log maintained by Sarah's first surrogate mother, and date from a time when Sarah was approximately 18 months old. "A visitor entered wearing a soft wool skirt; Sarah touched the skirt, looked at the visitor, then ran to the crib and felt her (similarly textured) blanket." ". . .Sarah, touching my tongue, looked at me, at her hand, and then stuck out her own tongue and touched it." (Premack, 1976). Do pigeons or other nonprimates engage in the spontaneous sorting of their environment? Are there any procedures that can teach such species the functional equivalent of those judgments that underlie sorting behavior and that in the chimpanzee are spontaneous? I think we must maintain at least tentative reservations about what training can accomplish in certain species.

VII. ACTION AND ABSTRACTION

In our limited examples, we have so far equated relational and abstract on the one hand, and absolute and concrete on the other, unduly narrowing the meaning of abstract. Abstract concepts are often relational to be sure, but the abstractness does not derive from this fact alone. Rather, a concept is abstract by merit of the fact that there are no limits on the possible realizations the concept can have.

Action is a domain which we seldom associate with abstractness, yet in this domain, too, comparisons between humans action and those of other species recall the extreme abstractness of human concepts. Consider, for example, *giving*, defined for the sake of this comparison simply as the transfer of an item from one creature to another. (I do not intend, by *giving*, the full human concept in which it is necessary to take into account the prerogative of ownership and whether prerogative is transferred along with the item, but only the purely behavioral matter of the transfer of an item from one agent to another.) In most species, even this physical relation is highly restricted. Characteristically it is confined to food and often, in addition, to caretaker and young. Some species expand on this narrow form, allowing food exchange between adults, as in the mating rituals of certain birds. But this is a minor elaboration compared to human giving.

What is distinctive about human giving is the *absence* of limitations on the possibilities; what is distinctive about pigeon giving is the *presence* of such limitations. Thus, in the human case, any agent can give anything to any other agent, including even other agents; whereas in the pigeon, only an agent that fulfills the prior specification of a caretaker can participate as a donor, and only one that fulfills the prior specification of a fledgling can participate as a recipient; moreover, food is the only item subject to transfer.

I suspect that the comparison in the case of giving is not special but representative of actions in general, both individual and social. If we were to sit by a stream, watching different species jump across, I think we would observe comparable differences. Sketches by van Lawick-Goodall (1968) of chimpanzees jumping a stream show them to land feet first and head first, as well as arms first. For man the list of jumping styles would be still longer. If we waited long enough, our patience would be rewarded by seeing someone jump across backwards. In the case of horse, dog, rabbit, etc., no matter how patient we were, I doubt we would ever observe any one of these animals jump the stream backwards. I suspect that in man, jump is as abstract a concept as is give, whereas in other species, jump and give, as indeed are all actions, are closed or bounded concepts.

Do the observable limitations in the pigeon's social behavior reflect conceptual limits or merely motivational ones? After all, pigeons may have no reason to give anything other than food. We might try to prove this motivational interpretation by showing that we could actually train the bird to respond in a manner quite unlike its normal one. For instance, we might shape adult males to give food to other adult males, or to transfer some item other than food. Yet, even if shaping of this kind were possible, it need neither disconfirm nor have any bearing on the conceptual view.

For, on the conceptual view, what counts is not what the bird can be shaped to do, but rather what items it can be taught to classify as equivalent. To answer this question we might present the bird with photographs of various exemplifications of giving, starting with those that show canonical or normal giving. Then we might show it acts of non-giving, for example, brooding, copulating, attack, nest building, and the like. Perhaps it could be taught to discriminate between the two, that is, between giving and not giving. If so, we could then introduce atypical or nonnormal instances of giving, the nonnormality lying either in the agent's participation, the items transferred, or both. If the birds could be taught not only to classify the nonnormal training cases as given, but also to show transfer in its classification, it would be clear that the limitation was not conceptual, and the motivational view would be upheld. Conversely, if the bird could not be taught to treat the noncanonical exemplars of giving the same way it treated the canonical ones — and could not despite the fact that with shaping the bird might actually be led to carry out some or all of the noncanonical cases — the motivational view could not be correct and the conceptual view would be upheld.

VIII. NATURAL CONCEPTS IN PIGEONS

Discrimination studies using photographs of natural objects have already shown that pigeons can discriminate man from nonman, water from nonwater, tree from nontree, and indeed a particular young woman from other people (Herrnstein et al., 1976; Malott et al., 1972; Siegel & Honig, 1970). Is the bird's success on these tasks not incompatible with the view we have taken here of the bird's limited capacity for abstraction? Indeed, does it not suggest that the limitations we have ascribed to the bird are based on laboratory or artificial cases? When tested on water, tree, and the like, the bird proves to have abstract classes — classes apparently as open as the corresponding human ones. It is only when tested on pairs of hues or brightnesses — laboratory cases — that the bird fails. If this were true, it would be instructive, for in the human case we do not appear to be able to draw a comparable distinction between natural and artificial. Quite possibly we may find differences in salience, even developmental differences — stages at which certain concepts can be exemplified with difficulty if at all — but the normal adult can make same-different judgments about pairs of hues as readily as he can identify instances of man or tree.

How shall we define natural objects? The attempt to find the features whose combinations will define either the bird's or our own concepts of water, tree, and the like have been unsuccessful. Those who have tried comment discouragingly (e.g., Herrnstein et al., 1976), they recommend instead an approach based on Wittgenstein's notion of "family resemblance" (Wittgenstein, 1953). Rosch's (1973) notion of prototype might also be tried although there has been no demonstration that the birds use prototypes, or that their categories have any internal structure.

The neonate pigeon evidently "knows what to do with water once it's in its beak," that is, it carries out motor responses appropriate to water from the start; yet it does not visually recognize water from birth and tries out various items, accepting some and rejecting others (e.g., Craig, 1912; both Hunt & Smith, 1967, and Fantz, 1957 have shown the same thing for chicks). Thus we cannot say the bird is born with a concept of water. Neither can we say, however, that it learns the concept of water, for all the learning parameters are wrong: the class is formed too fast, and we cannot state the defining properties of the class. At this point, the most we can say is that the pigeon is born with the possibility of the concept of water, and this concept can be activated by any of indefinitely many exemplars.

While it is premature to say whether the bird's concepts of tree, water, and the like are equivalent to ours, it is already clear that the concepts are perceptual classes and not stimulus—response associations. No motor pattern is associated with the sight of any of the classes. The bird does not respond in a fixed way when it sees a person, water, or a tree. These perceptual classes contrast therefore with, for example, the cichild's disposition to attack red, or the Greylag goose's disposition to retrieve egglike objects outside its nest. When brooding, the goose will retrieve any of a large class of objects; according to Lorenz and Tinbergen (1957) the items need merely have a continuous contour.

The goose, in all likelihood, has concepts like those of the pigeon, including water, tree, man, etc. Despite these concepts, the goose probably does not have a concept of the kind of item that can be used to induce egg retrieval in its species. That is, in all likelihood, the goose could not be taught to peck the left key when shown photos of items effective for egg retrieval, and the right key when shown photos of ineffective items. First, the goose must be in a special hormonal state for the stimuli to be effective, and when in this state it probably cannot associate arbitrary responses with the effective stimuli. Second, when it is not in a brooding mood, it probably cannot discriminate between items that do and do not elicit egg retrieval. In contrast, the identification of water, man, tree, and the like apparently does not depend critically upon thirst or on other special motivational states.

Stimuli that elicit fixed motor patterns — and whose efficacy depend on unique hormonal states — probably cannot be associated with arbitrary responses, and if not, the goose could not be said to have the concept of that which will elicit egg retrieval. Yet, it may very well have the concept of egg, in its own and/or other species, as a perceptual class independent of motivational state. Moreover, the properties that serve to define egg cannot be the same as those that release egg retrieval, the latter are far too broad or inclusive. Similarly, the goose may have the concept of gander, as a perceptual class, while not having the concept of "that which elicits mating behavior in me" and the stimuli that release mating behavior in the goose may play little, if any role, in the goose's definition of the perceptual class gander. You and I, however, can have both kinds of concepts, for example, egg, and that which releases egg-retrieval in the goose; gander, and that which releases mating behavior in the goose; etc. Why? First, because in us the efficacy of these stimulus classes does not depend upon unique hormonal states, and second, because we have totally abstract concepts of same-different, concepts that can take as their arguments items such as things that do and do not bring about egg retrieval in the goose. Are there perhaps stimuli that do rigidly control our behavior and for which we have no concept?

Ultimately we must determine whether the bird has only abstract non-relational classes, or abstract relational classes as well. Tree, water, man, and the like are absolute classes, whereas same-different, color of, giving (indeed, essentially all actions), are relational classes. This issue is important not only for the question of abstractness but even more so for sentences, for a sentence is inconceivable without a relational term. We could define a sentence in the weakest possible sense as a string of words not all of which are of the same status. Some words must be absolute and others relational, otherwise we end up with nonsentences of either of two kinds — tree, man, water — or equally a nonsentence — same, color of, give; rather than sentences such as, man give water, water same color of sky, and the like. A species' potential for sentences depends upon its having not only abstract absolute classes but also relational ones.

The evidence for perceptual classes in the bird suggests there may be a way to lead the bird to make judgments that have more of the character of human same-different judgments. Suppose we train the pigeon to respond in one way to two instances of water (W-W), and in another to an instance of water and nonwater (W-$\overline{\text{W}}$). Suppose further that the bird was able to respond correctly even when the two instances of water were not physically alike — in fact, when the physical difference between W_1 and W_2 was as great as that between W_3 and $\overline{W}_1$. Would this not bring the bird fully into line with the primate, canceling out those differences between the species that we claim to have found?

Even if the bird could respond in the proposed manner, which is a substantial extrapolation on its demonstrated performance, the difference between the bird and the primate would remain appreciable. This difference stems from the good possibility that the bird's perceptual classes are restricted, that is, not sufficient to sort the world exhaustively. For example, while the pigeon can recognize the equivalence between trees, water, and different photos of the same person, can it classify automobiles, typewriters, furniture, and the like? In addition, there is no reason to believe that the bird's perceptual deficiences are confined to human artifacts. The bird may be unable to recognize the equivalence between mountains, bolts of lightning, cow's udders, goat's eyes, termite mounds, and the like.

If the bird's ability to make same-different judgments were restricted to members of its perceptual classes, any limits on these classes would entail commensurate limits on the scope of its possible judgments. Notice that we are not so limited, but that we can make same-different judgments on all possible items. Why? Our unlimited ability could be accounted for in either of two ways.

1. We can make same-different judgments on items that are not classified.

2. The items we judge same-different *must* be classified, but this requirement does not restrict the scope of our judgments, for we have an infinite capacity for classification.

The second view is the most reasonable one, I think; in addition, it can serve to show that our original conclusion concerning limitations on the bird's perceptual classes was not itself misguided, based on having divided the world in a manner prejudicial to the bird. One may ask, "Does the bird really have fewer perceptual classes than we do, or only appear to because we have cut the world into pieces that disfavor the bird's perception while favoring our own?" That is, are there not alternative divisions of the world that would create the (no less mistaken) impression that the bird is more gifted than we are? Is there a way of testing these claims?

To test the claims we must divide the world in a way that is not prejudicial to either species. One way is to use a random procedure — presumably there are random procedures that would be entirely neutral — and to cut the world into random or noncanonical pieces. How would this affect the ability of pigeons and people to make same-different judgments?

There is no suggestion that the pigeon could make same-different judgments for such items (given that it cannot even make them for hues) and conversely, no suggestion that people would be unable to make such judgments. Having an infinite capacity for classification, we would first classify such items as, for example, "nonsense figures," "representations of snowflakes," "like the cookies

my daughter used to bake," and the like; and having devised a working perceptual class — one of the infinitely many we can tailor for any occasion — we
would then judge the items to be same or different.

IX. SECOND-ORDER RELATIONS

Another way of saying what I have said here in terms of abstract and circum-
scribed concepts, can be said in terms of first-order and second-order relations.
The pigeon's apparently limited concept of same-different is a first order relation
whereas the human concept is a second-order relation. The pigeon can treat the
relation between, say 500 and 500 mu as being the same as that between, say
560 and 560 mu, only insofar as 560 lies on the generalization gradient produced
by training at 500 (or vice versa). If 380 mu did not lie on the gradient, the bird
could not treat the relation between 380 and 380 mu as being the same as that
between the other values. Apparently it cannot treat two relations as being the
same except as the stimuli instancing the relations lie on the same generalization
gradient.

Primates are not limited in this way, nor apparently are the dolphins. The
dolphin, along with the primate, has been shown to do generalized match-to-
sample — and thus to recognize that the relation between A and A is the same as
that between B and B, despite the fact that A and B do not lie on a generalization gradient produced by training on either one of them (Herman & Gordon,
1974). For instance, primates can recognize that the relation between, say,
apple and apple is the same as that between, say toad and toad. To do so one
must first recognize that the relation between apple and apple is $same_1$; likewise
that the relation between toad and toad is $same_2$; and finally that $same_1$ is the
same as $same_2$. The abstract concept of same is therefore a second-order relation,
or a relation between relations. It is not only same-different that can be formulated in this way, but all relational terms or predicates in human language.

X. CONCLUSIONS

1. In learning or forming new associations, one does not either learn a
relation on the one hand, or associate a response with an absolute stimulus value
on the other. These alternatives are not mutually exclusive as they have classi-
cally been depicted. In fact, there is reason to believe that vertebrate species —
from pigeon to man — form both kinds of associations (relational and absolute)
more or less concurrently.

2. While all vertebrate species may learn both relational and absolute factors,
they appear to differ in the weight they assign to these factors. For instance,

pigeons assign so much greater weight to the absolute than to the relational factor that special designs are required to demonstrate the relational factor. On the other hand, chimpanzees assign so much greater weight to the relational factor that special designs are needed to show learning for the absolute factor.

3.   It is possible that in higher species the weights assigned these factors are flexible — influenced by experience — so that one can literally decide to concentrate on either the relational or absolute factor in a given situation. Lesser species, however, may lack this flexibility, and may divide their resources between the absolute and relational factors in a fixed and constant way.

4.   The assumption that relations are learned or abstractions are formed only when memory is burdened and individual exemplars can no longer be stored is false. Mnemonic factors of this kind *may* influence the human decision as to how to divide one's resources between relational and absolute factors, but a burdened memory is demonstrably not a necessary condition for perceiving relations or forming abstractions. For instance, after being taught no more than three different match-to-sample problems, young chimpanzees immediately passed transfer tests, indicating that they had not merely memorized the individual problems but had induced the matching principle. And it is certain that three problems do not tax chimpanzee memory.

5.   Without having been taught match-to-sample, chimpanzees give evidence for same-different judgments in their daily life: they spontaneously sort like objects into a common location or contact them in the same interval of time. The match-to-sample training does not instill the same-different judgment but simply gives it an unequivocally recognizable form.

6.   The pigeon's capacity for generalized match-to-sample has been underestimated by the use of test designs that oppose the absolute and relational factors, thereby obscuring learning for the relational factor.

7.   Chimpanzees match in their daily life without laboratory training, whereas pigeons (so far as we presently know) may not match in their daily life even with laboratory training.

8.   Although pigeons can be taught a form of differential responding that appears to be analogous to a same-different judgment, the analogy is misleading or at best incomplete. In the human and chimpanzee subject, a same-different judgment is of course categorical; once the difference between the items is suprathreshold, primates judge the pair as "different." Pigeons, however, treat difference in an analogue rather than digital fashion. When given pairs of different hues — all differences being suprathreshold — the frequency with which they use the nonidentity key increases with the magnitude of the difference.

9.   It is quite possible that in man and the ape, no less than in the pigeon, the latency of the judgment "different" will vary in an analogue fashion, being shorter as the magnitude of the difference between the stimuli is greater. How-

ever, in the primate the judgment itself will not vary in this analogue manner but will be categorical.

10.   In higher primates, latency of a judgment will reflect learning for the absolute factor, accuracy of the judgment learning for the relational factor. This should hold not only for same-different but for all other judgments, such as the relation between a color and an object that instanced it. Suppose a chimpanzee had been taught "color of" using red and apple and yellow and banana as exemplars (i.e., "red color of apple"). The animal's grasp of the relation will be shown in its ability to apply the word "color of" to new instances of the relation desite the considerable distance of the new instances from those used in training, for example, "red color of apple" versus "blue color of sky," etc. However, that the animal learned not only the relation but also the actual values in which it experienced the relation should be reflected in the latency of its judgment. Latency should be proportional to the similarity between the new instances and those used in training. In brief, the speed of the ape's judgment should reflect the relation between the training and test exemplars, whereas the accuracy of its judgment should be independent of this factor.

11.   The pigeon probably cannot be taught "color of"; but if it could we would expect it to behave differently from the ape. The pigeon's latency should vary in the same way as the ape's; however, its accuracy would also be expected to vary in an analogue fashion. Instances of "color of" distant from the training ones would not only be judged more slowly but also less accurately (being called "name of," "shape of," "not color of," etc. – even as the pigeon calls poor instances of "different" not different but "same").

12.   The analogue process that is reflected in the speed with which the individual makes a judgment is evidently a more primitive process than the digital judgment. Once the analogue information reaches a threshold or cutting point, higher primates impose a decision rule, thereby making categorical judgments. Pigeons seem incapable of processing the analogue information in this manner.

13.   There is a second reason for doubting the same-different character of the pigeon's differential responses to A-A versus A-B. If children and chimpanzees have first been taught to use the pieces of plastic as names for objects and/or actions, they they readily learn to use the pieces of plastic as "same-different." But if they have not first been taught to use the pieces of plastic in these other semantic functions, they seldom if ever learn to use them as "same-different." This fact, which is of interest in its own right, further differentiates the higher primate from the pigeon; for the pigeon learns to respond differentially to A-A versus A-B without first learning to peck keys that are differentially associated with either objects or actions.

14.   Although pigeons do not respond categorically to pairs of same and different stimuli, they give evidence of having perceptual categories such as that

of water, tree, and the like. There is no evidence, however, that pigeon's perceptual categories have any internal structure such as man's have been shown to have. That is, there is no evidence that pigeons learn to use prototypes in organizing information.

ACKNOWLEDGMENTS

Research reported here was supported by NSF grant CV-4377X, NIMH grant MH 15616, and a facilities grant from the Grant Foundation. A number of my colleagues either read an earlier draft of this article, or discussed parts of it with me, including R. C. Gallistel, R. Gelman, A. pPremack, E. Pugh, B. Rosner, and G. Woodruff. Their comments are gratefully acknowledged. A. Premack helped not only me but the reader in greatly improving the readability of the manuscript.

REFERENCES

Craig, W. Observations of doves learning to drink. *Journal of Animal Behavior,* 1912, *2,* 273–279.

Cumming, W. W., & Berryman, R. The complex discriminated operant: Studies of matching-to-sample and related problems. In D. I. Mostofsky (Ed.), *Stimulus generalization.* Stanford, Cal.: Stanford University Press, 1965.

Fantz, R. L. Form preference in newly hatched chicks. *Journal of Comparative and Physiological Psychology,* 1957, *50,* 422–430.

Farthing, G. W., & Opuda, M. J. Transfer of matching-to-sample in pigeons. *Journal of Experimental Analysis of Behavior,* 1974, *21,* 199–213.

Fodor, J. A. *The language of thought,* New York: Thomas Y. Crowell Co., 1975.

Hayes, K J., & Nissen, C. H. Higher mental functions of a home raised chimpanzee. In A. M. Schrier and F. Stollnitz (Eds.), *Behavior of Nonhuman Primates,* Vol 4. New York: Academic Press, 1971.

Herman, L. M., & Gordon, J. A. Auditory delayed matching in the dolphin. *Journal of Experimental Analysis of Behavior,* 1974, *21,* 19)26.

Herrnstein, R. J., Loveland, D. H., & Cable, D. Natural concepts in pigeons. *Journal of Experimental Psychology: Animal Behavior Processes,* 1976, *2,* 285–302.

Honig, W. K. Discrimination, generalization, and transfer on the basis of stimulus differences. In D. J. Mostofsky (Ed.) *Stimulus Generalization.* Stanford, Ca.: Stanford University Press, 1965.

Hunt, G. L., Jr., & Smith, W. J. Pecking and initial drinking responses in young domestic fowl. *Journal of Comparative and Physiological Psychology,* 1967, *64,* 230–236.

Köhler, W. *Gestalt Psychology.* New York: H. Liverright. 1929.

Lorenz, K., & Tinbergen, N. Taxis and instinctive action in the egg-retrieving behavior of the Greylag Goose. In Schiller, C. H. (Ed.), *Instinctive Behavior.* New York: International University Press, 1957.

Malott, R. W., & Siddall, J. W. Acquisition of the people concept in pigeons. *Psychological Reports,* 1972, *31,* 3–13.

McClure, M. *Chimpanzee's same-different judgments in the combined match-to-sample and oddity-learning paradigm.* Unpublished doctoral dissertation, University of California, Santa Barbara, 1975.

Moon, L. E., & Harlow, H. F. Analyses of oddity learning by rhesus monkeys. *Journal of Comparative & Physiological Psychology,* 1949, *42,* 454–462.

Posner, M. I., & Keele, S. W. On the genesis of abstract ideas. *Journal of Experimental Psychology,* 1968, *77,* 353–363.

Premack, D. Language in chimpanzee? *Science,* 1971, *172,* 808–822.

Premack, D. *Intelligence in ape and man.* Hillsdale, N.J.: Lawrence Erlbaum Associates, 1976.

Rosch, E. H. On the internal structure of perceptual and semantic categories. In T. E. Moore (Ed.), *Cognitive development and the acquisition of language.* New York: Academic Press, 1973.

Siegel, R. G., & Honig, W. K. Pigeon concept formation: successive and simultaneous acquisition. *Journal of Experimental Analysis of Behavior,* 1970, *13,* 385–390.

Smith, K. Grammatical intrusions in the recall of structured letter pairs: Mediated transfer or position learning? *Journal of Experimental Psychology,* 1966, *72,* 580–588.

Spence, K. W. The differential response in animals to stimuli varying within a single dimension. *Psychological Review,* 1937, *44,* 430–44.

Urcuioli, P. J. *Transfer of oddity-from-sample performance in pigeons.* Unpublished master thesis, Dalhousie University, 1977.

Urcuioli, P. J., & Nevin, J. A. Transfer of hue matching in pigeons. *Journal of the Experimental Analysis of Behavior,* 1975, *24,* 149–155.

van Lawick-Goodall, J. The behavior of free-living chimpanzees in the Gombe Stream Reserve. *Animal Behavior Monographs,* 1968, *1,* 161–311.

Wittgenstein, L. *Philosophical investigations.* (G. E. M. Ancombe, trans.) New York: Macmillan, 1953.

Zentall, T., & Hogan, D. Abstract concept learning in the pigeon. *Journal of Experimental Psychology,* 1974, *102,* 393–398.

Author Index

Subject Index